EMPIRICAL MODELS CHALLENGING BIBLICAL CRITICISM

ANCIENT ISRAEL AND ITS LITERATURE

Number 25

EMPIRICAL MODELS CHALLENGING BIBLICAL CRITICISM

Edited by

Raymond F. Person Jr. and Robert Rezetko

Atlanta

Library of Congress Cataloging-in-Publication Data

Names: Rezetko, Robert, editor. | Person, Raymond F., Jr., 1961– editor.
Title: Empirical models challenging biblical criticism / edited by Raymond F. Person Jr. and Robert Rezetko.
Description: Atlanta : SBL Press, [2016] | Series: Ancient Israel and its literature ; number 25 | Includes bibliographical references and index.
Identifiers: LCCN 2016011782 (print) | LCCN 2016012795 (ebook) | ISBN 9781628371321 (pbk. : alk. paper) | ISBN 9780884141501 (hardback : alk. paper) | ISBN 9780884141495 (ebook)
Subjects: LCSH: Bible—Criticism, Redaction—History. | Classical literature—History and criticism.
Classification: LCC BS500 .E78 2016 (print) | LCC BS500 (ebook) | DDC 220.6/6—dc23
LC record available at http://lccn.loc.gov/2016011782

Printed on acid-free paper.

Contents

Abbreviations

4QRP	4QReworked Pentateuch (4Q158, 4Q364–367)
AASF	Annales Academiae Scientiarum Fennicae
AB	Anchor Bible
AB	*Assyriologische Bibliothek*
ABRL	Anchor Bible Reference Library
AfO	*Archiv für Orientforschung*
AIL	Ancient Israel and Its Literature
AMD	Ancient Magic and Divination
ANEM	Ancient Near Eastern Monographs
AnSt	*Anatolian Studies*
AOAT	Alter Orient und Altes Testament
APB	*Acta Patristica et Byzantina*
ATD	Das Alte Testament Deutsch
AUMSR	Andrews University Monograph Studies in Religion
AuOr	*Aula Orientalis*
AuOrSup	Aula Orientalis Supplementa
AYBRL	Anchor Yale Bible Reference Library
b.	Babylonian Talmud
BaF	Baghdader Forschungen
BETL	Bibliotheca Ephemeridum Theologicarum Lovaniensium
BGE	*The Babylonian Gilgamesh Epic: Introduction, Critical Edition and Cuneiform Texts.* Andrew R. George. 2 vols. Oxford: Oxford University Press, 2003.
BH	*Book History*
BH	Biblical Hebrew
BHL	Blackwell Handbooks in Linguistics
BHS	*Biblia Hebraica Stuttgartensia.* Edited by Karl Elliger and Wilhelm Rudolph. Stuttgart: Deutsche Bibelgesellschaft, 1983.

BIAAOP	Occasional Publications of the British Institute of Archaeology at Ankara
Bib	*Biblica*
BIOSCS	*Bulletin of the International Organization for Septuagint and Cognate Studies*
BKAT	Biblischer Kommentar, Altes Testament
BMS	*Babylonian Magic and Sorcery: "Being The Prayers of the Lifting of the Hand"; The Cuneiform Texts of a Group of Babylonian and Assyrian Incantations and Magical Formulae Edited with Transliterations and Full Vocabulary from Tablets of the Kuyunjik Collections Preserved in the British Museum*. Edited by Leonard W. King. London: Luzac, 1896.
BSalmD	Bibliotheca Salmanticensis Dissertationes
BZ	*Biblische Zeitschrift*
BZAW	Beihefte zur Zeitschrift für die alttestamentliche Wissenschaft
ca.	circa
CahRB	Cahiers de la Revue biblique
CahTD	Cahiers du Groupe François-Thureau Dangin
CBET	Contributions to Biblical Exegesis and Theology
CBH	Classical Biblical Hebrew
CBQ	*Catholic Biblical Quarterly*
CBQMS	Catholic Biblical Quarterly Monograph Series
CHANE	Culture and History of the Ancient Near East
CM	Cuneiform Monographs
CNIP	Carsten Niebuhr Institute Publications
CP	The Carlsberg Papyri
CQS	Companion to the Qumran Scrolls
CRRAI	Compte Rendu de la Rencontre Assyriologique Internationale
CSASE	Cambridge Studies in Anglo-Saxon England
CUSAS	Cornell University Studies in Assyriology and Sumerology
DG	The Death of Gilgamesh
DJD	Discoveries in the Judaean Desert
DSS	Dead Sea Scrolls
DSSSE	*The Dead Sea Scrolls Study Edition*. Edited by Florentino García Martínez and Eibert J. C. Tigchelaar. 2 vols. Grand Rapids: Eerdmans; Leiden: Brill, 1999.
EANEC	Explorations in Ancient Near Eastern Civilizations

EBH	Early Biblical Hebrew
EstBib	*Estudios bíblicos*
ETL	*Ephemerides Theologicae Lovanienses*
ExpTim	*Expository Times*
FFC	Folklore Fellows Communications
FRLANT	Forschungen zur Religion und Literatur des Alten und Neuen Testaments
GA	Gilgamesh and Agga
GBH	Gilgamesh and the Bull of Heaven
GEN	Gilgamesh, Enkidu, and the Netherworld
GH	Gilgamesh and Huwawa
HBV	Hebrew Bible and Its Versions
HR	*History of Religions*
HS	*Hebrew Studies*
HSCL	Harvard Studies in Comparative Literature
HSM	Harvard Semitic Monographs
HThKAT	Herder Theologischer Kommentar zum Alten Testament
HTR	*Harvard Theological Review*
IBT	Interpreting Biblical Texts
ICC	International Critical Commentary
IEJ	*Israel Exploration Journal*
IIAS	International Institute of Advanced Studies
IOS	Israel Oriental Studies
IRT	Issues in Religion and Theology
ISBL	Indiana Studies in Biblical Literature
JAJSup	Journal of Ancient Judaism Supplements
JAOS	*Journal of the American Oriental Society*
JBL	*Journal of Biblical Literature*
JBS	Jerusalem Biblical Studies
JCS	*Journal of Cuneiform Studies*
JCSSup	Journal of Cuneiform Studies Supplement Series
JJS	*Journal of Jewish Studies*
JNES	*Journal of Near Eastern Studies*
JNSL	*Journal of Northwest Semitic Languages*
JR	*Journal of Religion*
JSHRZ	Jüdische Schriften aus hellenistisch-römisher Zeit
JSNTSup	Journal for the Study of the New Testament Supplement Series
JSOT	*Journal for the Study of the Old Testament*

JSOTSup	Journal for the Study of the Old Testament Supplement Series
JSPSup	Journal for the Study of the Pseudepigrapha Supplement Series
JSS	*Journal of Semitic Studies*
JTS	*Journal of Theological Studies*
KAL	Keilschrifttexte aus Assur literarischen Inhalts
KHC	Kurzer Hand-Commentar zum Alten Testament
LAI	Library of Ancient Israel
LBH	Late Biblical Hebrew
LDSS	Literature of the Dead Sea Scrolls
LHBOTS	Library of Hebrew Bible/Old Testament Studies
LSAWS	Linguistic Studies in Ancient West Semitic
LSS	Leipziger semitische Studien
LSTS	Library of Second Temple Studies
LXX	Septuagint
MC	Mesopotamian Civilizations
MCAAS	Memoirs of the Connecticut Academy of Arts & Sciences
MdB	Le Monde de la Bible
MES	Medieval European Studies
MF	Mandäistische Forschungen
MIFAO	Mémoires publiés par les membres de l'Institut français d'archéologie orientale
MS	Mnemosyne Supplementum
MSL	Materialien zum sumerischen Lexikon/Materials for the Sumerian Lexicon
MSU	Mitteilungen des Septuaginta-Unternehmens
MT	Masoretic Text
n(n).	note(s)
NA	Neo-Assyrian
NABU	*Nouvelles assyriologiques brèves et utilitaires*
Ned.	Nedarim
NETS	*A New English Translation of the Septuagint*. Edited by Albert Pietersma and Benjamin G. Wright. Oxford: Oxford University Press, 2007.
NICOT	New International Commentary on the Old Testament
NovT	*Novum Testamentum*
NovTSup	Supplements to Novum Testamentum
NS	New series

NT	New Testament
NTL	New Testament Library
NTT	New Testament Theology
OAC	Orientis Antiqvi Collectio
OB	Old Babylonian
OBO	Orbis Biblicus et Orientalis
obv.	obverse
OCTb	Oxford Centre Textbooks
OG	Old Greek
OHRT	Oxford Handbooks in Religion and Theology
OIS	Oriental Institute Seminars
OL	Old Latin
OPSNKF	Occasional Publications of the Samuel Noah Kramer Fund
Or	*Orientalia*
OTL	Old Testament Library
OTP	*The Old Testament Pseudepigrapha*. Edited by James H. Charlesworth. 2 vols. New York: Doubleday, 1983, 1985.
OtSt	Oudtestamentische Studiën
PFES	Publications of the Finnish Exegetical Society in Helsinki
PHSC	Perspectives on Hebrew Scriptures and Its Contexts
PIHANS	Publications de l'Institut historique-archéologique néerlandais de Stamboul
pl(s).	plate(s)
PTSDSSP	Princeton Theological Seminary Dead Sea Scrolls Project
Q	*Quelle* (German for source); the hypothetical written source for the material common to Matthew and Luke but absent from Mark
RA	*Revue d'assyriologie et d'archéologie orientale*
RB	*Revue biblique*
RBén	*Revue bénédictine*
RBL	*Review of Biblical Literature*
RBS	Resources for Biblical Studies
RelSoc	Religion and Society
repr.	reprint
rev.	reverse
RevQ	*Revue de Qumrân*
RILP	Roehampton Institute London Papers
RlA	*Reallexikon der Assyriologie*. Edited by Erich Ebeling et al. Berlin: de Gruyter, 1928–

RSRS	Routledge Studies in Rhetoric and Stylistics
SAA	State Archives of Assyria
SAL	Studies in Arabic Literature
SB	Standard Babylonian
SBLMS	Society of Biblical Literature Monograph Series
SBLStBL	Society of Biblical Literature Studies in Biblical Literature
SBS	Stuttgart Bibelstudien
SCL	Sather Classical Lectures
ScrHier	Scripta Hierosolymitana
SCS	Septuagint and Cognate Studies
SDSS	Studies in the Dead Sea Scrolls and Related Literature
SHBC	Smyth & Helwys Bible Commentary
SJOT	*Scandinavian Journal of the Old Testament*
SNTSMS	Society for New Testament Studies Monograph Series
SP	Samaritan Pentateuch
SPap	*Studia Papyrologica*
SSLL	Studies in Semitic Languages and Linguistics
SSN	Studia Semitica Neerlandica
SSU	Studia Semitica Upsaliensia
STDJ	Studies on the Texts of the Desert of Judah
StPohl	Studia Pohl
STT 1	*The Sultantepe Tablets*. Vol. 1. Oliver R. Gurney, and Jacob J. Finkelstein. BIAAOP 3. London: British Institute of Archaeology at Ankara, 1957.
STT 2	*The Sultantepe Tablets*. Vol. 2. Oliver R. Gurney and Peter Hulin. BIAAOP 7. London: British Institute of Archaeology at Ankara, 1964.
SVTG	Septuaginta: Vetus Testamentum Graecum Auctoritate Academiae Scientiarum Gottingensis editum
SymS	Symposium Series
TECC	Textos y estudios "Cardenal Cisneros"
Text	*Textus*
TSAJ	Texte und Studien zum antiken Judentum
TSHLRS	Texts and Studies in the Hebrew Language and Related Subjects
TZ	*Theologische Zeitschrift*
UAVA	Untersuchungen zur Assyriologie und vorderasiatischen Archäologie
VL	Vetus Latina: Die Reste der Altlateinischen Bibel

VT	*Vetus Testamentum*
VTSup	Supplements to Vetus Testamentum
VWGTh	Veröffentlichungen der wissenschaftlichen Gesellschaft für Theologie
WBC	Word Biblical Commentary
WC	Westminster Commentaries
WUNT	Wissenschaftliche Untersuchungen zum Neuen Testament
WVDOG	Wissenschaftliche Veröffentlichungen der deutschen Orient-Gesellschaft
ZAW	*Zeitschrift für die alttestamentliche Wissenschaft*
ZTK	*Zeitschrift für Theologie und Kirche*

Introduction: The Importance of Empirical Models to Assess the Efficacy of Source and Redaction Criticism

Raymond F. Person Jr. and Robert Rezetko

1. Introduction

The title of the present book clearly relates to Jeffrey Tigay's influential edited volume, *Empirical Models for Biblical Criticism*,[1] where we have changed *for* to *Challenging*. We view our book as both paying homage to the influence Tigay's volume has had on our own work and others' and correcting the current discussion of the efficacy of source and redaction criticism as is often practiced by biblical scholars, including those who may have been influenced by Tigay's book. In this introduction, we will discuss Tigay's publications concerning empirical models (including some before and after his influential volume) and the influence of Tigay's volume in biblical scholarship. We will then clarify why we think there is a need for reassessing the efficacy of source and redaction criticism on the basis of empirical models, which is the purpose of this volume. We will not only introduce the following chapters in this volume, but also summarize the collective force of the current volume as a whole on the efficacy of source and redaction criticism, arguing that too often biblical scholars make source and redactional arguments based on inappropriate criteria.

1. Jeffrey H. Tigay, ed., *Empirical Models for Biblical Criticism* (Philadelphia: University of Pennsylvania Press, 1985; repr. with a new foreword by Richard Elliott Friedman, Eugene, OR: Wipf & Stock, 2005).

2. Jeffrey Tigay and His "Empirical Models"

Tigay begins his 1975 *Journal of Biblical Literature* article "An Empirical Basis for the Documentary Hypothesis"[2] with a tribute to the 1890 *Journal of Biblical Literature* article by George Foot Moore, "Tatian's Diatessaron and the Analysis of the Pentateuch."[3] Moore was explicitly responding to critics of the Documentary Hypothesis who insisted that we have no evidence of such composite texts in the ancient world by showing how the four sources of the canonical gospels were combined in the Diatessaron analogous to the composite Pentateuch made up of JEDP.[4] Tigay wrote: "Although the *Diatessaron* has been ruled out of court because of its lateness, Moore's method in analyzing it was exemplary. He was able to demonstrate its literary background empirically because he had its sources as well as its final form before him."[5] Tigay adopted Moore's empirical method in his analysis of the Masoretic Text (MT) and the Samaritan Pentateuch (SP) and concluded as follows: "[W]e find that the documentary hypothesis presumes a method of composition which is empirically attested in ancient Israel, from a time close to that in which most of the biblical books attained their present form. The evidence here reviewed constitutes a type of documentary composition unfolding before our very eyes."[6] Thus Tigay understood that, like Moore but on the basis of earlier comparative data, he had defended the Documentary Hypothesis from its critics by providing "An Empirical Basis for the Documentary Hypothesis."

---

2. Jeffrey H. Tigay, "An Empirical Basis for the Documentary Hypothesis," *JBL* 94 (1975): 329–42; rev. Hebrew version, Tigay, "The Samaritan Pentateuch as an Empirical Model for Biblical Criticism," *BM* 22 (1977): 348–61; rev. English version, Tigay, "Conflation as a Redactional Technique," in Tigay, *Empirical Models for Biblical Criticism*, 53–95.

3. George Foot Moore, "Tatian's Diatessaron and the Analysis of the Pentateuch," *JBL* 9 (1890): 201–15.

4. The Diatessaron was produced by Tatian, an early Christian theologian, around the year 170 CE in Syriac or Greek. JEDP refers to the hypothesis that the first five books of the Bible, Genesis to Deuteronomy, developed into their present form from four sources of different dates and authorship which were gradually joined together (J = Jahwist or Yahwist, E = Elohist, D = Deuteronomist, P = Priestly source).

5. Tigay, "Empirical Basis for the Documentary Hypothesis," 330.

6. Ibid., 342.

A decade later in *Empirical Models for Biblical Criticism*,[7] Tigay's concern for providing an empirical basis for the Documentary Hypothesis against the criticism of the "harmonizers"[8]—that is, those who insisted

7. For the benefit of the reader who may be unfamiliar with Tigay's edited volume—others may skip this note—we summarize its basic content here as objectively as possible. It contains an introduction (1–20) and conclusion (239–41) by Tigay and eight other chapters by five scholars, three by Tigay (21–52, 53–95, 149–73), two by Emanuel Tov (97–130, 211–37), and one each by Alexander Rofé (131–47), Yair Zakovitch (175–96), and Mordechai Cogan (197–209). There is also an "Appendix: Tatian's Diatessaron and the Analysis of the Pentateuch" by George Foot Moore (243–56), and illustrations are inserted between 130 and 131. Most of the chapters were presented orally and/or published previously elsewhere (unnumbered page near the front and unnumbered notes on 1, 53, 131, 149, 197, 211, 243). Each chapter is preceded by a brief "Editor's Note" by Tigay that summarizes its content and significance (21–22, 53, 97–98, 131, 149–50, 175–76, 197, 211–12). The chapters cover a range of texts and topics, which are conveniently summarized in Tigay's introduction, editorial notes, and conclusion (19–22, 53, 97–98, 131, 149–50, 175–76, 197, 211–12, 239–40). We would outline those as follows: The *texts* come from Mesopotamian literature (Gilgamesh Epic, Laws of Hammurabi, etc.), biblical literature (Pentateuch, Josh 20, 1 Sam 16–18, Jeremiah, Chronicles, etc.) in the Bible's various textual traditions (MT, SP, biblical Dead Sea Scrolls [DSS], Septuagint [LXX]), and postbiblical Jewish and Christian literature (Jubilees, Temple Scroll, Talmudic literature, Tatian's Diatessaron, etc.). The principal *topics* are literary development; source and redaction criticism; composite documents, especially the Documentary Hypothesis; editorial techniques, including conflation, supplementation, and assimilation; phenomena such as anachronisms, inconsistencies, contradictions, repetitions, doublets, and thematic and stylistic variations; external or extrabiblical analogues or comparisons (e.g., Gilgamesh Epic); and internal or biblical duplicates or parallels (e.g., Samuel–Kings // Chronicles). The primary *objective* of his book relates to the phrase "empirical models." In its context that refers to the *analogues* and *duplicates* just mentioned. The aim is to offer tangible, observable, *empirical* evidence—versus hypotheses and theories—from ancient Near Eastern literature, nonbiblical and biblical, which illustrate and support—not prove—the assumptions, methods, and conclusions of critical scholarship about the literary formation of the Bible. In Tigay's own words: "Together these studies, based on texts whose evolution can be documented by copies from several stages in the course of their development—in other words, on *empirical models*—show that many literary works from ancient Israel and cognate cultures were demonstrably produced in the way critics believe that biblical literature was produced" (xi–xii, emphasis original). "The present volume brings together a number of studies that illuminate aspects of the development of the Hebrew Bible by means of comparison with analogues" (19).

8. Jeffrey H. Tigay, "The Stylistic Criterion of Source Criticism in the Light of Ancient Near Eastern and Postbiblical Literature," in Tigay, *Empirical Models for Biblical Criticism*, 149, 154; rev. from Tigay, "The Stylistic Criteria of Source-Criticism in

on the literary unity of the Pentateuch such as Umberto Cassuto, Cyrus Gordon, and Kenneth Kitchen—continued strongly as he not only provided *empirical models* but insisted that the nature of the Pentateuch itself is such that source criticism is efficacious. For example, in his "Editor's Note" to his own chapter "The Evolution of the Pentateuch Narratives in the Light of the Evolution of the *Gilgamesh Epic*," he wrote the following:

> Although we can see now that the epic was so extensively revised that no amount of critical acumen could have led critics to reconstruct its sources and early stages as they really were, we can also see that the general outline of development presumed by M. Jastrow on the basis of nineteenth-century critical suppositions was not very wide of the mark. The larger number of inconsistencies in the Torah indicates that it was not extensively revised; that is why it is more amenable to source criticism than is *Gilgamesh*.[9]

Later in the chapter "The Stylistic Criterion of Source Criticism in the Light of Ancient Near Eastern and Postbiblical Literature," he described two types of redactors, (1) those "who showed great deference toward their sources" and (2) those who "showed a greater willingness to revise the wording of their sources, and thereby produced smoother compositions."[10] He then concluded as follows:

> [T]he unevenness within the Torah shows its redactors to have been largely of the first type [that is, redactors who showed great deference toward their sources]. But even redactors who revised their sources extensively left some traces of the original wording, and where those traces occur in telltale combinations with each other or in association with other signs of compositeness, they can help guide the critic in identifying the components.[11]

---

the Light of Ancient Near Eastern Literature," in *Isac Leo Seeligmann Volume: Essays on the Bible and the Ancient World*, vol. 3: *Non-Hebrew Section*, ed. Alexander Rofé and Yair Zakovitch (Jerusalem: Rubinstein, 1983), 67–91. All subsequent references are to the 1985 version of the article from Tigay, *Empirical Models for Biblical Criticism*.

9. Jeffrey H. Tigay, "The Evolution of the Pentateuchal Narratives in the Light of the Evolution of the *Gilgamesh Epic*," in Tigay, *Empirical Models for Biblical Criticism*, 21–22.

10. Tigay, "Stylistic Criterion of Source Criticism," 172.

11. Ibid.

Thus it seems obvious that one of Tigay's objectives for his volume was to provide an empirical basis for the Documentary Hypothesis against its critics.[12] This appears to influence even his "Editor's Note[s]" introducing chapters that do not concern the Pentateuch. For example, he described Emanuel Tov's chapter "The Composition of 1 Samuel 16–18 in the Light of the Septuagint Version" as "[a]nother example of conflation,"[13] implying that Tov's chapter provides additional support to the examples in his own immediately preceding chapter "Conflation as a Redactional Technique" that is explicitly a defense of the Documentary Hypothesis.[14] In a similar fashion, he wrote the following in his "Editor's Note" to Alexander Rofé's chapter "Joshua 20: Historico-Literary Criticism Illustrated": "Rofé shows that the linguistic and conceptual inconsistencies in the chapter reflect differences between the two strata, thus validating the critical methods which take such differences as source-critical clues."[15] Significantly, Rofé's chapter immediately precedes Tigay's "The Stylistic Criterion of Source Criticism in the Light of Ancient Near Eastern and Postbiblical Literature" and in this way also prepares for Tigay's defense of the Documentary Hypothesis.[16]

When these conclusions are combined, the rhetorical force of *Empirical Models for Biblical Criticism* asserts the validity of the methods of source and redaction criticism. The ambiguity in the title itself—*Empirical Models for Biblical Criticism*—may have contributed to this influence. That is, although we will see below that Tigay may have understood the title to mean that biblical criticism should take more seriously the limitations that the empirical models place on the methods of biblical criticism (*Empirical Models for [Placing Limits on] Biblical Criticism*), the title has often been read as *Empirical Models for [the Validity of] Biblical Criticism*

12. Tigay himself states: "My interest in the subject of this volume derives ultimately from an early fascination with the documentary hypothesis" (Jeffrey H. Tigay, "Preface and Acknowledgements," in Tigay, *Empirical Models for Biblical Criticism*, xi).

13. Emanuel Tov, "The Composition of 1 Samuel 16–18 in the Light of the Septuagint Version," in Tigay, *Empirical Models for Biblical Criticism*, 97.

14. Tigay, "Conflation as a Redactional Technique."

15. Alexander Rofé, "Joshua 20: Historico-Literary Criticism Illustrated," in Tigay, *Empirical Models for Biblical Criticism*, 131. Furthermore, although Rofé's chapter does not deal with the Documentary Hypothesis per se, there is nevertheless a substantial discussion of the hypothesis in a section of his chapter, "Relevance for the Documentary Hypothesis" (143–47).

16. Tigay, "Stylistic Criterion of Source Criticism."

[*as Commonly Practiced by Source and Redaction Critics*]. As we have seen above, Tigay's earlier *Journal of Biblical Literature* article, his conclusions in *Empirical Models for Biblical Criticism* in his own chapters, and his "Editor's Note[s]" introducing others' chapters all seem to support this latter interpretation of the title.

However, in his introduction and conclusion, Tigay was somewhat more cautious. On the one hand, in his introduction he wrote the following, which is consistent with the above conclusions:

> Concrete analogues would enable the literary critic to base his work on something more than hypotheses about ancient literary techniques. They could function as models of literary development, providing the critic firsthand experience with compilers' and redactors' techniques, lending his observations a refinement they could never have so long as they were based entirely on hypotheses devoid of external controls.[17]

If one emphasizes only this conclusion, then one could easily conclude that the title should be read as *Empirical Models for* [*the Validity of*] *Biblical Criticism* [*as Commonly Practiced by Source and Redaction Critics*]. However, on the other hand, Tigay balanced this conclusion concerning such "external controls" for biblical criticism by cautioning against such a misreading in both his introduction and his conclusion as follows:

> This would be a fatal flaw in the use of such analogues if we imagined that analogues can confirm any particular theory about the development of an Israelite composition. That, however, is not the function of an analogue. Even another text by the same author cannot prove how a text was produced. Analogues can only serve to show what is *plausible* or *realistic* by showing what has happened elsewhere. Such a demonstration, if compatible with the evidence from within the biblical text being studied, can help critics evaluate the *realism* of an existing theory about the development of that text or it can suggest a new theory about it.[18]
>
> The preceding chapters have shown that many of the central hypotheses of biblical criticism are *realistic*. They do not prove that these hypotheses are correct, but they show that the processes of literary development

17. Jeffrey H. Tigay, "Introduction," in Tigay, *Empirical Models for Biblical Criticism*, 3.

18. Ibid., 17 (emphasis added).

> which critics inferred from clues within biblical literature are real phenomena, attested in the history of literature from ancient times down to our own. This conclusion is based on case studies of texts whose earlier stages are known and do not have to be hypothetically reconstructed; it is based, in other words, on empirical models.[19]

Tigay also noted that empirical models have potential "disadvantages"[20] and "might yield results at variance with certain critical hypotheses about biblical literature"[21] or "suggest explanations better than those currently preferred by critics."[22] Consequently, since empirical models only demonstrate what in general is "reasonable" or "plausible"[23] and cannot prove specific hypotheses or theories, there is also some justification in the book for giving it an alternative title along the lines of *Empirical Models for [Placing Limits on] Biblical Criticism.*

This tension in Tigay's edited volume continues in his more recent work. For example, in his 2012 essay "The Documentary Hypothesis, Empirical Models and Interpretations of Ancient Texts," he clearly continues to support the Documentary Hypothesis by referring to "empirical models":

> The examples we have reviewed here show that the process of redaction reconstructed by Biblical critics is realistic, that is, the redactorial combination of pre-existing written sources does indeed, at least sometimes, produce inconsistencies of fact and vocabulary, digression and non-sequiturs, of the type that provide the primary evidence for source criticism.... The examples reviewed above answer this question by demonstrating that redactors did not always allow themselves the freedom to rewrite their texts in order to resolve inconsistencies. Even if they resolved the inconsistencies exegetically in their own minds, in the written text they did not allow themselves to do much more than juxtapose or interweave the sources and add some transitional phrases.[24]

---

19. Jeffrey H. Tigay, "Summary and Conclusions," in Tigay, *Empirical Models for Biblical Criticism*, 239 (emphasis added).

20. Tigay, "Introduction," 15; see further 15–17.

21. Ibid., 9.

22. Tigay, "Summary and Conclusions," 240.

23. See also Tigay, "Introduction," 19–20; Tigay, "Evolution of the Pentateuchal Narratives," 26–27, 52.

24. Jeffrey H. Tigay, "The Documentary Hypothesis, Empirical Models and Holistic Interpretation," in *Modernity and Interpretations of Ancient Texts: The Collapse and*

There are hints in this essay, similar to his cautionary comments in the introduction and conclusion to his edited volume, that Tigay understands that empirical models cannot prove the Documentary Hypothesis. For example, in the quote above he includes "at least sometimes" and "did not always" as hedges. Furthermore, he identified three "difficulties and questions" raised by empirical models. First, "empirical models don't always explain themselves," which he illustrated by the debate between Tov and Rofé concerning whether or not the LXX of 1 Sam 16–18 represented the earliest source text that was conflated with another source to produce the MT of 1 Sam 16–18 (Tov) or the LXX was an abridgement of a (proto-) MT *Vorlage* (Rofé).[25] Second, "various versions of a text do not necessarily stand in a lineal relationship to each other. The earlier versions are not necessarily the direct or even indirect prototypes (*Vorlagen*) of the later ones."[26] Third, he acknowledged that there is some question about the appropriateness of using ancient Mesopotamian literature for the purpose of understanding the literary history of the Bible, "since we have no idea whether Israelite scribes had any knowledge at all of how scribe-authors worked in Mesopotamia, including how they edited and revised texts."[27] However, even after identifying these "difficulties and questions," he still understood empirical models to support the plausibility of the Documentary Hypothesis: "While the absence of a known analogue for a particular theory is not *ipso facto* an argument against its plausibility (what is unique is not implausible), the existence of an analogue can enhance the plausibility of a theory by showing that it is not out of line with types of literary development attested in other cases."[28] Thus, recently Tigay not only continued to insist that empirical models support the efficacy of source and redaction criticism as applied to (some) biblical texts but suggested that the empirical models support the plausibility of a specific theory, the Documentary Hypothesis.

Remaking of Traditions, ed. Jun Ikeda, IIAS Reports 1102 (Kyoto: International Institute of Advanced Studies, 2012), 125–26.

25. Ibid., 126. Tigay is referring to Tov, "Composition of 1 Samuel 16–18," and Alexander Rofé, "The Battle of David and Goliath: Folklore, Theology, Eschatology," in *Judaic Perspectives on Ancient Israel*, ed. Jacob Neusner, Baruch A. Levine, and Ernest S. Frerichs (Philadelphia: Fortress, 1987), 117–51.

26. Tigay, "Documentary Hypothesis, Empirical Models and Holistic Interpretation," 127.

27. Ibid.

28. Ibid., 128.

3. The Influence of Tigay's *Empirical Models for Biblical Criticism*

Tigay's edited volume has been cited often and widely discussed. Its significance and impact are evident merely by searching and perusing the results on, for example, Amazon or Google Books. Published reviews have generally agreed that the book accomplishes one of its main objectives, showing that the Documentary Hypothesis is "plausible" or "realistic" in the general sense described above.[29] Unsurprisingly, however, some so-called harmonizers and synchronic-readers of biblical literature have reacted less positively. Robert Polzin, for example, believes the book is both "important and trivial" and "[t]he use of external analogues to show how literary-historical research in biblical studies is, generally speaking, realistically motivated is mostly irrelevant, first, to the specific interpretation of specific texts, and, second, to one's ability to choose one specific genetic theory over its rival."[30] In short, the generally favorable response to Tigay's empirical models as well as some of his critics have often emphasized his conclusions concerning the plausibility of the Documentary Hypothesis, thereby to a large degree disregarding Tigay's cautionary comments. This is especially evident in Richard Elliott Friedman's new foreword in the 2005 reprinted edition of Tigay's book.[31]

Friedman is a recognized authority on and vocal proponent of the Documentary Hypothesis, and, indeed, Tigay cited him several times in the original book.[32] Friedman applauds the book, appropriately, for making "a significant contribution to our field in more ways than one when it first appeared" and which "remains now, a valuable response to claims

29. Adele Berlin, *JAOS* 107 (1987): 145–46; John A. Emerton, *VT* 37 (1987): 508–9; Richard Elliott Friedman, *JR* 67 (1987): 539–40; G. Lloyd Jones, *ExpTim* 98 (1986): 25; John W. Rogerson, *JTS* 39 (1988): 532–35; Henry W. F. Saggs, *JSS* 32 (1987): 196–99; however, the latter criticizes some examples as being not concerned with "empirical models."

30. Robert Polzin, *Samuel and the Deuteronomist: A Literary Study of the Deuteronomic History*, vol. 2: *1 Samuel*, ISBL (Bloomington: Indiana University Press, 1989), 228–29 n. 41; see also Robert P. Gordon, "Compositeness, Conflation and the Pentateuch," *JSOT* 51 (1991): 57–69.

31. Richard Elliott Friedman, "Foreword," in Tigay, *Empirical Models for Biblical Criticism* [1–10] (ten unnumbered pages).

32. Tigay, "Evolution of the Pentateuchal Narratives," 24 n. 12; Tigay, "Conflation as a Redactional Technique," 54 nn. 1, 3; Tigay, "Summary and Conclusions," 241 n. 6.

concerning the Documentary Hypothesis."[33] Furthermore in his view it is "a vindication of the process of the Documentary Hypothesis" and "a signpost, a contribution to our field's evolution."[34] His specific remarks range over and reiterate a number of topics, such as the general value of empirical models as well as specific issues such as doublets or dual variations of stories. Most of what Friedman says is quite in line with the contents of the chapters themselves, except that one senses that Friedman is more certain about specific facts of the Documentary Hypothesis than Tigay himself was willing to admit. On one point, though, Friedman goes far beyond what any of the authors in the volume actually assert or insinuate. We are referring to the issue of linguistic evidence and its relationship to the dating of biblical writings. Friedman speaks about the "more substantial … demonstrable, quantifiable … pervasive and concrete" linguistic data,[35] "linguistic evidence that [texts] are early," citing the publications of Avi Hurvitz and others,[36] and "linguistic evidence showing that the Hebrew of the texts corresponds to the stages of development of the Hebrew language in the periods in which the hypothesis [i.e., the Documentary Hypothesis] says those respective texts were composed."[37] Friedman may wish the linguistic evidence to carry this weight, but this desire on his part actually contradicts some of the arguments found within Tigay's book that he is supposedly supporting. For example, Rofé argued for a late fourth-century date for the supplements in MT Josh 20 but noted that the scribe that added this material imitated "ancient usage rather than writing in his own Second Commonwealth Hebrew" so that Rofé suggested that this empirical example and others "detract from the value of linguistic considerations in the dating of biblical passages."[38] Even more striking is Tigay's own observations concerning the linguistic evidence in the various versions of the Gilgamesh Epic: "[M]any of the late variants seem to employ language not less ancient than the language they replace."[39] That is, Rofé and Tigay seem to be suggesting the limited efficaciousness of language for the lin-

33. Friedman, "Foreword," [1].
34. Ibid., [8].
35. Ibid., [1, 6].
36. Ibid., [7] with n. 5.
37. Ibid., [1].
38. Rofé, "Joshua 20," 146 with n. 29.
39. Tigay, "Evolution of the Pentateuchal Narratives," 40–41.

guistic dating of biblical writings based on their own empirical evidence (contra Friedman).[40]

Although Tigay's volume has played a special role in discussions concerning pentateuchal sources, it would be a serious mistake to suggest that the volume has not influenced the study of the Bible more broadly. In fact, although as scholars we have tended to avoid discussions of pentateuchal sources, the influence of Tigay's volume has been evident in our own publications from the very beginning. We are confident that the following discussion of Tigay's influence on our own work represents the experience of many scholars of the Bible whose graduate training was contemporary to ours or later.

Person encountered Tigay's book during his doctoral studies and was especially influenced by the text-critical arguments in the volume. His first publication, an article in *Zeitschrift für die alttestamentliche Wissenschaft* that was a revision of a paper in a doctoral LXX seminar, was methodologically based on and drew from the conclusions of the chapters in *Empirical Models for Biblical Criticism* by Tov and Rofé as well as the work of other text critics.[41] This use of text-critical variants as providing empirical limitations on his redactional arguments continued to have a significant influence on his dissertation and later works.[42] He has also used other empirical models that are not found in Tigay's volume: the comparative study of oral traditions and the social scientific discipline of

40. See also the chapters in this volume by Person and by Rezetko.

41. Raymond F. Person Jr., "II Kings 24,18–25,30 and Jeremiah 52: A Text-Critical Case Study in the Redaction History of the Deuteronomistic History," *ZAW* 105 (1993): 174–205. Person referred to Tov, "Composition of 1 Samuel 16–18" (Person, "II Kings," 189 n. 45, 191 n. 51); Emanuel Tov, "The Literary History of the Book of Jeremiah in the Light of Its Textual History," in Tigay, *Empirical Models for Biblical Criticism*, 211–37 (Person, "II Kings," 176 n. 9, 180 n. 19, 186 n. 30, 187 n. 32, 189 n. 49); and Rofé, "Joshua 20" (Person, "II Kings," 175 n. 7, 185 n. 25, 186 n. 30, 189 n. 44, 191 nn. 51–52).

42. Raymond F. Person Jr., *Second Zechariah and the Deuteronomic School*, JSOTSup 167 (Sheffield: Sheffield Academic, 1993), esp. 43–54; Person, *The Kings–Isaiah and Kings–Jeremiah Recensions*, BZAW 252 (Berlin: de Gruyter, 1997); Person, *The Deuteronomic School: History, Social Setting, and Literature*, SBLStBL 2 (Atlanta: Society of Biblical Literature, 2002), esp. 34–50; and Person, *The Deuteronomic History and the Book of Chronicles: Scribal Works in an Oral World*, AIL 6 (Atlanta: Society of Biblical Literature, 2010), esp. 74–78, 87–129, 131–44.

conversation analysis.[43] Based on such empirical models, Person has concluded as follows:

> A new model of the development of literary texts in the ancient world is now necessary. This model should take seriously both the reality of textual plurality and the significant role of multiformity in primarily oral societies. Rather than envisioning one original, authoritative, determinant text, we should envision a collection of coexisting parallel editions, none of which preserves the tradition in its entirety and, therefore, none of which can be authoritative alone.[44]

The new model for which he advocated must include insights similar to empirical models found in Tigay's volume—that is, insights from "the reality of textual plurality"—as well as the empirical models from the study of oral traditions not found in Tigay's volume.

Rezetko also encountered Tigay's volume during his doctoral studies and was especially influenced by its text-critical arguments. In his dissertation, he used text-critical conclusions to inform his redactional arguments.[45] In his publications related to historical linguistics, he has applied analogous empirical models to critique the consensus model of Early Biblical Hebrew and Late Biblical Hebrew.[46] His work in histori-

---

43. For his use of the study of oral traditions, see especially Person, *Deuteronomic History and the Book of Chronicles*. For conversation analysis, see especially Raymond F. Person Jr., *In Conversation with Jonah: Conversation Analysis, Literary Criticism, and the Book of Jonah*, JSOTSup 220 (Sheffield: Sheffield Academic, 1996).

44. Person, *Deuteronomic History and the Book of Chronicles*, 171–72.

45. Robert Rezetko, *Source and Revision in the Narratives of David's Transfer of the Ark: Text, Language, and Story in 2 Samuel 6 and 1 Chronicles 13, 15–16*, LHBOTS 470 (New York: T&T Clark, 2007). Rezetko referred to Tigay's *Empirical Models for Biblical Criticism* (Rezetko, *Source and Revision*, 55 n. 52) and Tov's "Composition of 1 Samuel 16–18" (Rezetko, *Source and Revision*, 32 n. 106, 36 n. 131). See also Rezetko, "David over Saul in MT 2 Samuel 6,1–5: An Exercise in Textual and Literary Criticism," in *For and Against David: Story and History in the Books of Samuel*, ed. A. Graeme Auld and Erik Eynikel, BETL 232 (Leuven: Peeters, 2010), 255–71, which applies a similar sort of textual-exegetical argumentation.

46. The following contributions stress the relevance of *empirical* manuscript evidence when addressing linguistic developments in ancient Hebrew: Robert Rezetko, "Dating Biblical Hebrew: Evidence from Samuel–Kings and Chronicles," in *Biblical Hebrew: Studies in Chronology and Typology*, ed. Ian Young, JSOTSup 369 (London: T&T Clark, 2003), 242–45; Rezetko, "'Late' Common Nouns in the Book of Chronicles," in *Reflection and Refraction: Studies in Biblical Historiography in Honour of A. Graeme*

cal linguistics has found its most comprehensive expression in his publications coauthored with Ian Young and Martin Ehrensvärd. In *Linguistic Dating of Biblical Texts*, Young, Rezetko, and Ehrensvärd utilized as empirical controls data from different textual recensions and parallel biblical texts (especially Samuel–Kings and Chronicles) as well as various nonbiblical writings, such as Hebrew inscriptions and Qumran and rabbinic writings.[47] In *Historical Linguistics and Biblical Hebrew*, Rezetko and Young argued for the integration of linguistic, textual, and literary data when analyzing linguistic developments in Classical Hebrew, including also empirical ancient manuscript evidence and contemporary historical linguistic methodologies utilized in studies of premodern varieties of other languages such as English, French, and Spanish.[48] Based on their analysis of such empirical models for linguistic analysis, Young, Rezetko, and Ehrensvärd concluded that

> scholars of the language of the Hebrew Bible must take seriously the text-critical dimension in their research on chronological layers in BH [Biblical Hebrew] and in their efforts to date biblical texts on a linguistic basis. Linguistic analysis cannot afford to ignore scholarly consensuses about the Hebrew Bible's literary complexity and textual fluidity. Assigning dates to biblical *texts* on the basis of linguistic analysis stands at odds with text-critical perspectives on those *texts*. Textual stability is a fundamental premise of the linguistic dating of biblical texts, yet the extant evidence shows that ancient texts of the Bible were characterised by textual *instability*.[49]

Auld, ed. Robert Rezetko, Timothy H. Lim, and W. Brian Aucker, VTSup 113 (Leiden: Brill, 2007), 398; Rezetko, "What Happened to the Book of Samuel in the Persian Period and Beyond?," in *A Palimpsest: Rhetoric, Ideology, Stylistics and Language Relating to Persian Israel*, ed. Ehud Ben Zvi, Diana V. Edelman, and Frank H. Polak, PHSC 5 (Piscataway, NJ: Gorgias, 2009), 239–41; Rezetko, "The Spelling of 'Damascus' and the Linguistic Dating of Biblical Texts," *SJOT* 24 (2010), 124–26; Rezetko, "Diachrony in Biblical Hebrew: Review of an Approach from the Perspective of Paraleipomenon," *HS* 52 (2011): 402–5; Rezetko, "The Qumran Scrolls of the Book of Judges: Literary Formation, Textual Criticism, and Historical Linguistics," *JHS* 13 (2013): 1–68 (passim).

47. Ian Young, Robert Rezetko, and Martin Ehrensvärd, *Linguistic Dating of Biblical Texts*, 2 vols., BibleWorld (London: Equinox, 2008).

48. Robert Rezetko and Ian Young, *Historical Linguistics and Biblical Hebrew: Steps Toward an Integrated Approach*, ANEM 9 (Atlanta: SBL Press, 2014).

49. Young, Rezetko, and Ehrensvärd, *Linguistic Dating of Biblical Texts*, 1:359 (emphasis original).

This conclusion betrays the influence of the type of text-critical empirical models found in Tigay's volume and applies it to their criticism of the generally accepted approach to historical linguistic analysis of Biblical Hebrew for the purpose of dating biblical writings.[50]

Our own intellectual journey as influenced by Tigay's empirical models mirrors Tigay's own journey to some extent. That is, Tigay's own intellectual journey led him from providing in his earlier work "an empirical basis of the Documentary Hypothesis"—that is, providing external support for the Documentary Hypothesis by undercutting its critics' arguments—to reflecting more on the broader methodological implications of his empirical models. However, whereas Tigay continued to support the Documentary Hypothesis based on source criticism on the basis of his empirical models, we have been led to critique the efficacy of source and redaction criticism further, thereby directly challenging the methodological approaches used by biblical scholars. In other words, the rhetorical force of Tigay's volume, which seems to be confirmed in Tigay's later work and Friedman's foreword to the reprinted edition, understands the ambiguous title as *Empirical Models for [the Validity of] Biblical Criticism [as Commonly Practiced by Source and Redaction Critics]*. In contrast, we have emphasized Tigay's cautionary comments even further than Tigay himself, which can be represented as *Empirical Models for [Placing Limits on] Biblical Criticism*.

However, we are not alone in exploring further how empirical models suggest real limits on source and redaction criticism. Here we summarize what we understand as the two most significant publications that explicitly explore empirical models in an effort to refine source and redaction criticism within plausible limits, specifically David Carr's *The Formation of the Hebrew Bible* and Reinhard Müller, Juha Pakkala, and Bas ter Haar Romeny's *Evidence of Editing*.[51]

Part 1 of Carr's *The Formation of the Hebrew Bible* is an extensive review of documented transmission of ancient texts that have survived

50. Although Young, Rezetko, and Ehrensvärd refer to Tigay's volume only once (see ibid., 1:343 n. 7), elsewhere in their book they refer many times to the text-critical work of Cogan, Rofé, and Tov, who contributed to Tigay's volume.

51. David M. Carr, *The Formation of the Hebrew Bible: A New Reconstruction* (New York: Oxford University Press, 2011); Reinhard Müller, Juha Pakkala, and Bas ter Haar Romeny, *Evidence of Editing: Growth and Change of Texts in the Hebrew Bible*, RBS 75 (Atlanta: Society of Biblical Literature, 2014).

in multiple copies. Carr often cites Tigay's *Empirical Models for Biblical Criticism* and also his related volume *The Evolution of the Gilgamesh Epic*[52] on the general method of empirical study as well as on particular points of the texts that he studied. Analogues, duplicates, and indicators of textual growth (e.g., doublets) are the foundation of Carr's reconstruction of the Bible's formation. But he also recognizes some limitations to his method. For example, "documented cases of transmission history ... show that texts that are the result of textual growth do not consistently preserve enough traces of that growth in their final form for scholars to reconstruct each and every stage of that growth," because "their authors often worked from memory in incorporating earlier texts"[53] and "documented cases of transmission history also suggest that such indicators are easily lost in the process of gradual growth of texts, both in the initial processing of separate documents and in subsequent scribal smoothing of the marks that once indicated their separate existence."[54] That is, Carr argued that his empirical models strongly suggest that the efficacy of source and redaction criticism must be called into question.[55] However, he nevertheless identifies what he called a "trend toward expansion"—that is, in the long-duration literary texts he analyzed, he saw a tendency towards recording in the written tradition more and more of what earlier had been preserved primarily in the collective mind of the community.[56]

Müller, Pakkala, and Ter Haar Romeny's *Evidence of Editing* cited Tigay's book as the origin of "empirical" in connection with textual evidence.[57] They argued by way of fifteen sets of passages that are preserved

---

52. Jeffrey H. Tigay, *The Evolution of the Gilgamesh Epic* (Philadelphia: University of Pennsylvania Press, 1982; repr., Wauconda, IL: Bolchazy-Carducci, 2002).

53. Carr, *Formation of the Hebrew Bible*, 4.

54. Ibid., 106.

55. Despite his own conclusions, part 2 of Carr's work is his discussion of the formation of the Bible in the genre of a standard (German-style) introduction that describes in detail the historical origins of the biblical books or their constituent parts and how they changed over time. That is, although his stated method in part 1 undercuts conventional methods of source and redaction criticism, his conclusions concerning the literary history of the Bible continue to look very much like the results of source and redaction criticism, often without explicit empirical models as controls.

56. Carr, *Formation of the Hebrew Bible*, 65–72.

57. Müller, Pakkala, and Ter Haar Romeny, *Evidence of Editing*, 1 n. 1. Other works of interest by these authors are Juha Pakkala, *God's Word Omitted: Omissions in the Transmission of the Hebrew Bible*, FRLANT 251 (Göttingen: Vandenhoeck &

in more than one version that empirical evidence demonstrates substantial editing in the Bible's literary formation. When they focused on the methodological implications of their empirical models, they explicitly noted contradictory tendencies:

> In other words, the evidence points in two opposing directions. Some example texts show that it is possible to gain reliable results by using the literary-critical method. Other example texts, however, indicate that some editorial alterations would be very difficult or impossible to detect, especially many minor changes that nevertheless may affect the meaning substantially. These limitations should be acknowledged in all reconstructions of the literary prehistory.[58]

For example, they provide empirical examples that create "disturbing repetitions" but also those that reduce such repetitions from older versions by omission[59] as well as some examples that create inconsistencies but others that remove such inconsistencies.[60] They also provide examples in which the "rule" *lectio brevior potior* ("the shorter reading is stronger") applies or does not.[61] Despite such contradictory conclusions, their discussions remain chock-full of what they call "discernible traces"[62] of scribal techniques and editorial processes that provide "empirical evidence" for "reliable results." These discernible traces can be summarized in three main points, two specific and one general: (1) "disturbing repetitions" of words and phrases and especially *Wiederaufnahme*, or "resumptive repetition";[63] (2) "grammatical problems" and other linguistic phenomena that involve "unusual wording" or are "syntactically

---

Ruprecht, 2013); and Reinhard Müller and Juha Pakkala, eds., *Insights into Editing in the Hebrew Bible and the Ancient Near East: What Does Documented Evidence Tell Us about the Transmission of Authoritative Texts?*, CBET 84 (Leuven: Peeters, forthcoming).

58. Müller, Pakkala, and Ter Haar Romeny, *Evidence of Editing*, 222–23 (see further 221–25).

59. Ibid., e.g., 36 versus 68.

60. Ibid., e.g., 47–52 versus 184–87.

61. Ibid., 90, 98, 144 n. 4 versus 71, 76–77.

62. Ibid., "discernible traces" on 12, 177, 224–25; "trace(s)" on 15, 43–44, 85 n. 18, 144, 207, 221, 225.

63. Ibid., 21–25, 36–37, 66–68, 84, 103–5, 108, 112, 124, 131–32, 135–37, 139–40, 184–86, 216.

disturbing" or "stylistically awkward";[64] and, finally, (3) the two preceding "traces" and a large array of less well-defined phenomena upset the "literary unity" of the text under consideration.[65] Thus, even though they document empirical examples that provide contradictory conclusions concerning the efficacy of source and redaction criticism based on these discernible traces, the end result continues to be some faith in the very types of discernible traces in Tigay's empirical models, which have been used to support the efficacy of source and redaction criticism. Our estimation of this work by Müller, Pakkala, and Ter Haar Romeny is that, on the one hand, when they are explicitly discussing limitations of the efficacy of source and redaction criticism, they reach some extremely important insights concerning the contradictory evidence produced by their empirical models; however, on the other hand, they continue to apply the same criteria used in source and redaction criticism for many years as somehow supported by the contradictory evidence.

4. The Need for a Reassessment of the Efficacy of Source and Redaction Criticism

Often under the influence of Tigay's empirical models, a variety of scholars have recognized the need for a reassessment of the efficacy of source and redaction criticism and some (especially Carr and Müller, Pakkala, and

64. Ibid., 22, 33, 36–37, 43, 48, 56, 64–65, 72–74, 76–77, 79, 83–87, 107, 111–12, 115, 139–40, 146–47, 151, 157, 172, 174, 177, 182–83, 203, 221.

65. Müller, Pakkala, and Ter Haar Romeny do not use the phrase "literary unity"; however, they do mention "the unity of the text" (ibid., 65), "[t]he compositional unity" (ibid.), and "an integral unity" (166). They also speak once about the "uniformity ... of texts" (93). Nevertheless, the issue of "literary unity" is continuously under consideration on nearly every page of the volume. It is replete with nouns (and/or related adjectival or verbal forms) such as "confusion," "contradiction(s)," "digression(s)," "disturbance," "incoherence," "inconsistency(ies)," "interruption," "irregularity," "roughness," "tension(s)," and more general words such as "difference(s)" and "problem(s)," that are applied not only to the "disturbing repetitions" and "grammatical problems" of the texts under consideration, but also to other aspects of the texts such as their concepts (themes, topics), tendencies, perspectives, contexts, logic, theology, and so on. All of these phenomena which upset the "literary unity" of the text are described with adjectives and other words such as "abrupt," "awkward," "confusing," "different," "disturbing," "interrupted," "redundant," "sudden," "superfluous," "unnecessary," "unusual," and so on.

Ter Haar Romeny) have begun that reassessment. However, the results of these reassessments often seem to confirm the current practice of source and redaction criticism, if not in theory certainly in practice. This is especially the case with Müller, Pakkala, and Ter Haar Romeny, who continue to support the use of "discernible traces" as criteria for source and redaction criticism. Thus, the title of this volume eliminates the ambiguity in the title of Tigay's volume and explicitly focuses on *Empirical Models Challenging Biblical Criticism* [*as Commonly Practiced by Source and Redaction Critics*]. That is, the empirical models of the current volume, when taken together, caution against the kind of excessive conclusions often reached by source and redaction critics in the absence of such empirical controls and rather advocate for a much more modest expectation of the historical critical methods.

The empirical models found in Tigay's *Empirical Models for Biblical Criticism* and similar studies have clearly demonstrated that many ancient texts are composite texts with a complex literary history. That is, the vast majority of literary texts—that is, those writings that were written and transmitted as cultural objects rather than personal documents (such as contracts)—were the result of various authors and/or editors. Yet these same studies have also illustrated that the composition and transmission processes that produced such composite texts sometimes, even often, erased the types of visible signs that are necessary for the accurate application of the methods of source and redaction criticism. In some cases, short of conflicting textual data, we would not recognize that texts are actually composite. Furthermore, other empirical models have demonstrated that the types of visible signs that underlie literary-critical study can also be found in texts that are clearly produced by one writer, containing one source.

The chapters in this book explore various aspects of empirical models and their methods and conclusions. In some cases, well-known models are applied and vindicated, but at other times their efficacy is questioned. In a few cases new models are made use of or at least receive more attention than in previous studies. The studies as a whole are intended to complement and challenge previous studies, the latter in the sense that they contest a model's assumptions, methods, or conclusions or bring several different models into conversation and conflict with one another.

The ten chapters that follow relate to the literature of Mesopotamia, the Hebrew Bible, the sectarian Dead Sea Scrolls, and the New Testament, representing a similar breadth of studies as found in Tigay's earlier volume.[66] Regarding the Hebrew Bible, the major versions figure prominently (MT, SP, LXX, and the biblical DSS), and each major section of the canon is represented: Pentateuch (Schorch, Lemmelijn), Prophets (Trebolle Barrera, Person, Rezetko), and Writings (Person, Young). Some of the specific texts and topics addressed are described in the following abstracts. The chapters are organized generally in chronological and/or canonical order.

Sara Milstein, in "Outsourcing Gilgamesh," considers manuscript evidence for two originally independent Sumerian stories, Gilgamesh and Huwawa and Gilgamesh, Enkidu, and the Netherworld, which were incorporated at distinct points in the Standard Babylonian Gilgamesh Epic. She describes two different methods for the reuse of sources in an extended work, one where a source is transferred faithfully, only lightly revised, so that its content and wording may remain readily identifiable, and another where the source is radically transformed, very heavily revised, so that its independent origin and earlier wording may have vanished. She concludes by discussing several potential implications of her findings for understanding scribal methods in the production of biblical literature and the book of Judges in particular.

Alan Lenzi, in "Scribal Revision and Textual Variation in Akkadian *Šuila*-Prayers: Two Case Studies in Ritual Adaptation," examines manuscripts of two well-attested Akkadian religious texts, the "'hand-lifting' prayers" Gula 1a = Belet-ili 1 and Sîn 1. Though the surviving texts of these prayers are situated in time and place and though they furnish tangible evidence for scribal revision, an analysis of the textual variants and of other stylistic and theological phenomena proves inconclusive for determining exactly when, how, and why the texts were changed. He contrasts how much we know about the origins of these texts versus how little we know about the origins of the texts of the Bible, and he suggests that the results of the present study are a sobering caution to those who would engage in detailed reconstruction of the historical development of biblical writings.

Stefan Schorch, in "Dissimilatory Reading and the Making of Biblical Texts: The Jewish Pentateuch and the Samaritan Pentateuch," accentuates the complex interaction of textual and oral factors in the late stages of development of biblical texts. Not only were different written texts spoken

66. We deeply regret the absence of a chapter on postbiblical Jewish literature. That chapter was commissioned but, unfortunately, had to be dropped in order not to delay the publication of this book any longer.

differently, but different oral reading traditions of a single consonantal framework could bring about two different written texts. He illustrates this phenomenon in a selection of passages from the books of Genesis (and Exodus), especially Jacob's blessing in Gen 49:5–7. He argues that, in the examples under consideration, the readers who wrote the SP (and LXX), compared to the MT, read the consonantal framework differently, and this in turn led to a different written account arising from the same earlier written source.

Bénédicte Lemmelijn, in "Text-Critically Studying the Biblical Manuscript Evidence: An 'Empirical' Entry to the Literary Composition of the Text," elaborates a model for researching the history of biblical texts, one which rests first and foremost on textual criticism and which involves the collection, registration, description, and evaluation of the Hebrew and Greek witnesses to biblical texts. She argues that textual criticism should take priority over source and redaction criticism and that in fact a text-critical approach challenges the traditional view of distinctive phases in the literary production (composition and transmission) of texts. She illustrates the method in a discussion of a section of the Plague Narrative in Exodus (Exod 11:2–3). She concludes that in this text the MT contains the majority of preferable readings compared to the DSS, SP, and LXX. Furthermore, her text-critical analysis highlights some of the literary and theological concerns that led these other texts to diverge from the MT.

Julio Trebolle Barrera, in "Division Markers as Empirical Evidence for the Editorial Growth of Biblical Books," shows that the placements of these late markers in many places in these books frequently converge with the results of experienced literary-critical analysis, which concluded independently that a passage had been inserted in or after another one or moved to a different location. Consequently such concrete data for editorial activity in the formation of biblical writings should not be ignored in literary-critical research or by modern commentators and editors. More often than not, he underlines a late insertion or later arrangement in the MT compared to other textual witnesses.

Raymond Person, in "The Problem of 'Literary Unity' from the Perspective of the Study of Oral Traditions," contextualizes the formation of biblical literature in the comparative study of oral traditions and literary texts with roots in oral traditions, in particular Homeric and Serbo-Croatian epics. He argues that modern notions of literary unity that assume "linguistic unity" and "consistency of story" may be anachronistic when applied to ancient literary texts. He illustrates this in a discussion of several differences between the parallel passages 2 Sam 7 and 1 Chr 17, both of which can be regarded as incomplete instantiations of a selection of the broader tradition that was preserved in the collective memory of the ancient community that wrote those texts.

Robert Rezetko, in "The (Dis)Connection between Textual and Linguistic Developments in the Book of Jeremiah: Hebrew Bible Textual Criticism Challenges Biblical Hebrew Historical Linguistics," brings into conversation two research models, the first textual and the second linguistic, which seldom interact with one another and which have resulted in conflicting conclusions about the production of the book of Jeremiah, especially the time when that occurred. He argues that the surviving manuscript evidence favors the conventional literary-critical conclusion that the book gradually formed throughout the centuries of the Second Temple period. On the other hand, the efficacy of linguistic evidence for dating the production of this and other biblical writings is thrown into doubt, since observation of language usage in biblical and other literature suggests that late authors and editors could, and often did, use "early" language.

Ian Young's "The Original Problem: The Old Greek and the Masoretic Text of Daniel 5" evaluates three explanations for the highly variant Hebrew and Greek texts of Dan 5: the MT and the Old Greek (OG) are expansions of a common core text, the MT and/or the OG is a substantial rewrite of an earlier written version, or the OG and the MT are independent renditions of a common oral tradition. Based on, first, the recognized importance of oral traditions alongside written traditions for (preprinting press) story collections and, second, the small number of actual verbatim parallels between the two texts, the third explanation is preferred for the MT and OG of Dan 5. In other words, there may not be a direct relationship between the two texts of Dan 5; in effect there never was a common base text, each is a text without an original.

Maxine Grossman, in "Community Rule or Community Rules: Examining a Supplementary Approach in Light of the Sectarian Dead Sea Scrolls," considers three distinct types of textual variation in the eleven Qumran copies of the Serek Hayaḥad (1QS, 4QS255–264), and she ponders the significance of the differences between the manuscripts for our understanding of original texts and textual formation in an ancient Jewish setting. In particular, the textual profiles of the surviving copies of the Community Rule problematize any simplistic notion of linear evolutionary development from earlier texts to later ones, since the supplementation that is encountered is one of addition (or expansion) and subtraction (or contraction). More generally, the manuscripts of the Community Rule are evidence for a situation of simultaneous textual diversity in which it is possible that each distinct edition of the rule was understood as saying "the same thing."

Joseph Weaks, in "Limited Efficacy in Reconstructing the Gospel Sources for Matthew and Luke," evaluates the chance that the hypothetical source Q, which scholars have reconstructed from Matthew and Luke, is a reliable reconstruction. To test that possibility, he reconstructs Mark from Matthew and Luke—it is widely believed that Matthew and Luke used both Q and Mark as sources—and then compares the reconstructed MarQ to the actual Mark. It turns out that MarQ is a very poor representation of Mark. The reconstruction of a source, whether Q, MarQ, or otherwise, is a tenuous undertaking. In particular, the present analogy problematizes the way in which the reconstructed Q is used as a source for studying Christian origins.

5. Conclusions on the Efficacy of Source and Redaction Criticism

What follows is our assessment of the efficacy of source and redaction criticism based on our reading of previous studies as well as our synthesis of the individual chapters included in this volume. As such, we acknowledge that some of these conclusions may go further than the conclusions reached by some of the individual contributors to the volume. Nevertheless, these conclusions are our interpretation of the rhetorical force of our edited volume as a collective.

Like Tigay and other earlier studies using empirical models, many of the chapters provide empirical evidence for the composite character of texts in the Bible. This observation should not be the least bit surprising, since the composite character of biblical writings is widely accepted in scholarship. In fact, because of the strong influence of textual criticism on the contributors, none of them suggest that any of the extant texts can be understood as the original text and generally reject the very idea of ever constructing an original text, due to the characteristics of textual fluidity and textual plurality. This is especially obvious in the chapters by Milstein, Trebolle Barrera, and Grossman, all three of whom discuss how the textual fluidity of their respective texts allows for the transposition of entire passages into various locations within those texts in a modular fashion. Young goes one step further, suggesting that the most plausible explanation of the relationship of the OG and MT of Dan 5 is not to be found in a *literary* relationship based on one original text but on the basis of two independent textual traditions, both of which represent the oral tradition behind the texts.

Like Tigay and others, some of the chapters point to possible discernible traces of sources and redactional layers. However, none of the contributors explicitly suggest that any of these traces can be used without other empirical controls in the application of source and/or redaction criticism with any significant degree of certainty. For example, although Trebolle Barrera often refers to *Wiederaufnahme*, it is always in combination with the placement of the late markers dividing manuscripts into sections. Furthermore, nowhere does he conclude that the presence of any of these late markers, *Wiederaufnahme*, or the two combined necessarily indicates an insertion, because he notes the tremendous fluidity of the texts and the sometimes inconsistent use of such late markers in the different textual traditions. With this caveat, as will be discussed further below, we can conclude that even in these cases *Wiederaufnahme* cannot be understood as a discernible trace, if that term implies an objective criterion that necessarily identifies an insertion. In addition, although Lemmelijn points to literary problems similar to discernible traces, her explicit methodology requires not only a combination of textual criticism and redaction criticism but the priority of textual criticism as a control on redactional arguments.

Like Carr's assessment that "such indicators are easily lost in the process of gradual growth of texts,"[67] some of the chapters explicitly note the complexity of the literary history of the text, a complexity that would too easily eliminate many discernible traces. Of course, this problem was already implicit in Tigay's volume, especially in the chapter by Yair Zakovitch on assimilation and harmonization. That is, if a redactor's tendency for harmonization was especially high, then the very process of harmonization would eliminate many (if not, all) of the discernible traces assumed to be found in composite texts. In this volume, Lemmelijn also provides empirical evidence of harmonization, but she can only do so on the basis of textual variation—that is, any discernible traces were removed in the very process of harmonization. Milstein discusses the same process in the incorporation of the source Gilgamesh and Huwawa into the Gilgamesh Epic, leading her to conclude as follows: "Source content *could* be com-

67. Carr, *Formation of the Hebrew Bible*, 106.

pletely rewritten."[68] Thus, some of the empirical models suggest that discernible traces are sometimes lacking in composite texts.

Like Müller, Pakkala, and Ter Haar Romeny, some of the chapters point to "opposing directions."[69] As just noted, Lemmelijn points to harmonizing tendencies in the Plague Narrative in Exodus. In contrast, Schorch demonstrates the opposite tendency in the passage about Jacob's blessing in Genesis—that is, "dissimilatory reading" of even the exact same consonantal framework could lead to different vocalizing/pointing of the consonantal framework and/or changes in the consonantal framework itself. Certainly, Lemmelijn and Schorch allow for these opposing tendencies to occur in different texts and even within the same text within different communities in various historical periods of the texts' development. Nevertheless, the presence of these opposing tendencies creates problems for the efficacy of source and redaction criticism. Even more challenging are the conclusions by Grossman and Milstein, both of whom see opposing tendencies within the *same* textual tradition. Grossman's conclusion contradicts the often dichotomous assumption that redaction occurred according to a block/modular method of combining sources or according to a method of supplementation. Grossman gives evidence of both types of redactional development in her analysis of the Community Rule of Qumran: "Unlike my earlier examples, which reflected a practice of modular addition and subtraction, the form of supplementation that we encounter here is one of expansion and contraction, in which a simpler and a more complex version of the same text appears in parallel manuscript witnesses."[70] Note that even within both of these types of redactional development Grossman sees *opposing directions*, *addition and subtraction*, and *expansion and contraction*. Within the long literary history of the Gilgamesh Epic, Milstein concludes: "On the one hand, we have evidence of a source that has been transformed completely already in the first identifiable phase of transmission. Subsequently, however, that plotline became comparatively more stable. On the other hand, we have evidence of a source that is represented in near-identical form after a thousand years."[71] Thus, both Grossman and Milstein provide us with empirical evidence of opposing directions within the same literary text and its tradition. This should warn us against making

68. Milstein in this volume, 58 (emphasis added).

69. Müller, Pakkala, and Ter Haar Romeny, *Evidence of Editing*, 222.

70. Grossman in this volume, 314.

71. Milstein in this volume, 59.

too much of any such tendencies as providing us with any type of *objective* means to identify sources and redactional layers based on discernible traces and on our assumptions about scribal tendencies.

As noted above, despite such contradictory evidence in their empirical data, Müller, Pakkala, and Ter Haar Romeny nevertheless conclude that source and redaction criticism, at least for some texts, can be successfully applied when "discernible traces" are found, presumably even without (other) empirical evidence. Repeating what we said above, these discernible traces fall into three categories: (1) "disturbing repetitions" of words and phrases and especially *Wiederaufnahme* or resumptive repetition; (2) "grammatical problems" and other linguistic phenomena that involve "unusual wording" or are "syntactically disturbing" or "stylistically awkward"; and finally, (3) the two preceding "traces" and a large array of less well-defined phenomena upset the "literary unity" of the text under consideration. Therefore, even though in some ways Müller, Pakkala, and Ter Haar Romeny seem to undercut the efficacy of source and redaction criticism, they nevertheless conclude that these three types of discernible traces remain in some texts in the Bible, thereby defending the efficacy of source and redaction criticism as applied to these texts. Consequently, it seems appropriate for us to be explicit about these three types of what they identify as discernible traces in terms of how the collective voice of this volume critiques these discernible traces. Before turning to the evidence that challenges the efficacy of each of these three types, we should repeat that the contributors in this volume assert that most (if not all) of the books in the Bible are composite texts and provide empirical models that sometimes point to the possible efficacy of these discernible traces *when paired with text-critical variants and other empirical data*. However, as we will see, this does not suggest that these types of discernible traces alone—that is, without text-critical variants—can be successfully used to identify, with certainty, sources and redactional layers. Furthermore, even text-critical variants do not provide completely objective evidence, because there is always a certain degree of subjectivity to text-critical conclusions as well.

For over one hundred years, first in classical studies and later in biblical studies, *Wiederaufnahme*, or resumptive repetition, has been recognized as a practice used by ancient scribes to denote that an insertion has occurred.[72] An example confirmed by text-critical variants is found in the

72. For further critique of *Wiederaufnahme* as a discernible trace, see Raymond F.

comparison of the MT and LXX of Jer 27:19–22, where the editor of the (proto-)MT of Jeremiah inserted verses 19b–21 and repeated the phrase immediately preceding the insertion: "19 For thus said the Lord (of Hosts … 21 Thus said the Lord of Hosts, the God of Israel, concerning the vessels…)."[73] Tigay referred to *Wiederaufnahme* as empirical evidence and Müller, Pakkala, and Ter Haar Romeny make frequent use of *Wiederaufnahme* as a discernible trace.[74] Similarly, in this volume Trebolle Barrera uses *Wiederaufnahme* in combination with later division markers to suggest a possible insertion.[75] Their use of *Wiederaufnahme* has its roots in the study of the Greek classics but was used in biblical studies first in 1929 by Harold Wiener, who described "resumptive repetition" in his search for "discernible marks and signs," and was discussed systematically in 1952 by Curt Kuhl, who sought "somewhat objective aids."[76] Unfortunately, none of the chapters in this volume contain empirical models explicitly challenging *Wiederaufnahme*, but earlier publications have clearly addressed the problem of assuming that *Wiederaufnahme* alone can provide evidence of an insertion on the basis of what in hindsight fits Tigay's notion of *empirical* data. Therefore, we will review these previous studies briefly here. As early as 1962, Isac Leo Seeligmann posed the problem of how one could identify *Wiederaufnahme* from what he called "Pseudo-*Wiederaufnahme*," because he noted that such repetition can simply be a literary device of the original author, thereby complicating what had been seen as an objective criterion.[77] In his attempt to overcome this complication,

---

Person Jr., "A Reassessment of Wiederaufnahme from the Perspective of Conversation Analysis," *BZ* 43 (1999): 241–48.

73. This example is from Tov, "Literary History of the Book of Jeremiah," 235 and is cited by Trebolle Barrera in this volume, 181–82.

74. Tigay, "Evolution of the Pentateuchal Narratives," 48–49; Tigay, "Conflation as a Redactional Technique," 74 n. 46; Müller, Pakkala, and Ter Haar Romeny, *Evidence of Editing*, 22–25, 67–68, 103–4, 108, 131, 139–40, 186.

75. Trebolle Barrera in this volume, 174, 181–83, 189, 197, 201, 203, 205–6, 208.

76. Harold M. Wiener, *The Composition of Judges II 11 to I Kings II 46* (Leipzig: Heinrichs, 1929), 2; Curt Kuhl, "Die 'Wiederaufnahme'—ein literarkritisches Prinzip?," *ZAW* 64 (1952): 11.

77. Isac Leo Seeligmann, "Hebräische Erzählung und biblische Geschichtsschreibung," *TZ* 18 (1962): 305–25. See similarly, Henry Van Dyke Parunak, "Oral Typesetting: Some Uses of Biblical Structure," *Bib* 62 (1981): 153–68; Michael Fishbane, *Biblical Interpretation in Ancient Israel* (Oxford: Oxford University Press, 1985), 85–86.

Urban C. von Wahlde suggested four criteria that can be used to identify *Wiederaufnahme* as a redactional marker:

> Firstly, there is the presence of awkward repetition. The more extensive and the more awkward the repetition is, the more likely it is that we are dealing with redactional repetition. It is also significant if the repetition cannot be shown to serve some other clear function within the text. Secondly, the presence of phrases which have no other function than to resume or which are awkward in the text.... Thirdly, the intervening material contains "*aporiai*," literary features which are either inconsistent with or contradictory to the surrounding context. These can be "literary" in the general sense, or stylistic or theological. Fourthly, the "primitive" sequences attained by the excision of the supposed addition must make reasonable sense. In some cases, in fact, the resulting original sequence makes much better sense than the text as we now have it. In a given text, these factors will be present in varying degrees and so the text must be judged individually. However the presence of a majority of them would be a strong indication that the material has in fact been edited.[78]

Of course, von Wahlde's solution has effectively eliminated *Wiederaufnahme* as an efficacious discernible trace by itself—that is, as a discernible trace, it has no independence apart from using problems with literary unity as discernible traces. That is, *even without* the presence of *Wiederaufnahme*, many redaction critics would use von Wahlde's four criteria based on problems with literary unity to suggest a redactional insertion. Although Müller, Pakkala, and Ter Haar Romeny refer briefly to Kuhl's work on *Wiederaufnahme*, they appear to be unaware of Seeligmann's and others' critique of the efficacy of *Wiederaufnahme* as a reliable discernible trace.[79] However, in our judgment, *Wiederaufnahme* by itself cannot be understood as a reliable discernible trace. That is, although there is ample empirical evidence that *Wiederaufnahme* is sometimes such a discernible trace, there is also ample empirical evidence of what Seeligmann called "Pseudo-*Wiederaufnahme*" that was a literary device used by a single author.[80]

---

78. Urban C. von Wahlde, "Wiederaufnahme as a Marker of Redaction in Jn 6,51–58," *Bib* 64 (1983): 546.

79. Müller, Pakkala, and Ter Haar Romeny, *Evidence of Editing*, 22 n. 5, 67 n. 19, 103 n. 3.

80. For an analysis of how *Wiederaufnahme* is one of many similar so-called literary strategies, all of which are adaptations of a conversational practice called "restarts,"

At first glance the criterion of what Müller, Pakkala, and Ter Haar Romeny called "grammatical problems" seems to have a much better chance of control on our source and redactional conclusions, especially since historical linguistics has proven to be such a useful tool in other areas of literary study.[81] However, this criterion is challenged by some of the contributors in this volume. Rezetko, sometimes in collaboration with Young and Ehrensvärd, has published a variety of works criticizing the linguistic dating of biblical writings,[82] and his chapter in this volume continues to challenge the value of linguistic variation in Biblical Hebrew, especially between so-called early and late linguistic variants, as an empirical control for dating literary sources and redactional layers or establishing a relative chronology of biblical writings. Their challenge to linguistic dating has attracted its critics and one of the criticisms is that there is no evidence of literature produced by a single individual that contains such linguistic variety as found in the Bible, what Ziony Zevit labeled "an odd construct."[83] That is, Zevit and others assume that a high degree of linguistic variety within a text is often evidence of a composite text that lends itself well to analysis by source and redaction criticism in that early and late forms can help identify the relative chronology of the various redactional layers and sources. Person's chapter in this volume provides empirical evidence of just such "an odd construct" by drawing from the comparative study of oral traditions in which the traditional register of an oral tradition can actually be characterized by a blending of different linguistic forms (dialectical and historical) as a way of implying its universality within that tradition. Thus, if biblical texts have roots in oral traditions, then biblical texts may contain linguistic diversity that is the result of the same author or redactor using a traditional register. Such cases complicate the ability to discern different sources and redactional layers based on grammatical problems. Although

---

see Raymond F. Person Jr., *From Conversation to Oral Tradition: A Simplest Systematics for Oral Traditions*, RSRS 10 (London: Taylor & Francis, 2016).

81. We have chosen to focus here on the issue of language variation and change and linguistic diachrony, but there are other kinds of grammatical problems which we could address, such as the use of, for example, so-called Deuteronomistic or Priestly language in editorial adjustments and redactional layers. However, many of these such "problems" are also "problems" of literary unity.

82. Young, Rezetko, and Ehrensvärd, *Linguistic Dating of Biblical Texts*; Rezetko and Young, *Historical Linguistics and Biblical Hebrew*.

83. Ziony Zevit, review of *Biblical Hebrew: Studies in Chronology and Typology*, ed. Ian Young, *RBL* 8 (2004): 13.

it is certainly possible that sources and redactional layers in the composite texts of the Bible may have different linguistic profiles, Rezetko argues that our current insufficient knowledge of the linguistic history of ancient Hebrew[84] complicates this task, and Person argues that, even if we had sufficient knowledge, we must allow the possibility that the same author or redactor may use various linguistic forms for stylistic purposes. Therefore, grammatical problems are ineffective as discernible traces.[85]

As we noted above, von Wahlde's solution to the problem of "Pseudo-*Wiederaufnahme*" was simply to discern problems of literary unity created by an insertion. This tactic is very similar to Müller, Pakkala, and Ter Haar Romeny's, when they identify such *literary* problems as "contradictions," "digressions," "inconsistencies," "tensions," and so on. Of course, this is a common criterion used in source and redaction criticism and some contributors to this volume also note correctly how insertions may compromise the literary unity of a text. However, various contributors directly question the appropriateness of our modern notions of literary unity as a standard for discerning when the literary unity of an ancient text has been compromised. This is most explicit in the chapter by Person entitled "The Problem of 'Literary Unity' from the Perspective of the Study of Oral Traditions," but it is commented on by others as well. Lemmelijn notes as follows: "Our modern understanding of logicality need not square with that of the biblical authors and can often be extremely subjective."[86] Lenzi similarly observes: "[W]hen an argument for revision relies exclusively on some inconsistency, tension, or contradiction within the text and there is no other evidence to corroborate this perception, we run the risk of impos-

---

84. Our knowledge is insufficient, first, because of the absence of both early biblical manuscripts and an adequate control corpus of dated and localized extrabiblical sources, and second, because the actual distribution of linguistic data in the extant (late) texts of the Hebrew Bible (biblical DSS, MT, SP) resists an explanation along the lines of simple linear development from so-called Archaic to Early to Transitional to Late Biblical Hebrew. These issues are discussed at length in the volumes cited in n. 82.

85. Müller, Pakkala, and Ter Haar Romeny argue that "late" language betrays late editing (*Evidence of Editing*, 83, 85; see also 86 n. 23); however, elsewhere they argue that late use of "early" language is only "archaizing" rather than truly "archaic" (79 ["imitated older style"], 83-84, 87, 151 ["emulate older poetical texts"]; see also 65). In our opinion, they have not fully grasped the serious difficulty with using historical linguistics as a redactional criterion when late writers and editors could use either "early" or "late" language variants.

86. Lemmelijn in this volume, 132.

ing modern literary expectations on ancient texts and thereby inventing problems to which revision is the solution."[87] If our very notion of literary unity is anachronistic, then what we identify as discernible traces based on that anachronistic understanding not only does not provide some sort of *objective* means for identifying sources and redactional layers but at least in some cases also misleads us in that very effort.

Another of the observations made by Müller, Pakkala, and Ter Haar Romeny finds confirmation in some of the chapters in this volume—that is, their discussion of the important role of omissions in the literary history of the Bible, which undercuts at least to some degree Carr's notion of a "trend toward expansion," which is obviously closely related to the widely accepted principle of *lectio brevior potior* ("the shorter reading is stronger").[88] As Carr himself is aware, a trend is not a hard and fast rule, so the questions of "How strong is this trend?" and "Does this particular text exemplify this trend?" have always been implicit in this notion and the related principle of *lectio brevior potior*. However, drawing substantially from Pakkala's book *God's Word Omitted*, Müller, Pakkala, and Ter Haar Romeny's conclusions nevertheless bring some needed uncertainty to how effective one can be when assuming such a trend while making source-critical and redaction-critical arguments. That is, even if the trend is valid either for the majority of texts or even limited to the later periods of written transmission, the general validity cannot be easily applied to all cases of pluses and minuses in textual traditions. Much like Müller, Pakkala, and Ter Haar Romeny, both Milstein and Grossman provide additional empirical evidence of omissions in the literary history of the texts analyzed. Milstein observes "a major elimination of content," when the source Gilgamesh, Enkidu, and the Netherworld is incorporated into the Gilgamesh Epic.[89] Grossman, in her analysis of the various versions of the Community Rule and other rule texts at Qumran, concludes that

> 1QS appears to represent a more developed and more comprehensive witness to the Qumran Serek tradition than we find in our other key Serek manuscripts. From the perspective of textual transmission, it is therefore fascinating—and not a little bit confounding—to acknowledge

87. Lenzi in this volume, 68.

88. Müller, Pakkala, and Ter Haar Romeny, *Evidence of Editing*, 71, 76–77, 90, 98, 144 n. 4.

89. Milstein in this volume, 57.

> that 1QS has been identified as one of the *earliest* manuscript witnesses to the Serek tradition.[90]

That is, the earliest extant text in the Qumran Serek tradition is also the longest and most comprehensive. Thus, both Milstein and Grossman provide compelling nonbiblical empirical evidence similar to that of Müller, Pakkala, and Ter Haar Romeny concerning omissions.

Thus far, the above summary and conclusions have been structured primarily on the basis of conclusions by Carr and especially Müller, Pakkala, and Ter Haar Romeny in relationship to the efficacy of source and redaction criticism, but we think that the collective force of the volume has further implications, so we will discuss these further conclusions here.

In order for someone to begin to use empirical models, a scholar must first decide what extant texts to compare. Today the comparison of the MT and the LXX of Daniel (Young) or of the MT and SP of Genesis (Schorch), for example, seems rather obvious, but it was not too long ago when the use of the versions was typically dismissed as the versions were understood as "vulgar" or "sectarian" texts with little to contribute to the study of the Bible. That is, before the discovery of the biblical material in the Dead Sea Scrolls, the versions were often considered so aberrant to be generally unworthy of study for the source-critical and redaction-critical study of the Bible. Increasingly the division between *biblical* and *nonbiblical* scrolls at Qumran is being questioned. For example, was the so-called Reworked Pentateuch (4QRP = 4Q158, 4Q364–367) nonbiblical or biblical in the eyes of the Qumran community, especially if the types of variations—additions, omissions, substitutions, and different sequences—are similar to the variations between Exodus and Deuteronomy or between the MT and the SP? Some scholars, such as Eugene Ulrich, are now concluding that the Reworked Pentateuch may "constitute simply a variant literary edition of the Torah, alongside the MT and the SP."[91] This very

90. Grossman in this volume, 320 (emphasis original).

91. Eugene Ulrich, "The Text of the Hebrew Scriptures at the Time of Hillel and Jesus," in *Congress Volume: Basel 2011*, ed. André Lemaire, VTSup 92 (Leiden: Brill, 2002), 102. See also Sidnie White Crawford, *Rewriting Scripture in Second Temple Times*, SDSS (Grand Rapids: Eerdmans, 2008), 56–57; Sarianna Metso, "When the Evidence Does Not Fit: Method, Theory, and the Dead Sea Scrolls," in *Rediscovering the Dead Sea Scrolls: An Assessment of Old and New Approaches and Methods*, ed. Maxine L. Grossman (Grand Rapids: Eerdmans, 2010), 6.

issue is explicitly discussed by some of the contributors to this volume. Lenzi asks, "How do we know two tablets represent the same text?"[92] He then adds:

> [A]nd it admonishes us to own up to the fact that we are the ones who decide what counts as evidence of revision and what does not by deciding which texts to compare because they are *similar* enough to each other—despite some differences—to catch our eye and which to leave aside because they are *dissimilar* enough—despite some similarities—that we do not consider them relevant for our purposes.[93]

Similarly, Grossman recognizes our need to rethink "literary text":

> To the extent that a variety of very diverse manuscripts—with different wording, content, and character—can be recognized not only as examples of the same *textual tradition* but in fact as copies of the same *literary text*, it becomes necessary to rethink our larger understanding of original texts and textual formation in an ancient Jewish setting.[94]

For example, are 1QSa and 1QSb independent from or a part of the literary text the Community Rule (best preserved in 1QS)? These are the kinds of questions that led Person to question the consensus model's understanding of the relationship between Samuel–Kings and Chronicles as representing different literary texts that contain significantly different theologies.[95] Complicating the discussion of what is the *same* literary text and, therefore, by implication what constitutes a *different* literary text is Schorch's chapter in which he highlights how the exact same consonantal Hebrew text can nevertheless be read as different texts in various reading communities. Thus, the very notion of what a *literary text* is (complete with what are its sources and different redactional versions) that underlies

---

92. Lenzi in this volume, 68

93. Ibid., 65–66 (emphasis original)

94. Grossman in this volume, 329–30 (emphasis original).

95. Person in this volume. See also Person, *Deuteronomic History and the Book of Chronicles*; Raymond F. Person Jr., "Text Criticism as a Lens for Understanding the Transmission of Ancient Texts in Their Oral Environments," in *Contextualizing Israel's Sacred Writings: Ancient Literacy, Orality, and Literary Production*, ed. Brian B. Schmidt, AIL 22 (Atlanta: SBL Press, 2015), 193–211.

the current practice of source and redaction criticism requires much more serious thought based on empirical models.

One of the empirical models used in this volume that is not found in Tigay's volume comes from the comparative study of oral traditions. This should not be surprising, since the influence of the comparative study of oral traditions in biblical studies has expanded significantly since Tigay's volume appeared.[96] The challenge of the comparative study of oral traditions to source and redaction criticism has been recognized for some time. For example, in 1996, Susan Niditch acknowledged that understanding ancient Israel as a primarily oral society "forces us to question long-respected theories about the development of the Israelite literary traditions preserved in the Bible"—especially source criticism.[97] These earlier challenges have been too often and too quickly dismissed, especially by those who have made a reputation for themselves by defending the Documentary Hypothesis. For example, in his "Foreword" to the 2005 edition of Tigay's volume, Friedman explicitly proclaims Niditch's challenge as seriously flawed based on, in our opinion, his misunderstanding of Niditch's argument.[98] Nevertheless, some of the contributors to this volume bring additional insights to bear on source and redaction criticism based on the comparative study of oral tradition. Person draws from the study of oral traditions to critique the flawed assumptions concerning literary unity in the current practice of source and redaction criticism. Young concludes that, of the three models he evaluates to explain the relationship between the MT and the LXX of Dan 5, the best model is one that suggests that these two texts are independent literary traditions recording an earlier oral tradition of the character Daniel. Similarly, both Lenzi and Grossman imagine that the continuation of an oral tradition behind the texts they study helps to explain the textual plurality of the Akkadian "hand-lifting" prayers and the Serek texts of Qumran, respectively. In our opinion, like that of Niditch, the comparative study of oral traditions presents some

96. For recent reviews, see Raymond F. Person Jr., "Orality Studies, Oral Tradition: Hebrew Bible," in *The Encyclopedia of Biblical Interpretation*, ed. Steven L. McKenzie, 2 vols. (Oxford: Oxford University Press, 2013), 2:55–63; Raymond F. Person Jr. and Chris Keith, "Introduction," in *The Dictionary of the Bible and Ancient Media*, ed. Tom Thatcher et al. (London: Bloomsbury, forthcoming).

97. Susan Niditch, *Oral World and Written Word: Ancient Israelite Literature*, LAI (Louisville: Westminster John Knox, 1996), 134.

98. Friedman, "Foreword," [4–6].

serious challenges to biblical criticism, but also provides some empirical models for moving forward with a better understanding of the efficacy of source and redaction criticism, even if the influence is primarily limiting.

Our above summary and conclusions for the collective force of the volume has thus far not included comments on Weaks's insightful chapter. This is because it differs significantly from the other chapters in that it is a thought experiment in which he reconstructs a source based on the standard methods of source criticism of the gospels (although being in a real sense too generous), not because his chapter does not have much to contribute. In fact, in many ways it is a very fitting conclusion to the volume, so let us explicate here how we see Weaks's contribution in relationship to the conclusions we have given above, especially as it relates to the study of the Hebrew Bible. The reconstruction of the sayings source Q from Matthew and Luke is widely regarded as something highly plausible, even by those who might be skeptical about the application of source criticism to other texts based on discernible traces. This high degree of probability and plausibility is due to our ability to triangulate from Matthew and Luke to Q by using the material in the double tradition and by observing how the authors of Matthew and Luke used Mark as a source, since we have this source as a control on their redactional tendencies. Weaks's thought experiment explores how ineffective even this most probable reconstruction can be by reconstructing Mark on the basis of the triple tradition—that is, by triangulating from Matthew and Luke to his reconstructed Mark (what he calls MarQ). He can then compare Mark and MarQ. When he does, he concludes as follows: "A reconstructed text is unreliable in that it is missing the very features and structures characteristic of the actual source text and, further, it contains features and structures that originate not from the actual source text but from the reconstruction process itself."[99] He demonstrates that even with his most generous reconstruction, MarQ is only half the size of Mark and that this has tremendous consequences for the understanding of the literary and linguistic characteristics of the source text. Weaks's conclusions alone have wide implications for the efficacy of source and redaction criticism as valid methodologies. For example, our ability to describe the theology of the Priestly writer or the Succession Narrative or source A of Jeremiah poetry depends significantly on our ability to reconstruct these sources with a high degree of accuracy that

99. Weaks in this volume, 350.

preserves a significant majority of these sources. Weaks provides an example of why, at least in some cases, this standard cannot possibly be met. When we combine Weaks's conclusion with the above critique concerning the efficacy of source and redaction criticism on the basis of what have traditionally been understood as discernible traces that ensure some degree of plausibility, we must question even our ability to reconstruct sources and redactional layers with a high enough degree of plausibility *even when we have strong empirical evidence*. In other words, the most that source and redaction criticism may be able to do *even with empirical evidence* is help us understand in general ways the composite nature of the text with only sketchy notions of what sources and redactional layers may have contributed to the literary character of the text. Once we devote much time to analyzing these reconstructed sources and redactional layers themselves as literary objects worthy of close literary and theological study, we probably have crossed a line of plausibility that becomes much too speculative, at least in most cases. We certainly allow that there may be some limited cases in which the empirical controls appear to provide relatively sound judgments concerning sources and redactional layers—for example, the two sources behind 1 Sam 16–18. Nevertheless, we must acknowledge that even in these cases there are dissenting voices by respected scholars. Thus, in our opinion, future studies in source and redaction criticism must accept much more limited goals and objectives, primarily focused on the extant texts in their textual plurality and how that plurality may enlighten us on the prehistory of the chosen literary text, even if only faintly.

Outsourcing Gilgamesh*

Sara J. Milstein

1. Introduction

On paper—or more accurately, on tablets—the Gilgamesh Epic represents the ideal model for evidence of revision in ancient Near Eastern literature.[1] Not only is the Epic (or parts of it) attested in the Old Babylonian (OB), Middle Babylonian (MB), and Neo-Assyrian (NA) periods in a range of languages, tablet formats, and locations, but we also have apparent access to its *sources*.[2] Before the Epic emerged, the Urukean king Gilgamesh and

---

* I am grateful to Daniel Fleming for supplying me with swift and substantial feedback on multiple drafts of this chapter. The chapter also benefited from conversation with Paul Delnero, whose insights regarding issues of ancient Near Eastern textual transmission continue to inform and shape my perspective.

1. This is most famously demonstrated in Jeffrey H. Tigay, *The Evolution of the Gilgamesh Epic* (Philadelphia: University of Pennsylvania Press, 1982; repr., Wauconda, IL: Bolchazy-Carducci, 2002). Tigay presents a painstaking analysis of the "evolution" of the Gilgamesh Epic, tracking its growth from a handful of disparate Sumerian tales to an integrated epic in Akkadian in the Old Babylonian period and from there to its Middle Babylonian and Standard Babylonian (SB) versions. In Tigay, "The Evolution of the Pentateuchal Narratives in the Light of the Evolution of the *Gilgamesh Epic*," in *Empirical Models for Biblical Criticism*, ed. Jeffrey H. Tigay (Philadelphia: University of Pennsylvania Press, 1985), 21–52, Tigay then attempts to use these findings to test the plausibility of source-critical hypotheses for the Pentateuch.

2. For detailed descriptions of the Akkadian Gilgamesh evidence, see the tremendous two-volume edition of Andrew R. George, *The Babylonian Gilgamesh Epic: Introduction, Critical Edition and Cuneiform Texts*, 2 vols. (Oxford: Oxford University Press, 2003; henceforth *BGE*). George's edition includes all but one of the twelve Old Babylonian Akkadian Gilgamesh tablets and fragments that are now known. He published the twelfth in George, *Babylonian Literary Texts in the Schøyen Collection*, CUSAS 10 (Bethesda, MD: CDL, 2009), 37–41. The Middle Babylonian evidence

his trusty servant Enkidu starred in a set of five independent Sumerian tales: Gilgamesh and Huwawa (GH), Gilgamesh and the Bull of Heaven (GBH), Gilgamesh, Enkidu, and the Netherworld (GEN), Gilgamesh and Agga (GA), and The Death of Gilgamesh (DG).[3] Although these texts are

---

includes eighteen tablets and fragments from a variety of provenances, including Nippur, Ur, Boghazköy, Emar, and Megiddo (*BGE*, 1:287–384). A sizeable portion of the first-millennium BCE evidence derives from Assurbanipal's libraries at Nineveh. By that point, the Epic had assumed a standard form, known as the Standard Babylonian version. The Babylonian tradition of attributing the poem to Sîn-lēqi-unninni has led many to view him as the editor of the Standard Babylonian version, though it is difficult to determine the extent to which this individual shaped the Standard Babylonian version as we have it (for discussion, see *BGE*, 1:30). The Standard Babylonian version is represented by 116 fragments that have been assigned to seventy-three manuscripts (for use of the term *manuscript* as opposed to *tablet*, see *BGE*, 1:379). The differences among these manuscripts are relatively minor and pertain largely to orthography, grammar, and format (Tigay, "Evolution of the Pentateuchal Narratives," 43). There also exist fifteen other first-millennium Assyrian fragments; ten of these parallel the content and format of the Standard Babylonian version and five do not (*BGE*, 1:348).

3. These are all modern designations; as is widely known, Mesopotamian tales were typically identified by their opening lines. Early on, the Sumerian tales were likewise thought to have constituted a single epic. The argument for the independent nature of the Sumerian tales was first demonstrated by Samuel Noah Kramer, "The Epic of Gilgameš and Its Sumerian Sources: A Study in Literary Evolution," *JAOS* 64 (1944): 7–23, 83, and was met with widespread approval. In a different stance, Lubor Matouš argued that version A of GH, GBH, and DG constituted "a large epic composition" in Sumerian, while GEN and GA were independently copied (Lubor Matouš, "Les rapports entre la version sumérienne et la version akkadienne de l'epopée de Gilgameš," in *Gilgameš et sa légende*, ed. Paul Garelli, CRRAI 7, CahTD 1 [Paris: Klincksieck, 1960], 93). More recently, see Alhena Gadotti's nuanced argument in favor of a Sumerian Gilgamesh cycle, that is, a set of independent compositions that were arranged in a set order, as opposed to an epic or series (Alhena Gadotti, *"Gilgamesh, Enkidu, and the Netherworld" and the Sumerian Gilgamesh Cycle*, UAVA 10 [Boston: de Gruyter, 2014]). Gadotti asserts that this cycle would have included (in this order) GEN, GH (A and B), GBH, and DG (96). She bases this conclusion on a variety of evidence, including (1) the cosmological prologue of GEN; (2) the doxologies and colophons to the Sumerian tales; (3) the ending of GEN in the Ur tradition; (4) the catch-line in the Meturan version of GEN that links this tale to the first three lines of version A of GH; (5) the list of Gilgamesh's deeds in the Meturan version of DG; and (6) the archaeological context of certain tablets at Nippur (93–108). Antoine Cavigneaux interprets the Meturan catch-line as "a rather primitive, but very original attempt to connect the two stories … into a coherent literary unit" (Antoine Cavigneaux, "A Scholar's Library

almost entirely represented by Old Babylonian copies, the set of tales is widely considered to have originated in the Ur III period.[4] In the Old Babylonian period, long after Sumerian had died out as a spoken language, the tales belonged to a larger body of Sumerian literary texts that were copied with regularity in scribal schools.[5] It is thus not surprising that three of them—namely, GH, GBH, and GEN—would turn up later in the Epic, though all at different points.[6] In theory, this situation should allow us to

---

in Meturan?," in *Mesopotamian Magic: Textual, Historical, and Interpretative Perspectives*, ed. Tzvi Abusch and Karel van der Toorn, AMD 1 [Groningen: Styx, 1999], 256). Nonetheless, the Meturan text merely demonstrates that in this particular instance, GEN and GH were viewed as a pair to be copied in succession or perhaps simply as texts that were to be stored together. Given that Enkidu is a shade in GEN but alive in GH, it seems likely that the two were not integrated into anything we can call a Sumerian "Epic." See, however, Gadotti's persuasive argument that Enkidu does not in fact die in GEN (Gadotti, *"Gilgamesh, Enkidu, and the Netherworld,"* 83–91). Gadotti demonstrates that the understanding that Enkidu is a ghost is rooted in the Akkadian translation of the term *utukku* ("ghost" or "demon"). The Sumerian term *si-si-ig*, however, does not mean spirit or phantom. Instead she translates the relevant lines as follows: "He (Utu) opened a chink in the netherworld, and by means of his (Utu's) gust of wind, he sent his (Gilgamesh's) servant up from the netherworld" (lines 242–243).

4. This reflects broader notions regarding the origins of Sumerian "courtly literature" in King Šulgi's academies at Nippur and Ur in the Ur III period. Three fragments of Gilgamesh narrative do date to Ur III, however, including one fragment of GBH that was discovered at Nippur (*BGE*, 1:7–8). Tigay notes that a number of Ur III kings claimed Gilgamesh as their "brother" and that the Ur III dynasty appears to have seen itself as the legitimate successor of Uruk (Tigay, "Evolution of the Pentateuchal Narratives," 28).

5. The majority consensus is that Sumerian was a dead or dying language by the Ur III period (see especially Jerrold S. Cooper, "Sumerian and Akkadian in Sumer and Akkad," *Or* 42 [1973]: 239–46), though Christopher Woods considers the possibility that Sumerian was still spoken into the first centuries of the second millennium and perhaps beyond (Christopher Woods, "Bilingualism, Scribal Learning, and the Death of Sumerian," in *Margins of Writing, Origins of Cultures*, ed. Seth L. Sanders, OIS 2 [Chicago: Oriental Institute of the University of Chicago, 2006], 92).

6. To this list, one might add DG, which displays some links with material in SB IX–XI, as demonstrated in Kramer, "Epic of Gilgameš," 16–17. It is also evident that the Sumerian tale The Deluge served as a source (via the myth of Atrahasis) for SB XI, but the focus in this chapter is on the Sumerian Gilgamesh tales alone. The first attestations of GH, GBH, and GEN in the Epic range from the Old Babylonian period (GH) to the Middle Babylonian period (GBH) to the Neo-Assyrian period (GEN). GH and GEN will be discussed in detail below. The first evidence for GBH in the Epic comes from the Hittite paraphrase of the fourteenth and thirteenth centuries

evaluate the methods used to incorporate the Sumerian sources into the Epic and the degree to which the sources were preserved. These conclusions would then have the potential for application to the Bible. In practice, however, these pursuits are hindered by a number of obstacles:

- Even though we have Sumerian tales that are somehow related to the Epic, how do we know that these *specific* versions served as sources? Might there have been other versions of these tales (oral or written) that are more directly related?
- On a similar note, it is impossible to determine the extent to which copies of "the" Epic varied in the Old Babylonian period.[7] Of the twelve Akkadian tablets that date to the Old Babylonian period, only three overlap at all.[8] Among the four multicolumn tablets, while the Pennsylvania Tablet ("Penn") and the Yale Tablet ("Yale") clearly belonged to the same series and were even copied by the same scribe, the Sippar Tablet ("Sippar") diverges from these in both format and setting, thus providing some evidence for variation in transmission of the Epic.[9] Moreover, eight of the twelve tablets are single-column extracts that were likely produced

BCE. George observes that this episode "is not acknowledged by other Old Babylonian poems that cite Gilgameš's achievements, and occurs in art only from the Middle Assyrian period" (*BGE*, 1:23). He considers the date of its original incorporation into the Epic an open question.

7. George calls the term *epic* a "coinage of convenience" (*BGE*, 1:3) a coinage that I retain both here and in Daniel E. Fleming and Sara J. Milstein, *The Buried Foundation of the Gilgamesh Epic: The Akkadian Huwawa Narrative*, CM 39 (Leiden: Brill, 2010). George also refers to plural Old Babylonian "versions of the epic" in recognition of the variability in its form during this period (*BGE*, 1:23).

8. The six-column Yale Tablet overlaps in part with UM, a fragment of a multicolumn tablet of which eleven lines are visible, and to a limited degree with Schøyen-1, a single-column extract of which thirteen lines are preserved.

9. In referring to this tablet as "Sippar," I follow the justification laid out in Fleming and Milstein, *Buried Foundation of the Gilgamesh Epic*, 6 n. 14. Unlike the six-column tablets Penn and Yale, Sippar is a four-column tablet that appears to have been produced at Sippar, far from the likely origin of Penn and Yale at Larsa; it also displays a "north Babylonian" orthography (*BGE*, 1:272 n. 133). Penn and Yale are similar in clay, size, format (three columns per side), and orthographic conventions, and according to George, they are inscribed in "indistinguishable" hands (*BGE*, 1:159). Both also have the unusual trait of clay lumps on the edges.

in school settings. How representative would these extracts have been of "the" Epic in the Old Babylonian period?[10]

- Third, as Daniel Fleming and I have argued with regard to the transmission of GH, there may have been an intermediate literary stage between the Sumerian sources and the production of the Epic, what we call the "Akkadian Huwawa narrative." If so, then GH would be a source for the independent Akkadian rendition, which in turn would have served as the source for the Epic. If this scenario is correct, while GH would still represent a source for the Epic, it would be one step removed.
- Finally, although it is likely that the Sumerian tales predated the Akkadian Gilgamesh narrative, the bulk of the evidence is contemporaneous. Any arguments for the priority of Sumerian tales that are only attested in the Old Babylonian period must rely on logic beyond that of tablet chronology. Moreover, given that the Akkadian Gilgamesh narrative was newly emerging in the Old Babylonian period, it is possible that in the case of one or more tales, there was a mutual direction of influence. This has been suggested for GH, which exists in two substantially different versions, one of which (version A) shares closer affinities with the Akkadian material than the other (version B).

Despite these complications, certain data work in our favor. The first pertains to the pedagogical context of the tales. Drawing on a combination of literary catalogs and tablet typology, scholars have managed to reconstruct sets of texts that were learned at different phases in scribal training. One of these sets—the "Decad"—is a group of ten literary com-

10. As in *Buried Foundation of the Gilgamesh Epic*, I use the term *extract* to emphasize the potential parallels between these texts and the Sumerian Type III tablets with literary compositions, which have one column and represent extracts from longer texts. On the role of Type III tablets in scribal training, see Paul Delnero, "Sumerian Extract Tablets and Scribal Education," *JCS* 62 (2010): 53–69. Given that the average number of lines per Type III tablet is about 25 percent of the full composition and that Type III tablets outnumber the multicolumn Type I tablets by an average of 4:1, Delnero concludes that literary works were first learned in a series of four shorter sections that comprised the entire text. At a later point, the scribe would copy the entire composition on a Type I tablet (67). Although the Akkadian Gilgamesh extract tablets are attested in far fewer numbers than their Sumerian counterparts, they appear to reflect a similar practice.

positions that included version A of GH.[11] In total, eighty-five copies of version A have been discovered, along with five copies of the shorter version B, making GH the best attested of all the Gilgamesh tales.[12] It seems, moreover, that another set of literary texts held curricular status, at least at House F at Nippur, the scribal school that has yielded over 1,400 fragments.[13] This set, which includes GEN, has been identified by Eleanor

11. Much rests on the foundational work of Miguel Civil, who analyzed collections of tablets and divided them into four types of formats. Type I tablets, as noted above, are large multicolumned tablets; Type II are large "teacher-student" copies that contain extracts with one side inscribed by the teacher and the other inscribed by the student; Type III, again as noted, are single-column extracts of compositions; and Type IV are round tablets, or "lentils," that consist of 2–4 lines of a composition and show signs of inscription by teachers and students, like Type II (Miguel Civil, "Old Babylonian Proto-Lu: Types of Sources," in *The Series lu$_2$ = ša and Related Texts*, ed. Miguel Civil and Erica Reiner, MSL 12 [Rome: Pontifical Biblical Institute, 1969], 24–73). The first major application of these data was by Niek Veldhuis, who used it to reconstruct four phases in the elementary scribal curriculum at Old Babylonian Nippur (Niek Veldhuis, "Elementary Education at Nippur: The Lists of Trees and Wooden Objects" [PhD diss., Rijksuniversiteit Groningen, 1997], 40–63). Steve Tinney then determined that advanced scribes learned two sets of literary compositions: the "Tetrad," a group of four relatively simple hymns, and the "Decad," ten texts that were arguably learned in sequence (Steve Tinney, "On the Curricular Setting of Sumerian Literature," *Iraq* 59 [1999]: 159–72).

12. The numbers reflect the calculations in Paul Delnero, "Variation in Sumerian Literary Compositions: A Case Study Based on the Decad" (PhD diss., University of Pennsylvania, 2006), who follows collations and joins that reduce slightly the earlier number of ninety-two that was provided by Eleanor Robson, "The Tablet House: A Scribal School in Old Babylonian Nippur," *RA* 95 (2001): 54. Delnero's dissertation was revised and published as Paul Delnero, *The Textual Criticism of Sumerian Literature*, JCSSup 3 (Boston: American Schools of Oriental Research, 2012). See also the work of Dietz Otto Edzard, who includes eighty-two copies of version A (Dietz Otto Edzard, *"Gilgamesh und Huwawa": Zwei Versionen der sumerischen Zedernwaldepisode nebst einer Edition von Version "B"* [Munich: Bayerische Akademie der Wissenschaften, 1993], 14–15). Three of the five copies of version B come from Nippur, where fifty-nine of the version A texts were found.

13. The classic study of the House F evidence is Robson, "Tablet House." This scribal school is the most productive of all known Old Babylonian Nippur sites. Robson notes the extent to which the data from Nippur and from House F in particular "have contributed to our overall picture of Sumerian literature, and potentially skewed our understanding of what is normative within the corpus" (52). Over 25 percent of all Decad texts are from House F, and four-fifths of them are from Nippur. She

Robson as the "House F Fourteen."[14] This tale was also popular among Old Babylonian scribes, with seventy-four available tablets and fragments.[15] Notwithstanding some variation, these texts were relatively stable.[16] Thus, given the inclusion of version A of GH and GEN in the scribal curriculum and both the popularity and overall stability of these texts, it seems likely that the versions at our disposal were indeed sources for the production of Gilgamesh narrative in Akkadian.

Moreover, at House F, one piece of Akkadian literature was also found: a single-column tablet ("OB Nippur," in Andrew George's nomenclature) that pertains to Gilgamesh's dreams on the way to confront Huwawa, the fearsome guardian of the Cedar Forest. As such, this content is related to GH. The tablet has various erasures and spelling mistakes, prompting George to identify it as a school exercise.[17] Although this find is the only of its kind at Nippur, it reveals that the production of Gilgamesh content in Akkadian took place in the same location at which Sumerian Gilgamesh tales were learned and copied. While this phenomenon may have occurred at other sites during the Old Babylonian period, it is striking that only at Nippur do we find both Sumerian and Akkadian Gilgamesh texts. Given that OB Nippur was found in the company of twenty-one copies of version A of GH at House F, it is reasonable to consider that GH is related directly to OB Nippur and quite possibly to the other seven Old Babylonian Akkadian texts pertaining to the Huwawa episode.

---

notes further that the more varied evidence for the Tetrad suggests that Nippur may not be the prototype for the "Sumerian literary world" at large (52).

14. The number of sources for the Fourteen are comparable to that of the Decad, and like the Decad, the Fourteen are listed together on some Old Babylonian catalogs of Sumerian literature, though with some variation (Robson, "Tablet House," 54–57). This set included an array of *eduba* compositions (tales about school), hymns, laments, disputations, proverb collections, and myths, with GEN the only Gilgamesh tale in the group.

15. Here I follow the count and discussion in Gadotti, *"Gilgamesh, Enkidu, and the Netherworld,"* 129–51.

16. For a comprehensive analysis of variants in GEN, see ibid. Substantial differences will be discussed below. For the complete score of version A of GH, see Delnero, "Variation in Sumerian Literary Compositions," 2395–2473. The differences between versions A and B are a separate question and will be addressed in more detail below.

17. Nonetheless, it yields an oblique wedge at line 10 on the obverse, a feature that George notes is typically associated with library copies (*BGE*, 1:241).

Finally, it is important to note that while GH and GBH are wholly transformed in the Epic so that no two lines correspond directly, GEN overlaps substantially with its Akkadian counterpart in Tablet XII, the final tablet of the Standard Babylonian version. Although lines 1–171 of GEN are not attested in Tablet XII, lines 172–end of GEN (as per the version attested at Nippur) parallel SB XII 1–153 so closely that it is possible to speak of the latter in terms of a translation. In this case, then, while it is possible that a different version of GEN served as the source for Tablet XII, it is clear that at least part of GEN as we have it is related directly to Tablet XII. Unlike GH, at least some portion of the actual wording of GEN was preserved intact for over a millennium.

2. From Huwawa to the Netherworld: Two Case Studies

2.1. Introduction

Given the explicit ties that GH and GEN have to their Akkadian counterparts, it is worth probing the relationship between these two particular sources and their earliest attested Akkadian heirs. These pairs are at opposite ends of the spectrum, both with regard to the degree of preservation and to the date of first attestation in Akkadian. Moreover, while the Akkadian counterpart to GH is integrated seamlessly into the Epic, the latter half of GEN is tacked onto the end of the Standard Babylonian version, with no effort to smooth out the inconsistencies. They further differ in that GH is represented by two substantially different versions, while the copies of GEN are more closely aligned. Such variety makes this set of Sumerian/Akkadian cases the ideal *models* to bring to bear on questions of revision and preservation in the Bible.

2.2. Gilgamesh and Huwawa

Gilgamesh and Huwawa is a classic adventure tale that details Gilgamesh and Enkidu's journey to the highlands and their battle with Huwawa, the fearsome being that resides there. Notwithstanding a frightful lead-up, the two manage to dispose Huwawa of his "terrors," behead him, and present the head to Enlil at the story's end. Only the broad outlines of this conflict are represented in the Akkadian evidence, as will be clear below.

While there is a general consensus regarding the priority of the Sumerian tales, the relationships among versions A, B, and the Akkadian material remains an open question. Dietz Otto Edzard concludes that version A was developed from version B and that version A was possibly influenced by the contemporaneous Epic. This stance has been echoed by Tzvi Abusch, and Fleming and I argued along similar lines.[18] This theory accounts for the greater affinity between version A and the Akkadian material. It also helps explain why we have such different versions of GH in circulation—a rarity in the Sumerian evidence. At the same time, given that the copies of version A outnumber the Akkadian evidence by a factor of 7:1, it is uncertain as to whether nascent Akkadian material would have circulated widely enough so as to have such a major impact on GH. After all, it is version A, not B, that belongs to the Decad, and version A is much more widely attested than version B. There is also the question of the production of Sumerian literature in the Old Babylonian period. Would scribes have been inclined to revise heavily a "classic" Sumerian tale at that point, or was the instinct already to create new content in Akkadian? Given these issues, it seems more likely that the more popular version of GH that belonged to the Old Babylonian curriculum—version A—was the one that served as the source for the newly emerging Akkadian version. As such, I will treat version A as the source for the parallel Akkadian material.

The Old Babylonian Akkadian material includes four multicolumn tablets (Penn, Yale, UM, and Sippar) and eight scribal extracts of various lengths and states of preservation (Schøyen-1, Schøyen-2, Schøyen-3, Nippur, Harmal-1, Harmal-2, Ishchali, and IM).[19] The most well-preserved of these are Penn and Yale, two six-columned tablets that represent Tablets II and III in a series of at least four tablets that launched with the

18. See Edzard, *Gilgameš und Huwawa*, 53–59; Tzvi Abusch, "Hunting in the Epic of Gilgamesh: Speculations on the Education of a Prince," in *Treasures on Camels' Humps: Historical and Literary Studies from the Ancient Near East Presented to Israel Eph'al*, ed. Mordechai Cogan and Dan'el Kahn (Jerusalem: Magnes, 2008), 17; Fleming and Milstein, *Buried Foundation of the Gilgamesh Epic*, 83–90.

19. For discussion of the various find-spots and states of preservation of each of the Old Babylonian tablets, see *BGE*, 1:159–286. Schøyen-1, Schøyen-2, and IM lack provenance, though they appear to be from Babylonia, and no two are from the same setting. The best preserved among these is Schøyen-2, a completely preserved tablet of eighty-four lines. A more updated edition of it with commentary is published in George, *Babylonian Literary Texts*, 29–36, and pls. 13–16. Schøyen-3 is the name George gives to a collection of twenty fragments, eight of which are edited in ibid., 37–41, and pls. 17–18.

phrase *šūtur eli šarrī* ("Surpassing kings").[20] This is the best evidence for something that can be called an "epic" in the Old Babylonian period. Penn details the first encounter between Gilgamesh and Enkidu, and in Yale, Gilgamesh proposes that he and Enkidu head to the Cedar Forest to battle Huwawa. Though heavily broken, UM and Schøyen-1 overlap in limited part with Yale, and the remaining extract tablets cover different parts of the Huwawa adventure. The four-columned Sippar Tablet is then set in the period after Enkidu's death, with a woeful Gilgamesh mourning the loss. Notwithstanding its variation in format and style, the links between Penn and Sippar suggest that some version of the latter belonged to the *šūtur eli šarrī* series.[21] It is striking that of the twelve Old Babylonian Gilgamesh tablets, ten pertain to the Huwawa adventure. This seems to evince the parallel popularity of the Akkadian Huwawa episode in Old Babylonian scribal circles, albeit on a much smaller scale. The fact that eight of the tablets are in extract format suggests that the Akkadian version of this episode was also learned in Old Babylonian school settings.[22]

---

20. The colophon of Penn marks it as dub 2.kam.ma ("Tablet II") of the series *šūtur eli šarrī*. Although Tablet I is lost, the fact that this phrase is attested in SB I 29 suggests that some version of the contents of SB I from line 29 on may have occupied OB I. In SB I, the phrase belongs to a hymn to Gilgamesh that praises the king for his strength; this leads into Gilgamesh's oppression of the people of Uruk. However much of this might have belonged to OB I is complicated by the fact that a variant of the phrase appears in a Middle Babylonian copy of the prologue that was discovered at Ugarit (Middle Bronze Ugarit$_1$). The tablet is complete at thirty-eight lines and was evidently a school exercise (Daniel Arnaud, *Corpus des textes de bibliothèque de Ras Shamra-Ougarit [1936–2000] en sumérien, babylonien et assyrien*, AuOrSup 23 [Sabadell: AUSA, 2007], 14, 130; see also Andrew R. George, "The Gilgameš Epic at Ugarit," *AuOr* 25 [2007]: 238). George notes that the tablet is marked by corruption and "is garbled to the point of incoherence" (246). For a more forgiving stance, see Jack M. Sasson, "Prologues and Poets: On the Opening Lines of the Gilgamesh Epic," in *Beyond Hatti: A Tribute to Gary Beckman*, ed. Billie Jean Collins and Piotr Michalowski (Atlanta: Lockwood, 2013), 265–77. In Middle Bronze Ugarit$_1$, the phrase appears at line 17, where it launches a four-line hymn.

21. See Fleming and Milstein, *Buried Foundation of the Gilgamesh Epic*, 45–51 for a detailed discussion of the parallels between Penn and Sippar, as well as discussion regarding those features that may have been unique to the version represented by Sippar.

22. In *Buried Foundation of the Gilgamesh Epic*, Fleming and I argue that the Huwawa texts reflect remnants of a once-independent Akkadian Huwawa narrative that covered only Gilgamesh's plan, his attempt to persuade Enkidu and the elders of the merits of his plan, the pair's journey to the forest, and their battle with Huwawa.

At this point, let us turn to the relationship between GH and the Akkadian content. The following represent the key points of overlap and dissension between the two.

(1) *The Adventure in Context*: While GH was preserved as an independent episode in Sumerian, in the Old Babylonian Epic this episode is made to follow two six-column tablets, each of which must have numbered about 240–300 lines. Based on what we see in SB I and Penn, it appears that OB I introduced the key players: Gilgamesh, the aggressive king of Uruk; Enkidu, the wild "match" for Gilgamesh; and Shamkat, the harlot who propositions Enkidu. Tablet II then opens with Gilgamesh reporting a set of dreams to his mother that anticipate Enkidu's arrival. In columns ii–iii, Enkidu is copulating with Shamkat, who urges him to abandon his life in the steppe for Uruk. When Enkidu hears that Gilgamesh has been abusing his authority by coupling with the brides of Uruk, he heads to Uruk to confront the king. The two grapple at the doorway, and the tablet ends with Enkidu praising Gilgamesh. Yale then covers Gilgamesh's efforts to gain support for his charge against Huwawa. This must have been followed by at least one more tablet, given that Gilgamesh and Enkidu are just setting out for the Cedar Forest at the end of Yale. If some version of the contents of Sippar indeed belonged to this series, it appears that the Huwawa adventure in this series was followed at some point by Enkidu's death and Gilgamesh's subsequent grief and search for immortality.

(2) *The Period before the Journey*: In GH, the entire period leading up to the expedition occupies sixty lines. Gilgamesh announces his desire to enter the highlands, "since no man can elude life's end" (A:4). Upon Enkidu's insistence, Gilgamesh informs the sun god Utu of his plan. Utu resists at first but then furnishes Gilgamesh with seven cosmic warriors. Gilgamesh then amasses a small army as backup. The men prepare weapons and all set out for the highlands (A:60). This period is then expanded

---

The fact that these texts display features that distinguish them from Penn and Sippar suggests that the logic of the Akkadian Huwawa narrative was preserved even when the tale was taken up and expanded at both ends in the Epic. Whether these Huwawa tablets reflect copying from a separate tale or whether all of them belong to "the" Epic at this point is difficult to say, though one extract (Schøyen-1) does show signs of a distinct logic from the Epic, and the fact that all eight extracts derive from the Huwawa episode lends some support to the notion of an independent Huwawa tale (Fleming and Milstein, *Buried Foundation of the Gilgamesh Epic*, 92–95). In any case, it appears that GH serves as an indirect source for the Epic, with the Akkadian Huwawa narrative an intermediate step between the two.

considerably in the Epic, where about three-hundred lines cover the period between Gilgamesh's proposal and the actual expedition. In this case, Gilgamesh proposes from the outset to battle Huwawa, a detail that is absent from the Sumerian. The bulk of Yale is preoccupied with Gilgamesh's efforts to convince Enkidu and the elders of the merits of his plan. Unlike GH, here Enkidu does not join freely but instead must be persuaded by Gilgamesh. This reflects the fact that Enkidu is no longer Gilgamesh's servant but instead operates as a free agent from the steppe, one with firsthand knowledge of Huwawa. The bulk of columns i–iv is thus comprised of dialogue between the two men, with Gilgamesh using all sorts of rhetorical tactics to convince Enkidu to join him. Once Enkidu finally agrees, Gilgamesh then must convince the elders, who again resist the idea. After a broken section and Gilgamesh's plea before Shamash, the elders finally offer their blessings and advice before the men set out.

(3) *Heading to the Highlands/the Cedar Forest*: In GH, Gilgamesh and his companions cross seven ranges and reach the Cedar Forest. They then begin chopping and stacking the trees (A: 61–66). This prompts Huwawa to unleash his sleep-inducing terrors. Enkidu awakes in fear and tries to persuade Gilgamesh to abandon the project, but Gilgamesh refuses. Enkidu pleads again, but Gilgamesh insists that they will succeed if they proceed together. This is paralleled loosely in Schøyen-2, Schøyen-3, Nippur, and Harmal-1 by a set of dreams that Gilgamesh has along the way to the forest. Unlike GH, however, Gilgamesh's dreams are strictly anticipatory and precede any actual contact with Huwawa and/or his terrors. In this material, Gilgamesh repeatedly falls asleep and has terrifying dreams about Huwawa. Enkidu then interprets the dreams in terms of Gilgamesh's upcoming success. This content represents a second considerable expansion of the period before the actual confrontation.

(4) *Confronting Huwawa*: In GH, Gilgamesh encounters Huwawa and offers him his two sisters as wives in exchange for his terrors, to which Huwawa agrees. The loss of the terrors leaves Huwawa vulnerable to attack. Once captured, Huwawa weeps and pleads for clemency. Gilgamesh shows pity, but Enkidu refuses to release him. After Huwawa speaks disparagingly to Enkidu, Enkidu beheads Huwawa in a rage.[23] The two place the head

23. The corresponding section in version B is broken, though in version A, the same exchange between Gilgamesh and Enkidu leads to the death of Huwawa at the hands of Enkidu. However, Edzard argues that Gilgamesh may have permitted Huwawa to live in version B, whereas in version A Enkidu slays Huwawa (Edzard,

in a sack and deliver it to Enlil, who releases Huwawa's auras to recipients in the natural world. The tale concludes with a doxology to Gilgamesh, Huwawa, and Enkidu. In Ishchali, Enkidu likewise instructs Gilgamesh to smite Huwawa. Here, however, Gilgamesh is concerned that Huwawa's auras are escaping, but Enkidu insists that they focus first on capturing Huwawa. In this version, Gilgamesh agrees and smites Huwawa, and only then do the two begin to fell the cedar. In IM, the pair then select a tree to turn into a door for Enlil's palace.

While the Akkadian material retains certain general components of GH, it diverges in numerous respects.[24] Here I will highlight just a few. The Akkadian rendition expands massively the period before the encounter with Huwawa, including a long section before departure and a series of dreams leading up to the confrontation. With these additions, the old Huwawa episode becomes much less about conflict with Huwawa and much more about Gilgamesh and Enkidu and their *anticipation* of conflict. In addition, although Enkidu advises Gilgamesh in both sets of evidence, his role shifts from that of servant in GH to equal partner in the Akkadian texts. As such, Gilgamesh is thrust into the new position of having to persuade Enkidu of the merits of his mission. Finally, as is evident by Penn, Yale, and Sippar, we see that the Huwawa episode has not only been rewritten completely, but also has been supplemented massively at the front and back ends. In turn, Gilgamesh's quest becomes just one episode in an extended narrative about Gilgamesh's personal experience with intense love and loss.

2.3. Gilgamesh, Enkidu, and the Netherworld

After a cosmological prologue and a brief episode involving Enki on a boat, GEN zeroes in on Inanna, who has rescued and planted a tree that was battered by the Euphrates River. Various creatures settle in the tree,

---

Gilgameš und Huwawa, 11, 53–59). His argument is based on the observation that the damaged conclusion of version B preserves a dialogue between Huwawa and Gilgamesh that does not appear in version A (B: 151–156). According to Abusch, version A then reflects the same tradition as the Akkadian Epic: both make the defeat of Huwawa the central objective of the mission (Abusch, "Hunting in the Epic of Gilgamesh," 16–17).

24. For further discussion, see Fleming and Milstein, *Buried Foundation of the Gilgamesh Epic*, 69–90.

making it difficult for her to harvest the wood for a chair and bed. She seeks help from Utu; when he refuses, she turns to Gilgamesh, who dispels of the creatures and crafts furniture for the goddess. He then makes a ball and mallet for himself and plays a game with these on the backs of the city's orphans. When the people complain, the playthings fall into the netherworld. Gilgamesh is distraught, and Enkidu volunteers to retrieve them. Gilgamesh instructs Enkidu carefully with regard to his behavior in the netherworld, but Enkidu disobeys all of his instructions and becomes entrapped there for seven days. Then it is Gilgamesh's job to seek divine help, first from Enlil and Sîn, both of whom refuse, and finally from Enki, who brings Enkidu up as a phantom. Gilgamesh inquires about the various netherworld inhabitants and Enkidu responds. In all of the versions from Nippur, the tale apparently ends with one of these question/answer pairs, but in one text from Ur, Enkidu reports that Gilgamesh's father and mother are drinking contaminated water, and in another Ur text, Gilgamesh provides his parents with clean water to drink.

A total of seventy-four tablets and fragments of varying lengths and states of preservation are attested for this 300-line tale. The majority of tablets were found at Nippur, though other sites, such as Ur, Uruk, Sippar, Isin, and Meturan have also yielded tablets. Lines 172–end of the Nippur versions (beginning in the midst of Gilgamesh's lament about his fallen ball and mallet) are then represented closely in Akkadian translation in Tablet XII of the Standard Babylonian version, which is attested in nine manuscripts.[25] These constitute the earliest attestations of this part of GEN in Akkadian.

---

25. I follow George's system of numbering for GEN manuscripts, though George only transcribes line 172 onward (*BGE*, vol. 2). Lines 172–268 of the manuscripts largely agree, though see George's score for some minor differences (*BGE*, 2:748–63). At that point, the manuscripts vary with regard to the number and order of the lines. This pertains to a set of questions that Gilgamesh asks Enkidu about the status of various individuals in the netherworld. Rather than assign an "artificial line count," George instead groups the queries by theme and assigns each group a letter rather than a number (a–t). In referring to "GEN 172–end," I thus refer to 172–268 + a–t. At this point, there are several manuscripts that preserve unique sets of lines. Most significantly, there are two separate sections preserved in Ur MSS ll and nn. George continues the lettered system for MS ll (v–y), but for MS nn, a text that moves beyond the queries, he uses 1′–16′. The latter is the only manuscript to include a doxology to Gilgamesh.

Tablet XII has been viewed as an appendage to Tablets I–XI of the Standard Babylonian version for several reasons.[26] First, Tablets I and XI display a ring-like structure, with parallel references to circumambulating the walls of Uruk. George notes the symmetry of Tablets I–XI: Tablets I–V lead up to Gilgamesh's adventure in the Cedar Forest; Tablet VI details Gilgamesh and Enkidu at their peak; and Tablets VII–XI cover Enkidu's death and Gilgamesh's grief and subsequent search for immortality. Second, the fact that Enkidu is still alive in Tablet XII contradicts the preceding plotline. We may add to this the fact that Enkidu is represented as a servant only in Tablet XII and in the Sumerian tales. Third, as George explicates, the language and style of Tablet XII differ from those of the rest of the Epic.[27] Together, these inconsistencies indicate that the tablet is a secondary addition.

In this case, there is no question regarding the existence of a relationship between GEN 172–end and Tablet XII. There are, however, questions pertaining to other arenas. First, why is only the latter half of GEN preserved in the Akkadian? Did the scribe responsible for Tablet XII simply eliminate the first 171 lines, or did he only have access to a copy of GEN that started at line 172? If the former, why would this material have been eliminated? There is also a question concerning the "end" of GEN, as preserved at Ur. Did the scribe responsible for Tablet XII eliminate this ending, or did he only have access to the shorter version represented at Nippur? Second, what accounts for the appearance of GEN in Akkadian only in the first millennium? Does this merely reflect the luck of the finds, or does the available evidence reflect the actual point at which GEN was incorporated into the Epic? Third, given the inconsistencies between Tablets I–XI and Tablet XII, why was a translation of GEN 172–end even attached to the end of the Epic? We can only begin to pose answers to these questions

26. Even before the Sumerian tales were unearthed, Morris Jastrow had identified Tablet XII as an addition to the Epic (Morris Jastrow Jr., *The Religion of Babylonia and Assyria* [Boston: Ginn, 1898], 513). The first to adduce Sumerian evidence to explain Tablet XII as an "inorganic appendage" was Kramer, who contended that Tablet XII was attached "with complete disregard for the sense and continuity" of the Epic (Kramer, "Epic of Gilgameš," 23). See also Tigay, "Evolution of the Pentateuchal Narratives," 31; Tigay, *Evolution of the Gilgamesh Epic*, 27, 49; *BGE*, 1:47–54. Others have recognized the secondary origins of Tablet XII but have tried to argue for its essential contribution to the Epic; for a survey and critique of various views, see *BGE*, 1:50–52.

27. George cites the plain word order and vocabulary of GEN, among other less impressive features (*BGE*, 1:48).

once we outline the points of continuity and difference between GEN and Tablet XII. The following is an effort in that direction.

(1) *Inanna's Tree and Gilgamesh's Game* (GEN 1–171): The most evident difference between GEN and SB XII is the absence of lines 1–171 in the latter. In GEN, this material is highly repetitive. Lines 1–23 are comprised of a cosmological prologue and a short episode involving Enki, whose boat is battered by water. In lines 24–43, Inanna rescues a tree from the Euphrates, tends to it, and is prevented from using its wood by the creatures that settle in it. When she approaches Utu for help, she reiterates almost verbatim the bulk of the narrative thus far (lines 51–81 // lines 11–41). The same pattern follows in lines 90–122, where Inanna again recites the prologue, the Enki episode, and her incident with the tree, this time to Gilgamesh. Gilgamesh then destroys the creatures of the tree, provides the goddess with wood, and fashions a ball and mallet for himself. He and the men of the city play with the ball and mallet at the expense of a "team of orphans" (line 142). This prompts the items to fall into the netherworld. The king weeps to Enkidu about his loss.

(2) *Gilgamesh's Lament, Enkidu's Descent and Ascent, and Enkidu's Initial Report* (GEN 172–268 // SB XII 1–116): These sections overlap closely both in terms of content and line breaks. Gilgamesh laments the loss of his ball and mallet, and Enkidu offers to retrieve them. Gilgamesh provides Enkidu with strict instructions regarding his behavior in the netherworld (he must not dress in a clean garment, anoint with oil, wear sandals, etc.). Enkidu descends to the netherworld and promptly performs every forbidden action. The netherworld seizes him, and Gilgamesh weeps. After Enlil (and Sîn in Tablet XII) refuses to help, Gilgamesh gains support from Ea, who, with the assistance of Shamash, brings Enkidu up. The friends embrace and Enkidu begins to recount what he has witnessed. Gilgamesh inquires about the man who had one son up to the man who had seven sons, and Enkidu reports on each of their various states.

(3) *Enkidu's Continued Report of the Netherworld Inhabitants* (GEN a–t // SB XII 117–153): In this section, Enkidu reports further on the netherworld. This includes people who did not have sex or did not give birth, men who have been killed by various means (the man who fell off a roof, the man eaten by a lion, the leper, the man struck by the mooring pole, the man killed in battle, etc.), men who disrespected their parents or their god, stillborn babies, and the man who died a natural death. Although the corresponding section of SB XII is fragmentary, it is evident that this content overlapped at least in part with GEN a–t. A number of the same

individuals from GEN are represented (the palace eunuch, the man struck by a mooring pole, the one who died a natural death, the one whose corpse was left lying in the countryside, the one who is not provided with funerary offerings), though some of Enkidu's responses vary.[28]

(4) *More Reports and Gilgamesh and His Parents* (GEN, represented only in Ur MSS ll and nn): The two Ur texts include content that is absent both from the other copies of GEN and from Tablet XII. Manuscript ll includes five additional inquiries, the last of which pertains to Gilgamesh's parents, who are drinking dirty water. Manuscript nn concludes with Gilgamesh performing funerary rites for his parents, including the provision of clean water. Even though the content of MS nn is not represented in MS ll and vice versa, their shared concern with the quality of water for Gilgamesh's parents suggests that the two texts belonged broadly to the same tradition. The evidence would seem to suggest that this unit was unique to the tradition preserved at Ur.

This case study reveals a combination of overlap, variation, expansion, and possible elimination in the process of transmission. GEN 172–268 // SB XII 1–116 overlap closely, with only minor differences.[29] More substantial variation is then evident in the Sumerian and Akkadian content that follows (GEN a–t and what is visible of SB XII 117–153). Given that this material pertains to netherworld inhabitants that are not rooted in any particular sequence (vis-à-vis the men with one to seven sons), it was more susceptible to variation. The fact that GEN v–y and 1′–16′ are attested only in two manuscripts from Ur may suggest that these units represent an expansion in the Sumerian tradition. While it is possible that the scribe responsible for Tablet XII omitted this material, the limited number of attestations of this content in the Sumerian evidence suggests that the Sumerian source for Tablet XII more likely did not include this content. At the same time, it is worth adding that the focus in these lines on Gilgamesh's parents would have detracted from the unwavering focus on Gilgamesh in the Epic.

---

28. For details, see *BGE*, 1:735; 2:774–76.

29. The following slightly less minor variations are worth mentioning: the Mother of Ninazu is given further description only in GEN 204–205, yet only Tablet XII repeats its description of her in lines 48–50; only in Tablet XII does Gilgamesh turns to Sîn for help after Enlil refuses (lines 64–71); and only in Tablet XII does Enkidu first protest telling Gilgamesh about what he saw in the netherworld (line 92).

This leaves us with the largest difference between GEN and Tablet XII: the absence of GEN 1–171 in the latter. Broadly speaking, there are two possible explanations for this. The first is that the scribe responsible for Tablet XII only had at his disposal lines 172–end of GEN (the Nippur version). As such, Tablet XII would represent a faithful representation of the inherited material. This would account for the fact that the Akkadian version begins *in medias res*, omitting Gilgamesh's loss of the ball and mallet and even the beginning of Gilgamesh's speech. The copy available could have been an extract tablet that simply did not include the first half of the tale or even a broken tablet that was still deemed worth preserving. The second possibility is that the scribe responsible for Tablet XII knew the entire tale of GEN, either in oral or written form but opted only to include lines 172–end. As such, he would have preserved only the content pertaining to Gilgamesh and Enkidu.[30] Given that the Standard Babylonian Epic is concerned with Gilgamesh's love for Enkidu, his grief over losing Enkidu, and his subsequent struggle against the inevitability of mortality, it is fitting that the only GEN material represented in Tablet XII would pertain to Enkidu's loyalty to Gilgamesh, Gilgamesh's sorrow at losing Enkidu, his efforts to bring Enkidu back from the netherworld, and Enkidu's reports to Gilgamesh on the inhabitants of the netherworld. While this thematic overlap may be coincidental, it seems more likely that lines 1–171 were deemed extraneous in this context.

How GEN was preserved intact for a millennium and why it was attached to the Epic are two separate matters altogether. It is possible that GEN was preserved as a bilingual text before it was represented exclusively in Akkadian. Bilingual texts first started to appear in scribal schools in the Old Babylonian period, but at that point, as Jerrold Cooper notes, they were the products of individual scribes and bore no recognizable pattern in terms of format. After the Old Babylonian period, bilingual texts became more common, and standardized translation formats in the form

30. In addition, as Tigay notes, Gilgamesh's torment of the citizens of Uruk with the *pukku* ("ball") is already referenced in part in SB I 52–76 (Tigay, "Evolution of the Pentateuchal Narratives," 31). In this case, Gilgamesh's overly aggressive activity leads to the creation of Enkidu as a match for the king's restless energies. See also Gadotti, who considers that the omission of the *halub*-tree episode may have been due to redundancy with the Cedar Forest adventure (Gadotti, "*Gilgamesh, Enkidu, and the Netherworld*," 80).

of parallel columns or interlinear translations started to develop.[31] By the first millennium, Sumerian was preserved almost exclusively by bilingual texts, and Akkadian translations became standard accompaniments of Sumerian texts.[32] While we have no bilingual copies of GEN, the phenomenon of bilingual text production makes it possible that a bilingual version served as the source of Tablet XII. If this was indeed the case, it seems most likely that the complete tale would have been preserved as a bilingual text and that only the latter half was extracted and attached to the Epic in monolingual format.

Despite the fact that Tablet XII contradicts the events of Tablets I–XI and arguably detracts from the coherence of the Epic, it also provides an alternative ending of sorts, where in place of Gilgamesh's grief and search for immortality, we find the postnetherworld return of Enkidu and Gilgamesh's newfound knowledge about "life" after death. The juxtaposition is striking. After Gilgamesh's tormented and futile efforts to attain immortality, the Epic reverts abruptly to a Gilgamesh from a bygone era, one more preoccupied with the reality of ghosts in the netherworld than with the lofty pursuits of eternal life. While in the Epic Gilgamesh laments the loss of his dear friend Enkidu, Tablet XII brings it down a level (literally) in almost a comical way, with Gilgamesh lamenting the loss of his ball and mallet in the netherworld. For all that Tablets I–XI set Gilgamesh apart as the singular king who establishes his name through brave feats and building accomplishments, Gilgamesh wraps up his Epic role as one of "us," another Babylonian concerned with the comfort of the dead. While with our modern sensibilities and lofty aspirations we may relate more readily to the man in search of eternal life, it may well be that the average person in the first millennium BCE would have found Gilgamesh's preoccupations in Tablet XII more relevant. This is not to say that the addition of Tablet XII to the Epic was motivated by anything other than the impulse to find a decent home for additional Gilgamesh content, but only that this

---

31. See Jerrold S. Cooper, "*Bilinguals from Boghazköi. I*," *ZA* 61 (*1971*): 1–6.

32. Hannes D. Galter, "Cuneiform Bilingual Royal Inscriptions," in *Language and Culture in the Near East*, ed. Shlomo Izre'el and Rina Drory, IOS 15 (Leiden: Brill, 1995), 28–29. In this context, the fact that Tablet XII is a monolingual Akkadian translation as opposed to a bilingual text is rare. George notes that the only other extant monolingual Akkadian translation of a Sumerian literary text is a fragment of a MA recension of the Instructions of Šuruppak (*BGE*, 1:48).

combination may initially not have seemed the detraction that it appears to be through modern lenses.

In this light, it is finally worth exploring George's hypothesis that Tablet XII (or perhaps the complete Epic) may have been put to ritual use at funerals and in memorial cults. It is widely known that Gilgamesh was considered king and judge in the netherworld, and his presence at rituals of burial and commemoration is well-attested.[33] The focus of Tablet XII, moreover, is on the importance of commemorative ritual, even if it is not a ritual text per se. To some extent, the addition of Tablet XII is mirrored by the history of a text like Adapa (in its OB and NA versions), where the myth is followed by an incantation-like passage that pertains to the South Wind as an agent of disease. Like Tablet XII, there is no real transition between the end of the myth and the beginning of the incantation, and like Tablet XII, the incantation likely had some sort of independent life before it was attached to the myth. Whether or not the incantation reflects a cultic usage for the myth of Adapa itself is a matter of debate, but its inclusion points to another case where a narrative could attract material that touches broadly on the same theme but that preserves an altogether different style and focus.

3. Potential Applications to the Bible

3.1. Introduction

As is evident from recent works on ancient Near Eastern scribal culture, scribal practices attested in Mesopotamia belonged to a broader cultural landscape that included ancient Israel and Judah.[34] While this need not mean that these scribal cultures were identical, their numerous shared elements indicate much overlap and exchange. As such, I would like to draw some broad conclusions about what the two Gilgamesh cases may

---

33. *BGE*, 1:53–54. On the relationship between Tablet XII and Gilgamesh's role in the netherworld, see also Tzvi Abusch, "Ishtar's Proposal and Gilgamesh's Refusal: An Interpretation of the Gilgamesh Epic, Tablet 6, lines 1–79," *HR* 26 (1986): 184–87.

34. See especially Karel van der Toorn, *Scribal Culture and the Making of the Hebrew Bible* (Cambridge: Harvard University Press, 2007); David M. Carr, *Writing on the Tablet of the Heart: Origins of Scripture and Literature* (New York: Oxford University Press, 2005); Carr, *The Formation of the Hebrew Bible: A New Reconstruction* (New York: Oxford University Press, 2011), 11–149.

reveal (and conceal) about the reuse of sources in an extended work, with the hope that this may shed light on questions of textual transmission in ancient Israel.

3.2. Methods of Revision and Preservation of Sources

The following represents an effort to glean some basic principles of revision from the rather divergent cases of GH and GEN.

(1) Source content *could* be preserved verbatim for over a millennium. Evidently, at least in the case of GEN, it appears to have been transmitted in written form. This need not mean, however, that GEN was copied faithfully from one generation to the next. Only a single copy of GEN would have been required for this content to end up in the Epic. Although Israelite scribes utilized more perishable material than the Mesopotamians, it is theoretically possible that an old protobiblical document was likewise preserved and/or recopied when it became worn.

(2) In the case of GEN, this close preservation was apparently accompanied by a major elimination of content.[35] It appears that only the content that resonated with themes preserved in the Epic (in this case, the latter half of the tale) was retained. A similar phenomenon is evident in Tablet XI of the Standard Babylonian version, where only the latter half of the flood story is preserved.[36] It is possible that this "fracturing" of sources could take place precisely because these sources were composite in the first place, as appears to be the case for Atrahasis and GEN. In that sense, the

35. Carr, too, observes the phenomenon by which scribes tended not to reproduce their source compositions in full and often omitted their beginnings or endings (Carr, *Formation of the Hebrew Bible*, 88).

36. Ūta-napišti quickly sums up the events leading up to the flood before he delves into Ea's instructions to him to build a boat and save his life. In this case, too, it appears that the imported account was preserved closely. Tigay details the similarities between the account of the flood in Tablet XI and Atrahasis and concludes that the relevant portion of (a likely late version of) Atrahasis was preserved in Tablet XI with relatively little adjustment. This is most evident by the fact that while Gilgamesh calls the flood survivor Ūta-napišti, in the recounting of the flood story the protagonist is twice called Atrahasis (XI 187; Tigay, *Evolution of the Gilgamesh Epic*, 216–17). Tigay argues that the flood account was also added to the Epic at a late stage in transmission and that while Ūta-napišti is mentioned in the Sippar Tablet, his account of the flood was most likely not included in the Old Babylonian Epic (238–40).

omitted material may have been recognized as either inherently unnecessary or somehow separate.

(3) The best-preserved source (GEN) was tacked onto the end of the Epic as an appendix of sorts, with no effort made to ease the transition from the Epic to the source content. There was likewise no effort to smooth out the inconsistencies between the Epic and the source represented in Tablet XII. The common notion that the ends of biblical scrolls would have been a convenient place for additions of either new or old content thus finds support in the Akkadian evidence, and the case of GEN *may* suggest that sources affixed to the end of works are least likely to have been heavily revised.[37]

(4) Source content could be completely rewritten, as in the case of GH. This is also evident with regard to GBH. It is possible that in the case of GH, the source was first rendered in independent and radically different form (the Akkadian Huwawa narrative) before it was taken up and incorporated into the Epic. From that point on, however, the Huwawa episode underwent comparatively less change over the course of transmission, though it continued to accumulate accretions. As such, GH represents a complex case where the source was completely rewritten in the process of rendering it in Akkadian but then *that* version was retained somewhat more closely over a millennium, with at least several units represented in nearly identical terms.[38]

37. A number of biblical books are thought to have appendices or secondary conclusions (though not all are considered to preserve old content): for example, Deut 31–34 (see, e.g., Martin Noth, *The Deuteronomistic History*, trans. David J. A. Clines, JSOTSup 15 [Sheffield: JSOT Press, 1981], 13–17, 26–35; for a different take, see Van der Toorn, *Scribal Culture and the Making*, 151–72); Judg 17–21 (see, e.g., J. Alberto Soggin, *Judges: A Commentary*, OTL [Philadelphia: Westminster, 1981], 5); 2 Sam 20:23–24:25 (see, e.g., P. Kyle McCarter Jr., *II Samuel: A New Translation with Introduction, Notes, and Commentary*, AB 9 [Garden City, NY: Doubleday, 1984], 16–20); Isa 40–66, and within that, 55/56–66 (see, e.g., Marvin A. Sweeney, "Introduction to Isaiah," in *The New Oxford Annotated Bible, with the Apocryphal/Deuterocanonical Books: New Revised Standard Version*, ed. Michael D. Coogan et al., 3rd ed. [New York: Oxford University Press, 2001], 974); and Amos 9:11–15 (for bibliography, see Gerhard F. Hasel, *The Remnant: The History and Theology of the Remnant Idea from Genesis to Isaiah*, AUMSR 5 [Berrien Springs, MI: Andrews University Press, 1972], 207–8 n. 300, 473).

38. See, for example, the elders' response to Gilgamesh in OB II, col. v, lines 189–196 // SB II 287–295 or Gilgamesh's vanquishing of Huwawa in OB Ishchali rev. 19–23 // SB V 262–265.

(5) At least in the case of GH, the incorporation of source content into the Epic (whether directly or indirectly) was accompanied by massive additions at the front and back ends. In this case, in contrast to GEN, efforts were made to ease the transition between the new content and the beginning of the source.[39] In my *Tracking the Master Scribe* I detail the scribal practice of adding new material to the front of a work in order to change the reception of received material, something that is evident in both Mesopotamian and biblical texts.[40]

It is apparent that this pair of cases offers no simple confirmation of any extant scheme of Pentateuchal or Deuteronomistic compositional analysis. It is neither obvious that combining large documents was the standard method of choice nor that texts were written only by supplements, the addition of new material bit by bit. Rather, GH and GEN give glimpses into a complex process that reveals the use of a variety of techniques with a wide range of results. On the one hand, we have evidence of a source that has been transformed completely already in the first identifiable phase of transmission. Subsequently, however, that plotline became comparatively more stable. On the other hand, we have evidence of a source that is represented in near-identical form after a thousand years. In this case, one could easily identify Tablet XII as having had once-independent origins, and the fact that it starts *in medias res* already suggests that elimination has taken place. In terms of application to the Bible, it is possible that certain texts that appear to be tacked onto the ends of books not only originated independently, but also may represent old material. Sources that have been integrated into their surroundings, however, may have lost so much of their early formulations that their independent origins are no longer recognizable.

3.3. Back to School: The Possibility of Pedagogical Origins for Biblical Texts

At this point, I would like to consider whether the Gilgamesh evidence may provide us with insights of a different type, beyond questions of scribal method. For starters, it reveals that, at least in Mesopotamia, narrative school texts could have served as a pool of sources for incorporation into something

39. As noted above, however, this source may refer to the separate Akkadian Huwawa narrative.

40. See Sara J. Milstein, *Tracking the Master Scribe: Revision through Introduction in Biblical and Mesopotamian Literature* (New York: Oxford University Press, 2016).

different. This process was executed in various ways. The educational context for GH appears to have inspired the transition of the story from Sumerian to Akkadian, perhaps initially as an independent Huwawa narrative. If that Akkadian text was also copied in the Old Babylonian period as a school text, as suggested by the extract tablets, the larger Epic also would have been built from an Akkadian Huwawa narrative with reference to a pedagogical context. GEN instead reflects a situation where a popular school text was preserved independently for centuries before it was affixed to the end of the Epic. Each case thus reflects influence from the school context, even if the specific processes and circumstances differ.

While scholars have long conjectured that extended blocks about various figures in the Bible could have originated in independent episodes, the context for the preservation and transmission of these episodes has remained elusive. Gilgamesh provides a theoretical model for how and why such episodes could have been known and possibly preserved in writing. The extensive evidence available for Old Babylonian scribal training indicates that narratives had a role to play in the curriculum, alongside more obvious school texts such as proverbs or hymns.[41] Perhaps the scribes responsible for some extended sequences in the Bible likewise drew on narratives that they had learned as part of their training. The question remains, however, as to how one would nail down any possible contenders.[42] Any attempt to do so would have to draw not only on

41. Of course, there is another factor, in that these texts were copied as part of education in Sumerian, a language that would have been foreign to the students. Here, however, the Akkadian Huwawa narrative offers a more intriguing parallel, in that it would have been learned outside of the context of language acquisition. Cuneiform scribes were also skilled in writing legal texts, administrative texts, letters, divinatory texts, and so on, and yet unlike these, the Akkadian literary texts had no obvious practical application. The surprise of the Huwawa extracts, or even of Old Babylonian Gilgamesh tablets more generally, is that scribes in the Old Babylonian period learned literature as one part of education for writing in their own language.

42. I am speaking beyond the obvious school text candidates, such as acrostic compositions (Pss 9–10, 25, 34, 119, 145; Prov 31:10–31; Lam 1–4) or wisdom literature such as Proverbs, Job, and Qoheleth (see James L. Crenshaw, *Education in Ancient Israel: Across the Deadening Silence*, AYBRL [New York: Doubleday, 1998], 221–37, and Carr, *Writing on the Tablet of the Heart*, 126–34). Carr notes, however, that wisdom texts in Mesopotamia and Egypt were used alongside poetic texts and narrative texts and that we should be careful not to separate wisdom literature from other forms of literature in terms of educational usage in Israel (132; see also his n. 86). He then considers the possibility that a variety of other biblical texts were used in

internal data but also on broader ideas regarding the organizing principles behind an Israelite or Judahite scribal curriculum. Would the Israelite or Judahite scribes have likewise copied stories about kings, or would they have favored tales about patriarchs or military heroes? Would they have enjoyed stories about humor or tales marked by tragedy? Would they have copied and/or transformed narratives that originated in other cultures?

In this context, I would like to offer one theory for a biblical collection with possibly early pedagogical origins. The book of Judges has long stood out in the Bible for various reasons. All of its narratives take place in Israelite locales, not Judahite ones; it is mostly composed of separate narrative blocks that are only loosely drawn together; and it apparently includes the oldest poem in the Bible (Judg 5) as well as what many consider to be old narrative content (Judg 9).[43] Like the Gilgamesh Epic, it includes an "appendix" with two narrative blocks that are only tangentially joined (Judg 17–18 and 19–21); it contains colorful tales that pertain to adventure and combat; it includes tales of early kingship (Abimelech in Judg 9) and clusters of episodes about heroes (e.g., Samson in Judg 13–16). The reference in 1 Sam 12:9–11 to tales known from Judges (Judg 4–5, 9, 10–12, 13–16) could indicate knowledge of a pedagogical collection. Without pushing the evidence too far, the interest in "Israel" in "Judah's Bible" could mirror the celebration of Sumer by the Babylonians in the Old

---

or related to education, including, for example, Deuteronomy and the Deuteronomistic History, prophetic books, and Gen 1–11 (126–56). Van der Toorn likewise treats Deuteronomy, Isaiah, and Psalms as likely candidates for texts in the Second Temple scribal curriculum and notes the preponderance of these three books among the Dead Sea Scrolls (Van der Toorn, *Scribal Culture and the Making*, 101–4).

43. See, for example, Christoph Levin, "Das vorstaatliche Israel," *ZTK* 97 (2000): 385–403, esp. 398–401. Levin notes: "Wir haben es mit authentischer altisraelitischer Überlieferung zu tun, für die Zeit vor Saul mit einer der wenigen regelrechten Quellen überhaupt" (400). He adds that the Abimelech account is "das Bindeglied" between the Amarna letters and the emergence of the Israelite kingdom (401). Walter Groß considers the Abimelech account to date to the twelfth century BCE, even if the actual text must date to the early monarchic period (Walter Groß, *Richter*, HThKAT [Freiburg: Herder, 2009], 87). Brendon C. Benz highlights the features of Judg 9 that resonate with details found in the Amarna evidence: the depiction of collective leadership (the "seventy sons of Jerubbaal"), the rule of an individual over multiple urban centers, and the notion of a collective body taking action against the king (Brendon C. Benz, "The Varieties of Sociopolitical Experience in the Late Bronze Age Levant and the Rise of Early Israel" [PhD diss., New York University, 2012], 496–99).

Babylonian period.[44] While pedagogical origins need not account for all of the content in Judges, they would offer a realistic model for how and why some of these narratives (and other biblical tales for that matter) could have been preserved over centuries and then expanded or combined. If we have anything to learn from Gilgamesh beyond the inevitability of our own mortality, it may be to keep the scribal origins of the Bible in full view.

44. I draw on the distinctions highlighted in Daniel E. Fleming, *The Legacy of Israel in Judah's Bible: History, Politics, and the Reinscribing of Tradition* (Cambridge: Cambridge University Press, 2012).

Scribal Revision and Textual Variation in Akkadian *Šuila*-Prayers: Two Case Studies in Ritual Adaptation*

Alan Lenzi

1. Introduction

If one talks with someone who has spent an extended time in another culture, one will inevitably hear about the different customs encountered in the foreign land and the new perspectives developed on that person's own cultural conventions upon returning home. The purpose of this study is to provide biblicists an analogous opportunity: to gain a new perspective on their own material after seeing familiar questions posed to a foreign body of evidence, that is, Akkadian religious texts.[1] As wonderfully important and variously relevant as is Assyriology for biblical interpretation,[2] the present study limits itself to several case studies on textual variation and scribal revision in the textual witnesses to two *šuila*-prayers, Gula 1a =

* This chapter was first presented at a session of the Hebrew Scriptures and Cognate Literature section of the Society of Biblical Literature's Annual Meeting in San Diego, CA (November 24, 2014). I thank Sara J. Milstein for inviting me to participate. I also wish to thank her, the other participants, and those in attendance for their valuable feedback.

1. I do not intend to imply that the Hebrew Bible is just like Akkadian religious texts. The cultures are different. Further, the textual evidence from each is different, especially with regard to the duration of the scribal transmission of the texts. The latter comes into strong relief in the epilogue of this chapter.

2. See Alan Lenzi, "Assyriology and Biblical Interpretation," in *The Oxford Encyclopedia of Biblical Interpretation*, ed. Steven L. McKenzie (New York: Oxford University Press, 2013), 42–52.

Belet-ili 1 and Sîn 1.[3] In the epilogue, I reflect on how the findings may relate to the diachronic study of the biblical text.[4]

2. Preliminary Thoughts about Scribal Revision

Imagine an ancient Babylonian scribe who composes a new text and another who carefully transcribes a previously existing text verbatim to a new tablet.[5] Somewhere between these two ideal scribal activities is *revision*—an activity in which a scribe transmits a preexisting text from one material support to another but makes changes during the process so that the product is an altered text that remains similar enough to the earlier text that we recognize a genetic relationship between the two.[6]

---

3. For a brief introduction to Akkadian *šuila*-prayers, see Christopher Frechette's discussion in Alan Lenzi, Christopher Frechette, and Anna Elise Zernecke, "Introduction," in *Reading Akkadian Prayers and Hymns: An Introduction*, ed. Alan Lenzi, ANEM 3 (Atlanta: Society of Biblical Literature, 2011), 24–35. I present detailed information on the two prayers below.

4. I am not the first to consider the use of Mesopotamian materials as a potential means to illuminate scribal activities in the biblical text. See, for example, Sara J. Milstein, "Reworking Ancient Texts: Revision through Introduction in Biblical and Mesopotamian Literature" (PhD diss., New York University, 2010), to be published as Milstein, *Tracking the Master Scribe: Revision through Introduction in Biblical and Mesopotamian Narratives* (New York: Oxford University Press, forthcoming). Also worthy of note are two other studies that look at manuscript evidence for various Akkadian compositions in order to understand textual variation in transmission. They then use these results to reflect on the transmission of the biblical text. The two studies are: Russell Hobson, *Transforming Literature into Scripture: Texts as Cult Objects at Nineveh and Qumran*, BibleWorld (Sheffield: Equinox, 2012), which considers the textual variation between manuscripts for the Akkadian compositions Enuma Anu Enlil Tablet 63, MUL.APIN, the Laws of Hammurabi, and Tablet XI of the Standard Babylonian (SB) version of the Epic of Gilgamesh (I thank Robert Rezetko for this reference); and Mordechai Cogan, "Some Text-Critical Issues in the Hebrew Bible from an Assyriological Perspective," *Text* 22 (2005): 1–20, which considers the textual variations in and revisions between editions of Assurbanipal's royal annals, limiting itself to editions B (649 BCE), F (646 BCE), and A (643 BCE). The present study intends to complement these by using *šuila*-prayers as the corpus of Assyriological evidence.

5. The latter, it seems, is asserted by the common colophonic refrain *šaṭir-ma bari* (*kīma labīrīšu*), "written and checked (according to its original)" on some tablets. See Hermann Hunger, *Babylonische und assyrische Kolophone*, AOAT 2 (Kevelaer: Butzon & Bercker; Neukirchen-Vluyn: Neukirchener, 1968), 175–76 (s.v. *šaṭāru*).

6. My perspective is explicitly textual in orientation, but this should not imply that it is the only possible perspective.

From the outset, this definition runs into a very common problem of definition making: it assumes we already know how to quantify key components in the definition, in this case, sameness and difference. Thus, we are confronted by a question: when does scribal activity produce a duplicate of a text, a revised text (i.e., a different edition/recension), or, due to the quantity and quality of changes, a discrete text?[7] As is often the case in taxonomies, the precise boundaries are a matter of judgment.[8] One might suggest that such a question derives from our own cultural fascination (or anxiety?) with copyright, textual fixity, and library cataloging. Yet making distinctions between a duplicate, a revision, and a discrete text may be a matter of practicality, especially when organizing and editing, for example, Assyrian royal inscriptions, but also, as my last case study shows, incantation-prayers, of which *šuila*s are a subset. Moreover, poor classification practices may deprive us of useful historical-cultural information.[9]

I raise this preliminary concern, because it problematizes a fundamental classificatory scheme upon which the exploration of scribal revision relies, and it admonishes us to own up to the fact that we are the ones who decide what counts as evidence of revision and what does not by deciding which texts to compare because they are *similar* enough to each other—despite some differences—to catch our eye and which to leave

7. I wish to thank Jamie Novotny for thinking with me about these matters in an engaging personal correspondence.

8. In its discussion of how much revision constitutes a new edition of a book, *The Chicago Manual of Style* defines a new edition "as one in which a *significant or substantial change* has been made in one or more of the essential elements of the work" (emphasis original). It then goes on to note that "[s]omething subjective and unquantifiable persists in this definition, but that is because the decision is ultimately judgmental, not mathematical" (*The Chicago Manual of Style*, 14th ed. [Chicago: University of Chicago Press, 1993], §1.21). I suggest the same standard and caveat apply to the distinctions between a duplicate of a text, a revised text, and a discrete or unique text. Interestingly (and illustrating both the point of this footnote and our general anxiety over textual fixity), subsequent editions of the *Manual* have arbitrarily quantified the amount of revision necessary to qualify a text as a new edition to 20 percent; see §1.22 in the 15th (2003) and §1.26 in the 16th (2010) editions.

9. See, for example, Mario Liverani, "Critique of Variants and the Titulary of Sennacherib," in *Assyrian Royal Inscriptions: New Horizons*, ed. Frederick Mario Fales, OAC 17 (Rome: Istituto per l'Oriente, 1981), 225–31 for reflections on the importance of identifying and presenting compositional variants in Neo-Assyrian royal inscriptions as a means of acquiring evidence to understand the historical and political dynamics of the empire.

aside because they are *dissimilar* enough—despite some similarities—that we do not consider them relevant for our purposes.[10]

But an even more fundamental issue than quantifying sameness and difference between two texts in order to identify evidence of scribal revision is the fact that our definition requires us to know what we hardly ever know when it comes to ancient texts, namely, the precise conditions in which scribes worked and the materials they had in hand as they worked to produce the texts that lie before us today. We can be sure, however, that scribes in ancient Mesopotamia revised texts, not only because we think we can find evidence of it in the manuscripts they left behind (often a very subjective enterprise) but also, more importantly, because they sometimes explicitly write about revising texts.[11] I offer a pertinent example below.

Although such scribal notices prove in principle that scribes revised texts, in order to understand how a *particular* text was in fact revised, we would ideally like to have the original text, the revised text, and a clear indication that this is in fact their relationship (that is, that one existed before the other and that the later text was in fact based on and worked from the earlier one). This is an evidentiary standard that is rarely met in Assyriology.[12] Short of this kind of evidence, I would argue, we must

---

10. It is worth noting that the issues surrounding the identification of revision are similar to those of identifying allusion and influence. Benjamin Sommer provides a useful introduction (Benjamin D. Sommer, *A Prophet Reads Scripture: Allusion in Isaiah 40–56*, Contraversions [Stanford, CA: Stanford University Press, 1998], 6–20).

11. Editorial notes are sometimes included on texts that have been edited; see, for example, Irving L. Finkel, "Adad-apla-iddina, Esagil-kīn-apli, and the Series SA.GIG," in *A Scientific Humanist: Studies in Memory of Abraham Sachs*, ed. Erle Leichty, Maria de Jong Ellis, and Pamela Gerardi, OPSNKF 9 (Philadelphia: University Museum, 1988), 149.

12. Neo-Assyrian royal inscriptions offer important exceptions. See Marc Van De Mieroop, *Cuneiform Texts and the Writing of History* (London: Routledge, 1999), 40–52, who provides an overview with examples of how these texts could be revised from year to year. See also Cogan, "Some Text-Critical Issues," who discusses variations between editions of Assyrian royal annals and provides references to other studies that do likewise. I am aware of various studies of, for example, Akkadian narrative poetry—one could cite a litany of studies for omen and ritual series as well—that compare a late version of the text with an Old or Middle Babylonian (or Assyrian) version of the same text; for example, W. G. Lambert and Alan R. Millard, *Atra-ḫasīs: The Babylonian Story of the Flood* (Oxford: Clarendon, 1969; repr., Winona Lake, IN: Eisenbrauns, 1999), 31–39 (implicit in their discussion of the manuscripts of Atrahasis); Jerrold S. Cooper, "Symmetry and Repetition in Akkadian Narrative," *JAOS* 97

always admit that our judgment about textual revision exists at best in the graded shadows of historical plausibility or at worst in the murky margins of historical speculation. In other words, we must humbly admit that we are likely never to have certainty about the process of textual revision in most texts (i.e., how a text changed through time and why)—even if we can decide the percentage of change required to qualify a text as presenting such—because we hardly ever have the required evidence to make the judgment with unqualified confidence. This leaves two options, it seems to me. Option one: abandon the diachronic study of texts entirely. Or, as the first option is unappealing and overly cautious, option two: leave certainty behind, embrace plausibility as our inescapable companion, and refine our methodology so that speculation is minimized.[13]

3. The Method

How, then, do we minimize speculation? I think speculation and thus the tentativeness of our conclusions about scribal revision increase in direct

(1977): 508–12; Cooper, "Gilgamesh Dreams of Enkidu: The Evolution and Dilution of Narrative," in *Essays on the Ancient Near East in Memory of Jacob Joel Finkelstein*, ed. Maria de Jong Ellis, MCAAS 19 (Hamden, CT: Archon Books, 1977), 39–44; Jeffrey H. Tigay, *The Evolution of the Gilgamesh Epic* (Philadelphia: University of Pennsylvania Press, 1982); Tigay, "The Evolution of the Pentateuchal Narratives in the Light of the Evolution of the *Gilgamesh Epic*," in *Empirical Models for Biblical Criticism*, ed. Jeffrey H. Tigay (Philadelphia: University of Pennsylvania Press, 1985), 21–52; Marianna E. Vogelzang, "Repetition as a Poetic Device in Akkadian," in *Mesopotamian Poetic Language: Sumerian and Akkadian*, ed. Marianna E. Vogelzang and Herman L. J. Vanstiphout, CM 6 (Groningen: Styx Publications, 1986), 167–82; and Vogelzang, *Bin Šar Dadmē: Edition and Analysis of the Akkadian Anzu Poem* (Groningen: Styx Publications, 1988), 190–224. But these studies cannot always demonstrate conclusively that the scribes of the SB versions used the older versions of the poem currently known to us rather than some other older version. Tigay, for example, cannot identify the version of Atrahasis from which SB Gilgamesh took the flood story (Tigay, *Evolution of the Gilgamesh Epic*, 216–18; Tigay, "The Stylistic Criterion of Source Criticism in the Light of Ancient Near Eastern and Postbiblical Literature," in Tigay, *Empirical Models for Biblical Criticism*, 160–61), and Vogelzang must admit that her *comparanda* could "go back to similar but different OB [Old Babylonian] recensions or that they are genetically related" (Vogelzang, *Bin Šar Dadmē*, 198). Needless to say, such comparisons between late and older versions can be quite useful and provide interesting results, even if the precise genetic connection between editions of the poems is currently indiscernible (see Cooper, "Symmetry and Repetition," 508 n. 2).

13. Or, at least, duly noted as such.

proportion to our reliance upon internal (intratextual) evidence. That is, when an argument for revision relies exclusively on some inconsistency, tension, or contradiction within the text and there is no other evidence to corroborate this perception, we run the risk of imposing modern literary expectations on ancient texts and thereby inventing problems to which revision is the solution.[14] This problem is exacerbated when the texts are also undated and unprovenanced. Due to a dearth of ancient manuscripts, internal evidence from manuscripts copied long after the presumed time of the text's origin is often the only kind of evidence available to the biblical scholar interested in the development of, for example, the Masoretic Text.[15] Assyriologists, however, have another option, one that is possible due to the common state of evidentiary affairs for first millennium Akkadian compositions, namely, the existence of ancient, excavated tablets that show slightly different texts of the same Akkadian compositions. Thus, we can compare witnesses of the same composition to see how scribes may have changed/revised its texts during the course of its ramified transmission. Of course, the issue of quantification arises here again. How do we know two tablets represent the same text? Aside from cases in which copies present identical contents (i.e., they are simple duplicates), which would make such textual witnesses useless for our present purpose, how much deviation does it take to disqualify a text as a duplicate or to qualify it as a revision? Again, this is a matter of judgment that is not easily quantifiable (as will be seen below). The other issue that arises is chronological ordering of the manuscripts. Can we set the manuscripts into a chronological order so we can retrace the revision process?

As illustration is the goal of this study, I begin with the manuscript evidence identified by the most recent editors of the two *šuila*-prayers chosen for my case studies, Gula 1a = Belet-ili 1 and Sîn 1 in Werner Mayer's catalog. I have chosen these compositions for test cases, because they are well attested, I know them well, and we have a good deal of informa-

---

14. I am not implying that such readings *always* foist modern literary expectations on the ancient text, only that there is a higher risk of doing so in such situations.

15. Of course, biblical scholars can compare versions (e.g., Masoretic Text versus Septuagint versus Samaritan Pentateuch) and material from the Dead Sea, as does Tigay at times in *Empirical Models for Biblical Criticism* (for example, in Jeffrey H. Tigay, "Conflation as a Redactional Technique," in Tigay, *Empirical Models for Biblical Criticism*, 53–83), but such does not always help in the explanation of perceived tensions or contradictions within one of the versions (e.g., MT).

tion about several of their textual witnesses. (The latter point is of great importance and in striking contrast to our knowledge about most of the textual witnesses to the Hebrew Bible.) The information we have on the witnesses for these two *šuila*s allows us to ask an important question: what may we learn about scribal revision and textual variation when we are on the firmest of textual ground? That is, what can we learn when we are able to compare closely textual witnesses of the same composition from a genre *known* to have been revised (see below) *and* the witnesses of the composition are also dated, provenanced, and, in some cases, plausibly contextualized within a ritual setting?

This study therefore begins in the exact opposite manner as did Jeffrey Tigay's in *Empirical Models for Biblical Criticism*. Tigay went looking for texts, in many cases, Mesopotamian texts, that "confirm established hypotheses of biblical criticism."[16] That is, he went looking for comparative evidence to support a previously obtained result in the Bible. In distinction, this study begins with a broad category of texts, incantation-prayers labeled *šuila* (i.e., used in a *šuila*-ritual), that we know for certain were at times revised in order to adapt them to new situations. It examines two representatives from this category by way of several of their textual witnesses to determine what we can learn about the scribal revision process from a close, empirical comparison. Only with these results in hand does the present study consider briefly how its results might impact our expectations of the textual evidence provided in the biblical text.

4. The Results Anticipated

The results of the comparison ought to give all diachronic interpreters of ancient documents some pause. For while it is quite easy to describe the differences between the witnesses of the same composition and to establish broad ideas about how the revision/adaptation process was implemented, in some cases there is no clear way to explain the differences in detail and in all of the cases there is no clear way to establish a textual development among the manuscripts—and this despite all that we know about each witness. And, let us be clear, as historians interested in the dynamic of textual production and its implications for and within the social formations

16. Jeffrey H. Tigay, "Summary and Conclusions," in Tigay, *Empirical Models for Biblical Criticism*, 240. See especially Tigay, "Evolution of the Pentateuchal Narratives," 21–52; and Tigay, "Stylistic Criterion of Source Criticism," 149–67.

we study, *the explanation of differences* is why we pursue the question of scribal revision and textual variation in the first place.[17]

5. *Šuila*-Prayers and Ritual Adaptation: A Reason for Scribal Revision and Textual Variation

Before I turn to the case studies, I want to establish that the *šuila*-prayer genre was in fact a genre subject to scribal revision for the purposes of ritual adaptation. The most convincing and objective way to prove this would be to find a statement along these lines from a scribe. We could hardly ask for better evidence than the following letter from an Assyrian scholar to his king:

> The "farmer" [i.e., the king's title during the substitute king ritual] should perform the apotropaic ritual against evil of any kind; the "farmer" should (also) perform the penitential psalms for Nergal and the "hand-lifting" prayer [*šuila*] for Nergal. Let them write in the apotropaic ritual and the prayer as follows: "In the evil of the planet Mars which exceeded its term and ap[peared] in the constellation Aries: may its evil not [approach], not come near, not press up[on (me)], not affect me, my country, the people of [my pal]ace and my army!" Let them write like this in the apotropaic ritual and the "hand-lifting" prayer.[18]

---

17. Liverani makes the same point with regard to variants in royal inscriptions. He writes: "[S]ometimes we meet changes of historical interest. These variations are generally analysed with the aim of pointing out the more 'reliable' formulation. This is clearly a transfer to the historical level of the philological aim in the critical edition, namely to point out the 'best' variant reading (the original one). But, as we noted in the beginning of our study, since the texts are generally dated, since it is known that the later derive from the former ones, the result of such an analysis is disconcerting in its obviousness: the 'best' recension is the first one! Less banal and less obvious and less mechanical would be the further step to be accomplished (and rarely accomplished): the individuation of the *reason* for the variation, a reason that must have an historical setting. Also this kind of analysis is the transfer to the historical level of a philological interest: the interest to follow the manuscript tradition not only in order to reconstruct the original reading, but also as a study in culture of the time to which later manuscripts and their variants belong" (Liverani, "Critique of Variants," 252, emphasis original).

18. SAA 10 381, obv. 1–rev. 6 (= Simo Parpola, *Letters from Assyrian and Babylonian Scholars*, SAA 10 [Helsinki: Helsinki University Press, 1993], no. 381). For a discussion of the ritual situation, see Christopher Frechette, *Mesopotamian Ritual-Prayers of "Hand-Lifting" (Akkadian* Šuillas*): An Investigation of Function in Light*

Here a scholar advises King Assurbanipal how to revise and thereby adapt certain ritual-prayers (both a *namburbî*, "apotropaic ritual,"[19] and a *šuila*, "'hand-lifting' prayer") for the situation he faces by inserting specific words into the prayers' texts. As this letter was part of the royal archive and not part of the literary or scribal tradition, it is first hand evidence of an actual intention to revise a prayer in order to adapt it to a new situation and for a specific ritual performance.[20] Moreover, the words that are suggested for insertion sound very similar to some of the formulaic expressions we find in the prayers considered below. There can be no question that we are warranted to look for scribal revision in *šuila*-prayers.

6. The Comparison of Textual Witnesses to *Šuila*-Prayers: Two Case Studies

6.1. Introduction

In considering each prayer's data, I first offer a description of the witnesses used in the study, the find spot of these witnesses (if known), the content of each tablet on which our prayer occurs and what that may tell us about the prayer's ritual context,[21] and finally, if possible, the relative chronology of the witnesses vis-à-vis one another. This information establishes date, provenance, and use. After this preliminary presentation, I then offer a synoptic comparison of the four witnesses to the prayer chosen for careful scrutiny in this study, none of which is identical, to determine how and, if possible, why each witness bears the text that it does. The comparison works at the level of words, phrases, and lines. Orthographic variations, which are commonplace in witnesses of the same Akkadian text, and obvious scribal errors (dittography, mistaken or misshaped signs, omission of signs, additions of signs, spelling errors, etc.) are not considered pertinent data for the present purposes. In keeping with the editorial policy of this book, the synoptic Akkadian text of the prayers are presented only in English translation.

---

of the Idiomatic Meaning of the Rubric, AOAT 379 (Münster: Ugarit-Verlag, 2012), 184–85.

19. For a brief introduction to *namburbîs*, see my discussion in Lenzi, Frechette, and Zernecke, "Introduction," 36–40. Essential secondary literature is cited there.

20. See also SAA 10 177, obv. 15–rev. 6 and SAA 10 373, rev. 4–14.

21. The prayers under consideration are not always the only composition on the tablets that bear them.

6.2. Gula 1a = Belet-ili 1

6.2.1. Witnesses

The *šuila*-prayer designated Gula 1a = Belet-ili 1 in Mayer's catalog is attested in nine manuscripts (tablets), two of which preserve ritual instructions.[22] Three of these manuscripts direct the prayer to Belet-ili (B, E, H). Five direct it to Gula (A, C, F, G, I). One manuscript (D) is not sufficiently preserved to determine its divine addressee. Among these nine manuscripts, the most interesting witnesses for the present purpose are known in the most recent edition by the sigla:

A = K.2106 + K.2384 + K.3393 + K.3605 + K.6340 + K.7146 + K.8605 + K.8983 + K.9576 + K.9688 + K.9754 + K.11589 + K.12911 + K.13792 + K.13800
B = K.3330 + Sm.394 + 81-2-4,244
E = Rm.96
H = Si.6

Of these, only MS A attests ritual instructions, which for this reason are left out of our textual comparison in table 1.[23]

Caveat: Modern scholars have grouped the nine textual witnesses to Gula 1a = Belet-ili 1 together, despite the different divine names used in various manuscripts, because of the otherwise quite marked textual similarities among the witnesses (as will be seen below). This recognition of

22. For the most recent and complete edition of the prayer, see Werner R. Mayer, *Untersuchungen zur Formensprache der babylonischen "Gebetsbeschwörungen,"* StPohl Series Maior 5 (Rome: Pontifical Biblical Institute, 1976), 450–54, but he does not include ritual instructions. For an introduction to the prayer and an annotated, pedagogical treatment of the prayer (Akkadian vocabulary and grammar notes are supplied), see Alan Lenzi, "A Shuilla: Gula 1a," in Lenzi, *Reading Akkadian Prayers and Hymns*, 243–56. For a list of manuscripts, see Mayer, *Untersuchungen*, 450, and Frechette, *Mesopotamian Ritual-Prayers of "Hand-Lifting,"* 255, both of whom also list citations of the prayer's incipit as a catch-line or as part of ritual instructions. Add now to the list BM 38537 (= MS I), published in Lenzi, "A New Akkadian Shuila-Prayer to the Three Paths of Heaven and the Third Tablet of *Bīt salā᾿ mê*," *Or* NS 82 (2013): 1–10 (available at http://cdli.ucla.edu/P453575). Only Mayer's MSS A and G attest ritual instructions.

23. For the tablets' contents and essential publication information, see below.

modern scholars as outsiders to the ancient tradition, however, does not take away from the likelihood that the Mesopotamian scribes themselves saw two prayers, distinguished by divine name, rather than one among the witnesses that I am considering together here.

6.2.2. Discovery

Manuscripts A, B, and E come from Nineveh, the last Assyrian capital, and are presently part of the famous Kuyunjik Collection at the British Museum. As is well known, tablets from Nineveh are notoriously difficult to place in their proper find spots within the city,[24] though most of the tablets were found somewhere in Sennacherib's South-West Palace or Assurbanipal's North Palace.[25]

Sm.394, excavated by George Smith in 1874, is one of three fragments that comprise MS B of Gula 1a = Belet-ili 1. This suggests that the fragments comprising K.3330 + were probably (not certainly) excavated at the South-West Palace, though not at the same time.[26]

---

24. See Jeanette C. Fincke, "The Babylonian Texts of Nineveh: Report on the British Museum's Ashurbanipal Library Project," *AfO* 50 (2003/2004): 114–15 for a succinct summary of the archaeological and museological reasons for this difficulty. For a full list of the various groups of tablets in the Kuyunjik collection, see Fincke's helpful web page, "The List of Nineveh Joins: Description and Explanation," http://tinyurl.com/SBL2628a.

25. See Julian E. Reade, "Ninive (Nineveh)," *RlA* 9:421–22. Some of the tablets were brought to the collection from elsewhere (see, for example, Simo Parpola, "Assyrian Library Records," *JNES* 42 [1983]: 1–29). But this does not seem to be the case with any of the Ninevite tablets treated in this study. For an overview of the collection, see Reade, "Ninive (Nineveh)," 421–27, and the less technical presentation in Eleanor Robson, "Reading the Libraries of Assyria and Babylonia," in *Ancient Libraries*, ed. Jason König, Katerina Oikonomopoulou, and Greg Woolf (Cambridge: Cambridge University Press, 2013), 41–45. One should note that not all of the tablets in the Kuyunjik collection are from Nineveh. Walker estimates that about 1–2 percent of tablets in the collection were excavated elsewhere and lumped in with the Ninevite tablets upon their arrival at the British Museum (Christopher B. F. Walker, "The Kouyunjik Collection of Cuneiform Texts: Formation, Problems, and Prospects," in *Austen Henry Layard tra l'Oriente e Venezia: Symposium Internazionale, Venezia, 26–28 Ottobre 1983*, ed. Frederick Mario Fales and Bernard J. Hickey, La Fenice 8 [Rome: "L'Erma" di Bretschneider, 1987], 186).

26. See Julian E. Reade, "Archaeology and the Kuyunjik Archives," in *Cuneiform Archives and Libraries: Papers Read at the 30e Rencontre Assyriologique Internationale,*

Manuscripts E and A (Rm.96 and K.2106 +, respectively) both bear Assurbanipal colophon c.[27] But, as noted by Julian Reade, this is not unimpeachable proof of a tablet's find spot in the North Palace.[28] Based on archaeological and museum records, Reade believes Rm.96 (MS E) came from the South-West Palace, "probably [from within the] south-central area."[29] The precise find spot in Nineveh for K.2106 + (MS A) is still unclear.

Manuscript H (= Si.6) comes from Sippar, excavated by M. Vincent Scheil in 1894. Based on a few hints in Scheil's narrative, I surmise the tablet was found with some other religious texts in what Scheil called area N of the temple.[30] But this is not entirely clear.[31] It certainly dates to the reign of Shamash-shum-ukin in Babylonia (667–648 BCE) since the tablet names the king as the supplicant in its text.

In sum, we know that all four witnesses date to the seventh century BCE. Three of them came from Nineveh (A, B, E), two of which (B, E) are very likely from the South-West palace. Of the three from Nineveh, two (A, E) were written by Assurbanipal himself (thus sometime between 668–627 BCE), if the colophon is to be believed. One witness (H), probably from the vicinity of a temple in Sippar, was prepared during the reign of Shamash-shum-ukin (667–648 BCE).

Leiden, 4–8 July, 1983, ed. Klaas R. Veenhof, PIHANS 57 (Leiden: Nederlands Instituut voor het Nabije Oosten, 1986), 214, and Reade, "Ninive (Nineveh)," 422 (with more details of the location) for the origin of most Sm. tablets in the South-West Palace, though some Sm. tablets came from elsewhere. Given its accession number, (18)81-2-4,244 must have been excavated in late 1880 by Rassam's workers.

27. See Hunger, *Babylonische und assyrische Kolophone*, no. 319c. For a discussion of Assurbanipal's personal tablet collection, see Stephen J. Lieberman, "Canonical and Official Cuneiform Texts: Towards an Understanding of Assurbanipal's Personal Tablet Collection," in *Lingering Over Words: Studies in Ancient Near Eastern Literature in Honor of William L. Moran*, ed. Tzvi Abusch, John Huehnergard, and Piotr Steinkeller, HSM 37 (Atlanta: Scholars Press, 1990), 305–36.

28. Reade, "Archaeology and the Kuyunjik Collection," 218.

29. Reade, "Ninive (Nineveh)," 422.

30. See M. Vincent Scheil, *Une Saison de Fouilles à Sippar*, MIFAO 1 (Le Caire: Imprimerie de Institut français d'archéologie orientale, 1902), 71.

31. As Olof Pedersén notes, "[i]t will never be possible to sort out which texts were found in this room [Room 55], in other rooms of the temple, or in other houses in the city" (Olof Pedersén, *Archives and Libraries in the Ancient Near East: 1500–300 B.C.* [Bethesda, MD: CDL, 1998], 193).

6.2.3. Tablet Contents

The prayers under consideration are not always the only composition on the tablets bearing them. A quick review of the contents further contextualizes each witness.

Manuscript A (K.2106+) contains several *šuila*-prayers in succession. The obverse bears Anu 1, Nusku 3, Sîn 3, and the beginning of Gula 1a. The reverse completes Gula 1a and then continues with Shamash 1.[32] Each prayer is followed by a standard *šuila* rubric. After the rubric for Gula 1a, there is in addition a one-line ritual (not set off from the rubric by a ruling). An incipit to the *šuila* Papsukkal 1 and Assurbanipal colophon c concludes the tablet.[33] The order of the *šuila*s on this tablet is the exact order prescribed by a ritual tablet for *Bīt salā' mê*, a complex royal ritual, suggesting this witness belongs to that series.[34] The presence of the common placeholder phrase *anāku annanna mār annanna* ("I, so-and-so, son of so-and-so") in obv. 27 of the tablet (in a prayer to Nusku) suggests the prayers were not copied for a specific ritual performance, which we could have surmised since Assurbanipal, the most likely ritual patient of *Bīt salā' mê*, copied the tablet himself.

Manuscript B (K.3330 +) contains parts of three *šuila*-prayers. The obverse has a very fragmentary prayer to Nabu (6) followed by a standard *šuila* rubric, both of which precede our prayer—here directed to Belet-ili. A standard *šuila* rubric follows the prayer. The reverse preserves part of

---

32. See Mayer, *Untersuchungen*, 379, 406, 408, 410, and 407–8, and Frechette, *Mesopotamian Ritual-Prayers of "Hand-Lifting,"* 252, 267, 268, 270, and 271 for more information about Anu 1, Nusku 3, Sîn 3, Shamash 1, and Papsukkal 1 (mentioned presently above), respectively.

33. See Leonard W. King, "BMS 06," Cuniform Digital Library Initiative, http://cdli.ucla.edu/P394195 for a photograph; and King, ed., *Babylonian Magic and Sorcery: "Being The Prayers of the Lifting of the Hand"; The Cuneiform Texts of a Group of Babylonian and Assyrian Incantations and Magical Formulae Edited with Transliterations and Full Vocabulary from Tablets of the Kuyunjik Collections Preserved in the British Museum* (London: Luzac, 1896) (henceforth *BMS*), no. 6, which does not include K.3605, K.7146, and K.9754 since they were joined later.

34. See Claus Ambos, *Der König im Gefängnis und das Neujahrsfest im Herbst: Mechanismen der Legitimation des babylonischen Herrschers im 1. Jahrtausend v.Chr. und ihre Geschichte* (Dresden: ISLET, 2013), 162, 203–11 for this fact and a new edition of the tablet in the context of that ritual.

a prayer to Išḫara (1).[35] This prayer breaks off before its completion. The presence of *ina arḫi annanna ūmi annanna* ("in month so-and-so, day so-and-so") in the *attalû* formula in the final prayer (see rev. 27) indicates it was not copied in response to a specific lunar eclipse (and thus made for an actual ritual performance),[36] though the formula itself suggests the prayers might have been prepared for a *namburbî* or *Bīt rimki* (i.e., another complex royal ritual for purifying the king).[37]

The broken obverse of MS E (Rm.96) contains part of our prayer, directed again in this case to Belet-ili, until the tablet breaks off. The reverse contains the end of Assurbanipal c. Since obv. 15 contains the generic *ina arḫi annanna ūmi annanna* phrase within the *attalû* formula, it was probably not composed in response to a specific lunar eclipse and a particular ritual performance, though the formula itself suggests, again, that this copy could have been a part of *Bīt rimki* or a *namburbî*.[38]

I cannot yet verify the contents of MS H (Si.6), which is housed in the Istanbul Archaeological Museums. I know the tablet only from Scheil's and Mayer's transliterations,[39] with reference to Frederick W. Geers's notebook (Ac 2).[40] From what I can determine, the obverse preserves only a part of our prayer, directed to Belet-ili. Geers notes that there are traces of twelve lines on the reverse, but he gives no transliteration or clue about their identity. As this would be about the number of lines needed to finish out the prayer according to some of the other manuscripts of the prayer

35. See Mayer, *Untersuchungen*, 400–401, 388, and Frechette, *Mesopotamian Ritual-Prayers of "Hand-Lifting,"* 264, 255, respectively, for more information about Nabu 6 and Išḫara 1.

36. The *attalû* formula or lament gives expression to anxieties surrounding the evil announced by a lunar eclipse. See Mayer, *Untersuchungen*, 100–102.

37. Frechette, *Mesopotamian Ritual-Prayers of "Hand-Lifting,"* 193. For a copy of the tablet, see *BMS*, no. 7. A public photograph is not available.

38. Frechette, *Mesopotamian Ritual-Prayers of "Hand-Lifting,"* 193. For a photograph, see "Rm 0096," Cuniform Digital Library Initiative, http://cdli.ucla.edu/P424619. For a copy, see Oswald Loretz and Werner R. Mayer, *Šu-ila-Gebete: Supplement zu L. W. King; Babylonian Magic and Sorcery*, AOAT 34 (Kevelaer: Butzon & Bercker; Neukirchen-Vluyn: Neukirchener, 1978), no. 19.

39. See Scheil, *Une Saison de Fouilles à Sippar*, 96, no. 6, and Mayer, *Untersuchungen*, 450–54, but the latter is not an independent source since he relies on Scheil and Geers.

40. Available here: Frederick W. Geers, "Heft Ac," Cuniform Digital Library Initiative, http://www.cdli.ucla.edu/tools/cdlifiles/geers_ac.pdf.zip.

(with a couple of lines to spare for a rubric and one-line ritual), the reverse may have simply contained the rest of the prayer's text. The presence of the *attalû* formula that also names Shamash-shum-ukin in it suggests the prayer was prepared for *Bīt rimki* (or a *namburbî*) for that king.[41]

6.2.4. Relative Chronology

We have three manuscripts—A, E, and H—that come from the reigns of Assurbanipal or Shamash-shum-ukin. The other manuscript, B, dates to sometime in the seventh century. Despite what we know about these tablets, it is impossible to arrange our witnesses in a more precise chronological order or declare one confidently as the oldest. As the next section demonstrates, we must treat our evidence for all practical purposes as contemporary copies of the same prayer, each bearing slight variations in its wording.

6.2.5. Synoptic Comparison

Table 1: Gula 1a = Belet-ili 1[42]

MS A = K.2106+	MS B = K.3330+	MS E = Rm.96	MS H = Si.6
(Nineveh)	(Nineveh)	(Nineveh)	(Sippar)
o71. O <u>Gula</u>, most exalted lady, merci[ful] mother, [who d]wells in the pure heavens,	o9′. O <u>Belet-ili</u>, [most ex]alted lady, [merci-ful mother, who dwells in the pure heavens,]	o1. [O <u>Belet-ili</u>, most exalted lady, merciful mother, who dwells in the pure heavens,]	o1′. [O <u>Belet-ili</u>, most exalted lady, me]rciful [mother, who dwells in the pure heavens],

41. See Frechette, *Mesopotamian Ritual-Prayers of "Hand-Lifting,"* 193, and Jørgen Læssøe, *Studies on the Assyrian Ritual and Series Bit Rimki* (Copenhagen: Munksgaard, 1955), 95, who confidently assigns the tablet to *Bīt rimki*, though he seems to believe that the prayer is directed to Gula in this witness rather than Belet-ili. The latter is not listed in the ritual tablet among the deities to receive a prayer (25).

42. The texts behind the translations of MSS A, B, and E were collated against photographs of the tablets, which I took at the British Museum. The transliteration behind the translation of MS H is only based on Scheil's and Mayer's, with reference to Geers's notebook (Ac 2). I have not yet seen a copy, a photograph, or the tablet itself.

o72. I call out to you, my lady, stand nearby and [liste]n to me!	o10′. I call out to you, my lady, stand nea[rby and listen] to me!	o2. [I call out to you, my lady, stand ne]arby and listen [to me]!	ø?
o73. I seek you out, I turn to you, as the he[m of my god('s) (and)? godde]ss('s garment), I lay hold of your (garment's) hem,	o11′. I seek you out, I turn to you, as the he[m of my god('s) (and)? goddess('s garment), I lay hold of your (garment's) hem],	o3. [I seek you out, I turn to you, as the h]em of my god('s) and goddess('s garment), [I lay hold of your (garment's) h]em,	o2′. [I seek you out, I turn to you, as the hem of] my god('s) (and) goddess('s garment), [I lay hold of your (garment's) hem],
o74. Because jud[ging] a case, handing down the decision,	o12′. Because judging a case, [handing down the decision],	o4. [Because judg]ing a case, hand[ing down] the decision,	o3′. [Because judging a case], handing down the decision,
o75. Because restoring and mai[ntaining] well-being are within your power,	o13′. Because restoring (and) maintain[ing well-being are within your power],	o5. [Because restoring and] maintaining well-being are [within your power],	o4′. [Because rest]oring and maintaining well-being are within your power,
o76. Because you know how to save, to sp[are], and to [r]escue.	o14′. Because [you know how] to save, to spare, (and) to rescue.	o6. [Because] you know [how to save, to spare, and to rescue].	o5′. [Because you know how to s]ave, to spare, and to rescue.
o77. O Gula, most [exalted] lady, merciful mother,	o15′. O Belet-ili, sublim[e] lad[y, merciful mother],	o7. [O Belet-ili, sublime/most exalted? lady], merciful mother,	o6′. [O Belet]-ili, sublime lady, merciful mother,
r1. [Among the myri]ad stars of the hea[vens],	o16′. Among the myriad stars of the heavens,	o8. [Among the m]yriad stars of the heavens,	o7′. Among the myriad stars of the heavens,
r2. [O lady, to you] I turn; [my ears] are attentive to you.	O lady, to/in y[ou I turn/trust?; my ears are attentive to you].	o9. [O lady,] in you [I] trust; my ears are attentive to you.	o8′. O lady, in you I trust; my ears are attentive to you.
ø	ø	ø	o9′. I, Shamash-shum-ukin, the king, the son of his god,

ø	ø	ø	o10′. whose god (is) Marduk, goddess (is) Zarpanitu,
ø	ø	ø	o11′. on account of the evil of a lunar eclipse, which occurred on the fifteenth day of the month Shabbatu,
ø	ø	ø	o12′. (and) the evil of portents (and) omens, unpleasant (and) unfavorable,
ø	ø	ø	o13′. which are present in my palace and (throughout) my land,
ø	ø	ø	o14′. am afraid, in fear, and constantly frightened.
ø	ø	ø	o15′. May its evil, to me and my house,
ø	ø	ø	o16′. not draw near, approach, advance, (or) arrive.
r3. [Rece]ive [my flour offering], accept my pra[yer].	o17′. Receive my flour offering, [accept my prayer].	o10. [Rece]ive [my flour offering], accept my prayer.	o17′. Receive my flour offering, accept my prayer.
r4. [Let me send you] to my angry (personal) god (and)[my angry] (personal) go[ddess],	o18′. Let me send you to my an[gry (personal) god (and) my angry (personal) goddess],	o11. [Let me send you to] my angry (personal) god (and) my angry (personal) goddess,	o18′. Let me send you to my angry (personal) god (and) my angry (personal) goddess,

r5. [To the god of my city who] is furious and enrage[ed with me].	o19′. To the god of my city who is furious and en[raged with me].	o12. [To the god of my city who] is furious and enraged with me.	o19′. To the god of my city who is furious and enraged with me.
r6. [On account of oracles and dre]ams that are [hounding me],	ø	o13. [On account of oracles and dr]eams that are hounding me,	o20′. On account of oracles and dreams that are hounding me,
r7. [I am afraid and] constantly [anxious].	ø	ø	ø
ø	ø	o14. [I so-and-so, son of so-and-so] whose god (is) so-and-so (and) goddess (is) so-and-so,	ø
ø	o20′. on account of the evil of a lunar eclipse, which [occurred in month…],	o15. [on account of the evil of a lunar eclipse, which] occurred in so-and-so month (on) so-and-so day,	ø
ø	o21′. (and) the evil of portent[s (and) omens, unpleasant (and) unfavorable],	o16. [(and) the evil of portents (and) omens, unp]leasant (and) unfavorable,	ø
ø	o22′. which are present in my palace [and (throughout) my land—]	[x]. [which are present in my palace and (throughout) my land—]	ø
r8. [O G]ula, most exalted lady, through the word of your [august] command, [which is supreme in Ekur],	o23′. O Belet-ili, [most exalted?] lady, [through the word of your august command,] which is supreme in Ekur,	[The remainder is broken away.]	o21′–22′. O Belet-ili, merciful lady, through the word of your august command, which is supreme in Ekur,

r9. And your sure approval, whi[ch cannot be altered],	o24′. And your sure approval, whi[ch cannot be altered],	o22′. And your sure approval, which cannot be alte[re]d,
r10. May my furious god turn back to me; may my ang[ry] goddess [turn again to me with favor].	o25′. May my furious [god turn back to me; may my angry goddess turn again to me with favor].	[The remainder is broken away.]
r11. May the god of my city who is furious and enrage[ed with me],	o26′. [May] the god of my city who is furio[us and enraged with me],	
r12. Who is in a rage, relent; who is incen[sed, be soothed].	o27′. Who is in a rage, rel[ent; who is incensed, be soothed].	
r13. O Gula, most exalted lady, who inter[cedes on behalf of the powerless],	o28′. O Belet-ili, most ex[alted] lady, [who intercedes on behalf of the powerless],	
r14. With Marduk, king of the gods, merciful lord, Inter[cede! Speak a favorable word!]	o29′. With Marduk, king of the gods, [merciful] lo[rd, Intercede! Speak a favorable word!]	
r15. May your wide canopy (of protection), your noble forgiveness [be with me].	o30′. May your wide canopy (of protection), [your noble] fo[rgiveness be with me].	
r16. [Provide] a requital of favor and life fo[r me],	o31′. Provide a requital of favor and [life for me],	

r17. That I may proclaim your greatness (and) [resound your] praises!	o32′. That I may procla[im] your greatness [(and) resound your praises]!
r18. It is the wording of a lifted-hand prayer for <u>Gula</u>. [Its] ritual: […].	o33′. It is the wording of [a lifted-hand prayer for <u>Belet-ili</u>].

One of the most striking and obvious variations in the prayer as it is preserved in the manuscripts is its divine addressee. As stated above, five manuscripts are addressed to Gula whereas three are addressed to Belet-ili. Of course, many Mesopotamian gods have multiple names or are synchronized with other gods. But such is not the case here; these deities are not related.[43] Unless we are willing to suppose the unlikely possibility that two prayers were created independently with, coincidentally, nearly identical wording, someone has revised this prayer to adapt it at some point in its transmission for use with a different goddess than the original one.[44]

It is even more striking, though perhaps not as obvious, that the wording of the hymnic introduction and laments, aside from some formulaic insertions (see below),[45] were not substantially altered when this prayer

43. For recent overviews of the goddesses, see Nicole Brisch, "Mother Goddess (Ninmah, Nintud/r, Belet-ili)," *Ancient Mesopotamian Gods and Goddesses* (Oracc and the UK Higher Education Academy, http://oracc.museum.upenn.edu/amgg/listofdeities/mothergoddess/), and Barbara Böck, *The Healing Goddess Gula: Towards an Understanding of Ancient Babylonian Medicine*, CHANE 67 (Leiden: Brill, 2014), 7–44 (for Gula), and see Yağmur Heffron, "Gula/Ninkarrak (Goddess)," in *Ancient Mesopotamian Gods and Goddesses*; http://oracc.museum.upenn.edu/amgg/listofdeities/gulaninkarrak/ (for Belet-ili).

44. Logically, one could also entertain the idea that both prayers were created independently on the basis of another lost written text (or oral tradition) and adapted to fit two different goddesses.

45. I leave aside the possibility that MS H omitted the second line of the prayer as presented in the other witnesses (see MS A obv. 72, MS B obv. 10′, and MS E obv. 2), because I cannot exclude the possibility that this second poetic line was written in the breaks at the end of the first and/or beginning of the second lines on the tablet. Mayer tentatively suggests this line of the prayer was left out (see Mayer, *Untersuchungen*, 451, note [4] on line 71).

was refit for an entirely different goddess.[46] We have disagreement in the verb of the ninth line: *asḫurki*, "I turn to you" (Gula MS A r.2)[47] versus *atkalki*, "I trust in you" (Belet-ili MSS E obv. 9 and H obv. 8′; the verb in MS B obv. 16b′ is not preserved in this line). We have variants in some adjectives that describe the goddesses: *šurbûtu*, "most exalted," in Gula MS A obv. 77 versus *šaqûtu*, "sublime, most exalted," in Belet-ili MSS B obv. 15′ and H obv. 6′ (MS B is broken here);[48] and *šurbûtu*, "most exalted," in Gula MS A r.8 versus *rēmēnītu*, "merciful," in Belet-ili MS H obv. 21′ (MSS B and E are broken here).[49] But as these are semantic variants and common descriptors of deities, none of them tells us anything that helps determine the original goddess to which this prayer was directed.[50] Moreover, since MSS B and E (from Nineveh) agree with MS H (from Sippar) in one or the other of these variants and there are no clear patterns among the variants when the other preserved manuscripts are considered,[51] we are probably not dealing with local recensions of the same prayer. In other words, the prayers seem quite obviously related though they differ in small ways, but we cannot determine anything about their relative chronological position vis-à-vis one another by means of these variants, and thus we cannot determine anything of much use with regard to the prayer's revision history, including which version revised which, aside from the fact that the prayer was viewed as suitable for both goddesses without substantial alteration and adapted to that purpose through the insertion of the other goddess's name.

One might go hunting for distinctive phrases that point to attributes that are most closely associated with one of the goddesses, thereby showing her to be the original addressee. In other words, stylistic criteria or theology (i.e., internal evidence) may help us tease out the original addressee. But there is, in my opinion, insufficient evidence in the text of

---

46. See Joel H. Hunt, *Mesopotamian Šuilla Prayers to Ea, Marduk, and Nabû: Exegetical Studies* (Lewiston, NY: Mellen, 2010), who investigates the manner in which introductions to *šuila*s were tailored to specific deities.

47. Manuscripts C (rev. 2; Nineveh), F (obv. 10; Assur), G (rev. 8; Huzirina), and I (obv. 8; Babylon) agree with MS A.

48. Manuscripts G (rev. 6) and I (obv. 7) show *šurbûtu* whereas C (obv. 9′) and F (obv. 8) have *šaqûtu*.

49. Manuscript H is unique of the six manuscripts that preserve the adjective here.

50. Furthermore, these kinds of variants are expected in manuscripts of the same composition. See Cogan, "Some Text-Critical Issues," 7–8.

51. See nn. 47–48.

the prayer to make a judgment on this matter. The phrase *aššum bulluṭu u šullumu bašû ittīki, aššum eṭēru gamālu u šūzubu tīde*, "because restoring and maintaining well-being are within your power, because you know how to save, to spare, and to rescue," may seem like promising evidence that points to Gula, a healing goddess, especially since the phrase occurs in another Gula *šuila*. But it also occurs in other prayers; thus, it is not manifestly distinctive to Gula.[52] On the other hand, one could counter this evidence for Gula with phrases from the opening line of the prayer that point to Belet-ili. For example, *beltu šurbûtu*, "exalted lady," could be construed as a translation of the name of the mother goddess in Sumerian, Ninmaḫ, who shared features with Belet-ili; and *āšibat šamê ellūti*, "who dwells in the pure heavens," in the first line of our prayer recalls the opening line of another prayer to Belet-ili, where she is *nūru ina šamê*, "the light in the heavens."[53] A careful look through the remainder of the prayer does not produce any clear stylistic or theological indications, to my knowledge, that would allow us to discern which goddess was original and which was inserted into the text secondarily.[54]

This leaves, as far as I can see, the formulaic expressions mentioned above as the remaining possibility for giving some insight into the revision and adaptation process, though these will not inform us about the matter of which goddess was the original recipient of the prayer. *Šuila*-prayers, as Mayer has shown exhaustively,[55] are highly formulaic texts. They are

52. See Mayer, *Untersuchungen*, 166–67 (note, however, that the wording of Gula 1a and 1b is quite close and may simply be free variations of the same prayer, a point already noted by Walter G. Kunstmann, *Die babylonische Gebetsbeschwörung*, LSS NS 2 [Leipzig: Hinrichs, 1932], 90—a point that is quite in keeping with the conclusions of this study of a more limited textual base). The point above may prove incorrect if lines 79-7-8,50: 15′ and IV R^2 60, obv. 36–38 are proven to be part of prayers directed to Gula.

53. See Mayer, *Untersuchungen*, 380.

54. The Assyrian recension of Enuma Elish may be the best known example in which we can have a very high level of confidence, even certainty, that it is a product of revision based on the replacement of one divine name (Marduk) for another (Assur). Our certainty on this matter is due to the facts that we know the Babylonian version existed prior to the Assyrian and the change that the Assyrian scribes made was superficial and half-hearted, thus making its identification and interpretation rather simple. See W. G. Lambert, *Babylonian Creation Myths*, MC 16 (Winona Lake, IN: Eisenbrauns, 2013), 4–6.

55. Mayer, *Untersuchungen*.

chock full of stock phrases and well-worn expressions. What I intend here by "formulaic expressions" are specifically self-presentation formulas and lament formulas that mention evil or troubling signs. (The latter also often elicit the use of other formulaic phrases about the supplicant's fear or petitions for deliverance from the signs, as will be noted in MSS A and H.) These formulas typically do not occur in all of a prayer's textual witnesses, and when they are included, they are sometimes placed in a different position within the prayer compared to the other textual witnesses that include them.[56] Some deployed formulas use the generic term NENNI/*annanna*, "so-and-so," as a placeholder for names of supplicants in the self-presentations and for the names of months and the number of the day in the lament formulas while others specify these details. Given these features, the formulas are certainly evidence of revision; that is, the prayers have been adapted for new situations (i.e., a new supplicant or a new ritual use) with their insertion.[57]

The four witnesses for Gula 1a = Belet-ili 1 considered here contain one or more of these formulas. No two witnesses agree about which formulas to include; each witness presents a unique combination. But there is one occasion when three witnesses, sharing the same formula, have put it in the same place within the prayer, and another when three witnesses, sharing another formula, have agreed two out of three times about its placement. Further, two witnesses put the same two formulas in sequence but place them in different places within the prayer. All of this suggests there may have been a general sense about which formula goes where or how they should be related to one another. But there are no easily formulated rules, as Mayer has shown.[58] The following discussion illustrates this

---

56. See ibid., 46 for the self-presentation formulas; 100 n. 64 and 101 for the *attalû* formula; and 73 n. 16 for a list of *šuila*s that include a formulaic expression of fear attested in a witness of both Gula 1a = Belet-ili 1 and Sîn 1. For the latter two formulas, see also Frechette, *Mesopotamian Ritual-Prayers of "Hand-Lifting,"* 138.

57. For the general point, see Mayer, *Untersuchungen*, 72 and 99. Mayer supports his opinion that these formulas were inserted into prayers by pointing out with regard to the *attalû* formula that it is sometimes placed rather awkwardly within the prayer and can therefore disrupt the flow of the text (101). But this latter point is a subjective stylistic evaluation that is unnecessary, given the fact that the formulas occur in only some of the manuscripts of many different prayers.

58. See ibid., 47, for example, for Mayer's generalization about the placement of self-presentation formulas. Although there are common and rare placements, the self-

with both Gula 1a = Belet-ili 1 and, in the next section, with Sîn 1 (see tables 1 and 2).

Reverse 6 in MS A, though quite fragmentary now, contains a lament formula about troubling signs (i.e., oracles and dreams),[59] which is followed by a stock expression of the supplicant's fear (rev. 7).[60] The latter expression occurs five times in *namburbî* incantation-prayers but only once in a prayer designated a *šuila* (here) and, as far as MS A is concerned, probably to be used in *Bīt salā᾿ mê*.[61]

MS A rev.
6. [On account of oracles and dre]ams that are [hounding me],
7. [I am afraid and] constantly [anxious].

The very same phrase that is found in rev. 6 of MS A is cited in obv. 13 of MS E and obv. 20′ of MS H in the same position within the prayer (after the line that reads "To the god of my city who is furious and enraged with me"). But neither of these other manuscripts includes the expression of fear that follows (i.e., results) from this lament as in MS A. It is impossible on present evidence to know why this is.

Manuscript B includes the so-called *attalû* formula, a lament concerning the evil of a lunar eclipse and the attendant unfavorable portents associated with it, directly after the same line that preceded the previously discussed formula in MSS A, E, and H (i.e., "To the god of my city"). In other words, all four manuscripts agreed to insert a formula after the same line: three chose the same formula (cited above); MS B went its own way. To complicate matters, MS E also includes this generic *attalû* lament but does so only after adding a generic self-presentation[62] just before it in obv. 14,

presentation formula is attested at most of the major structural transition points in one incantation-prayer or another.

59. See ibid., 106, for this lament formula. The phrase occurs in seven witnesses of Gula 1a = Belet-ili 1 (MSS A, C, E, F, G, H, and I). Manuscript D does not preserve the text this far into the prayer. The phrase only occurs elsewhere, though transposing the terms for dream and oracle, in three witnesses to Gula 1b (MSS A, B, and C, the only witnesses extant in these lines; see ibid., 106, 455, 457). See, however, n. 52 for the likely genetic relationship between Gula 1a and Gula 1b.

60. This expression is only preserved in MSS A, F, and G.

61. See Mayer, *Untersuchungen*, 73 with n. 17.

62. For this common self-presentation formula, see ibid., 51.

so that the self-presentation comes between the previous lament formula (about oracles and dreams) and the *attalû* lament.

MS E obv.
13. [On account of oracles and dr]eams that are hounding me,
14. [I so-and-so, son of so-and-so] whose god (is) so-and-so (and) goddess (is) so-and-so,
15. [on account of the evil of a lunar eclipse, which] occurred in so-and-so month (on) so-and-so day,
16. [(and) the evil of portents (and) omens, unp]leasant (and) unfavorable,
[x]. [which are present in my palace and (throughout) my land—]

A similar self-presentation formula as appears in MS E is inserted earlier in the prayer in MS H, namely, at the conclusion of the hymnic introduction (obv. 8′ in MS H, that is, the line that reads, "O lady, in you I trust/turn; my ears are attentive to you"), though in this case the supplicant's name, royal designation, and personal deities are specified.[63] Directly after this self-presentation is an *attalû* lament, which also fills in its generic placeholders: the month and day of the lunar eclipse are stated. In other words, though these formulas have been filled out for a particular performance in MS H, they are the same as those in MS E and appear in the same order *but* they are placed earlier in the prayer. Unlike MS E, MS H also includes a stock expression of fear that has resulted from this celestial harbinger, "I am afraid, in fear, and constantly frightened" (obv. 14′),[64] followed by a stock petition that the evil not draw near to the supplicant.[65] Thus, MS H is a longer text.

MS H obv.
9′. I, Shamash-shum-ukin, the king, the son of his god,
10′. whose god (is) Marduk, goddess (is) Zarpanitu,

63. For this self-presentation with royal epithet, see ibid., 52.

64. For this expression in incantation-prayers, see ibid., 73 with n. 16; and Frechette, *Mesopotamian Ritual-Prayers of "Hand-Lifting,"* 138 n. 55. This phrase is comparable but slightly different from the relatively rare one in MS A rev. 7.

65. See Mayer, *Untersuchungen*, 265–66 with n. 61 for this expression and its attestations in *šuila*s. It is most commonly found in *namburbî*s.

11′. on account of the evil of a lunar eclipse, which occurred on the fifteenth day of the month Shabbatu,
12′. (and) the evil of portents (and) omens, unpleasant (and) unfavorable,
13′. which are present in my palace and (throughout) my land,
14′. am afraid, in fear, and constantly frightened.
15′. May its evil, to me and my house,
16′. not draw near, approach, advance, (or) arrive.

What does all of this tell us about scribal revision and adaptation? I think it clearly shows that although we can be confident about the scribal adaptation of Gula 1a = Belet-ili 1 to a royal or an apotropaic ritual (either *Bīt rimki* or a *namburbî*),[66] it is important to note that all three manuscripts bearing witness to this adaptation do so in a unique manner, despite being addressed to the same deity (Belet-ili) and, in two cases, coming from the same city. Since we are dealing with the insertion of formulas, we may have to reckon with the fact that these insertions were likely done in an ad hoc manner or perhaps only under rather loose guidelines or general notions of which formulas should be included and where they should go. In other words, textual fluidity and flexibility seem to be the rule, even when we can identify scribal revisions in individual witnesses and explain their common ritual adaptive purpose.

6.3. Sîn 1

6.3.1. Witnesses

The *šuila*-prayer designated Sîn 1 in Mayer's catalog is attested in nine manuscripts, three of which preserve ritual instructions.[67] Among the

---

66. We do not, however, have any evidence for such a ritual use aside from the internal evidence of these three witnesses (MSS B, E, and H) to Belet-ili 1.

67. For the most recent and complete edition of the prayer that includes various ritual instructions, see Sally A. L. Butler, *Mesopotamian Conceptions of Dreams and Dream Rituals*, AOAT 258 (Münster: Ugarit-Verlag, 1998), 379–96. Mayer's older edition (Mayer, *Untersuchungen*, 490–94) remains useful. For an introduction and an annotated, pedagogical treatment of the prayer (Akkadian vocabulary and grammar notes are supplied to a rather eclectic text), see Alan Lenzi, "A Shuilla: Sin 1," in Lenzi, *Reading Akkadian Prayers and Hymns*, 385–402. For a list of manuscripts, see Butler, *Mesopotamian Conceptions of Dreams*, 380, and Mayer, *Untersuchungen*, 490, the latter

nine manuscripts, the most interesting witnesses for the present purpose are known in the most recent edition by the sigla:

A_1 = K.155
C_1 = S.U. 51/107
F_1 = VAT 13854 (+) 14060
A = BM 78432

Of these, only MS A attests ritual instructions, which for this reason are left out of our textual comparison in table 2.[68]

6.3.2. Discovery

The four manuscripts considered here in detail were not all scientifically excavated. Manuscript A_1 (= K.155) was excavated at Nineveh. According to its colophon, King Assurbanipal (668–627 BCE) copied the tablet himself. As noted previously, the presence of an Assurbanipal colophon does not indicate that a tablet came from the North Palace.[69] In fact, it probably was excavated in the South-West Palace since MS A_1 bears a low Kuyunjik Collection number (K.155), and, as Reade notes, "the great majority

of whom also lists citations of the prayer's incipit as a catch-line or as part of ritual instructions. Note that K.17283, joined to other fragments comprising Butler's MS B_1, is published in Werner R. Mayer, "Sechs Šu-ila-Gebete," *Or* NS 59 (1990): 486 (for photo see Leonard W. King, "BMS 01 K 03332 dupl," Cuniform Digital Library Initiative, http://cdli.ucla.edu/P394701), and her MS F_1 comprises VAT 14060 and VAT 13854, the latter of which is now published in Stefan M. Maul, Rita Strauß, and Daniel Schwemer, *Ritualbeschreibungen und Gebete I*, WVDOG 133, KAL 4 (Wiesbaden: Harrassowitz, 2011), no. 66, who note the high probability that the two fragments are originally from the same tablet (123). Only Butler's MSS A, b, and c attest ritual instructions. For an important study of how Sîn 1 was adapted into different ritual contexts, see Frechette, *Mesopotamian Ritual-Prayers of "Hand-Lifting,"* 201–8. Alongside comparing ritual instructions attached to the manuscripts of the prayer, Frechette also includes the ritual instructions in a scholar's letter (Butler's MS G_1, for which see Butler, *Mesopotamian Conceptions of Dreams*, 396–97, and SAA 10 298, obv. 9–17 = Parpola, *Letters from Assyrian and Babylonian Scholars*, no. 298) and those for a lunar eclipse *namburbî*, which cites the incipit to Sîn 1 (for which see Stefan M. Maul, *Zukunftsbewaltigung: Eine Untersuchung altorientalischen Denkens anhand der babylonish-assyrisches Löserituale [Namburbi]*, BaF 18 [Mainz: von Zabern, 1994], 458–60).

68. For the tablets' contents, see below.

69. See Reade, "Archaeology and the Kuyunjik Collection," 218.

of tablets bearing the low [K.] numbers were found during Layard's 1851 excavations in the South-West Palace at Kuyunjik, notably in the area of Rooms XL and XLI."[70]

Manuscript C_1 (S.U. 51/107), excavated at Sultantepe (ancient Huzirina), was part of a collection of just over four hundred literary and scholarly tablets and fragments belonging to one Qurdi-Nergal, a *shangu*-priest, and his family.[71] Dates on the tablets suggest they were written between the years 718 and 612 BCE. The tablets were found outside the family's house, heaped up against one of the walls. But this is generally taken to be a secondary placement. The tablets were probably kept inside the house.[72] Given the poor quality of the script and the naming of numerous "(junior) apprentices," *šamallû* (*seḫrūtu*), in the colophons of the tablets, this collection is probably the remains of a provincial scribal school.[73]

As for MS F_1 (= VAT 13854 [+] 14060), German archaeologists excavated hundreds of scholarly and literary tablets from a private house belonging to a family of exorcists in Assur, who flourished in the late eighth and the first half of the seventh centuries BCE.[74] Manuscript F_1 is certainly

70. Ibid., 213; see also Reade, "Ninive (Nineveh)," 422.

71. For an overview of the tablet collection from this site, see Robson, "Reading the Libraries of Assyria and Babylonia," 48–51. Line drawings of all the tablets are provided in Oliver R. Gurney and Jacob J. Finkelstein, *The Sultantepe Tablets*, vol. 1, BIAAOP 3 (London: British Institute of Archaeology at Ankara, 1957) (= *STT* 1), and Oliver R. Gurney and Peter Hulin, *The Sultantepe Tablets*, vol. 2, BIAAOP 7 (London: British Institute of Archaeology at Ankara, 1964) (= *STT* 2).

72. See Pedersén, *Archives and Libraries in the Ancient Near East*, 178–79, *STT* 1:iv, and Robson, "Reading the Libraries of Assyria and Babylonia," 48–49 for the archaeological context. A map is available in Seton Lloyd and Nuri Gokçe, "Sultantepe: Anglo-Turkish Joint Excavations, 1952," *AnSt* 3 (1953): 30. For the family, see Oliver R. Gurney, "Scribes at Huzirīna," *NABU* 1997/17.

73. Robson, "Reading the Libraries of Assyria and Babylonia," 49–50.

74. The collection was found in a room of the house located within the excavation area hD8I. Pedersén designated the library N4 (= Assur 20) in his studies of the tablets (Olof Pedersén, *Archives and Libraries in the City of Assur: A Survey of the Material from the German Excavations*, vol. 1, SSU 6 [Uppsala: Acta Universitatis Upsaliensis, 1986], 41–76, with map on 42; Pedersén, *Archives and Libraries in the Ancient Near East*, 135–36, also with map). For a more recent overview of this collection, see Stefan M. Maul, "Die Tontafelbibliothek aus den sogenannten 'Haus des Beschwörungspriesters,'" in *Assur-Forschungen: Arbeiten aus der Forschungsstelle "Edition literarischer Keilschrifttexte aus Assur" der Heidelberger Akademie der Wissenschaften*, ed. Stefan M. Maul und Nils P. Heeßel (Wiesbaden: Harrassowitz, 2010), 189–228.

from Neo-Assyrian Assur and may have come from the same exorcists' house. This location will be treated here as a reasonable suggestion for the tablet's source,[75] but we cannot be certain about this on present evidence.

Sally Butler's MS A (= BM 78432 = Bu. 88-5-12, 335) certainly dates to the reign of Assurbanipal's brother Shamash-shum-ukin in Babylonia (667–648 BCE) since the tablet shows Neo-Assyrian ductus and mentions the king by name in a formulaic statement in the text. Its provenance, however, is rather problematic. During Budge's visit to Egypt and the Near East in 1887–1888, he collected (i.e., bought from dealers) and sent back to the British Museum hundreds of tablets. The lot labeled Bu. 88-5-12, which includes our tablet (no. 335), is a rather mixed group. We cannot be sure whence our tablet came, though the environs of Sippar is a tenable but tentative suggestion.[76]

In sum, we know the general date—seventh century BCE—of all four witnesses and the city of origin for three. Further, we know precise find spots for two of the witnesses (C_1 and A_1), the copyist of one of the witnesses (A_1), the scribal family to which one of them belonged (C_1), and the likely family that owned the last witness (F_1).

6.3.3. Tablet Contents

After the wording of the prayer to Sîn, MS A_1 bears a standard *šuila*-rubric and then shows the text of a *šuila* to Ishtar (Mayer's Ishtar 1).[77] The tablet breaks off in the middle of this prayer. The text on the reverse begins in the middle of a *šuila* to Tashmetu (Mayer's Tashmetu 1),[78] which is followed by a standard *šuila*-rubric. The tablet concludes with a catch-line to the *šuila*

---

75. Maul and Strauß, *Ritualbeschreibungen und Gebete I*, 22.

76. See Erle Leichty, Jacob J. Finkelstein, and Christopher B. F. Walker, *Catalogue of the Babylonian Tablets in the British Museum*, vol. 8: *Tablets from Sippar 3* (London: British Museum Publications, 1988), xvi–xvii for information about Budge's tablet collecting with regard to lot Bu. 88-5-12.

77. See Mayer, *Untersuchungen*, 388, and Frechette, *Mesopotamian Ritual-Prayers of "Hand-Lifting,"* 255–56, for more information. Butler's MS B_1 (= K.2823 +), which also bears the *šuila* to Sîn and follows the text of A_1 very closely (it differs in only three signs), gives the first line of Ishtar 1 as a catch-line after the rubric. See Loretz and Mayer, *Šu-ila-Gebete*, IX and the copy of K.2823 +, which is their text no. 1.

78. See Mayer, *Untersuchungen*, 423–24, and Frechette, *Mesopotamian Ritual-Prayers of "Hand-Lifting,"* 273–74, for more information.

Madanu 1 = Nusku 1[79] and a colophon that identifies the tablet as part of the seventh house of *Bīt rimki* and belonging to Assurbanipal (Assurbanipal colophon c).[80] The fact that this same series of prayers was used in the *Bīt rimki* ritual ceremony is confirmed by a ritual tablet that prescribes in its ritual agenda the recitation of our prayers in the order they appear on the tablet.[81] But the presence of the phrase *ina arḫi annanna ūmi annanna* ("month so-and-so, day so-and-so") in obv. 12 suggests the tablet was not copied for a particular ritual performance in response to an actual (datable) lunar eclipse (as Assurbanipal colophon c confirms).

Manuscript C_1 begins with a *šuila* to Ea (Ea 2),[82] though its text ends at the end of the hymnic introduction. There is a catch-line to an otherwise unknown prayer and then, after a single ruling, the *šuila* to Sîn begins. It continues onto the reverse but its text, like the first prayer on the tablet, does not go beyond the hymnic introduction. Another incipit to an otherwise unknown prayer may follow the text of the prayer.[83] After a single ruling, a colophon, scratched into the tablet after it had dried, follows,[84] dedicating the tablet to Adad for the life of a certain Aplaya, who is known only from this colophon.[85] We do not know why these partial

79. See Mayer, *Untersuchungen*, 394, and Frechette, *Mesopotamian Ritual-Prayers of "Hand-lifting,"* 259.

80. See Hunger, *Babylonische und assyrische Kolophone*, no. 319c. For a photo of the tablet, see Leonard W. King, "BMS 01." Cuniform Digital Library Initiative. http://cdli.ucla.edu/P393771. A copy is available in *BMS*, no. 1.

81. See Læssøe, *Studies on the Assyrian Ritual and Series Bit Rimki*, 25; Heinrich Zimmern, *Beiträge zur Kenntnis der Babylonischen Religion*, AB 12 (Leipzig: Hinrichs, 1901), 128–29; and Frechette, *Mesopotamian Ritual-Prayers of "Hand-Lifting,"* 177–78. The *šuila* Nabu 2 (see Mayer, *Untersuchungen*, 400, and Frechette, *Mesopotamian Ritual-Prayers of "Hand-Lifting,"* 263) is lost in the gap between obverse and reverse. Because MS B_1 shows part of this same order (that is, it moves from Sîn 1 to Ishtar 1), Frechette notes the possibility that MS B_1 (which is almost identical to A_1, see n. 77) was also used in *Bīt rimki* (Frechette, *Mesopotamian Ritual-Prayers of "Hand-Lifting,"* 202 n. 87).

82. See Mayer, *Untersuchungen*, 381, and Frechette, *Mesopotamian Ritual-Prayers of "Hand-Lifting,"* 253, for more information.

83. This interpretation is wholly dependent on reading the first extremely broken sign as the superscript ÉN, which marks the beginning of most incantation-prayers.

84. See Hunger, *Babylonische und assyrische Kolophone*, no. 407.

85. See Karen Radner, *The Prosopography of the Neo-Assyrian Empire*, vol. 1.1 A (Helsinki: Neo-Assyrian Text Corpus Project, 1998), 119, no. 53. A copy of the tablet is available in *STT* 1, no. 56. An edition by Greta Van Buylaere is available in Eleanor

prayers occur on this tablet in this order with catch-lines to other prayers. I offer a very tentative suggestion below.

The wording of the prayer to Sîn in MS F_1 starts mid-prayer on the obverse of VAT 14060 and continues on VAT 13854 to its bottom edge. The reverse of VAT 13854 continues the prayer and then the reverse of VAT 14060 follows. After the wording of the prayer, VAT 14060 bears a partial *šuila*-rubric and then the fragment ends.[86] Stefan Maul and Rita Strauß suggest that it is reasonable to think this witness, which names Assurbanipal, was prepared for one of his *Bīt rimki* ritual ceremonies. But this is uncertain.[87]

Because the top of MS A's obverse is broken, the text also begins mid-prayer (to Sîn) in this witness. The prayer continues without interruption onto the reverse. A standard *šuila*-rubric stands at the prayer's conclusion, and then a long ritual that seems to have the purpose of securing a favorable dream (in which Anzagar assures the supplicant of his release from guilt via a revelatory dream)[88] continues until the tablet breaks off. Sîn 1 (wording and ritual) is the only composition on the tablet.[89] The prayer mentions Shamash-shum-ukin in its text (obv. 5′), which is otherwise quite short in comparison to the other witnesses compared here.[90] Since

Robson's CAMS/Geography of Knowledge Corpus project (University of Pennsylvania Museum of Archaeology and Anthropology, http://oracc.museum.upenn.edu/cams/gkab/).

86. A copy of VAT 14060 is available in Erich Ebeling, Franz Köcher, and Liane Rost, *Literarische Keilschrifttexte aus Assur* (Berlin: Akademie, 1953), no. 39, and a copy of VAT 13854 is in Maul and Strauß, *Ritualbeschreibungen und Gebete I*, no. 66. As to whether the rubric on the reverse of VAT 14060 belongs to the prayer Sîn 1, see Frechette, *Mesopotamian Ritual-Prayers of "Hand-Lifting,"* 269.

87. Maul and Strauß, *Ritualbeschreibungen und Gebete I*, 22. Note how MS A_1, which explicitly names that ceremony in its colophon, includes an *attalû* formula in its text. As far as we can determine, MS F_1 does not.

88. Note how the supplicant is to speak additional words, according to the ritual instructions, imploring his ears to be opened (only in MS A rev. 9: GESTUG.II.MEŠ BAD.MEŠ [*uznā liptettâ*], "let him continually open [my] ears").

89. A copy of the tablet is available in Butler, *Mesopotamian Dream Conceptions*, pls. 1–2.

90. But MS A is quite similar to MS b (from Sippar), in that it omits a significant part of the hymnic introduction (attested in other witnesses), inserts the self-presentation of Shamash-shum-ukin (in obv. 4′), and includes (the early part of) the ritual instructions.

parts of the ritual instructions are cited in a scholar's letter to the king,[91] it is possible that this (or some very similar) ritual-prayer to secure a favorable dream was actually performed.

6.3.4. Relative Chronology

Three manuscripts, A, A_1, and F_1, come from the reigns of Assurbanipal or Shamash-shum-ukin. The other manuscript, C_1, dates to sometime in the seventh century. Despite what we know about these tablets, it is impossible to arrange our witnesses in a more precise chronological order and declare one the oldest with confidence. But a comparison of the contents across witnesses does reveal some points of interest in terms of scribal revision and adaptation of the prayer to different ritual settings. Still, we are left with many unexplained differences between versions of the prayer.[92]

6.3.5. Synoptic Comparison

Table 2: Sîn 1

MS A_1 = K.155	MS C_1 = SU 51/107	MS F_1 = VAT 13854 (+) 14060	MS A = BM 78432
(Nineveh)	(Huzirina)	(Assur)	(Sippar?)
o1. Incantation: O Sîn, resplendent luminary, [foremost of the gods!]	o19. Incantation: O Sîn, resplendent luminary, [foremost of the go]ds!	[The beginning of the text is broken.]	[The beginning of the text is broken.]
o2. O Sîn, perpetually renewing one, who illumina[tes the darkness],	o20. [O Sîn], perpetually renewing one, who illuminates the darkness,		

91. See Butler's MS G_1 (*Mesopotamian Dream Conceptions*, 396–97) and SAA 10 298, obv. 9–17 (= Parpola, *Letters from Assyrian and Babylonian Scholars*, no. 298).

92. The texts behind the translations of MSS A and A_1 were collated against photographs of the tablets that I took at the British Museum in London. The text behind the translation of MS F_1 was collated against photographs of the tablet that I took at the Vorderasiatisches Museum in Berlin. And the text behind the translation of MS C_1 was collated against photographs that I took at the Anatolian Civilizations Museum in Ankara.

o3. Provides light for the [teeming] people!	o21. [Provides l]ight for the teem[ing] people!		
o4. To the black-headed people, [your] ra[ys] are sent forth.	o22. Your shining appearance [is b]right in the p[ure hea]vens,		
o5. Your shining appearance is bright in the [pure] heavens.	o23. [To the] black-headed [peop]le, [your] rays are sent forth,		
o6. Your torch is magnificent, [your] bur[ning?] like Girra.	o24. Your shining appearance [is magni]ficent,… […] like Girra,		
o7. Your awe-inspiring luminosity fills the wide [earth].	o25. Your awe-inspiring luminosity [fill]s the wid[e] earth.		o1′. [Your awe-inspiring luminosity fills the wid]e [ea]rth.
o8. With pride, the people vie with one another to gaze up[on you].	ø		o2′. [With pride, the people vie with one another] to gaze upon you.
ø	o26. […] heed(s) your divinity const[antly].		ø
o9. O Anu of the heavens, whose advice no [one] can learn,	o27. [O Anu of the heavens], whose advice [no] … ca[n learn],	VAT 14060	ø
o10. Your shining appearance is supreme, like Shamash, [your] son.	o28. Your [shining] appearance [is supreme], like S[hamas]h, [your son].	o1′. Your [shining appearance is supreme], like S[hamash, your son].	ø
o11. The great gods kneel before you. The decision of the lands is set before [you].	r1.–2. The grea[t] gods [kneel befo]re you. [The decision of the lands] is set before [you].	o2′. [The great gods kneel before you. The de]cision of the lands is set [before you].	ø

o12. On account of the evil of a lunar eclipse, which occurr[ed] in so-and-so month, (on) so-and-so day,	ø	ø	ø
o13. (And) the evil of portents (and) omens, unpleasant (and) unfavorable, which are present in my house and (throughout) my land.	ø	ø	ø
ø	ø	o3′. [I, Assurb]a-nipal, the king, the so[n of his god],	ø
ø	ø	o4′. [whose god (is) Assur], goddess (is) Assuri[tu,]	ø
ø	ø	o5′. [am afraid, in] fear, and constantly fright[ened].	ø
o14. The great gods inquire of you, and you give advice.	r3. [The grea]t [god]s inquire of you, and you giv[e advice].	o6′. [The great gods in]quire of you, and you give [advice].	ø
o15. They are seated in their assembly; they discuss (it) at your feet.	ø	o7′. [They are seated in the]ir [assembly] and discuss (it) at [your] fe[et].	ø
ø	r4. [The Anun-naki] and the Igigi grant you […].	ø VAT 13854	ø

o16. O resplendent Sîn of Ekur, they inquire of you, and you giv[e] the oracle of the gods.	ø	o1′. [O resplendent Sîn of Ekur], they [inquire of you, and you give the oracle of the gods].	ø
o17. The day of the new moon (is) the day of your oracle, the secret of the great gods.	r5. [The day of the new moon] (is) the day of the decision of the [great] gods.	o2′. [The day of the new moon (is) the d]ay of your oracle, the se[cret of the great gods].	ø
ø	r6. […] renewal they take notice of you.	ø	ø
ø	r7. […]	ø	ø
ø	r8. [I ca]ll to you, O lord, in the mi[dst of the pure heavens.]	ø	ø
ø	r9. [Incantation:?] To the gods this … […]	ø	ø
o18. The thirtieth day (of the month) (is) your festival, the day for celebrating [your] divinity.	[This is the end of the text. A colophon follows on the tablet.]	o3′. [The thirtieth day (of the month) (is) your [f]estival, the day for ce[lebrating your divinity].	ø
o19. O Namraṣit, unrivalled in strength, whose advice [no o]ne can learn,		o4′.–5′. [O Nam]raṣit, [unrivalled] in strength, [whos]e advice [no one c]an learn,	o3′–4′. [O Namraṣit], unrivalled in [str]ength, [whose] advice no one [can lear]n,
ø		ø	o5′. [I am Shamash-sh]umukin, your servant.

o20. I offered to you a pur[e] flour-offe[ring] of the night. I libated for you first class beer (and) honey.	o6′–7′. [I offered] to you a [pure] flour-offeri[ng of the night]. [I libated for you] first class beer [(and) honey].	o6′–7′. [I offered to you] a pure flour-offering of the night. [I libated for you f]irst class beer (and) honey.
ø	ø	o8′. [With the consecrate]ed […] I (hereby) invoke your name.
ø	ø	o9′. [I call to you, O lo]rd, in the midst of the pure heavens.
o21. I am kneeling (and) I stand. I (hereby) seek y[ou].	o8′. [I am kneeling (and) I st]and. I (hereby) seek [you].	o10′. [I am kneeling (and) I sta]nd. I (hereby) seek you.
o22. Establish for [me] a propitious and just oracular utterance.	r1. Establish [for me] a [pr]opitious and just [oracular utterance].	o11′. [Establish for me a propitious] and just oracular utterance.
o23. My god and my goddess, who have been angry [with me] for many days,	r2.–r3. [My god and] my goddess, who have been ang[ry with me] f[or man]y [days],	o12′. [My god and my goddess, who] have been angry with me for many days,
o24. Through truth and justice, may they be at peace with me. May my path be favorable, may my way [be straight].	r4.–r5. [Through tru]th and justice, may they be [at peace with me], [May my path be favorab]le, [may] my way [be straight].	o13′–14′. [Through truth and jus]tice, may they be at peace with me. [May my path be favorable], may my way be straight.
o25. I (hereby) send Anzagar, god of dream[s].	[The remainder of the fragment is broken.]	o15′. [I (hereby) send] Anzagar, gods! of dreams.

o26. Let him absolve my sins at night. Let me hear. Let me [myself] be purified of my punishment.		r1–2. [Let him absol]ve my sins [at night. Let me hear.] [Let] me myself [be] purified [of my punishment].
o27. Let me proclaim [your] praises forever!	VAT 14060	r3. [Let me] proclaim your praises [forever]!
o28. [It is] the wording of a lifted-hand prayer to Sîn.	r1′. [It is the wording of] a lifted-hand prayer to S[in].	r4. [It is the wording of] a lifted-hand prayer to Sîn.
		[The rest of the reverse preserves a ritual.]

A synoptic comparison shows that the texts from Nineveh (MS A_1) and Assur (MS F_1) are verbatim (aside from orthographic differences) in almost the entire preserved portions of the text. The two prayers differ only in which formulaic expressions they include, though they both place their respective formulas after the same line in the hymnic introduction (that is, after the line "The great gods kneel before you. The decision of the lands is set before you" [obv. 11 in MS A_1 and obv. 2′ in MS F_1]). Manuscript A_1 attests an *attalû* lament formula.[93]

> MS A_1 obv.
> 12. On account of the evil of a lunar eclipse, which occurr[ed] in so-and-so month, (on) so-and-so day,
> 13. (And) the evil of portents (and) omens, unpleasant (and) unfavorable, which are present in my house and (throughout) my land.

Manuscript F_1, in distinction, shows a self-presentation formula that names Assurbanipal as the supplicant and Assur and Assuritu as his per-

93. The placement of the formula is rather awkward here. Mayer's evaluation is stronger. He believes the formula is "an unpassender Stelle eingeschoben" (Mayer, *Untersuchungen*, 100). For more on the formula, see 100–102.

sonal gods.[94] The text in MS F_1 also moves directly on from the self-presentation to a stock expression about the supplicant's fear already seen in Gula 1a = Belet-ili 1 above, namely, "I am afraid, in fear, and constantly frightened."[95] This latter expression is usually accompanied by a reason for the fear.[96] But this does not occur in MS F_1, which reads:

MS F_1 obv.
3′. [I, Assurb]anipal, the king, the so[n of his god],
4′. [whose god (is) Assur], goddess (is) Assuri[tu,]
5′. [am afraid, in] fear, and constantly fright[ened].

It is reasonable to suggest that the *attalû* lament in MS A_1 is an insertion into the prayer to bring its concerns into line with those of the *Bīt rimki* series, of which, as indicated in the colophon, our witness A_1 is a part.[97] We cannot interpret the absence of the *attalû* lament as evidence against MS F_1 being used in *Bīt rimki*, as some Assyriologists suspect,[98] since not all *šuila*s used in that series always showed the lament formula.[99] The expression of fear may hint at this concern. But we can say nothing more with the present evidence.[100] What is clear is that we have two versions (from two different Assyrian cities) of essentially the same prayer, each being slightly revised via the insertion of *different* formulas—which, it should be noted, we could not have predicted—in the same exact place within their shared text. This finding is quite in line with the findings of the previous case study.

Manuscript A from Sippar differs significantly from the previous two witnesses. First, it leaves out a large chunk of the hymnic introduction; in comparative terms, MS A has no parallel to MS A_1 obv. 9–11 and 14–18. If the broken top of the obverse of MS A included the first six lines as attested

94. See ibid., 52 for this formula.

95. See ibid., 73 with n. 16, and Frechette, *Mesopotamian Ritual-Prayers of "Hand-Lifting,"* 138 n. 55.

96. As it does in Gula 1a = Belet-ili 1 MS H obv. 14′.

97. See likewise Frechette, *Mesopotamian Ritual-Prayers of "Hand-Lifting,"* 202.

98. See n. 87.

99. See Frechette, *Mesopotamian Ritual-Prayers of "Hand-Lifting,"* 193.

100. The lack of ritual instructions at the conclusion of the prayer may be taken as offering some support for the prayer's use in a *namburbî* or in *Bīt rimki*, as argued in ibid., 207.

in MS A_1, and presently there is no such proof for this,[101] the hymnic introduction would have read as follows:

Presumed lost at the top of the obverse of MS A:
[Incantation: O Sîn, resplendent luminary, foremost of the gods!
O Sîn, perpetually renewing one, who illuminates the darkness,
Provides light for the teeming people!
To the black-headed people, your rays are sent forth.
Your shining appearance is bright in the pure heavens.
Your torch is magnificent, your burning like Girra.]

What is attested in MS A obv.

1′. [Your awe-inspiring luminosity fills the wid]e [ea]rth.
2′. [With pride, the people vie with one another] to gaze upon you.
3′–4′. [O Namraṣit], unrivalled in [str]ength, [whose] advice no one [can lear]n…

Even if we assume those six lines were on MS A before it was broken, the hymn in MS A_1 is still twice as long as the one in MS A. Further differences in the text include the facts that MS A bears no *attalû* lament in its text but does insert a brief self-presentation formula after its obv. 3′–4′ (= MS A_1 obv. 19; and MS F_1 obv. 4′–5′), naming Shamash-shum-ukin (obv. 5′). And after a couple of lines (obv. 6′–7′) paralleled in MSS A_1 (obv. 20) and F_1 (obv. 6′–7′ in VAT 13854), MS A also includes in obv. 8′–9′ two lines unique to this manuscript.

MS A obv.
8′. [With the consecrate]ed […] I (hereby) invoke your name.
9′. [I call to you, O lo]rd, in the midst of the pure heavens.

Obviously, the self-presentation formula has been included in MS A to adapt the prayer to Shamash-shum-ukin's participation. Beyond this, it is difficult to understand the shorter hymnic introduction and the inclusion of two extra lines describing the supplicant's actions in the witnesses

101. The introduction was, at least, known in Sippar, as attested by Butler's MS d_1 (= Si.884).

from Sippar (MS b, also from Sippar, follows A in all three differences). One might suggest the shorter hymn has omitted the material about Sîn's important position among the celestial court of the gods (obv. 9–11, 14–16 in MS A_1 and parallels in MS F_1) and the emphasis on the new moon (obv. 17–18 in MS A_1 and parallels in MS F_1), because it was irrelevant to securing a favorable dream.[102] Given the fact, however, that *attalû* formulas are frequently *added* to *šuila*s to adapt them to the purpose of addressing the evil of a lunar eclipse, one may be (more?) warranted to argue the exact opposite: MS A's shorter hymn is more original and the longer hymnic material in MSS A_1 and F_1 was added by Assyrian scribes to make the text more relevant to the new lunar eclipse concern.[103] Clearly, then, we can see that scribes were adapting texts to particular purposes. But how this happened (i.e., which text was revised and which was the revision) is not clear.[104] In light of the very different shape of the opening hymns, we might be led to ask, should we even assume a common original text in this case? The shared ending to the prayer in MS A_1 and MS A is probably the best argument to maintain that these two prayers are variations of a common composition; that is, we are probably justified in thinking in terms of differing editions.[105] But the question of quantification does not want to go away: how much text is enough to differentiate two witnesses currently considered revisions/adaptations of the same composition into two discreet texts? Or, from a different angle, when are we inventing a revised text out of two independent ones?

These questions are brought into high relief with the very different hymnic material presented in MS C_1, which falls into three categories: (1)

102. Though she does not give the reason stated above, Butler does seem to think the development of Sîn 1 went from lunar eclipse incantation to favorable dream incantation (Butler, *Mesopotamian Dream Conceptions*, 139, 149).

103. This seems to be Kunstmann's view since he describes MS A (designated simply as BM 78432) as providing the prayer in its original purpose, to secure a favorable dream (Kunstmann, *Babylonische Gebetsbeschwörung*, 103).

104. Manuscript C_1 from Sultantepe also attests a number of the "added" lines in MS A_1 (but also leaves out some and adds others; see below). Since, however, MS C_1 only copied the hymnic introduction to the prayer, we cannot look to it for any help in adjudicating our problem because the *attalû* formula may or may not have been part of the posthymnic text on the tablet from which MS C_1 was copied—presuming there was such text.

105. The discovery of the beginning of the hymnic introduction in MS A from Sippar could substantially strengthen or weaken this point.

transposition of lines, (2) small textual differences, and (3) major additions and omissions vis-à-vis the other witnesses.

First, the transposition: MS C_1 from Sultantepe transposes the order of the fourth and fifth lines of the prayer vis-à-vis the four other manuscripts that attest these lines: MSS A_1, B_1, d_1, and E_1. I cite MS A_1 for comparison.

MS A_1 obv.
4. To the black-headed people, [your] ra[ys] are sent forth.
5. Your shining appearance (*ṣētka*) is bright in the [pure] heavens.

MS C_1 obv.
22. Your shining appearance (*ṣētka*) [is b]right in the p[ure hea]vens,
23. [To the] black-headed [peop]le, [your] rays are sent forth,

Obviously, this could be a scribal mistake. But apart from simply accepting the majority of witnesses as the correct text, we cannot be sure.

Second, MS C_1 shows several small textual variations in lines that it shares with other witnesses. The first two variations appear in obv. 24. In the first half of this line, C_1 has "shining appearance" (*ṣētka*), used previously in the lines cited above, instead of "your torch" (*dipāraka*), as attested in the other two manuscripts showing this part of the line, A_1 and B_1. Manuscript C_1 also seems to have a different word in the second half of the same line than the two witnesses preserving the latter half of the line (MSS A_1 and d_1). That is, MS A_1 shows the ḪI sign, thus providing a basis for Mayer to suggest *ḫi*[*miṭka*], "your burning," at the end of the line. (MS d_1 may show a partial TAB sign, which can also be read *ḫ*[*imiṭka*].) But MS C_1 has a SU sign, which suggests an entirely different (and still unrecognized) word in this position in the line.[106] In sum, MS C_1 obv. 24–25 compares with the parallel lines in MS A_1 (and d_1) as follows:

MS A_1 obv.
6. Your torch is magnificent, [your] bur[ning?] like Girra.
7. Your awe-inspiring luminosity fills the wide [earth].

106. But these readings remain uncertain, since they are all based on conjectured restorations following the initial sign of the final word in each of the three witnesses. See Mayer, *Untersuchungen*, 491, n. (2) on line 6.

MS C_1 obv.
24. Your shining appearance [is magni]ficent, … […] like Girra,
25. Your awe-inspiring luminosity [fill]s the wid[e] earth.

Manuscript C_1 also differs in a small way in obv. 27 vis-à-vis the only other witness to this part of the line, MS A_1 obv. 9. Where A_1 reads "no [one]" (*ma-a*[*m-man*]), C_1 reads inexplicably *kab*-[…].

MS A_1 obv.
9. O Anu of the heavens, whose advice no [one] can learn,

MS C_1 obv.
27. [O Anu of the heavens], whose advice [no] … ca[n learn],

Another small difference occurs in MS C_1 rev. 5 compared to MSS A_1 obv. 17 and F_1 obv. 2′. The latter two read "the day of your oracle, the secret of the great gods" (*ūm tamitīka pirišti ilī rabûti*) while MS C_1 reads "the day of the decision of the [great] gods" (*ūm purussê ilī rabûti*). Though both phrases refer to the revelation of the new moon, MS C_1's is more direct.

One might explain these small differences by various appeals to scribal mistakes, stylistic preferences, semantic variants, or lapses in memory. In fact, these are the kinds of variants one expects to find in copies of the same composition.[107]

But the final category of differences may call into question our assumption that MS C_1 is a copy of the same composition as the other witnesses, because MS C_1 lacks some lines attested in other manuscripts and includes others not attested in them. Manuscript C_1 lacks the line "with pride, the people vie with one another to gaze upon you" (MSS A_1 obv. 8 and A obv. 2′; also partially attested in MSS b and B_1) but includes, apparently in its place, a line that reads partially "[…] heed(s) your divinity const[antly]." Manuscript C_1 also lacks the line that reads "they are seated in their assembly; they discuss (it) at your feet" in MSS A_1 obv. 15 and F_1 obv. 7′ (probably also attested in MSS B_1) and reads in its place "[the Anunnaki] and the Igigi grant you […]." Next, MS C_1 lacks the line "O resplendent Sîn of Ekur, they inquire of you, and you give the oracle of the gods" preserved in MSS A_1 obv. 16 and F_1 obv. 1′ (of VAT 13854) without a substitute and

107. See similarly Cogan, "Some Text-Critical Issues," 7–8.

adds at least three, perhaps four, more lines to its conclusion in rev. 6–8 (or 9)[108] between what A_1 and F_1 have as adjacent lines in obv. 17–18 (A_1) and obv. 2′–3′ (F_1).[109] Thus, C_1 reads:

MS C_1 rev.
6. [...] renewal they take notice of you.
7. [...]
8. [I ca]ll to you, O lord, in the mi[dst of the pure heavens.]
9. [Incantation:?] To the gods this ... [...]

Reverse 8, interestingly, is one of the added lines in MS A from Sippar (obv. 9′). This led Butler to suggest that "Assyrian and Babylonian versions of the same incantation have been merged."[110] But given the many differences between the Sultantepe manuscript and MS A (from Sippar) as well as the rather formulaic character of the phrase in question, this seems highly unlikely.

What then can we say about MS C_1 and its relationships to the other witnesses? The big picture about the shape and purpose of the text in C_1 is much easier to guess at—and I use that word deliberately—than the details of its relationship to the other witnesses. As for the big picture, given the fact that the first two lines on the tablet are clumsily and almost certainly mistakenly repeated (including the ÉN superscript from line 1 in line 3) and given the late addition of a colophon to the dried tablet (scratched onto its surface), I suspect the tablet started out as a kind of scribal exercise (in keeping with the proposed purpose of the collection from which it came) that was then turned into a votive object—deemed appropriate by virtue of the two hymns (stubs of a prayer) inscribed on it—for some individual named Aplaya. This seems to me a reasonable inference based on the location of the tablet and some distinctive features on it—but, significantly, not features within the part containing the prayer we are dealing with. But this does not address the quite divergent content of our prayer when compared to other witnesses of Sîn 1. In fact, the differences are so great, especially with regard to the differences in whole lines, that we are probably warranted in questioning whether MS C_1 should even be

108. The number of lines turns on how one reads the first sign of MS C_1 rev. 9 (as [ÉN], thereby signifying a catch-line, or something else).

109. B_1 (from Nineveh) shows the same text as these two witnesses.

110. Butler, *Mesopotamian Dream Conceptions*, 381.

considered a witness to Sîn 1 at all. This recognition leads us back to the issue of how to decide when similar texts are *not* slightly deviating duplicates or revisions/adaptations of the same prayer but rather *different texts* altogether. Given our earlier difficulty in determining the original hymnic introduction, whether the longer hymn in MS A_1 or the shorter one as is presented in MS A, perhaps we should be talking about three different texts (editions?) that share a lot of material, but whose precise genealogical relationship is indeterminable.

Walter Kunstmann, in fact, divided the witnesses to this prayer into two groups Sîn 1a and 1b, grouping the two text witnesses available to him at the time with the short hymnic introduction and long ritual instructions, that is, Butler's MSS A and b from Sippar, together as Sîn 1b, and labeling the one witness with the *Bīt rimki* colophon, that is, Butler's MS A_1 from Nineveh as Sîn 1a.[111] The positing of different recensions in Sippar and Nineveh/Assur seems quite reasonable. I cannot determine why Mayer did not follow Kunstmann in this classification, when he did in several other similar situations.[112] In any case, reinstating Kunstmann's typology and extending it to include a Sîn 1c, represented by Butler's MS C_1 from Sultantepe, may be worth considering, especially if new information (e.g., the first part of the hymnic introduction of MS A) comes to light as the recovery of these texts proceeds.

7. Conclusions

I have tried to illustrate what we can learn about scribal revision and textual variation that results from ritual adaptation of prayers to new circumstances. I have done this by working from the ground up. That is, I have compared broadly dated, provenanced, and in some cases ritually contextualized witnesses to (presumably) the same prayer (within a genre known to have been revised and adapted for ritual performances) to establish empirical data about how each differs vis-à-vis the others and then to explore, based on what we know about each witness, possible explanations for these differences. The results are mixed. We can

111. Kunstmann, *Babylonische Gebetsbeschwörung*, 103.

112. Mayer preserved Kunstmann's distinction between Adad 1a and 1b (Kunstmann, *Babylonische Gebetsbeschwörung*, 83; Mayer, *Untersuchungen*, 378), Ea 1a and 1b (Kunstmann, 85; Mayer, 380–81), Enlil 1a and 1b (Kunstmann, 88; Mayer, 384), and Gula 1a and 1b (Kunstmann, 89–90; Mayer, 387).

clearly see how formulas were inserted into both prayers to adapt them to certain ritual contexts or for specific ritual participants. But where these formulas were inserted and why in one specific place in this manuscript but in another in some other manuscript remains rather unclear. One gets a sense that there was some general notion of where formulas could be inserted and the order in which they could occur, but we can say little more. Also, small variations in the wording were apparently easily accommodated by scribes, though why these differences exist is unknown. No clear explanation arises by an appeal to scribal revision or adaptation for these minor textual variations. The same is true about disagreements in the divinity addressed. Why one deity's name was switched with another (and which was the original) could not be determined, despite all that we know about the tablets bearing the prayer directed to them. More difficult was the prayer (or prayers?) to Sîn. These texts seem to be related on first glance but not nearly as closely as the witnesses to the prayers to Gula/Belet-ili. Perhaps they represent local recensions in three different cities. Still, we have little to go on aside from speculations based on internal evidence alone. Overall, the results are sobering for those who would detect scribal revision or development in these ancient documents. For even if we attempt to minimize speculation by comparing multiple manuscripts of the same composition from a genre known to have been subject to scribal revision/adaptation and these manuscripts can be dated, provenanced, and in some cases ritually contextualized, we still cannot put these manuscripts into any kind of chronological order and we still cannot divine in detail the reasons for and placement of the textual variations we can see among the witnesses. The evidence simply will not cooperate.

8. Epilogue: Implications for Biblical Studies

We know these two Akkadian prayers were revised and adapted. We know some broad aspects of why (e.g., specific ritual performances) and even how (i.e., insertion of formulas, change of deities names, addition/omission of lines), but we cannot know why *in detail* and we cannot establish the chronological priority of specific variants to retrace the genealogy of revision. And yet these are the very kinds of things scholars often do with the biblical text. They explain minute details in terms of scribal revision/activity (i.e., insertions, explanations, clarifications, corrections, corruptions, polemics, etc.), and they posit textual priority (i.e., the original material) for one variant over another or some portion (or version) of a passage within a larger whole in order to trace revisions/interpolations within it on the basis of what *they* perceive to be the internal logic of the text or the aesthetically better phrasing. Yet we know next to nothing about what the scribes actually had at hand at the time of writing, revising, or copying most biblical texts!

There can be no doubt that the biblical text underwent revision/development, and there can be no doubt that the ancient scribal cultures in ancient Mesopotamia and Israel/Judah were different in various respects. I do not intend to overstate the implications of the findings here. Indeed, a similar study as the present one in different genres in either culture would produce slightly different kinds of results with regard to textual variation versus stabilization.[113] Yet it still seems to me that the present study commends greater caution and a more explicit recognition of the limits of our textual evidence when trying to trace in detail the revisions we suspect lie buried in an ancient text, including the biblical one.

113. See, for example, Hobson, *Transforming Literature into Scripture*, 130, 170 n. 19.

Dissimilatory Reading and the Making of Biblical Texts: The Jewish Pentateuch and the Samaritan Pentateuch

Stefan Schorch

1. Introduction

Both in literary and textual history, the evolution of biblical texts has been described mainly from the perspective of textual composition and transmission in writing. Jeffrey Tigay's important collection of empirical models is here no exception. However, it seems obvious that the formation of ancient Hebrew texts was heavily influenced by oral performance and oral traditions, not only in the early stages, but throughout the whole literary process until the emergence of texts regarded as authoritative and fixed, from the late second century BCE onwards.

One aspect of this interplay of oral and literary textual representation and transmission is that the orally realized reading of written records in different contexts, as well as the subsequent emergence of oral reading traditions, influenced and shaped the written transmission of biblical texts and became a most influential factor in their multiplication and dissimilation, leading to diverging written consonantal frameworks. It will be shown that the emergence of both the Samaritan Pentateuch (SP) and the Jewish Pentateuch should at least partly be understood as resulting from divergent reading traditions, which had been orally transmitted in different contexts and by different communities.

The model of textual dissimilation laid out in the following on the basis of textual evidence gathered mainly from the SP (as opposed to the Masoretic Text [MT]) challenges, opposes, and complements the model of textual assimilation as described by Yair Zakovitch in Tigay's volume.[1] Although literary and textual transmission may indeed involve phenomena of textual assimilation as described by Zakovitch, leading to the rapprochement of two texts, it may equally include dissimilatory phenomena, which drive texts apart from one another and may create a multitude of texts, all proceeding from one and the same written record.

Proceeding from this perspective, the comparison between parallel passages from the SP and the MT of the Torah demonstrates that the differences between these two textual corpora as they appear in the two written traditions were at least partly caused by dissimilatory reading, supplementing Tigay's analysis of the text-historically secondary conflationist expansions within the SP as opposed to an earlier unexpanded text preserved in the MT.[2]

2. The Problem: Texts as Products of Reading

The construction of literary history is based on the observation that a given earlier text [T^a] is different from a given later text [T^b] and the assumption that [T^a] was transformed into [T^b]. This transformation and textual change may concern all the parameters that determine a text, especially its form, function, and meaning, and it may be induced by different factors. Reading is one of the most important of them, because if [T^b] is related to [T^a], the former is obviously based on a reading of the latter.

In order to fully realize the influence imposed by the reading of a text on its transmission, the following should be kept in mind: reading usually proceeds from a written record. The written record of [T^a], however, is obviously not quite identical with [T^a] itself, since most writing systems, the Hebrew script included, only partially encode the information by which texts are determined. Therefore, in order to retrieve a text from a given written document, the reader is expected and required to provide additional information not found in the written record but drawn from his own experience and cultural knowledge. If a specific reader is fully aware of the cultural codes and horizons of [T^a], he might be able to supply the

1. Yair Zakovitch, "Assimilation in Biblical Narratives," in *Empirical Models for Biblical Criticism*, ed. Jeffrey H. Tigay (Philadelphia: University of Philadelphia Press, 1985), 175–96.

2. Jeffrey H. Tigay, "Conflation as a Redactional Technique," in Tigay, *Empirical Models for Biblical Criticism*, 61–83.

necessary details and to apply them on the written document in the way required to (re-)create [T$^{a(1)}$] as a full equivalent of the original [T^{a}]. If this is not the case, however, he is likely to produce [T^{b}] in a way only partially compliant with [T^{a}].

This problem, inherent to script and the written transmission of documents in general as mentioned before, seems to have been even more grave with regard to the Hebrew Bible. The reason is that the Hebrew script is not able to record vowels, with the exception of the so-called vowel letters (*matres lectionis*),[3] although the distinctiveness of a certain vocalization may carry important semantic information.[4] As a result, the Hebrew Bible contains in fact a large number of words with different meaning, which had been homographs before the invention of the masoretic pointing. For example:

> מטה: (1) מִטָּה ("bed," Gen 37:1); (2) מַטֶּה ("staff," Gen 38:25); (3) מַטָּה ("below," Deut 28:43); (4) מֻטֶּה ("corruption," Ezek 9:9)

In the following case, the number of homographs is even higher:

> וישב: (1) וַיֵּשֶׁב ("and he dwelt," imperfect consecutive, Num 25:1); (2) וְיָשַׁב ("and he shall dwell," perfect consecutive, Num 32:17); (3) וְיֹשֵׁב ("and he who is sitting," Ps 50:20); (4) וַיֹּשֶׁב ("and he placed them," 2 Kgs 17:6); (5) וַיָּשָׁב ("and he returned," Gen 37:29); (6) וְיָשֹׁב ("and he should go back," Deut 20:5); (7) וַיָּשֶׁב ("and he brought back," Gen 14:16); (8) וַיָּשֵׁב ("and he drove away," Gen 15:11); (9) וַיִּשְׁבְּ ("and he took captive," Num 21:1); etc.

The multitude of homographs means that the way a reader vocalizes a given written consonantal framework can lead to a meaning of the whole passage that is deviant from the meaning originally intended to be encoded in writing; that is, the reading might easily produce a text [T^{b}] that is significantly different from the text [T^{a}] intended to be transmitted by the

3. See James Barr, "Reading a Script without Vowels," in *Writing without Letters*, ed. William Haas (Manchester: Manchester University Press; Totowa, NJ: Rowman & Littlefield, 1976), 74–79.

4. The same is true for further phonetic features, which find no expression in Hebrew writing, as for instance doubling of consonants (as required in the distinction of *qal* versus *piel*, etc.) or stress (as required for the distinction of segolate nouns, etc.).

scribe of the respective manuscript. The textual consequences of this problem can be demonstrated with the following example from Gen 15, which involves the readings (1) and (8) of the consonantal cluster וישב from the above list, as well as the homograph אִתָּם/אֹתָם. In the course of the story, Abraham slaughters animals and cuts them into pieces in preparation for a covenant ceremony. When birds of prey start to approach the carcasses, Abraham shoos them away, as told in the MT of Gen 15:11:

> And when the vultures came down on the carcasses,
> MT: וַיַּשֵּׁב אֹתָם אַבְרָהָם (Abraham drove them away.)

The Septuagint (LXX), however, contains a very different account of that moment:

> LXX: *καὶ συνεκάθισεν αὐτοῖς* Αβραμ (Abraham sat down together with them.)

Although the latter text thus presents a different story, the variant in the underlying Hebrew reading is rather minor: both versions, the MT and the LXX, proceeded from the same written consonantal framework. The masoretic vocalization reads וַיַּשֵּׁב אֹתָם ("he drove them away"), interpreting the verbal form וישב on the basis of the root נש"ב (*hiphil*, "to frighten away"). The Greek translator, on the other hand, obviously read וַיֵּשֶׁב אִתָּם* ("he sat down together with them"), proceeding from the root יש"ב ("to sit"). Accordingly, the following word had to be read as the preposition אִתָּם ("with them"), instead of the *nota accusativi* אֹתָם ("them"). From a text-historical point of view, there is not much doubt that it is the masoretic reading that correctly renders the text originally encoded in the consonantal framework.[5] In other words, [T^a] and [T^b] are equal in the case of the masoretic reading: [T^a] = [$T^{b\,(MT)}$].

The Greek translator, on the other hand, seems to have been unaware of the rare verb נש"ב, which is a *hapax legomenon* in the Pentateuch, and

5. See James Barr, "Vocalization and the Analysis of Hebrew among the Ancient Translators," in *Hebräische Wortforschung: Festschrift zum 80. Geburtstag von Walter Baumgartner*, ed. Benedikt Hartmann et al., VTSup 16 (Leiden: Brill, 1967), 4; Stefan Schorch, "The Septuagint and the Vocalization of the Hebrew Text of the Torah," in *XII Congress of the International Organization for Septuagint and Cognate Studies: Leiden 2004*, ed. Melvin K. H. Peters, SCS 54 (Atlanta: Society of Biblical Literature, 2006), 43–44.

he therefore resorted to the most current vocalization of the very frequent consonantal sequence ו-י-ש-ב. As a consequence of this reading, however, he created a text $[\mathrm{T}^{\mathrm{b}}]$ which is different from $[\mathrm{T}^{\mathrm{a}}]$: $[\mathrm{T}^{\mathrm{a}}] \neq [\mathrm{T}^{\mathrm{b\ (LXX)}}]$.

Most obviously, therefore, the reading, which supplied vocalization, had a dissimilatory influence on the transmission of Gen 15. Instead of one text, which was the point of departure, two different readers (or groups of readers) created two different texts. The Hebrew and the Greek account are different from one other, although they both originate in the same source. It is exactly this phenomenon which is called here "dissimilatory reading."

3. Biblical Texts and the History of Reading in Ancient Israel

3.1. Synthesis

In light of the high importance of the reading, it is of course a very problematic fact that the reading was not always part of the written transmission of the biblical text. It was only after the invention of masoretic punctuation, apparently in the sixth–seventh centuries CE,[6] that the reading became codified within the written tradition.

This relatively late inclusion in the corpus of written tradition does not mean, however, that the reading before that time had no part in the transmission of the biblical text at all. Rather, the reading was transmitted orally prior to that time, and the high measure of stability of this way of transmission, be it in the context of the regular and public reading of Scripture in the synagogues or in the context of the study of Scripture, should not be underestimated.[7] The classical rabbinic tradition even regarded the reading as having the same origin and authority as the written tradition of the biblical text, as can be learned from the following quo-

6. See Emanuel Tov, *Textual Criticism of the Hebrew Bible*, 3rd ed. (Minneapolis: Fortress, 2012), 36–47. For an inquiry into the problems involved with the early history of reading from the Torah see Lawrence H. Schiffman, "The Early History of Public Reading of the Torah," in *Jews, Christians, and Polytheists in the Ancient Synagogue: Cultural Interaction during the Greco-Roman Period*, ed. Steven Fine (London: Routledge, 1999), 38–49.

7. Among modern scholars of the Hebrew Bible, this was most prominently stressed by James Barr in his studies cited here.

tation from the Babylonian Talmud, attributed to a rabbi from the late third century CE (b. Ned. 37b):[8]

אמר רבי יצחק מקרא סופרים ועיטור סופרים וקריין ולא כתיבן וכתיבן ולא קריין הלכה למשה מסיני.

Rabbi Yishaq said: "The correct reading of the words, the omissions as well as the words which are to be read although they are not written or the words which are not to be read although they are written were handed down as Law to Moses at Sinai."

Of course, this mythological claim cannot be justified from a scholarly point of view. Rather, it seems likely that the reading of the Torah gained stability only from the late second century BCE onwards, when distinctive liturgical readings emerged as part of the identities of different groups of the Israelite-Jewish tradition, like the Samaritans and the protorabbinic movement.[9] Therefore, although the reading codified in the MT is certainly considerably older than the first written witnesses that preserve it, it still seems to have originated at a substantially later time than the consonantal framework of the Torah.

Prior to the fixation of reading traditions, therefore, the reader of a given Hebrew text from the Torah had to provide the required information with regard to the vocalization and punctuation of the written consonantal framework in front of him from different sources other than the written record itself, and the available evidence suggests that readers were often influenced by paratextual traditions, that is, narrative accounts, which covered the stories contained in the biblical texts, although they did not render them in a literal way. The main characteristics of these parabiblical retellings are as follows:

---

8. This opinion dominated the traditional Jewish perception of the biblical text in general and the vocalization in particular at least until Elijahu Bakhur (Elia Levita, 1469–1549), and it became part of the general views of Lutheran scholars in the late sixteenth century. See Stefan Schorch, *Die Vokale des Gesetzes: Die samaritanische Lesetradition als Textzeugin der Tora*, vol. 1: *Das Buch Genesis*, BZAW 339 (Berlin: de Gruyter, 2004), 1–2; Schorch, "Which Bible, Whose Text? Biblical Theologies in Light of the Textual History of the Hebrew Bible," in *Beyond Biblical Theologies*, ed. Heinrich Assel, Stefan Beyerle, and Christfried Böttrich, WUNT 295 (Tübingen: Mohr Siebeck, 2012), 359–64.

9. Schorch, *Vokale des Gesetzes*, 55–61.

- They seem to have provided no full coverage of the Torah but pertained only to parts of it. Therefore, besides passages whose content was familiar to the reader, he might have met passages that he did not know beforehand and consequently would have had to resort to guessing.
- They seem to have covered mostly the narrative passages of the biblical text, while the poetical parts are often without parabiblical traditions. This feature is mainly due to the fact that within poetical texts form and meaning are often closely intertwined, which impedes a simple narrative retelling.
- They seem to have been exposed to further literary influences, leading to the contamination, expansion, or the introduction of other literary and semantic changes of the account.

All these different phenomena pertaining to the reconstruction of the early history of Hebrew reading are well attested in the Greek translation of the book of Genesis, which originated in the third century BCE and was therefore carried out without access to a firm vocalization tradition attached to the consonantal framework. Being most probably the first translation ever of a biblical book,[10] the Greek book of Genesis seems to be free from influences by earlier translations and most probably preserves a genuine product of reading the consonantal framework of Hebrew Genesis in a third century BCE setting.[11]

3.2. The Partial Coverage of the Biblical Text by Parabiblical Traditions

There is clear evidence that the Greek translator of the book of Genesis was not always successful in reconstructing the text [T^{a}] originally encoded by the Hebrew scribe of the consonantal framework of his *Vorlage*. One of these cases is preserved in the Greek translation of Gen 15 shown above, which is most probably the result of an educated guess, that is, the product of a reader, who of course knew Biblical Hebrew, but did not know the story told in Gen 15 and probably had a vocabulary more

---

10. "Genesis was, in fact, the first attempt by the Alexandrians to translate parts of the Torah" (John William Wevers, *Notes on the Greek Text of Genesis*, SCS 35 [Atlanta: Scholars Press, 1993], ix); see also Martin Rösel, *Übersetzung als Vollendung der Auslegung: Studien zur Genesis-Septuaginta*, BZAW 223 (Berlin: de Gruyter, 1994), 11.

11. See Schorch, "Septuagint and the Vocalization."

limited than or at least different from the one contained in Hebrew Genesis.[12] A further case would be Gen 47:31, a detail in the account of Jacob's parting from Joseph:

> And (Israel) said: "Swear to me." And he swore to him. Then Israel bowed himself
>
> MT: at the head of the bed. (עַל־רֹאשׁ הַמִּטָּה)
>
> LXX: at the top of his staff. (ἐπὶ τὸ ἄκρον τῆς ῥάβδου αὐτοῦ = על ראש הַמַּטֶּה*)

Most obviously, the Greek translation is based on the reading *הַמַּטֶּה ("the staff") instead of הַמִּטָּה ("the bed"), as presented by the masoretic vocalization, and the context makes it highly unlikely that this is a correct rendering of the text [T[a]] originally encoded in the consonantal framework.[13] The general narrative is concerned with Jacob's illness and impending death, and the act of prostration can hardly be carried out on the tip of a staff. Thus, although the Greek rendering was ultimately understood as a meaningful text [T[b]] as proven by its quotation in Heb 11:21,[14] the underlying Hebrew reading is clearly erroneous in terms of transmission, since it did not retrieve the original message in the right way. This could have been possible only under the condition that the translator did not know

---

12. See James Barr, "'Guessing' in the Septuagint," in *Studien zur Septuaginta: Robert Hanhart zu Ehren; Aus Anlaß seines 65. Geburtstages*, ed. Detlef Fraenkel, Udo Quast, and John William Wevers, MSU 20 (Göttingen: Vandenhoeck & Ruprecht, 1990), 19–34.

13. Schorch, "Septuagint and the Vocalization," 44–45; Barr, "Vocalization and the Analysis of Hebrew," 3–4; Emanuel Tov, "Did the Septuagint Translators Always Understand Their Hebrew Text," in *The Greek and Hebrew Bible: Collected Essays on the Septuagint*, VTSup 72 (Leiden: Brill, 1999), 213. Raymond de Hoop tried to show that the vocalization הַמַּטֶּה is text-historically preferable and should be understood as "and Israel bowed down to the head of the tribe," but he failed to give a sufficient explanation of how the use of the preposition על could be reconciled with this interpretation. See Raymond de Hoop, "'Then Israel Bowed Himself…' (Genesis 47.31)," *JSOT* 28 (2004): 467–80.

14. "By faith Jacob, when dying, blessed each of the sons of Joseph, bowing in worship over the top of his staff" (NRSV).

the story written down by the Hebrew scribe, since otherwise he certainly would not have misread the consonantal framework.

In other cases, however, the Greek translator was much more successful in retrieving the originally encoded text [T^a], although the consonantal framework was equally ambivalent and therefore potentially misleading, as can be demonstrated by the following case from Gen 45, the passage in which Joseph reveals himself to his brothers who had come to Egypt and approached him to buy food. According to 45:2 in the MT, Joseph "wept so loudly

> MT: that the Egyptians heard it, and the house of Pharaoh heard it. (וַיִּשְׁמְעוּ מִצְרַיִם וַיִּשְׁמַע בֵּית פַּרְעֹה)

Thus, the MT reads both forms of the verb שמ"ע in the *qal*, attributing to them the same meaning. The LXX, however, proceeds in each of the two instances from a different vocalization, leading to a somewhat different version of the story, namely

> LXX: all the Egyptians heard it, and it came to be heard in the house of Pharaoh. (ἤκουσαν δὲ πάντες οἱ Αἰγύπτιοι καὶ ἀκουστὸν ἐγένετο εἰς τὸν οἶκον Φαραω)

The Greek translation is clearly based on more or less from the same consonantal framework as attested in the MT, but it seems to have read two different vocalizations for the two verbal forms of שמ"ע, since it renders them differently. A Hebrew vocalization that could justify and accommodate the Greek rendering is indeed attested in the SP:

> SP: the Egyptians heard it and let it hear the house of Pharaoh. (וַיִּשְׁמְעוּ מצרים וַיְשַׁמְעוּ בית פרעה*)[15]

---

15. The SP has been published in transcription by Zeev Ben-Hayyim, עברית וארמית נוסח שומרון, כרך ד': מלי תורה [*The Literary and Oral Tradition of Hebrew and Aramaic amongst the Samaritans*, vol. 4: *The Words of the Pentateuch*] (Jerusalem: The Academy of the Hebrew Language, 1977). In this version, the passage in question reads as follows: *wyišmā'u miṣrəm wyešammā'u bit fāru*. The first verb, *wyišmā'u*, is in the *qal* stem (= *וַיִּשְׁמְעוּ), while the second one, *wyešammā'u*, is in the *piel* (= *וַיְשַׁמְעוּ). The reconstruction of the vocalization in Tiberian signs is for the sake of comparison, as explained in Schorch, *Vokale des Gesetzes*, 79–80.

It thus seems likely that the Greek translator vocalized the consonantal framework in a way similar to the Samaritan reading tradition. Representing the *lectio difficilior* as opposed to the masoretic vocalization, this vocalization seems to have been the one intended by the scribe of [T^a], and therefore the LXX in this case attests an example for successful transmission. In other words, [T^a] was faithfully preserved. The question is, however, why the Greek translator successfully retrieved [T^a] in this case, but failed in other places? Most probably, the present story was known to him beforehand, apparently from a parabiblical narrative. Since the parabiblical accounts the translator had access to did not cover the whole book of Genesis, he failed with regard to other stories.

3.3. The Limited Value of Parabiblical Traditions in the Reading of Poetical Texts

Unlike the firm vocalization traditions of the consonantal framework of biblical texts, which emerged from the second century BCE onward, parabiblical retellings and paraphrases of biblical texts cover mainly the narrative passages of the biblical text and were therefore often not available or not helpful for the translation of poetic passages. This is mirrored by the fact that the number of Greek translations based on erroneous vocalization of the consonantal framework is much higher in poetical passages of the biblical text than in prose. An example of this is the saying to Simeon and Levi in Jacob's blessing in Gen 49:6:

> MT: Let not *my honor* [כְּבֹדִי] be united to their assembly.
>
> LXX: Let not *my livers* [τὰ ἥπατά μου = *כְּבֵדַי] contend in their assembly.

In this passage, the MT and LXX attest two different vocalizations of the consonantal cluster כבדי. Because the masoretic vocalization is supported by the Samaritan reading *kābūdi* (= כְּבֹדִי),[16] it is more likely to preserve the reading that was intended by the scribe of this passage. However, both readings seem to fit the general message encoded in this passage, namely, that the poetical "I" does not support the joint actions of Simeon

16. See Schorch, *Vokale des Gesetzes*, 225–26.

and Levi.[17] In any case, one of the two readings, either that of the Greek translator or that of the MT, did not successfully retrieve [T^a] and instead created an alternative [T^b]. The reason, therefore, is that neither the consonantal framework itself nor a parabiblical account could have provided the necessary information for the preservation of the vocalization of [T^a].

3.4. Influences from Other Traditions

In many cases, parabiblical accounts contain different versions of a story than that encoded in the MT, which then influenced the reader. In addition, readers of a given consonantal framework were sometimes influenced by traditions, which before that had not been in immediate contact with the biblical account. In some cases, this influence left traces in the interpretation of the consonantal framework and resulted in the emergence of a new text [T^b]. One well known example is found in Gen 6:4:

> There were נפילים/γίγαντες on the earth in those days, and also afterward, when the sons of God came in to the daughters of men
>
> MT: who bore them offspring. (וְיָלְדוּ לָהֶם)
>
> LXX: and produced offspring for themselves. (καὶ ἐγεννῶσαν ἑαυτοῖς = *וְיוֹלִידוּ לָהֶם)

Most probably, the masoretic vocalization corresponds to the text [T^a], which was originally intended by the scribe of the consonantal framework.[18] The Greek translator, however, read the verb in the *hiphil* instead in the *qal*, since he was apparently influenced by a parabiblical story similar or identical to the one preserved in the Ethiopic Enoch.[19] This story identifies the נפילים as giants and provides a much more detailed account of the sexual relations between human women and heavenly beings than the MT. Although the translator, who generally kept to his

17. See Claus Westermann, *Genesis*, BKAT 1 (Neukirchen-Vluyn: Neukirchener Verlag, 1982), 256, who leaves the question of the correct vocalization open, since both readings carry the same message.

18. See Schorch, *Vokale des Gesetzes*, 102–3.

19. See 1 En. 6:2; 7:1–2. See Siegbert Uhlig, *Das äthiopische Henochbuch*, JSHRZ 5.6 (Gütersloh: Mohn, 1984), 519–20; and Devorah Dimant, "1 Enoch 6–11: A Fragment of a Parabiblical Work," *JJS* 53 (2002): 231.

Hebrew *Vorlage* quite closely, made no exception in this case and therefore certainly did not rewrite the story, his vocalization of the consonantal framework still means that it makes the intercourse much more explicit than the MT. However, since the SP contains exactly the Hebrew text which should be reconstructed as the *Vorlage* of the Greek translator, it might well be that this textual change entered the consonantal framework, expressed by *matres lectionis*, already before the Greek translation.

The aforementioned examples demonstrated that historical readers of the consonantal framework of the biblical texts created in many instances a new text in the course of reading that was different from the text the scribe of that framework had intended to codify, that is, $[T^a] \neq [T^b]$. Since the Greek translation of the LXX seems generally to originate in a singular, individual, and transitory reading act of the translator and not in a repeated and repeatable reading of the consonantal framework of the Hebrew *Vorlage*, this reading usually left no traces in the Hebrew transmission of the biblical text. It was only through the codification of the translation that this reading was preserved, although solely in a Greek version. Nevertheless, we still can conclude on the basis of this evidence that a given consonantal framework could potentially serve as the point of departure for different texts, even if in many cases they may have existed only temporarily in the mind of the reader, or in the act of reading itself.

In some cases, however, specific readings of the Hebrew consonantal framework did develop into fixed traditions, which were handed down and perpetuated by a community. The implication of that development is that $[T^b]$ coagulates and becomes stable. Therefore, with the fixation of the reading, the latter cannot be regarded anymore as one single event in the unconnected sequence of original reading acts, each of which potentially produces a new text ($[T^b]$, $[T^c]$, $[T^d]$, $[T^e]$, etc.). Rather, the original reading is simply repeated on the basis of a tradition, which means that $[T^b]$ is faithfully reproduced consistently, although at different points of time: $[T^{b(1)}] = [T^{b(2)}] = [T^{b(3)}] = [T^{b(4)}]$, and so on. Moreover, if in addition to one reading producing $[T^b]$, another reading which produces another text $[T^c]$ develops into a fixed and stable tradition ($[T^{c(1)}] = [T^{c(2)}] = [T^{c(3)}]$, etc.), two different texts come into perpetual existence: $[T^{b(x)}] \neq [T^{c(x)}]$, instead of one which was originally codified by the scribe of the consonantal framework, that is, $[T^a]$. Unlike in the instances quoted from the LXX tradition, which were analyzed above where $[T^b]$ is preserved only in a Greek rendering, in these cases both $[T^b]$ and $[T^c]$ are Hebrew texts, the results of dissimilatory reading.

4. Dissimilatory Reading and the Emergence of the Samaritan Pentateuch

Most obviously, one of the several readings that became fixed in the context of a tradition is preserved in the masoretic vocalization. A second reading tradition, different from the MT, is preserved in the SP.[20] Thus, there are two Hebrew textual witnesses extant for the Torah as a whole, and both of them are fully vocalized, although this fact is often overlooked. The comparison of these two textual traditions reveals quite a substantial number of cases for dissimilatory reading and, as a consequence, the parallel emergence of two different Hebrew texts.[21] It seems that it was in fact at least partially the differences in the respective readings that drove not only the Jews and Samaritans apart from one other,[22] but the two textual corpora as well.

One illustrative example, based on the *divergent vocalization* of one word, can be found in Gen 2:7 in the account of God's creation of man from dust. After the introductory "Then the Lord God formed man from the dust from the earth," the MT continues:

> MT: וַיִּפַּח באפיו נשמת חיים (and breathed into his nostrils the breath of life.)

While the masoretic reading is based on the vocalization of the verb ויפח in the *qal* stem, the SP contains a different vocalization, proceeding from a *hiphil* of the same word:[23]

> SP: וַיַּפַּח באפיו נשמת חיים (and let breathe in his nostrils the breath of life.)

20. See Schorch, *Vokale des Gesetzes*, 7–10.

21. For a comprehensive treatment of the reading differences between the MT and the SP traditions in Genesis, see Schorch, *Vokale des Gesetzes*.

22. See Stefan Schorch, "The Construction of Samari(t)an Identity from the Inside and from the Outside," in *Between Cooperation and Hostility: Multiple Identities in Ancient Judaism and the Interaction with Foreign Powers*, ed. Rainer Albertz and Jakob Wöhrle, JAJSup 11 (Göttingen: Vandenhoeck & Ruprecht, 2013), 138.

23. The word is pronounced *wyabba* in the SP, presenting the Samaritan Hebrew equivalent to the MT וַיִּפַּח; see Ben-Hayyim, *Literary and Oral Tradition*, 183, and Schorch, *Vokale des Gesetzes*, 87.

Thus, although both texts present God as the creator of man from dust, they imply different anthropological concepts. According to the MT, the first men consisted of two clearly distinctive components: a body made from dust, and "the breath of life," which originated directly with God. According to the SP, however, "the breath of life" is not a separate entity, but merely a function of the body, which was commenced by God.[24] Thus, the different vocalization of one word of the consonantal framework led to two distinct texts, which both continue to exist side by side.

That divergent vocalization is only one way of dissimilative reading is demonstrated by the following case, where the emergence of the MT and the SP as two different and distinctive accounts was motivated by *divergent punctuation*. In Exod 19:23–24, the MT reads:

> 23 Moses said to the LORD: "The people cannot come up to Mount Sinai; for you yourself warned us, saying: 'Set bounds around the mountain and keep it holy.'" 24 The LORD said to him: "Go down, and come up, you and Aaron with you. But the priests and the people, let them not break through to come up to the LORD; otherwise he will break out against them."

Thus, according to 19:24, Moses is commanded to ascend Mount Sinai, bringing Aaron with him, while the priests and the people are forbidden to come too close to the summit of Mount Sinai. A different version of that part of the story, however, is contained in many manuscripts of the SP, which read as follows:

> 24 The LORD said to him, "Go down, and come up, together with Aaron and the priests. But the people, let them not break through to come up to the LORD."[25]

---

24. See Schorch, "Which Bible," 361–62.

25. The translation follows some of the most ancient manuscripts of the SP that are preserved: MSS Cambridge University Library Add. 713 (before 1213 CE), Add. 714 (1219), Dublin Chester Beatty Library 751 (1225), Manchester John-Rylands Library Sam 1 (1211), Leipzig Universitätsbibliothek Vollers 1120 (ca. 1345), etc. Other ancient manuscripts contain a different version, reading והעלית ("and bring an offering") instead of ועלית ("and come up"): MSS Nablus Synagogue 6 (1204), Cambridge University Library Add. 1846 (12th century), Leiden Or. MS 6 (1350), etc. In fact, the reading as heard today in the Samaritan community has *wāllīta*, that is, the *hiphil* (= והעלית). See Ben-Hayyim, *Literary and Oral Tradition*, ad loc.

According to the Samaritan version, therefore, God commands Moses to ascend Mount Sinai not only together with Aaron, as in the MT, but together with Aaron and the priests, while only the common people are not allowed to ascend Mount Sinai.

The difference between the MT and the SP is based on a different punctuation. The MT has an *atnach* after וְאַהֲרֹן עִמָּךְ ("and Aaron with you"), separating it from the following וְהַכֹּהֲנִים וְהָעָם ("But the priests and the people"):

וַיֹּאמֶר אֵלָיו יְהוָה לֶךְ־רֵד וְעָלִיתָ אַתָּה וְאַהֲרֹן עִמָּךְ
וְהַכֹּהֲנִים וְהָעָם אַל־יֶהֶרְסוּ לַעֲלֹת אֶל־יְהוָה פֶּן־יִפְרָץ־בָּם׃

The SP, on the other hand, has the stop not after עמך, but after והכהנים, constructing the phrase אתה ואהרן עמך והכהנים as one syntactical unit:[26]

ויאמר אליו יהוה לך רד ועלית אתה ואהרן עמך והכהנים:
והעם אל יחרסו לעלות אל יהוה פן יפרץ בם:

26. Most manuscripts have at this place an *afsaq* ("full stop"); among the manuscripts mentioned previously in n. 25 only MS Cambridge University Library Add. 713 has a different stop, namely *arkenu* (/). The apparatus of punctuation variants in von Gall's edition lists two manuscripts with a *turu* (ı:), which is yet another stop sign (see August Freiherr von Gall, ed., *Der hebräische Pentateuch der Samaritaner* [Giessen: Töpelmann, 1914–1918], ad loc). Note however, that there is at least one manuscript without a stop sign, Leiden Or. MS 6 (1350). Possibly, this deviation reflects a different reading, since today two ways of reading this verse are attested side by side in the Samaritan community, one with a stop after "and the priests" [והכהנים:], as in the vast majority of manuscripts, and the other with a stop after "with you" [עמך:], as in the MT. This phenomenon is even reflected in modern editions of the SP, which were produced by Samaritans. The Torah written by Tsedaka follows the "priestly" reading, having a stop after "and the priests" (Israel Tsedaka, *Samaritanische Tora* [Holon: A. B. Institute of Samaritan Studies, 1998], ad loc.) while the edition of A. and R. Sadaqa contains a stop after "with you" (Abraham Sadaqa and Ratzon Sadaqa, *Jewish and Samaritan Version of the Pentateuch: With Particular Stress on the Differences between Both Texts* [Tel Aviv: Mass, 1961–1965], ad loc.). Apparently, the parallel existence of these two readings is the expression of a certain tension between the Samaritan priests and the Samaritan people; see Stefan Schorch, "Gemeindeopfer oder Priesteropfer? Die späte Deuteronomisierung des samaritanischen Passaopfers," in *"Und das Leben ist siegreich!": mandäische und samaritanische Literatur; Im Gedenken an Rudolf Macuch (1919–1993)*, ed. Rainer Voigt, MF 1 (Wiesbaden: Harrassowitz, 2008), 244–46.

Most obviously, the two versions imply two different concepts of priesthood, especially with respect to the two questions, whether the priests had immediate access to the revelation at Mount Sinai and whether they are to be regarded as part of the Israelite people in general or as a separate group. As in the case of the creation of man told in Gen 2:7, the divergence of the SP versus the MT reading had a dissimilatory effect and in fact produced two distinct Hebrew texts.

In both examples presented so far in this chapter, the consonantal framework is ambiguous and could accommodate both readings, while the textual dissimilation was expressed only through the fixation of the reading involving a certain vocalization or a certain punctuation. The following example, however, shows a different phenomenon of textual dissimilation generated in the course of reading.

In the passage devoted to the brothers Simeon and Levi from Jacob's blessing in Gen 49:5–7, the different ways of reading a given consonantal framework not only became fixed through the emergence of two distinctive reading traditions, but also had repercussions on the consonantal framework itself and finally reshaped it in a dissimilatory way, as the following synoptic translation of the two versions will demonstrate:[27]

<table>
<tr><th>MT</th><th>SP</th></tr>
<tr><td colspan="2">Simeon and Levi are brothers;</td></tr>
<tr><td>their swords are</td><td>their covenant-making</td></tr>
<tr><td>weapons of violence.</td><td>brought violence to an end.</td></tr>
<tr><td colspan="2">Let not my soul enter their council;</td></tr>
<tr><td colspan="2">with their assembly let not my glory</td></tr>
<tr><td>be united.</td><td>be angry.</td></tr>
<tr><td colspan="2">For in their anger they slew a man,</td></tr>
<tr><td colspan="2">And in their self-will they hamstrung an ox.</td></tr>
<tr><td>Cursed be</td><td>Mighty is</td></tr>
</table>

27. The passages, which are identical in both versions are printed in the middle of the two columns, while diverging passages appear side by side in their respective columns. Additionally, differences between the two texts are underlined.

their anger, for it is fierce;

and their wrath,	and their company,

for it is strong!

Most obviously, the SP and the MT traditions contain a different text of this passage, which is based on the following Hebrew texts:[28]

MT	SP
שִׁמְעוֹן וְלֵוִי אַחִים	שמעון ולוי אחים
כְּלֵי חָמָס מְכֵרֹתֵיהֶם׃	כַּלּוּ חמס מַכְרֵתֵיהֶם
בְּסֹדָם אַל תָּבֹא נַפְשִׁי	בסודם אל תבוא נפשי
בִּקְהָלָם אַל תֵּחַד כְּבֹדִי	ובקהלם אל יִחַר כבודי
כִּי בְאַפָּם הָרְגוּ אִישׁ	כי באפם הרגו איש
וּבִרְצֹנָם עִקְּרוּ שׁוֹר׃	וברצונם עקרו שור
אָרוּר אַפָּם כִּי עָז	אָדִיר אפם כי עז
וְעֶבְרָתָם כִּי קָשָׁתָה	וְחֶבְרָתָם כי קשתה

Besides the divergent reading being employed, the comparison between the two consonantal frameworks reveals some significant differences. It is most obvious, however, that these two consonantal frameworks are very close to one another and in fact represent two different text-historical developments of one and the same consonantal framework, which served as point of departure for both from a diachronic perspective.

Some of the differences exhibited in the present forms of the MT versus the SP are based on interchanges between similar consonants, namely, ו/י and ר/ד, respectively. Within both pairs the signs were graphically almost indistinguishable in the Aramaic and/or Hebrew script of the

28. As above, the rendering of the Samaritan vocalization follows the orally transmitted reading of the Torah, as published by Zeev Ben-Hayyim, but it was transcribed with the help of the vowel signs from the Tiberian Masorah in order to facilitate the comparison between the SP and the MT; see above, and Schorch, *Vokale des Gesetzes*, 76–79.

Hellenistic period.[29] Therefore, the written shapes of the two word pairs כלי/כלו ("they brought to an end" versus "their weapons") and ארור/אדיר ("mighty" versus "cursed") must have been more or less identical. The same holds true for יחר and תחד, although these two forms involve an additional change in the verbal preformative, as a response to the otherwise masculine gender of כבוד.[30]

A different issue is the interchange between עברתם ("their wrath") and חברתם ("their company"), involving an interchange between ע and ח. Although these two consonants are not identical with regard to their shape, they were phonologically identical in some Hebrew dialects of the Second Temple period, including Samaritan Hebrew.[31] Therefore, the two words עברתם and חברתם became homophones; that is, they sounded identical.

A further textual difference involves vocalization alone: the last word of 49:5 is vocalized מְכֵרֹתֵיהֶם by the Masoretes. This reading poses serious problems for explanation, but it most probably means "their swords." The Samaritans vocalized the same consonants in a very different way: מַכְרֵתֵיהֶם is a noun of the root כר"ת ("to cut"), and accordingly the form has been understood in the Samaritan tradition as "covenant making."

Therefore, if we look at the two texts as a whole, it is clear that the basic version, common to both subsequent versions, had been open to different readings. The MT tradition chose one of these options, proceeding from

---

29. Note, however, that the interchangeability caused by graphical similarities allows for historical conclusions: "The only interchanges which occur frequently in most books of the LXX are ד/ר and ו/י.... In view of the lack of distinction between *waw* and *yod* in most of the Qumran scrolls, it seems that the books of the LXX which show a preponderance of ו/י interchanges would reflect a relatively late stage of the textual transmission.... On the other hand, all other books display earlier stages in the development of the Hebrew script, as the interchange ד/ר is possible in both the square Aramaic script and the earlier paleo-Hebrew script, and is actually more likely in the paleo-Hebrew script" (Emanuel Tov, "Interchanges of Consonants between the Masoretic Text and the *Vorlage* of the Septuagint," in *Sha'arei Talmon: Studies in the Bible, Qumran, and the Ancient Near East Presented to Shemaryahu Talmon*, ed. Michael Fishbane and Emanuel Tov [Winona Lake, IN: Eisenbrauns, 1992], 264–66).

30. The difference with regard to the preformative of the verbal form, however, has a different reason, as it seems to have been caused by the adaptation of the verbal form to the masculine use of כבוד.

31. Zeev Ben-Hayyim and Abraham Tal, *A Grammar of Samaritan Hebrew: Based on the Recitation of the Law in Comparison with the Tiberian and Other Jewish Traditions* (Winona Lake, IN: Eisenbrauns, 2000), 38–43.

a negative view of the deeds of Simeon and Levi. The SP tradition chose another option, taking as its starting point a positive appraisal of what Simeon and Levi did according to the story told in Gen 34, when they took revenge on the inhabitants of Shechem for the rape of their sister Dinah. Since the Samaritan reading of Gen 49:5–7 is fully in line with the general tendency of Gen 34, it implies harmonization, which is one of the characteristic features of the SP.[32]

The example of Gen 49:5–7 demonstrates that the written transmission of Hebrew texts is full of gaps that had to be filled in during the course of reading in order to create a text in the proper sense of the word out of the written framework. If so, the reading was an essential factor in the creation of a given Hebrew text. Moreover, the text which was orally created in the course of reading had a strong influence on the shape of the written tradition. For example, once the reading אדיר ("mighty") had been established in the tradition, there was no way back to ארור ("cursed") in a script which made a clear difference between י/ו and ר/ד, respectively. Thus, it was not only the written tradition that determined the reading, but, conversely, the influence worked in the opposite direction as well, when the reading shaped the written framework. Most obviously, therefore, in Gen 49:5–7 the reading not only drove the SP and the MT apart from one other by way of dissimilatory reading, but it led in fact to the inscription of the reading into the consonantal framework.

32. See Esther Eshel and Hanan Eshel, "Dating the Samaritan Pentateuch's Compilation in Light of the Qumran Biblical Scrolls," in *Emanuel: Studies in Hebrew Bible, Septuagint, and Dead Sea Scrolls in Honor of Emanuel Tov*, ed. Shalom M. Paul et al., VTSup 94 (Leiden: Brill, 2003), 215–40; Tov, *Textual Criticism of the Hebrew Bible*, 82–83.

Text-Critically Studying the Biblical Manuscript Evidence: An "Empirical" Entry to the Literary Composition of the Text

Bénédicte Lemmelijn

1. Introduction

Within the context of the present book on *Empirical Models Challenging Biblical Criticism*, this contribution focuses on the way in which textual criticism as the study of the multiple and pluriform manuscript evidence represents a concrete model of empirical research into the biblical text. Proceeding from the illustrative study of the so-called Plague Narrative in Exod 7:14–11:10,[1] it will be demonstrated that the study of the multiple physical texts in textual criticism essentially contributes to the subsequent literary and redactional study of the text. It not only offers a critically assessed textual basis on which the literary and redactional study can work; it also reveals that studying the empirical material of the multiple texts, as a first phase in research, brings to the fore elements that assist in the interpretation of the textual and literary growth (literary and redaction criticism) and even with respect to the theological concerns of the text.

More precisely, the study of manuscript evidence as an empirical way of analyzing the text(s), and especially within the context of an intertwined textual and literary-critical approach, indeed challenges the traditional view of a distinctive phase in the production of the text (which used to be called the domain of diachronic exegesis and, more concretely, redaction

1. The development of the argumentation and the elaboration of the methodological options taken in this contribution are mainly based on Bénédicte Lemmelijn, *A Plague of Texts? A Text-Critical Study of the So-Called "Plague Narrative" in Exodus 7:14–11:10*, OtSt 56 (Leiden: Brill, 2009).

criticism) and in the transmission of the text (the study of which would be the task for textual criticism). Moreover, studying the phenomena observed in the textual evidence within the framework of an intersection between textual and literary criticism questions the traditional description of the activities of scribes and authors/redactors respectively.[2]

Already quite some years ago, Julio Trebolle Barrera firmly stated the following:

> *Textual criticism* studies the process of transmission of the text from the moment it is put into writing or its first edition. Its aim is to determine the oldest biblical text witnessed by the manuscript tradition. *Literary criticism* (in the sense of the German term *Literarkritik*) studies instead the process before the formation of the biblical writings in order to determine their author and date. Even though in theory the domains and methods of these two disciplines are quite separate, in practice they often overlap. The meeting point causing friction between them is in the editorial process where the previous process of collecting material and of composition and of editing the text ends and the next process, textual transmission, begins.[3]

Further along in the same book, he states even more explicitly: "In theory the distinction between these disciplines is clear, but in practice the boundary separating them is very movable making necessary the use of both methods in combination."[4] Until recently, and unfortunately sometimes even still today, the generally accepted position was indeed that textual criticism as the study of the transmission of the complete literary work began where literary criticism as the study of the history of origin and literary formation of the text left off.

However, empirically speaking, a clear distinction between these two processes simply cannot be satisfactorily made.[5] First, the two aforemen-

---

2. Bénédicte Lemmelijn, "Influence of a So-Called P-Redaction in the 'Major Expansions' of Exodus 7–11? Finding Oneself at the Crossroads of Textual and Literary Criticism," in *Textual Criticism and Dead Sea Scrolls Studies in Honour of Julio Trebolle Barrera: Florilegium Complutense*, ed. Andrés Piquer Otero and Pablo A. Torijano Morales, JSJSup 157 (Leiden: Brill, 2012), 203–22.

3. See Julio Trebolle Barrera, *The Jewish Bible and the Christian Bible: An Introduction to the History of the* Bible, trans. Wilfred G. E. Watson (Leiden: Brill; Grand Rapids: Eerdmans, 1998), 370 (emphasis original).

4. Ibid., 390.

5. See also Lemmelijn, *Plague of Texts*, 3–7, and passim.

tioned stages in the creation of texts do in fact overlap. Indeed, it is highly likely that the textual transmission of certain biblical texts was already underway prior to the literary completion of the composition in question, if such a completion was ever reached consciously or intentionally at all. Second, it is clear that, when textual and literary criticism empirically "cooperate" in their study of the text, literary irregularities and problems are often discovered precisely at those places and instances where, text-critically speaking, textual variants are observed.[6]

Following this observation, it is very clear that there is only one way to start the study of biblical texts, and that is by the *facts*. Indeed, and as Marc Vervenne sometimes expresses it,[7] biblical scholars are the "engineers" of theology. Exegetes start with the facts; they work with "physical material" to be explored, to be analyzed, and to be evaluated in an empirical way. Our facts are the texts, indeed in the plural. The absolute text simply does not exist. With this in mind, it becomes clear that the presupposition behind the search for an *Urtext*, which was once considered as the ultimate goal of textual criticism, is no longer valid. Even more uncritical is the implicit acceptance of such a principle by scholars who, in the context of their literary, structural, diachronic, or synchronic study of a specific pericope, simply point to the Masoretic Text (MT) as if it were the *original* text. Indeed, talking about the canon of *the* Old Testament and a fortiori talking about a normative *standard* text of the Old Testament—sometimes for confessional reasons—cannot be unequivocally maintained in the present framework of a growing consciousness of multiple and manifold textual evidence.

So, if we have to start with the textual facts, that implies that we start—indeed empirically—by collecting, describing, and evaluating the textual material. In other words, we begin by studying the text-critical situation of the text we aim to study. In what follows, I will first present an empirical working model for text-critical research (§2). After introducing each phase of the model, I will offer an illustration of its application from the so-called Plague Narrative in Exod 7:14–11:10. Afterwards, I will demonstrate that,

6. See also Bénédicte Lemmelijn, "The So-Called 'Major Expansions' in SamP, 4QpaleoExod^{m} and 4QExod^{j} of Exod 7:14–11:10: On the Edge between Textual Criticism and Literary Criticism," in *X Congress of the International Organization for Septuagint and Cognate Studies, Oslo 1998*, ed. Bernard A. Taylor, SCS 51 (Atlanta: Society of Biblical Literature, 2001), 429–39, and Lemmelijn, *Plague of Texts*, 197–207.

7. See Kolet Janssen and Rebekka Jonkers, *Mondeling Examen: Marc Vervenne* (Leuven: Acco, 2010), 20.

within such an empirical approach, substantial data, important to the literary study of the text, indeed come to the fore (§3).

2. An Empirical Working Model for Text-Critical Research

2.1. Introduction

Anyone planning to engage in serious critical research into a particular biblical pericope must begin by determining his or her methodological strategy.[8] Biblical scholars are at odds in this regard, as to whether the study of a text should begin with literary criticism or textual criticism. I think, however, that serious literary criticism cannot be done without a detailed prior study of the textual material available to us with reference to the passage in question. Those who begin immediately with literary analyses run the risk of appealing to the internal dynamics of the narrative and the generally accepted principles of logic whereby a particular narrative is branded as illogical or inconsistent. The use of such arguments, however, has its limits. Our modern understanding of logicality need not square with that of the biblical authors and can often be extremely subjective. For this reason, it seems better to begin empirically with the textual evidence of the narrative in question. Strange and apparently illogical passages should first be accepted as they are, without any endeavor to explain them on the basis of the literary context. In addition, no single solution can be offered that covers every problem. A text-critical decision must be made on the basis of preestablished priorities. It is thus advisable to begin with the solution to textual problems before one endeavors to explain potential literary problems. As a consequence, this immediately locates us within the domain of textual criticism, which is responsible for the collection, description, and evaluation of the textual data.

2.2. Collecting the Textual Material: Synopsis and Registration

Thus, I prefer to begin research with the material form of the text, the text as "physical product," before moving on to its literary study.[9] As a

---

8. This working model was presented briefly in Bénédicte Lemmelijn, "What Are We Looking for in Doing Text-Critical Research?" *JNSL* 23 (1997): 69–80, and was developed further in Lemmelijn, *Plague of Texts*, 22–28.

9. See Lemmelijn, "So-Called 'Major Expansions,'" 429–39; see also Marc Ver-

matter of fact, the textual data ultimately represent the factual basis upon which research as such is based. The collection and registration of these data must serve, in my opinion, as the primary and empirical point of departure for any well-founded textual study. Literary criticism has to base itself on a critical text—and that can only be determined after painstaking text-critical analysis. For this reason, I favor the close examination of the formal and factual characteristics of the text as an initial step in the methodological process. The evaluation of the said textual phenomena must ultimately be postponed at this juncture. In this regard, I define the term *variant* as referring to every different reading evident between the textual witnesses, without giving priority per se to the MT as the standard text with which the remaining witnesses should be compared.[10] In other words, I consider a variant reading to be a variant with respect to any other extant textual witness and not only when compared with the MT. This necessarily implies, however, that text-critical research should not only focus attention on the major pluses and/or minuses evident in the text,[11] but should also examine the minor, often minute details or at least take note of them.[12] To this end, a synoptic survey of the textual versions under analysis has proven to be useful and appropriate.[13] A synoptic survey offers a number of clear advantages. In the first instance, it offers an excellent introduction to and exploration of the textual material. Second, it provides

venne, "Tekst en teksten," in *Inleiding in het Oude Testament*, ed. Henk Jagersma and Marc Vervenne (Kampen: Kok, 1992), 38; Bénédicte Lemmelijn, "Current Tendencies and Developments in the Study of the Book of Exodus," in *Studies in the Book of Exodus: Redaction, Reception, Interpretation*, ed. Marc Vervenne, BETL 126 (Leuven: Peeters, 1996), 33.

10. See Lemmelijn, *Plague of Texts*, 13–15.

11. It should be noted that the terms *minus* and *plus* are purely descriptive. They simply state that a verse or verse segment is missing or supplementary without implying any evaluation of it. See also Emanuel Tov, *The Text-Critical Use of the Septuagint in Biblical Research*, JBS 3 (Jerusalem: Simor, 1981), 127–33, esp. 130.

12. See also Emanuel Tov, "The Nature of the Differences between MT and the LXX in 1 Sam. 17–18," in *The Story of David and Goliath: Textual and Literary Criticism*, ed. Dominique Barthélemy, OBO 73 (Fribourg: Editions Universitaires; Göttingen: Vandenhoeck & Ruprecht, 1986), 22–23.

13. See Lemmelijn, *Plague of Texts*, 219–357. See also, for example, the method in Tov, "Nature of the Differences," 24–33; and Pierre-Maurice Bogaert, "Les deux rédactions conservées (LXX et MT) d'Ézéchiel 7," in *Ezekiel and His Book: Textual and Literary Criticism and Their Interrelation*, ed. Johan Lust, BETL 74 (Leuven: Peeters, 1986), 26–27, 35–36.

a convenient arrangement of the textual material, making it immediately accessible. Third, it allows for all the variants, however small, to be noted and registered. This registration thus implies the noticing of all variants.

Making concrete what is said above, I refer to my exhaustive text-critical synopsis of the Plague Narrative in Exod 7:14–11:10.[14] The complete survey itself is subdivided as follows: the first column contains the MT (*BHS*); the second column the eclectic Septuagint (LXX) text of John Wevers (Göttingen Edition);[15] the third one the text of the Samaritan Pentateuch (SP) based on the diplomatic text edition of Abraham Tal.[16] Next to these three complete texts, a variety of textual fragments preserved in several different manuscripts from Qumran relating to the Plague Narrative have been employed. The first one is 4Q22 (4QpaleoExod[m]), a scroll providing one of the best-preserved Exodus texts from Qumran and exhibiting a number of unusual pluses in the Plague Cycle.[17] It is presented in the fourth column and is based on DJD 9.[18] The fifth column presents 4Q11 (4QpaleoGen–Exod[l]), which has preserved five passages from Exod 7–11 and is likewise based on DJD 9.[19] The sixth column presents 2Q2 (2QExod[a]) (two preserved fragments), following the text edition of DJD 3.[20] The seventh column offers the text of 4Q14 (4QExod[c]) (thirty fragments), based on DJD 12. The eighth column contains 4Q1 (4QGen–Exod[a]) (three fragments). Finally, the ninth column presents 4Q20 (4QExod[j]) (two identified fragments), both likewise based on DJD 12.[21] A few symbols are used

14. Lemmelijn, *Plague of Texts*, 219–357.

15. John William Wevers, ed., *Septuaginta: Vetus Testamentum Graecum*, vol. 2.1: *Exodus*, SVTG (Göttingen: Vandenhoeck & Ruprecht, 1991).

16. Abraham Tal, *The Samaritan Pentateuch: Edited according to Ms 6(C) of the Shekhem Synagogue*, TSHLRS 8 (Tel-Aviv: Tel Aviv University, 1994).

17. The pluses in question exhibit numerous similarities with the SP: they are called "major expansions." See below.

18. Patrick W. Skehan, Eugene Ulrich, and Judith E. Sanderson, eds., *Qumran Cave 4:IV: Palaeo-Hebrew and Greek Biblical Manuscripts*, DJD 9 (Oxford: Clarendon, 1992), 53–71, 72–85, and pls. VII–XI.

19. Ibid., 17–26, 28–33, and pl. II.

20. See Maurice Baillet, Józef T. Milik, and Roland de Vaux, eds., *Les "Petites Grottes" de Qumrân: Exploration de la falaise: Les grottes 2Q, 3Q, 5Q, 6Q, 7Q à 10Q: Le rouleau de cuivre*, 2 vols., DJD 3 (Oxford: Clarendon, 1962), 1:50–51; 2: pl. X.

21. For the last three manuscripts referred to in the text, see Eugene Ulrich and Frank M. Cross, eds., *Qumran Cave 4:VII: Genesis to Numbers*, DJD 12 (Oxford: Clarendon, 1994), 7–10, 28, 97–113, 149–50, and pls. IV, XVI, XVII.

in the synoptic survey. A combination of three short hyphens (---) designates a minus. Exclamation marks (!) point to a different location of words in the respective columns. Slashes (/) divide the distinctive segments in Hebrew words.

From the above described exhaustive synopsis, I simply offer a sample below, just to make clear how it looks and how it works. It is taken from Exod 11:2–3 and will serve as the basis of the discussion below as well. Since five of the Qumran texts have not survived for these verses and for the sake of brevity in the present context, I have excluded their respective columns from the following synopsis (4Q22, 4Q11, 4Q14, 4Q1, 4Q20).

	MT	LXX	SP	2Q2
11:2				
	דבר	λάλησον	דברו	
	נא	οὖν	נא	
	---	κρυφῇ	---	
	ב/אזני	εἰς τὰ ὦτα	ב/אזני	
	ה/עם	τοῦ λαοῦ	ה/עם	
	ו/ישאלו	καὶ αἰτησάτω	ו/ישאלו	
	איש	ἕκαστος	איש	
	מ/את	παρὰ	מ/את	
	רע/הו	τοῦ πλησίον ---	רע/הו	
	ו/אשה	καὶ γυνὴ	ו/אשה	
	מ/את	παρὰ	מ/את	
	רעות/ה	τῆς πλησίον ---	רעות/ה	
	כלי	σκεύη	כלי	
	כסף	ἀργυρᾶ	כסף	
	ו/כלי	καὶ ---	ו/כלי	
	זהב	χρυσᾶ	זהב	
	---	καὶ ἱματισμόν	ו/שמלות	
11:3				
	! ו/יתן	!	! ו/נתתי	[! ו/יתן
	יהוה	κύριος δὲ !	---	יהוה
	!	ἔδωκεν	!	!
	את חן	τὴν χάριν	את חן	את חן
	ה/עם	τῷ λαῷ	ה/עם	ה/עם
	---	αὐτοῦ	ה/זה	---
	ב/עיני	ἐναντίον	ב/עיני	ב/עיני

מצרים	τῶν αἰγυπτίων	מצרים	מצרים
---	καὶ ἔχρησαν αὐτοῖς	ו/השאילום	---
גם	καὶ	!	גם
ה/איש	ὁ ἄνθρωπος	!	ה/איש
משה	μωυσῆς	!	מושה
גדול	μέγας	!	גדול
---	ἐγενήθη	---	---
מאד	σφόδρα	!	מאד
ב/ארץ	---	!	בתו]ך ארץ
---	ἐναντίον	---	---
מצרים	τῶν αἰγυπτίων	!	[מצרים
---	καὶ ἐναντίον	---	---
---	φαραὼ	---	---
ב/עיני	καὶ ἐναντίον	!	ב/עיני
---	πάντων	---	---
עבדי פרעה	τῶν θεραπόντων αὐτοῦ	!	עבדי פרעה
ו/ב/עיני	---	!	ו/ב/עיני
ה/עם	---	!	ה/עם]
11:3b			
---	---	ו/כ/חצית	---
---	---	ה/לילה	---
---	---	אני	---
---	---	יצא	---
---	---	ב/תוך	---
---	---	ארץ	---
---	---	מצרים	---
---	---	ו/מת	---
---	---	כל	---
---	---	בכור	---
---	---	ב/ארץ	---
---	---	מצרים	---
---	---	מ/בכור	---
---	---	פרעה	---
---	---	ה/ישב	---
---	---	על	---
---	---	כסא/ו	---
---	---	ו/עד	---
---	---	בכור	---

---	---	ה/שׁפחה	---
---	---	אשר	---
---	---	אחר	---
---	---	ה/רחים	---
---	---	ו/עד	---
---	---	בכור	---
---	---	כל	---
---	---	בהמה	---
---	---	ו/היתה	---
---	---	צעקה	---
---	---	גדלה	---
---	---	ב/מצרים	---
---	---	אשר	---
---	---	כמ/וה	---
---	---	לא	---
---	---	נהיתה	---
---	---	ו/כמ/וה	---
---	---	לא	---
---	---	תוסף	---
---	---	ו/ל/כל	---
---	---	בני	---
---	---	ישׂראל	---
---	---	לא	---
---	---	יחרץ	---
---	---	כלב	---
---	---	לשנ/ו	---
---	---	ל/מ/איש	---
---	---	ו/עד	---
---	---	בהמה	---
---	---	ל/מען	---
---	---	תדע	---
---	---	אשר	---
---	---	יפלא	---
---	---	יהוה	---
---	---	בין	---
---	---	מצרים	---
---	---	ו/בין	---
---	---	ישׂראל	---

!	! ---	ו/גם	!
!	!	ה/איש	!
!	!	משה	!
!	!	גדל	!
!	!	מאד	!
!	---	ב/ארץ	!
!	!	מצרים	!
!	!	ב/עיני	!
!	!	עבדי	!
!	---	פרעה	!
!	---	ו/ב/עיני	!
!	---	ה/עם	!
---	---	ו/יאמר	---
---	---	משה	---
---	---	אל	---
---	---	פרעה	---
---	---	כה	---
---	---	אמר	---
---	---	יהוה	---
---	---	בני	---
---	---	בכורי	---
---	---	ישׂראל	---
---	---	ו/אמר	---
---	---	אל/יך	---
---	---	שׁלח	---
---	---	את בני	---
---	---	ו/יעבד/ני	---
---	---	ו/תמאן	---
---	---	ל/שׁלח/ו	---
---	---	הנה	---
---	---	יהוה	---
---	---	הרג	---
---	---	את בנ/ך	---
---	---	בכור/ך	---

2.3. Registration and Description of the Textual Variants

On the basis of the synopsis, all variants are marked and registered, and following that initial exploration, all variants should also be described in detail. Indeed, during the phase of description, which is the second phase in my working model, a list and a meticulous description of all textual differences, evident when comparing the various textual forms, is presented. If we return to the example we are using, we observe that the text-critical comparison of the textual witnesses to the Plague Narrative of Exod 7:14–11:10 in the exhaustive synopsis exposes a significant number of textual variants representing a wide spectrum of characteristics.[22]

The majority of variants exhibit only minor differences that mostly possess little if any text-critical relevance. It is difficult to determine with respect to such variants which one is to be taken as the preferable reading. Where variants in the Greek text are concerned, one is often embroiled in the challenging question of whether they should be traced back to a different *Vorlage* or understood as stemming from the translator.[23] Such so-called minor variants are not text-critically evaluated in my working model. A detailed registration and description of them suffices. Indeed, and often, they can be explained as a question of translation technique or on the basis of the grammatical demands of the Hebrew and Greek language systems.

In addition to the minor variants, however, there are also a number of more extensive or more striking differences. Some of the latter change aspects of the narrative at the level of content, others reveal significant expansions. These major or text-relevant variants should be studied and evaluated carefully in the third phase of my working model (see below). In this context, one tries to establish whether the *preferred* variant or *preferable* reading can be determined or whether we are dealing with *synonymous* readings.[24] The latter can be understood as variants, of which the degree in terms of relatively "more original" cannot be defined and neither can one establish the direction of any possible interdependence.

---

22. See also the succinct preliminary description of the results in Bénédicte Lemmelijn, "As Many Texts as Plagues: A Preliminary Report of the Main Results of the Text-Critical Evaluation of Exod 7:14–11:10," *JNSL* 24 (1998): 111–12; Lemmelijn, "So-Called 'Major Expansions,'" 429–39. A complete description can be found in Lemmelijn, *Plague of Texts*, 33–95.

23. See Anneli Aejmelaeus, "What Can We Know About the Hebrew *Vorlage* of the Septuagint?," *ZAW* 99 (1987): 67–68. For a more accurate characterization and evaluation of the translation technique of the LXX see §2.4, below.

24. For the terminology of *preferable variants*, *synonymous readings*, and *unique readings*, see Lemmelijn, *Plague of Texts*, 20–22.

In what follows, I again present a sample from the registration and description of the Plague Narrative. For each variant, I begin with a biblical reference followed by a snapshot of the relationship between the textual witnesses as far as the respective variant is concerned. Thereafter, I make note of the variant itself whereby, with respect to the so-called smaller textual differences, the nature of the said variant is described in brief.[25] In the event that a given variant represents a plus with respect to one or more of the other textual versions, a plus sign (+) is placed next to the sigla designating the text in which the variant in question is found. The Hebrew text is presented in its unvocalized form and the Greek text without accents.[26] The sample is again taken from Exod 11:2–3.[27]

Verse	Variation	Comment
11:2	MT, SP ≠ LXX	κρυφῃ = LXX +[28]
11:2	MT, SP ≠ LXX	וישאלו - και αἰτησατω: difference in number, third-person plural versus third-person singular
11:2	MT, SP ≠ LXX	ו in רעהו = MT and SP +: possessive suffix
11:2	MT, SP ≠ LXX	ה in רעותה = MT and SP +: possessive suffix
11:2	MT, SP ≠ LXX	כלי = MT and SP +

25. The more text-relevant variants are described and evaluated in greater detail in the next phase of the working model.

26. Only the *spiritus asper* and *lenis* are employed.

27. This presentation is excerpted from Lemmelijn, *Plague of Texts,* 89–91. One may refer to the synopsis above in order to situate the described variants more easily. In my original study, the MT is designated with the letter M, the LXX with the letter G, and the SP with the siglum SamP. 2Q2 is referred to as 2Q[a]. Also, in the complete study described above, 4Q22 is referred to as 4Q[m], 4Q11 as 4Q[l], 4Q14 as 4Q[c], 4Q1 as 4Q[a], and 4Q20 as 4Q[j].

28. "Exod also adds κρυφῃ, i.e. 'speak secretly,' though MT simply has דבר נא. The translator thereby makes explicit what is implicit in MT" (John William Wevers, *Notes on the Greek Text of Exodus*, SCS 30 [Atlanta: Scholars Press, 1990], 162). See also Alain Le Boulluec and Pierre Sandevoir, *L'Exode: Traduction du texte grec de la Septante*, BA 2 (Paris: Cerf, 1989), 141.

11:2	MT ≠ LXX, SP	και ἱματισμον, ושמלות = LXX and SP + (compare with 3:22 and 12:35!)[29]
11:2	LXX ≠ SP	και ἱματισμον - ושמלות: difference in number, (collective) singular versus plural
11:3	MT, SP, 2Q2 ≠ LXX	ו in ויתן, ונתתי, ויתן - δε: different location
11:3	MT, SP, 2Q2 ≠ LXX	ויתן, ונתתי, ויתן - ἔδωκεν: different location[30]
11:3	MT, LXX 2Q2 ≠ SP	ויתן, ἔδωκεν, ויתן - ונתתי: different verb form, third-person singular versus first-person singular. The third-person singular in the MT, LXX, and 2Q2 agrees with the account of the "despoiling motif" in 12:36. The first-person singular of the SP is parallel with the version of 3:21.
11:3	MT, LXX, 2Q2 ≠ SP	יהוה, κυριος, יהוה = MT, LXX, and 2Q2 +: the subject of the third-person singular is expressed, while the SP had already implied the first-person singular as subject in the form of the verb. Parallel once again with 12:36 and 3:21, respectively.
11:3	MT, SP, 2Q2 ≠ LXX	την = LXX +: definite article. The Hebrew, however, is also defined on account of the *nota accusativi*.
11:3	MT, 2Q2 ≠ LXX ≠ SP	αὐτου = LXX +: possessive pronoun ("his people")[31]; הזה = SP +: demonstrative pronoun ("this people")
11:3	MT, SP, 2Q2 ≠ LXX	בעיני - ἐναντιον: different formulation for the same semantic datum
11:3	MT, 2Q2 ≠ LXX, SP	και ἔχρησαν αὐτοις, והשאילום = LXX and SP + (see also 12:36)[32]

29. "Selon sa tendance harmonisante, la LXX introduit ici les 'vêtements' (*και ἱματισμον*): cf. Ex 3,22 et 12,35" (Le Boulluec and Sandevoir, *Exode*, 141).

30. "Exod has changed the usual order: verb–subject, with *κυριος* standing first, thereby paralleling the second clause pattern where *ὁ ἄνθρωπος* Μωυσης also precedes the predicate" (Wevers, *Notes on the Greek Text of Exodus*, 162).

31. "La LXX précise: '*son* peuple'" (Le Boulluec and Sandevoir, *Exode*, 142).

32. "The clause *και ἔχρησαν αὐτοις* is based on והשאלום: see Sam and 12:36" (Wevers, *Notes on the Greek Text of Exodus*, 163); "The fact is that all of v. 3a is based

11:3	MT, LXX, 2Q2 ≠ SP	The second part of 11:3, from גם האיש to ובעיני העם and in the Greek from και ὁ ἄνθρωπος to των θεραποντων, is in a different location in the SP, namely, at the end of the larger plus 11:3b. The text of this expansion (SP 11:3b) is identical to the textual versions of the MT and 2Q2 in 11:3 and exhibits the same differences with respect to the LXX.[33]
11:3	MT, SP, 2Q2 ≠ LXX	ἐγενηθη = LXX +: The LXX expresses the verb γιγνεσθαι in contrast to the Hebrew nominal clause.
11:3	MT, SP ≠ 2Q2 ≠ LXX	בארץ = MT and SP +, בתוך ארץ = 2Q2 +. The MT/SP and 2Q2 contain different prepositions: ב (MT, SP) and בתוך (2Q2).
11:3	MT, SP, 2Q2 ≠ LXX	*ἐναντιον* = LXX +: preposition
11:3	MT, SP, 2Q2 ≠ LXX	מצרים - των αἰγυπτιων: The Hebrew מצרים would appear to be geographical (בארץ מצרים and בתוך ארץ מצרים), while the Greek employs των αἰγυπτιων to refer to the inhabitants of Egypt. Note also the preposition ἐναντιον, a plus that arises from this variant interpretation.[34]
11:3	MT, SP, 2Q2 ≠ LXX	και ἐναντιον φαραω = LXX +
11:3	MT, SP, 2Q2 ≠ LXX	παντων = LXX +: adjective
11:3	MT, SP, 2Q2 ≠ LXX	פרעה - αὐτου: substantive versus possessive pronoun
11:3	MT, SP, 2Q2 ≠ LXX	ובעיני העם = MT, SP, and 2Q2 +[35]

on a parent text equaling 12:36a" (ibid., 162–63); "La LXX précise: '*son* peuple,' et insère dans ce contexte la formule, absente ici du TM, d'Ex 12,36: 'et ils leur prêtèrent' (*και ἐχρησαν αὐτοις*)" (Le Boulluec and Sandevoir, *Exode*, 142).

33. For this reason, the variants—including those in relation to the SP—have already been registered here.

34. See Le Boulluec and Sandevoir, *Exode*, 142.

35. "Un écart plus important par rapport au TM est l'absence dans la LXX de toute mention du 'peuple,' comme si la célébrité de Moïse était limitée à la cour de

11:3b MT, LXX, 2Q2 ≠ SP, 4Q22	11:3b = SP and 4Q22 +: larger plus.[36] From the beginning, וכחצית הלילה to ובין ישׂראל, 11:3b in the SP agrees with 11:4b–7 in the MT, LXX, SP, 4Q11, and 2Q2. What follows, from וגם האיש to ובעיני העם, agrees with the end of 11:3 in the MT, LXX, and 2Q2, which is in a different location in the SP. Finally, the last part of the larger plus in 11:3b, from ויאמר משה to the end את בנך בכורך, exhibits much similarity with 4:22–23 in the MT, LXX, and SP.[37]

If we take a closer look at this short sample of the second phase in the working model, we observe that the accurate registration and description of all the variants, based on the empirical survey of the text-critical synopsis, starts serving as the basis for establishing the difference between *grammatical* variants, to which a meticulous description suffices, and *text-relevant* variants, which need a serious text-critical evaluation in the third phase of my working model.

Pharaon: il est peu vraisemblable que cela soit intentionnel; c'est peut-être le témoin d'une lecture ancienne, plus brève, déjà inconnue du Targum" (ibid., 142).

36. The text of 11:3b has not been preserved in 4Q22. On the basis of a reconstruction of 4Q22, however, it has been suggested that 4Q22, in line with the SP, contained such an expansion (see Skehan, Ulrich, and Sanderson, *Qumran Cave 4:IV*, 67, 84–85). With respect to 4Q11, which has not preserved a text of 11:3, it has been suggested nonetheless on the basis of information gleaned from 11:4 that the manuscript in question did not contain the larger plus in 11:3b ("The fact that 11:4 begins on the right margin suggests that the preceding line ended with an interval, a possible indication that the major expansion 11:3^{b} of 4QpaleoExod^{m} and [SP] was not present in this MS"; ibid., 32).

37. The Qumran manuscripts (4Q22, 4Q11, 2Q2, 4Q14, 4Q1, and 4Q20) have not preserved the text of 4:22–23.

2.4. Discussion and Text-Critical Evaluation of the Variants

2.4.1. Introduction

Having collected, registered, and described the objective evidence and textual variants on the basis of a clear synoptic presentation, thereby establishing the point of departure upon which literary, redactional, and theological research should be based, we are now ready to make a careful transition to the discussion and evaluation of text-critical issues based on the material at hand, such as questions relating to textual corruption, expansion, abbreviation, or harmonization.[38]

At this point, a preliminary point of caution should first be mentioned. Whenever the textual forms employed in a text-critical study include one or other of the so-called *versions*, as it is the case in the study of the Plague Narrative with respect to the LXX, a comprehensive study must also be made of the translation technique of the text in question. This implies that an analysis is made of the contribution of the translator where variants present themselves. Not all of the variants in the LXX, registered on the basis of a synoptic comparison of the textual forms, came into existence on the basis of a variant in the consonantal text of the *Vorlage*. As a matter of fact, variants in the textual forms might be the result of the conscious or unconscious activities of the translator. The study of so-called translation technique,[39] which is necessary in order to trace the various factors that lie at the origins of textual "deviations," includes, among other things, research into the linguistically and contextually exegetical renderings the translator may have brought about, the study of word sequence, a detailed analysis of the quantitative representation of the various words in the differing versions, and the consistency of translation equivalents.[40] In this

38. See Johan Lust, "The Story of David and Goliath in Hebrew and Greek," in Barthélemy, *Story of David and Goliath*, 6, 8–11; see also Lemmelijn, "What Are We Looking for," 75–77.

39. See, for example, Bénédicte Lemmelijn, "Two Methodological Trails in Recent Studies on the Translation Technique of the Septuagint," in *Helsinki Perspectives on the Translation Technique of the Septuagint*, ed. Raija Sollamo and Seppo Sipilä, PFES 82 (Helsinki: The Finnish Exegetical Society; Göttingen: Vandenhoeck & Ruprecht, 2001), 43–63; Lemmelijn, *Plague of Texts*, 96–125.

40. See, for example, Tov, *Text-Critical Use of the Septuagint*, 20–24; Tov, "Nature of the Differences," 33–39; see also Lemmelijn, "Two Methodological Trails"; Lemmelijn, *Plague of Texts*, 108–14.

vein, it focuses often on the so-called literalness of the translation in its different aspects. At the same time, however, a systematic survey also has to be made on the basis of typical Hebrew grammatical constructions in order to determine the extent to which the Greek translator exercised his *freedom* as a translator.[41] Moreover, both the translator's freedom and literalness should be nuanced by other categories, such as *faithfulness*.[42]

Complementing the latter aspects, reference should be made to a quite recent emphasis not only on the translators' freedom as such, but equally on their *creativity*.[43] Indeed, when the LXX translations are to be evaluated in an adequate way, it is only the detailed and painstaking research into the character of the translation that will offer a serious assessment. In this respect, and together with Hans Ausloos, I have developed an approach that focuses on what has been called "content-related" criteria, or perhaps even more appropriately, "content- and context-related criteria."[44] These criteria complement the traditional approach from the specific angle of

---

41. See, in particular, the collected contributions of Anneli Aejmelaeus in Anneli Aejmelaeus, *On the Trail of the Septuagint Translators Translators: Collected Essays*, CBET 50 (Kampen: Kok Pharos, 1993); the most prominent contributions of Ilmari Soisalon-Soininen, collected in *Ilmari Soisalon-Soininen: Studien zur Septuaginta-Syntax; zu seinem 70. Geburtstag am 4. Juni 1987*, ed. Anneli Aejmelaeus and Raija Sollamo, AASF Series B 237 (Helsinki: Suomalainen Tiedeakatemia, 1987); and the contributions of Raija Sollamo, including *Renderings of Hebrew Semiprepositions in the Septuagint*, AASF Dissertationes Humanarum Litterarum 19 (Helsinki: Suomalainen Tiedeakatemia, 1979); Sollamo, "The LXX Renderings of the Infinitive Absolute Used with a Paronymous Finite Verb in the Pentateuch," in *La Septuaginta en la investigación contemporanea: V Congreso de la IOSCS*, ed. Natalio Fernández Marcos, TECC 34 (Madrid: Instituto "Arias Montano," 1985), 101–13.

42. This term has been most prominently suggested by Aejmelaeus: "A distinction should be made between literalness and faithfulness," in Anneli Aejmelaeus, "The Significance of Clause Connectors in the Syntactical and Translation-Technical Study of the Septuagint," in *VI Congress of the International Organization for Septuagint and Cognate Studies, Jerusalem 1986*, ed. Claude E. Cox, SCS 23 (Atlanta: Scholar's Press, 1987), 378; see also Lemmelijn, *Plague of Texts*, 114.

43. See Hans Ausloos and Bénédicte Lemmelijn, "Faithful Creativity Torn between Freedom and Literalness in the Septuagint's Translations," *JNSL* 40 (2014): 53–69. The following paragraphs build on this contribution.

44. For a description of the content- and context-related criteria in the characterization of translation technique, see, for example, Hans Ausloos and Bénédicte Lemmelijn, "Content Related Criteria in Characterising the LXX Translation Technique," in *Die Septuaginta: Texte, Theologien, Einflüsse; 2. Internationale Fachtagung veranstaltet von Septuaginta Deutsch (LXX.D), Wuppertal 23.–27. Juli 2008*, ed. Wolf-

research into the way that the LXX translator has dealt with very specific questions related to the content of the Hebrew/Greek text. Examples of these criteria can be found in the analysis of how the translator rendered into Greek the Hebrew jargon-defined vocabulary,[45] Hebrew wordplay in the literary context of etiologies (for example, with respect to the rendering of proper names for persons or toponyms),[46] Hebrew wordplay in the context of parallelism,[47] peculiar stylistic elements, and Hebrew absolute *hapax legomena*.[48]

---

gang Kraus, Martin Karrer, and Martin Meiser, WUNT 252 (Tübingen: Mohr Siebeck, 2010), 357–76.

45. See, for example, Bénédicte Lemmelijn, "Flora in Cantico Canticorum: Towards a More Precise Characterisation of Translation Technique in the LXX of Song of Songs," in *Scripture in Transition: Essays on Septuagint, Hebrew Bible and Dead Sea Scrolls in Honour of Raija Sollamo*, ed. Anssi Voitila and Jutta Jokiranta, JSJSup 126 (Leiden: Brill, 2008), 27–51.

46. See, for example, Hans Ausloos, "LXX's Rendering of Hebrew Proper Names and the Characterization of the Translation Technique of the Book of Judges," in Voitila and Jokiranta, *Scripture in Transition*, 53–71; Ausloos, "The Septuagint's Rendering of Hebrew Toponyms as an Indication of the Translation Technique of the Book of Numbers," in Piquer Otero and Torijano Morales, *Textual Criticism and Dead Sea Scrolls*, 35–50. See also the studies of, and together with, our former doctoral student, Valérie Kabergs: Hans Ausloos, Bénédicte Lemmelijn, and Valérie Kabergs, "The Study of Aetiological Wordplay as a Content-Related Criterion in the Characterisation of LXX Translation Technique," in *Die Septuaginta: Entstehung, Sprache, Geschichte; 3. Internationale Fachtagung veranstaltet von Septuaginta Deutsch (LXX.D), Wuppertal 22.–25. Juli 2010*, ed. Siegfried Kreuzer, Martin Meiser, and Martin Sigismund, WUNT 286 (Tübingen: Mohr Siebeck, 2012), 273–94; Valérie Kabergs and Hans Ausloos, "Paronomasia or Wordplay? A Babel-Like Confusion: Towards a Definition of Hebrew Wordplay," *Bib* 93 (2012): 1–20; Kabergs, "Puns within the Context of Name Explanations in MT and LXX Exodus," in *Die Septuaginta: Text, Wirkung, Rezeption; 4. Internationale Fachtagung veranstaltet von Septuaginta Deutsch (LXX. D), Wuppertal 19.–22. Juli 2012*, ed. Wolfgang Kraus and Siegfried Kreuzer, WUNT 325 (Tübingen: Mohr Siebeck, 2014), 215–33; see also Kabergs, "Creativiteit in het spel? De Griekse weergave van expliciet Hebreeuws woordspel op basis van eigennamen in Pentateuch en Twaalf Profeten" (PhD diss., Katholieke Universiteit Leuven, 2015).

47. In this respect, another doctoral research project is ongoing and will soon be defended by Marieke Dhont focusing on the Greek rendering of Hebrew wordplay in the specific literary context of the parallelism within the book of Job, as a content-related criterion in the characterization of the LXX's translation technique.

48. See Hans Ausloos and Bénédicte Lemmelijn, "Rendering Love: Hapax Legomena and the Characterisation of the Translation Technique of Song of Songs," in *Translating a Translation: The LXX and Its Modern Translations in the Context of Early*

Each of the criteria mentioned confronts the translator with a choice: whatever direction his rendering may take, the very act of translation requires him to give a specific answer to each of these particular problems as they arise. Thus, the use of the content- and context-related approach could be compared to an artificially created laboratory situation in which a specific test is set up in order to elicit a reaction: specific textual data are isolated in order to be able to describe and interpret the reaction of the translator. Against the background of this—again rather empirical—research focus, we are neither interested in the study of wordplay or etiology as a literary characteristic in itself nor do we seek to define the problem of *hapax legomena* as such, and we do not want to become involved in discussions about the uses of parallelism as a stylistic device. The intention is rather to carefully and systematically observe particular situations in which the translator was forced to make a decision in one way or the other. Studying these reactions of the translator could indeed offer more accurate information about his way of handling both his source and his target text, in other words, his translation technique.

This kind of approach not only yields a more precise characterization of the translation in terms of its literalness, freedom, or faithfulness. Rather, and in addition, it reveals specific aspects of an extraordinary *creativity* on the side of the translator. In managing the above-mentioned difficult semantic or stylistic situations, the LXX translators sometimes produce wonderfully creative solutions to render their Hebrew text by a meaningful Greek equivalent.

Judaism, ed. Hans Ausloos et al., BETL 213 (Leuven: Peeters, 2008), 43–61; Hans Ausloos, "The Septuagint's Rendering of Hebrew Hapax Legomena and the Characterization of its 'Translation Technique': The Case of Exodus," *APB* 20 (2009): 360–76; Hans Ausloos and Bénédicte Lemmelijn, "Characterizing the LXX Translation of Judges on the Basis of Content-Related Criteria: The Greek Rendering of Hebrew Absolute Hapax Legomena in Judg 3:12–30," in *After Qumran: Old and Modern Editions of the Biblical Texts; The Historical Books*, ed. Hans Ausloos, Bénédicte Lemmelijn, and Julio Trebolle Barrera, BETL 246 (Leuven: Peeters, 2012), 171–92. See also the contributions of another former doctoral research fellow: Elke Verbeke, "The Use of Hebrew Hapax Legomena in Septuagint Studies: Preliminary Remarks on Methodology," in *Florilegium Lovaniense: Studies in Septuagint and Textual Criticism in Honour of Florentino García Martínez*, ed. Hans Ausloos, Bénédicte Lemmelijn, and Marc Vervenne, BETL 224 (Leuven: Peeters, 2008), 507–21; Verbeke, "Hebrew Hapax Legomena and Their Greek Rendering in LXX Job" (PhD diss., Katholieke Universiteit Leuven, 2011).

When the translation technique of the versions, such as the LXX, is studied carefully, the results can offer indications as to whether the variants have originated in the process of translation or rather in a different *Vorlage*. Only then, the character of the variant can be evaluated text-critically. In so doing, one remains, again, grounded in a textual basis that offers objective, *empirical* facts, and having studied the latter, one can endeavor to make a judgment about the nature of the textual version in question as well as an evaluation of the individual variants. The point of departure is thus to be found again in the *facts* at the textual level.

When coming to the text-critical evaluation proper, I hold the view that the discussion of variant readings ought to pay due attention to the classical internal criteria, with the emphasis firmly focused on the appropriateness of a reading in its immediate and broader context, and to the distinctive characteristics and demands of each individual textual variant. In this way, the primary point of departure, as well as the fundamental basis on which evaluative judging is done, is again the empirical starting point of the text and its context. Other formal criteria, such as the study of established narrative patterns and the early or late character of the Hebrew usage, can also facilitate the evaluation of textual variants.[49] A balanced evaluation of the various possibilities remains, nevertheless, a complex and delicate task leading to tentative decisions that ultimately involve a certain degree of subjectivity.

In what follows, I present some examples of how text-relevant variants and larger pluses within the Plague Narrative can be evaluated, taking into account the above-mentioned aspects. To offer the possibility of linking them up to the previous phases in the working model, the sample is again taken from Exod 11:2–3.[50]

---

49. See Johan Lust, "The Use of Textual Witnesses for the Establishment of the Text: The Shorter and Longer Texts of Ezekiel; An Example: Ez 7," in *Ezekiel and His Book: Textual and Literary Criticism and Their Interrelation*, ed. Johan Lust, BETL 74 (Leuven: Peeters, 1986), 17–19; Lust, "Story of David and Goliath," 123–26.

50. These examples are taken from Lemmelijn, *Plague of Texts*, 190–94. In order to be able to adequately understand the character of the variants, one can look again at the synopsis presented above.

2.4.2. Example 1: Exod 11:2: MT, SP ≠ LXX; κρυφη = LXX +

No evidence can be found in the context of the Plague Narrative that can explain the presence of the Greek plus in 11:2, κρυφη ("secretly"). Given the lack of a contextual explanation for the variant and bearing in mind that scribal error, in my opinion, is equally unlikely at this juncture, one might be inclined to conclude that this plus in the LXX reflects a different *Vorlage* to that of the MT.[51]

Nevertheless, as Wevers argues, it is also possible that the LXX's more elaborate expression simply represents an endeavor on its part to give explicit formulation to what is already implicitly expressed in דבר נא באזני העם ("speak now in the ears of the people").[52] As a matter of fact, the modern English expression "whisper something in someone's ear" also connotes a degree of secrecy. In this case, the plus κρυφη should be understood to stem from the translator and his desire to write fluent and idiomatic Greek, which led him to explain the Hebrew expression.

Given the fact that both readings ultimately relate the same content and that any attempt to determine the origin of the Greek plus in 11:2 would be nothing more than guesswork, I prefer to designate the Hebrew and Greek readings as *synonymous* variants.

2.4.3. Example 2: Exod 11:2: MT and SP ≠ LXX; כלי = MT and SP +

In 11:2 reference is made to the lending and borrowing of silver and golden objects. The Hebrew texts of the MT and SP explicitly state the same subject כלי ("objects") twice, in each instance in a *status constructus* with the material nouns כסף ("silver") and זהב ("gold"). The Greek, by contrast, only mentions the substantive σκευη ("object") once, in combination with two adjectives agreeing in gender and number, linked by the conjunction και ("and"). A minus is thus evident in the LXX where the Hebrew texts repeat the substantive כלי.

In my opinion, the variant in question has its roots in grammar and linguistic feeling. The Greek translator of Exodus sought to provide fluent and idiomatic Greek. This is evident from the fact that he avoided the

51. See, for example, Nina L. Collins, "Evidence in the Septuagint of a Tradition in which the Israelites Left Egypt without Pharaoh's Consent," *CBQ* 56 (1994): 444–45, 447–48.

52. See Wevers, *Notes on the Greek Text of Exodus*, 162.

unnecessary repetition of the substantive *σκευη* as equivalent for the twofold כלי. For this reason, I am inclined to designate the variant readings in 11:2 as *synonymous* variants.

2.4.4. Example 3

Exod 11:3: MT, SP, and 2Q2 ≠ LXX; *και ἐναντιον φαραω* = LXX +
Exod 11:3: MT, SP, and 2Q2 ≠ LXX; בעיני העם = MT, SP, and 2Q2 +

One encounters further differences in the final part of 11:3 when the Hebrew and Greek textual witnesses are compared. With the help of the prepositions ב and בעיני ("in the sight") the MT and 2Q2 state that Moses was great "in the land of Egypt, in the sight of Pharaoh's servants and in the sight of the people." The SP relates precisely the same thing and in precisely the same fashion but in a different location, namely, toward the end of the major expansion in 11:3b.[53] With the help of the preposition *ἐναντιον* ("before"), the LXX, by contrast, also speaks of the Egyptians (quasi-parallel with ארץ מצרים ["the land of Egypt"]) and then refers to Pharaoh and the servants of Pharaoh (equivalent of עבדי פרעה ["the servants of Pharaoh"]).

In this text fragment, the Hebrew texts thus have a minus with respect to the Greek text's *και ἐναντιον φαραω* ("and before Pharaoh") and the Greek text has a minus with respect to the Hebrew text's בעיני העם ("in the sight of the people"). With respect to the Hebrew minus, one might suggest that Pharaoh is intentionally not mentioned in the MT, SP, and 2Q2 for theological reasons. The Hebrew text thus shows that all Egypt, the servants of Pharaoh and the people, recognized Moses and YHWH. Pharaoh himself, however, does not capitulate, refusing to recognize either Moses or YHWH. The Hebrew text makes no reference to Pharaoh in order to show the extent of his uncompromising obduracy.[54] While such an explanation is attractive, it nevertheless remains speculative. An alternative is possible, however. The plus in the LXX is not unusual in the context of the Plague Narrative. When similar summarizing statements in the narrative are compared, it is remarkable that Pharaoh is often if not always included.[55] As a consequence, it is possible that the *Vorlage* of the LXX harmo-

53. This major expansion is discussed in more detail in §3.3.2, below.

54. See also 11:10. The final words of the Plague Narrative continue to describe Pharaoh's hardening.

55. See, by way of example, 7:20 (MT, LXX, SP), 28 (MT, LXX, SP); 8:5 (MT, LXX,

nized with the context and made explicit reference to Pharaoh on the basis of the formulation frequently employed in the Plague Narrative.[56] If this explanation is correct, then the Hebrew textual witnesses should be understood as having preserved the *preferable* variant in the present instance.

With respect to the minus in the Greek in contrast to the Hebrew בעיני העם, reference should be made to the fact that the LXX has already made explicit reference to the Egyptians in this verse and even placed them in the first position: *ἐναντιον των αἰγυπτιων* ("before the Egyptians"). The latter formula is parallel with the same expression a little earlier in the same verse in both the LXX (*ἐναντιον των αἰγυπτιων*) and the MT, SP, and 2Q2 (בעיני מצרים). It is probable that the LXX's *Vorlage* harmonized with this expression, perhaps even consciously. As a consequence, given the fact that the Egyptian people had already been mentioned, the *Vorlage* of the LXX saw no reason to mention them again. However, given the fact that the Hebrew בארץ מצרים has geographical significance (in contrast to the above mentioned בעיני מצרים), the explicit formulation of בעיני העם in the Hebrew text, an element that occurs with relative frequency in the context of the Plague Narrative, is not superfluous. Bearing this in mind, one can argue that the *Vorlage* of the LXX manipulated its text and that the existing Hebrew textual witnesses probably preserved the *preferable* variant in this instance.

If we take a look at the examples above, we indeed observe that the careful observation of variants in their context and the text-critical evaluation of those offers a clear exploration of the text, and it prevents rash literary and theological speculation. In what follows, I will demonstrate in which way such a working model is helpful to the adequate interpretation of biblical texts, thereby entering into the second main part of this contribution.

SP), 7 (MT, LXX, SP), 17 (MT, LXX, SP, 4Q14), 25 (MT, LXX, SP), 27 (MT, LXX, SP); 9:14 (MT, LXX, SP).

56. Wevers likewise suggests that the *Vorlage* of the LXX is responsible for this plus in the Greek text: "only explicable on the basis of a different parent text" (Wevers, *Notes on the Greek Text of Exodus*, 163).

3. Empirical Textual Criticism: A Gateway to Literary and Redactional Analysis

3.1. Introduction

Following the above working model and getting back to the starting point of this contribution, I hold the view that textual criticism has indeed a role of utmost importance to play as the empirical basis on which one can build the accurate literary study of biblical texts, and this in a double way. First of all, as already indicated from the outset, textual criticism is indispensable as a first phase in the study of a biblical pericope in order to evaluate the value of the textual witness chosen to be used as a basis for the literary study. Second, a text-critical study can often contribute to the recognition of fundamental data, important to the literary study of a text. The latter aspect functions again in a double way. First, it tracks down literary irregularities in the text, and, second, it reveals the contextual framework.

As mentioned at the beginning, this contribution aims at substantiating these theses, basing itself on and referring to the main results of the exhaustive study of the Plague Narrative in Exod 7:14–11:10, when studied along the lines of the above-described working model. Within the framework of this contribution, it is, of course, impossible to repeat all of the detailed results in this respect.[57] However, in what follows, I want to point out some of the main results both regarding each of the phases in the working model in particular as well as regarding the literary and redactional study of the pericope in general.[58]

3.2. Critically Choosing and Evaluating a Textual Witness as a Basis for Literary Study

At the level of the collection and interpretative description of the variants, I observed that the MT was not the only text to have preserved the narrative found in Exod 7–11. This implied ipso facto that the MT should not be considered *the* text without a prior critical study of the other textual material at our disposal. The MT is merely *a* text. In addition to the MT, there

57. For the detailed study see Lemmelijn, *Plague of Texts*; see also preliminary survey results in Lemmelijn, "As Many Texts as Plagues."

58. See also Lemmelijn, *Plague of Texts*, 209–18.

is a completely preserved text of Exod 7:14–11:10 in the LXX, SP, and fragments of the narrative in question in 4Q22, 4Q11, 2Q2, 4Q14, 4Q1, and 4Q20. A significant number of textual differences were registered when these textual witnesses were compared with one another. Many variants could be explained on the basis of grammatical and linguistic characteristics peculiar to the Hebrew and Greek languages. I provided a detailed description and explanation of this category of grammatical or stylistic variants. In addition, however, a number of other textual differences became apparent. They were referred to as *text-relevant variants*. In this regard, we can speak of variants that expand the text with a single word or a few words and variants that abbreviate the text in the same fashion. Other text-relevant differences reveal variant presentations of content. The so-called major expansions in the SP, 4Q22, and 4Q20 are of particular interest in this regard.

Within the framework of the third phase of my text-critical analysis—the text-critical evaluation of text-relevant variants in Exod 7:14–11:10—a study of the translation character of the Greek text of Exodus and of 7:14–11:10 in particular was made, prior to the assessment, including the adequate interpretation and correct evaluation, of the registered Greek textual differences. This study revealed that the Greek translator of Exodus should be characterized as a competent translator with a concern for the provision of idiomatic Greek. He can thus be described as free in his relationship to his *Vorlage*, although he remains precise in providing a faithful rendering of his original.[59] With the aforesaid characterization of the translation technique of LXX Exodus in mind, the study can then proceed to the concrete text-critical evaluation of the text-relevant variants in 7:14–11:10. This evaluation gave rise to a number of findings. In the first instance, it became clear that the majority of variants in the textual witnesses to the Plague Narrative could be explained on the basis of contextual arguments. The different readings in 7:14–11:10 mostly came into existence via recapitulation of or harmonization with the (immediate or wider) context in which they were encountered. A review of the concrete results of the evaluation reveals that a *preferable variant* is suggested in fifty-four instances, while the different readings in the remaining instances are designated as *synonymous variants*. It is striking that the MT—together

59. See ibid., 126–50; Lemmelijn, "Free and Yet Faithful: On the Translation Technique of LXX Exod 7:14–11:10," *JNSL* 33 (2007): 1–32; Ausloos, "Septuagint's Rendering of Hebrew Hapax Legomena."

with or without other textual witnesses—was found to have preserved the preferable variant in forty-seven of these fifty-four instances. The remaining seven preferable variants have been preserved by the LXX—likewise together with or without other textual witnesses but in contrast to the MT.[60]

Based on these results, it has become apparent that the customary use of textual variants from other text witnesses as a means to "correct" (by way of conjecture) Exod 7:14–11:10 in the MT is seldom justifiable.[61] Indeed, the vast majority of the textual variants in which a preferable variant could be established are to be found in the MT, albeit together with other textual witnesses. The LXX, on the other hand, appears to have preserved the preferable variant in twenty instances, of which only seven contrast with the reading in the MT. These seven variants could only be evaluated as preferable on the basis of a thorough text-critical analysis. The preferable variants found exclusively in the LXX are given precedence on the basis of scribal error (parablepsis) in the MT and SP (8:13), an addition for the purposes of emphasis in the MT, SP, and 4Q22 (9:10), and the observation of harmonizations in the MT and SP (9:20, 21, 25; 10:13; 11:1). As a consequence, one is clearly not at liberty to make use of the textual variants arbitrarily or when one considers it appropriate.

The fact that the majority of preferable variants are to be found in the MT, however, need not imply that the MT should immediately be considered the best text without reserve. It is only on the basis of a detailed text-critical study of the individual variants in the MT of Exod 7:14–11:10 that the epithet "best text" or "more original text" can be applied to it.[62] Each evaluation focuses attention on one specific, individual variant, whereby—strictly speaking—only the variants in question can be described as preferable. Nevertheless, taken as a whole, the readings evaluated as preferable variants on the basis of text-critical evaluation ultimately make it possible to provide a global appreciation of the entire text.[63]

---

60. See also Lemmelijn, "So-Called 'Major Expansions,'" 431–33.

61. As it is sometimes done in literary studies on biblical pericopes. In this regard, see Lemmelijn, "What Are We Looking for," 69–70.

62. "It is generally thought that the MT represents a well preserved and in most cases the original text. It must, however, be realized that a generalization like this is only valid if it is based on observations made on the details of the text" (Aejmelaeus, "What Can We Know," 88).

63. "The general probability of a text preserving original readings is the sum of individual cases of original readings. Before the details have been studied, there can hardly be any reliable general idea of the value of a certain textual witness" (ibid.).

The emphasis on preferable variants, however, should not gloss over the presence of synonymous variants and even secondary variants in the various textual witnesses. In spite of the fact that they often revolve around textual minutiae, such readings should not be ignored. While the variants in question are frequently based on textual details that may not be particularly relevant for the evaluation of one or another textual witness as such, they nevertheless have an important value in themselves.[64] In some places they betray the intention of the author or scribe; in others they bear witness to the creativity of the biblical authors. This fact should likewise encourage scholars to be cautious in granting monopoly status to a particular text whereby many significant minutiae are simply ignored. In the evaluation as presented above, I have therefore endeavored to approach each variant in itself and evaluate it in the first instance on the basis of contextual clues and indications and not on the purported value of the manuscript as a whole. Moreover, even if the MT ultimately appears to contain the majority of preferable variants, thus allowing us to describe it as the best text with respect to Exod 7:14–11:10, one should not forget that the MT frequently shares these preferable variants with various other textual witnesses, which, as a consequence, can be designated as equally original.

Against the background of these considerations and in service of the literary study of the Plague Narrative, it is important that a single working text be established. Theoretically speaking, one might argue that the extreme consequence of a text-critical evaluation of the variants in the Plague Narrative should lead, of necessity, to a new, eclectic text containing all of the preferable variants from the various textual witnesses. In such an instance, however, one would be basing oneself on a text that does not actually exist, a text that would be based on a hypothetical reconstruction of a number of fortuitously surviving manuscripts and of which the evaluation of the variants has been unable to avoid a degree of subjectivity.[65] The alternative is to opt for one single well-defined, albeit imperfect textual witness that is objectively extant. In such an instance, one is obliged to take the available material as one's point of departure, bearing in mind the marginal observations associated with it.

Based on the evaluation of the textual material of the Plague Narrative, I am of the opinion that the MT of Exod 7:14–11:10 can function in

64. See also, for example, Tov, *Text-Critical Use of the Septuagint*, 9.

65. For a more elaborate discussion of this topic see Lemmelijn, "Influence of a So-Called P-Redaction," 205–6.

this regard as a practical working text for the literary study of this intriguing narrative. In the first instance, only three complete texts are available to us, namely, the MT, LXX, and SP. While the materials stemming from Qumran are informative and interesting for the study of individual variants, they cannot serve as the point of departure of a literary study of the text in question on account of their fragmentary character. Of the three aforementioned complete textual witnesses, I have demonstrated that the MT contains the preferable variant in forty-seven of the fifty-four registered cases, although not always as the only textual witness to it. The MT, in addition, exhibits a number of synonymous variants. In the seven instances in which the LXX provided the preferable reading in contrast to the MT (8:13; 9:10, 20, 21, 25; 10:13; 11:1), the literary analysis of the text in question will be obliged to bear this in mind and include it as part of the literary discussion.

The above short presentation of the textual materials of 7:14–11:10 provides, in my view, enough proof to substantiate the first thesis mentioned above. Taking into consideration the factual multiplicity of textual witnesses of, for example, 7:14–11:10, textual criticism, as an empirical entry to the text, *has shown itself to be an indispensable first phase* in the research of a biblical pericope in order to evaluate the value of the textual witness chosen to be used as a basis for its literary study.

3.3. Contributing to the Recognition of Fundamental Data in the Literary Study of the Text

3.3.1. Introduction

Against this background, it is time to demonstrate that the empirical entry to the text, via the text-critical analysis of 7:14–11:10, has indeed produced results that are of essential importance for the literary study of the Plague Narrative,[66] thereby substantiating the second thesis of this contribution. The textual variants are of potential relevance in a double way. First, they can be very helpful in the recognition and explanation of irregularities in the final text. Second, they also reveal the contextual framework in which the text functions, both literarily and theologically.

66. In this regard see also Lemmelijn, "So-Called 'Major Expansions,'" 429–39.

3.3.2. Tracking Down Structural Patterns and Irregularities in the Text

3.3.2.1. Introduction

When one reads the Plague Narrative in Exod 7–11, one immediately notices that the story proceeds in a very stereotypical way. In general, one observes that YHWH commands Moses and/or Aaron to speak to Pharaoh and announce a plague. At other times, he orders them to produce the plague immediately. These commands are followed by the description of their execution and its consequences (e.g., 7:19–21; 8:1–2, 12–13). Now, when one begins the study of the Plague Narrative with a text-critical examination of the extant witnesses, this structural pattern of command and execution is immediately detectable on that level, that is, even before the content of the story is at stake. Indeed, a large number of variants in the textual witnesses of this narrative can be explained and evaluated when the literary context is carefully observed.[67] It then becomes clear that many of these have originated out of a tendency to harmonize their readings to the literary context and thereby to create greater internal consistency in the text.[68] This is particularly the case in the so-called major expansions within the Plague Narrative of the SP, 4Q22, and 4Q20. They seem to have attempted to complete the scheme of command and execution when it was not strictly applied, thereby showing the scholar, already at this stage of research, that the text of 7:14–11:10 contains some literary irregularities in its structure. By way of example, I refer to the textual situation of the two major expansions in 11:3b.[69]

3.3.2.2. Example 1: Exod 11:3b^1: SP[70]

Within the first expansion of 11:3b, which I refer to here as 11:3b^1, we are dealing with an expansion that formulates a command prior to the execution of it as related in the other textual witnesses. The larger plus repeats

67. See Lemmelijn, *Plague of Texts,* 150–207.

68. See similarly Emanuel Tov, “Textual Harmonizations in the Ancient Texts of Deuteronomy,” in *Hebrew Bible, Greek Bible, and Qumran: Collected Essays*, TSAJ 21 (Tübingen: Mohr Siebeck, 2008), 271. On the phenomenon of biblical harmonizations in general, see also Tov, “The Nature and Background of Harmonizations in Biblical Manuscripts,” *JSOT* 31 (1985): 3–29.

69. See Lemmelijn, *Plague of Texts*, 205–6.

70. As indicated in n. 36, 4Q22 originally bore witness to both expansions in 11:3b; however, they have not been preserved in the extant text fragments.

the words of the execution in precisely the same fashion in order to demonstrate that YHWH de facto commanded what was being executed.

Against this background, one notes that the expansion found in 11:3b[1], from the beginning of וכחצית הלילה ("and about midnight") up to and including ובין ישראל ("and between Israel"), agrees word-for-word with the text of 11:4–7 (MT, LXX, SP, 4Q11, 2Q2). In this way, the expansion demonstrates that the words addressed by Moses to Pharaoh in 11:4–7 are from YHWH. Exodus 11:3b[1] thus formulates a command prior to the execution of it in 11:4–7.

On the other hand, the continuation of 11:3b[1], from וגם האיש ("and also the man") up to and including ובעיני העם ("and in the sight of the people"), is identical to the end of 11:3 (MT, LXX, 2Q2), to which the SP does not bear witness at that location. In other words, the expansion would appear to hark back at this juncture to that which precedes it, although the textual basis of the expansion found in the SP (and 4Q22) remains unclear. Given the fact that the MT, LXX, and 2Q2 have preserved identical phraseology in 11:3, however, it is clear that the words found in 11:3b[1] are not an invention of the SP and 4Q22, and it is probable that this segment of the expansion came about as a result of harmonization.

3.3.2.3. Example 2: Exod 11:3b[2]: SP

The concluding portion of the expansion found in 11:3b, which I refer to here as 11:3b[2], is very special. The portion of 11:3b in question repeats the command of YHWH from 4:22–23 with exactly the same words.[71] In 4:22–23, YHWH commands Moses to announce to Pharaoh that all the firstborn of Egypt will die if he refuses to let Israel, YHWH's firstborn, go. In the expansion of 11:3b[2], Moses addresses Pharaoh with the words commanded to him in 4:22–23.

One observes in this regard that both passages employ precisely the same words, with the exception that the command ואמרת ("and you will say") becomes narrative ויאמר ("and he said") in the execution and the subject משה ("Moses") is made explicit where this was not necessary in the context of YHWH's address to Moses in 4:22–23. In addition, where

71. See also Edward L. Greenstein, "The Firstborn Plague and the Reading Process," in *Pomegranates and Golden Bells: Studies in Biblical, Jewish, and Near Eastern Ritual, Law, and Literature in Honor of Jacob Milgrom*, ed. David P. Wright, David Noel Freedman, and Avi Hurvitz (Winona Lake, IN: Eisenbrauns, 1995), 561.

YHWH speaks in the first-person singular (אנכי ["I"]) before the verb הרג ("to kill") in 4:22–23, Moses, who repeats these words to Pharaoh, speaks of יהוה ("YHWH") in the third person. Nevertheless, suffixes in the first-person singular are maintained a little earlier in the text.

Against this background, it is also clear that the structure of the beginning of Exod 11 in the SP is different from the one in the other textual witnesses. In the various textual witnesses, 11:1 begins with a direct address of YHWH that continues to the end of 11:2. In 11:3, we then find a narrative passage concerning the people and Moses. In 11:4–7, Moses then announces YHWH's words concerning the death of the firstborn of Egypt to Pharaoh, without making any reference to a command in the same words. In the SP, by contrast, YHWH's direct address does not end after 11:2. By analogy with 3:21, 11:3 continues in the first-person singular, such that YHWH's direct address is continued. The expansion found in 11:3b¹ continues the said address in which YHWH commands Moses to announce the death of the firstborn to Pharaoh in precisely the same words as those found in 11:4–7. After YHWH's direct address in which the command is formulated, the remainder of 11:3b¹ continues with the narrative passage concerning Moses, which the other textual witnesses relate at the end of 11:3. Exodus 11:3b² then begins with the account of the execution of YHWH's commands. The second expansion found in 11:3b relates the execution of the command from 4:22–23 in precisely the same terms. Exodus 11:4–7 then recapitulates the command given in 11:3b¹. The SP thus constructs a corresponding parallel pattern of command and execution via the two expansions found in 11:3b. Where the other textual witnesses begin the execution (of a command not explicitly mentioned) in 11:4, the SP begins the execution of YHWH's commands in 11:3b² and shapes the remainder of the execution in agreement with the harmonized expansion of the command in 11:3b¹. One thus observes a harmonization of command and execution in 11:3b², albeit based on words that are not found in the immediate context but hark back rather to a much earlier pericope.

3.3.3. Revealing the Contextual Framework

3.3.3.1. Introduction

Directly related to what has just been said, it becomes clear that the empirical text-critical study of the textual materials prior to any so-called literary study, helps to reveal the contextual framework in which the literary text functions. This is not only true for the major expansions[72] and especially for the second plus in 11:3b that reiterates the command of YHWH from 4:22–23, as I just demonstrated above. It is equally true for minor variants. By way of an example, I refer to the minor variants in the context of the literary motif of the so-called despoiling of the Egyptians in 11:2–3, in which the LXX and SP seem to have harmonized their story to the other pericopes on the despoiling in 3:21–22 and 12:35–36. I will give three examples.[73]

3.3.3.2. Example 1: Clothes

Concerning the motif of the so-called despoiling of the Egyptians in 11:2–3, the taking away of "clothes" (*και ἱματισμον*, ושמלות) next to silver and gold, whereas the MT says nothing about clothes. At first sight, one could think that this variant might stem from a different *Vorlage*, because of the fact that one does not find an explanation in the immediate context. If one studies the broader context, however, and looks for the way in which the motif of the despoiling is described, it would be seen that in 3:22 as well as in 12:35, these clothes are mentioned in the MT as well. In other words, the textual variant of 11:2 is a harmonization of the story with the other pericopes on the despoiling in 3:21–22 and 12:35–36.[74]

3.3.3.3. Example 2: Lending

The same is true for another variant from the same context in 11:3. All textual witnesses narrate that YHWH gave the people favor in the sight of the Egyptians, but only the LXX and SP tell us why this favor was needed, namely, so that they would lend their things. They read *και ἔχρησαν αὐτοις* and והשאילום ("and they lent to them"), respectively. Again, the explanation can be found in the broader context, since the plus of the LXX and

72. I have discussed these instances in detail elsewhere: Lemmelijn, "So-Called 'Major Expansions'"; Lemmelijn, *Plague of Texts*, 197–207; and more recently and extensively in Lemmelijn, "Influence of a So-Called P-Redaction."

73. See also Lemmelijn, *Plague of Texts*, 191–92, 195.

74. With respect to the harmonizations in the textual witnesses of 11:1–10 with 3:21–22; 4:22–23; and 12:35–36, see especially Bénédicte Lemmelijn, "Setting and Function of Ex 11:1–10 in the Exodus Narrative," in *Studies in the Book of Exodus: Redaction, Reception, Interpretation*, ed. Marc Vervenne, BETL 126 (Leuven: Peeters, 1996), 443–60.

SP in 11:3 is identical to the same words in 12:36. Thus, the *Vorlage* of the LXX and SP seems to have been harmonized with Exod 12.

3.3.3.4. Example 3: Signs

A final example is taken from the end of Exod 11. In 11:9–10 all the extant textual witnesses mention מופתי ("my wonders") and *τερατα* ("wonders") respectively. Only the LXX has a plus, *τα σημεια και* ("the signs and"), which is the common equivalent of the Hebrew אות ("signs"). It is remarkable that YHWH's action is generally described precisely with the terms אות and *σημεια* (see also 8:19, MT, LXX, SP; 10:1, MT, LXX, SP; 10:2, MT, LXX, SP). Nevertheless, the terminology מופתי and *τερατα* in 11:9–10 seems to be original, because all the extant witnesses have it that way. By reading *σημεια και τερατα*, the LXX could have aimed at conformity in the terminology. In addition, however, attention must be drawn to the fact that 11:9–10 functions as the conclusion of the Plague Narrative. When these verses are compared to 7:3, which formulates a kind of prologue to the plagues, then it is striking that in the latter verse precisely the same double formula is used in a similar context, also in the MT. Thus, it is likewise possible that the LXX's *Vorlage* intended to harmonize its conclusion of the plagues with its prologue to this narrative.

3.3.4. Summary of Overall Findings for the Plague Narrative

Taking into account my thesis above, I will sum up more generally what the empirical, text-critical entry to the Plague Narrative has brought in service of the literary and theological understanding of the text:[75]

- Generally speaking, the harmonizations of command (or announcement) and execution that were more explicitly sought after and implemented in various textual witnesses, different from the MT, draw the attention of the scholar to this structural design of the Plague Narrative. In addition, the harmonizing variants that were uncovered in various textual witnesses to Exod 11, reveal contextual relationships between the Plague Narrative and 3:21–22; 4:22–23; 7:2–4, 6; and 12:35–36.

75. This summary is based on that of the exhaustive analysis in Lemmelijn, *Plague of Texts*, 209–18.

- Content related and structural irregularities in the literary final text of 7:14–11:10 are marked by variant readings, which endeavor to iron them out with the help of supplementary additions and harmonizations. Particular reference should be made in this regard to the major expansions found in 7:18b, 29b; 8:1b, 19b; 9:5b, 19b; 10:2b; and 11:3b, each of which renders a command or execution where this has not been related and where the narrative becomes uneven.
- The secondary character of the reference to Aaron in some places in the Plague Narrative (e.g., 8:4, 8, 21; 9:27, 28; 10:3, 8–11, 16) is confirmed by the addition of them in 7:29b (LXX, SP, 4Q22); 9:5b (SP); 9:19b (SP, 4Q22); 10:24 (LXX, SP, 4Q22), for example, where the verb forms are also adapted.[76]
- Within the same context of the command and execution pattern, variations with respect to the command to stretch out the hand and/or staff, which lead to unevenness between command and execution (e.g., 7:19; 8:1, 2, 12, 13), are harmonized in a variety of textual witnesses. The LXX, SP, and 4Q14 adapt 8:12 on the basis of 8:13. The LXX harmonizes 9:23 with 9:22. The SP brings 10:12 into agreement with 10:13. These textual emendations provide evidence of the observation of (literary) irregularities.
- Finally, if we take a walk through the text from beginning to end, we observe a number of other more particular characteristics, which can only be summarized here.[77] I will recap a number of remarkable results:
    - The content related irregularities found in 8:12 with respect to 8:13 are harmonized in the LXX via an adaptation of the command in 8:12 to the command in 8:13 and 8:14.
    - The irregularities that arise from the lack of complete agreement between the announcement and the description of the consequences of the given plague in 9:9 and 9:10 are disguised in the LXX by way of harmonization. The variant ויעמדו ("and they stood") in the MT, SP, and 4Q22, which likewise disrupts

76. There is much to be said on the presence of the character of Aaron in the "major expansions." Studying this specific issue led to the conclusion that said additions reveal links with the theological concerns of a Priestly-oriented redaction. In this regard see Lemmelijn, "Influence of a So-Called P-Redaction."

77. They are dealt with extensively in Lemmelijn, *Plague of Texts*, 150–96.

agreement between the various elements of 9:9 and 9:10, appears on the basis of text-critical evaluation to be secondary. In this instance, the LXX is taken to represent the preferable variant.

- The evaluation of the LXX as the preferable variant in 9:20, 21 is of importance for distinguishing the redactional layers of the verses in question.
- The harmonization of 9:28–29 with 9:18 and 9:23 emphasizes and confirms the relationship between them.
- The association between 10:5 and 10:15 is likewise underlined by harmonizations in the SP and 4Q22. Indeed, it becomes evident on that basis that the description of the consequence of the given plague in 10:14–15 not only ties in with 10:12–13 but also with the announcement of the plague in 10:3–6.

4. Conclusion

Reaching the end of this contribution, I hope to have illustrated that textual criticism as an empirical entry to the texts can indeed complement literary and redactional study, and does so by detecting and explaining textual variants that contribute to the literary and theological understanding of the text. Harking back to the concrete study of the Plague Narrative, which functioned as an example of the applied approach, we can conclude that the primary result of the text-critical analysis of the Plague Narrative is the provision of a critically evaluated textual basis for the literary study of Exod 7:14–11:10, namely, the MT. In addition, the analysis of the text-critical variants in the various textual witnesses to 7:14–11:10 has already drawn attention to a significant number of literary irregularities. What is very remarkable in the Plague Narrative is the general tendency to harmonize literary and structural irregularities in the text in order to make it smoother, one could say. Precisely the study of those variants reveals the structural pattern to the scholar, indicates the literary and contextual problems, and hints at the way in which the scribe, redactor, or translator has tried to solve them.[78]

78. On the activities of scribes, redactors, and translators, see Lemmelijn, "Influence of a So-Called P-Redaction," 219–21.

Following that trail and elaborating on it beyond the initial analysis, the study of the extant witnesses for 7:14–11:10 leads to the question of the interrelation between the different texts. Indeed, combining textual and literary criticism demonstrates that *textual* variants often reveal *literary* and *theological* concerns. And this in turn leads to a reassessment of traditional opinions within literary and redaction criticism proper. Contrasting the source-critical division of Exod 7–11 at the heyday of the Documentary Hypothesis, newer redaction criticism resulting from the above-mentioned intertwinement with the empirical text-critical approach demands a comprehensive view of the concept of redaction[79] and especially challenges the concept of the "Priestly" redaction of/in this narrative[80] and probably by extension also in the Pentateuch as a whole. All that, however, is beyond the scope of this contribution. I only hope that it invites the reader to further explore, to further reflect, to further apply, and certainly to further develop the path of research presented above.

79. See, in this regard, Bénédicte Lemmelijn, "The So-Called 'Priestly' Layer in Exod 7:14–11:10: 'Source' and/or/nor 'Redaction'?," *RB* 109 (2002): 481–511.

80. See Lemmelijn, "Influence of a So-Called P-Redaction."

Division Markers as Empirical Evidence for the Editorial Growth of Biblical Books

Julio Trebolle Barrera

1. Introduction

Phenomena as late in the Hebrew textual transmission as the *petuhah* (פ) and *setumah* (ס) divisions in the masoretic medieval manuscripts and as early as the *vacats* (uninscribed or empty surfaces) in Qumran biblical scrolls are connected with two main phenomena that occurred in the editorial process of the Hebrew Bible: the different arrangement of pericopes in the Masoretic Text (MT) and the Septuagint's (LXX) *Vorlage* and the literary units inserted in either text. According to David Carr, in the "Hellenistic-period authors limited themselves to rearranging older materials (e.g., Psalms and parts of prophetic books) and/or expanding on older material."[1] "Editors" is surely a better designation than "authors" here.

Late passages in the Pentateuch are marked by division signs as, for example, the pericopes of Num 20:1–13 framed by *petuhah* and *setumah*, Num 20:22–29 between *petuhah* and *setumah*, Num 27:12–14 between *setumah* and *petuhah*, and Num 27:15–23 preceded and followed by *petuhot*. Deuteronomy 32:48–52 framed by *petuhah* and *setumah* is also a late unit, a possible resumptive repetition of Num 27:12–14.[2]

The pericope Num 10:35–36, between *setumah* and *petuhah*, is

1. David M. Carr, *The Formation of the Hebrew Bible: A New Reconstruction* (Oxford: Oxford University Press, 2011), 191.

2. Ibid., 138–39; Christophe Nihan, "La mort de Moïse (Nb 20,1–13; 20,22–29; 27,12–23) et l'édition finale du livre des Nombres," in *Les dernières rédactions du Pentateuque, de l'Hexateuque et de l'Ennéateuque*, ed. Thomas Römer and Konrad Schmid, BETL 203 (Leuven: Peeters, 2007), 145–82.

> set off by inverted *nuns*, which indicates an awareness on the part of the ancient Jewish scribes that these two captioned verses were either out of place here or, as is more likely, that they were cited from an independent source. This scribal convention parallels the practice of the Alexandrian scribes in their copies of Greek texts, where similar markings are evident.[3]

In the Greek version, 10:34 is after 10:36, thus framing the addition of 10:35–36:

> MT Num 10:34 (> LXX) The cloud of the Lord being over them by day when they set out from the camp.
> ׆ (*inverted nun*) 35 ס Whenever the ark set out, Moses would say,
> "Arise, O Lord, let your enemies be scattered,
> And your foes flee before you."
> 36 And whenever it came to rest, he would say,
> "Return, O Lord of the ten thousand
> Thousands of Israel." ׆ (*inverted nun*) פ
> LXX (> MT) The cloud of the Lord being over them by day when they set out from the camp.

Numbers 21:17–20, delimited by *setumah* and *petuhah*, is introduced by אז ("then"), a particle frequently used to interpolate a clearly recognizable pericope, a song in this case:[4] "Then it was that Israel sang this song: 'For the well. Sing out for the well.'" In 21:21 a new unit begins.[5]

On numerous occasions, the masoretic divisions *petuhah* and *setumah* and the *vacats* in Qumran manuscripts indicate the points at which a pericope appears transposed to a different location in the MT and LXX or at which a pericope is inserted into another or added after another.[6] Signs of division of the text into pericopes are empirical evidence of the process of literary formation of certain books of the Hebrew

---

3. Baruch A. Levine, *Numbers 1–20*, AB 4A (New York: Doubleday, 1993), 317–18; Levine, "More on the Inverted *Nuns* of Num. 10:35–36," *JBL* 95 (1976): 122–24.

4. Jan Dus, "Gibeon: Eine Kultstätte des Šmš und die Stadt des benjaminitischen Schicksals," *VT* 10 (1960): 358 n. 1.

5. Baruch A. Levine, *Numbers 21–36*, AB 4B (New York: Doubleday, 2000), 99.

6. A *petuhah* (פ) or "open" paragraph, as in modern paragraphing, had to commence at the beginning of a new line. Furthermore, the preceding line had to be left partially or wholly blank. On the other hand, a *setumah* (ס) or "closed" paragraph had to commence at a point other than the beginning of a line. See Page H. Kelley, Daniel

Bible. These books are those in which the Qumran manuscripts as well as the LXX and its secondary versions contribute to identifying two or more editions, including:

Exodus: The Old Latin (OL) (Codex Monacensis), LXX, MT, 4Q22 (4QpaleoExod[m]), 4Q158 (4QRP[a]), and the Samaritan Pentateuch (SP) attest six successive stages, respectively, in the edition of this book. The OL knew a different version of chapters 36–40, where the LXX lacks some sections of the MT, and in a few places it also adds details.[7]

Joshua: 4Q47 (4QJosh[a]) and Josephus represent an early form of the narrative of chapter 4, which appears transposed in chapter 8 in the MT and LXX.[8] The Old Greek (OG) reflects a level of the oldest Hebrew text and possibly better than the one transmitted by the MT.[9] The MT edition expanded a shorter one reflected in the LXX.[10]

Judges: 4Q49 (4QJudg[a]) ignores the literary piece of MT 6:7–10 and shows significant points of contact with the pre-Lucianic and OL texts. The book has several starting points through which it links with Joshua.[11] It also presents various endings, one of them in 16:31 (LXX^L, OL), located before the appendixes which form chapters 17–21. These textual and liter-

S. Mynatt, and Timothy G. Crawford, *The Masorah of Biblia Hebraica Stuttgartensia: Introduction and Annotated Glossary* (Grand Rapids: Eerdmans, 1998), 155.

7. Pierre-Maurice Bogaert, "L'importance de la Septante et du 'Monacensis' de la Vetus Latina pour l'exégèse du livre de l'Exode (Chap. 35–40)," in *Studies in the Book of Exodus: Redaction, Reception, Interpretation*, ed. Marc Vervenne, BETL 126 (Leuven: Peeters, 1996), 401; Molly M. Zahn, *Rethinking Rewritten Scripture: Composition and Exegesis in the 4QReworked Pentateuch Manuscripts*, STDJ 95 (Leiden: Brill, 2011), 74.

8. Eugene Ulrich, "4QJosh[a]," in *Qumran Cave 4:IX: Deuteronomy, Joshua, Judges, Kings*, ed. Eugene Ulrich et al., DJD 14 (Oxford: Clarendon, 1995), 146; Ulrich, "The Old Latin, Mount Gerizim, and 4QJosh[a]," in *Textual Criticism and Dead Sea Scrolls Studies in Honour of Julio Trebolle Barrera: Florilegium Complutense*, ed. Andrés Piquer Otero and Pablo A. Torijano Morales, JSJSup 157 (Leiden: Brill, 2012), 361–75.

9. Harry M. Orlinsky, "The Hebrew *Vorlage* of the Septuagint of the Book of Joshua," in *Congress Volume: Rome, 1968*, ed. John A. Emerton, VTSup 17 (Leiden: Brill, 1969), 187–95.

10. Emanuel Tov, "The Growth of the Book of Joshua in Light of the Evidence of the Septuagint," in *Studies in the Bible*, ed. Sara Japhet, ScrHier 31 (Jerusalem: Magnes, 1986), 321–39.

11. Alexander Rofé, "The End of the Book of Joshua according to the Septuagint," *Henoch* 4 (1982): 17–36.

ary data can only be explained by assuming a complex editorial process that resulted in both the LXX and MT.[12]

Samuel: 4Q51 (4QSam[a]) retains a portion of text missing in the MT and LXX at the beginning of chapter 11, which has a parallel in the text of Josephus.[13] The story of David and Goliath (1 Sam 17–18) appears transmitted in two editions, a short one reflected by the LXX and a longer one preserved by the MT.[14] The OL translates a Greek pre-Lucianic text close to the OG and is preferable sometimes to the known Hebrew text.[15]

Kings: The MT and LXX and the Hebrew text of Chronicles represent different arrangements of the text in 1 Kgs 2–12 and also throughout Kings in connection with diverging chronological systems.[16]

Jeremiah: The LXX, 4Q71 (4QJer[b]), and 4Q72a (4QJer[d]) transmit a first edition of this book, and the MT, together with 4Q70 (4QJer[a]) and 4Q72 (4QJer[c]), transmit a second augmented edition.[17] The OG was revised from 29:1 onwards (following the LXX order) on the basis of the MT. The

12. Julio Trebolle Barrera, "Textual Variants in 4QJudg[a] and the Textual and Editorial History of the Book of Judges," *RevQ* 14 (1989): 229–45; Emanuel Tov, *Textual Criticism of the Hebrew Bible*, 3rd ed. (Minneapolis: Fortress, 2012), 344–45.

13. Frank M. Cross, "The Ammonite Oppression of the Tribes of Gad and Reuben: Missing Verses from 1 Samuel 11 Found in 4QSamuel[a]," in *History, Historiography, and Interpretation*, ed. Hayim Tadmor and Moshe Weinfeld (Jerusalem: Magnes, 1983), 148–58.

14. Dominique Barthélemy, ed., *The Story of David and Goliath: Textual and Literary Criticism*, OBO 73 (Fribourg: Editions Universitaires; Göttingen: Vandenhoeck & Ruprecht, 1986); Stanley D. Walters, "Hannah and Anna: The Greek and Hebrew Texts of 1 Samuel 1," *JBL* 107 (1988): 385–412.

15. Eugene Ulrich, "The Old Latin Translation of the LXX and the Hebrew Scrolls from Qumran," in *The Hebrew and Greek Texts of Samuel, 1980 Proceedings IOSCS—Vienna*, ed. Emanuel Tov (Jerusalem: Academon, 1980), 121–65; Ulrich, *The Qumran Text of Samuel and Josephus*, HSM 19 (Missoula, MT: Scholars Press, 1978).

16. Julio Trebolle Barrera, *Salomón y Jeroboán: Historia de la recensión y redacción de I Reyes 2–12, 14*, BSamD 3 (Salamanca: Universidad Pontificia, 1980).

17. Emanuel Tov, "4QJer[a-e]," in *Qumran Cave 4:X: The Prophets*, ed. Eugene Ulrich et al., DJD 15 (Oxford: Clarendon, 1997), 145–207; Tov, "Exegetical Notes on the Hebrew *Vorlage* of the LXX of Jeremiah 27 (34)," *ZAW* 91 (1979): 73–93; Pierre-Maurice Bogaert, "Le livre de Jérémie en perspective: Les deux rédactions antiques selon les travaux en cours," *RB* 101 (1994): 363–406; Anneli Aejmelaeus, "Jeremiah at the Turning-Point of History: The Function of Jer. XXV 1–14 in the Book of Jeremiah," *VT* 52 (2002): 460–61, 479–80; Andrew G. Shead, *The Open Book and the Sealed Book: Jeremiah 32 in Its Hebrew and Greek Recensions*, JSOTSup 347, HBV 3 (London: Sheffield Academic, 2002).

OL (Codex Wirceburgensis) omits MT 39:1–2. These verses were not part of the LXX.[18]

Ezekiel: The long MT edition depends on the short one represented by the LXX. The minuses present in 12:26–28 and 32:25–26, as well as considerable differences between the two texts in chapter 7, reflect two different Hebrew forms.[19] The OL (Codex Wirceburgensis) and Greek papyrus 967 are the only witnesses preserved which show that the oldest text followed the sequence 38, 39, 37, and omitted 36:23c–28.[20] The OL and the Coptic version frequently follow the text of 967.

To these books three others are to be added that also developed editorially through various textual forms, including:

Job: The Hebrew *Vorlage* of the LXX differed from the preserved Hebrew text. To the shorter text, closer to the Greek original (attested by the OL and the Sahidic Coptic version), were added a series of passages

---

18. Pierre-Maurice Bogaert, "De Baruch à Jérémie: Les deux rédactions conservées du livre de Jérémie," in *Le livre de Jérémie: Le prophète et son milieu; Les oracles et leur transmission*, ed. Pierre-Maurice Bogaert, BETL 54 (Leuven: Peeters, 1981), 168–73; Bogaert, "La libération de Jérémie et le meurtre de Godolias: Le texte court (LXX) et la rédaction longue (TM)," in *Studien zur Septuaginta: Robert Hanhart zu Ehren: Aus Anlaß seines 65. Geburtstages*, ed. Detlef Fraenkel, Udo Quast, and John William Wevers, MSU 20 (Göttingen: Vandenhoeck & Ruprecht, 1990), 312–22; Bogaert, "La *vetus latina* de Jérémie: Texte très court, témoin de la plus ancienne Septante et d'une forme plus ancienne de l'hébreu (Jer 39 et 52)," in *The Earliest Text of the Hebrew Bible: The Relationship between the Masoretic Text and the Hebrew Base of the Septuagint Reconsidered*, ed. Adrian Schenker, SCS 52 (Atlanta: Society of Biblical Literature, 2003), 51–82.

19. Emanuel Tov, "Recensional Differences between the MT and the LXX of Ezekiel," *ETL* 62 (1986): 89–101; Johan Lust, "The Use of Textual Witnesses for the Establishment of the Text: The Shorter and Longer Texts of Ezekiel; An Example: Ez 7," in *Ezekiel and His Book: Textual and Literary Criticism and Their Interrelation*, ed. Johan Lust, BETL 74 (Leuven: Peeters, 1986), 7–20; Lust, "Major Divergences between the LXX and the MT in Ezekiel," in Schenker, *Earliest Text of the Hebrew Bible*, 83–92.

20. Pierre-Maurice Bogaert, "Le témoignage de la Vetus Latina dans l'étude de la tradition des Septante: Ézéchiel et Daniel dans le Papyrus 967," *Bib* 59 (1978): 384–95; Bogaert, "Montagne sainte, jardin d'Éden et sanctuaire (hiérosolymitain) dans un oracle d'Ézéchiel contre le prince de Tyr (Éz 28,11–19)," in *Le Mythe, son langage et son message: Actes du Colloque de Liège et Louvain-la-Neuve de 1981*, ed. Henri Limet and Julien Ries, Homo religiosus 9 (Louvain la-Neuve: Centre d'Histoire des Religions, 1983), 131–53; Johan Lust, "Ezekiel 36–40 in the Oldest Greek Manuscript," *CBQ* 43 (1981): 517–33.

taken from Theodotion's version, aimed at bringing the Greek version closer to the MT.

Song of Songs: In 4Q106 (4QCant^{a}), 6:11 follows 4:7. Also 4Q107 (4QCant^{b}) goes from 4:3 to 4:8, and in the previous column it might also go from 3:5 to 3:9 (at least there is text missing between 3:2 and 3:10). All the missing passages are "complete literary units."[21] Emanuel Tov considers the Qumran text an abbreviated form, while Eugene Ulrich assumes that the poetic units absent in the two manuscripts may have been located at other places in a book that consisted of brief single units with a structure and logical order difficult to discern; they may even have been simply ignored by the editor responsible for the textual form transmitted in the Qumran manuscripts.[22] The OL presents the same verse order in chapter 5 as Greek manuscript R 952 (5:12, 14b, 13, 14a, 15).[23]

Daniel: The MT, together with 1Q71–72 (1QDan^{a,b}), 4Q112–116 (4QDan^{a-e}), 6Q7 (6QpapDan), and, on the other side, the LXX, represent two editions, the former shorter and the later characterized saliently by the Greek additions to this book.[24] The LXX represents a form of tradition that is earlier than the Aramaic of Dan 2–7. Papyrus 967 represents the more original form of the Greek text, showing the order of chapters 1–4, 7–8, 5–6, and 9–12, followed by the stories of Bel and the Dragon and Susanna. This arrangement is also found in the Latin writer Quodvultdeus.[25]

Other books transmitted in various textual forms are:

---

21. Emanuel Tov, "Introduction to 4QCant^{a-c}," *Qumran Cave 4:XI: Psalms to Chronicles*, ed. Eugene Ulrich et al., DJD 16 (Oxford: Clarendon, 2000), 195.

22. "If the first scenario obtained, these MSS would be analogous to the rearranged Book of Jeremiah; if the second obtained, they would be analogous to the longer vs. shorter forms of the Book of Daniel" (Eugene Ulrich, "The Text of the Hebrew Scriptures at the Time of Hillel and Jesus," *Congress Volume: Basel 2001*, ed. André Lemaire, VTSup 92 [Leiden: Brill, 2002], 105).

23. Donatien De Bruyne, "Les anciennes versions latines du Cantique des Cantiques," *RBén* 38 (1926): 97–122; Francesco Vattioni, "Osservazioni ai papiri greci del Cantico dei Cantici," *SPap* 17 (1978): 89–95.

24. Eugene Ulrich, "The Parallel Editions of the Old Greek and Masoretic Text of Daniel 5," in *A Teacher for All Generations: Essays in Honor of James C. VanderKam*, ed. Eric F. Mason et al., 2 vols., JSJSup 153 (Leiden: Brill, 2012), 1:201–17.

25. Pierre-Maurice Bogaert, "Job latin chez les Pères et dans les Bibles: D'une version courte à des versions longues sur le grec et sur l'hébreu," *RBén* 122 (2012): 48–99, 366–93; Olivier Munnich, "Texte massorétique et Septante dans le livre de Daniel," in Schenker, *Earliest Text of the Hebrew Bible*, 93–120.

Minor Prophets: The LXX order seems to have been modified to the proto-MT order.

Psalms: The MT and 11Q5 (11QPs[a]) represent two different editions. Some authors consider that 11Q5 would be a liturgical scroll.[26]

Proverbs: The LXX and the MT represent different editions, neither of which is clearly prior to the other.

Esther: The first Greek translation, whose text is attested exclusively in the OL, was revised with the MT, producing the traditional Greek text. Some of the six major additions to the Greek version appear to have been done in Hebrew or Aramaic.[27]

Ezra: Ezra–Nehemiah and 1 Esdras (LXX) represent two editions, each with its own distinct literary shape.[28]

The OG text of the books of Exodus, Joshua, Judges, Samuel, Kings, Jeremiah, and Ezekiel reflects a Hebrew text different from the MT and was revised by the group or school that undertook the *kaige* recension.[29] This recension was conducted in the first half of the first century BCE with the purpose of bringing the OG text closer to the proto-MT that was considered authoritative in certain rabbinic circles. The most significant characteristic of this recension is the translation of the particle וגם by καὶ γε. Theodotion's later recension had a similar goal as the *kaige* recension, so that these two recensions can be grouped together. These recensions affect the following books:[30]

Exodus: Theodotion's version in Exodus occupies a position in the textual tradition analogous to that of the *kaige* recension in other books. "It depends on a form of the OG that had already undergone partial revision towards a Hebrew text, but did not differ from the original OG on the form and general content of chapters 36–40."[31]

---

26. Peter W. Flint, *The Dead Sea Psalms Scrolls and the Book of Psalms*, STDJ 17 (Leiden: Brill, 1997), 202–27.

27. Jean-Claude Haelewyck, "The Relevance of the Old Latin Version for the Septuagint, with Special Emphasis on the Book of Esther," *JTS* 57 (2006): 439–73.

28. Robert Hanhart, *Text und Textgeschichte des 2. Esrabuches*, MSU 25 (Göttingen: Vandenhoeck & Ruprecht, 2003), 290.

29. Dominique Barthélemy, *Les devanciers d'Aquila: Première publication intégrale du texte des fragments du Dodécaprophéton trouvés dans le désert de Juda*, VTSup 10 (Leiden: Brill, 1963), 47.

30. Ibid.

31. Kevin G. O'Connell, *The Theodotionic Revision of the Book of Exodus: A Con-*

Joshua: Readings attributed to Theodotion represent the *kaige* recension that brings the LXX closer to a Hebrew text nearly identical to the MT.[32]

Judges: The text attested by the groups of Greek manuscripts Irua$_2$ and Befsz transmits the text of the *kaige* recession, while LXX^A and LXX^L text groups retain the OG text.[33]

Samuel–Kings: Based on the different characteristics of translation, Thackeray established a division of the text into five sections, whose version would have been the work of as many translators (α 1 Sam 1–31; ββ 2 Sam 1:1–11:1; βγ 2 Sam 11:2–1 Kgs 2:11; γγ 1 Kgs 2:12–21:43; γδ 1 Kgs 22:1–2 Kgs 25:30).[34] However, the Greek text of these books can be traced back to a single translation, while the LXX^B text of sections βγ and γδ is part of the *kaige* recension.[35]

Jeremiah: The original Greek translation was revised from 29:1 onwards (following the order of the LXX). This revision was based on the Hebrew of the masoretic tradition.[36] The Theodotionic additions of the LXX belong to the *kaige* group.

Ezekiel: The original translation underwent a revision that affected chapters 28–39 (36:23c–38 were missing in the OG). The transition from

---

tribution to the Study of the Early History of the Transmission of the Old Testament in Greek, HSM 3 (Cambridge: Harvard University Press, 1972), 292.

32. "Th[eodotion] in Joshua is indeed a revision of an older Greek in the direction of the developing MT text" (Leonard J. Greenspoon, "The Kaige Recension: The Life, Death, and Postmortem Existence of a Modern—and Ancient—Phenomenon," in *XII Congress of the International Organization for Septuagint and Cognate Studies, Leiden, 2004*, ed. Melvin K. H. Peters, SCS 54 [Atlanta: Society of Biblical Literature, 2006], 9); Greenspoon, *Textual Studies in the Book of Joshua*, HSM 28 (Chico, CA: Scholars Press, 1983).

33. Barthélemy, *Devanciers d'Aquila*, 34–35, 47; Walter R. Bodine, *The Greek Text of Judges: Recensional Developments*, HSM 23 (Chico, CA: Scholars Press, 1980); Bodine, "Kaige and Other Recensional Developments in the Greek Text of Judges," *BIOSCS* 13 (1980): 45–57.

34. Henry St. John Thackeray, "The Greek Translators of the Four Books of Kings," *JTS* 8 (1907): 277.

35. James Donald Shenkel, *Chronology and Recensional Development in the Greek Text of Kings*, HSM 1 (Cambridge: Harvard University Press, 1968); Ralph W. Klein, "New Evidence for an Old Recension of Reigns," *HTR* 60 (1967): 93–105.

36. Emanuel Tov, *The Septuagint Translation of Jeremiah and Baruch: A Discussion of an Early Revision of the LXX of Jeremiah 29–52 and Baruch 1:1–3:8*, HSM 8 (Missoula, MT: Scholars Press, 1976), 199.

the text of the first translator to the second takes place between chapters 25 and 26.[37]

Similarly the Song of Songs, Job, and Daniel were transmitted in various textual forms in Qumran and the LXX. The Greek version of the Song of Songs is the work of the *kaige* group. The Theodotionic text of Daniel and the Theodotionic additions of Job are also related to the activity of this group.[38]

Thus the *kaige* recension affected the books whose Greek text differed from the proto-MT. Therefore, it provides empirical evidence on the plurality of textual forms or editions in which these books were circulating at the turn of the era. It should also be remembered that the historical books and Jeremiah underwent one or more "Deuteronomistic" redactions, which undoubtedly contributed very early to an increasing fluidity in the textual transmission of these books.

This chapter presents cases mainly from the aforementioned books (Exodus, Joshua–Kings, Jeremiah–Ezekiel) in which a transposed or inserted pericope is framed between masoretic divisions or *vacats*. This is not a systematic study. It mainly intends to point out a line of research that relates lower with higher criticism, the history of the textual transmission with the history of the literary formation of these books. More examples can also be found in other books. Outstanding cases are the transpositions in Proverbs of 30:1–14, enclosed by *petuhot*, that appears in the LXX after the interval (*setumah*) following 24:22; of MT 30: פ 15–30 (+ 31: ס 1–8) transposed in the LXX after 24:34 פ; and of MT 31: פ 10–31 placed in the LXX after 29:27 פ.

This research has important ramifications that would benefit from a more comprehensive statement and discussion than is possible in the present context:

(1) The most extensive and significant textual variants tend to be produced at the points where a transposition or addition has been produced, for example, before and after the *petuhah* (missing in 4Q51) between chapters 10 and 11 of 1 Samuel.

37. Leslie John McGregor, *The Greek Text of Ezekiel: An Examination of its Homogeneity*, SCS 18 (Atlanta: Society of Biblical Literature, 1986).

38. Barthélemy, *Devanciers d'Aquila*, 47; Natalio Fernández Marcos, *The Septuagint in Context: Introduction to the Greek Versions of the Bible*, trans. Wilfred G. E. Watson (Leiden: Brill, 2000), 141–54.

(2) *Vacats* indicating the division between literary units are the points where transpositions or additions usually are to be found. In 4Q106 6: ס 11 comes after 4:7 ס. In 4Q107 4:3 (*vacat* in the manuscript) is followed by 4: ס 8 and possibly 3: ס 9 comes after 3:5 ס.

(3) Additions are often produced by means of a linking repetition (*Wiederaufnahme*); textual variants in one part or another of the repetition can often be observed.

(4) Explicit quotations of biblical passages in later writings often reproduce an entire pericope (an oracle, for example) or the first verse of the pericope, thus signifying that the quote does not refer only to the first verse but to the whole unit, often framed by a *vacat* or a masoretic sign(s) of division.

(5) Literary units added or transposed in the Hebrew tradition and marked by the corresponding signs of division often coincide with sections delimited in the Greek text with an asterisk (indicating a passage absent in the *Vorlage* of the LXX) or an obelus (indicating a passage absent in the MT and added in the Hebrew underlying the Greek version). Thus the signs of the asterisk and the obelus also become empirical evidence of the growth of the biblical books. The Hexaplaric additions correspond to additions produced in the proto-MT or in the *Vorlage* of the LXX.

In mishnaic times, the introduction of changes in the *petuhot* and *setumot* system in Torah manuscripts for liturgical usage was forbidden. Qumran manuscripts as well as the Ugaritic tablets attest the existence of such divisions in far earlier times.[39] The masoretic divisions and the *vacats*

39. Emanuel Tov, "Sense Divisions in the Qumran Texts, the Masoretic Text, and Ancient Translations of the Bible," in *The Interpretation of the Bible: The International Symposium in Slovenia*, ed. Jože Krašovec, JSOTSup 289 (Sheffield: Sheffield Academic, 1998), 121–46; Tov, *Scribal Practices and Approaches Reflected in the Texts Found in the Judean Desert*, STDJ 54 (Leiden: Brill, 2004), 143–62; Eugene Ulrich, "Impressions and Intuition: Sense Divisions in Ancient Manuscripts of Isaiah," in *Unit Delimitation in Biblical Hebrew and Northwest Semitic Literature*, ed. Marjo C. A. Korpel and Josef M. Oesch, Pericope 4 (Assen: Van Gorcum, 2003), 279–307; Joachim Conrad, "Die Entstehung und Motivierung alttestamentlichen Paraschen im Licht der Qumranfunde," in *Bibel und Qumran: Beiträge zur Erforschung der Beziehungen zwischen Bibel und Qumranwissenschaft; Hans Bardtke zum 22.9.66*, ed. Siegfried Wagner (Berlin: Evangelische Haupt-Bibelgesellschaft, 1968), 47–56; Josef M. Oesch, "Textgliederung im Alten Testament und in den Qumranhandschriften," *Henoch* 5 (1983): 289–321; Ernst Kutsch, "Die Textgliederung im hebräischen Ijobbuch sowie in 4QTgJob und in 11QTgJob," *BZ* 27 (1983): 221–28; Jesper Hoegenhaven, "The First Isaiah Scroll from

in Qumran manuscripts correspond to what is usually called "sense divisions," which means that the divisions of literary units are made *ad sensum* as based on *impressions* or *intuitions*, without it being possible to recognize a system that can give a reason for their existence and distribution.[40]

Charles Perrot's explanation according to which there is a connection between the masoretic divisions and the liturgical readings of the Torah does not seem applicable in general and to other books.[41] It is very easy to see that they often begin with verbs of speaking (e.g., "So says the Lord"), but this does not explain many other divisions, especially those enclosing simple sentences or short sections of text.

Jozef Oesch raised the question of whether in order to establish the function of the masoretic signs of division it would be possible to relate them to the structuring of the text as proposed by literary critics.[42] Also François Langlamet wondered if the *parashiyyot* division "has the function of maintaining a system prior to the current division," and he added that confirmation of the hypothesis could come from what I have called the method of "recension-redaction criticism."[43] The analysis of the recensional history of the LXX is a necessary step that is methodologically prior

---

Qumran (1QIs^{a}) and the Massoretic Text: Some Reflections with Special Regard to Isaiah 1–12," *JSOT* 28 (1984): 17–35; Marjo C. A. Korpel, "Unit Delimitation in Ugaritic Cultic Texts and Some Babylonian and Hebrew Parallels," in *Layout Markers in Biblical Manuscripts and Ugaritic Tablets*, ed. Marjo C. A. Korpel and Josef M. Oesch, Pericope 5 (Assen: Van Gorcum, 2005), 141–60.

40. "My closer analysis of the Isaiah sense divisions for this article confirms my general impression gained by studying all the biblical manuscripts over the past thirty years: there was no 'system' of sense divisions" (Ulrich, "Impressions and Intuition," 301).

41. Charles Perrot, "*Petuhot* et *Setumot*: Étude sur les alinéas du Pentateuque," *RB* 76 (1969): 84–89.

42. "Weiters wären die ältesten Gliederungszeichen auch mit jenen Textstrukturen zu vergleichen, die mit Hilfe der traditionellen exegetischen (Literarkritik, Formkritik, Redaktionskritik) oder neuerer linguistischer Methoden zu erheben sind, und es wäre in Diskussion mit ihnen ihre nähere Funktion und ihr genaueres 'Gewicht' zu bestimmen" (Jozef M. Oesch, *Petucha und Setuma: Untersuchungen zu einer überlieferten Gliederung im hebräischen Text des Alten Testaments*, OBO 27 [Fribourg: Editions Universitaires; Göttingen: Vandenhoeck & Ruprecht, 1979], 366).

43. "Mais ce complément d'information est à demander pour une large part à l' 'histoire de la recension-rédaction' dont les résultats prometteurs sont connus des lecteurs de la RB" (François Langlamet, "Les divisions massorétiques du livre de Samuel: À propos de la publication du Codex du Caire," *RB* 91 [1984]: 484 n. 10; he

to the study of the composition and redaction of books transmitted in plural textual forms.[44] The history of the Greek text and of the secondary versions reflects the previous history of the Hebrew text: Hexaplaric additions relate to additions in the Hebrew text, both in the proto-MT (sections marked with an asterisk) and in the *Vorlage* of the LXX (sections marked with an obelus). This chapter reassesses the masoretic tradition of *parashiyyot* division, not taken into account by modern criticism, and consequently it serves as a challenge to methods of literary criticism that ignore empirical data.

2. The Contributions of Jeffrey Tigay, Emanuel Tov, and Alexander Rofé in *Empirical Models for Biblical Criticism*

In *Empirical Models for Biblical Criticism*, Jeffrey Tigay gives several examples of conflation—the joining of two preexistent versions of a text—as a redactional technique. One of them refers to the pericope Esth 2:21–23, duplicated in the LXX A:12–16:

> A narrative doublet resulting from conflation is found in the LXX of Esther, in one of the six additional passages not found in the Hebrew text. One of these describes an incident that duplicates another found later in both the Hebrew and LXX, at 2:21–23. In the LXX these are presented as two separate episodes. Their similarities are such that source criticism of the LXX would recognize them as two variants of the same episode even if we did not have documentary evidence to that effect.… Indeed, in the "Lucianic" revision of the LXX of Esther the entire incident in 2:21–23 is omitted.…[45] This implies that 2:21–23 was already recognized in antiquity as a doublet of A:12–16.[46]

cites Julio Trebolle Barrera, "Testamento y muerte de David: Estudio de historia de la recensión y redacción de 1 Reyes II," *RB* 87 [1980]: 87–103).

44. Julio Trebolle Barrera, "Redaction, Recension, and Midrash in the Books of Kings," *BIOSCS* 15 (1982): 12–35.

45. Here Tigay cites Emanuel Tov, "The 'Lucianic' Text of the Canonical and the Apocryphal Sections of Esther: A Rewritten Biblical Book," *Text* 10 (1982): 11–12.

46. Jeffrey H. Tigay, "Conflation as a Redactional Technique," in *Empirical Models for Biblical Criticism*, ed. Jeffrey H. Tigay (Philadelphia: University of Philadelphia Press, 1985), 57, 60–61.

The literary unit duplicated and transposed, 2:21–23, appears framed by signs of *petuhah* and *setumah*.

Several additions to the book of Esther appear inserted into an interval indicated by a sign of division. In 3:7, followed by *setumah*, the Lucianic text introduces a paraphrasis: "Haman in his jealousy and shaken to the core went red." After 3:15, followed by *petuhah*, the OL inserts a prayer of the Jews, expressing sorrow for the sins of the nation (H 1–5, La-Greek III).[47] At the end of 4:17, marked by *setumah*, the Greek presents additions C and D, the prayers of Mordechai and Esther. The OL addition presupposes a now lost Greek passage which, in turn, was based on either a Hebrew or Aramaic text. The pericope of 5:1–3, enclosed by *setumot*, is much longer in the Greek (addition D). At the end of 9:18, the Lucianic text introduces a short thanksgiving: "And all the people cried aloud and shouted, 'Be blessed, O Lord, for you are mindful of the covenants made with our ancestors! Amen.'" After 9:19, followed by *petuhah*, the Greek adds "whereas for those who live in the cities the day of rejoicing … is the fifteenth day of Adar." If 9:19 is to be considered as an addition, both additions were introduced at the end of the appendix formed by 9:1–19, followed by *petuhah*; the two appendixes that follow, 9:20–32 and 10:1–3, are also marked by masoretic divisions (9: פ 20, 10:1–3 פ end of the book). The unit 9:5–9, between *petuhot*, was not part of the Latin version and of its original Greek.[48]

Tigay points out the composite version of the motive clause for the Sabbath command present in 4Q41 (4QDeut^{n}). This Qumran manuscript adds the version found in Exod 20:11 (citing the creation) after that found in Deut 5:15 (citing the exodus).[49] The insertion occurs at a point that is signaled with a *vacat* after the unit Deut 5:12–15, which is enclosed by *petuhot*:

> MT Deut 5:12–15 פ Observe the Sabbath day, to keep it holy, as the Lord your God commanded you. Six days you shall labor … therefore the Lord your God commanded you to observe the Sabbath day to keep it

47. Jean-Claude Haelewyck, *Hester*, VL 7.3 (Freiburg: Herder, 2003), 77–94.

48. Ibid., 405; Haelewyck, "Relevance of the Old Latin Version," 465–67.

49. Tigay, "Conflation as a Redactional Technique," 55–57; Sidnie White Crawford, *Rewriting Scripture in Second Temple Times*, SDSS (Grand Rapids: Eerdmans, 2008), 30–32.

holy. פ + Exod 20:11 *for in six days the Lord made the heaven and earth.... Therefore the Lord blessed the Sabbath day to keep it holy.*

In this same volume, Tov presents evidence about the composition of 1 Sam 16–18 in light of the LXX version.[50] In the story of David and Goliath, the pericopes missing in the LXX are signaled by a previous *petuhah* and/or *setumah* and also by the corresponding asterisk, even in the case of a single verse that is missing in the Greek, 18:30.[51]

MT 17:1–11	פ 12–31	32–54	ס 55–18:5	פ 6–9	ס 10–11	12–16	פ 17–19	20–29	ס 30 ס
LXX 17:1–11	> *	32–54	> *	6–9	> *	12–16	> *	20–29	> *

Tov also analyzes an exemplary case study in the editing process of the biblical books: the two editions of Jeremiah. His conclusion that the shorter text translated in the LXX is earlier than the longer version of the MT is confirmed by the Qumran manuscript 4Q71, which "resembles the LXX of Jeremiah in the two major features in which the reconstructed *Vorlage* of that translation differs from the Masoretic Text, namely, the arrangement of the text and its shortness compared to the Masoretic Text."[52] One of the largest pluses of Edition II (MT) is the prophecy in 33:14–26 on the "true branch" and the durability of the covenant.[53] This pericope appears embraced by *setumot*. It is absent from the LXX and may have been added secondarily on the basis of the oracle about the Davidic king in Jer 23:5–6, which is also enclosed by *setumot*.[54] The unit MT 33:14–26 appears in LXX 40:14–26 marked with an asterisk as a Hexaplaric addition.[55] Furthermore,

50. Emanuel Tov, "The Composition of 1 Samuel 16–18 in the Light of the Septuagint Version," in Tigay, *Empirical Models for Biblical Criticism*, 97–130.

51. Emanuel Tov, "The Nature of the Differences between MT and the LXX in 1 Sam. 17–18," in Barthélemy, *Story of David and Goliath*, 19–46.

52. Emanuel Tov, "The Literary History of the Book of Jeremiah in the Light of Its Textual History," in Tigay, *Empirical Models for Biblical Criticism*, 213; see also Yohanan Goldman, *Prophétie et royauté au retour de l'exil: Les origenes littéraires de la forme massorétique du livre de Jérémie*, OBO 118 (Fribourg: Editions Universitaires; Göttingen: Vandenhoeck & Ruprecht, 1992).

53. Tov, "Literary History of the Book of Jeremiah," 214.

54. According to Adrian Schenker, the oracle about the Davidic king in Jer 23:5–6 was revised in the proto-MT plus of Jer 33:14–26 (see also 33:15–16), missing in the Greek version (Adrian Schenker, "La rédaction longue du livre de Jérémie doit-elle être datée au temps des premiers Hasmonéens?," *ETL* 70 [1994]: 286–89).

55. Joseph Ziegler, ed., *Septuaginta: Vetus Testamentum Graecum*, vol. 15: *Ier-*

MT 31:35–37 appears in the LXX with the order 37, 35, 36. The transposition in the MT is signaled with an additional *setumah* placed between 31:36 and 31:37. In this way, 31:37 becomes in the MT an independent oracle introduced by the formula "Thus says the Lord," missing in the LXX.

Tov also notes that MT 23:7–8 occur in the LXX after 31:40 and that MT 31:35–37 are placed in the LXX in chapter 38 in the order of verses 37, 35, 36. The oracle of MT 23:7–8, framed by *setumot* and marked in the Greek with an asterisk,[56] is a doublet of the pericope in MT 16:14–15, also marked with *setumot*. This passage appears in the LXX after 23:40 ס. According to J. Gerald Janzen, the oracle was originally between 23:1–4 and 23:ס 5–6 ס.[57] The pericope of MT 31:35–37 on Israel's endurance is also enclosed by *setumot*. The LXX has MT 31:35–36 in chapter 38 after 38:37 as two secondary units (the MT introduces 31:7 with the formula "Thus says the Lord," missing in the LXX).[58] In MT 7:1–2, editor II expanded the short heading of LXX 7:1, "Hear the word of the Lord, all you of Judah," with information from 7:10 and the parallel passage in chapter 26.[59]

> MT Jer 7:1–2 פ (* [asterisk] The word which came to Jeremiah from the Lord: "Stand at the gate of the house of the Lord, and there proclaim this word" : [obelus]) "Hear the word of the Lord, all you of Judah (who enter these gates to worship the Lord)." ס

This expansion of MT 7:1–2 is preceded by *petuhah* and followed by *setumah*. The Greek text of these verses is marked with an asterisk.[60] Tov notes also that in Edition II (and not in Edition I) several sections are duplicated: 15:13–14, followed by *setumah*, is found also in 17:3–4, verses followed by *setumah* and missing in the LXX;[61] the unit 46:27–28, enclosed

---

emias, Baruch, Threni, Epistula Ieremiae, SVTG (Göttingen: Vandenhoeck & Ruprecht, 1957), 379–80; Hermann-Josef Stipp, *Das masoretische und alexandrinische Sondergut des Jeremiabuches: Textgeschichtlicher Rang, Eigenarten, Triebkräfte*, OBO 136 (Fribourg: Editions Universitaires; Göttingen: Vandenhoeck & Ruprecht, 1994), 133.

56. Ziegler, *Ieremias*, 263.

57. J. Gerald Janzen, *Studies in the Text of Jeremiah*, HSM 6 (Cambridge: Harvard University Press, 1973), 92–93, 220–21.

58. William L. Holladay, *Jeremiah 2: A Commentary on the Book of the Prophet Jeremiah, Chapters 26–52*, Hermeneia (Minneapolis: Fortress, 1989), 170.

59. Stipp, *masoretische und alexandrinische Sondergut*, 109.

60. Ziegler, *Ieremias*, 183.

61. Ibid., 233.

by *setumot*, is duplicated in 30:10–11, verses placed between *setumah* and *petuhah*.[62]

The duplicate 6:13–15 // 8:10b–12 includes also 6:12 as well as 8:10a, as confirmed by the *parashiyyah* which is delimited by *setumot* at the beginning and end of 8:10–12 and the concluding *setumah* in 6:12–15.

Jer 8:10–12	Jer 6:12–15
ס 10 So I will give their wives to other men, their fields to new masters,	12 Their houses shall pass to other men, so also their fields and their wives. Yes, I will stretch my hand over those living in this land—it is Yahweh who speaks.
for all, least no less than greatest, all are out for dishonest gain; prophet no less than priest, all practice fraud… —says Yahweh. ס	13 For all, least no less than greatest, all are out for dishonest gain; prophet no less than priest, all practice fraud… —says Yahweh. ס

Edition II duplicates also 15:13–14 in 17:3–4. Both passages end with *setumah*. The omission in the LXX of 17:1–4 proves that this whole unit, marked with an asterisk in the Greek,[63] is an addition to the MT enclosed by *setumot*.

The pericope 46:27–28, enclosed by *setumot* and missing in the LXX, duplicates 30:10–11, also delimited by *setumot* and marked with an asterisk.[64]

The doublet of 49:22 in 48:40b, 41b also includes 48:40a, which marks the beginning of the unit, preceded by *setumah* before 48:40 and ending with *setumah* after 49:22.

Jer 48:40b, 41b	Jer 49:22
40a ס For Yahweh says this:	
40b (“Here is one who hovers like an eagle, who will spread his wings over Moab.)	“Here is someone who soars and hovers like an eagle, who will spread his wings over Bozrah.
41a The towns will be captured, The strongholds seized.	

62. Tov, “Literary History of the Book of Jeremiah,” 219.

63. Ziegler, *Ieremias*, 175, 233.

64. “[I]n plerisque codicibus vulgatae editionis sub asteriscis de Theodotione addita est” (ibid., 351–52).

41b (And the heart of Moab's warriors that day will be like the heart of a woman in labor pains.)	And the heart of Edom's warriors that day will be like the heart of a woman in labor pains." ס
42 Moab will be destroyed, no longer a people ..."	

Edition II "added many Deuteronomistic phrases ... and also complete sections that abound with Deuteronomistic phraseology such as 11:7–8; 29:16–20, and sections of chap. 27 (vv. 7, 13–14a, 17)."[65] Of these, the pericope 29:16–20 that is missing in the LXX (36:16–20 with an asterisk) appears between *setumot*. According to Tov, "[t]he greatest contextual difficulty caused by the insertion is that the verse before the insert (v. 15) has its direct continuation in verse 21 and that verses 16–20 have no connection at all with that verse."[66] But 29:8–9, signaled by *petuhah* and *setumah*, are to be placed after 29:15. In this way, 29:15 has its continuation in 29:8–9 and thereafter also in the added unit of 29:16–20.

Tov signals the numerous additions present in MT 27:19–22 (27:19–20 between *petuhah* and *setumah* and 27:21–22 between *setumah* and *petuhah*). He points to the technique termed *Wiederaufnahme* or "resumptive repetition" in 27:21: "After the long additions in vv. 19 and 20, ed. II felt the need to repeat the introductory formula of the prophecy as well as the object of the prophecy: [19]For thus said the Lord (of Hosts ... [21]Thus said the Lord of Hosts, the God of Israel, concerning the vessels...)."[67]

LXX Jer 34:16–18	MT Jer 27:19–22 (LXX 34:19–22, Hexaplaric)
16 For thus said the Lord	פ 19 For thus said the Lord
	(of Hosts concerning the columns, the tank, the stands and)
concerning the rest of the vessels	concerning the rest of the vessels
	(which remain in this city),
17 which the king	20 which (Nebuchadnezzar) the king
of Babylon did not take	of Babylon did not take
when he exiled Jeconiah	when he exiled Jeconiah
	(son of Jehoiakim, king of Judah)
from Jerusalem.	from Jerusalem

65. Tov, "Literary History of the Book of Jeremiah," 220.

66. Ibid., 226; Stipp, *Masoretische und alexandrinische Sondergut*, 121–22.

67. Tov, "Literary History of the Book of Jeremiah," 235.

	(to Babylon, with all the nobles of Judah and Jerusalem ס
	21 For thus said the Lord of Hosts, the God of Israel, concerning the vessels remaining in the House of the Lord, in the royal palace of Judah and Jerusalem):
18 They shall be brought to Babylon	22 They shall be brought to Babylon (and there they shall remain until I take not of them)
—declares the Lord.	—declares the Lord— (and bring them up and restore them to this place). פ

The mechanism of resumptive repetition (*Wiederaufnahme*) indicates that the material interposed between the repeated terms has been added. However 27:19–20a (except additions in parentheses) are found in the short version of the LXX. The material really added to the long version of the MT is that which follows in 27:21, parallel to 27:20: "concerning the rest of the vessels (which remain in this city) … concerning the vessels remaining in the House of the Lord." The resumptive repetition works well between "Jerusalem … Jerusalem" or "of Judah and Jerusalem … of Judah and Jerusalem." In any case the presence of a *setumah* between 27:20 and 27:21 seems to be indicative of an insertion at that point.

In the same volume, Alexander Rofé shows how a Priestly source text has been supplemented by a later Deuteronomistic writer.[68] In this case, there are no signs of masoretic division corresponding to the Deuteronomistic addition of Josh 20:4–5, missing in the LXX. But Rofé published another important article on the end of the book of Joshua according to the LXX, concluding

> that the sequence reflected in the LXX at the end of the book of Joshua—the death of Joshua and the elders, the beginning of the people's sin, the submission of Eglon (and the appearance of Ehud)—is most likely the original sequence of an ancient scroll of the books of Joshua–Judges, remnants of which still existed in Second Temple times.[69]

68. Alexander Rofé, "Joshua 20: Historico-Literary Criticism Illustrated," in Tigay, *Empirical Models for Biblical Criticism*, 131–47.

69. Rofé, "End of the Book of Joshua according to the Septuagint," 32.

According to Rofé, LXX Josh 24:33a, b is connected with Judg 3: פ 12–30 ס, skipping the material between, largely Deuteronomistic (1:1–3:11) (see the discussion of Joshua in §5, below).[70]

3. *Vacats* in the Qumran Manuscripts and the Transposition or Addition of Literary Units in Qumran writings

The plurality of editions spreads to the Apocrypha and Pseudepigrapha as well as to Qumran writings such as 4QReworked Pentateuch, the Temple Scroll, the Community Rule, the Damascus Document, and the Hodayyot. The study of the composition techniques in these writings, especially those of transposition and ring composition (*Wiederaufnahme*), contribute greatly to the study of the formation and growth of the biblical books.[71]

The transposed pericopes in the biblical books appear frequently marked by signs of *petuhah* or *setumah*. According to the editors of 4Q51:

> [O]ut of seventy-six occurrences of paragraph-divisions in 4QSam[a] [4Q51], 𝔐 [MT] has paragraph-divisions at the same place in the text on forty occasions, or slightly more than fifty percent of the time. This statistic is evidence that no fixed tradition of paragraphing reflecting the tradition of intervals fixed in the Rabbinic Recension existed in the scribal tradition found in 4QSam[a]. The roughly half of the intervals in agreement are sufficiently explained by sense breaks in the narrative or in the poetry.[72]

The SP and 4Q22, the Temple Scroll (11Q19–20), and 4QReworked Pentateuch (4Q158, 4Q364–366) show significant cases of transposition

---

70. Ibid.

71. "The Dead Sea Scrolls can offer material evidence and criteria for the sort of literary processes in the Hebrew Bible that critical biblical scholarship hypothesizes. But the mutual relationship possibly extends further than that. Several contributors argue for understanding the compositional history of the Hebrew Bible and Second Temple texts as one of continual exegetical reflection and textual growth" (Reinhard Kratz and Mladen Popovic, "Editorial Note," *DSD* 20 [2013]: 347; see also Sarianna Metso, "Methodological Problems in Reconstructing History from Rule Texts Found at Qumran," *DSD* 11 [2004]: 315–35).

72. Frank M. Cross et al., eds., *Qumran Cave 4:XII: 1–2 Samuel*, DJD 17 (Oxford: Clarendon, 2005), 19.

of literary units from one context to another or of insertion of biblical or "new" material at points signaled by masoretic divisions.

Samaritan Pentateuch: In the SP, the instructions for the making of the incense altar, Exod 30:1–10 enclosed by *petuhot*, are relocated to after Exod 26:35.[73] The same rearrangement is partially extant in the proto-Samaritan manuscript 4Q22. The pericope 30:1–10 is an appendix to chapters 25–31.[74] 4Q22 ends at Exod 37:16, a verse followed by *petuhah*.

Temple Scroll: The Temple Scroll "collects together a variety of laws pertaining to sacrifice and indeed TS proceeds topically, rather than according to the pentateuchal sequence, from this point [Deut 17:1] all the way through 55:13, where it finally arrives back at Deut 17:2 (Deut 17:1 occurs at TS 52:4)."[75] Deuteronomy 17:1 is a good example of a movable unit framed by signs of *setumah*.

4QReworked Pentateuch: In 4Q158 frags. 1–2 (4QRP[a]) the episode of Gen 32:25–32 on Jacob's wrestling with the angel and the one of Exod 4:27–28 on Moses's meeting with Aaron appear juxtaposed at a point marked with *petuhah* at the beginning of the inserted section, before Exod 4:27.[76]

In 4Q364 15 (4QRP[b]), in the *vacat* (*petuhah*) between Exod 24:18 and 25:1–2, a "new text" was inserted:

> The two lines of additional text after v 18 (lines 3–4) may have described what God showed Moses during the forty days and forty nights before His speech (chap. 25) at the end of that period. A similarly dated revelation to Moses is recorded in *Jub.* 1:4ff.: "And Moses was on the Mount

73. Judith E. Sanderson, *An Exodus Scroll from Qumran: 4QpaleoExod[m] and the Samaritan Tradition*, HSS 30 (Atlanta: Scholars Press, 1986), 11–13, 310; Patrick W. Skehan, Eugene Ulrich, and Judith E. Sanderson, eds., *Qumram Cave 4:IV: Palaeo-Hebrew and Greek Biblical Manuscripts*, DJD 9 (Oxford: Clarendon, 1992), 109–30; Zahn, *Rethinking Rewritten Scripture*, 159; J. Gerald Janzen, *Exodus*, WC (Louisville: Westminster John Knox, 1997), 216.

74. Bogaert, "Importance de la Septante," 401; George J. Brooke, "The Temple Scroll and the LXX Exodus 35–40," in *Septuagint, Scrolls and Cognate Writings: Papers Presented at the International Symposium on the Septuagint and Its Relationship to the Dead Sea Scrolls and Other Writings*, ed. George J. Brooke and Barnabas Lindars, SCS 33 (Atlanta: Scholars Press, 1992), 81–106; John I. Durham, *Exodus*, WBC 3 (Waco, TX: Word, 1987), 351.

75. Zahn, *Rethinking Rewritten Scripture*, 222.

76. Crawford, *Rewriting Scripture in Second Temple Times*, 52–53.

> forty days and forty nights and God taught him the earlier and the later history of the division of all the days of the law and of the testimony."[77]

Exodus 24:18 informs that Moses was with God on Mount Sinai for forty days and nights. Following this, 4Q364 XV 3–4 includes a two line addition before Exod 25:1: "] … he made known to him everything […] he did at the time of assembly [." The impulse for this addition would seem to be similar to that in Jubilees (1:4): to expand on what God revealed to Moses during that time.[78]

In 4Q365 36 (4QRP^c^), Num 27:11 is followed immediately (without even a paragraph break) by Num 36:1–2, showing that the two passages had been joined.[79] The two pericopes concern the inheritance of the daughters of Zelophehad. The end of the first unit, 27:11, is pointed out by a *setumah*, as well as the beginning of the added pericope, 36:1–2, which is marked with a *petuhah*. According to Sidnie White Crawford, "Since 4Q365 is fragmentary it is impossible to tell if the passage from ch 36 has been transferred to the middle of ch. 27 or whether 27:1–11 has been transferred to the beginning of ch. 36."[80] This unit, 27:1–11, appears enclosed by *setumot*.

According to Crawford, 4Q365 28

> contains the text of Num 4:47–49 (the end of ch. 4), followed by a blank line, then continuing with Num 7:1. The blank line may be a signal to the reader that an exegetical change has occurred, but we cannot be certain. The reason for the joining of these two passages is that both concern the service of the tabernacle; ch. 4 ends with the census of the Levites to determine who was eligible to serve in the tabernacle; ch. 7 begins with

---

77. Emanuel Tov and Sidnie A. White, "4QRP[b] (4Q364)," in *Qumran Cave 4:VIII: Parabiblical Texts, Part 1*, ed. Harold Attridge et al., *DJD* 13 (Oxford: Clarendon, 1997), 223; see also Christoph Berner, "The Redaction History of the Sinai Pericope (Exod 19–24) and Its Continuation in 4Q158," *DSD* 20 (2013): 400 n. 42.

78. Daniel K. Falk, *The Parabiblical Texts: Strategies for Extending the Scriptures among the Dead Sea Scrolls*, CQS 8, LSTS 63 (London: T&T Clark, 2007), 117; Michael Segal, "4QReworked Pentateuch or 4QPentateuch?," in *The Dead Sea Scrolls: Fifty Years after Their Discovery: Proceedings of the Jerusalem Congress, July 20–25, 1997*, ed. Lawrence H. Schiffman, Emanuel Tov, and James C. VanderKam (Jerusalem: Israel Exploration Society, 2000), 391–99.

79. Emanuel Tov and Sidnie A. White, "4QRP[c] (4Q365)," in Attridge, *Qumran Cave 4:VIII*, 255–318.

80. Crawford, *Rewriting Scripture in Second Temple Times*, 45–46.

> the completion of the tabernacle. The intervening material in chs. 5 and 6 is a miscellaneous collection of laws not relating to the service of the tabernacle; therefore it makes exegetical sense to join the end of ch. 4 with the beginning of ch. 7.[81]

This joining occurs precisely at a point marked by a blank line. The first unit Num 4:47–49 ends with a *petuhah* and the beginning of the added unit also follows a sign of *petuhah*.

4Q365 6a II and 6c contains also a large addition of new material, inserted after Exod 15:21 at a point marked with *setumah* and a blank line.[82] After Exod 15:21, "Sing to the Lord, for he has triumphed gloriously; horse and rider he has thrown into the sea," 4Q365 attempts to supply Miriam's song in full, distinct from Moses's song. A somewhat expanded version appears in Targum Pseudo-Jonathan and Targum Neofiti to Exod 15:21.[83]

In the same way 4Q366 4 (4QRP[d]) relocates Deut 16:13–14 to after Num 29:32–30:1, thus bringing into proximity two laws on the festival of Sukkot. The unit Num 29:32–30:1 appears between *petuhah* and *setumah*. The transposition occurs at a *vacat* signaled by *setumah*.

4QRP juxtaposes pericopes brought from different contexts, including:

4Q365 36 groups together the story about an inheritance claim by Zelophehad's daughters (Num 27:1–11, enclosed by *setumot*) with what appears to be an appendix to the story at the end of the book (Num 36:1–11, preceded by *petuhah*). 4Q366 IV, 1 brings together laws concerning Sukkot from Num 29:32–30:1, enclosed by *petuhot* and Deut 16:13–14, preceded by *petuhah*.

---

81. Ibid., 46.

82. "The first [addition] occurs in frgs. 6a–c, col. ii, in the text of Exodus 15. Frg. 6b (part of col. i) of 4Q365 contains Exod 15:16–20 in its extant text. Since we do not have the bottom of the fragment, it is likely that the text continued through v. 21. Verse 22 begins on line 8 of frg. 6a, col. ii. Between v. 21, which begins at the end of col. i, and v. 22, which commences on line 8 of col. ii, intervene at least seven lines of text not found in any other witness to the text of Exodus.… The additional material draws on the Song of Moses as its primary inspiration" (ibid., 48–49).

83. Falk, *Parabiblical Texts*, 116; George J. Brooke, "Power to the Powerless: A Long-Lost Song of Miriam," *BAR* 20 (1994): 62–65.

4Q385 1 (4QpsEzek[a]) paraphrases the oracle against Egypt in Ezek 30:1–5,[84] enclosed by *petuhot*, perhaps a late complement to the preceding text. Two *parashiyyot* delimit two literary units: 30:1–5 and 30:6–9. Verse 5, constructed in prose, may be a later addition,[85] inserted between both pericopes.

Equally in 4Q524 (4QT[b]) the laws governing sexual relations are followed by the law of levirate marriage, Deut 25:5–10. According to the editor, Émile Puech, "Après un petit *vacat* commencerait une citation apparemment complète de Dt 25:5–9 (10?), le paragraphe concernant la loi ou le devoir du lévirat" ("After a small *vacat* begins a seemingly complete citation of Deut 25:5–9 [10?], the paragraph about the law and the duty of the levirate").[86] Puech's doubt regarding the inclusion of 25:10 is solved if we take into account that the pericope is completed with this verse as shown by the masoretic division that includes Deut 15:5–10 between two *setumot*.

Testimonia, tefillim, and phylacteries link various biblical passages one after another. The units quoted are marked by masoretic signs of division.

4Q175 (4QTest) contains four excerpts: (1) Exod 20:18, preceded by *petuhah*, + Deut 5:28–29 + 18:18–19; (2) a quotation from Num 24:15–17, part of the oracle of Balaam (the same scriptural passage is used in the Damascus Document 7:19–20 and the War Scroll 11:6–7); (3) a quotation of Deut 33:8–11, enclosed by *setumot*; and (4) a quotation of Josh 6:26 (following the LXX *Vorlage*), preceded by *petuhah* and followed by *setumah*.[87]

The passages to be included in the tefillim were standardized by the rabbinic period to four: Exod 13:1–10, included between *petuhah* and *setumah*; Exod 13:11–16, between *setumot*; Deut 6:4–9 (*shema*ʿ), enclosed by *petuhah* and *setumah*; and Deut 11:13–21, also marked by *setumot*.[88]

84. Monica Brady, "Biblical Interpretation in the 'Pseudo-Ezekiel' Fragments (4Q383–391) from Cave Four," in *Biblical Interpretation at Qumran*, ed. Matthias Henze, SDSS 6 (Grand Rapids: Eerdmans, 2005), 95.

85. Daniel I. Block, *The Book of Ezekiel: Chapters 25–48*, NICOT (Grand Rapids: Eerdmans, 1998), 158.

86. Émile Puech, ed., *Qumrân Grotte 4:XVIII: Textes hébreux (4Q521–4Q528, 4Q576–4Q579)*, DJD 25 (Oxford: Clarendon, 1998), 107.

87. Crawford, *Rewriting Scripture in Second Temple Times*, 35; George J. Brooke, "Thematic Commentaries on Prophetic Scriptures," in Henze, *Biblical Interpretation at Qumran*, 138–40; David Katzin, "The Use of Scripture in 4Q175," *DSD* 20 (2013): 223.

88. Crawford, *Rewriting Scripture in Second Temple Times*, 33.

The Qumran tefillim contain a wider array of passages beyond those mandated by the rabbis, including Deut 5:1–6:9; 10:12–11:21; and Exod 12:43–13:16; and all three sections are framed by *petuhah* and *setumah*.

The phylactery 4Q134 (4Qphyl G) contains Deut 5:1–21 on the *recto* and Exod 13:11–12 on the *verso*. "The governing text of the Decalogue is clearly Deuteronomy, since it begins with Deut 5:1."[89] Both passages are the starting points of important pericopes marked with masoretic divisions.

4. Exodus

The order of the text of Exodus presents considerable differences between the MT and LXX. Chapters 25–31 on the building of the sanctuary and on its ministers have their counterpart in chapters 35–40, an almost word for word repetition of chapters 25–31. The orders given in the first section are carried out in the second. Suffice it here to note the signs of masoretic division delimiting the transposed units between the LXX and the MT (→) and the doublets present in the MT (//).[90]

LXX	MT	Subject	Doublet
(cf. 37:1–2)	ס 36:8–19 ס	Tabernacle	//MT ס 26:1–11, 14 פ
(cf. 38:18–21)	ס 36:20–34	Framework	//MT פ 26:15–29, 30 ס
37:3–6	→ (-) 36:35–38 פ	Veil	//MT ס 26:31–32, 36–37 ס
38:1–8	→ פ 37:1–9 פ	Ark	//MT פ 25:10–20 (-)
38:9–12	→ פ 37:10–16 פ	Table for the offertory bread	//MT פ 25:23–29 פ
38:13–17	→ פ 37:17–24 פ	Lamp-stand	//MT פ 25:31–39 [40 ס]
> LXX OL	פ 37:25–28 (-)	Altar of incense	//MT פ 30:1–5 (-)
38:25	(-) 37:29 פ	Altar of incense	//MT פ 30:22–33 ס 34–38 פ
(cf. 38:22–24)	פ 38:1–7 ס	Altar of holocaust	//MT ס 27:1–8 ס

89. Ibid., 34.

90. Samuel R. Driver, *An Introduction to the Literature of the Old Testament*, 5th ed. (Edinburgh: T&T Clark, 1894), 37–38. On the Greek textual tradition and its relation with the Hebrew text, see Anneli Aejmelaeus, "Septuagintal Translation Techniques: A Solution to the Problem of the Tabernacle Account," in Brooke and Lindars, *Septuagint, Scrolls and Cognate Writings*, 381–402; Martha Lynn Wade, *Consistency of Translation Techniques in the Tabernacle Accounts of Exodus in the Old Greek*, SCS 49 (Atlanta: Society of Biblical Literature, 2003).

→ 38:26	→ ס 38:8 ס	Bronze basin	//MT פ 30:17–18a (-)
→ 37:7–18	→ ס 38:9–20 ס	Court	//MT ס 27:9–19 ס
→ 37:19–21	→ ס 38:21–23 ס	Amount of metal used	
→ 39:1–10	→ ס 38:24–31 (-)	Amount of metal used	cf. MT פ 30:11–16 פ
→ 36:8b–40	→ 39:1–31 ס	Ephod	//MT ס 28:1–43 ס
→ 39:11, 14–23	→ ס 39:32–43 פ	Finished work presented	

In Exod 6:12 פ … 30 פ a *Wiederaufnahme* defines the extent of the insertion between the repeated sentence: "And Moses spoke in front of the Lord, '…How will Pharaoh listen to me, poor speaker that I am?'… And Moses spoke in front of the Lord, '…How will Pharaoh listen to me, poor speaker that I am?'"

5. Joshua

Joshua 6: פ 26 // 1 Kgs 16:34 ס (> LXX^{L}, Josephus): Verse 26, preceded by *petuhah* ("Cursed be the man who proceeds to rebuild this city, Jericho…)," corresponds to 1 Kgs 16:34, followed by *setumah*: "It was in his time that Hiel of Bethel rebuilt Jericho…, just as Yahweh had foretold through Joshua son of Nun." This verse is omitted in the Lucianic text. This implies that it was not part of the OG and of its Hebrew *Vorlage*. The presence of this verse in 4Q175 proves the independent and mobile character of this unit (see §3, above).

Joshua 8: פ 30–35 פ: This pericope is introduced by the particle אז, frequently used to unite a pericope to the context: "*Then* Joshua built an altar to Yahweh." 4Q47 presents this pericope before 5:2–7, preceded by *setumah*, whereas the LXX has this passage after the unit 9:1–2, also between *petuhot* in the MT.[91] A repetition in the OL frames the pericope 9:1–2. The first form of the text follows the order of the LXX. It appears between 8:1–29 and 8:30–35. The second form is located, according to the MT, between 8:30–35 and 9:3–27.[92] In this way, it underscores the mobile character of this literary piece, which is out of place in its present context in

91. Ulrich, "4QJosh[a]." For an up-to-date detailed study of this passage, with discussion and critique of the different scholarly positions (Emanuel Tov, A. Graeme Auld, Aaron Kempinski, Eugene Ulrich, Alexander Rofé, Ed Noort), see Michaël N. van der Meer, *Formation and Reformulation: The Redaction of the Book of Joshua in the Light of the Oldest Textual Witnesses*, VTSup 102 (Leiden: Brill, 2004), 479–522.

92. Ulysse Robert, ed., *Heptateuchi partis posterioris versio latina antiquissima e Codice Lugdunensi* (Lyon: Rey, 1900).

the MT and can appear in three different locations, either after the report of the conquest of Ai (MT); after 9:2 and before the story of the Gibeonites (LXX); or before 5:2–7, the account of the circumcision at Gilgal (4Q47).

OL	LXX	4Q47	MT	Subject
	5:1	5:1	ס 5:1	Kings of the Amorites
		8:30–35		Altar on Mount Ebal
	5:2–12	5:X, 2–7…	ס 5:2–12 ס	Circumcision at Gilgal
	8:1–29		פ 8:1–29 פ	Conquest of Ai
	>		פ *8:30–35* פ	Altar on Mount Ebal
9:1–2	9:1–2		פ 9:1–2 פ	Six–seven peoples
8:30–35	*8:30–35*			Altar on Mount Ebal
9:1–2				Six–seven peoples
	9:3–27		פ 9:3–27 פ	Gibeonites in the camp of Gilgal

Joshua 10: ס 12–14 פ: Here also the particle אז is used to introduce a passage, in this case a poetic text: "*Then* Joshua spoke to Yahweh … 'Sun, stand still over Gibeon.'" In 10:15, omitted in the LXX, "[t]he glossator did not recognize the disgressionary character of vv 12–14."[93]

Joshua 10: פ 33: The pattern אז + perfect tense "must be seen as disjunctive and disgressionary within a series of converted imperfects that unite the entire section, vv. 29–43."[94]

Joshua 16:10 פ: After the *petuhah*, the LXX contains an added verse about the conquest of Gezer by Pharaoh. This verse is almost identical with 1 Kgs 9:16 (LXX 5:14).

Joshua 19:47–48 פ. After the *petuhah*, elements have been added in the *Vorlage* of the LXX describing the migration of the Danites to the North. These elements run parallel to Judg 1:34–35. Furthermore the LXX transposes 19:48 at the end of 19:46 and after 19:46, 48, 47 adds a text corresponding to Judg 1:35, followed by *petuhah*.

Joshua 19: פ 49–50 blank line (*seder*) 51 פ: The masoretic divisions distinguish two units, each of which represents a different end of the preceding section on the division and distribution of the land. The first unit, 19:49–50, between *petuhah* and a blank line (*seder*), focuses on Joshua and the legitimation of his personal fief. In the second unit, 19:51, enclosed by a blank line and *petuhah*, Joshua takes second place, between Eleazar

93. Robert G. Boling, *Joshua: A New Translation with Notes and Commentary*, AB 6 (Garden City, NY: Doubleday, 1982), 277.

94. Ibid., 282.

the priest and the patriarchal chiefs. The whole opens and closes with two parallel expressions with some textual variants: "49 They completed the distribution of the land … 51 … They completed the apportionment of the land."[95]

Joshua 20: פ 1–9 פ: The LXX preserves a late ("P-like") version of the law regarding cities of refuge that lacks the addition of the MT in 20:4–6.[96] This addition is to be related with Num 35:9–34, enclosed by *petuhah*, and with Deut 19:1–13, between *setumot*. The long text of the MT reflects the terminology and quotations from both the Priestly Code in Num 35:9–34 and Deut 19:1–13. In the LXX, on the other hand, the quotation from Deuteronomy is lacking in 20:4–6. An earlier stage of Joshua referred only to the Priestly formulation of the law of the cities of refuge. The later edition added the terminology of, and a quote from, Deuteronomy.[97]

Joshua 21:42 ס: In the *vacat* after 21:42, the LXX (21:42a–d) places the passage of MT 19:49b–50, which is an editorial addition preceded and followed by *petuhah* and followed by the sign *seder*.[98]

Joshua 21: ס 43–45 פ (end of the apportioning): This seems to be an ancient ending of Joshua to be connected with Judg 2:8–10.*[99] The various endings of the book of Joshua and connections with Judges can only be explained by supposing variant editions of these books (see below).[100]

Joshua 24:28 פ 31: The text of Josh 24:28–31 appears in the LXX with verses in the following order: 28, 31, 29–30, coinciding with the order of Judg 2:6–9. The *petuhah* between 24:28 and 24:29 defines two pericopes: 24:28, 31 ("Then Joshua sent the people away)" and 24:29–30 ("After these things Joshua … died)."

---

95. Ibid., 469–70.

96. Carr, *Formation of the Hebrew Bible*, 171; Rofé, "Joshua 20."

97. Rofé, "Joshua 20"; Tov, "Growth of the Book of Joshua," 325.

98. "A long gap in the MT is here filled from the LXX" (Boling, *Joshua*, 483).

99. Uwe Becker, *Richterzeit und Königtum: Redaktionsgeschichtliche Studien zum Richterbuch*, BZAW 192 (Berlin: de Gruyter, 1990), 68–72; Erhard Blum, "Der kompositionelle Knoten am Übergang von Josua zu Richter: Ein Entflechtungsvorschlag," in *Deuteronomy and Deuteronomic Literature: Festschrift C. H. W. Brekelmans*, ed. Marc Vervenne and Johan Lust, BETL 133 (Leuven: Peeters, 1997), 181–212.

100. Books of the Pentateuch conclude also with different appendixes. See Eep Talstra, "Deuteronomy 31: Confusion or Conclusion? The Story of Moses' Threefold Succession," in Vervenne and Lust, *Deuteronomy and Deuteronomic Literature*, 87–110.

LXX Josh 24:28, 31, 29–30 (MT 24:28–31)	MT Judg 2:6–7, 8–9
(28) Joshua dismissed the people, each man to his patrimony.	(6) פ Joshua dismissed the people, and the Israelites went off to occupy the country, each man to his allotted portion.
(31) Israel served the Lord during the lifetime of Joshua and of the elders who outlived him and who well knew all that the Lord had done for Israel. פ	(7) The people worshiped the Lord as long as Joshua was alive and the elders who survived him, who had witnessed the whole great work which the Lord had done for Israel.
(29) After these things, Joshua son of Nun the servant of the Lord died; he was a hundred and two years old. (30) They buried him within the border of his own patrimony…	(8) Joshua son of Nun, the servant of the Lord, died at the age of a hundred and ten years. (9) And they buried him within the border of his own property…

Joshua 24:33 (the end of the book): According to Rofé, LXX Josh 24:33b is connected with Judg 3:12–30, skipping the material between, which is largely Deuteronomistic (1:1–3:11).[101] Going further beyond the proposal made by Rofé, LXX Josh 24:33b contains three elements that are not directly connected with Judg 3:12, but instead mark three different links: with 2:6 (MT "the Israelites went each man to his allotted portion)," with 2:11–13 (MT "they worshipped the Baalim)," and with 3:12–14. (MT "and the Lord gave Eglon king of Moab power over them)." The extent of the literary units and the points of insertion are marked by signs of division.

Joshua (Linking with Judges)	Judges	Interposed Unit
24:33b$^{\alpha}$ LXX οἱ δὲ υἱοὶ Ισραηλ ἀπήλθοσαν ἕκαστος εἰς τὸν τόπον αὐτῶν… ("the Israelites went each man to his place…")	= פ 2:6 ילכו בני ישראל איש לנחלתו… ("the Israelites went each man to his allotted portion…")	ס 1:1–2:5 פ
24:33b$^{\beta}$ LXX καὶ ἐσέβοντο οἱ υἱοὶ Ισραηλ τὴν 'Αστάρτην… ("they worshiped the Ashtoreth…")	= פ 2:11 ויעבדו את הבעלים + καὶ τῇ 'Αστάρτῃ (L) ("they worshiped the Baalim")	ס 1:1–2:10 ס

101. Rofé, "End of the Book of Joshua according to the Septuagint," 32.

24:33b^{γ} LXX καὶ παρέδωκεν αὐτοὺς Κύριος εἰς χεῖρας Εγλωμ τῷ βασιλεῖ Μωαβ… ("and the Lord put them in the hands of Eglon…)	= ויחזק יהוה את עגלון 3:12 פ מלך מואב… ("and the Lord gave Eglon king of Moab power over them…")	ס 1:1–3:11 ס

These duplicates betray a complex editorial process that left its traces in the two editions or textual forms in which the end of Joshua and the beginning of Judges have been transmitted (MT, LXX). They differ mainly in how the Deuteronomistic materials inserted in Judg 1–3 as well as the stories added at the end of Judges (chs. 16 and 17–18) were integrated.

6. Judges

Judges 6: **פ** 7–10 **פ** (> 4Q49): 4Q49 is the only extant witness which does not include the literary unit found in 6:7–10 of the MT and LXX, although Hebrew manuscripts and the *kaige* LXX^{B} text also omit 6:7a. Verses 8–10 have been generally recognized by modern critics as a literary insertion attributed in the past to an Elohistic source and now generally considered a piece of early Deuteronomistic (Dtr^{1}),[102] late nomistic (Dtr^{N}),[103] or post-Deuteronomistic redaction.[104]

4Q49 is "manifestly non-aligned, and actually independent" and "may reflect a different literary edition."[105] This manuscript represents "a

102. Robert G. Boling, *Judges: Introduction, Translation, and Commentary*, AB 6A (Garden City, NY: Doubleday, 1975), 30, 36, passim.

103. Rudolf Smend, "Das Gesetz und die Völker: Ein Beitrag zur deuteronomistischen Redaktionsgeschichte," in *Probleme biblischer Theologie: Festschrift für Gerhard von Rad zum 70. Geburtstag*, ed. Hans Walter Wolff (Munich: Kaiser, 1971), 494–509; Smend, *Die Entstehung des Alten Testaments*, 4th ed. (Stuttgart: Kohlhammer, 1989), 116; Walter Dietrich, *Prophetie und Geschichte: Eine redaktionsgeschichtliche Untersuchung zum deuteronomistischen Geschichtswerk*, FRLANT 108 (Göttingen: Vandenhoeck & Ruprecht, 1972), 133; Timo Veijola, *Das Königtum in der Beurteilung der deuteronomistischen Historiographie: Eine redaktionsgeschichtliche Untersuchung*, AASF Series B 198 (Helsinki: Suomalainen Tiedeakatemia, 1977), 43–48; J. Alberto Soggin, *Judges: A Commentary*, OTL (Philadelphia: Westminster, 1981), 112.

104. Anthony F. Campbell and Mark A. O'Brien, *Unfolding the Deuteronomistic History: Origins, Upgrades, Present Text* (Minneapolis: Fortress, 2000), 183; Becker, *Richterzeit und Königtum*, 144–45; Walter Groß, *Richter*, HThKAT (Freiburg: Herder, 2009), 369–70, 389, 396.

105. Emanuel Tov, "The Biblical Texts from the Judaean Desert: An Overview

form of the text independent from any other known text type, although it shares readings with the pre-Lucianic text and the OL," and "can confidently be seen as an earlier literary form of the book than our traditional texts."[106] "The convergence here of experienced literary-critical methodology applied to the composition and redaction of Judges plus the new manuscript evidence documenting those critical results strongly argues that 4QJudg[a] [4Q49] displays, if not an earlier edition of the entire book of Judges, at least an 'earlier literary form' for this passage."[107]

According to Richard Hess, it is unlikely that the minus in 4Q49 is related either to inadvertent loss due to haplography or intentional omission for theological reasons. But observing that Judg 6:7–10 is placed between *petuhot*, Hess attributes the omission in 4Q49 to "a tendency to insert, omit and change sections or paragraphs of biblical text at what would become the masoretic *parashoth* divisions of text," and he asserts, "the fragment is part of a larger manuscript that … may have been a collection of biblical texts serving a particular liturgical purpose for the community who read it."[108] Natalio Fernández Marcos supports the arguments by Hess and sustains that there is not "sufficient textual evidence to postulate two editions or different literary strata for the book of Judges."[109] According to Rofé, Hess's hypothesis is "farfetched" and Trebolle Barrera's "peremptory verdict has not been backed up by a minute examination of the style and the contents of the reproach."[110] The minus in 4Q49 is simply

---

and Analysis of the Published Texts," in *The Bible as Book: The Hebrew Bible and the Judaean Desert Discoveries*, ed. Edward D. Herbert and Emanuel Tov (London: The British Library; New Castle, DE: Oak Knoll, 2002), 156.

106. Julio Trebolle Barrera, "4QJudg[a]," in Ulrich et al., *Qumran Cave 4:IX*, 162.

107. Eugene Ulrich, "Deuteronomistically Inspired Scribal Insertions into the Developing Biblical Texts: 4QJudg[a] and 4QJer[a]," in *Houses Full of All Good Things: Essays in Memory of Timo Veijola*, ed. Juha Pakkala and Martti Nissinen, PFES 95 (Helsinki: Finnish Exegetical Society; Göttingen: Vandenhoeck & Ruprecht, 2008), 492.

108. Richard S. Hess, "The Dead Sea Scrolls and Higher Criticism of the Hebrew Bible: The Case of 4QJudg[a]," in *The Scrolls and the Scriptures: Qumran Fifty Years After*, ed. Stanley E. Porter and Craig A. Evans, JSPSup 26, RILP 3 (Sheffield: Sheffield Academic, 1997), 126–27.

109. Natalio Fernández Marcos, "The Hebrew and Greek Texts of Judges," in Schenker, *Earliest Text of the Hebrew Bible*, 1, 16.

110. Alexander Rofé, "Studying the Biblical Text in the Light of Historico-Literary Criticism: The Reproach of the Prophet in Judg 6:7–10 and 4QJudg[a]," in *The Dead Sea Scrolls in Context: Integrating the Dead Sea Scrolls in the Study of Ancient Texts,*

an accidental omission due to parablepsis. MT 6:7–10 is not post-Deuteronomistic or even Deuteronomistic but actually pre-Deuteronomistic, a text written in the eighth century BCE.[111]

However, the omissions and transpositions of pericopes placed between masoretic divisions are rather frequent. They are not "anomalies" (as Hess asserts) of texts other than the MT. In fact, many such omissions and transpositions are to be attributed to the activity of composers or editors in the period of the formation of the textual forms of the MT, 4Q49, and the LXX, rather than to scribes of a later period.

Judges 3: ס 31 ס: This verse framed by *setumot* is placed in the OG (LXX^{L}, OL) after 16:31, followed by *petuhah*: "After him came Shamgar son of Anath. He routed six hundred of the Philistines with an ox-goad; he too was a deliverer of Israel." This mobile unit is better placed at the end of chapter 16 because of the common reference to the Philistines rather than in chapter 3 where it interrupts the narratives of chapters 3 and 4. Just as it has different beginnings, so also Judges has three different endings: the first in 15:20, "Samson was judge in Israel in the days of the Philistines for twenty years"; the second in 16:31, where the previous ending is repeated, "He [Samson] was judge in Israel for twenty years" and followed by "After him came Shamgar…; he too was a deliverer of Israel"; and the third and actual ending includes the "appendixes" inserted in chapters 17–21.[112]

7. 1 Samuel

1 Samuel 1:1–28 פ + 2:11 (Codex Aleppo: פ 1–10 ס): This is a typical case in which the insertion of a literary unit has caused various textual variants in each textual form at the points of contact between the units that compose the text. At the point where the Song of Hannah (1:1–20) is inserted, several masoretic signs of division accumulate. At the end of 1:28, Codex Leningrad has a *petuhah*. 4Q51 presents a *vacat* after 1:28a, "is dedicated to Yahweh" ("middle of line blank") and another after "and she said" (2:1,

Languages, and Cultures, ed. Armin Lange, Emanuel Tov, and Matthias Weigold, 2 vols., VTSup (Leiden: Brill, 2011), 1:113 n. 5, 114.

111. Ibid., 121–22.

112. Julio Trebolle Barrera, "Samuel/Kings and Chronicles: Book Division and Text Composition," in *Studies in the Hebrew Bible, Qumran, and the Septuagint Presented to Eugene Ulrich*, ed. Peter W. Flint, Emanuel Tov, and James C. VanderKam, VTSup 101 (Leiden: Brill, 2006), 96–108.

"remainder of line blank"). The next line (line 17) begins with another *vacat* before the beginning of the Song of Hannah ("My heart exults…").[113] A repetition in 1:28b and 2:11a frames the inserted song. 4Q51 yields a meaningful variant, to be added to those in the MT and LXX.

1 Sam 1:28b
MT: וישתחו שם ליהוה, And (Elkanah) worshiped there the Lord
4Q51: ותעזבהו שם ותשתחו ליהוה, And (Hannah) left him there and worshiped the Lord
LXX^B: omitted; + *καὶ προσεκύνησεν* (-*αν* z) (*ἐκεῖ* N) *τῷ κυρίῳ* Ncgxz
LXX^L: + *καὶ προσεκύνησαν τῷ κυρίῳ* boc_2e_2 Arm

1 Sam 2:11
MT: וילך אלקנה הרמתה על ביתו, Then Elkanah went home to Ramah
LXX^B: *καὶ κατέλιπεν αὐτὸν ἐκεῖ ἐνώπιον κυρίου καὶ ἀπῆλθεν εἰς αρμαθαιμ* = ותעזבהו שם ל(פני) יהוה ותלך הרמתה, And Hannah left him there before the Lord and went home to Ramah
LXX^L: *καὶ κατέλιπον αὐτὸν ἐνώπιον κυρίου ἐκεῖ καὶ προσεκύνησαν τῷ κυρίῳ καὶ ἀπῆλθον εἰς αρμαθαιμ εἰς τὸν οἶκον αὐτῶν*

OL (MS 115)	LXX^B (Rahlfs)	LXX^L, Syriac, Vulgate	4Q51	MT
		And they	And (Hannah) left him there	28b פ/ס And (Elkanah)
		worshiped	and worshiped	worshiped there
		the Lord:	the Lord.	the Lord.
et dixit Anna	And Hannah said:			2:1 Hannah offered this prayer and said:
[…]	["Song"]	["Song"]	["Song"]	[פ Song of Hannah]
et reliquit ibi puerum ante dominum	And Hannah left him there before the Lord	And they left him before the Lord there,		2: פ 11 Then Elkanah

113. Cross et al., *Qumran Cave 4:XII*, 31.

		and worshiped the Lord,		
et abit in Armathem	and went home to Ramah	and went home for Ramah		went home to Ramah *vacat* (4Q51)

In 4Q51 and the LXX, the subject of the feminine verb form is Hannah, "and (Hannah) left him there" (ותעזבהו, *καὶ κατέλιπεν*),[114] as is the verb that follows, "and (Hannah) went home to Ramah" (*καὶ ἀπῆλθεν*, ותלך). In the MT, the subject seems to be Elkanah (וישתחו ... וילך). According to the narrative beginning with 2:24, Hannah is the main character of the actions narrated down to the end of the original story: "And Hannah left him there and went home to Ramah." The first of those two expressions appears in 4Q51 in 1:28b before the Song of Hannah, whereas in the LXX it appears after it, in 2:11a. Besides, the MT presents the reading וישתחו שם ליהוה, "And (Elkanah) worshiped there the Lord," which in 4Q51 appears in the feminine and without the reference to the sacred place (שם): "And (Hannah) worshiped the Lord," ותשתחו ליהוה. This expression facilitated the insertion of the song, and therefore it would be an addition to the expressions that concluded the narrative: "And (Hannah) left him there and went home to Ramah."

1 Samuel 2: *vacat* 11b–17 *vacat*: This literary unit concerning Eli's children was inserted in the preceding Samuel narrative at points probably marked by *vacats* in 4Q51 before 2:11b and before 2:18.[115] The sentence of 2:11a, "And Hannah left him there before the Lord and went home to Ramah" (LXX), concludes the story of chapter 1. The sentence of 2:11b, "and the boy was ministering to the Lord in the presence of Eli the priest," constitutes the transition to the episode on the sons of Eli. The pericope of 2:12–17 was inserted by the procedure of resumptive repetition (*Wiederaufnahme*).[116]

---

114. The verb κατελίπειν translates עזב, as also in 1 Sam 30:13; 31:7; 1 Kgs 11.33; 19:20; 2 Kgs 8:6.

115. Cross, *Qumran Cave 4:XII*, 32, 39; Andrew Fincke, *The Samuel Scroll from Qumran: 4QSam^a Restored and Compared to the Septuagint and 4QSam^c*, STDJ 43 (Leiden: Brill, 2001), 9–10.

116. Julio Trebolle Barrera, "Textual Criticism and the Composition History of Samuel: Connections between Pericopes in 1 Samuel 1–4," in *Archaeology of the Books of Samuel: The Entangling of the Textual and Literary History*, ed. Philippe Hugo and Adrian Schenker, VTSup 132 (Leiden: Brill, 2010), 261–86.

> *vacat* (4Q51) 2:11b *And the boy was in the service of the Lord* in the presence of Eli the priest
> 2:12–17 (pericope on the sons of Eli)
> *vacat* (4Q51) 2:18 *And Samuel was in the service of the Lord…*

1 Samuel 2: ס 22–26 ס: This unit also concerning the sons of Eli was inserted by *Wiederaufnahme* at points marked by *petuhot.*

> 2:21b *The boy Samuel grew up* with the Lord [MT עם יהוה]/in the presence of the Lord (4Q51, LXX).[117] ס [2:22–25 Eli, now a very old man, had heard how his sons were treating all the Israelites…] 2:26 *The boy Samuel grew up…* [והנער שמואל הלך וגדל … עם יהוה].

1 Samuel 2: ס 27–36 ס: This pericope is enclosed by repetitions linking the episodes about the birth and consecration of Samuel at Shiloh and those about Eli and his children (2:21 // 2:26 and 3:1 // 2:18).

1 Samuel 3: ס 2–3 פ: These verses are a parenthetical text ("At that time Eli was lying down in his room") linking the story of Eli and his sons (chs. 1–3) with that of the ark (chs. 4–6). The traces left in the syntax of the sentence in 3:2 betray an interpolation that begins with the initial formula ...ויהי ביום ההוא, "At that time…," which finds no continuation until 3:4: "(At that time) Yahweh called…"[118]

1 Samuel 6: ס 15–16 ס: Verse 15 interrupts the narrative and introduces the Levites in order that profane hands not touch the ark. The interpolation is produced by the usual *Wiederaufnahme*: "14 and offered … as a burnt-offering to the Lord … 15 … offered burnt-offerings … to the Lord."[119] After the insertion of 6:15, the story concludes in 6:16, followed by *setumah* (Codex Aleppo *petuhah*): "When the five lords of the Philistines saw it, they returned that day to Ekron." Verse 17, enclosed by *setu-*

117. MT ויגדל הנער שמאל עם יהוה, to be corrected with 4Q51 לפני יהוה and LXX ἐνώπιον κυρίου, "in the presence of the Lord"; see also Syriac and Targum.

118. A. Graeme Auld, *I and II Samuel: A Commentary*, OTL (Louisville: Westminster John Knox, 2011), 53.

119. Julio Trebolle Barrera, *Centena in libros Samuelis et Regum: Variantes textuales y composición literaria en los libros de Samuel y Reyes*, TECC 47 (Madrid: Consejo Superior de Investigaciones Científicas, 1989), 60–62.

mot, is also a parenthetical addition: "These are the gold tumors, which the Philistines returned as a guilt-offering to the Lord."

1 Samuel 8: ס 10 ס: This verse introduces into the text the reference to the people "asking" (שאל) for a king, who turns out to be Saul (שאול). The story uses a more common expression, "appoint [שים] a king for us," and goes directly from 8:9 to 8:11: "'you shall show them the ways of the king who shall reign over them.' Samuel said: 'These will be the ways of the king who will reign over you.'"

1 Samuel 10: line break 27 פ 11:1: At the intersection between the previous story about the election of Saul by lot and the next about the victory over the Ammonites, a number of variants in the MT, LXX, 4Q51, and Josephus occur. The Qumran text also has a long text and even a supralinear correction.[120]

1 Samuel 13: ס 19–23 ס: The notice of 13:19–22 ("There was not blacksmith to be found…") is also a parenthetical insertion.[121]

1 Samuel 15: ס 16 ס: This verse is omitted in Greek manuscript a_2 and by Lucifer of Cagliari. The insertion has occurred again using the procedure of *Wiederaufnahme*: "*Samuel said* to Saul, 'Stop! I will tell you what the Lord said to me last night.' He replied, 'Speak' 17 *Samuel said…*"

1 Samuel 15: ס 24–26 ס: These verses enclosed by *setumot* seem to be an addition introduced once more by resumptive repetition (*Wiederaufnahme*):

> *Because you have rejected the word of the Lord, he has also rejected you from being king.* ס
>
> > 24 Saul said to Samuel, "I have sinned; for I have transgressed the commandment of the Lord and your words, because I feared the people and obeyed their voice…" 26 …
>
> *Because you have rejected the word of the Lord, the Lord has rejected you from being king over Israel.* ס

1 Samuel 20: ס 11–17 ס: This pericope is an addition that anticipates the transfer of power from Saul to David. "Jonathan's plea for his family is

120. Cross et al., *Qumran Cave 4:XII*, 65; Alexander Rofé, "The Acts of Nahash according to 4QSam[a]," *IEJ* 32 (1982): 129–33; Auld, *I and II Samuel*, 118.

121. Trebolle Barrera, *Centena in libros Samuelis et Regum*, 71; P. Kyle McCarter Jr., *I Samuel: A New Translation With Introduction, Notes and Commentary*, AB 8 (Garden City, NY: Doubleday, 1980), 238.

probably a secondary interpolation in the narrative … Verses 11–17, with their emphasis on David's loyal treatment of Jonathan's descendants, are editorial anticipation of the Mephibosheth episode in II Samuel 9."[122]

1 Samuel 22: ס 5 ס: It is surprising to find Gad with David this early. On other hand, the area of the Forest of Hereth is mentioned nowhere else.[123]

1 Samuel 23:11b ס 12 ס: The juxtaposition of two oracular inquiries has produced different textual forms (4Q52 [4QSam^b], MT, the *Vorlage* of the LXX, and the Greek and Latin recensions). 4Q52 preserves better the beginning of the text corresponding to the second query (ועתה הירד שאול ויאמר יהוה ירד …). This interpolation triggered the repetition present in the MT, which editors, following Julius Wellhausen, consider a dittography. In fact, it would be a linking repetition that took place in a textual layer prior to the preserved manuscript tradition.[124]

1 Samuel 24: פ 17–18: 4Q51 presents the remainder of a blank line before 24:17, a *vacat* after האלה אל שאול, the beginning of a blank line before 24:18, and a *vacat* at the beginning of the line before 24:19:

> *petuhah/blank line* 17 When David had finished speaking these words to Saul *vacat* Saul said, "Is that your voice, my son David?" Saul lifted up his voice and wept. *vacat* 18 He said to David, "You are more righteous than I, for you have repaid me good, whereas I have repaid you evil. *vacat* 19 Today you have explained how you have dealt well with me."

These divisions seem to be an indication of the ornate character of this section of the text, which, as on other occasions, contains a double discourse by Saul: "Saul said … He said …"

1 Samuel 26: פ 10–11a: Verse 10 is secondary in my opinion, because its references go beyond the narrative in which it is inserted. The insertion occurred by *Wiederaufnahme* of "raise (his) hand against the Lord's

122. McCarter, *I Samuel*, 342, 344.

123. Ibid., 357.

124. Julio Trebolle Barrera, "Textual and Literary Criticism on Passages Attested by 4QSam^a,b (1 Sam 6:4–5 and 1 Sam 23:11–12)," in *The Hebrew Bible in Light of the Dead Sea Scrolls*, ed. Nóra Dávid et al., FRLANT 239 (Göttingen: Vandenhoeck & Ruprecht, 2012), 82.

anointed (26:9) … raise (my) hand against the Lord's anointed (26:11)" so that "and be guiltless" (26:9) is also part of the addition.

1 Samuel 30: פ 26–31 פ: The pericope contains a list of cities to which David sends the booty. The previous unit concludes with the phrase "it continues to the present day," which marks an end and a clear separation from the following pericope.

8. 2 Samuel

2 Samuel 3: פ 33–34: These verses, preceded by *petuhah*, form a poem inserted into the narrative by repeating (*Wiederaufnahme*) the terms "and all the people wept [ויבכו כל העם] … and all the people wept over him again [ויספו כל העם לבכות; 4Q51 omits כל העם]."

2 Samuel 4: ס 4: This verse contains information outside the immediate context relative to Mephibosheth who was crippled in his feet.

2 Samuel 5: פ 4–5 + 6–10 פ: The unit about the years of David's reign in Hebron and Jerusalem, 2 Sam 5:4–5, is preceded by *petuhah*. It is missing in Chronicles as well as in 4Q51. Its absence also from the OL and Josephus probably reflects an omission in the OG.[125] Karl Budde placed in chapter 8 the whole of 5:4–5 with 3:2–4 preceded by *setumah* and 5:13–16 framed by *petuhah* and *setumah*, thus attributing to this pericope a "mobile" quality.[126] There should be a division after 5:5 since the following unit 5:6–10 is well defined by the parallel of 1 Chr 11:4–9, in which this unit is framed between *setumah* and *petuhah*.

2 Samuel 5: פ 11–12 ס: In Chronicles, 1 Chr 11:4–9 to 14:1–2 stands between 5:4–10 and 5:11–12 in Samuel. This means that in Chronicles these two units of 2 Samuel between which the material of 1 Chr 11:10 is inserted at the end of chapter 13 were independent pericopes.

2 Samuel 11: פ 1 ס + 12: פ 26, 30–31 פ = 1 Chr 20: פ 1–3 פ: 2 Samuel 11:1 is the point of insertion for the story of David and Bathsheba, 2 Sam 11:1*–12:25.[127] This verse closes the non-*kaige* section (1 Sam 1–2 Sam 11:1) and opens the *kaige* section that runs as far as 1 Kgs 2:11. Chronicles

---

125. Ulrich, *Qumran Text of Samuel and Josephus*, 60–61; Dominique Barthélemy, "La qualité du texte massorétique de Samuel," in Tov, *Hebrew and Greek Texts of Samuel*, 1–14; Julio Trebolle Barrera, "El estudio de 4QSam^{a}: Implicaciones exegéticas e históricas," *EstBib* 39 (1981): 5–18.

126. Karl Budde, *Die Bücher Samuel* (Tübingen: Mohr Siebeck, 1902), 219.

127. Stefan Seiler, *Die Geschichte von der Thronfolge Davids (2 Sam 9–20; 1 Kön*

reproduces the text of 2 Sam 11:1* + 12:26, 30–31 in 1 Chr 20:1–3, without the interposed story of David and Bathsheba. The texts of Samuel and Chronicles contain significant variants.[128]

1 Chr 20:1–3	2 Sam 11:1 + 12:26, 30–31
פ 20:1 וַיְהִי לְעֵת תְּשׁוּבַת הַשָּׁנָה לְעֵת צֵאת הַמְּלָכִים	פ 11:1 וַיְהִי לִתְשׁוּבַת הַשָּׁנָה לְעֵת צֵאת הַמַּלְאכִים
וַיִּנְהַג יוֹאָב אֶת־חֵיל הַצָּבָא	וַיִּשְׁלַח דָּוִד אֶת־יוֹאָב וְאֶת־עֲבָדָיו עִמּוֹ וְאֶת־כָּל־יִשְׂרָאֵל
וַיַּשְׁחֵת אֶת־אֶרֶץ בְּנֵי־עַמּוֹן וַיָּבֹא וַיָּצַר אֶת־רַבָּה וְדָוִיד יֹשֵׁב בִּירוּשָׁלִָם	וַיַּשְׁחִתוּ אֶת־בְּנֵי עַמּוֹן וַיָּצֻרוּ עַל־רַבָּה וְדָוִד יוֹשֵׁב בִּירוּשָׁלִָם: ס
וַיַּךְ יוֹאָב אֶת־רַבָּה וַיֶּהֶרְסֶהָ:	12:26 וַיִּלָּחֶם יוֹאָב בְּרַבַּת בְּנֵי עַמּוֹן וַיִּלְכֹּד אֶת־ עִיר הַמְּלוּכָה:
20:2 וַיִּקַּח דָּוִיד אֶת־עֲטֶרֶת־מַלְכָּם מֵעַל רֹאשׁוֹ וַיִּמְצָאָהּ מִשְׁקַל כִּכַּר־זָהָב וּבָהּ אֶבֶן יְקָרָה וַתְּהִי עַל־רֹאשׁ דָּוִיד וּשְׁלַל הָעִיר הוֹצִיא הַרְבֵּה מְאֹד:	12:30 וַיִּקַּח אֶת־עֲטֶרֶת־מַלְכָּם מֵעַל רֹאשׁוֹ וּמִשְׁקָלָהּ כִּכַּר זָהָב וְאֶבֶן יְקָרָה וַתְּהִי עַל־רֹאשׁ דָּוִד וּשְׁלַל הָעִיר הוֹצִיא הַרְבֵּה מְאֹד:
20:3 וְאֶת־הָעָם אֲשֶׁר־בָּהּ הוֹצִיא וַיָּשַׂר בַּמְּגֵרָה וּבַחֲרִיצֵי הַבַּרְזֶל וּבַמְּגֵרוֹת	12:31 וְאֶת־הָעָם אֲשֶׁר־בָּהּ הוֹצִיא וַיָּשֶׂם בַּמְּגֵרָה וּבַחֲרִצֵי הַבַּרְזֶל וּבְמַגְזְרֹת הַבַּרְזֶל וְהֶעֱבִיר אוֹתָם בַּמַּלְכֵּן
וְכֵן יַעֲשֶׂה דָוִיד לְכֹל עָרֵי בְנֵי־עַמּוֹן וַיָּשָׁב דָּוִיד וְכָל־הָעָם יְרוּשָׁלִָם: פ	וְכֵן יַעֲשֶׂה לְכֹל עָרֵי בְנֵי־עַמּוֹן וַיָּשָׁב דָּוִד וְכָל־הָעָם יְרוּשָׁלִָם: פ

20:1 פ In the spring of the year, the time when kings go out to battle, Joab led out the army, ravaged the country of the Ammonites, and came and besieged Rabbah. But David remained at Jerusalem.	11:1 פ In the spring of the year, the time when kings go out to battle, David sent Joab with his officers and all Israel with him; the ravaged the Ammonites, and besieged Rabbah. But David remained at Jerusalem. ס
Joab attacked Rabbah, and overthrew it.	12:26 Now Joab fought against Rabbah of the Ammonites, and took the royal city.
20:2 David took the crown of Milcom from his head; he found that it weighed a talent of gold, and in it was a precious stone; and it was placed on David's head.	12:30 He took the crown of Milcom from his head; the weight of it was a talent of gold, and in it was a precious stone; and it was placed on David's head.

1–2): Untersuchungen zur Literarkritik und Tendenz, BZAW 267 (Berlin: de Gruyter, 1998), 223–40.

128. Sara Japhet, *I and II Chronicles: A Commentary*, OTL (London: SCM, 1993), 361–65.

He also brought out the booty of the city, a very great amount.	
20:3 He brought out the people who were in it, and set them to work with saws and iron picks and axes. Thus David did to all the cities of the Ammonites. Then David and all the people returned to Jerusalem. פ	12:31 He brought out the people who were in it, and set them to work with saws and iron picks and iron axes, or sent them to the brickworks. Thus he did to all the cities of the Ammonites. Then David and all the people returned to Jerusalem. פ

In 2 Samuel, the action concerns David and his veterans: "David sent Joab.... They ravaged ... and laid siege..." (11:1), and then Joab: "Joab attacked ... and conquered..." (12:26). The same action, with the same verbs, is then attributed to David: "David ... attacked it and conquered it" (12:29b). The result is a linking repetition (*Wiederaufnahme*), "attacked and conquered ... attacked and conquered," which marks the addition of the subparagraph formed by 12:27–29a. This insertion ascribes to Joab the wish to leave to David the honor of having conquered the city of Rabbah. As a result there is an inconsistency in the text, for the same verbs "attacked and conquered" first have Joab as their subject and then David.

In 1 Chr 20:1, Joab instead is the only protagonist: "Joab led the troops ... reduced Rabbah and destroyed it." Chronicles does not know of Joab's message to David, in which he offered him the honor of taking the city (2 Sam 12:26–29). Chronicles does not omit this passage, which would have supposed an intervention typical of modern "Literarkritik." It reproduces a text that did not know the passage 2 Sam 12:26–29. The text of 1 Chr 20:1 reproduces the words of 2 Sam 11:1 in line with its own *Vorlage*, which represents here a text earlier than the MT. Joab was the protagonist both in this verse and throughout the account of the campaign against the Ammonites, 2 Sam 10:1–14 + 11:1 + 12:30–31 // 1 Chr 19: פ 1–15 פ + 20: פ 1–3 פ. The pericope about the victory over the Arameans, 2 Sam 10:15–19 פ, is an independent unit as attested by the *petuhot* enclosing the parallel text in 1 Chr 19: פ 16–19 פ. It was inserted in the narrative of the war against the Ammonites. Second Samuel 11:1 (1 Chr 20:1) connects directly to 2 Sam 10:14 (1 Chr 19:15). David's role is reduced to sending Joab into battle and collecting the booty at the end of the battle.

2 Samuel 14: ס 25–27 פ: This short unit was inserted in the narrative by means of repetition (*Wiederaufnahme*): "and [Absalom] did not come into the king's presence [ופני המלך לא ראה, 14:24] ... and did not come into the king's presence [ופני המלך לא ראה, 14:28]." After the addition

of 14:25–27, the composer returned to the previous narrative thread by adding "So Absalom lived two full years in Jerusalem" (14:28), meaning that the anger of David lasted two years during which Absalom had to stay in his home away from the king. At the end of the unit, the Hebrew underlying the LXX adds a datum taken from 1 Kgs 15:2: "and [Maacah; LXX^L, OL] became (the) woman of Rehoboam, son of Solomon, and gave birth to Abiathar/Abias" (καὶ γίνεται γυνὴ τῷ Ροβοαμ υἱῷ Σαλωμων καὶ τίκτει αὐτῷ τὸν Αβιαθαρ/Αβια).

2 Samuel 16: ס 12b פ: This subsection located between intervals (many manuscripts do not contain the second) is an element related to the Benjaminite sections of the book: "Shimei went along on the hillside opposite him and cursed as he went, throwing stones and flinging dust at him." It returns to the beginning of the story ("he came out cursing and throwing stones at David," 16:6), expanding Shimei's curse to the path followed by David.

2 Samuel 18: ס 18 ס: This short notice is found also between intervals (the second is omitted by some manuscripts): "Absalom in his lifetime had taken and set up for himself a pillar … It is called Absalom's Monument to this day." The final expression, "to this day," along with the closing expression of the previous story, "all the Israelites fled to their tents," define the extent of this secondary subclause.

2 Samuel 19: ס 10–11 ס: The interval after 19:11 is surrounded by several repetitions and transpositions in the MT and LXX with other variants ("Why should you be the last to bring the king back to his house," "The talk of all Israel has come to the king, to his house)." The text is overloaded as shown also by the repetition of the discourse "Say to … Say to…," addressed first to the elders of Judah and afterwards to Amasa.

2 Samuel 21: ס 6b–7: The interval is omitted by many medieval manuscripts. It may mark the beginning of a clause inserted in the text, alluding to Mephibosheth/Meribbaal and to the "oath of Yahweh" between David and Jonathan.

2 Samuel 21: פ 15–17 פ: This episode of the Philistine wars is without parallel in Chronicles.

2 Samuel 21: פ 18 פ 19 ס 20–22 פ//1 Chr 20: 4 פ–8 פ: Three independent units of 2 Samuel are brought together in a single block in the parallel of Chronicles.

9. 1 Kings

The two editions of Kings represented by the MT and LXX as well as the edition represented by Chronicles are especially open to a study of the division of pericopes that takes into account the presence of the masoretic signs of division *petuhah* and *setumah.* In 1 Kgs 3–10, the MT and LXX present numerous cases of transposition with extensive parallels in Chronicles.[129] Movable pieces placed in one place or another in the MT and LXX are 3:1b; 5:1a–4; 5:31–32a; 6:37–38; 7:1–12; 9:16–17a; 9:15, 17b–22; and 9:24a.

1 Kings 2: ס 7, 8–9 + 2:36–46: The MT divides the narrative about Shimei in two parts placed in different contexts: the first, 2:8–9, as part of David's testament; the second, 2:36–46, after the execution of Adonijah and Joab. The first part, together with 2:7 dealing with the sons of Barzillai, is a clear addition to David's testament, inserted between a *Wiederaufnahme* (underlined) and preceded by *setumah*:

6 "Act therefore according to *your wisdom,*	ועשית כחכמתך
but do not let *his gray head go down to Sheol in peace.*	ולא תורד שיבתו בשלם שאל ס
[2:7–9a, Shimei's story]	[2:7–9a, Shimei's story]
You will know what you ought to do to him,	וידעת את אשר תעשה לו
and you must bring *his gray head down with blood to Sheol*"	והורדת את שיבתו בדם שאול

The LXX keeps the two parts of the narrative together, 2:35l–o, 36–46, forming a literary unit clearly delimited by an introduction (OG καὶ ἐν τῷ ἔτι Δαυιδ ζῆν ἐνετείλατο τῷ Σαλωμων λέγων) and by the material of the supplement following thereafter: 2:46a–l.

1 Kings 2: ס 26–27 פ: This Deuteronomistic addition lacks the narrative style of the context in which it is inserted and disrupts the story between 2:25 and 2:28.[130]

1 Kings 3: פ 16–28 ס: The story of Solomon's judgment framed by *petuhah* and *setumah* begins also with the particle אז: "Then two harlots came to the king." This narrative is inserted between the story of Solomon's

---

129. Adrian Schenker, *Une Bible archétype? Les parallèles de Samuel-Rois et des Chroniques*, ed. Michaël Langlois, L'Écriture de la Bible 3 (Paris: Cerf, 2013).

130. Ernst Würthwein, *Die Bücher der Könige, 1. Könige 1–16*, ATD 11.1 (Göttingen: Vandenhoeck & Ruprecht, 1977), 23.

prayer in Gibeon (3:4–15) and the list of his officials (4:1–19). This unit is missing in Chronicles and appears enclosed by a kind of *Wiederaufnahme*. In 1 Chr 1:13, it is preceded by "And he reigned over Israel," and in 1 Kgs 4:1 it is followed by "Solomon was king over Israel" (see also the LXX).

1 Kings 4: ס 1–6 ס: The list of Solomon's ministers forms a literary unit missing in Josephus.[131]

1 Kings 4: *seder* 20–5:14 ס. The material of MT 1 Kgs 4:20–5:14, preceded by the sign indicating the beginning of a *seder* ("order, sequence") and followed by *setumah*, appear in the LXX in the order 5:5, 7–8, 2–4, 9–14 (LXX omits 4:20). The unit of 4:2–4 is preceded by *petuhah* as the unit of 4:9–14 is by *setumah*.

1 Kings 5: ס 9–14 ס: This pericope about Solomon's wisdom is an independent unit, situated in different contexts in the MT and LXX. In the MT it follows 5:7–8; in the LXX it is found between short movable units: 5:2–4 (// 2:46b^{b}) and 3:1b (// 2:35c^{a}).

1 Kings 5: פ 15 ס: At the end of this verse, clearly delimited by masoretic divisions, 2 Chronicles inserts 1:18–2:1 (Solomon's preparations for the temple construction) framed by *petuhot*. Afterwards, both texts run in parallel in 1 Kgs 5:16 // 2 Chr 2:2.

1 Kings 6: פ 11–14 ס: This pericope framed by *petuhah* and *setumah* is absent from the OG and Josephus. It contains the oracle of an anonymous prophet, a late addition which is strange in the context.[132]

1 Kings 7:1–12 פ: This passage about the construction of the royal palace is marked at its end with *petuhah*. It is omitted in Chronicles and appears in the LXX after the unit 7:21–51, whose end is also marked by *petuhah*.

1 Kings 7: פ 27–37 ס: This literary unit about the ten stands of bronze, placed between *petuhah* and *setumah*, is missing in the parallel text of 2 Chr 4 between 4:5 and 4: 6. At this point a *setumah* in Chronicles and a *petuhah* in Kings marks the end of the previous unit 2 Chr 4:1–5 // 1 Kgs 7:22–26. At the same point, between 1 Kgs 7:26 and 7:27, meaningful variants are produced. The OG omits the last words of MT 1 Kgs 7:26, יכיל בת אלפים.

---

131. Josephus, *Les antiquités juives*, trans. Etienne Nodet, Yohanan Lederman, and Serge Bardet, 5 vols. (Paris: Cerf, 2005), 4:44.

132. "Der Text setzt also die späteste Formationsphase des Pentateuchs sprachlich und konzeptionell voraus" (Reinhard Achenbach, "Der Pentateuch, seine theokratischen Bearbeitungen und Josua–2 Könige," in Römer and Schmid, *Dernières rédactions du Pentateuque*, 253).

Likewise in the parallel text of 2 Chronicles, the Syriac version omits the last words of 4:5, מחזיק בתים שלשת אלפים יכיל. The literary unit 1 Kgs 7:27–37 which is wanting in Chronicles is delimited by a ring repetition at its beginning and end: "He also made the ten stands of bronze" (7:27) and "After this manner he made the ten stands" (7:37).

1 Kings 8:53 פ: The unit 2 Chr 6:41–42, located between *petuhah* and *setumah* and added to the end of Solomon's prayer (1 Kgs 8:53 פ), inserts at this point verses 8–10 + 1 of Ps 132.

The presence of the *petuhah* and *setumah* divisions is especially worthy of consideration when examining units introduced by אז, a particle frequent in the insertion of glosses.

1 Kings 8: פ 1 and 9: פ 2–9 פ: The pericope about the dedication of the temple starts with אז: "Then Solomon assembled the elders of Israel." In the OG this is the apodosis of the protasis: "And it came to pass when Solomon had finished building the house of the Lord and his own house after twenty years, then king Solomon assembled all the elders." This protasis repeats expressions of 9:1, "When Solomon had finished building the house of the Lord and the king's house," and 9:10, "At the end of twenty years, in which Solomon had built the two houses, the house of the Lord and the king's house." These two parallel verses enclose the unit about the Lord's second appearance to Solomon (9:2–9), which is framed by *petuhot*.

1 Kings 8: פ 12–13 // 2 Chr 6: פ 1–2: These verses contain a poem introduced with אז after *petuhah* in both books: "Then Solomon said: 'The Lord has said that he would dwell in thick darkness.'" This is a movable unit placed in the LXX after 8:53 and followed in the MT by *petuhah*.

1 Kings 9:16–17a + 3:1: These verses form a movable unit located in the LXX after 5:14 in a *vacat* marked with *setumah* (see above on 1 Kgs 5: ס 9–14 ס). The Lucianic text preserves the OG reading τότε (LXX^{B} οτε) at the beginning of the unit: MT: "Pharaoh, king of Egypt, had gone up and captured Gezer."; OG: "Then [τότε, אז] went up Pharaoh the king of Egypt, and took Gazer."

1 Kings 9:24a (LXX): This is also a short movable unit that appears in the LXX after 9:9 at a point signaled with *petuhah*: "But [MT אך] Pharaoh's daughter went up from the city of David to her own house." The Greek reading τότε (אז) instead of the MT אך betrays also the secondary character of this notice: "Then [τότε] Solomon brought up the daughter of Pharaoh out of the city of David."

1 Kings 10 (MT, LXX) // 2 Chr 9: In 1 Kgs 10 two movable units are found. The material of MT 1 Kgs 9:15, 17b–22 appears in the LXX after

MT 10:18–22. Also MT 5:1a is located in the LXX after MT 10:26. Chronicles has the same order: 2 Chr 9:25, 26a. These transpositions as well as the masoretic divisions contribute to delimit the units of this passage. The parallel units in Kings and Chronicles appear marked by masoretic divisions as follows:

2 Chr 9	LXX 1 Kgs 10	MT 1 Kgs 10
פ 9:13–16	10:14–17	ס 10:14–17 Solomon's gold
פ 9:17–21	10:18–22	פ 10:18–22 Solomon's throne, vessels and fleet
	9:15, 17b–22	
פ 9:22–24	10:23–25	10:23–25 Solomon's wisdom
פ 9:25	10:26	ס 10:26 Solomon's chariots and horses
9:26a	5:1a	
9:27–28 פ	10:27–29	10:27–29 פ Silver, cedar, horses and chariots

1 Kings 11: ס 7–8, 6, 9–10 פ (following the LXX order of verses): This unit begins with אז: "Then Solomon built a high place for Chemosh." Verse 7 is preceded by *setumah* and 11:10 is followed by *petuhah*. This pericope is also framed by a *Wiederaufnahme*, 11:4b repeated in 11:10 according to the LXX: "and his heart was not wholly true to the Lord his God, as was the heart of David his father" (οὐκ ἦν ἡ καρδία αὐτοῦ … οὐκ ἦν ἡ καρδία αὐτοῦ).

1 Kings 14: פ 1–20 פ: The long literary unit about Ahijah's judgment upon Jeroboam is framed by *petuhot* in the MT and is wanting in the OG which reproduces an alternative story.

1 Kings 16: פ 21–22 פ: This unit framed by *petuhot* is also inserted by means of the particle אז, "Then the people of Israel were divided into two parts." It is furthermore placed outside the regnal formulas of Zimri and Omri, breaking in this way a composition rule of Kings. This small unit is probably an interpolation related to the chronological system of Kings as differently attested in the MT and LXX.[133]

1 Kings 16:28 פ 29: In the interval signaled with *petuhah* the OG (LXX^{B,L}) presents the regnal formulas of Jehoshaphat (16:28a–h) after the previous reign of Omri. In the MT they appear in 1 Kgs 22: פ 41–51 ס, behind Ahab's reign.

---

133. Ronald S. Hendel, "The Two Editions of the Royal Chronology in Kings," in Piquer Otero and Torijano Morales, *Textual Criticism and Dead Sea Scrolls Studies in Honour of Julio Trebolle Barrera*, 103.

1 Kings 18: פ 9–12 פ: This pericope, framed by *petuhot*, is a summary or duplicate of 1 Kgs 17:5–6, inscribed also between *petuhot*.

1 Kings 22: פ 41–51 ס: The unit 22:41–51, delimited by *petuhah* and *setumah*, is found in the OG in 1 Kgs 16:28a–h.

10. 2 Kings

2 Kings 1:17a[a] פ a[b]: The masoretic sign of division interrupts the sentence "His brother Jehoram succeeded him as king פ in the second year of." This *petuhah* denotes here the beginning of the usual regnal formula as attested by the OG: "In the second year of King Jehoram son of Jeshoshaphat of Judah became king Johoram son of Ahab in Samaria" (LXX[L] 1:17–18).[134]

2 Kings 12: ס 1 פ: This short notice, enclosed by *setumah* and *petuhah*, is out of place: "Johoash was seven years old when he began to reign." In the OG attested by the Lucianic text this sentence appears integrated in the usual clause: "In the seventh year of Jehu, Jehoash began to reign; he was seven years old when he began to reign" (12:1–2). According to Ernst Würthwein, LXX[L] could have transposed the clauses because of "Angleichung an das gewöhnliche Schema" ("alignment with the ordinary scheme"), but the usual pattern was a rule for the composer or editor and not so much for later scribes not attentive to old formal patterns.[135]

2 Kings 12: פ 18–19: This notice is introduced also with אז and preceded by *petuhah*: "Then Hazael king of Syria went up." In a similar way the notice of 2 Kgs 16:5, which is introduced by אז, "Then Rezin king of Syria," is probably an insertion.[136]

---

134. Julio Trebolle Barrera, "Textual Criticism and the Literary Structure and Composition of 1–2 Kings/3–4 Reigns: The Different Sequence of Literary Units in the MT and the LXX," in *Die Septuaginta: Entstehung, Sprache, Geschichte; 3. Internationale Fachtagung veranstaltet von Septuaginta Deutsch (LXX.D), Wuppertal 22.–25. Juli 2010*, ed. Siegfried Kreuzer, Martin Meiser, and Martin Sigismund, WUNT 286 (Tübingen: Mohr Siebeck, 2012), 55–78.

135. Ernst Würthwein, *Die Bücher der Könige, 1. Kön. 17—2. Kön. 25*, ATD 11.2 (Göttingen: Vandenhoeck & Ruprecht, 1984), 353.

136. "[*A*]*z* ersetzt kaum ein genaues Datum, das in einem vorliegenden Archivtext gestanden hat. Vielmehr weist der lose Anschluss auf eine interpolation hin, die nicht von vornherein als Archivmaterial beurteilt werden sollte" (Würthwein, *1. Kön. 17—2. Kön. 25*, 387).

2 Kings 13: פ 10–11, 12–13 פ: In the MT, the initial and final regnal formulas of Jehoash's reign appear one after the other framed by *petuhot*. These formulas are followed by the prophetic narratives around Elisha's death (13:14–21) and the Aramean wars (13:22–25). Both units, signaled by *petuhot*, stand outside any regnal frame, breaking a law that governs the composition of Kings.

2 Kings 13: פ 14–21 פ: Transpositions attested by the OL and LXX^L in the *kaige* section correspond also to literary units marked by masoretic divisions. The narrative of Elisha's death and burial in 2 Kgs 13:14–21 is placed between *petuhot*. The OL (Codex Vindobonensis) places this narrative in an earlier location, in chapter 10, between 10:30 and 10:31, after the initial formula of Jehu's reign and the Deuteronomistic judgment at the end of the narratives about Elisha and his disciples. The strange location of some division signs seems to be related to a transposition or interpolation in the text. Thus in MT 2 Kgs 1:17b the location of *petuhah* disrupts the course of the clause at the point in which a transposition has been produced: the clause "in the second year of king Jehoram" of 1:18a (LXX^L = OG) was relocated to 1:17 (MT).

LXX^L (OG)	LXX^B (*kaige*)	MT
καὶ ἐβασίλευσεν Ἰωρὰμ ... ἀντ' αὐτοῦ	>	וימלך יהרם תחתיו פ
	>	בשנת שתים ליהורם בן יהושפט מלך יהודה
ὅτι οὐκ ἦν αὐτῷ υἱός	>	כי לא היה לו בן
And Jehoram became king in his place	>	And Jehoram became king in his place
	>	in the second year of Jehoram son of Jehoshaphat king of Judah
because he did not have a son	>	because he did not have a son

2 Kings 15: ס 16 פ: This is another inserted verse introduced with אז and framed by *setumah* and *petuhah*: "Then Menahem sacked Tiphsah." This notice is also placed outside any regnal frame, breaking once more a composition rule of Kings.

2 Kings 25: פ 27–30: This unit preceded by *petuhah* is a final note about Jehoiachin's release written by a scribe in the exile (Noth) and perhaps even as a new conclusion of the book (Römer).[137]

137. Martin Noth, *Überlieferungsgeschichte des Pentateuchs*, 2nd ed. (Stuttgart:

11. Jeremiah

Besides the cases reported by Tov and others discussed in section 2, above, are to be added further instances of transpositions between Edition I (LXX) and Edition II (MT), additions in the MT, and duplicates or redactional interventions in both editions.

11.1. Transpositions (→): From Edition I (LXX) to Edition II (MT)

Edition I (LXX)	Edition II (MT)	Subject
32:15–38	→ ס 25:15–38 ס	Judgment on the nations
51:1–30	→ ס 44:1–30 ס	Jeremiah's last words
51:31–35	→ ס 45:1–5 ס	Consolation of Baruch
26:2–28	→ ס 46:1–28 ס	Against Egypt
26:2–12	46: 2–12[138]	Battle of Carchemish
26:13–28	46:13–28	Invasion of Egypt
29:1–7	→ ס 47:1–7 ס[139]	Against Philistia
31:1–40	→ ס 48:1–47 ס	Against Moab
30:1–5	→ ס 49:1–6 ס	Against Ammon
29:8–23	→ ס 49:7–22 ס	Against Edom
30:12–16	→ ס 49:23–27 ס	Against Damascus
30:6–11	→ ס 49:28–33 ס	Against Arabia
25:14–26:1	→ ס 49:34–39 ס	Against Elam
27:1–28:58	→ ס 50:1–51:58 ס	Against Babylon
28:59–64	→ ס 51:59–64 ס	Oracle in the Euphrates

11.2. Additions in Edition II (MT) to Edition I (LXX)

Jeremiah 8: ס 10–12 ס: These verses, absent in the LXX, are a secondary doublet of 6:13–15.[140]

Kohlhammer, 1948), 87; Thomas Römer, "La construction du Pentateuque, de l'Hexateuque et de l'Ennéateuque: Investigations préliminaires sur la formation des grands ensembles littéraires de la Bible hébraïque," in Römer and Schmid, *Dernières rédactions du Pentateuque*, 31.

138. The LXX omits 46: ס 1.

139. Pierre-Maurice Bogaert, "Relecture et déplacement de l'oracle contre les Philistins: Pour une datation de la rédaction longue (TM) du livre de Jérémie," in *La vie de la parole: De l'Ancien au Nouveau Testament; Études d'exégèse et d'herméneutique bibliques offertes à Pierre Grelot* (Paris: Desclée, 1987), 139–50.

140. William L. Holladay, *Jeremiah 1: A Commentary on the Book of the Prophet*

Jeremiah 10: ס 6–8.10 ס: These verses are not present in the Greek version (Theodotion*). The OL confirms the short text of the LXX and of the Hebrew attested by 4Q71.[141] According to Pierre Bogaert, the joint evidence of the OL and the LXX (10:9 after 10:5 "they shall not walk") allows us to identify the textual development from a short form to the longer one of the MT:

> OL: (ס 1) 2 Thus says the Lord: "According to the ways of the nations do not go [*ne ambulaueritis*],[142] and of the signs of the sky do not be afraid, because they fear their faces, 3 because the laws of nations are vain.
>
> It is a tree cut from the forest, the work of craftsmen and molten metal, 4 with silver and gold they are embellished; with hammers and nails they have been fixed—they shall not move. 5a They are of beaten silver—they shall not walk. 9 Silver is brought from Tarsis and gold from Uphaz, and the hands of the goldsmith. All are the work of the artisan. Their clothing is blue and purple. 5b They have to be carried,—for they shall not march.
>
> Do not be afraid of them, for they cannot do evil, nor it is in them to do good ס."

The structure of the unit is clear: between the expressions "do not be afraid of them" there are descriptions of the idols made of wood, metal, and cloth, with reference to each material enclosed by a variant of the same refrain: "they shall not move … they shall not walk … they shall not march." The long MT follows a different order and inserts several doxological additions in the central section (10:6–8) and end (10:10) of the unit. The structure becomes more complex and the content enriched. The oracle is not focused any longer on the idolatry of the nations but on the king of nations.[143]

Jeremiah, Chapters 1–25, Hermeneia (Philadelphia: Fortress, 1986), 215, 275; Janzen, *Studies in the Text of Jeremiah*, 95–96.

141. The OL text has been edited by François Dolbeau, "Nouveaux sermons de saint Augustin pour la conversion des païens et des donatistes," *REAug* 37 (1991): 49–51.

142. The OL reading *ambulaueritis* translates the Greek πορεύεσθε which represents the OG text. The reading chosen in Ziegler's edition, μανθάνετε, follows the MT *tilmādû* (Ziegler, *Ieremias*, 199).

143. Pierre-Maurice Bogaert, "Les mécanismes rédactionnels en Jér 10,1–16

Jeremiah 17: ס 1–4 ס: This unit, characteristic of the long redaction, is missing in the LXX. Furthermore, 17:3–4 are duplicated in 15:13–14 ס.

Jeremiah 23: ס 7–8 ס = 16: ס 14–15 ס: This passage is found in the LXX in chapter 23 after verse 40 ס and omitted in chapter 16. The oracle is related to the preceding unit 23: ס 5–6 ס = 33:15–16 ס.

Jeremiah 25:14 ס: This secondary addition is omitted in the LXX.

Jeremiah 29: ס 16–20 ס: This addition, missing in the LXX, is marked with an asterisk in the Hexaplaric text.[144]

Jeremiah 33: ס 14–26 ס: This proto-MT plus, the longest passage of the book that is missing in the Greek version, is generally considered a secondary addition. The Hebrew style is careless and inelegant. The content of the passage constitutes a revision of the oracle about the Davidic king in Jer 23: ס 5–6 ס = 33:15–16 ס.[145]

Jeremiah 38 (LXX 45): ס 28b פ: The terms "When Jerusalem was taken" are absent in the LXX and a few Hebrew medieval manuscripts.[146]

Jeremiah 39 (LXX 46): פ 1 ס 2: These verses were not part of the OG, as they are marked with an asterisk. The LXX also omits 39:4–13 ס. The Hebrew of this added passage is markedly late, when compared to the rest of the book.[147] The OL (Codex Wirceburgensis) does not contain 39:1–2 and attests a very brief text (38:28a; 39:3, 14):

(LXX et TM) et la signification des suppléments," in Bogaert, *Livre de Jérémie*, 222–38.

144. Ziegler, *Ieremias*, 346–47; Stipp, *Das masoretische und alexandrinische Sondergut*, 128.

145. Pierre-Maurice Bogaert, "*Urtext*, texte court et relecture: Jérémie xxxiii 14–26 TM et ses préparations," in *Congress Volume: Leuven 1989*, ed. John A. Emerton, VTSup 43 (Leiden: Brill, 1991), 236–47; Schenker, "Rédaction longue du livre de Jérémie," 286–89; Robert P. Carroll, *Jeremiah: A Commentary*, OTL (London: SCM, 1986), 637.

146. Ziegler, *Jeremiah*, 411.

147. Jan Joosten, "L'excédent massorétique du livre de Jérémie et l'hébreu post-classique," in *Conservatism and Innovation in the Hebrew Language of the Hellenistic Period: Proceedings of a Fourth International Symposium on the Hebrew of the Dead Sea Scrolls and Ben Sira*, ed. Jan Joosten and Jean-Sébastien Rey, STDJ 73 (Leiden: Brill, 2008), 93–108; Hermann-Josef Stipp, "Zur aktuellen Diskussion um das Verhältnis der Textformen des Jeremiabuches," in *Die Septuaginta: Texte, Kontexte, Lebenswelten; Internationale Fachtagung veranstaltet von Septuaginta Deutsch (LXX.D), Wuppertal 20.–23. Juli 2006*, ed. Martin Karrer and Wolfgang Kraus, WUNT 219 (Tübingen: Mohr Siebeck, 2008), 630–53.

(MT 38 / LXX 45:28) פ And Jeremiah remained in the court of the prison until the day that Jerusalem was taken. ס (39 / 46:3) And all the officials of the king of Babylon came and [names of the officials] and all the officials of the king of Babylon sat in the middle gate. [> 39:4–13] 14 And they sent to take Jeremiah from the court of the prison and they entrusted him to Gedaliah son of Ahikam son of Shaphan and they brought him to Tafret [OL *in iafret*] and he stood in the middle of his people ס.

12. Ezekiel

The OL (Codex Wirceburgensis) can be considered an independent witness to the order preserved in Greek papyrus 967. Both manuscripts show a different arrangement of chapters 36–40. Chapter 36 is followed by chapters 38 and 39, and chapter 37 is inserted between chapters 39 and 40, making the order 36:1–23b; 38–39; 37; 40. Papyrus 967 lacks counterparts to passages found as late additions in the proto-MT.[148]

Ezekiel 12: פ 26–28 ס: "The section is probably an insert."[149]

Ezekiel 36:23b–38 ס: Both manuscripts omit this passage not found in the earliest text of the LXX, nor in its *Vorlage*, as shown by the special linguistic character of these verses.[150] The MT appears to reflect a more developed textual stage of Ezekiel beyond that of the OG.[151]

Ezekiel 36: ס 37–38 ס: Yahweh's restoration of Israel (36:36 is followed by 37:15).

Ezekiel 37: ס 1–14 פ: The pericope on the dry bones.

Ezekiel 37: פ 15–28: On the recreation of a unified Israel.

148. Bogaert, "Témoignage de la Vetus Latina"; Ashley S. Crane, *Israel's Restoration: A Textual-Comparative Exploration of Ezekiel 38–39*, VTSup 122 (Leiden: Brill, 2008) 207–25.

149. Lust, "Major Divergences Between the LXX and the MT in Ezekiel," 86.

150. Bogaert, "Témoignage de la Vetus Latina"; Ingrid I. Lilly, *Two Books of Ezekiel: Papyrus 967 and the Masoretic Text as Variant Literary Editions*, VTSup 150 (Leiden: Brill, 2012), 125.

151. Daniel M. O'Hare, *"Have You Seen, Son of Man?" A Study in the Translation and Vorlage of LXX Ezekiel 40–48*, SCS 57 (Atlanta: Society of Biblical Literature, 2010), 17.

13. Conclusion

The substantial catalog of texts I have provided above could be enlarged by including other secondary passages in biblical books marked with masoretic signs of division, quotations, or developments in postbiblical literature of literary units delimited by masoretic signs of division and Hexaplaric signs as empirical evidence of transpositions and additions in the proto-MT or in the *Vorlage* of the LXX. However, to bring this chapter to a conclusion, and summarizing the overall significance of the texts I have discussed above, late phenomena in textual transmission, including the *petuhah* and *setumah* divisions in the masoretic medieval codices, the *vacats* in Qumran biblical manuscripts, and the Hexaplaric additions in the LXX, can be connected with phenomena that occurred in the editorial process of the biblical books, such as the different arrangement of pericopes in the MT and LXX and the interpolations inserted in either text. Bible commentaries and editions of the Hebrew text should pay more attention to these signs of division and their implications for the study of the textual growth of the biblical books. The empirical evidence provided here is not isolated or anomalous and does not relate only to the occasional biblical pericope or book, and consequently it serves as a challenge and correction to literary(-critical) approaches which neglect empirical evidence for the development of the biblical writings.

The Problem of "Literary Unity" from the Perspective of the Study of Oral Traditions

Raymond F. Person Jr.

1. Introduction

The methods of source criticism and redaction criticism are based on certain assumptions about the literary unity of a text produced by a single author, as illustrated well in the following quote from Joel Baden's *The Composition of the Pentateuch*, which is explicitly a defense of these methods as well as the Documentary Hypothesis:

> The hallmark of a unified composition, one created by a single author, is internal consistency: consistency of language and style, consistency of theme and thought, and above all, consistency of story. Every narrative makes certain claims about the way events transpired—who, what, when, where, how, and why. When these elements are uniform throughout a text, there is no pressing need to inquire as to its unity.[1]

When these elements are not uniform—that is, repetitions and inconsistencies occur in the narrative—the text is generally assumed to be a composite text ripe for analysis by source and redaction criticism.

In the early years of the development of source and redaction criticism, there was a lot of crossover between biblical studies, ancient Near Eastern literature, and classics, so that the methods being applied to the Bible, Gilgamesh, and Homer, for example, were very similar; therefore, the conclusions concerning the efficacy of the methodologies were mutually reinforcing. Although that continued to some degree, some recent discussions in

1. Joel S. Baden, *The Composition of the Pentateuch: Renewing the Documentary Hypothesis*, AYBRL (New Haven: Yale University Press, 2012), 16.

Homeric studies diverge significantly from that of biblical studies and provide an excellent test case for the validity of the assumptions concerning "literary unity" in source and redaction criticism of the Bible.

In the nineteenth and early twentieth centuries, the Homeric Question—that is, whether the *Iliad* and the *Odyssey* were composite texts written by many "Homers" or were the result of one literary genius named Homer—resulted in two opposing schools of thought. The Analysts insisted that repetitions and inconsistencies in the texts allowed the application of source and redaction criticism to uncover the literary work of the various Homers. The Unitarians insisted that Homer was a historical literary genius who produced these two great epics. A major advancement occurred when Milman Parry and Albert Lord changed the debate between these two schools significantly. By using their recordings of Serbo-Croatian bards to demonstrate how oral traditional epic can be produced by a single performer using a traditional register, they explained the existence of certain repetitions and inconsistencies within the work of a single performer and by implication within a single literary text like the *Iliad* or the *Odyssey*.[2] Despite the influence Parry and Lord have had in biblical studies, many source and redaction critics of the Bible nevertheless continue to assume that literary unity necessarily betrays a single author and that repetitions and inconsistencies necessarily betray a composite text—that is, a text with multiple authors/editors. In this chapter, I will elaborate upon current discussions of Homeric epic in light of Parry and Lord's Serbo-Croatian analogue as an empirical control, especially as continued in the work of John Miles Foley and Gregory Nagy. I will then be able to draw some conclusions about the nature of literary unity in ancient literature that requires us to look at the biblical text differently. I will illustrate this different perspective by a discussion of the relationship between Samuel–Kings and Chronicles, showing how the inconsistencies emphasized by the consensus model's use of source and redaction criticism can be explained in ways so that both texts can be understood as faithful representations within the literary unity of the broader tradition.

2. For the most comprehensive history of scholarship, see John Miles Foley, *The Theory of Oral Composition: History and Methodology*, Folkloristics (Bloomington: Indiana University Press, 1988).

2. The Linguistic Arguments of the Homeric Analysts and the Empirical Counter-Evidence of Serbo-Croatian Epic

The strongest arguments made by the Analysts that the Homeric epics must be composite texts were linguistic—that is, a single Greek author would not mix both Ionic and Aeolic forms of Greek and would not include both archaisms and neologisms.[3] Therefore, the Homeric epics must be composite texts from different geographical areas and historical periods. Parry was significantly influenced by this argument, because there was no denying the existence of what seemed to be linguistic inconsistencies in the epics; however, his sympathies were with the Unitarians, and he was convinced that the study of living oral traditions could help him explain how these supposed linguistic inconsistencies could nevertheless occur within the work of a single Homer.

In 1934–1935, Parry with his doctoral student Lord and a native assistant Nikola Vujnovic conducted fieldwork in the former Yugoslavia among the *guslari*, the Serbo-Croatian oral poets who performed traditional Muslim epics. After Parry's untimely death, Lord continued his teacher's project comparing Serbo-Croatian epic to Homeric epic. In fact, Lord expanded the discussion by including other ancient and medieval literature. The Serbo-Croatian evidence demonstrated that the mere presence of linguistic inconsistencies can be understood as a result of an oral traditional linguistic register—that is, a *guslar* may combine both the Ijekavski and Ekavski dialects of Serbo-Croatian and use archaisms, such as Turkish vocabulary and the rarely used aorist verb form, within the special epic language he uses to compose the traditional epics.[4] In fact, based on much more comparative data from other living oral traditions, Foley later concluded as follows: "Often an epic language will mix dialect forms from various geographical regions, as well as preserve archaic words and forms that long ago dropped out of the quotidian register used outside the performance arena."[5] That is, traditional verbal art uses what Lord called

3. For a recent view, see Geoffrey Horrocks, "Homer's Dialect," in *A New Companion to Homer*, ed. Ian Morris and Barry Powell, MS 163 (Leiden: Brill, 1997), 193–217.

4. John Miles Foley, *Homer's Traditional Art* (University Park: Pennsylvania State University Press, 1999), 76–86.

5. John Miles Foley, "Analogues: Modern Oral Epic," in *A Companion to Ancient Epic*, ed. John Miles Foley (Oxford: Blackwell, 2005), 202.

a "special grammar" and what Foley called a "traditional register,"[6] which because of its traditional character may conservatively preserve archaic linguistic features (both vocabulary and grammar) as well as draw from various regional dialects as a way of establishing an aesthetic that communicates its traditional character as transcending time and space to competent audiences. Nevertheless, this special grammar continues as a contemporary linguistic register, so that the addition of neologisms may occur within this living language.

Within the context of the Homeric question, Lord concluded as follows:

> The formulaic techniques, therefore, in the Greek and South Slavic poetries are generically identical and operate on the same principles. This is the surest proof now known of oral composition, and on the basis of it alone we should be justified in the conclusion that the Homeric poems are oral compositions.[7]

More recent Homer scholars are much more cautious concerning such matters of oral composition, including Foley and Nagy, both of whom are successors of the Parry-Lord approach to oral traditions. Their hesitancy for such a strong conclusion that Homer was definitely a single oral poet is based on their understanding of the complexity of the text-critical evidence for the Homeric epics and how this textual complexity interacted with what was certainly a living oral tradition out of which the Homeric epics were composed, received, and transmitted, both orally and in written texts, as well as a much fuller understanding of oral traditions and literature with roots in oral traditions in general, since so much more comparative work has occurred since Lord's groundbreaking *Singer of Tales*.

3. From the "Orally Dictated Texts" of Homer to Living Traditional Texts of Homers

If Homer was a single literary genius who composed orally, then, in Lord's judgment, the *Iliad* and the *Odyssey* were "orally dictated texts," the "nearest" type of written composition to "an actual performance without the

6. Albert B. Lord, *Singer of Tales*, HSCL 24 (Cambridge: Harvard University Press, 1960), 35–36; Foley, *Homer's Traditional Art*, 65–88.

7. Lord, *Singer of Tales*, 144–45.

use of a recording machine."[8] A major problem with this thesis is that the earliest complete texts of the Homeric epics are much later than their purported time of composition. Although Homer may have lived in the eighth century BCE, the earliest complete extant texts of the epics are Byzantine.[9] Moreover, the text-critical evidence strongly suggests that "both oral composition, the craft of the *aoidos* [bard], and a creative brand of memorization, the province of the rhapsode (*rhapsôidos*), contributed to the early transmission of Homer."[10] This reality greatly complicates any reconstruction of the earliest texts of Homer. In fact, the "Homeric textual evidence clearly points toward the reality of 'multitextuality,'"[11] something that even Parry suggested as early as 1932 based on the variety of the Ptolemaic fragments.[12]

In *Multitextuality in the Homeric Iliad*, Graeme Bird analyzed the Ptolemaic papyri fragments of the *Iliad*, which are among the earliest fragments of Homeric epic but nevertheless were copied centuries after Homer. He concluded that the many "plus verses" in these fragments, which became part of the later vulgate editions of the *Iliad*, do not betray their later origins. Rather,

> the nature of the variation is "organic"—lines have not been "dropped" into place arbitrarily; rather, they give the appearance of having "grown" in their current locations, in the process modifying their surroundings and resulting in a coherent "version" of an episode that is no less "Homeric."[13]

This is clear text-critical evidence that hexameter lines of Homeric poetry continued to be composed throughout the transmission of the epics for centuries and these "new" lines were composed in the same linguistic register, complete with its "archaisms," so that lacking text-critical evidence

8. Ibid., 149.

9. John Miles Foley, *Traditional Oral Epic: The Odyssey, Beowulf, and the Serbo-Croatian Return Song* (Berkeley: University of California Press, 1990), 20–21.

10. Ibid., 21–22.

11. Graeme D. Bird, *Multitextuality in the Homeric Iliad: The Witness of the Ptolemaic Papyri*, Hellenic Studies 43 (Washington, DC: Center for Hellenic Studies, 2010), 60.

12. Ibid., 32.

13. Ibid., viii.

these "new" lines appear to have been a part of the tradition from the beginning. Thus, Nagy could conclude as follows:

> [C]omposition and proliferation need not necessarily be related to an *event* followed by a *process*: the evolution of the fixed texts that we know as the *Iliad* and the *Odyssey* may be envisaged as a cumulative process, entailing countless instances of composition/performance in a tradition that is becoming streamlined into an increasingly rigid form as a result of ever-increasing proliferation.[14]

Therefore, we cannot (easily, if at all) determine how the "special grammar" of Homer's "original" composition differs from the "special grammar" of the later "Homers" who simply "transmitted" the text, because this very distinction depends on an assumed dichotomy that does not apply well to the composition/performance/transmission of the Homeric epics in its first five or more centuries.[15]

4. "Literary Unity" and "Incompleteness": The Problem of Oral Performances of Epics and the Public Reading of Texts

As illustrated in the above quote from Baden, the common assumption of "literary unity" includes "consistency of story"—that is, the literary narrative has a clear beginning and end, the events narrated within the time frame have a consistently logical temporal sequence, and the development of the characters has a consistent progression. Therefore, the failure to narrate certain events or the relationships between specific characters, for example, as well as the addition of elements from other versions of what is presumed to be the same narrative distracts significantly from the literary unity, thereby creating significant gaps in the narrative as well as inconsistencies or needless repetitions. Thus, any *literary text* should evince such *literary unity*. The comparative study of oral traditions challenges this notion of literary unity, at least when considering individual

14. Gregory Nagy, *The Best of the Achaeans: Concepts of the Hero in Archaic Greek Poetry*, rev. ed. (Baltimore: Johns Hopkins University Press, 1999), 8.

15. See Nagy's discussion of the various "Homers" during the "six ages of Homeric reception" from the Bronze Age to the time of Virgil (Gregory Nagy, *Homer: The Preclassic*, SCL 67 [Berkeley: University of California Press, 2010], 1; Nagy, *Homer: The Classic*, Hellenic Studies 36 [Washington, DC: Center for Hellenic Studies, 2009], 2).

oral performances of traditional epic and by implication even in the public reading of written texts.[16]

Based on his knowledge of numerous studies, Foley concluded as follows: "Internationally, the common practice in oral epic is for bards to perform 'part' of what we would consider the 'whole' tale."[17] He provided examples from singers of *Mwindo* epic from the Congo, the *Epic of Son-Jara* of Nigeria, *Pabuji* epic from India, and Serbo-Croatian epic of the former Yugoslavia. "In these and so many other cases, the bard performs *pars pro toto*, the part implying the whole, without rehearsing the entire linear compass of the implied traditional context."[18] Since the bards do not perform the entire epic in any one setting, the learning process by which someone becomes a bard also does not involve learning the entire epic in sequence from a single teacher. This is illustrated well in the following interview by Lauri Honko of Gopala Naika, a bard of the Indian *Siri Epic*:

> Q: That means, you cannot learn under only one person.
> A: It is not possible. That is what I am saying now. I had my teacher only for two years. He was there in Belaalu. I was here in Kaarinja. Under him I could not learn very many things, you see. I mean, then I was young, too. Had I an opportunity to learn with him? He would sing a little. After this, as I go round one corner, another person will be there singing and I will take a bit of that. Just this is the skill. As I go round another corner, a woman will be there singing, like this and like that. In this case I cannot consider them as teachers. I cannot call all of them teachers. For me only one man is teacher. Yet what he has got, out of that I have learned very little. Under whom? Under this Soomayya Naika, the wisdom I learned was minimal during that period of two years. I cannot say that is much, it may be little.[19]

16. See Raymond F. Person Jr., "Biblical Historiography as Traditional History," in *Oxford Handbook of Biblical Narrative*, ed. Danna Fewell (Oxford: Oxford University Press, 2016), 73–83. Drawing from the study of Greek historiography, I argue that ancient historiography was read aloud in public performances and, therefore, shared some characteristics, such as multiformity, with the oral performance of epic.

17. Foley, "Analogues," 204.

18. Ibid.

19. Lauri Honko, *Textualizing the Siri Epic*, FFC 264 (Helsinki: Suomalainen Tiedeakatemia, Academia Scientiarum Fennica, 1998), 527.

Not only did Gopala Naika not have only one teacher, but his source for the *Siri Epic* was likewise multiple sources, as illustrated in the following statement from his interview: "Also in what way this [Siri sandhi] was little by little sung by other people, some of that knowledge might have entered my head. Yet for me it is something coming by itself, it is something mine."[20] Thus, Honko concluded as follows: "The secret of Gopala Naika's learning the Siri epic is that he never acquired it as a whole from anyone. Instead, the sources were multiple and the process of compositions and mental editing long."[21] Foley applied these insights from the comparative study of living epic traditions to ancient epics, explicitly referring to Homeric epic and the Epic of Gilgamesh, both of which existed in textual plurality. "Seeing the ancient epics only as singular, always fossilized artifacts or items may lead us to expect prior transmission processes that, while comfortably familiar in the modern western world of fixity and print, amount to untenable impositions."[22] Therefore, we must explore the possibility that ancient written texts, especially epics but other genres as well, are written *pars pro toto*. That is, analogous to any particular oral performance of an epic, any specific manuscript is a written instantiation of a much broader tradition so much so that the manuscript is necessarily understood as an imperfect and partial representation of the whole. If this is the case, then literary unity may be anachronistic when applied to ancient literary texts, even though the broader tradition preserved in the collective memory of the community would have something analogous to a literary unity. Such a possibility would certainly be another explanation for why much of ancient and medieval literature exists in multiple versions, at least whenever it exists in more than one manuscript.[23]

---

20. Ibid., 524.

21. Ibid., 527.

22. Foley, "Analogues," 204.

23. See Raymond F. Person Jr., "Text Criticism as a Lens for Understanding the Transmission of Ancient Texts in Their Oral Environments," in *Contextualzing Israel's Sacred Writings: Ancient Literacy, Orality, and Literary Production*, ed. Brian B. Schmidt, AIL 22 (Atlanta: SBL Press, 2015), 193–211. Here I discuss text-critical evidence from Homeric epic, Old English literature, *Thousand and One Nights*, and the Dead Sea Scrolls, all of which suggests that manuscripts were imperfect instantiations that represent the broader tradition.

5. The Relationship of Samuel–Kings and Chronicles and the Problem of "Literary Unity": 2 Sam 7 // 1 Chr 17 as a Case Study

The consensus model concerning the relationship of Samuel–Kings and Chronicles assumes that the Chronicler(s) used Samuel–Kings as the main source with additions, omissions, and substitutions sometimes influenced by other authoritative sources, especially the Pentateuch. These additions, omissions, and substitutions are often understood to detract from the "literary unity" that should have been or would have been, if Chronicles was an original literary creation rather that a derived work. This assumption is illustrated well in the following quote from Sara Japhet:

> [I]t seemed that a better explanation of the book's variety and composition is the view that it is one work, composed essentially by a single author, with a very distinct and peculiar literary method. The author's penchant for citing existing texts, and his being influenced by both the Pentateuch, the Deuteronomistic historiography and a plethora of earlier sources, yet going his own way, account best for the varieties of the book. It is doubtful whether a rational, meticulous harmony of all the possible details was ever aimed at by the Chronicler.[24]

Japhet is reacting against another "explanation of the book's variety and composition" in the secondary literature—that is, the notion that Chronicles has undergone various redactions, that there are two or more Chroniclers. However, both of these explanations share the same understanding of literary unity as produced by a single author—that is, in order for Japhet to reject the notion of multiple Chroniclers, she must conclude that the one and only Chronicler has a "very distinct and peculiar literary method," which accounts better for the lack of literary unity that both explanations attempt to resolve. It is almost as if she wished that the Chronicler had undertaken "a rational, meticulous harmony," which is what any good author should do. Nevertheless, no matter which explanation one adopts in the consensus model, the actual writing of the Chronicler himself is assumed to have, in Gary Knoppers's words, a "distinctive Chronistic

24. Sara Japhet, *I and II Chronicles: A Commentary*, OTL (London: SCM, 1993), 7. See also Isaac Kalimi, *The Reshaping of Ancient Israelite History in Chronicles* (Winona Lake, IN: Eisenbrauns, 2005), 7; Kalimi, *An Ancient Israelite Historian: Studies in the Chronicler, His Time, Place, and Writing*, SSN 46 (Assen: Van Gorcum, 2005), 10.

vocabulary, style, or themes"[25] that can be discerned in order to distinguish between source material and/or post-Chronistic additions, on the one hand, and the Chronicler's own redactional material, on the other. Moreover, Chronistic additions generally contain the type of "literary unity" lacking in the whole of Chronicles.

In *The Deuteronomic History and the Book of Chronicles: Scribal Works in an Oral World*, I argued against the consensus model and proposed that these two historiographies are contemporary literary works that are both faithful representations of the broader tradition, despite what from our modern perspective appear to be two theologically divergent literary works from different historical periods. Two crucial insights for my arguments there were the textual plurality in which these ancient texts survive and the characteristic of multiformity in oral traditions and texts with roots in oral traditions. Here I draw from that monograph, making more explicit how our typical notion of literary unity is anachronistic when applied to the Deuteronomic History and the book of Chronicles. I will illustrate this approach with a selective discussion of God's covenant with David (2 Sam 7 // 1 Chr 17), first concerning linguistic unity and then concerning consistency of story.

6. "Literary Unity" and "Linguistic Unity" in 2 Sam 7 // 1 Chr 17

The consensus model concerning the historical linguistics of Biblical Hebrew assumes the conclusions reached by the consensus model concerning the relationship of Samuel–Kings and Chronicles, which in turn points to the linguistic model for confirmation—that is, the preexilic/exilic Samuel–Kings, which contains Early Biblical Hebrew (EBH), has been revised by the postexilic Chronicler who used Late Biblical Hebrew (LBH). The consensus model of historical linguistics as applied to ancient Hebrew has been seriously challenged by Ian Young, Robert Rezetko, and Martin Ehrensvärd,[26] and I drew extensively from their work in *The Deuteronomic History and the Book of Chronicles*. Here I discuss only one of

25. Gary N. Knoppers, *1 Chronicles 10–29*, AB 12A (New York: Doubleday, 2004), 662.

26. See especially Ian Young, Robert Rezetko, and Martin Ehrensvärd, *Linguistic Dating of Biblical Texts*, 2 vols., BibleWorld (London: Equinox, 2008). See also Robert Rezetko and Ian Young, *Historical Linguistics and Biblical Hebrew: Steps Toward an Integrated Approach*, ANEM 9 (Atlanta: SBL Press, 2014).

their many examples, the variation between the first-person pronouns (אנכי and אני, which are assumed to be EBH and LBH, respectively), since this variation occurs in 2 Sam 7 // 1 Chr 17. The following quote from a chapter by Rezetko shows the fallacy in any argument that assumes that the LBH form replaced the EBH form in Chronicles.

> [I]t is misleading to claim that אנכי in Samuel and Kings is "systematically" replaced by אני in Chronicles "wherever" the former is found. In fact, if one considers synoptic passages, אנכי occurs in both Samuel–Kings and Chronicles on a single occasion; אני occurs in both Samuel–Kings and Chronicles on eight occasions; אנכי occurs in Samuel–Kings and אני occurs in Chronicles on *only four* occasions. Interestingly, all three situations appear in 2 Sam 7 // 1 Chr 17. Finally, in the Bible as a whole I am aware of 14 occasions on which both forms occur side by side in the same verse.[27]

Here are the four instances of the first-person pronoun in the Masoretic Text (MT) of 2 Sam 7 // 1 Chr 17, in which "all three situations appear":

MT 2 Sam 7	MT 1 Chr 17
2 I [אנכי] am living in a house of cedar	1 I [אנכי] am living in a house of cedar
8 I [אני] took you from the pasture	7 I [אני] took you from the pasture
14 I [אני] will be to him a father	13 I [אני] will be to him a father
18 Who am I [אנכי]?	16 Who am I [אני]?

If we assume that "literary unity" includes "linguistic unity," then the presence of both so-called EBH and LBH linguistic forms in both texts is problematic. One might assume that the Chronicler should have consistently changed the EBH form of אנכי to the LBH form of אני. However, the fact that both Samuel and Chronicles contain both forms creates problems, in the sense that neither text preserves such a linguistic unity, thereby suggesting a lack of literary unity. Furthermore, the fourteen other verses that

27. Robert Rezetko, "Dating Biblical Hebrew: Evidence from Samuel–Kings and Chronicles," in *Biblical Hebrew: Studies in Chronology and Typology*, ed. Ian Young, JSOTSup 369 (London: T&T Clark, 2003), 225–26 (emphasis original).

Rezetko referred to in which "both forms occur side by side" demonstrate this point.[28]

Linguistic arguments certainly cannot be made on the basis of one such example, and the arguments made by Young, Rezetko, and Ehrensvärd must be critiqued as a collective.[29] However, this one example helps us to see how assumptions about linguistic unity often contribute to assumptions about literary unity. As discussed above, such a lack of supposed linguistic unity often occurs within the work of a single composer of traditional epic—that is, linguistic forms from different dialects or historical periods are mixed together. In other words, the linguistic register for some speech events and by implication some written genres may be special grammars or traditional registers that combine linguistic forms that would not generally be used by the same speakers or writers when they engage in the register of everyday conversation in the same language. Therefore, in some sense the literary unity of such works is created by the traditional register that from another perspective contains a lack of linguistic unity. If this is the case, then the assumption of a literary unity based on linguistic unity within source and redaction criticism is undermined, at least to some degree, as illustrated by this one example. Such an assumption can be seen in Ziony Zevit's review of some of the early work by Young and Rezetko, in which he dismissed their critique and proposal, because they assumed that "there were people writing texts in both a living language and an archaic form of the same language, though they provide no reason for such an odd construct."[30] By extension, Zevit presumes that a single author would produce a text with a literary unity, including linguistic uniformity—that is, consistent use of either EBH, LBH, or some transitional mixture of the two. However, as we have seen above, the study of oral traditional epic provides an empirical model for just "such an odd construct." Of course, the previous possible explanations remain valid for some linguistic differences—that is, like any other language, ancient Hebrew existed in different

28. See further Rezetko and Young, *Historical Linguistics and Biblical Hebrew*, 310–12. Here Rezetko and Young provide all of the extant variants between the Qumran manuscripts of Samuel and the MT of Samuel for first-person pronouns.

29. For my discussion of the work of Young, Rezetko, and Ehrensvärd, see Raymond F. Person Jr., *The Deuteronomic History and the Book of Chronicles: Scribal Works in an Oral World*, AIL 6 (Atlanta: Society of Biblical Literature, 2010), 23–40.

30. Ziony Zevit, review of *Biblical Hebrew: Studies in Typology and Chronology*, by Ian Young, ed., *RBL* 8 (2004): 13.

dialects and underwent historical change, and this may account for some linguistic variations; however, the mere presence of linguistic variations cannot always be explained by insisting on a composite text, because the mixing of linguistic forms can be a characteristic of some traditional registers. Thus, the use of linguistic variation in source and redaction criticism becomes much more complicated, because without some other type of empirical evidence the mere presence of different linguistic forms does not necessarily suggest a composite text.

7. "Literary Unity" and "Consistency of Story" in 2 Sam 7 // 1 Chr 17

In *The Deuteronomic History and the Book of Chronicles*, I drew extensively from Graeme Auld's thesis of a shared common source, even though I clearly share some of the critiques of his position. One of the critiques of Auld's thesis that I do not share—that is, the synoptic material shared by Samuel–Kings and Chronicles requires knowledge of sections of the written text that the Chronicler omitted—betrays a flaw in the consensus model's approach related to its notion of "literary unity" requiring "consistency of story." Here I review this critique of Auld, and my defense of his thesis in relationship to this particular critique by focusing on two examples in 2 Sam 7 // 1 Chr 17 used by scholars in the consensus model to argue against Auld's thesis—that is, the reference to the period of the judges (2 Sam 7:7, 10–11 // 1 Chr 17:6, 9–10) and the reference to David being anointed by Samuel and as a shepherd (2 Sam 7:8 // 1 Chr 17:7).

Auld's critics have compiled lists of verses "where the Chronicler alludes to or presupposes knowledge of passages in the books of Samuel that he did not include in his own narration of history."[31] These "omissions" by the Chronicler create "awkwardness"[32] in the narrative and are described as "completely inexplicable."[33] In other words, the Chronicler's omissions have destroyed the consistency of story and the literary unity found in Samuel–Kings; thus, the Chronicler necessarily presupposed that his readers were

31. Ralph W. Klein, *1 Chronicles*, Hermeneia (Minneapolis: Fortress, 2006), 31–32. See also Gary N. Knoppers, *1 Chronicles 1–9*, AB 12 (New York: Doubleday, 2003), 67; Steven L. McKenzie, "The Chronicler as Redactor," in *The Chronicler as Author: Studies in Text and Texture*, ed. M. Patrick Graham and Steven L. McKenzie, JSOTSup 263 (Sheffield: Sheffield Academic, 1999), 80–86.

32. Klein, *1 Chronicles*, 407.

33. Japhet, *I and II Chronicles*, 362.

familiar with the narrative as preserved in Samuel–Kings, in order for them to make sense of his own narrative with all of its awkward gaps.[34] Now we will see how this argument has been applied to 2 Sam 7 // 1 Chr 17.

According to the consensus model, the references to the period of judges in 2 Sam 7 does not create any problems, because Samuel is a part of the larger literary work, the Deuteronomistic History; however, since the Chronicler omitted all stories of the judges, preferring to begin his narrative with David, any references to the judges complicates his narrative. The only references to the judges in Chronicles occur in the following:

MT 2 Sam 7:7, 10–11a	MT 1 Chr 17:6, 9–10a
7 In every place that I have walked	6 In every place that I have walked
with all the sons of Israel,	with all Israel,
did I speak a word with any of	did I speak a word with any of
the tribal leaders of Israel,	the judges of Israel,
whom I commanded to shepherd	whom I commanded to shepherd
my people Israel, "Why have you	my people, "Why have you
not built me a house of cedar?" …	not built me a house of cedar?" …
10 I will appoint a place for my people	9 I will appoint a place for my people
Israel, and will plant them, so that they	Israel, and will plant them, so that they
may dwell in it and tremble no more;	may dwell in it and tremble no more;
and evildoers shall not afflict them	and evildoers shall not wear them down
anymore, as they did formerly,	anymore, as they did formerly,
11 from the day when I appointed	10 from the days when I appointed
judges over my people Israel; and I	judges over my people Israel; and I
shall give you rest from all your enemies.	shall subdue all your enemies.

34. For my summary and critique of similar arguments concerning other passages in Chronicles, see Person, *Deuteronomic History and the Book of Chronicles*, 101–3, 111, 114–15, 134–38.

(Although there are various differences between 2 Sam 7 and 1 Chr 17, I will refrain from commenting on all of them here and focus simply on the references to the judges in Chronicles.)

Proponents of the consensus model note that 1 Chr 17 is "virtually identical in length and content" to 2 Sam 7.[35] This is important to their argument for explaining these references to the judges. For example, Ralph Klein wrote, "Because he sticks relatively close to his *Vorlage* in this chapter, he retains aspects of Israel's history that he downplayed elsewhere."[36] It is as if the Chronicler should have consistently omitted references to the judges, but slipped up occasionally when he is following his source in Samuel–Kings (too) closely. This is even more obvious in the following quote concerning 1 Chr 17 from Japhet:

> In general, there are very few references in Chronicles to pre-monarchical times, and in these the period is represented by the figure of the prophet Samuel (I Chron. 26.28; II Chron. 35.18). This chapter, on the other hand, mentions the judges twice … and these references have been left unchanged by the Chronicler. This is a clear example of the problematics of a historiography based on ready-made building blocks rather than on the raw material of original composition, or of the working of divergent tendencies within one world-view. The major significance of this chapter in the Chronicler's historical-theological world-view leads him to introduce his source-material virtually unaltered. Thus, he retains some aspects of Israel's history which are played down elsewhere in his work.[37]

Here Japhet clearly contrasts the Chronicler's literary ability with what she assumes as the norm—that is, the norm is a single-authored "original" composition based on "raw material" and, if an author is going to use "ready-made building blocks," he (or she) should edit those building blocks with their "divergent tendencies" into a literary unity that is characterized by only "one world-view," so that there is a consistency of

35. Klein, *1 Chronicles*, 374. See similarly Steven L. McKenzie, "Why Didn't David Build the Temple? The History of a Biblical Tradition," in *Worship and the Hebrew Bible: Essays in Honour of John T. Willis*, ed. M. Patrick Graham, Rick R. Marrs, and Steven L. McKenzie, JSOTSup 284 (Sheffield: Sheffield Academic, 1999), 217.

36. Klein, *1 Chronicles*, 378. See similarly, Knoppers, *1 Chronicles 10–29*, 668–69; McKenzie, "Why Didn't David Build the Temple?," 218.

37. Japhet, *I and II Chronicles*, 330.

story. Although her remarks are more explicit here about the failings of the Chronicler, they nevertheless represent well the assumptions of literary unity within the consensus model.

According to the consensus model, since the Chronicler began his narrative by copying from his source of Samuel at 1 Sam 31:1, references to material in 1 Sam 1–30 create gaps that readers necessarily must fill based on their knowledge of the full text of 1 Samuel. The reference to Samuel's anointing of David and the boy David as a shepherd in 1 Chr 17:7 (//2 Sam 7:8) creates such a problem.

MT 2 Sam 7:8	MT 1 Chr 17:7
I took you from the pasture, from following the flocks, to be ruler over my people, over Israel.	I took you from the pasture, from following the flocks, to be ruler over my people Israel.

(Although there are minor differences between 2 Sam 7 and 1 Chr 17, I will refrain from commenting on them here and focus simply on the reference in Chronicles to the narrative of David's early life as preserved in 1 Sam 16:1–13.)

Once again, according to the consensus model, the Chronicler's closely following his source in Samuel explains the allusion to material omitted elsewhere by the Chronicler. For example, Klein wrote the following:

> [T]he Chronicler has Yahweh allude to David's anointing by Samuel in 1 Sam 16:1–13 and David's occupation as a shepherd at that time, although he chose not to include that passage in his own narrative. He could presuppose, of course, that his readers would understand the allusion.[38]

Therefore, the Chronicler's work does not evince the consistency of story expected for obtaining a good literary unity.

The problem of such a lack of consistency of story and therefore literary unity requires an explanation that solves this problem. The consensus model approaches this problem with two possible solutions, both described well by Japhet. Her description of the first follows: "The exegete may assume that, in spite of the contradictory elements in the editing process, the author succeeded in producing a fully coherent story, and that

38. Klein, *1 Chronicles*, 378. See also Knoppers, *1 Chronicles 10–29*, 668.

the present text is therefore a result of corruption and does not faithfully represent the Chronicler's original composition."[39] This is the approach taken by those scholars who apply source and redaction criticism (and sometimes text criticism) to remove post-Chronistic intrusions that detract from the Chronicler's original. Japhet illustrated this approach with a discussion of Rudolph's commentary in which he often emended the text of Chronicles before interpreting his reconstructed original. Her description of the second option follows: "The exegete may also adopt a less interventive mood, and accept the present text as authentic, observing that its adaptation did not reach perfection because of the natural mutual interference of the two tendencies: literary adherence and theological adaptation."[40] Japhet prefers the second option, especially since she advocates for a single author for Chronicles.[41] Many in the consensus model combine these two options—that is, even those scholars who argue for multiple Chroniclers or significant post-Chronistic material (the first option) nevertheless explain the type of problems caused by the so-called omissions in Chronicles (for example, the references to the judges) as creating a lack of literary unity (the second option).

Both of these options, however, make the same assumptions about literary unity—that is, they both imagine that a single author necessarily creates an original text that has the consistency of story according to our modern notions of literary unity. In the first option, we can only understand the work of a single author once we have reconstructed his material with the use of source and redaction criticism, so that the reconstruction will necessarily have a greater literary unity than the present composite text of Chronicles. In the second option, especially if, like Japhet, we limit ourselves to that option, we have to accept the presumed imperfections of the present text of Chronicles and hope to find some explanation for why the single author of Chronicles (or even just one of the Chroniclers) left such a mess in his text—that is, the mutually exclusive tendencies of "literary adherence and theological adaptation" interfered with the notion of literary unity, because the Chronicler did not adequately smooth out the rough edges.

The comparative study of oral traditions and literary texts with roots in oral traditions suggests a third option that has rarely been considered

39. Japhet, *I and II Chronicles*, 362.

40. Ibid., 363.

41. Ibid., 7.

in biblical studies—that is, any specific manuscript of a literary text is a written instantiation of a much broader tradition so much so that any manuscript is necessarily understood as an imperfect and partial representation of the whole, *pars pro toto*. This insight is expressed well in the words of Joyce Tally Lionarons, a scholar of medieval manuscripts in Old English:

> The familiar concept of the literary text, defined as an autonomous arrangement of words shaped by an individual writer and reflecting that writer's authorship, is taken for granted in most contemporary scholarship. In recent years, however, the applicability of the idea of the text to medieval literary works has been challenged by scholars studying the manuscript culture of the Middle Ages. Medievalists have argued convincingly that it was only "the development of printing with moveable type" that created the conditions that allowed the literary texts as such to come into existence in the first place. …
>
> Nevertheless, the language [that] scholars have traditionally used to describe manuscripts and their contexts carries with it an assumption of textuality born in a print culture—we speak of textual "archetypes" and "variants;" we identify scribal "corruption" and "errors," just as if a separate, uncorrupted master text did in fact exist outside of and prior to the manuscript work.[42]

Since Lionarons is speaking of medieval manuscripts that often were bound in codices, her insights would apply that much more to the scrolls of ancient Israelite literature.[43] For example, even a public reading of the entire scroll of the book of Samuel (something I think unlikely) would create the same problems relating to consistency of story and literary unity—that is, the references to the judges in 2 Sam 7 would be read aloud

---

42. Joyce Tally Lionarons, "Textual Appropriation and Scribal (Re)Performance in a Composite Homily: The Case for a New Edition of Wulfstan's *De Temporibus Anticristi*," in *Old English Literature in Its Manuscript Context*, ed. Joyce Tally Lionarons, MES 5 (Morgantown: West Virginia University Press, 2004), 67–68.

43. Here I do not intend to promote an evolutionary model that necessarily assumes that reading strategies changed significantly with the invention of the codex, but rather simply that codices were an innovation that allowed more text to be recorded within one artifact when compared to scrolls. For an excellent discussion of the material culture of scrolls and codices, see Eva Mroczek, "Thinking Digitally about the Dead Sea Scrolls: Book History Before and Beyond the Book," *BH* 14 (2011): 241–69.

without the reading of the book of Judges, which would be on another scroll. Therefore, the public reading of 2 Sam 7 would, according to the same logic of the consensus model, require its hearers, most of whom would be illiterate, to possess this assumed knowledge. That is, the public reading of 2 Sam 7 and 1 Chr 17 would be "virtually identical,"[44] at least in relationship to the references to the judges, and both would necessarily be *pars pro toto*. This situation would obtain for any reading of any scroll containing only a portion of the Deuteronomic History or the book of Chronicles, whether that reading was done in silence by one individual (something rare in the ancient world) or was read aloud in public. That is, even if we imagined the reference to David being a shepherd (2 Sam 7:8) and 1 Sam 16:1–13 being on the same scroll, the principle of *pars pro toto* remains for any particular reading of portions of the Samuel scroll and, therefore, is not a problem unique to the shepherd reference in 1 Chr 17:7.

If this is the case, then literary unity may be anachronistic when applied to ancient literary texts, first because no specific scroll could possibly be the original or uncorrupted master text (something that even text critics have abandoned[45]) and second because the literary unity that we moderns seek in literary texts existed in the collective memory of the community of the ancients, which was certainly supported by the existence of manuscripts. That is, the literary unity, including the consistency of story, did not exist primarily in literary texts, but rather in the broader tradition that existed in communal memory. Any performance of this broader tradition, whether orally composed or based on a public recitation of a text by memory or the public reading of a text, was necessarily *pars pro toto*, only an imperfect instantiation of a selection of the broader tradition that nevertheless represented the broader tradition in its fullness.

8. Conclusion

I want to close with a discussion of Isaac Kalimi's work on the literary artistry of the Chronicler, because I think that he has expressed well an uneasiness with the presumed notion of literary unity that underlies the consensus model—that is, all of the scholars in the consensus model strive to resist imposing modern standards on the ancient literature that are

44. Klein, *1 Chronicles*, 374.

45. See Person, "Text Criticism as a Lens."

anachronistic and rather try to understand the literature on its own terms, but our modern notions of "literary unity" often conflict with what we find in the biblical text. More than other scholars, Kalimi has striven to elucidate the literary artistry of the Chronicler. In *The Reshaping of Ancient Israelite History in Chronicles*, he provides exhaustive lists of the various literary techniques he identified in Chronicles and concludes as follows: "I consider the Chronicler to be a creative artist, a *historian* who selected the material he desired out of his sources and edited it in the order, the context, and the form he found fitting, thus creating a literary composition comprising part of late biblical historiography."[46] Because of his exhaustive treatment, his last chapter contains his discussion of those passages that are problematic to his thesis, what he refers to as inconsistencies, disharmonies, and historical mistakes.[47] The following two quotes strongly suggest that Kalimi himself is uncomfortable with how his assumptions about literary unity and historical accuracy have necessarily led him to a conclusion in which the Chronicler's literary artistry and historical acumen are less than desired.

> It may even be possible for other scholars who read this book to be able (to some degree) to use the data presented below in analyzing the work of other biblical writers, instead of subjecting them to the usual Greek-Western criteria of consistency and absolute conformity.
>
> [W]e may draw an analogy, even if it is limited, between the Chronicler's work, which shows inconsistency in its methodologies, and the works of other biblical authors, which frequently are inappropriately criticized by scholars on the basis of Greek/Western criteria that demand completeness and consistency.[48]

That is, Kalimi acknowledged that the notion of literary unity that complicated his conclusions concerning the Chronicler is a greater problem in that it complicates our understanding of biblical literature as a whole and that he hoped for some other scholar to discover a way out of the "usual Greek-Western criteria of consistency and absolute conformity" that defines our inappropriate notion of literary unity. Hopefully, the notion

---

46. Kalimi, *Reshaping of Ancient Israelite History in Chronicles*, 7 (emphasis original).

47. Ibid., 381–403.

48. Ibid., 381, 411.

of literary unity derived from the comparative study of oral traditions and literary texts with roots in oral traditions has at least opened up a path to a better, more appropriate understanding of literary unity for ancient texts, including the Bible, that exists within the context of a broader tradition preserved in the memory of the community. However, if this notion of literary unity is more appropriate for ancient literature, it undercuts the efficacy of source and redaction criticism, at least as typically practiced, by increasing the uncertainty of the results, when those results are based on notions of *linguistic unity* and *consistency of story* as essential to literary unity. Therefore, for example, some defenses of the Documentary Hypothesis—such as Baden's emphasis on how the Pentateuch could not possibly have been "a unified composition, one created by a single author," because it lacks a consistent literary unity—fail and other arguments, based on sound empirical models, become more necessary.

The (Dis)Connection between Textual and Linguistic Developments in the Book of Jeremiah: Hebrew Bible Textual Criticism Challenges Biblical Hebrew Historical Linguistics

Robert Rezetko

1. Introduction

The fundamental argument of *Empirical Models for Biblical Criticism* is that external analogues, such as biblical textual traditions, Mesopotamian literature, and postbiblical Jewish and Christian literature, "whose evolution can be documented by copies from several stages in the course of their development—in other words, on *empirical models*—show that many literary works from ancient Israel and cognate cultures were demonstrably produced in the way critics believe that biblical literature was produced."[1] So, for example, it is concluded that such analogues supply evidence that the Documentary Hypothesis is a realistic and persuasive theory of the formation of the Pentateuch. A key focus of the chapters in *Empirical Models for Biblical Criticism* is the many divergences between the various Hebrew and Greek versions of the Bible, including the the Masoretic Text (MT), the Samaritan Pentateuch (SP), the biblical Dead Sea Scrolls (DSS), and the Septuagint (LXX).

Along the way, several contributors to *Empirical Models for Biblical Criticism* comment briefly on language issues and the relationship between textual and linguistic developments in ancient Near Eastern writings. Yair Zakovitch, for instance, points to some late language as corroborative evi-

1. Jeffrey H. Tigay, "Preface and Acknowledgements," in *Empirical Models for Biblical Criticism*, ed. Jeffrey H. Tigay (Philadelphia: University of Pennsylvania Press, 1985), xi–xii (emphasis original).

dence for the late insertion of verses 21–22 in Isa 38 (both MT and 1QIsa[a]) in comparison with the parallel in 2 Kgs 20:7–8.[2] Two other authors, however, offer an alternative perspective on the text-language issue. According to Alexander Rofé, the late fourth century BCE author of the supplements in MT Josh 20 (compared to the shorter LXX edition of the story)

> phrased his innovation in the familiar language of the sources, imitating ancient usage rather than writing in his own Second Commonwealth Hebrew; thus he was successful in hiding his origins and date.... Phenomena such as these detract from the value of linguistic considerations in the dating of biblical passages.[3]

In a similar way, Jeffrey Tigay underscores in his discussion of the versions of the Gilgamesh Epic that many late variants do not employ late language:

> A few of the changes in wording seem to be chronologically conditioned, with the late version adopting language which is especially prevalent in late sources. However, the number of late variants using demonstrably late language does not seem extensive, and many of the late variants seem to employ language not less ancient than the language they replace. The changes may therefore be based largely on the subjective artistic judgment or taste of the later editors, not new linguistic developments.[4]

---

2. Yair Zakovitch, "Assimilation in Biblical Narratives," in Tigay, *Empirical Models for Biblical Criticism*, 183 with n. 16; see also Jeffrey H. Tigay, "The Evolution of the Pentateuchal Narratives in the Light of the Evolution of the Gilgamesh Epic," in Tigay, *Empirical Models for Biblical Criticism*, 25 with n. 14.

3. Alexander Rofé, "Joshua 20: Historico-Literary Criticism Illustrated," in Tigay, *Empirical Models for Biblical Criticism*, 146 with n. 29.

4. Tigay, "Evolution of the Pentateuchal Narratives," 40–41. For additional discussion of this issue, he refers to Jeffrey H. Tigay, *The Evolution of the Gilgamesh Epic* (Philadelphia: University of Pennsylvania Press, 1982; repr. Wauconda, IL: Bolchazy-Carducci, 2002), 55–72. Kouwenberg comes to a similar conclusion, arguing that Akkadian literary writings show little internal linguistic evolution over time, and consequently the date of composition of a literary work cannot be established on the basis of linguistic criteria; see N. J. C. Kouwenberg, "Diachrony in Akkadian and the Dating of Literary Texts," in *Diachrony in Biblical Hebrew*, ed. Cynthia Miller-Naudé and Ziony Zevit, LSAWS 8 (Winona Lake, IN: Eisenbrauns, 2012), 433–51. Similarly, in his chapter in the present volume, Alan Lenzi does not identify any stylistic criteria for sequencing the manuscripts of the two *šuila*-prayers that he studies.

The quotations in the preceding paragraph illustrate two possible relationships between textual and linguistic data: late textual developments and late linguistic developments may be consistent with one another (Zakovitch) in the sense that both are considered to represent *late* phenomena, or they may not correspond, in which case late linguistic developments may not characterize or even appear in late textual developments (Rofé, Tigay). The principal aim of the present chapter is to explore in more depth the (dis)connection between textual and linguistic developments in the writings of the Hebrew Bible.[5] My main conclusions are that textual and linguistic developments in biblical writings ordinarily do not intersect, and traditional arguments for (late) literary developments that incorporate textual evidence rest on a firmer foundation and are more conclusive than some contemporary historical linguistic and linguistic dating arguments against such (late) literary developments. In other words, contemporary textual criticism of the Hebrew Bible challenges contemporary historical linguistics of Biblical Hebrew insofar as practitioners of the latter seek to undermine the conventional view that "early" sources and books were edited and/or authored in the Second Temple period.

This chapter will proceed along the following lines. First, I will illustrate the crux of the problem by surveying the incompatible conclusions reached by contemporary textual critics and historical linguists on the formation of the biblical book of Jeremiah. Second, I will show that while there is a substantial empirical basis for the conclusions reached by textual critics of the Hebrew Bible, the conclusions reached by historical linguists of Biblical Hebrew are not based on recognizable analogues or conventional historical linguistic sources and methods. Third, I will strengthen the argument in the previous point by reviewing two illustrative case studies of language variation in the Hebrew Bible in general and in the short (LXX) versus the long (MT) editions of Jeremiah in particular: "cry" (צעק/זעק) and "I" (אני/אנכי).

5. Previous work on the text-language issue by me, Ian Young, and others is cited and/or discussed in Ian Young, Robert Rezetko, and Martin Ehrensvärd, *Linguistic Dating of Biblical Texts*, 2 vols., BibleWorld (London: Equinox, 2008), esp. vol. 1, ch. 13; and more recently and in much more depth in Robert Rezetko and Ian Young, *Historical Linguistics and Biblical Hebrew: Steps Toward an Integrated Approach*, ANEM 9 (Atlanta: SBL Press, 2014), esp. chs. 3–6 and appendixes 1–2.

2. Formation of the Book of Jeremiah

2.1. Text-Critical Perspective

The book of Jeremiah situates the prophet in the late seventh and early sixth centuries BCE.[6] The dated events in the book begin with the prophet's call (or perhaps birth) in 627/626 (1:1–19), continue through the destruction of Jerusalem and its aftermath in 586–585 (chs. 39–44, 52), and end with a final portrait of King Jehoiachin of Judah in exile in Babylon in 560 (52:31–34). The scholarly consensus, however, is that the production of the book was long and complex, lasting beyond the exile into the postexile, reaching as a minimum into the Persian period (538–332) and probably into the Hellenistic period (332–63). For example, and with an eye on the text-critical evidence especially (on which I will say more), Marvin Sweeney states, "[b]oth versions [MT and LXX] point to an interest in shaping the books of Jeremiah, including the extensive material that appears to go back to the prophet himself, in order to serve competing interests in the Persian period and perhaps also in the Hellenistic period,"[7] and David Carr comments, "[c]ritical evaluation of early manuscript evidence suggests that the book of Jeremiah was significantly expanded and reordered during the late Hellenistic (including Hasmonean) period, including the addition of numerous passages composed in semi-Deuteronomistic diction … and smaller glosses with similar features."[8] Similar perspectives on the book's production are argued or assumed in the bulk of entries in dictionaries and encyclopedias, introductions to the Hebrew Bible/Old Testament, critical commentaries, and so on.[9]

Assorted considerations serve as evidence for the protracted and complicated process through which numerous authors, editors, and scribes

6. It would be more correct to talk about the "books," plural, of Jeremiah, but for consistency's sake I will speak about the "book," singular.

7. Marvin A. Sweeney, *The Prophetic Literature*, IBT (Nashville: Abingdon, 2005), 94.

8. David M. Carr, *The Formation of the Hebrew Bible: A New Reconstruction* (Oxford: Oxford University Press, 2011), 318.

9. See the excellent survey of research with abstracts of most of the major publications in Marvin A. Sweeney, "Jeremiah," in *Oxford Bibliographies Online: Biblical Studies* (http://www.oxfordbibliographies.com/view/document/obo-9780195393361/obo-9780195393361-0060.xml). In his chapter in the present volume, Julio Trebolle Barrera also describes many examples of secondary and late elements in MT Jeremiah.

produced the book of Jeremiah.[10] These include "distinctive interests ... identified with various social circles active after the fall of Jerusalem and during the Persian period,"[11] certain historical allusions (e.g., "the nobles of Judah" in 27:20 [MT]; 39:6 [MT]; "the kings of the Medes" in 51:11), various scrolls mentioned within the book itself (30:2; 36; 45:1; 51:59–64), interlaced first- and third-person speech (e.g., 1:4 versus 7:1 [MT]), interwoven poetry and prose (passim), frequent repetitions (e.g., 6:12–15 // 8:10–12),[12] and diverse innerbiblical relationships (e.g., Deuteronomistic language, 2 Kgs 24–25 // Jer 39, 52 // 2 Chr 36).[13] To these considerations I would add the generalization that the biblical writings, collectively and individually, and like many other premodern literary, especially religious writings, are analogous specimens of long-duration scribally formed literature that evolved through a complex process of composition and transmission until they reached their final form(s), as argued throughout Tigay's *Empirical Models for Biblical Criticism* and the present book.[14] However, I would prefer to focus my remarks in the remainder of this section on the observable textual evidence for Jeremiah's production history.

---

10. A helpful summary of most of the following issues is given in Terence E. Fretheim, *Jeremiah*, SHBC (Macon, GA: Smyth & Helwys, 2002), 22–29.

11. Robert P. Carroll, *Jeremiah: A Commentary*, OTL (Philadelphia: Westminster, 1986), 69–70.

12. See, in particular, Geoffrey H. Parke-Taylor, *The Formation of the Book of Jeremiah: Doublets and Recurring Phrases*, SBLMS 51 (Atlanta: Society of Biblical Literature, 2000).

13. See, for example, Reinhard Müller, Juha Pakkala, and Bas ter Haar Romeny, *Evidence of Editing: Growth and Change of Texts in the Hebrew Bible*, RBS 75 (Atlanta: Society of Biblical Literature, 2014), chs. 9–11; Raymond F. Person Jr., *The Kings–Isaiah and Kings–Jeremiah Recensions*, BZAW 252 (Berlin: de Gruyter, 1997), 80–113; see also Person, *Second Zechariah and the Deuteronomic School*, JSOTSup 167 (Sheffield: JSOT Press, 1993), 62–78; Person, *The Deuteronomic School: History, Social Setting, and Literature*, SBLStBL 2 (Atlanta: Society of Biblical Literature, 2002), 9–13.

14. This is the conventional view in critical introductions to the Hebrew Bible/Old Testament such as Carr, *Formation of the Hebrew Bible*; Jan Christian Gertz, Angelika Berlejung, Konrad Schmid, and Markus Witte, *T&T Clark Handbook of the Old Testament: An Introduction to the Literature, Religion, and History of the Old Testament* (London: T&T Clark, 2012); Alexander Rofé, *Introduction to the Literature of the Hebrew Bible*, JBS 9 (Jerusalem: Simor, 2009); Thomas Römer, Jean-Daniel Macchi, and Christophe Nihan, eds., *Introduction à l'Ancien Testament*, 2nd ed., MdB 49 (Geneva: Labor et Fides, 2009); Konrad Schmid, *The Old Testament: A Literary History* (Minneapolis: Fortress, 2012).

Emanuel Tov's *Textual Criticism of the Hebrew Bible*, widely considered to be the authoritative standard handbook in the field, provides a concise summary of the consensus view on the textual situation of the book of Jeremiah that is held by the bulk of text-critical experts.[15] First, the differences between the texts are recognizable in two main areas: length and order. The LXX, reflected also in 4Q71 and 4Q72a (4QJer^{b,d}) is shorter by about one-sixth (others: one-seventh or one-eighth) than the MT, reflected also in 2Q13, 4Q70, 4Q72, and 4Q72b (2QJer, 4QJer^{a,c,e}). The LXX lacks words, phrases, and entire sections that are found in the MT. The LXX also deviates from the order of the MT in several sections and chapters. Second, despite an occasional dissenting voice, the "scholarly consensus"[16] holds that the LXX and MT represent two literary editions of the book of Jeremiah; the LXX was translated from a Hebrew text close to 4Q71 and 4Q72a, and the translation did not abridge its Hebrew source; the LXX reflects a first, short, literary edition (Edition I); and the MT is a second, long, literary edition (Edition II), whose supplements date to the postexilic period.[17] In the words of Sidnie White Crawford, LXX Jeremiah falls within "the conservative scribal tradition," but MT Jeremiah comes within "the revisionist scribal tradition."[18] It is notable that Tov speaks

15. Emanuel Tov, *Textual Criticism of the Hebrew Bible*, 3rd ed. (Minneapolis: Fortress, 2012), 286–94; see also 20–21, 137, 168, 189.

16. Ibid., 288 n. 11.

17. Eugene Ulrich also holds the "scholarly consensus." See, for example, Eugene Ulrich, *The Dead Sea Scrolls and the Origins of the Bible*, SDSS (Grand Rapids: Eerdmans, 1999), passim (e.g., 6, 9–10, 13–14). John Quant interacts with Tov's and Ulrich's slightly different perspectives on the formation of the book of Jeremiah and comes to something of an in-between stance; see John F. Quant, "Rewriting Scripture Inside and Out: A Typology of Rewriting in Variant Editions and Rewritten Scripture" (PhD diss., Emory University, 2014), 125–60. His main conclusion is: "The shorter and longer extant texts are two surviving moments of an ongoing process, like the tip of an iceberg that does not show the full extent of the picture" (159–60). Incidentally, Quant also recognizes that attention to textual criticism introduces obstacles to theories of linguistic development and methods of linguistic dating (9–10).

18. Sidnie White Crawford, "Understanding the Textual History of the Hebrew Bible: A New Proposal," in *The Hebrew Bible in Light of the Dead Sea Scrolls*, ed. Nóra Dávid et al., FRLANT 239 (Göttingen: Vandenhoeck & Ruprecht, 2012), 67; see also 69. The editorial, exegetical, and other changes that are observable in the MT are described in Emanuel Tov, "The Literary History of the Book of Jeremiah in the Light of Its Textual History," in Tigay, *Empirical Models for Biblical Criticism*, 211–37; revised from Tov, "Some Aspects of the Textual and Literary History of the Book of

unequivocally about the "post-exilic date" (once) and "post-exilic additions" (twice) of Edition II (= MT).[19] Other text-critical experts concur with Tov's assessment, arguing that the revisions exhibited in the MT date to the Persian and/or Hellenistic period—not to the sixth-century—that is, to the milieus of the writers of Chronicles and/or Daniel, for example.[20] In short, "the two editions represent the accumulation of centuries of development, reflection, supplementation and variation."[21] This perspective is especially evident in William McKane's now widely accepted "rolling corpus" theory of the book's composition.[22] "In general, the theory is bound up with the persuasion that the rolling corpus 'rolled' over a long period of time and was still rolling in the post-exilic period,"[23] and "the corpus of the book of Jeremiah grew over the centuries"—not "over the decades" of the sixth century.[24]

2.2. Historical Linguistic Perspective

Compared to the extensive text-critical work on the book of Jeremiah, there has been very little historical linguistic work on its language.[25] In

---

Jeremiah," in *Le livre de Jérémie: Le prophète et son milieu, les oracles et leur transmission*, ed. Pierre-Maurice Bogaert, BETL 54 (Leuven: Peeters, 1981), 145–67; revised in Tov, *The Greek and Hebrew Bible: Collected Essays on the Septuagint*, VTSup 72 (Leiden: Brill, 1999), 363–84.

19. Tov, *Textual Criticism of the Hebrew Bible*, 288. In fact, Tov does not use "post-exilic" anywhere else in his book. Elsewhere Tov comments: "[T]he Masoretic edition of Jeremiah is post-exilic, as opposed to the edition included in the LXX" (Emanuel Tov, "The Dead Sea Scrolls and the Textual History of the Masoretic Bible," in Dávid et al., *Hebrew Bible in Light of the Dead Sea Scrolls*, 50).

20. Tov cites numerous scholars whose publications espouse this view, including Aejmelaeus, Bogaert, Janzen, Joosten, Lange, Lust, Schenker, Stipp, Stulman, Weis, and Wells (Tov, *Textual Criticism of the Hebrew Bible*, 286). See also the citations above of Carr and Sweeney.

21. Carroll, *Jeremiah*, 54.

22. William McKane, *A Critical and Exegetical Commentary on Jeremiah*, vol. 1: *Introduction and Commentary on Jeremiah I–XXV*, ICC (Edinburgh: T&T Clark, 1986); McKane, *A Critical and Exegetical Commentary on Jeremiah*, vol. 2: *Commentary on Jeremiah XXVI–LII*, ICC (Edinburgh: T&T Clark), 1996.

23. Ibid., 1:lxxxiii.

24. Ibid., 2:clxxiv.

25. Other short surveys of historical linguistic work on Jeremiah's language are available in Aaron D. Hornkohl, *Ancient Hebrew Periodization and the Language of the*

this context, I will briefly summarize the contributions of four scholars (Guenther, Stipp, Smith, and Joosten). Then I will examine more deeply (and critically) the work of a fifth individual (Hornkohl).

Allen Robert Guenther's PhD dissertation analyzes differences in the syntax of verbal clauses in Jer 37–45 and Esth 1–10.[26] He studies fifteen items in which there is a difference between (*Classical* Biblical Hebrew) Jeremiah and (Late Biblical Hebrew) Esther and concludes that twelve are the outcome of language change, perhaps due to some extent to contact with Aramaic. Significant presuppositions behind his analysis are that each text constitutes a compositional unity, the book of Jeremiah is a sixth-century composition and an interval of one to three or four centuries separates it from the book of Esther—that is, these books represent milestones on either side of the exile—and his analysis is based on the MT only.

Hermann-Josef Stipp's work highlights 130 cases of 37 linguistic items that occur only in the readings (mostly surpluses) particular to the MT edition of Jeremiah.[27] In his estimation, "[t]his material appears to pose a major challenge to theories favouring the priority of the Masoretic edition over the Alexandrian one."[28] While Stipp says relatively little in his article on the subject of dating, making only a passing reference to "post-exilic Jerusalem,"[29] he clearly expresses his view in his monograph

---

Book of Jeremiah: The Case for a Sixth-Century Date of Composition, SSLL 74 (Leiden: Brill, 2014), 52, 358–59 n. 8; Young, Rezetko, and Ehrensvärd, *Linguistic Dating of Biblical Texts*, 2:36–37 (see the index, 2:345, for references to discussions of specific linguistic features of the book).

26. Allen Robert Guenther, "A Diachronic Study of Biblical Hebrew Prose Syntax: An Analysis of the Verbal Clause in Jeremiah 37–45 and Esther 1–10" (PhD diss., University of Toronto, 1977). Additional discussion of Guenther's dissertation is available in Young, Rezetko, and Ehrensvärd, *Linguistic Dating of Biblical Texts*, 1:27–29; 2:37.

27. Hermann-Josef Stipp, "Linguistic Peculiarities of the Masoretic Edition of the Book of Jeremiah: An Updated Index," *JNSL* 23 (1997): 181–202. This article updates the discussion of the same issue in Stipp, *Das masoretische und alexandrinische Sondergut des Jeremiabuches: Textgeschichtlicher Rang, Eigenarten, Triebkräfte*, OBO 136 (Fribourg: Editions Universitaires; Göttingen: Vandenhoeck & Ruprecht, 1994), 77–82, 142. There are some brief remarks on Stipp's work in Carr, *Formation of the Hebrew Bible*, 97–98; Hornkohl, *Ancient Hebrew Periodization*, 358 n. 8. The thirty-seven items which Stipp discusses are divine epithets (1–5), formulas marking divine speech (6–8), human titles (9–14), various other phrases (15–32) and lexemes (33–36) restricted to the MT edition of Jeremiah, and *Atbash*-type cryptoscripts (37).

28. Stipp, "Linguistic Peculiarities," 181.

29. Ibid., 197.

that the origin of the special MT material was in the fourth and third centuries BCE.[30]

Colin Smith's PhD dissertation examines forty-eight morphological features of pronouns, nouns, and verbs.[31] He concludes, first, the lack of a more widespread Aramaic influence in Jeremiah reinforces the evidence of a late monarchical/early exilic date for the book, and, second, the book's blend of linguistic peculiarities reflects a regional dialect of Benjamin with elements from Judahite Hebrew to the south and Israelian Hebrew to the north and east. Smith frames his results as a challenge to "source criticism," to a "post-exilic date for Jeremiah," and to "one author/s for both books" of Deuteronomy and Jeremiah. Finally, a significant presupposition of Smith's analysis is that it is based on the MT only, since "[r]ecent approaches in biblical scholarship have emphasized the study [of] the books based upon *actual* texts, not hypothetical sources or reconstructed texts."[32]

Jan Joosten's chapter examines nine linguistic features in MT pluses vis-à-vis the LXX, arguing that the MT has elements of postclassical Hebrew.[33] He accepts the consensus view on the textual situation of the book of Jeremiah that is held by the bulk of text-critical experts (see §2.1, above). Consequently, late language in the MT edition of Jeremiah accords well with the revision of the book in the Persian and/or Hellenistic period.[34]

---

30. Stipp, *Masoretische und alexandrinische Sondergut*, 142–43.

31. Colin J. Smith, "'With an Iron Pen and a Diamond Tip': Linguistic Peculiarities of the Book of Jeremiah" (PhD diss., Cornell University, 2003). There are a few remarks on Smith's dissertation in Hornkohl, *Ancient Hebrew Periodization*, 52, 62–64; Young, Rezetko, and Ehrensvärd, *Linguistic Dating of Biblical Texts*, 2:37.

32. Smith, "With an Iron Pen and a Diamond Tip," 10 (emphasis original); see also 6–17.

33. Jan Joosten, "L'excédent massorétique du livre Jérémie et l'hébreu postclassique," in *Conservatism and Innovation in the Hebrew Language of the Hellenistic Period: Proceedings of a Fourth International Symposium on the Hebrew of the Dead Sea Scrolls and Ben Sira*, ed. Jan Joosten and Jean-Sébastien Rey, STDJ 73 (Leiden: Brill, 2008), 93–108. For additional discussion of Joosten's chapter see Hornkohl, *Ancient Hebrew Periodization*, 314–15 n. 52, 318 n. 64, 358–59 n. 8; Robert Rezetko, "The Qumran Scrolls of the Book of Judges: Literary Formation, Textual Criticism, and Historical Linguistics," *JHS* 13 (2013): 68; Rezetko and Young, *Historical Linguistics and Biblical Hebrew*, 94–95; Young, Rezetko, and Ehrensvärd, *Linguistic Dating of Biblical Texts*, 2:158.

34. Jan Joosten, "Excédent massorétique du livre Jérémie," 95 n. 11, 98, 101–2, 104, 108.

In summary, whereas Guenther and Smith dismiss text-critical evidence and consider that (proto-)MT Jeremiah is a product of the sixth century, Stipp and Joosten embrace textual data, the scholarly consensus on the (earlier, shorter) LXX and (later, longer) MT editions of Jeremiah, and the dating of (proto-)MT Jeremiah to the (late) postexilic period.

Another perspective is evident in the work of other scholars. They assume the framework of the conventional periodization of Biblical Hebrew in which a preexilic Early (or Classical or Standard) Biblical Hebrew phase (EBH, CBH, or SBH) developed into a postexilic Late Biblical Hebrew phase (LBH), and they regard Jeremiah's language (in the MT) as a specimen of exilic or transitional Biblical Hebrew (TBH).[35] The most recent and thorough argument for this view is Aaron Hornkohl's *Ancient Hebrew Periodization and the Language of the Book of Jeremiah: The Case for a Sixth-Century Date of Composition*. As indicated in the book's subtitle, Hornkohl's argument is that the bulk of (proto-)MT Jeremiah is the product of the sixth-century. Hornkohl's principal *objective* is the linguistic dating of the book of Jeremiah: "to situate the language of the book of Jeremiah within the broader history of the Hebrew language."[36] His *methodology* is Avi Hurvitz's four criteria of linguistic distribution, opposition, extrabiblical attestation, and accumulation.[37] In particular, he clearly and consistently applies the conventional Hurvitzian methodology in his investigation of more than forty linguistic features—related to orthography, phonology, morphology, syntax, and the lexicon—in Jeremiah and other biblical and extrabiblical sources.[38] Hornkohl arrives at three main *conclusions*.[39] First, a "mixture," "admixture," or "mixed usage"

35. For proponents of this view see the references in Hornkohl, *Ancient Hebrew Periodization*, 15 n. 39; Young, Rezetko, and Ehrensvärd, *Linguistic Dating of Biblical Texts*, 1:51; 2:36.

36. Hornkohl, *Ancient Hebrew Periodization*, 51.

37. For summaries of these criteria see Hornkohl, *Ancient Hebrew Periodization*, 6–8; Young, Rezetko, and Ehrensvärd, *Linguistic Dating of Biblical Texts*, 1:20–23.

38. The case studies comprise the bulk of Hornkohl's book (Hornkohl, *Ancient Hebrew Periodization*, 72–355). For summaries of the individual studies see ibid., 53–62, 361–65.

39. For his clearest statements of these results see ibid., 363–69. In particular, observe particularly his comments on the language of Jeremiah in comparison to the language of Ezekiel, Haggai, Zechariah, and Malachi (367, 371). The language of Jeremiah is more classical or conversely the language of Ezekiel, Haggai, Zechariah, and Malachi is typologically later.

of early/classical and late/postclassical linguistic elements characterizes both the "short edition" (text in both the MT and LXX) and the "supplementary material" (text in the MT but absent from the LXX). Second, the supplementary material has a slightly later linguistic profile than the short edition. Third, both editions of Jeremiah should be dated to the sixth century, because neither has the concentration of late linguistic elements that characterizes the early postexilic works of Haggai, Zechariah, and Malachi (ca. 500 BCE) or the later works of Esther, Daniel, Ezra–Nehemiah, and Chronicles (after ca. 450 BCE).

As just remarked, Hornkohl believes that the bulk of (proto-)MT Jeremiah is to be dated to the sixth century, because the book lacks the accumulation of late language which characterizes books like Haggai–Malachi, Esther–Chronicles, and other post-sixth-century writings. Throughout the book, he consistently talks about the time of the book's composition in the sixth century,[40] prior to the rise of LBH (ca. 500–450) and LBH in its purest form (ca. 450 onwards).[41] Nevertheless, on the final page, in the final paragraph, and in the final footnote of the main body of the book, immediately preceding the conclusion, he offers several remarks which are in tension with ideas expressed elsewhere. First, he grants the possibility of literary developments in the Persian and/or Hellenistic period, that is, after the sixth century, but these are "unlikely to have involved the addition of more than short interpolations."[42] Basically, therefore, in Hornkohl's mind the book of Jeremiah was written and revised during the sixth century, but in the following centuries, that is, from ca. 500 to the third–first centuries BCE (the dates of the biblical Dead Sea Scrolls of Jeremiah: 2Q13, 4Q70–72b), the two editions of Jeremiah remained more or less untouched by the hands of editors. Second, he comments:

> It should be noted that the position advocated in this study regarding the dating of Jeremiah in general and the short edition and supplementary material more specifically in no way contradicts McKane's … now widely accepted "rolling corpus" theory of the book's composition. It is generally accepted that the bulk of this process of accretion took place over an extended period during the years of the Exile. This conclusion is very much in line with the results of the present study, according to which

40. Ibid., 14, 52, 66, 369–71.
41. Ibid., 10–11, 46, 66, 367.
42. Ibid., 369.

the book's principal literary components were by and large complete by 500–450 BCE.

Several comments can be made about this statement by Hornkohl. First, the period 500–450 in relation to the book of Jeremiah is one which Hornkohl has not given elsewhere in the book where he has spoken consistently about the sixth century. Second, Hornkohl's assertion that his results cohere well with McKane's theory of a corpus that rolled "over an extended period during the years of the Exile" is a claim that fits poorly both with the scholarly consensus on the book's long and complex formation and with even McKane's own view that the book continued to develop in the "post-exilic period" and "over the centuries" (see §2.1, above). In short, the conclusions reached by Hornkohl, on the one hand, and textual critics, on the other, are incompatible. Since Hornkohl's book is until now by far the most thorough investigation of Jeremiah's language, and because it is a consistent application of the conventional Hurvitzian methodology for the linguistic dating (or "historical linguistic" investigation) of biblical literature, in the remainder of this chapter I will regard it as the representative of the consensus view on the historical linguistic situation of the book.[43] The question therefore arises: which approach and conclusion rests on a firmer foundation, that of textual critics or historical linguists?

3. Empirical Models for Textual and Linguistic Developments

3.1. Text-Critical Model

Textual criticism has a long history in classical, medieval, and biblical studies. The practice of textual criticism of the Hebrew Bible begins with the empirical data: variations between parallel passages (e.g., 2 Sam 22 // Ps 18 in the MT) and between textual traditions (MT, SP, DSS, LXX, etc.).[44] Variants are collected, compared, and evaluated in order to determine relationships between readings and manuscripts and, ideally, an

43. Hornkohl's thesis might be described as an attempt to reach a compromise between the conservative dating of the entire book of Jeremiah adopted by Guenther and Smith (and several others) and the compositeness and secondariness of the MT book of Jeremiah accepted by Stipp and Joosten (and most others).

44. Müller, Pakkala, and Ter Haar Romeny, *Evidence of Editing*, 1–17; Tov, *Textual Criticism of the Hebrew Bible*, 1–22.

account of a writing's composition and transmission. Similar to other premodern literatures the textual evidence for the Hebrew Bible is problematic because of its sparseness and lateness. The Dead Sea Scrolls (third century BCE–first century CE) are nearly a thousand years older than medieval MT and SP manuscripts, but even they are incomplete and distant witnesses to "original" biblical writings.[45] By the same token, the Hebrew Bible was translated into Greek in the third and second centuries BCE, but the most important manuscripts containing all or almost all the books of the LXX date to the fourth and fifth centuries CE.[46] Scholars have formulated various procedures and guidelines for evaluating textual differences, but the only real rules are that each textual problem is intrinsically unique and textual evaluation is inherently subjective.[47] Given such problems of sources and methodology and other theoretical difficulties, the most constructive approach will focus on tangible examples and probable causal relationships.[48]

As an illustration of the empirical model for textual development, I will briefly sketch the example of Gedaliah's murder in MT/LXX 2 Kgs 25:25, LXX Jer 48:1–3, and MT Jer 41:1–3. My remarks closely follow Juha Pakkala's excellent work on this example, and in this context I must refer the reader to his publications for detailed discussions of the individual variants.[49]

After the destruction of Judah, the Babylonians appointed Gedaliah as governor over the remaining population. Soon afterward he was murdered by Ishmael, one of the military commanders who came to Mizpah. The following parallel layout and translation highlight the considerable

---

45. The Hebrew witnesses are described in Tov, *Textual Criticism of the Hebrew Bible*, 23–115.

46. The Greek witnesses are described in ibid., 127–47.

47. On the latter, see the discussion of the evaluation of readings in ibid., 269–82.

48. "Once the basic principles have been apprehended, what is needed is observation and practice, not research into the further ramifications of theory" (Martin L. West, *Textual Criticism and Editorial Technique: Applicable to Greek and Latin Texts*, Teubner Studienbücher: Philologie [Stuttgart: Teubner, 1973], 5.)

49. Juha Pakkala, "Gedaliah's Murder in 2 Kings 25:25 and Jeremiah 41:1–3," in *Scripture in Transition: Essays on Septuagint, Hebrew Bible, and Dead Sea Scrolls in Honour of Raija Sollamo*, ed. Anssi Voitila and Jutta Jokiranta, JSJSup 126 (Leiden: Brill, 2008), 401–11; revised as "Evidence for the Literary Growth of Gedaliah's Murder in 2 Kings 25:25, Jeremiah 41:1–3 MT, and Jeremiah 48:1–3 LXX," in Müller, Pakkala, and Ter Haar Romeny, *Evidence of Editing*, 127–41.

differences between the editions of the story in the Hebrew and Greek versions of Kings and Jeremiah. A reconstruction of the Hebrew *Vorlage* is given for LXX Jeremiah. The pluses shared by LXX and MT Jeremiah in relation to Kings are single underlined, and the additional pluses in only MT Jeremiah are double underlined. Relocated words are marked with a dashed underline.

Jer 41:1–3 (MT)	Jer 48:1–3 (LXX)	2 Kgs 25:25 (MT/LXX)
ויהי בחדש השביעי	ויהי בחדש השביעי	ויהי בחדש השביעי
בא ישמעאל	בא ישמעאל	בא ישמעאל
בן־נתניה בן־אלישמע	בן־נתניה בן־אלישמע	בן־נתניה בן־אלישמע
מזרע המלוכה	מזרע המלך	מזרע המלוכה
ורבי המלך		
ועשׂרה אנשים אתו	ועשׂרה אנשים אתו	ועשׂרה אנשים אתו
אל־גדליהו	אל־גדליהו	
בן־אחיקם		
המצפתה	המצפתה	
ויאכלו שׁם לחם יחדו	ויאכלו שׁם לחם יחדו	
במצפה		
ויקם ישמעאל	ויקם ישמעאל	
בן־נתניה		
ועשׂרה אנשים אשר־היו אתו	ועשׂרה אנשים אשר־היו אתו	
ויכו את־גדליהו	ויכו את־גדליהו	ויכו את־גדליהו
בן־אחיקם בן־שׁפן בחרב		
וימֶת		וימֹת
אתו		
אשר־הפקיד מלך־בבל	אשר־הפקיד מלך־בבל	
בארץ	בארץ	
ואת־	ואת־	ואת־
כל־	כל־	
היהודים	היהודים	היהודים
		ואת־הכשׂדים
אשר־היו אתו	אשר־היו אתו	אשר־היו אתו
את־גדליהו		
במצפה	במצפה	במצפה
ואת־הכשׂדים	ואת־הכשׂדים	
אשר נמצאו־שם	אשר נמצאו־שם	

את אנשי המלחמה הכה
ישמעאל

In the seventh month Ishmael, son of Nethaniah, the son of Elishama, who was of royal seed and one of the king's high officers, came with ten men to Gedaliah, son of Ahiqam, to Mizpah. When they were eating a meal together at Mizpah, Ishmael, son of Nethaniah, and the ten men who were with him, stood up and struck down Gedaliah, the son of Ahiqam, the son of Shaphan, with the sword so that he died and thus killing him, whom the king of Babylon had appointed as governor over the land, and all the Judeans and Chaldeans who were with him, with Gedaliah, at Mizpah, and the Chaldeans who were found there, the soldiers, Ishmael struck down.

Pakkala's detailed discussions of the individual variants are clearly presented and reasonably argued, and in general I, and I believe other textual/literary critics, will agree with his critical assessments. In the context of the present chapter the following larger conclusions are relevant:

- *Development through supplementation*: The story grew through successive expansions by later editors (a rolling corpus). MT Jeremiah is the latest stage in the development of the story. The story was *not* abridged in LXX Jeremiah and then further in MT/LXX Kings.
- *More than doubled in size*: The oldest literary stage is less than half the size of the youngest. The oldest text has 22 words and 124 characters, the intermediate text has 39 words and 225 characters, and the youngest text has 54 words and 308 characters. "This means that the oldest text was radically and substantially expanded."[50]
- *Mainly spontaneous and unrelated additions*: "Many of the additions are glosses, short explanatory additions, inspired by factors in the older text, or additions that increase details. Many of them may be unrelated to each other and may have been spontaneous additions by copyist-editors. There is no evidence of a comprehensive redaction in any of the additions."[51]

50. Pakkala, "Gedaliah's Murder," 406; see also Müller, Pakkala, and Ter Haar Romeny, *Evidence of Editing*, 140.

51. Pakkala, "Gedaliah's Murder," 410; see also Müller, Pakkala, and Ter Haar Romeny, *Evidence of Editing*, 139.

- *At least two and perhaps five to seven different editors*: "It is unlikely that the additions in the present text example were all written by two editors only. Three stages of the development have been preserved in these witnesses, but they are only glimpses of some arbitrary points in the development of the text. On the basis of the discussed documented evidence, one could assume that the text now preserved in Jer 41:1–3 MT is the result of at least five to seven different editors, which corresponds to some of the most radical redaction-critical models."[52]
- *Development over several centuries and into a relatively late period*: It is probable that the story was constantly expanded by different hands over several centuries and into a relatively late period. The story arguably did *not* develop through a period of decades in the sixth century.[53]
- *Probability of earlier undocumented developments*: "It is possible that the shortest text, reconstructed by using such 'empirical evidence,' is not the original text, because texts of the Hebrew Bible also developed in the earlier stages of transmission of which we possess no textual evidence."[54]

Before concluding this discussion of the empirical model for textual development, I would like to highlight one more feature of the extant versions of Gedaliah's murder in Kings and Jeremiah. I referred earlier to Rofé's and Tigay's assertion that late linguistic developments may not characterize or even appear in late textual developments (see §1, above). In the present case, we are dealing with a small quantity of text, which however grew considerably over the centuries, but in any case we should proceed cautiously without exaggerating the significance of the evidence. What I therefore want to underline is that MT Jeremiah (and presumably also the *Vorlage* of LXX Jeremiah), which has the youngest and in all probability a late Second Temple edition of Gedaliah's murder, is *unmarked* by so-called late language. Again, I repeat, the data are scanty, but at any rate we find in MT Jeremiah such conventional Classical Hebrew language as *waw* con-

52. Müller, Pakkala, and Ter Haar Romeny, *Evidence of Editing*, 140–41; see also Pakkala, "Gedaliah's Murder," 411.

53. Pakkala, "Gedaliah's Murder," 410–11.

54. Ibid., 401; see also 411; Müller, Pakkala, and Ter Haar Romeny, *Evidence of Editing*, 141 n. 26.

secutive verb forms (41:1, 2), directive *he* (41:1),[55] and *-yahu* names (41:1, 3; see also 41:2).[56] At the very least, the language of the (latest) revision is based on the familiar language of the (earlier) source, and so, against what many biblicists and Hebraists often presume, there is not a one-to-one correspondence between late textual/literary developments and "late" language.[57]

3.2. Historical Linguistic Model

I recently published a book on the historical linguistics of Biblical Hebrew in relation to general historical linguistic theory and method that examines in detail traditional work by Hebraists on diachronic development in Biblical Hebrew.[58] My objective therefore in this section is to sketch briefly what constitutes empirical data and an empirical approach in conventional historical linguistic research. Then in the following section, I will give several examples that illustrate shortcomings in Hornkohl's work on the linguistic dating of the book of Jeremiah and more generally in the use of Biblical Hebrew linguistic data in historical linguistic research.

The selection and evaluation of the sources of linguistic data have fundamental importance in conventional historical linguistics.[59] Ideally the sources should be authentic (original), noncomposite (unedited), dated (situated in time), and localized (situated in place). As a rule, historical linguists prefer to work with documentary sources, such as letters, rather than literary sources which often have a long and complex history of pro-

---

55. מצפתה is also used in MT 1 Sam 7:5, 6, 7; Jer 40:6, 8, 12, 13. Contrast the usage of מצפה in MT Judg 11:34; 20:1, 3; 21:5, 8; 1 Sam 10:17; 22:3; 2 Kgs 25:23.

56. גדליהו is also found in MT 2 Kgs 25:22, 23 (x 2), 24, 25; Jer 38:1; 39:14; 40:7, 9, 11, 12, 13, 14, 15, 16; 41:2, 4, 6, 9, 10, 18; 43:6; 1 Chr 25:3, 9. Contrast גדליה in MT Jer 40:5, 6, 8; 41:16; Zeph 1:1; Ezra 10:18. In contrast, נתניה is found in MT Jer 41:1, 2, and also in MT 2 Kgs 25:23, 25; Jer 40:14, 15; 41:6, 7, 10, 11, 12, 15, 16, 18; 1 Chr 25:2. Contrast נתניהו in MT Jer 36:14; 40:8; 41:9; 1 Chr 25:12; 2 Chr 17:8.

57. This outcome matches the result of my previous work on the textual developments and linguistic contours of Judges and Samuel. See Rezetko, "Qumran Scrolls of the Book of Judges"; Robert Rezetko, *Source and Revision in the Narratives of David's Transfer of the Ark: Text, Language and Story in 2 Samuel 6 and 1 Chronicles 13, 15–16*, LHBOTS 470 (New York: T&T Clark, 2007), passim; Rezetko and Young, *Historical Linguistics and Biblical Hebrew*, 171–210, 453–591, and elsewhere on Samuel.

58. Rezetko and Young, *Historical Linguistics and Biblical Hebrew.*

59. Ibid., 21–45.

duction in the hands of numerous editors and scribes who lived in various times and places. Close attention should be given especially to independent variables (e.g., dialect) when seeking to explain the distribution of linguistic features (dependent variables). Unfortunately, however, the sources available for historical linguistic research often fall short of the ideal, yet in such cases the researcher should offer an explanation about why certain texts and not others were chosen as the sources of data, and he or she should discuss possible flaws in the research due to the paucity of suitable texts. In short, philological analysis plays a chief role in conventional historical linguistics. I hardly need to call attention to the poor quantity and quality of sources for historical linguistic research on ancient (Biblical) Hebrew or the fact that Hebraists rarely contemplate the nature of the sources.[60]

Historical linguistics is a major field of research with a diversity of methods for documenting and explaining variation and change in language over time, including the comparative method, internal reconstruction, and so on.[61] Anita Auer and Anja Voeste, in a chapter on grammatical variables, describe three conventional methods of "data capture" for historical linguistic research.[62] The first method, "*intra*-textual" variable analysis, "examines the frequency and range of variants in one text or a corpus of texts that has been compiled for this purpose and is treated as a single text," such as the Nuremberg chronicle or a corpus of texts such as the *lettres provinciales*.[63] The second method, "*inter*-textual" variable analysis, compares "the results of two or more intra-textual investigations," such as the Nuremberg chronicle and other incunabula, "thereby changing the external determinants such as time or place."[64] The third method, "*cross*-textual" variable analysis, "compares the variants in different versions of the same text."[65]

---

60. Ibid., 61–71, 83–110, 115–16, where I discuss such matters at length.

61. Brian D. Joseph and Richard D. Janda, eds., *The Handbook of Historical Linguistics*, BHL (Malden, MA: Blackwell, 2003), 181–310; Silvia Luraghi and Vit Bubenik, eds., *Continuum Companion to Historical Linguistics* (London: Continuum, 2010), 37–86.

62. Anita Auer and Anja Voeste, "Grammatical Variables," in *The Handbook of Historical Sociolinguistics*, ed. Juan Manuel Hernández Campoy and Juan Camilo Conde Silvestre, BHL (Chichester: Wiley-Blackwell, 2012), 259–61.

63. Ibid., 259 (emphasis original).

64. Ibid., 260 (emphasis original).

65. Ibid., 260 (emphasis original).

In the following section, I will make use of intratextual variable analysis to study the distributions of two sets of linguistic variables in Biblical Hebrew and related writings: צעק and זעק for "cry" and אנכי and אני for "I." A premise of the analysis is that these writings are considered to be a single (complete and closed) corpus, though the individual constituents obviously do not come from the same time and place. The particular approach I will use is variationist analysis, by which a comparison is made of changing proportions of occurrence in different writings of two or more language variables or different ways of saying the same thing.[66] My analysis is descriptive,[67] adheres to the principles of synonymy (forms studied have the same meaning), accountability (all occurrences of relevant forms are recorded), and individuality (occurrences in individual writings rather than groups of writings are considered),[68] and recognizes the problems of sources (see above) and periodization.[69]

4. Illustrations of Language Variation

4.1. "Cry" (זעק/צעק)

Hornkohl argues, first, that the book of Jeremiah should be dated to a sixth century transitional period because of its mixture of early (preexilic) and late (postexilic) language, and, second, that the supplementary material (MT) has a slightly later profile and should be dated somewhat later than the short edition (MT // LXX) (see §2.2, above). One feature that he discusses in support of his arguments is the distribution of the variants צעק and זעק for the variable "cry" in Biblical Hebrew generally and Jeremiah specifically.[70] MT Jeremiah has seven occurrences of צעק and

66. For a thorough introduction to variationist analysis, see Rezetko and Young, *Historical Linguistics and Biblical Hebrew*, 6, 45–49, 211–403.

67. Ibid., 14–21.

68. Ibid., 227–32.

69. Ibid., 49–56, 318–25, 395–402. I cannot discuss the matter further in this context (see the discussions in the previously cited pages), but I should at least point out that the notion of language periodization, that is, language states and transitions, is highly problematic both theoretically and methodologically, and with very few exceptions this has been overlooked by Hebraists who seek to date biblical writings to particular historical periods on the basis of linguistic criteria.

70. Hornkohl, *Ancient Hebrew Periodization*, 78–82; see also 53, 55, 58–59, 62, 69, 362, 365.

fourteen of זעק (66.7 percent זעק). The figures are seven צעק/twelve זעק in the short edition (63.2 percent זעק) and zero/two in the supplementary material (100 percent זעק). "From the perspective of use and distribution, then, Jeremiah's language patterns as a form of TBH [Transitional Biblical Hebrew], linking the CBH [Classical Biblical Hebrew] best exemplified by the Pentateuch and the LBH [Late Biblical Hebrew] of the distinctively late books."[71] And זעק is a "late phenomen[on] especially characteristic of the supplementary material."[72]

The following figures give the frequencies of the roots צעק and זעק, and the percentage of זעק relative to צעק and זעק, in the Hebrew Bible (MT), the book of Ben Sira, the nonbiblical Dead Sea Scrolls, and the Mishnah.[73] Space does not permit a full discussion of the distribution and usage of צעק and זעק in the variationist framework.[74] However, it seems to me that Hornkohl's method is neither objective nor empirical. This is largely because he examines the data only in relation to groups of biblical books, though he does in fact present the data for individual books in a table. The particular groups of books he discusses are the Pentateuch (Genesis–Deuteronomy), Prophets (Joshua–Malachi), Former Prophets (Joshua–Kings), Latter Prophets (Isaiah–Malachi), and "the distinctive LBH corpus" (Esther–Chronicles). Hornkohl, therefore, is effectively discussing, and attempting to date, the individual book of Jeremiah relative to large groups of books whose constituents are undifferentiated. There is no basis for such an approach in conventional historical linguistic theory and method. Furthermore, as the figures above indicate, other "early" and "late" books have comparable mixtures of צעק and זעק and similar rates of

71. Ibid., 82.

72. Ibid., 361–62.

73. The books are organized according to the hypothetical dates of biblical books and then in canonical order as described in Rezetko and Young, *Historical Linguistics and Biblical Hebrew*, 248–50. These roots are unattested in Hebrew inscriptions. To minimize the complexity of the figures, the Dead Sea Scrolls and Mishnah are each presented as an undifferentiated whole, but the result of the analysis is uncompromised since the main objective here is to describe the place of the book of Jeremiah within the corpus of the MT Bible. The figures for non-P and P in the Torah are from Francis I. Andersen and A. Dean Forbes, *The Vocabulary of the Old Testament* (Rome: Pontifical Biblical Institute, 1992), 312, 407. The figures for the short and supplementary editions of Jeremiah are from Hornkohl, *Ancient Hebrew Periodization*, 82, 362.

74. For additional discussion see Rezetko and Young, *Historical Linguistics and Biblical Hebrew*, 278–83.

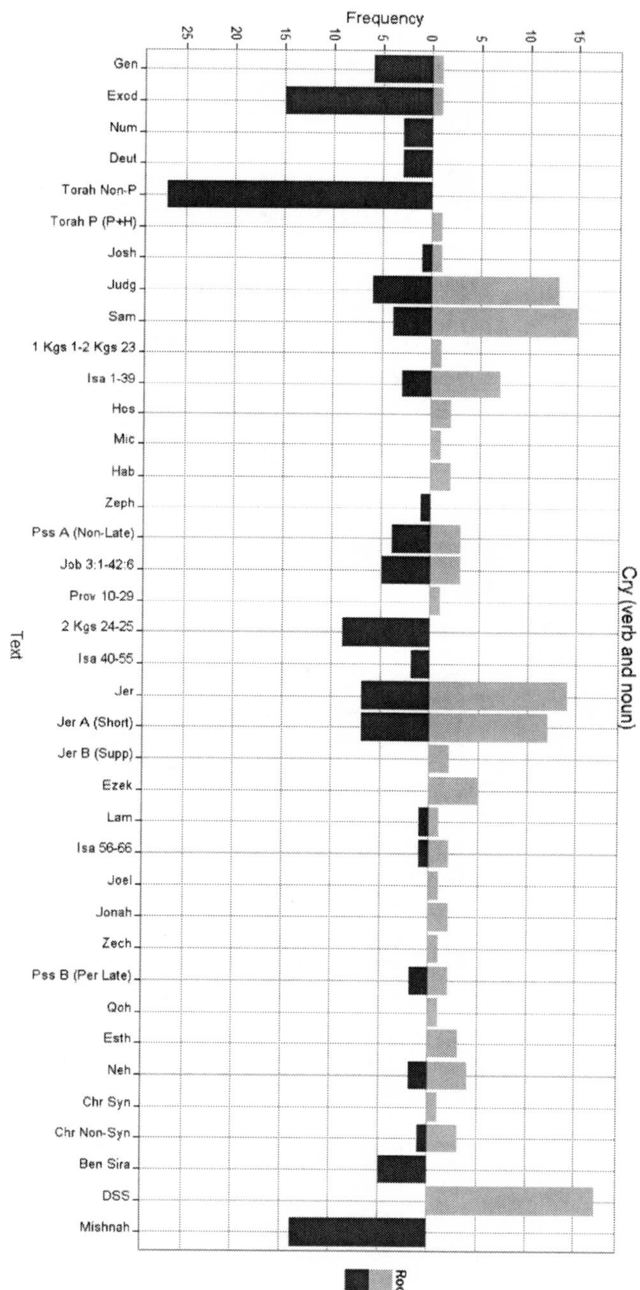
Cry (verb and noun)
Frequency
25
20
15
10
5
0
5
10
15
Text
Gen
Exod
Num
Deut
Torah Non-P
Torah P (P+H)
Josh
Judg
Sam
1 Kgs 1-2 Kgs 23
Isa 1-39
Hos
Mic
Hab
Zeph
Pss A (Non-Late)
Job 3:1-42:6
Prov 10-29
2 Kgs 24-25
Isa 40-55
Jer
Jer A (Short)
Jer B (Supp)
Ezek
Lam
Isa 56-66
Joel
Jonah
Zech
Pss B (Per Late)
Qoh
Esth
Neh
Chr Syn
Chr Non-Syn
Ben Sira
DSS
Mishnah
Root
z'q
s'q

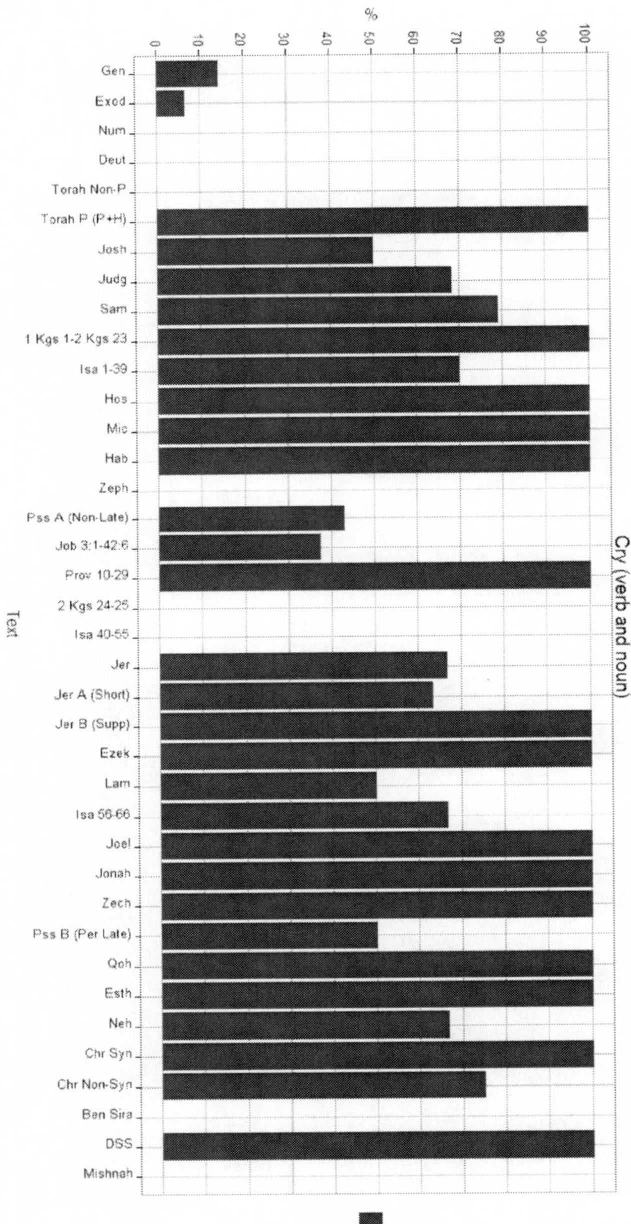
Cry (verb and noun)
%
0
10
20
30
40
50
60
70
80
90
100
Text
Gen
Exod
Num
Deut
Torah Non-P
Torah P (P+H)
Josh
Judg
Sam
1 Kgs 1-2 Kgs 23
Isa 1-39
Hos
Mic
Hab
Zeph
Pss A (Non-Late)
Job 3:1-42:6
Prov 10-29
2 Kgs 24-25
Isa 40-55
Jer
Jer A (Short)
Jer B (Supp)
Ezek
Lam
Isa 56-66
Joel
Jonah
Zech
Pss B (Per Late)
Qoh
Esth
Neh
Chr Syn
Chr Non-Syn
Ben Sira
DSS
Mishnah
Percent z'q

usage of "late" זעק. Compare, for example, "early" Judges (six צעק/thirteen זעק, 68.4 percent זעק) and "late" Nehemiah (two צעק/four זעק, 66.7 percent זעק) with "transitional" Jeremiah (seven צעק/fourteen זעק, 66.7 percent זעק). Consequently, while Biblical Hebrew may attest ongoing change related to צעק and זעק during the biblical period, the data fail to support the conventional linguistic dating approach and the transitional dating of the book of Jeremiah that Hornkohl advocates.

4.2. "I" (אני/אנכי)

Another feature that Hornkohl discusses in support of his arguments is the distribution of the variants אנכי and אני for the first common singular independent subject pronoun "I" in Biblical Hebrew generally and Jeremiah specifically.[75] MT Jeremiah has twenty-seven occurrences of אנכי and fifty-four of אני. The figures are twenty-one אנכי/forty-six אני in the short edition (68.7 percent אני) and six/eight in the supplementary material (57.1 percent אני). Hornkohl argues the following points: (1) אנכי and אני were both used in the preexilic and exilic periods, but אנכי fell into disuse in the postexilic period and thus אני became predominant; (2) the mixed usage of both forms in the book of Jeremiah is indicative of its transitional language; (3) the mixed usage characterizes both the short edition and the supplementary material; (4) the use of אנכי in the book is archaistic and conditioned primarily in divine speech. "On the evidence of certain key linguistic features [n. 13: 'Especially the use of אֲנִי and אָנֹכִי "I"'], it emerges that both the short edition and the supplementary material are characterized by admixtures of classical and post-classical tendencies that point rather decisively to a shared linguistic background in the transitional period between CBH and LBH proper."[76]

The following figures give the frequencies of אנכי and אני, and the percentage of אני relative to אנכי and אני, in the Hebrew Bible (MT), the book

75. Hornkohl, *Ancient Hebrew Periodization*, 108–11; see also 15, 34–35, 51, 53, 55, 58–59, 62, 65, 144, 361, 363–64, 366.

76. Ibid., 366. The two other "key" or "decisive" linguistic features that he cites are theophoric names ending in *–yah*/*–yahu* and the prepositions *ʾet*/*ʿim* (366 n. 13). Elsewhere in the book he underlines the importance of these same three linguistic features, saying: "A few cases of mixed usage also appear to be particularly characteristic of compositions from the transitional period" (15).

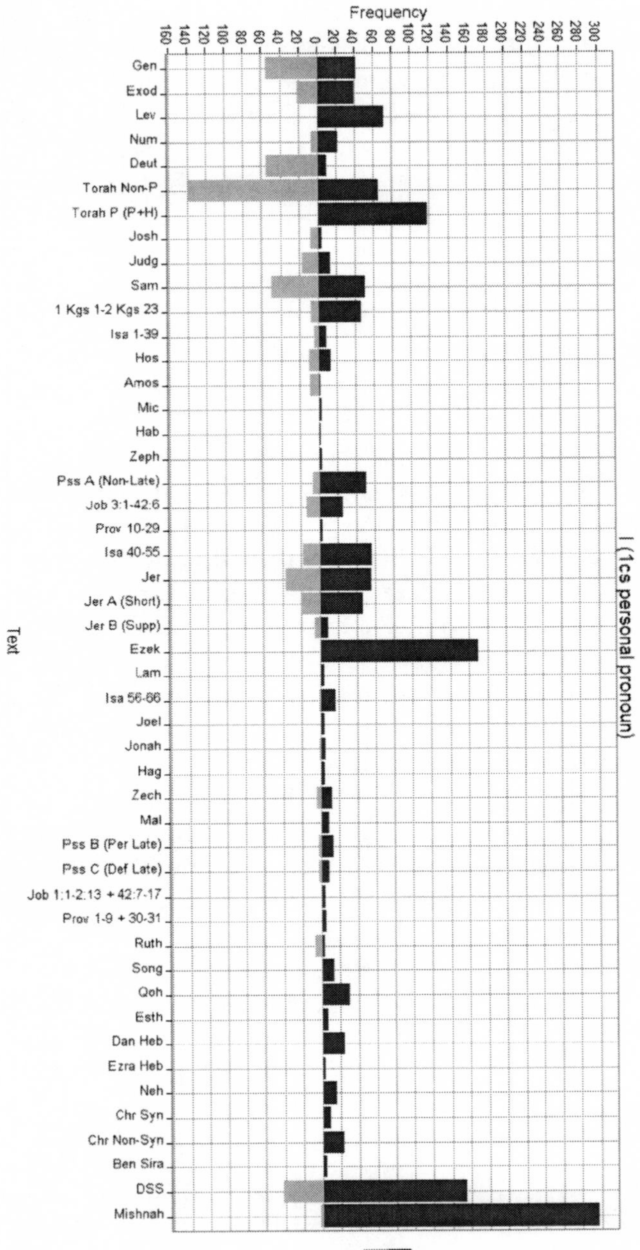
Frequency
160
140
120
100
80
60
40
20
0
20
40
60
80
100
120
140
160
180
200
220
240
260
280
300
Text
Gen
Exod
Lev
Num
Deut
Torah Non-P
Torah P (P+H)
Josh
Judg
Sam
1 Kgs 1-2 Kgs 23
Isa 1-39
Hos
Amos
Mic
Hab
Zeph
Pss A (Non-Late)
Job 3:1-42:6
Prov 10-29
Isa 40-55
Jer
Jer A (Short)
Jer B (Supp)
Ezek
Lam
Isa 56-66
Joel
Jonah
Hag
Zech
Mal
Pss B (Per Late)
Pss C (Def Late)
Job 1:1-2:13 + 42:7-17
Prov 1-9 + 30-31
Ruth
Song
Qoh
Esth
Dan Heb
Ezra Heb
Neh
Chr Syn
Chr Non-Syn
Ben Sira
DSS
Mishnah
I (1cs personal pronoun)
ʾani
ʾanoki

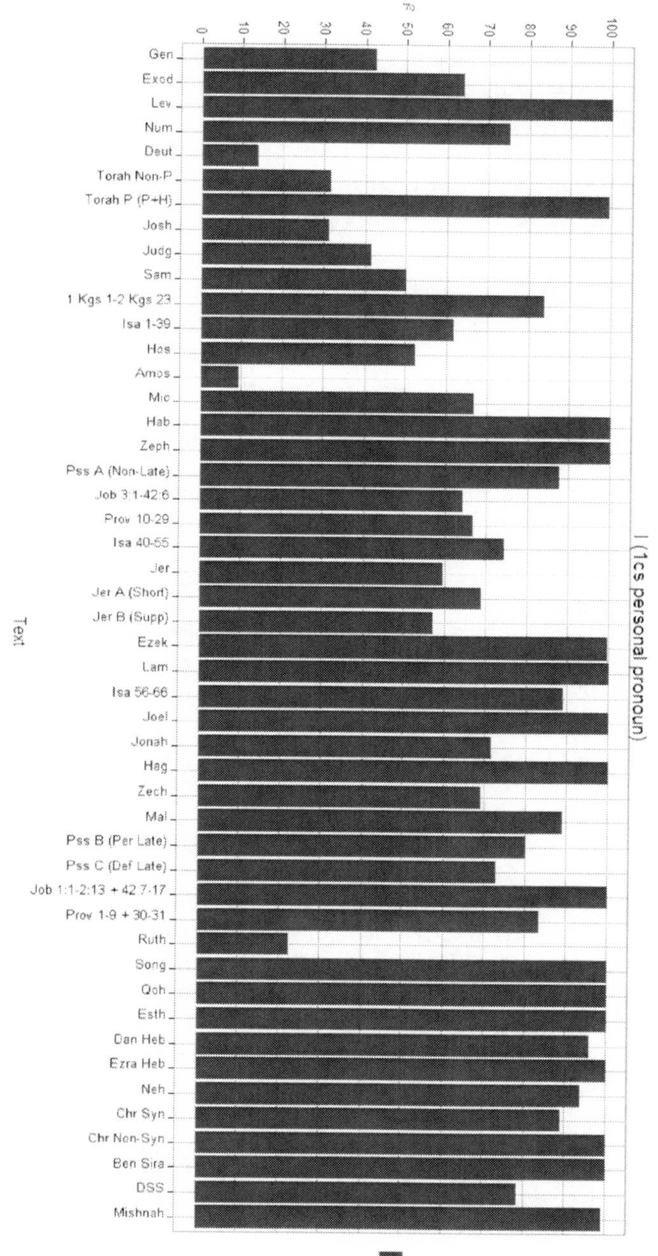
%
0
10
20
30
40
50
60
70
80
90
100
Gen
Exod
Lev
Num
Deut
Torah Non-P
Torah P (P+H)
Josh
Judg
Sam
1 Kgs 1-2 Kgs 23
Isa 1-39
Hos
Amos
Mic
Hab
Zeph
Pss A (Non-Late)
Job 3:1-42:6
Prov 10-29
Isa 40-55
Jer
Jer A (Short)
Jer B (Supp)
Ezek
Lam
Isa 56-66
Joel
Jonah
Hag
Zech
Mal
Pss B (Per Late)
Pss C (Def Late)
Job 1:1-2:13 + 42:7-17
Prov 1-9 + 30-31
Ruth
Song
Qoh
Esth
Dan Heb
Ezra Heb
Neh
Chr Syn
Chr Non-Syn
Ben Sira
DSS
Mishnah
Text
I (1cs personal pronoun)
% 'ani

of Ben Sira, the nonbiblical Dead Sea Scrolls, and the Mishnah.[77] Again, space does not permit a full discussion of the distribution and usage of אנכי and אני in the variationist framework.[78] Hornkohl's study of this variable is commendable compared to that of "cry," because in this case he discusses the book of Jeremiah in comparison to individual books instead of groups of books. All things considered, and as he himself indicates on several occasions (see above), this is one of the strongest examples in support of his arguments. However, the devil is in the details, and various facts cast doubt upon his dating of the entire book to a sixth century transitional period on the basis of this "key" linguistic criterion (and others).

To begin, Hornkohl argues that the language of Jeremiah is transitional, and Hurvitz and Rooker argue that the language of Ezekiel is also transitional.[79] The usage of אני/אנכי is considered in all three of their discussions.[80] Hornkohl is aware of this issue,[81] but, strikingly, in this context he casually brackets off Ezekiel with "other late material" like Daniel, Nehemiah, and Chronicles.[82] Again, it seems to me that Hornkohl's method is

77. Again, the books are organized according to the hypothetical dates of biblical books and then in canonical order as described in Rezetko and Young, *Historical Linguistics and Biblical Hebrew*, 248–50. Hebrew inscriptions have limited data: אני in Arad 88:1 and (probably) אנכי in Lachish 6:8–9. Again, to minimize the complexity of the figures, the Dead Sea Scrolls and Mishnah are each presented as an undifferentiated whole, but the result of the analysis is uncompromised since the main objective here is to describe the place of the book of Jeremiah within the corpus of the MT Bible. The figures for non-P and P in the Torah are from Andersen and Forbes, *Vocabulary of the Old Testament*, 280. The figures for the short and supplementary editions of Jeremiah are from Hornkohl, *Ancient Hebrew Periodization*, 361.

78. For additional discussion, though not in the variationist framework, see Robert Rezetko, "Dating Biblical Hebrew: Evidence from Samuel–Kings and Chronicles," in *Biblical Hebrew: Studies in Chronology and Typology*, ed. Ian Young, JSOTSup 369 (London: T&T Clark, 2003), 225–26; Rezetko, "The Spelling of 'Damascus' and the Linguistic Dating of Biblical Texts," *SJOT* 24 (2010): 127–28; Rezetko and Young, *Historical Linguistics and Biblical Hebrew*, 465–67.

79. Avi Hurvitz, *A Linguistic Study of the Relationship between the Priestly Source and the Book of Ezekiel: A New Approach to an Old Problem*, CahRB 20 (Paris: Gabalda, 1982); Mark F. Rooker, *Biblical Hebrew in Transition: The Language of the Book of Ezekiel*, JSOTSup 90 (Sheffield: JSOT Press, 1990).

80. Hurvitz, *Linguistic Study of the Relationship*, 169 n. 35; Rooker, *Biblical Hebrew in Transition*, 72–74.

81. Hornkohl, *Ancient Hebrew Periodization*, 14–15.

82. Ibid., 108.

neither objective nor empirical. He would like us to believe that Jeremiah is transitional with a 37/54 ratio, and Ezekiel is transitional with a 1/169 ratio, and somehow both these roughly contemporary books sit chronologically between books with mixed usage of אני/אנכי and books with predominant or exclusive usage of אני. Hornkohl may be right, but he has not argued the case objectively or empirically. In addition, Hornkohl considers that the language of earlier books like Judges, Samuel, First Isaiah, and Hosea is "fairly balanced."[83] However, the language of these books is not regarded as transitional, yet the rates of usage of אני in Samuel (50 percent), Hosea (52.2 percent), especially First Isaiah (61.5 percent), and Jeremiah (59.3 percent; short edition: 68.7 percent; supplementary material: 57.1 percent [!]) are quite similar. Also, the individual books of the Former Prophets or Deuteronomistic History have considerably different rates of usage of אני: Deuteronomy (13.8 percent), Joshua (30.8 percent), Judges (41.4 percent), Samuel (50 percent), Kings (83.6 percent). Hornkohl does not indicate this or mention the elevated figure in Kings. Furthermore, the usage in Kings is "natural" (that is, not "conditioned" by divine speech; see below), and thus this book in this regard looks even later or further along the "transitional path" than Jeremiah. Turning to P, Hornkohl downplays its virtually exclusive use of אני (x 117 to אנכי once).[84] Of course, others such as Samuel Driver have considered this a decisive indication that P originated in a later period when אנכי had fallen into disuse.[85] Finally, looking at usage, Hornkohl compares Jeremiah and the Temple Scroll, both of which, he believes, use אנכי mainly in archaistic and conditioned divine speech,[86] but it comes as a surprise, at least to me,

83. Ibid., 108.

84. Ibid., 51, 108–9 n. 4.

85. Samuel R. Driver, *An Introduction to the Literature of the Old Testament*, 9th ed. (Edinburgh: T&T Clark, 1913). He says: "The writer [that is, Driver] is also now of opinion that, although in particular cases P's use of אני might be explained consistently with an early date, yet his all but *uniform* preference for it above אנכי, taken in conjunction with his resemblance in this respect to Ez. … and other later writers (as Lam., Zech 1-8, Hag, Est, Eccl, Dan, Ezr, Neh, Chr…), constitutes a presumption, difficult to neutralize, that he wrote in the later period of the language" (155–56 n. †, emphasis original).

86. Hornkohl, *Ancient Hebrew Periodization*, 111, 363. Actually, the Temple Scroll is slightly more flexible than Jeremiah in this regard. See 11Q19 XXIX, 7 (אני), 9 (אנכי); XLVI, 4 (אנכי), 12 (אני); LI, 7 (אנכי; x2), 16 (אני); LIII, 8 (אנכי), 21 (אני); see also אנכי elsewhere only in II, 1; XLV, 13 (x 2).

that P and Ezekiel, however they are dated, show a similar inclination only once (Ezek 36:28).[87] Therefore, while Biblical Hebrew may attest ongoing change related to אנכי and אני during the biblical period, the data fail to support the conventional linguistic dating approach and the transitional dating of the book of Jeremiah that Hornkohl advocates.[88]

5. Conclusions

In the preceding sections, I have presented two descriptions of the production of the book of Jeremiah and the data said to support those scenarios. One model, which I have called the text-critical model, examines extant and reconstructed texts of the book in Hebrew, Greek, Latin, and other languages. The practitioner of this approach compares textual variants and seeks to establish a sequence of changes in regard to individual variants, groups of variants, and then entire manuscripts. The result of this approach is that the book of Jeremiah was produced over a long period of time, beginning in the late First Temple period and ending in the late Second Temple period. The other model, which I have called the historical linguistic model—though it might more appropriately be called the linguistic dating model[89]—examines linguistic features of the book in mainly, but not exclusively, the MT. The practitioner of this approach traces linguistic forms or uses across the Hebrew Bible and several extra-biblical sources and tries to situate the particular characteristics of Jeremiah's language within a continuum of other, presumably, early and late writings or groups of writings. The result of this approach is that the book of Jeremiah was produced in a relatively short period of time in roughly the sixth century BCE. Therefore, in the first model, the language of (MT) Jeremiah is understood to represent a variety of language that was written during the very long span of time through which the book was produced

87. Abraham is the speaker in Gen 23:4 (P).

88. Three more of Hornkohl's examples are studied in the variationist framework in Rezetko and Young, *Historical Linguistics and Biblical Hebrew*, 329–94. See also the discussion of the prepositions אֵת and עִם in Dong-Hyuk Kim, review of *Ancient Hebrew Periodization and the Language of the Book of Jeremiah: The Case for a Sixth-Century Date of Composition*, by Aaron D. Hornkohl, *RBL* 3 (2016): 7–8.

89. For example, Hornkohl briefly mentions historical linguistics in only four contexts (Hornkohl, *Ancient Hebrew Periodization*, 36, 48–49, 52, 231), and he does not cite any related literature or offer any relevant discussion linked to this field of study. His theoretical and methodological framework is the conventional Hurvitzian approach.

(preexilic, exilic, and postexilic periods), while in the second model the language of (MT) Jeremiah is understood to represent the variety of language that was written during only the relatively short span of time in which the book was produced (roughly the sixth century BCE).

My evaluation of the two models has interacted with the work of scholars such as Tov, Pakkala, and others, on the one hand, and Hurvitz, Hornkohl, and others, on the other. In my estimation, while neither approach is watertight,[90] largely due to the nonexistence of securely dated and localized textual sources at numerous points in (the second half of) the first millennium BCE—an unsurmountable obstacle which seriously weakens *both* models—the text-critical model as presently advanced by textual critics of the Hebrew Bible has the edge over the historical linguistic (that is, linguistic dating) model as currently practiced by Hebraists. My judgment is based on two premises. First, the text-critical model approximates a conventional text-critical approach but the historical linguistic (that is, linguistic dating) model does not come near to any conventional historical linguistic approach. More specifically, for example, Hornkohl's linguistic dating approach is contraindicated by the outcome of variationist analysis, a well-established historical (socio-)linguistic technique, and his approach overlooks scholarly theorizing on the notion of language periodization (states and transitions, including so-called transitional language), the principles of accountability and individuality, and so on. Second, I am able to grasp the linguistic profile of (MT) Jeremiah in the conventional text-critical context because of the training of ancient scribes in standard literary Hebrew, but I cannot really understand the text-critical situation in the conventional historical linguistic (that is, linguistic dating) framework. Furthermore, I think it is rather unlikely that the content of the book of Jeremiah was highly variant for a relatively short period and then suddenly became very stable for a long

90. Nor objective. Textual critics of the Hebrew Bible usually admit the subjectivity inherent to text-critical work (see §3.1, above), but, and curiously from a historical linguistic stance, Hebraists often stress the supposed objectivity, or the greater objectivity, of the conventional linguistic dating approach. Hornkohl repeats the sentiment: "Finally, while no approach to the dating of ancient texts is free of subjective judgment, the accepted linguistic approach to dating BH [Biblical Hebrew] texts arguably provides more objective controls than non-linguistic [i.e., textual and literary] alternatives" (Hornkohl, *Ancient Hebrew Periodization*, 371). See the discussion of such claims in Young, Rezetko, and Ehrensvärd, *Linguistic Dating of Biblical Texts*, 1:3, 16–17, 20, 60–68, 81, 341.

time. I suspect that if it really were Hornkohl's and others' idea that the (short and long) texts of Jeremiah were variant in the sixth century BCE, but then were copied faithfully during the whole of the Second Temple period, this would be seen as rather bizarre by textual and literary scholars of biblical and other ancient Near Eastern literatures.[91]

---

91. Hornkohl inherited his approach from Hurvitz. Hurvitz's argument is simple: late (postexilic) writings inevitably have some degree (allowing for differences of consistency and frequency) of late language, hence writings without late language are dated early (preexilic). Furthermore, this explanation applies to the entire production history of biblical writings, including their original composition and subsequent editing and copying. So, for example, in a chapter on the terminology of genealogical records in Genesis–Joshua, Hurvitz says: "In conclusion: Whatever editorial activities and literary modifications the Priestly genealogy-related accounts and records in Genesis–Joshua may have undergone during the process of their transmission, all these textual developments must have come to an end *prior* to the emergence of the distinctive LBH corpus as laid before us in its presently extant version. Or, in a slightly different formulation, the linguistic formation and consolidation of the Priestly genealogical and other similar material preserved in the books of the Pentateuch and Joshua *predate* the time period that shaped our LBH corpus as found in the MT. The language of this material should therefore be categorized typologically as Classical Biblical Hebrew and assigned historically to the preexilic period" (Avi Hurvitz, "Terminological Modifications in Biblical Genealogical Records and Their Potential Chronological Implications," in *Hebrew in the Second Temple Period: The Hebrew of the Dead Sea Scrolls and of Other Contemporary Sources*, ed. Steven E. Fassberg, Moshe Bar-Asher, and Ruth A. Clements, STDJ 108 [Leiden: Brill, 2013], 116, emphasis original). In other publications, Hurvitz has extended this specific remark on genealogical material to the language of P as a whole (e.g., Hurvitz, "The Evidence of Language in Dating the Priestly Code: A Linguistic Study in Technical Idioms and Terminology," *RB* 81 [1974]: 24–56; Hurvitz, *Linguistic Study of the Relationship*). Philip Davies points out, correctly, the circularity in Hurvitz's approach: "*Since* Judaean scribes of the Persian period cannot have written CBH—*ergo* they didn't: the theory is driving the data, and the argument is completely circular; it is a version of the absurd claim that we can always detect a forgery because forgers always make mistakes!" (Philip R. Davies, "Biblical Hebrew and the History of Ancient Judah: Typology, Chronology and Common Sense," in Young, *Biblical Hebrew: Studies in Chronology and Typology*, 154 [emphasis original]; see also 154–55; on the circularity of Hurvitz's method, see Young, Rezetko, and Ehrensvärd, *Linguistic Dating of Biblical Texts*, 1:65–68, 92–93 with n. 22 on 93–94). There are other points against Hurvitz's approach, such as the accumulation of "late" language in some "early" writings and the nonaccumulation of "late" language in some late writings, as discussed, for example, in Young, Rezetko, and Ehrensvärd, *Linguistic Dating of Biblical Texts*, 1:111–42; Rezetko and Young, *Historical Linguistics and Biblical Hebrew*, 196–202. My main point here, however, is

Another important outcome of the present discussion is that it is *usual* to find literary writings in which nonlinguistic and linguistic criteria are at variance with one another.[92] In other words, it is generally *untrue* that textual/literary developments and linguistic developments coincide in the sense that the latter characterize the former. Consequently, the use of (historical) linguistic criteria to identify source and redaction layers is far more problematic than is generally presumed in conventional biblical criticism.

In conclusion, and repeating my words at the start of this chapter, contemporary textual criticism of the Hebrew Bible challenges contemporary historical linguistics (that is, linguistic dating) of Biblical Hebrew insofar as practitioners of the latter seek to undermine the conventional view, based on empirical textual data, that "early" sources and books were edited and/or authored in the Second Temple period.[93] At this point, I am very happy to end my chapter as Pakkala ended his:

> The comparison of these three witnesses [of Gedaliah's murder] once again confirms that because of the massive and constant editing, textual and literary criticism must be the basis of any scientific use of Biblical texts for historical [and I would add: historical linguistic] purposes. As noted by Hugo Gressmann already in the 1920's, "without them, one is only building fairytale castles in the air, hypotheses without scientific importance."[94]

---

that empirical textual data, which corroborate the long production history of biblical writings (for example, the books of Samuel or Jeremiah, including their composition, editing, and copying), undercut the efficacy of Hurvitz's and Hornkohl's conjectural explanation of the linguistic data.

92. I refer the reader once again to Rofé's conclusion on biblical writings and Kouwenberg's and Tigay's conclusions on Akkadian writings (§1, above) and to the results of my own work on Judges and Samuel (§3.1, above). Other examples related to other languages and literatures are cited in Rezetko and Young, *Historical Linguistics and Biblical Hebrew*, especially in chapter 4 on the theory and method of cross-textual variable analysis.

93. Never mind Richard Elliott Friedman's remarks in his new "Foreword" to the reprinted Tigay volume of *Empirical Models for Biblical Criticism* (Eugene, OR: Wipf & Stock, 2005), [1, 6–7, 9]. He repeatedly extols the power of linguistic data for dating biblical writings.

94. Pakkala, "Gedaliah's Murder," 411, citing Hugo Gressmann, "Die Aufgaben der alttestamentlichen Forschung," *ZAW* 42 (1924): 3. On the relationship between textual criticism and historical linguistics, see Rezetko and Young, *Historical Linguistics and Biblical Hebrew*, 26–33.

The Original Problem: The Old Greek and the Masoretic Text of Daniel 5

Ian Young

1. The Problem

It is well known that the Old Greek (OG) and the Masoretic Text (MT) contain highly variant versions of Dan 4, 5, and 6.[1] In Dan 5, the subject of this chapter, the OG evidences a much shorter text, most obvious in those cases where blocks of verses in the MT have no parallel in the OG, 5:13b–16a, and 5:18–22. In addition, there are many cases where parallel verses are formulated quite differently. One example of this is the description of the entry of the queen and her speech in 5:10–12. Nevertheless, there is no question that the same basic storyline is present in both versions. King Belshazzar makes a feast at which wine is drunk. Then the sacred vessels of the temple are brought in and wine is drunk from them, while pagan gods are praised. A hand appears and writes on the wall of the palace, startling the king. The king offers a reward, but none of his specialists can interpret the writing. The queen enters and suggests that Daniel be called to give the interpretation of the writing on the wall, and she describes some of Daniel's special gifts. At the king's request, Daniel interprets the significance of the writing, which involves the loss of the kingdom to the Medes and Persians due to the king's disrespect for God shown by his misuse of the temple vessels. Daniel is rewarded, and Belshazzar suffers his fate.

Scholars have proposed competing theories to explain the relationship between the OG and the MT in this chapter (and elsewhere in Daniel).

1. Even this numbering of chapters conceals a variation, since in the OG papyrus 967 what are MT chapters 7–8 appear between MT chapters 4 and 5, giving the chapter order, according to the MT numbering: 1–4, 7–8, 5–6, 9–12.

A further complication is the presence in the OG of a third version of at least part of the story, the OG Preface, which although it will not be my main concern in this chapter, still needs to be borne in mind.[2] In older scholarship, the tendency was to argue for the priority of one text over the other, either that the MT was (virtually) the original text, which was subsequently shortened and rewritten by the OG translator or his *Vorlage*, or that the OG's *Vorlage* was the more original text, which was expanded and rewritten as in the MT. More recently, more sophisticated theories have begun to dominate the field, according to which both the OG and the MT are developments of an earlier common text. An assumption of many of these theories, nevertheless, is that there was one original *text*, the contours of which can more or less be successfully recovered by scholarly methods used on the existing texts, and that therefore the developments that the texts have undergone away from this earlier text can be outlined. This chapter explores other models of the relationship between the OG and the MT of Dan 5, which have received more attention from scholars in recent years. These include the suggestion that the earlier forms of the text which are developed in the OG and the MT were already parallel renditions of a common oral tradition, and thus there never was a common base *text* of Dan 5.

---

2. The Preface is not a summary of either the OG or the MT in the forms we have them, including extra or variant details such as the occasion of the feast ("on the day of the dedication of his palace") or the description of the guests ("two thousand men of his nobles"). In the translation of R. Timothy McLay, "Daniel," in *A New English Translation of the Septuagint*, ed. Albert Pietersma and Benjamin G. Wright (Oxford: Oxford University Press, 2007), 1007, the Preface reads: "King Baltasar gave a great reception on the day of the dedication of his palace, and he invited two thousand men of his nobles. On that day, Baltasar, in high spirits from the wine and boasting in his drink, praised all the molten and carved gods of the nations, and he did not give praise to the Most High God. On that same night, fingers, as though of a human, came forth and inscribed on the wall of his house, on the plaster, opposite the light: MANE PHARES THEKEL. Their translation is: MANE, it has been numbered; PHARES, it has been taken away; THEKEL, it has been established."

2. The Data: The OG and the MT in Parallel Columns

Here are the data of both texts in English translation arranged according to common material (center column),[3] parallel material (//), related material (cf.), and pluses of each text.[4]

Verse	OG Pluses/Variants	Common	MT Pluses/Variants
1		King Belshazzar made a great feast	
	for his associates	//	for a thousand of his lords
	and		and before the thousand
		he drank wine.	
2	And his heart was exalted, and he said	//	Belshazzar said, under the influence of the wine
		to bring the vessels of gold and silver	
	of the house of God		[cf. MT later in this verse: from the temple that is in Jerusalem]
		which Nebuchadnezzar his father had brought (out)	
	from Jerusalem	//	from the temple that is in Jerusalem
	and to pour wine in them	//	that they might drink from (literally: in) them

3. Material in brackets or separated by a forward slash in this shared material indicates slight variants.

4. The English translation of the Aramaic is mine, aiming to reflect the syntax of the Aramaic rather than produce a smooth English translation. For the Greek, I modified the *NETS* translation as necessary, in particular to bring out cases of agreement/disagreement with the Aramaic text. I do not here go into complicated questions such as the reliability of our witnesses for the OG of Daniel (see §6, below) but simply rely on the work of McLay, "Daniel," which is largely a translation of the critical text of Munnich in Joseph Ziegler and Olivier Munnich, eds., *Septuaginta: Vetus Testamentum Graecum*, vol. 16.2: *Susanna, Daniel, Bel et Draco*, 2nd ed., SVTG (Göttingen: Vandenhoeck & Ruprecht, 1999). The arrangement of the material into three columns and the judgments implied by the arrangement are my own.

	for his companions.	//	the king and his lords, his wives and his concubines.
3		Then they (were) brought	
	[cf. v. 2]		the vessels of gold that they brought out from the temple of the house of God which is in Jerusalem
		and they drank from them	
			the king and his lords, his wives and his concubines.
4			They drank the wine
		and they praised	
	their handmade idols	//	the gods of gold and silver, bronze, iron, wood, and stone
	and they did not bless the eternal God who had authority over their spirit.		[cf. both texts in v. 23: and the God who/and your breath is in his hand (and) {you did} not honor (him)]
5		In that same moment went forth fingers	
	as though of a	//	of the
		hand of a man and they wrote	
	on the wall of his house, on the plaster opposite the light, facing King Baltasar	//	opposite the lampstand upon the plaster of the wall of the palace of the king
	and		and the king
		(he) saw	
			the palm of
	a hand writing.	//	the hand that was writing.

6	And	//	Then the king
		his appearance changed (upon him?) and (his) thoughts dismayed/ hastened him	
			and the joints of his loin were loosened and his knees one to another knocked together.
	Therefore, the king hastened and stood up and kept looking at that writing, and his companions spoke loudly around him.		[cf. MT v. 9: Then the king was greatly alarmed and his appearance changed upon him, and his lords were perplexed.]
7		(And) the king cried out in a loud voice to bring in/call the enchanters, (the magicians), the Chaldeans and the diviners	
	to tell the interpretation of the writing.		[cf. MT later in this verse: this writing and its interpretation he will make known to me]
	And they came to the spectacle to see the writing, and they were unable to interpret the meaning of the writing for the king.		
	Then the king published a declaration, saying:	//	The king answered and said to the wise men of Babylon:
	"Anyone who can show the interpretation of the writing	//	"Any man who can read this writing and its interpretation he will make known to me

	he will dress him in purple, and the gold torque he will put on him, and authority over a third of the kingdom will be given to him."	//	he will be clothed in purple and a chain of gold upon his neck, and he will rule as third in the kingdom."
8	And	//	Then
		they entered	
	the enchanters and sorcerers and	//	all the wise men of the king
	Gazarenes		
		and they were not able (none of them)	
	to tell the interpretation of the writing.	//	the writing to read, and its interpretation [*ketiv*: the interpretation.] to make known to the king.
9		Then the king	
			Belshazzar
	[cf. OG v. 6: Therefore, the king hastened and stood up and kept looking at that writing, and his companions spoke loudly around him]		was greatly alarmed and his appearance changed upon him, and his lords were perplexed.
	summoned the queen about the sign, and he explained to her how large it was and that no person was able to tell the king the meaning of the writing.		
10	Then		
		the queen	
	reminded him concerning Daniel who was among the captives of Judea.		[cf. MT v. 13: Daniel, who is from the sons of the exile of Judah]

			because of the words of the king and his lords entered the banqueting house.
	(OG v. 11) And she said to the king	//	The queen answered and said: "O king live forever! Do not let your thoughts alarm you, and let not your appearance change.
11	"That person was prudent and wise and surpassed all the sages of Babylon,	// (vv. 11–12)	There is a man in your kingdom who has a spirit of holy gods in him and in the days of your father enlightenment, and understanding and wisdom like the wisdom of gods was found in him, and king Nebuchadnezzar your father made him chief of the magicians, enchanters, Chaldeans (and) diviners; your father the king.
12	and a holy spirit is in him. And in the days of your father the king he explained difficult meanings to Nabouchodonosor your father."	// (vv. 11–12)	because an excellent spirit and knowledge and understanding for interpreting dreams and explaining riddles, and solving problems (literally: unbinding knots) was found in him, in Daniel, whom the king made his name Belteshazzar
			Now, let Daniel be called, and he will explain the interpretation."

13		Then Daniel was brought in before/to the king (and) the king answered (and) said	
	to him [cf. OG v. 10: Daniel who was among the captives of Judea]	//	to Daniel "You are Daniel who is one of the sons of the exile of Judah, whom the king my father brought from Judah.
14	[cf. both texts in vv. 11–12]		And I have heard concerning you that a spirit of gods is in you, and enlightenment and understanding and excellent wisdom is found in you.
15	[cf. both texts in v. 8]		And now, the wise men, the enchanters have been brought before me that they might read this writing and its interpretation to make known to me, but they were not able to make known the interpretation of the thing (word).
16			And I have heard concerning you that you are able interpretations to interpret and puzzles to solve (literally: knots to untie). [cf. MT v. 12]
	"O Daniel		
			Now if
	are you able to show me the interpretation of the writing?	//	you are able to read the writing and its interpretation to make known to me

	And I will dress you in purple, and the gold torque I will put on you, and you will have authority over a third of my kingdom."	//	you will wear purple, and a chain of gold on your neck, and third in the kingdom you will rule."
17		Then Daniel	
	stood before the writing and read		
	and thus he answered the king	//	answered and said before the king
			"Let your gifts be for yourself, and give your rewards to another. However, I will read the writing to the king and the interpretation I will make known to him.
	"This is the writing: it has been numbered; it has been reckoned; it has been taken away. And the writing hand ceased		[cf. MT v. 25: And this is the writing that was inscribed: MENE, MENE, TEKEL and PARSIN]
	and this is their interpretation.		[cf. MT v. 26a: this is the interpretation of the matter (word)]
18			You, O king, the Most High God gave kingship and greatness and glory and honor to Nebuchadnezzar your father
19			and because of the greatness that he gave him, all peoples, nations, and tongues were trembling and fearing before him. Whomever he wished, he would kill, and whomever he wished he

			would keep alive, and whomever he wished he would exalt, and whomever he wished he would bring low.
20			But when his heart was lifted up and his spirit was hardened (strengthened) to act proudly, he was brought down from the throne of his kingdom and glory was taken (they took) from him.
21			And from humans he was driven away and his heart was made like a beast and with the wild asses was his dwelling place. Grass like oxen they fed him, and by the dew of heaven his body was wet, until he knew that the Most High God is ruler in the kingdom of men, and whomever he wishes he raises up over it.
22			And you, his son Belshazzar, you did not humble your heart, though you knew all this.
23			But you lifted yourself up against the Lord of Heaven
	O King, you made a feast for your friends, and you were drinking wine		
		and the vessels of	
	the house of the living God	//	his house

		they (were) brought before you	
		and you and your lords [OG: following “and you drank from them”]	
			your wives and your concubines
		drank (wine) from them	
	and you (plural) praised	//	(and) you (singular) praised [MT: after object “and the gods of…”]
	all the idols made by human hands	//	the gods of silver and gold, bronze, iron, wood, and stone who do not see and do not hear and do not know
		and the God	
	the living (God) you did not praise		
		who/and your breath is in his hand	
	and he himself gave your kingdom to you		
			and all your ways are his
	and		
		[you did] not	
	you (did not) bless him nor		
		honor (him).	
24			Then from before him the hand (literally: the palm of the hand) was sent and this writing was inscribed.
25	[cf. OG v. 17: This is the writing: it has been numbered; it has been reckoned; it has been taken away]		And this is the writing that was inscribed: MENE, MENE, TEKEL and PARSIN.

26		This is the interpretation of	
	the writing	//	the matter (word)
	the time of your kingdom has been reckoned; your kingdom is coming to an end.	//	MENE: God has reckoned (i.e., the value of) your kingdom and has brought it to an end [or: paid it out, handed it over].
27	It has been cut short, and it has finished.		
			TEQEL: You have been weighed in the scales and you have been found wanting.
28			PERES: (Your kingdom) is divided [or: is assessed]
		your kingdom (and) is given to the Medes and Persians."	
29	Then Baltasar the king clothed	//	Then Belshazzar commanded (said) and they clothed
		Daniel in purple and a chain of gold	
	around him, and he gave him authority over a third part of his kingdom.	//	upon his neck, and they proclaimed concerning him that he would be third ruler in the kingdom.
30	And the interpretation came upon Baltasar the king, and the rule was taken away from the Chaldeans and was given to the Medes and to the Persians.		
			In that very night, Belshazzar king of the Chaldeans was killed.

31/ 6:1a	And Xerxes [Greek MS 88 and Syro-Hexapla: Artaxerxes] the king of the Medes	//	And Darius the Mede
	received the kingdom.		

3. Preliminary Options for Interpreting the Data: The OG and the MT as Parallel Texts

From the data as presented above, it has been evident to scholars that suggesting a direct development of one text to the other, by simply adding material, for example, is not plausible. It is certainly the case that there are sections that can be explained as simple pluses against the other text. These are most evident in the MT. For example, there are the major pluses of material in MT 5:13b–16a (the king's speech to Daniel) and 5:18–22 (reference to the events of Dan 4 to contrast Nebuchadnezzar with Belshazzar). On the other hand, there are various pluses in the OG that, while not as extensive as the pluses of the MT, are no less real. For example, note the extra references to, or emphasis on the God of Israel in 5:2 (OG + "the house of God"), 5:4 (OG + "and they did not bless the eternal God who had authority over their spirit"), 5:23a (OG + "[the house of] the living God"), and 5:23b (OG + "the living [God] you did not praise").

However, beyond material that can be interpreted as simple pluses, it is regularly the case that parallel material in both texts is phrased differently. For example, the description of where the hand wrote the message is quite similar in both texts in 5:5, but the order of the components of the description is different. While the MT has the components in the order A: opposite the lampstand, B: upon the plaster, C: of the wall, D: of the palace, E: of the king, the OG has parallels to these elements in the order: C-D-B-A-E: C: on the wall, D: of his house, B: on the plaster, A: opposite the light, (facing) E: King Baltasar. Therefore even if one text is a direct development of the other text, we have a case of rewriting, not a case of more simple linear text development.

If a simple linear text development from one to another does not fit the evidence, the next most simple theory about the relationship between the OG and the MT in Dan 5 is that one text is a substantial rewrite of a version of the story largely the same as one of the current versions. Thus, the most commonly held scholarly view over the last century and a half is that the OG of Dan 5, or its *Vorlage*, is an abbreviation of an earlier text represented by the MT. One influential voice in favor of this theory is that of James Montgomery in his classic 1927 ICC commentary on Daniel.[5] Montgomery's judgment on the value of the OG of this chapter is brutal: "In no respect is 𝔊 [OG] preferable to 𝔐 [MT]; it appears to be an intentional abstract."[6] He considers the relationship of the OG to the MT that: "The text of X is considerably abbreviated."[7] In fact, however, most of Montgomery's arguments boil down to explanations of what the OG was doing on the *assumption* that the MT was the earlier text, rather than actual arguments for MT priority. For example, in regard to the major pluses of material I mentioned in MT 5:13b–16a and 5:18–22, Montgomery comments rather lamely: "The omission of both these passages is evidently due to economy; the first of them is a repetition [for example, of material in the queen's speech], the second reviews the well-known story in c[hapter] 4."[8] On the contrary, it has seemed more likely to recent scholars that these are MT pluses intended, among other purposes, to make the link between chapters 4 and 5 more explicit.[9] While it is possible that only one of the two texts of Dan 5 represents substantial rewriting, given what we now know of the prevalence of variant literary editions of biblical books and passages, the burden of proof should surely be on any claim that the author of one text had close to exactly the current form of the other text in front of him when he rewrote it. It seems more plausible on general grounds, as seems to be the developing consensus, that both the OG and the MT represent somewhat independent developments of the basic story of Dan 5.

An emerging consensus on the relationship between the OG and the MT of Dan 5, therefore, is that both are parallel developments of an earlier,

5. James A. Montgomery, *A Critical and Exegetical Commentary on the Book of Daniel*, ICC (Edinburgh: T&T Clark, 1927).

6. Ibid., 267.

7. Ibid.

8. Ibid.

9. See, for example, Johan Lust, "The Septuagint Version of Daniel 4–5," in *The Book of Daniel: In the Light of New Findings*, ed. Adam S. van der Woude, BETL 106 (Leuven: Peeters, 1993), 40–41; Olivier Munnich, "Texte massorétique et Septante dans le livre de Daniel," in *The Earliest Text of the Hebrew Bible: The Relationship between the Masoretic Text and the Hebrew Base of the Septuagint Reconsidered*, ed. Adrian Schenker, SCS 52 (Atlanta: Society of Biblical Literature, 2003), 107–16.

no longer extant, text. This has been forcefully argued by Eugene Ulrich.[10] He states:

> Thus, the claim of this essay is that the [shared material between the OG and the MT] contains an earlier, no longer extant, complete core form of the story of Belshazzar's feast that served as the basis for the two separate, more developed forms of the story transmitted in the MT and the OG. To that common narrative core the MT and the OG (*Vorlage*) each added or emphasized distinctive story-telling embellishments to produce their divergent editions. In the few seemingly missing spots, especially at verse 9, the core narrative was replaced in both by their distinctive expansions.[11]

> The most cogent explanation seems to be that there was an earlier version of the narrative that was shorter than the preserved forms and that the OG (or probably the Aramaic *Vorlage* of the OG) expanded the narrative in certain ways, whereas the precursor of the MT expanded it even more fully with different insertions. It seems quite unlikely that either would have been produced by excising the pluses in the other.[12]

Ulrich makes it clear that he means that an earlier written text was expanded/reworked in two different ways. For example, he puts these texts in the context of other variant literary editions and describes the core narrative as part of the earliest known of four editions of the book of Daniel.[13] However, he emphasizes that these texts are different to most variant editions, which are usually successive editions, whereas here we have two parallel editions expanded from an earlier common core.[14]

---

10. Eugene Ulrich, "The Parallel Editions of the Old Greek and Masoretic Text of Daniel 5," in *A Teacher for All Generations: Essays in Honor of James C. VanderKam*, ed. Eric F. Mason et al., 2 vols., JSJSup 153 (Leiden: Brill, 2012), 1:201–17. In his chapter, Ulrich follows a similar path to his PhD student Dean O. Wenthe, "The Old Greek Translation of Daniel 1–6" (PhD diss., University of Notre Dame, 1991), but his views are, as might be expected after further reflection, more clearly expressed and the data more clearly presented.

11. Ulrich, "Parallel Editions," 205.

12. Ibid., 208–9.

13. Ibid., 205. In fact there are five, since Theodotion's MT-like text plus the Greek additions is clearly a different edition to the OG plus additions.

14. Ibid., 203–4.

4. Empirical Models for the Parallel Texts in Daniel 5

In the rest of this chapter, I would like to suggest that empirical models exist that indicate three somewhat different ways we might understand the idea that the OG and the MT of Dan 5 are parallel versions of the story of Daniel and King Belshazzar.

The first is the one implied by Ulrich's work, where both texts of Dan 5 are later developments of an earlier, shorter written text. According to this theory, we can recover an earlier written form of the story from the common material shared by the OG and the MT, and this is what Ulrich does in his chapter. By comparison of the later texts with the earlier text they were working on, we can see clearly what changes each made to the base text and hence hopefully reveal the purposes behind their rewriting. Such a model is well-established among biblical scholars, where it is common to see one text as a development of another (for example, the view that the longer MT Jeremiah is a later literary edition than the shorter *Vorlage* of the Septuagint [LXX] of Jeremiah)[15] or two texts using an earlier text as a base (for example, the view that the Gospels of Matthew and Luke were using Mark as a major source). Since this is so widely accepted among mainstream biblical scholars, I am going to concentrate my attention on two other models for the relationship of the OG and the MT in Dan 5.

These two other models build on recent work that emphasizes the importance of oral traditions alongside written traditions in ancient Israel.[16] The first of these is the situation where an author or editor has access to a written version of a story and uses it as a source for a new writing of the story, a new writing which might draw on other versions of the story known to the writer, in oral or written form. Thus, this model, if applied to Dan 5, would indicate that either the OG or the MT was based on a known written version of the story similar to what is found in the other text, but

---

15. Emanuel Tov, *Textual Criticism of the Hebrew* Bible, 3rd ed. (Minneapolis: Fortress, 2012), 286–94. In fact, examples such as this are probably closer to Ulrich's example than first appears, since it would usually be admitted that even in such a case the LXX's *Vorlage* is not identical to the ancestor of the MT but has itself undergone later development away from that common ancestor. For this view see, for example, Andrew G. Shead, *The Open Book and the Sealed Book: Jeremiah 32 in Its Hebrew and Greek Recensions*, JSOTSup 347, HBV 3 (London: Sheffield Academic, 2002).

16. See, for example, Raymond F. Person Jr., *The Deuteronomic History and the Book of Chronicles: Scribal Works in an Oral World*, AIL 6 (Atlanta: Society of Biblical Literature, 2010), and the works referred to there.

that that text was completely rewritten, most likely under the influence of other oral versions of the story. So, for example, the MT could have been based on something like the OG version of the story, but it was rewritten with a view to other traditions (such as the story now in Dan 4) into the form we now have it. Alternatively, the OG could represent a rewrite of something like the MT version of the story (see Montgomery's view). Or both the OG and the MT could be rewrites of an earlier written version. This latter situation is like what Ulrich has proposed, with the key difference that we would not be able to recover a core text shared by the two, since one or both texts has been completely rewritten, not simply expanded, thus leaving no core intact as Ulrich suggests.

The final model is where the OG and the MT of Dan 5 are both simply parallel renditions of a common oral tradition, two attempts to create a written version of the story with no shared literary history. This would be analogous to hearing two versions of the story of Snow White and the Seven Dwarfs told by storytellers well-informed about the story. The basic storyline would be the same, but the details of each "performance" would be different.[17] In this case, there would be no chance to discover a common text behind the two versions, simply because there was none. They would be two texts without an "original."[18]

I will now look further into the empirical evidence for these latter two models, beginning with a discussion of some recent scholarly work on the topic, and then ask the question of which of the three models mentioned in this section best fits with the data from the two texts of Dan 5.

Some significant work has been done on the relevance of a continued interaction between oral traditions and the written texts of Daniel. Thus, in his study of Dan 4, Matthias Henze says:

> I would like to propose, then, that neither the MT nor the Old Greek has served as the *Vorlage* for the other. Instead, both versions have preserved

17. Snow White came to me, I think, due to the presence in various versions of the magic words to the mirror on the wall, which must have triggered an association with the writing on the wall in Dan 5.

18. "The answer to the question of how the [divergent manuscripts] arose may possibly be found in some cases in the fact that one is dealing with two oral texts rather with a text modified by a scribe or by a second poet working from an already written text" (Albert B. Lord, *Singer of Tales*, HSCL 24 [Cambridge: Harvard University Press, 1960], 63). On the absence of an original in oral tradition see, for example, 100–101.

> double literary editions, or duplicate narratives, of the same story. They developed independently out of a common form of the story no longer extant. Whether this "proto-form" of the story existed in a written *or in an oral form* is, of course, no longer possible to establish with any degree of certainty.[19]

Henze thus at least raises the possibility that the OG and MT versions of Dan 4 are two renditions of an oral tradition. He draws an analogy between the Daniel literature as a whole and the work of Peter Schäfer on the *hekhalot* literature, which is, according to Schäfer, "an extremely fluid literature which has reached different literary expressions in different manuscripts at different times and in different places."[20] Henze concludes that

> a comparison of the MT and the Old Greek of Dan 4 has shown that these versions are not reducible to a linear chain of development.... [T]hese are duplicate narratives which developed independently of each other.... [T]he MT and the Old Greek of Dan 4 should not be arranged in form of a stemma, but as a synopsis.[21]

Another important example of scholarship on the relevance of a continued interaction between oral traditions and the written texts of Daniel is the chapter of Edgar Kellenberger.[22] He argues that scholars of Daniel need to get away from a fixation on just literary transmission of texts, with the associated search for an Ur-text. Instead, he explains variants from various parts of Dan 1–6 as due to the continued interaction of oral and written traditions with each other.

The most important recent work on the narratives in the book of Daniel is that of Tawny L. Holm, who discusses them in the context of the empirical evidence for story collections in the ancient Near East and

---

19. Matthias Henze, *The Madness of King Nebuchadnezzar: The Ancient Near Eastern Origins and Early History of Interpretation of Daniel 4*, JSJSup 61 (Leiden: Brill, 1999), 40 (emphasis added).

20. Peter Schäfer, "Tradition and Redaction in Hekhalot Literature," *JSJ* 14 (1983): 180; Henze, *Madness of King Nebuchadnezzar*, 44–46.

21. Henze, *Madness of King Nebuchadnezzar*, 47.

22. Edgar Kellenberger, "Textvarianten in den Daniel-Legenden als Zeugnisse Mündlicher Tradierung," in *XIII Congress of the International Organization for Septuagint and Cognate Studies: Ljubljana, 2007*, ed. Melvin K. H. Peters, SCS 55 (Atlanta: Society of Biblical Literature, 2008), 207–23.

beyond.[23] She demonstrates that the stories in various story collections regularly display textual variability.[24] In this context, she states: "Compilers of story-collections are also authors in that they rarely simply collect stories without writing or rewriting them to their satisfaction and purpose and with a new context in mind."[25] Specifically in regard to Dan 4–6, Holm states: "[C]hs. 4–6—which vary so widely between MT/Th[eodotion] and the OG—are best seen as duplicate editions of the same three tales rather than part of a reconstructed *stemma*,"[26] and, "[t]he OG tales were written down as a fresh telling of three stories that were already known."[27]

Holm gives three options for the OG's relationship with the MT in Dan 4–6: MT priority, OG priority, or "that both are independent literary traditions of a common core story."[28] As I have indicated above, in fact this third option actually can itself be understood in at least three ways. Holm does not commit herself to any one of these three ways and thus simply discusses work such as Ulrich's, which presumes a literary relationship of both texts to an earlier core text, along with other theories. In this, she seems to have not fully defined the differences between Ulrich's position and other positions, for example, when she says: "Eugene Ulrich in particular has argued for a pluriformity, or multiple literary editions, of certain biblical texts that cannot be traced back to an original as such and that likely existed alongside each other from earliest times and did not develop from each other."[29] On the contrary, Ulrich's main model is of successive linear development of literary editions.[30] His suggested model for Dan 5 is

23. Tawny L. Holm, *Of Courtiers and Kings: The Biblical Daniel Narratives and Ancient Story-Collections*, EANEC 1 (Winona Lake, IN: Eisenbrauns, 2013).

24. Ibid., 41.

25. Ibid., 4.

26. Ibid., 330.

27. Ibid., 490; see also 4, 220, 239, 483, and 211 on the oral register of the Daniel stories.

28. Ibid., 226–27.

29. Ibid., 232.

30. "[I]t seems increasingly clear that the text of each book developed through successive revised literary editions, whereby an earlier form of the book was intentionally revised to produce a newer revised edition" (Eugene Ulrich, "Clearer Insight into the Development of the Bible: A Gift of the Scrolls," in *The Dead Sea Scrolls and Contemporary Culture: Proceedings of the International Conference held at the Israel Museum, Jerusalem [July 6–8, 2008]*, ed. Adolfo D. Roitman, Lawrence H. Schiffman, and Shani Tzoref, STDJ 93 [Leiden: Brill, 2011], 128).

a departure from his more common model. Even here, Ulrich is clearly not arguing that the two texts of Dan 5 "cannot be traced back to an original." Thus, Holm is actually describing a different model when she suggests: "It is possible that no single original ever existed and that the MT and the OG represent parallel developments."[31]

Despite this imprecision in separating the various options, Holm presents a great deal of empirical evidence that "[s]tory-collections indeed often do contain stories that have variant editions elsewhere, each maintaining the central core common to all but lacking a fixed text."[32] There is much evidence referenced by her or others, which fully substantiates this statement. I mention here a few illustrative examples.[33]

A rich source of information about the textual fluidity of stories in story-collections is found in the Arabian Nights. Variant forms of stories are found both in different manuscripts of the Arabian Nights and in stories and story-collections found in other sources, which David Pinault describes as "analogue manuscripts." Pinault points out that redactors of the manuscripts retold the stories, in other words acting as the latest in a long line of reciters and professional storytellers.[34] "Each redaction, each analogue-manuscript can be seen as another telling of the given tale."[35] Thus, different manuscripts of The Fisherman and the Genie,[36] The Enchanted Prince,[37] The Three Apples,[38] The False Caliph,[39] or The City of Brass[40] agree in the general progression of events but differ from each other in wording, description of events, and presentation of details. Pinault regularly suggests that the variant versions go back to earlier common manuscript versions but that the earlier versions are rewritten by later redactors

---

31. Holm, *Of Courtiers and Kings*, 234. Similarly, 238–39 also seems to me to reflect an imprecise understanding of Ulrich's and Wenthe's position in relation to other options.

32. Ibid., 235.

33. See also the reference to the *hekhalot* literature above.

34. David Pinault, *Story-Telling Techniques in the Arabian Nights*, SAL 15 (Leiden: Brill, 1992), 249–50.

35. Ibid., 251.

36. Ibid., 35; see also 31–81.

37. Ibid.

38. Ibid., 86; see also 86–99.

39. Ibid., 100–101; see also 99–138.

40. Ibid., 155; see also 148–239.

who retell the stories using the traditional formulaic repertoire used by earlier storytellers.[41]

Siegfried Neumann describes the methods used by the Brothers Grimm in collecting and editing the various editions of their Fairy Tales.[42] The brothers noted that no two versions of any tale were the same, although they had a stable core.[43] Furthermore, they themselves produced new editions of the tales by not only choosing what they considered better versions of the tales but by modifying them stylistically.[44] An example of this are the three different versions of the introduction to The Frog King where, as Holm notes, "by the final edition of the story, the core remained stable but the style in which the story was written by Wilhelm Grimm evolved remarkably."[45] In fact, there are almost no verbal parallels between the three versions, even though key features appear in all of them. This is presumably an example of a storyteller both interacting with different versions available orally and also rewriting the story according to his own literary taste.

In her study of ancient novels and Apocryphal Acts of the Apostles, Christine M. Thomas notes an "impulse to create a new version of the story with each retelling of it,"[46] not only "including or deleting entire episodes,"[47] but also "surprisingly numerous variants, mostly on the level of phrasing and word-order."[48] Christoph Burchard describes a similar situation in the manuscripts of Joseph and Asenath, which present

---

41. See especially ibid., 113–14. This is analogous to the situation where oral poets consider written texts to be simply another performance of a song, not to possess any special authority. See, for example, Lord, *Singer of Tales*, 79.

42. Siegfried Neumann, "The Brothers Grimm as Collectors and Editors of German Folktales," in *The Reception of Grimms' Fairy Tales: Responses, Reactions, Revisions*, ed. Donald Haase (Detroit: Wayne State University Press, 1993), 24–40.

43. Ibid., 31. Despite the "fluidity" of oral tradition, the stability of the basic skeleton of the stories is noted by Lord, *Singer of Tales*, 99, 113, 123.

44. Neumann, "Brothers Grimm," 29–30.

45. Holm, *Of Courtiers and Kings*, 235–36, quote on 236; Neumann, "Brothers Grimm," 29–30.

46. Christine M. Thomas, "Stories Without Texts and Without Authors: The Problem of Fluidity in Ancient Novelistic Texts and Early Christian Literature," in *Ancient Fiction and Early Christian Narrative*, ed. Ronald F. Hock, J. Bradley Chance, and Judith Perkins, SymS 6 (Atlanta: Scholars Press, 1998), 289.

47. Ibid., 280.

48. Ibid., 281.

manuscripts "very different in both wording and length," even though Burchard considers that "all textual witnesses known to date go back to a common archetype."[49]

Scholars of medieval literature have likewise stressed the performative nature of preprinting manuscript production. Joyce Tally Lionarons points out that "[t]extual indeterminacy … is a hallmark of manuscript culture"[50] and summarizes a widely held view among medievalists that each manuscript was a unique performance of the work it contained.[51] Katherine O'Brien O'Keeffe describes the situation in regard to Old English poetry thus: "Surviving Old English verse texts, whatever the circumstances of their composition, are collaborative products whose scribes have not merely transmitted the texts but have actually taken part in shaping them."[52]

Graeme D. Bird has discussed the interaction between oral performances and the manuscript tradition of Homer's *Iliad*. He argues that "the variation in our surviving manuscripts of Homer (and other sources) is inconsistent with a single archetype, but rather points back to a multiplicity of archetypes, a situation which arises from the oral nature of the transmission of Homeric epic."[53] Thus, "a manuscript of Homer could be derived from an oral performance which was more or less different from any other performance, thus giving rise to 'variants' which would be inexplicable if one were to depend solely on the canons of textual criticism as applied to written works."[54] Examination of the text of early papyri shows not only the presence of "extra" lines, when compared to the later received text, but also that shared lines appear in different forms. Thus in the text of *Il.* 3:302–12, not only does papyrus 40 have five extra lines, several lines are formulated differently. For example, line 302 in the standard version is "Thus they spoke, but the son of Kronos would not yet grant them fulfil-

49. Christoph Burchard, "Joseph and Asenath," *OTP* 2:180–81.

50. Joyce Tally Lionarons, "Textual Appropriation and Scribal (Re)Performance in a Composite Homily: The Case for a New Edition of Wulfstan's *De Temporibus Anticristi*," in *Old English Literature in Its Manuscript Context*, ed. Joyce Tally Lionarons, MES 5 (Morgantown: West Virginia University Press, 2004), 70.

51. Ibid., 69–70.

52. Katherine O'Brien O'Keeffe, *Visible Song: Transitional Literacy in Old English Verse*, CSASE 4 (Cambridge: Cambridge University Press, 1990), 193.

53. Graeme D. Bird, *Multitextuality in the Homeric Iliad: The Witness of the Ptolemaic Papyri*, Hellenic Studies 43 (Washington, DC: Center for Hellenic Studies, 2010), 28.

54. Ibid., 29; see also 44, 100.

ment," while in the papyrus it is "[Thus they spoke, pray]ing, and Zeus the counsellor thundered greatly."[55]

My final examples come from Egyptian literature. Kim Ryholt discusses two written versions of the Egyptian story of The Imprisoned Magician, suggesting that since "[t]he two versions of this story are not only set in an entirely different wording, but the name of the magician as well as the setting of the story also differ," that "it seems likely that we might be dealing with a story which had been orally transmitted and was committed to writing at different localities and, perhaps, at different times."[56] Another example that Ryholt discusses is the story of 'Onch-Sheshonqy where "the Tebtunis manuscript is presented in an entirely different wording from that of the B[ritish] M[useum] manuscript," which he understands as a case of the Tebtunis manuscript revising the version found in the British Museum manuscript.[57] A third example, which Ryholt also considers as a case of reworking of an older version in a later one, is where the Saqqara manuscript of the Story of Petese "is presented in an entirely different wording from that of the two Tebtunis manuscripts, which date about 500 years later."[58]

5. Examining the Data

We are therefore presented with a number of models for the relationship between the OG and the MT in Dan 5. These are: (1) the MT and the OG are expansions of a common core text in different ways that, nevertheless, left the core text basically intact (see Ulrich's view); (2) the MT and/or the OG is a substantial rewrite of an earlier written version to such an extent that the earlier version is no longer recoverable; (3) the OG and the MT are independent renditions of a common oral tradition, with no shared ancestor text, or at least no significant controlling influence of a single

55. Ibid., 86–89.

56. Kim Ryholt, *The Story of Petese, Son of Petetum and Seventy Other Good and Bad Stories (P. Petese)*, CP 4, CNIP 23 (Copenhagen: University of Copenhagen, Museum Tusculanum Press, 1999), 89.

57. Kim Ryholt, "A New Version of the Introduction to the Teachings of 'Onch-Sheshonqy," in *A Miscellany of Demotic Texts and Studies*, ed. Paul John Frandsen and Kim Ryholt, CP 3, CNIP 22 (Copenhagen: University of Copenhagen, Museum Tusculanum Press, 2000), 114; see also 120, 134–36.

58. Ibid., 114 n. 7; Ryholt, *Story of Petese*.

written text. These models merely expand the possible ways that the relationship between the OG and the MT might be understood in Dan 5. They do not compel us to choose one of them without considering the evidence.

How could we decide which of these models best explains the evidence of the current OG and MT versions of Dan 5? It seems likely that the product of each of these models would be most clearly distinguishable by the proportion of verbatim parallels between the two texts. If the two texts are independent renditions of a common oral tradition, we would expect a quite low proportion of verbatim parallels between the two texts. A substantial rewrite of an earlier written text might still exhibit a higher proportion of verbatim parallels. However, this would depend on how substantial the rewrite was, and thus in practice it might not be possible to tell the difference between this model and the model of independent renditions of a common oral tradition. A rewrite of an earlier written text could take into account other oral versions and end up not too far from an independent version of the story. Finally, if both texts are an expansion of an earlier common text, we should expect a high amount of verbatim parallels, focused on the parallel sections. This is what Ulrich has argued is the case with Dan 5. We will now investigate this model to see whether Ulrich has established his case beyond question.

Ulrich sets out his data in an appendix.[59] He admits that there are certain points where the common text is missing something and we have only the parallel texts, such as in 5:9, although he considers these to be few.[60] In fact there are thirteen occasions where Ulrich's core narrative requires the insertion of a word on the basis that "a similar expression [was] probably in the original because both MT and OG use it."[61] Beyond these cases, there are quite a few examples where Ulrich's common material includes text that could be interpreted instead as parallel. Thus, in 5:2 he has "under the influence of the wine" (בטעם חמרא) in his common material, whereas the OG has "his heart was exalted"; he places the MT's "from the temple that is in Jerusalem" in his common material, whereas the OG has only "from Jerusalem"; and he has the MT's "that they might drink from them"

59. Ulrich, "Parallel Editions," 211–17; see also Wenthe, "Old Greek Translation of Daniel 1–6," 167–79. Ulrich's work is more clearly done than the similar section of Wenthe's work, since he does not conflate OG and MT pluses to the same extent and is less willing to place parallel but different material in his "core narrative" column.

60. Ulrich, "Parallel Editions," 205.

61. Ibid., 205 n. 20.

in the common material where the OG has "to pour wine in them." In 5:5, his common material is the MT's "fingers *of* a man's hand," whereas the OG has "fingers *as though* of a hand of a man"; he has the MT's "opposite the lampstand upon the plaster of the wall" as common material, whereas the OG has these in a different order; and has the king seeing "the palm of the hand that was writing" whereas the OG has just that he saw "a hand writing." In 5:7 and 5:16 (see also 5:29), he takes the MT's "he will be clothed in purple and a chain of gold upon his neck, and he will rule as third in the kingdom" as common text, even though the OG differs in detail on all three points: "he will dress him in purple, and the gold torque he will put on him, and authority over a third of the kingdom will be given to him." A similar expression leads him to obscure the text in 5:29, giving as his common text of the beginning of the verse, "Then Belshazzar and they dressed," which is not comprehensible as it stands and reflects only some of the words of the MT's "then Belshazzar commanded (said) and they clothed," influenced by the parallel but different OG "then Baltasar the king clothed." Ulrich's core of the queen's speech in 5:11–12 is just short fragments, and it is arguable whether even these match up, for example, the MT's "chief of the magicians" is extracted from a longer list and considered the same as "surpassing all the sages of Babylon" and "an excellent spirit" in the MT is considered the same as the OG's "a holy spirit." In 5:23, "the vessels of his house" is put in the common text, although the OG has the different and longer "the house of the living God." Finally, in 5:26 "God has reckoned your kingdom and has brought it to an end" is considered common with OG's "the time of your kingdom has been reckoned; your kingdom is coming to an end."

When one reviews Ulrich's core narrative in its details and as a whole, it is not necessary to agree that he has been able to reconstruct a "complete" narrative as he set out to do,[62] especially after the first few verses. It is true that he succeeds in showing that the same basic outline is followed in both the OG and the MT. However, one could argue that, rather than stripping away both texts to such an extent, it is better to admit that there is no common core but simply the basic outline of a single story told in two different ways.

62. "[T]he claim of this essay is that the central column of the Appendix contains an earlier, no longer extant, complete core form of the story of Belshazzar's feast that served as the basis for the two separate, more developed forms of the story transmitted in the MT and in the OG" (ibid., 205).

This argument is further backed up by an investigation of the proportion of verbatim parallels between the two texts. To get a firmer grasp of this, I used the Aramaic graphic units of the MT as the basic unit and divided them into groups according to the table in section 2, above.[63] There are 528 Aramaic graphic units in Dan 5:1–6:1a. Of these, 265, or 50.19 percent, or almost exactly a half, are classified as "unparalleled" in the presentation of the texts in section 2. In comparison, 156 of the 515 Greek words are without MT parallel, or 30.29 percent, or between a quarter and a third. This backs up the observation that the MT has more pluses than the OG but that the OG still has a significant number. In contrast to these large numbers, of the 528 graphic units, only 81 are treated as verbatim parallels in section 2 by both texts being placed together in the central column. This is 15.34 percent of the total, or if we remove the unparalleled MT material, still only 81/263 or 30.80 percent. Note that a different definition of "verbatim parallel," which was less tolerant of minor variations and did not include some of the more isolated elements, would reduce the number of verbatim parallels further. This leaves 182 Aramaic graphic units that are in some way parallel without being verbatim parallels, which is 34.42 percent of the total or, removing the unparalleled MT material, 182/263 or 69.20 percent. In other words, even with this generous definition of a verbatim parallel and removing all of the MT plus material, less than a third of the OG and the MT of Dan 5 is similar in wording.

In summary, Ulrich has made a strong case that the OG and the MT of Dan 5 are parallel versions of a tradition, rather than that one text is directly dependent on the other. However, the suggestion that the two texts are expansions of an earlier text that can be reconstructed from the common material may be questioned on the basis of the many places where parallel material is presented in both texts but in different forms and with different wording. The low amount of verbatim parallels between the two texts and the fact that those that do exist are largely confined to the most basic elements of the story (e.g., "they brought … they drank … they praised") would in fact tend to argue against significant use of any earlier

63. Due to the nature of the decisions that are involved in sorting some items into various groupings such as "unparalleled," plus issues with the textual evidence discussed in the following section, the numbers here cannot hope to be definitive, but rather give a solid general indication of the overall trends readily observable from scrutiny of the texts as presented in §2, above.

written text.[64] This material much more easily fits in with the model of two independent renditions of a common oral tradition without any significant guiding influence from a common written text—which would explain why major elements of the storyline are shared by both versions, but the wording of each version, even in parallel sections, is different.[65]

6. Issues Interpreting the Data of the OG

The data discussed in the previous section are, however, not a clear refutation of Ulrich's approach. Ulrich has, of course, thought about these issues and suggests an alternative interpretation in line with his approach. This is that the many cases of verbal variation are due to "free" translation by the OG translator of a *Vorlage* similar to the Aramaic of the MT. The alternative is that the OG translator gave a less free translation of an Aramaic text that differed in detail in all of these cases. This would indicate that rather than sharing a common written text, the similarity between the two texts is a shared storyline only, and that they are two renditions of a common oral tradition.

There is not space here to give a full discussion of the OG translation of Daniel.[66] What I do aim to do in this section, however, is to raise some of the issues that must be resolved before we can definitely decide the question about the nature of the OG's *Vorlage*.

The first question that has to be discussed is whether the OG translator translated a variant Semitic *Vorlage* or whether the translator was himself responsible for the variations, which never existed in any Semitic text. Here a broad scholarly consensus exists that the OG translator translated a variant Semitic text. Thus, Timothy McLay can sum up the state of the question as follows: "Scholars are agreed that the differing version of chapters iv–vi in the OG is based on a Semitic *Vorlage*."[67] Although Hebrew has

64. By "significant," I mean to exclude the situation where a written text was used but did not provide the basis for the subsequent edition of the story.

65. For the stability of the basic storyline in oral traditions, see n. 43.

66. As more work is done on this by myself and others, we might hope to give a clearer answer to the issues raised in this section.

67. R. Timothy McLay, "Old Greek Translation of Daniel IV–VI and the Formation of the Book of Daniel," *VT* 55 (2005): 304–5. See also, for example, Montgomery, *Daniel*, 37; John J. Collins, *Daniel: A Commentary on the Book of Daniel*, Hermeneia (Minneapolis: Fortress, 1993), 6; Eugene Ulrich, "The Text of Daniel in the Qumran Scrolls," in *The Book of Daniel: Composition and Reception*, ed. John J. Collins and

been suggested for the language of this *Vorlage*,[68] Aramaic seems the most likely language, the same as the MT.[69]

A major issue in describing the translation technique of the OG translator is the scope of the corpus, or put differently, how many translators were involved. Scholars are divided on this question into two camps: those who see the same translator as responsible for the whole book[70] and those who consider that the translation of chapters 4–6 was done by a different translator than the rest of the book.[71] This is often related to the highly variant character of the OG of those chapters compared to the MT.

The question of whether Dan 4–6 had a separate translator than the rest of the book is a very important question for translation technique. Was the translator so "free" in his translation style that he would, for example, rearrange the elements in the description of the location of the writing on the wall, or give only the sense, not the exact details, in the description of the clothing of Daniel in purple as Ulrich necessarily implies? If the same translator translated all of the book, then we can say that other chapters,

---

Peter W. Flint, 2 vols., VTSup 83 (Leiden: Brill, 2001), 2:582; Ulrich, "Parallel Editions," 205; Timothy J. Meadowcroft, *Aramaic Daniel and Greek Daniel: A Literary Comparison*, JSOTSup 198 (Sheffield: Sheffield Academic, 1995), 25–26.

68. For example, Pierre Grelot, "Le Chapitre V de *Daniel* dans la Septante," *Sem* 24 (1974): 45–66.

69. Apart from the fact that the only known Semitic version of the story is in Aramaic, there are other indications. For example, it is a characteristic of the Aramaic chapters of Daniel to begin sentences with באדין and אדין ("then") as opposed to the normal Hebrew style of beginning with the simple conjunction *waw* (Lust, "Daniel 4–5 LXX," 42–43 with n. 12). In line with this, the OG uses clause initial τότε ("then") six times in chapter 5 (both in verbatim and nonverbatim sections) and regularly (a further twenty-eight times) in the other Aramaic chapters (except ch. 4) but never when translating the Hebrew sections. This would seem to indicate that for chapter 5 at least, the OG's *Vorlage* was Aramaic, not Hebrew.

70. For example, Montgomery, *Daniel*, 37; Ulrich, "Parallel Editions," 205 n. 17.

71. For example, Rainer Albertz, *Der Gott des Daniel: Untersuchungen zu Daniel 4–6 in der Septuagintafassung sowie zu Komposition und Theologie des aramäischen Danielbuches*, SBS 131 (Stuttgart: Katholisches Bibelwerk, 1988), 161–65; Albertz, "Bekehrung von oben als 'messianisches Programm': Die Sonderüberlieferung der Septuaginta in Dan 4–6," in *Theologische Probleme der Septuaginta und der hellenistischen Hermeneutik*, ed. Henning Graf Reventlow, VWGTh 11 (Gütersloh: Kaiser; Gütersloher Verlaghaus, 1997), 47–50; R. Timothy McLay, *The OG and Th Versions of Daniel*, SCS 43 (Atlanta: Scholars Press, 1996), 109, 145; McLay, "Old Greek Translation of Daniel IV–VI," 306–7.

such as chapter 1, which are evidently much more closely related to the MT, do not exhibit the same amount of freedom in translation.[72] If only chapters 4–6 were translated by this translator, however, our arguments become much more circular, since we have no point of reference to decide to what extent the deviations from the MT are due to a variant *Vorlage* or the translation technique of the translator. Scholars are, however, mostly agreed that the OG translator, whether of the whole book or of Dan 5 specifically, translated "exactly" or at least "faithfully."[73]

In regard to verbatim parallels between the OG and the MT, an important issue is the reliability of our current limited evidence for the OG translation. In particular, it is acknowledged that all of our major witnesses to the OG—papyrus 967, manuscript 88, and the Syro-Hexapla—have been corrupted by readings from the MT-related Theodotion Greek translation of Daniel.[74] Thus, such verbatim parallels as do exist in Dan 5 must be investigated under the suspicion that they represent subsequent corruptions rather than evidence of the original relationship of the OG (*Vorlage*) and the (proto-)MT.

In general, scholars discuss corruptions of the OG toward the MT. However, in an earlier period, it is likely that there was already a "complex intertextuality"[75] between the texts where not only did the proto-MT influence the OG's *Vorlage*, but also the OG's *Vorlage* exerted an influence

72. Disregarding minor variations as I did for Dan 5, there is a direct reflection of about 90 percent of the Hebrew words of MT Dan 1 in the OG.

73. For example: "La version grecque de Dan 5 LXX est la traduction servile d'un original sémitique" (Grelot, "Chapitre V," 63); the translator "mit ein größeren Genauigkeit gearbeitet haben, als bislang angenommen," including in chapters 4–6: "auch hier um Genauigkeit gegenüber seiner aramäischen *Vorlage* bemüht hat" (Ziegler and Munnich, *Susanna Daniel Bel et Draco*, 90); "the probability is that the LXX translates the text in front of it relatively literally" (Meadowcroft, *Aramaic Daniel and Greek Daniel*, 263). For Ulrich's and his students' judgment of "faithful but free," see, for example, Ulrich, "Parallel Editions," 205; Wenthe, "Old Greek Translation of Daniel 1–6," 21, 181, 194, 247; Sharon Pace Jeansonne, *The Old Greek Translation of Daniel 7–12*, CBQMS 19 (Washington, DC: Catholic Biblical Association of America, 1988), 49, 56, 69, 112, 131–32.

74. McLay, *OG and Th Versions of Daniel*, 14, 109, 214–15, 242; Ziegler and Munnich, *Susanna Daniel Bel et Draco*, 76; Munnich, "Livre de *Daniel*," 94–95. For a detailed introduction to papyrus 967 see Ziegler and Munnich, *Susanna Daniel Bel et Draco*, 63–76.

75. For the term see, for example, Person, *Deuteronomic History and the Book of Chronicles*, 8.

on the proto-MT.[76] Given these factors that likely brought the two texts together, it is perhaps remarkable that so few verbal parallels between the current texts exist.

7. Conclusion

In conclusion, let us remind ourselves of the three models for the composition of Dan 5 that have been the focus of this discussion. The first is that the MT and the OG are expansions of a common core text in different ways that, nevertheless, left the core text basically intact. The second is that the MT and/or the OG is a substantial rewrite of an earlier written version to such an extent that the earlier version is no longer recoverable. The third is that the OG and the MT are independent renditions of a common oral tradition, with no shared ancestor text.

As I have discussed above, all three models remain potentially valid, although I have provided further data here for the second and third options. A key aspect of evaluating them further is the continued growth of our understanding of the nature of the OG translation of Daniel. This gives even more reason to study this fascinating and important ancient text. It should be noted also that all three models, not just the last two, assume that the two texts of Dan 5 reflect access to a variety of traditions. Either an earlier common written text was expanded on the basis of such traditions or variant oral traditions provided the major impetus for the varying OG and MT texts, whether or not written text(s) were also involved. The representation of yet other variant traditions in the OG Preface[77] serves to further emphasize this point.

The major implication of this study for approaches to the variant texts of Dan 5 is the suggestion that there is not necessarily any direct relationship between the two texts. Rather than discussing how each text developed from an earlier known version of the story, we would simply have two versions of the story, each told in different ways.[78] In a sense, however, this "major implication" is hardly new. Even scholars like Montgomery who argued for the priority and originality of the MT version of the story realized that there was not a simple literary relationship with the OG but

76. Holm, *Of Courtiers and Kings*, 191–92, 330.

77. See n. 2, above.

78. For the different emphases of the two texts, see especially Meadowcroft, *Aramaic Daniel and Greek Daniel*, 57–84.

that (for them) the translator of the OG had substantially and creatively rewritten the (proto-)MT. Perhaps a more important "major implication" of the study of this text is the suggestion that Dan 5 is just a more obvious example of a widespread phenomenon in the ancient world. Rather than being the exception, it may provide clear evidence that those who handled the biblical texts regularly had knowledge of alternative versions of the traditions, even when such large-scale variations as in Dan 5 are not evidenced in our texts. This in turn would remind us to constantly bear in mind that even when texts are generally a lot closer to each other than the MT and OG of Dan 5, variant texts are not necessarily to be directly related to each other or derived from each other but that the potential for creative adaptation of variant traditions was always present.

Community Rule or Community Rules: Examining a Supplementary Approach in Light of the Sectarian Dead Sea Scrolls

Maxine L. Grossman

1. Introduction

In *Empirical Models for Biblical Criticism*, Jeffrey Tigay argues for "common-sense techniques" for understanding the development of biblical texts,[1] urging scholars to ask: "Is this really the way that literature grew in the ancient Near East?"[2] At the end of his introduction, he expresses the hope that, in light of the examples provided there, "readers will be encouraged to seek more such models, especially for genres of biblical literature not covered in this volume."[3] The present study reflects one such effort, to consider the genre of "sectarian rule documents," specifically those found among the Dead Sea Scrolls. The association of such rule texts with a sectarian religious community makes the question of their composition particularly interesting.

Especially relevant for a discussion of the social and literary development of the rule texts is Alexander Rofé's contribution to *Empirical Models for Biblical Criticism*, "Joshua 20: Historico-Literary Criticism Illustrated."[4] Rofé identifies three questions that stand at the center of a

1. Jeffrey H. Tigay, "Introduction," in *Empirical Models for Biblical Criticism*, ed. Jeffrey H. Tigay (Philadelphia: University of Pennsylvania Press, 1985), 18.

2. Jeffrey H. Tigay, "The Evolution of the Pentateuchal Narratives in the Light of the Evolution of the *Gilgamesh Epic*," in Tigay, *Empirical Models for Biblical Criticism*, 26.

3. Tigay, "Introduction," 20.

4. Alexander Rofé, "Joshua 20: Historico-Literary Criticism Illustrated," in Tigay, *Empirical Models for Biblical Criticism*, 131–47.

historico-literary critical approach to a given textual composition. The first concerns the nature of the text and in particular the diverse dynamics that may lie behind its composition: "Is it a combination of various oral traditions? a redaction of several documents? an accumulation of layers of revisions and recensions? Does it incorporate the marginal notes of late scribes? Does it reflect some other form of authorship?"[5] Rofé's second point of consideration is the origin of the text: where and when it was composed, in what social milieu, and for what particular functions.[6] His third concern is for the historical evidence provided by the text, in which category he includes not only the historical claims made in the text itself, but also the information that the text provides—perhaps inadvertently—about the particular social and intellectual world of its authors.

Rofé goes on to explore a particular mode of textual development, which he frames as a *supplementary hypothesis*. In contrast with a documentary hypothesis (which imagines the editing-together of separate, complete texts), Rofé argues that some texts display evidence for dynamics of supplementation, "the formation of biblical literature as a gradual developmental process: layer on layer, stratum on stratum, continuing until the works reached their canonical form."[7] As in the case of a documentary model, particular authors and settings can be associated with the various stages of development. In contrast with a documentary model, however, a supplementary approach aims to identify the evolutionary development of a single text and not a combination of multiple texts.

The case of the sectarian Dead Sea Scrolls provides a context for putting Rofé's approach to the test, with results that both support his general perspective and sharpen or challenge aspects of it. In this context, a discussion of the Rule of the Community, or Serek Hayaḥad (S), is particularly apt. The manuscript witnesses for this sectarian rule provide evidence for a complex dynamic of textual development whose precise stages are still a matter of scholarly debate. A discussion of social milieu and historical setting is similarly challenging. Taken as a whole, this discussion clarifies the literary and social understanding of the genre of sectarian rule texts, while also further challenging our understanding of dynamics of textual formation.

---

5. Ibid., 132.
6. Ibid., 133.
7. Ibid., 144.

2. Textual Diversity and the Genre of the Sectarian Rule

In the late 1940s, when the Dead Sea Scrolls were first discovered in a series of eleven caves in the Judean desert near the site of Khirbet Qumran, scholars were quick to identify their authors with the ancient Essenes, an ascetic Jewish sect described in the writings of Philo, Josephus, and Pliny the Elder.[8] This identification has been critiqued in the intervening decades, and current scholarship is sensitive to the dangers of a harmonistic reading (both of the classical sources for the Essenes and within the scrolls corpus itself), but the fact remains that a subset of the scrolls does indeed bear the marks of a particular religious communal perspective.[9] Among these so-called sectarian scrolls,[10] we find diverse scriptural interpretations, hymns and liturgies, and especially the rule texts that will be the subject of my discussion here. The Damascus Document, the Community Rule, the Rule of the Congregation, and other texts share a particular interest in everyday collective matters—the structures of rituals and rules

8. A recent discussion of these and other classical sources for the Essenes appears in Alison Schofield, *From Qumran to the Yaḥad: A New Paradigm of Textual Development for* The Community Rule, STDJ 77 (Leiden: Brill, 2009), 191–218; see also Todd S. Beall, *Josephus' Description of the Essenes Illustrated by the Dead Sea Scrolls*, SNTSMS 58 (Cambridge: Cambridge University Press, 1988). The major classical sources are compiled in Géza Vermes and Martin Goodman, eds., *The Essenes according to the Classical Sources*, OCTb 1 (Sheffield: JSOT Press, 1989).

9. Much has been written on the texts and cultural setting of the Dead Sea Scrolls. An excellent short introduction is James C. VanderKam, *The Dead Sea Scrolls Today*, 2nd ed. (Grand Rapids: Eerdmans, 2010). A good place to begin for a more expansive treatment is Timothy H. Lim and John J. Collins, eds., *The Oxford Handbook of the Dead Sea Scrolls*, OHRT (Oxford: Oxford University Press, 2012). For the scrolls texts themselves, with translation, see Florentino García Martínez and Eibert J. C. Tigchelaar, eds., *The Dead Sea Scrolls Study Edition*, 2 vols. (Grand Rapids: Eerdmans; Leiden: Brill, 1999), henceforth *DSSSE*.

10. The terms *sect* or *sectarian literature* are sometimes used in a very general sense to refer to any small religious group and its writings. My use of these expressions reflects a more specific sociological framing for such a small group, characterized by dynamics of social boundary-formation and competition with regard to a shared religious heritage. See David J. Chalcraft, ed., *Sectarianism in Early Judaism: Sociological Advances*, BibleWorld (London: Equinox, 2007); for discussion and additional bibliography, see Schofield, *From Qumran to the Yaḥad*, 21–33; and Charlotte Hempel, "Rewritten Rule Texts," in *The Qumran Rule Texts in Context*, TSAJ 154 (Tübingen: Mohr Siebeck, 2013), 137–50, esp. 141. Further discussion and bibliography follow below.

for participation in a given group—interspersed with sermonic and occasional narrative material. The combination of ritual, legal, and sermonic material is characteristic of these rule texts, which are well represented among the scrolls. At least eleven copies of the Community Rule were discovered, as well as ten of the Damascus Document, more than the number of scrolls for all but six books of the canonical Hebrew Bible.[11] They are notable both for their thematic consistency and for important variants among their manuscript witnesses.

The variations within the Serek Hayaḥad, or Community Rule, text tradition are of particular interest for my discussion of textual formation. The Cave 1 witness to the Community Rule (1QS) is particularly well preserved. Its eleven columns contain an introduction, the description of a covenant renewal ceremony, a philosophical meditation (the so-called Doctrine of the Two Spirits), and a series of sections describing rules for membership, group meetings, and a penal code. The manuscript ends with the first-person Hymn of the Maskil ("instructor"), a recitation of his devotion to God and his community, with emphasis on the passing of proper times and seasons.[12] The Cave 4 witnesses, in contrast, are much more fragmentary.[13] Nevertheless, they provide evidence

---

11. Psalms and Deuteronomy, with more than thirty manuscripts each, are the most common texts from the Hebrew Bible. Genesis and Isaiah are represented by at least twenty manuscripts each, while Exodus and Leviticus are in the teens. Note that Jubilees (with fourteen or fifteen manuscripts) and 1 Enoch (twenty manuscripts) are similarly well represented. See VanderKam, *Dead Sea Scrolls Today*, 48 (chart), 191–93. The Damascus Document is also represented by two medieval witnesses from the Cairo Geniza (CD A and B).

12. The first publication of the Community Rule was that of Millar Burrows, *The Dead Sea Scrolls of St. Mark's Monastery: 2.2. Plates and Transcription of the Manual of Discipline* (New Haven: American Schools of Oriental Research, 1951), and a number of major publications followed; an accessible publication with translation is Elisha Qimron and James H. Charlesworth, "Rule of the Community (1QS)," in *The Dead Sea Scrolls: Hebrew, Aramaic, and Greek Texts with English Translations*, vol. 1: *Rule of the Community and Related Documents*, ed. James H. Charlesworth, PTSDSSP (Louisville: Westminster John Knox; Tübingen: Mohr Siebeck, 1994), 1–107. For a brief but thorough introduction to the Community Rule and its textual tradition, see Sarianna Metso, *The Serekh Texts*, CQS 9, LSTS 62 (New York: T&T Clark, 2007).

13. The manuscript witnesses to 4QS are 4Q255–264 (4QS^{a-j}). The editio princeps of the Cave 4 Serek material is Philip S. Alexander and Géza Vermes, eds., *Qumran Cave 4:XIX: Serekh ha-Yaḥad and Two Related Texts*, DJD 26 (Oxford: Clarendon, 1998); for information on the textual witnesses and the identification of other small

for parallels to all the major sections of 1QS, with sometimes significant textual divergences.[14]

Textual variation within the Serek tradition occurs at every level, from the structure of the composition itself, to the content and wording of specific sections, and even down to the level of orthography. In this brief discussion, I will consider three different examples of textual variation across the manuscript tradition: (1) the presence or absence of textual materials beyond a shared textual core, (2) language of leadership in two key passages, and (3) variations in the details of the penal code.[15]

3. Modular Differences in the Serek Manuscripts

Variation within the Serek tradition begins at the level of the text as a whole, with respect to the presence or absence of major sections of textual material. We might think of these differences as *modular* in effect, with large sections of the text appearing in some manuscript witnesses and not in others. Notable variations of this sort are connected especially with the opening of the text, its closing hymn, and the supplementary material associated with it.

As noted above, 1QS begins with an introduction, a covenant ceremony of blessings and curses, and the much-discussed Doctrine of the Two Spirits, whose radical dualism has often been treated as one of the characteristic qualities of Qumran religious thought. This material makes up the first four columns (roughly one-third) of 1QS. Column five of 1QS

Serek fragments, see 1–3, esp. 1 n. 1; Metso, *Serekh Texts*, 1–6. Three important early studies on the 4QS material are James H. Charlesworth and Brent A. Strawn, "Reflections on the Text of *Serek ha-Yaḥad* Found in Cave IV," *RevQ* 17 (1996): 403–35; Philip S. Alexander, "The Redaction-History of *Serekh ha-Yaḥad*: A Proposal," *RevQ* 17 (1996): 437–56; and Sarianna Metso, *The Textual Development of the Qumran Community Rule*, STDJ 21 (Leiden: Brill, 1997).

14. See especially the helpful charts in Alexander and Vermes, *Qumran Cave 4:XIX*, 2–3; Metso, *Serekh Texts*, 1–2, and bibliography at xi–xiii. Note the appendix plates at the end of Schofield, *From Qumran to the Yaḥad*, which provide a line-by-line text of the Serek, with the major witnesses in parallel format.

15. Parallels to the Serek penal code are found in the rule traditions of the Damascus Document (CD, 4Q266–273 [4QD^{a-h}]) and 4Q265 (4QMiscellaneous Rules). The discussion of textual diversity within the Serek tradition should also be carried outward into a comparative discussion of the sectarian rule texts more generally (see below).

then proceeds with a new discussion, on the structures and values of the *yaḥad* community, which reads like a new opening to the text as a whole. This repetition of content is provocative for readers in search of evidence for composite text formation. Alongside it we find paratextual evidence that is similarly interesting. The manuscript of 1QS is marked with marginal section breaks throughout, which take the form of horizontal lines or "fishhook" marks, as well as paleo-Hebrew letters.[16] A major section-break marker is found in the margin opposite 1QS V, 1.

These data gain interest when read against the textual evidence of 4Q258 (4QS[d]), a manuscript of the Community Rule that preserves substantial parallels to seven of the eleven columns of 1QS. What 4Q258 does not preserve is any evidence for the first four columns of the manuscript. To be clear, this is not to say that the first four columns have been lost, but rather that they were never part of the manuscript to begin with. 4Q258 is unusual among the scrolls in that it preserves a right-hand (or starting) margin for the manuscript. This margin is without stitching (thus indicating that it was not preceded by another leather sheet), and it is particularly wide (2.2 cm, as opposed to the more usual 1–1.2 cm).[17] Extra-deep margins are common at the beginnings and ends of scrolls manuscripts (sometimes accompanied by or instead of blank handle-sheets sewn onto the margin of the opening leather sheet).[18] The material evidence for 4Q258 thus reflects a witness to the Serek tradition that begins in parallel with 1QS V, 1, precisely where that manuscript indicates a major section break.[19]

Endings are as significant as beginnings in this textual tradition. I have noted already that 1QS ends with a lengthy hymn (1QS IX, 26–XI, 22). In

---

16. On section breaks in 1QS and other Qumran scrolls, see Emanuel Tov, *Scribal Practices and Approaches Reflected in the Texts Found in the Judean Desert*, STDJ 54 (Leiden: Brill, 2004), esp. 178–81. For a close look at the manuscript itself, see the "Digital Dead Sea Scrolls" website of the Israel Museum, http://dss.collections.imj.org.il/community.

17. Alexander and Vermes, *Qumran Cave 4:XIX*, 85; see also Metso, *Serekh Texts*, 4.

18. Tov, *Scribal Practices*, 99–118, esp. 113.

19. Five other fragmentary 4QS manuscripts lack evidence for a text paralleling 1QS I–IV (4Q259–261, 263–264). Of these, 4Q259 (4QS[e]) preserves the most substantial textual material, and Metso observes that "it is unclear whether the material of 1QS I–IV was included in this manuscript." Alexander and Vermes, *Qumran Cave 4:XIX*, 131, describe this line of thinking as "rather speculative." For a number of other differences between 4Q259 and 1QS, see Metso, *Serekh Texts*, 4–5. See below for further discussion of 4Q259.

this first-person song, the narrator pledges to praise God during the cycles of day and night, the seasons, months, festivals, and sabbatical years. Sacrificial language combines with references to judgment and righteousness in this hymn, which also dwells upon binaries of wickedness and righteous behavior and upon the ultimate power of God to know all and control all things. The concluding lines of the hymn praise God in language that is representative of the major theological themes within the sectarian scrolls: God shares secret divine knowledge only with a chosen few, and nothing comes about in the world except by God's will; humans left to their own devices are imperfect, lowly, and incapable of true understanding.

Textual evidence for this final hymn appears in four Cave 4 manuscripts, while five others lack information to indicate the presence or absence of the hymn.[20] In two of the manuscripts that contain the hymn, we find hints that the end of the hymn does not mark the end of that particular Serek manuscript.[21] More dramatically, though, one manuscript, 4Q259, contains an entirely different text in the place where the other manuscripts have this hymn.

4Q259 is an interesting manuscript in its own right. It preserves no evidence for the text paralleling 1QS I–IV (but neither does it preserve evidence for its absence in the manuscript's original form), and it appears to have lacked the material paralleling 1QS VIII, 15–IX, 11 (regulations for conduct and repentance) outright.[22] In place of the concluding hymn, the editors of this manuscript argue, 4Q259 contained a calendrical text, preserved today in fragmentary form as 4Q319 (4QOtot).[23] This calendri-

20. Evidence is present in 4Q256 (4QS^{b}), 258, 260 (4QS^{f}), 264 (4QS^{j}); we have no information from 4Q255 (4QpapS^{a}), 257 (4QpapS^{c}), 261–263 (4QS^{g-i}).

21. The final fragment of 4Q256 contains the final lines of the concluding hymn, but the text then continues with additional, otherwise unknown material. The editors of 4QS observe that this fragment may not belong to this manuscript "or even to S," but that if it does, it indicates the presence of additional material immediately after the concluding hymn. See Alexander and Vermes, *Qumran Cave 4:XIX*, 63. The editors also note the presence of stitching to the left of the final column of 4Q264, thus indicating a second instance in which a Serek manuscript might have continued on past the conclusion of the hymn; see ibid., 202. Note further discussion below.

22. See ibid., 11, 134, 148. Note that this is not the Qumran penal code (found in 1QS VI, 24–VII, 25), with its specific listing of transgressions and punishments, but instead a more discursive treatment of a particular two-year punishment cycle, framed in terms of sacrifice and repentance.

23. Although preserved under a separate manuscript number, 4Q319 is a physical continuation of the 4Q259 manuscript; see ibid., 150–51.

cal text is of a genre that is familiar among the Qumran manuscripts. It lines up the calendrical signs ("Otot") of the year with standard cycles of priestly service in the temple (priestly courses), including references to sabbatical years, jubilees, and holidays. Its place at the end of this rule text is a bit curious, but scholars have speculated that it serves a similar purpose to the first portion of the 1QS concluding hymn: underscoring the importance of the sacred calendar and the perpetuity and universality of the secret knowledge provided by God only to the faithful of his covenant.[24]

A final example of material that is present only in some Serek manuscripts is found in the texts of 1Q28a (1QSa) and 1Q28b (1QSb), so-called supplements to the major Cave 1 Serek manuscript. 1Q28a, the Rule of the Congregation (or Messianic Rule), represents another composite rule text. It is much shorter than 1QS and provides rules for a marrying congregation (or *edah*), such as we find in the Damascus Document (neither *edah*-language nor references to marrying sectarians appear in the text of 1QS). 1Q28a compiles short collections of rules, an accounting of the life-cycle stages of congregation members from childhood through old age, and accounts of a messianic banquet to be held in the end times. 1Q28b, the Blessings Rule, contains an expansive blessings liturgy not unlike that found at the opening of 1QS.

The texts of 1Q28a and 1Q28b fit within the Serek tradition, making use of its distinctive language (references to the *yaḥad* and to Zadokite authority), but 1Q28a also uses language found in the Damascus Document and absent from the Community Rule, as noted above.[25] The manuscripts of 1Q28a and 1Q28b were attached to 1QS in antiquity,[26] and the

---

24. Robert Kugler has explored the relationship of the hymn and the Otot text. See Robert Kugler, "Of Calendars, Community Rules, and Common Knowledge: Understanding 4QS^{e}–4QOtot, with Help from Ritual Studies," in *Rediscovering the Dead Sea Scrolls: An Assessment of Old and New Approaches and Methods*, ed. Maxine L. Grossman (Grand Rapids: Eerdmans, 2010), 215–28.

25. The text opens with reference to "all the *congregation* of Israel" (1Q28a I, 1, emphasis added) but then refers also to "the sons of Zadok, the priests, and the men of their covenant" (1Q28a I, 2). A later section makes extensive references to the "council of the community," a term more often associated with 1QS. Charlotte Hempel observes that 1Q28a must have undergone a "Zadokite recension," which brought together these diverse sectarian concepts. See Charlotte Hempel, "The Earthly Essene Nucleus of 1QSa," *DSD* 3 (1996): 253–69; updated as Hempel, "The Damascus Document and 1QSa," in Hempel, *Qumran Rule Texts in Context*, 47–62.

26. Metso states that 1Q28a was "physically stitched to 1QS" (Metso, *Serekh Texts*,

same scribe copied all three texts.[27] At the same time, the three manuscripts represent independent compositions with developmental histories of their own. Each works as a stand-alone text, and there is tentative evidence for additional copies of the Rule of the Congregation among some extremely fragmentary papyrus manuscripts from Cave 4, written in a cryptic script.[28] But among the Cave 4 Serek manuscripts, we find no indications of any material from either 1Q28a or 1Q28b.

At a macrolevel, then, the text of the Community Rule is thoroughly composite. More than composite, it appears to reflect a modular quality, in which portions of the composition can be present in some manuscripts and absent in others, and it is even possible to replace one textual section with a quite different textual composition.

4. Language and Authority in the Serek Tradition

Scaling down from large sections to the level of the wording in particular sections, we also find significant variations in the Serek tradition. Perhaps the most famous such variant from the Cave 4 Serek material concerns the textual framing of communal authority. At the beginning of 1QS V, a passage that we have already identified as paralleling the opening section of at least one of the Cave 4 Serek manuscripts, we read: "This is the rule for the men of the Community who freely volunteer to convert from all evil and to keep themselves steadfast in all he commanded in compliance with his will" (1QS V, 1).[29] The text goes on to state that the members of the *yaḥad*

---

51); see also Tov, *Scribal Practices*, 77, citing Józef T. Milik, "Annexes à la Règle de la Communauté (1QS)," in *Qumran Cave 1*, ed. Dominique Barthélemy and Józef T. Milik, DJD 1 (Oxford: Clarendon, 1955), 107. Tov disagrees and instead argues that the three scrolls were rolled up together in antiquity and that 1Q28a and 1Q28b may have been stitched to each other. See Tov, *Scribal Practices*, 110–12, esp. nn. 147, 149.

27. Although there is surprisingly little evidence for individual scribes copying more than one manuscript among the scrolls, the scribe associated with 1QS, 1Q28a, and 1Q28b apparently also copied 4Q53 (4QSam[c]) and added corrections to 1QIsa[a]. See Tov, *Scribal Practices*, 23; for further discussion and bibliography, see Charlotte Hempel, "'Haskalah' at Qumran: The Eclectic Character of Qumran Cave 4," in Hempel, *Qumran Rule Texts in Context*, 312.

28. See Stephen J. Pfann, "Cryptic Texts," in *Qumran Cave 4:XXVI: Cryptic Texts and Miscellanea Part 1*, ed. Stephen J. Pfann et al., DJD 36 (Oxford: Clarendon, 2000), 515–74; Metso, *Serekh Texts*, 51.

29. Translations of 1QS follow *DSSSE*, 1:79–81.

community will keep themselves separate from their opponents and will form "a Community in law and possessions, and acquiesce to the authority of the sons of Zadok, the priests who safeguard the covenant /and/ to the authority of the multitude of the men of the Community, those who persevere steadfastly in the covenant" (1QS V, 2–3). Similar language appears a few lines later, in connection with the oath that new sectarians must make

> to revert to the Law of Moses, according to all that he commanded, with whole heart and whole soul, in compliance with all that has been revealed of it to the sons of Zadok, the priests who keep the covenant and interpret his will and to the multitude of the men of their covenant who freely volunteer together for his truth and to walk according to his will. (1QS V, 8–9)

This language of authority—combined with a very different set of references to the Zadokite priesthood in the Damascus Document (or Zadokite Fragments)[30]—has contributed to an understanding of the scrolls community as priestly in character and helped to shape one of the early historical theories of scrolls origins (in a community of disaffected Zadokite priests, driven from power by the Hasmonean usurpation of the Jerusalem temple).[31]

Interestingly, though, a very different picture of communal authority appears in the Cave 4 Serek scrolls. The parallel passage in 4Q258 contains many variants in comparison with 1QS,[32] beginning with its opening words: "A sermon [*midrash*] for the Maskil concerning the men of the Torah." The lines that follow assign communal leadership simply to "the authority of the many," without any reference to the Zadokite priests.[33] The second passage, describing the oath of admission, is fragmentary but appears to make reference to "the authority of the council of the men of

30. The relevant passages include CD III, 21–IV, 4 and possibly V, 1–5; for a contrasting perception of group identity, see CD VI, 2–12.

31. A classic treatment of this theory appears in Géza Vermes, "The History of the Community," in *The Complete Dead Sea Scrolls in English* (New York: Penguin, 1997), 49–66, esp. 50–53.

32. Note the editors' comment, that "the text in this column differs so much from 1QS that it is impossible to insert the 1QS line numbers" (Alexander and Vermes, *Qumran Cave 4:XIX*, 93 n. 3).

33. See 4Q258 I, 1–2. For text, translation, and comments, see ibid., 93–96.

the community," again without any mention of Zadokites.[34] Direct and indirect confirmation of this wording is found in the fragmentary text of 4Q256.[35]

A few observations with regard to this passage are particularly relevant to my discussion. First, the language of 1QS here is much more expansive and "wordy" than that of the 4Q manuscripts. For example, 4Q258 has, "no man shall walk in the stubbornness of his heart to go astray, but rather he shall lay a [foundation of] truth for Israel as a community for everyone who freely pledges himself to holiness in Aaron, and a house of truth for Israel and (for) those who joi[n] th[e]m for community."[36] In contrast, the parallel text in 1QS has (italics represent pluses):

> no man shall walk in the stubbornness of his heart to go astray *following his heart and his eyes and the musings of his inclination* but rather he shall *circumcise in the Community the foreskin of his tendency and of his stiff neck in order to* lay a foundation of truth for Israel as a community, *an eternal covenant, to repent* for everyone who freely pledges himself to holiness in Aaron, and a house of truth for Israel and (for) those who join them for community, *lawsuit, and judgment, to proclaim as guilty all those who trespass the decree. These are the regulations of their behavior concerning all these decrees when they are enrolled in the Community.*[37]

The material that follows in 1QS also includes a number of scriptural citations, each of which supports and expands on a given injunction in the shorter text. Thus, the sectarian is not to associate with outsiders in matters of work, because, "you shall remain at a distance from every lie" (Exod 23:7, at 1QS V, 15), and he is not to share their food or drink without paying for them, "as it is written, 'shun the man whose breath is in his nostrils, for how

34. 4Q258 I, 7; see ibid., 93–96.

35. 4Q256 IX preserves the full reference to "the authority of the many" (at 4Q256 IX, 3). The manuscript fragment breaks off before the location of the reference to "the authority of the council of the men of the community." The editors observe that "the recension of S in this column of 4QS[b] appears to be the same as that in 4QS[d], but differs markedly from that in 1QS." They are able to use the text of the latter manuscript (4Q258 = 4QS[d]) to fill in the missing wording from the former (4Q256 = 4QS[b]). See the discussion in ibid., 54; for text, translation, and comments, see 53–55.

36. 4Q258 I, 4–5; see ibid., 93–97.

37. 1QS V, 4–7, see *DSSSE*, 1:80–81; 4Q258 I, 4–5, see Alexander and Vermes, *Qumran Cave 4:XIX*, 93–97. Translation is harmonized in the direction of Alexander and Vermes, *Qumran Cave 4:XIX*.

much is he worth?'" (Isa 2:22, at 1QS V, 17). In each case, the 4QS tradition contains the injunction but lacks the scriptural reference.[38]

In these selected passages of the Serek tradition, then, we find a more expansive text in 1QS than appears in the parallel 4QS material. Unlike my earlier examples, which reflected a practice of modular *addition* and *subtraction*, the form of supplementation that we encounter here is one of expansion and contraction, in which a simpler and a more complex version of the same text appears in parallel manuscript witnesses.

5. Penal Code Variations

Textual variation also extends beyond the boundaries of the Serek tradition to include overlaps with other Qumran rule texts. I have noted that the Serek tradition has a modular aspect to it, with some manuscripts containing sections or even entire works that are absent from other manuscripts. A curious fact of the Qumran corpus is that some compositions also appear to cross the boundaries *between* texts. The Qumran penal code is one such example. The penal code of the Community Rule (1QS VI, 24–VII, 25 and 4Q parallels)[39] delineates a series of transgressions against communal authority and the decorum of community gatherings and indicates the penalties associated with them.[40] Evidence for this code has been found not only in the Serek tradition but also in manuscripts of the Damascus Document, the Miscellaneous Rules (4Q265), and an additional fragment from Cave 11.[41] The presence of this composition in the manuscripts of a variety of distinct Qumran texts complicates our picture of textual variation and text formation. It indicates the possibility that shared oral (or written?) traditions could be incorporated into distinct sectarian texts,

38. 1QS V, 14–17, *DSSSE*, 1:80–81; 4Q258 I, 7–10, see Alexander and Vermes, *Qumran Cave 4:XIX*, 93–97.

39. Evidence for the penal code appears in 4Q258 V, 1; 4Q259 I, 4–15; II, 3–8; 4Q261 III, 2–4; IVa–b, 1–7; Va–c, 1–9; VIa–e, 1–5.

40. See Metso, *Serekh Texts*, 12; Schofield, *From Qumran to the Yaḥad*, 180–83; and more comprehensively, Joseph M. Baumgarten, "The Cave 4 Versions of the Qumran Penal Code," *JJS* 43 (1992): 268–76; and Charlotte Hempel, "The Penal Code Reconsidered," in *Legal Texts and Legal Issues: Proceedings of the Second Meeting of the International Organization for Qumran Studies, Cambridge 1995*, ed. Moshe J. Bernstein, Florentino García Martínez, and John Kampen, STDJ 23 (Leiden: Brill, 1997), 337–48.

41. The text preserved in 11Q29 is not directly relevant to my discussion, although it is worth noting its presence among the material evidence.

in ways that might seek to retain content and structure, while seeming to demonstrate less concern for specific wording or presentation.

The 1QS penal code makes reference to both *punishments* and *exclusions*. The text itself is elliptical, beginning with a rather fully worded statement about punishment and exclusion and then successively dropping words from the statements that follow in a way that shifts the tone toward greater and greater brevity. The text then pauses and draws breath before beginning again with a series of more fully worded statements. It will be useful to briefly summarize this material, to set the scene for what follows.

The opening case within the penal code of 1QS states that community members who knowingly lie about a matter connected with personal property are "*excluded* from the purity of the many for one year and are *punished* (with the reduction of) one quarter of their bread" (VI, 25, emphasis added). A community member who is disrespectful toward a higher-ranking member "is punished" for one year (VI, 27); a member who utters the name of God "is excluded" permanently from the council of the community (VII, 1–2). One who speaks against an authoritative priest is punished for one year and excluded "alone" from the purity of the many (VII, 2–3);[42] if his statement is unintentional, his punishment is only for six months (VII, 3). An intentional lie is punished for six months (VII, 4), while a member who engages in intentional and unjustified rudeness toward a fellow member is punished for a year and excluded (VII, 4–5). The transgressions in the next series are punished but not connected with exclusion: deceptive speech is punished for six months (VII, 5); negligence toward a fellow member is punished for three months (VII, 6); negligence with communal property requires replacement of the property or a punishment of sixty days (VII, 6–8); baseless animosity is punished for six months (corrected to one year, VII, 8). The text then becomes even more elliptical, dropping the word "punish" and merely indicating the length of time of the penalty: with reference to retaliation, "likewise" (= six months or one year?) (VII, 9); pointless speech, three months (VII, 9); interrupting a fellow member, ten days (VII, 9–10); lying down and sleeping in a meeting, thirty days (VII, 10).

The text at this point becomes a bit less elliptical, stating that "the same [penalty] applies" to someone who leaves the meeting without permis-

42. The text here reads ומובדל על נפשו, which may be understood as "excluded alone" or "by himself" (see Qimron and Charlesworth, "Rule of the Community," 30–31 n. 175) or "excluded, under sentence of death" (see *DSSSE*, 1:86–87).

sion or falls asleep three times in a given meeting: he shall be punished for ten days; but if he leaves while they are standing, he is punished for thirty days (VII, 10–12). Unnecessary public nakedness is punished for six months, while spitting in the meeting is punished for thirty days (VII, 12–13); indecent exposure is punished for thirty days (VII, 13–14); frivolous laughter is punished for thirty days (VII, 14–15); and rude gestures (with "the left hand") are punished for ten days (VII, 15).

At this point in the penal code, the rhetoric of the text returns to a more full or wordy presentation, with the assertion that a member who goes around defaming his fellow within the group "is excluded for one year from the purity of the many and is punished" (VII, 15–16); if he defames the group as a whole, he is permanently expelled from the group (VII, 16–17); if he complains about the foundation of the community, he is permanently expelled (VII, 17); if he complains baselessly about his fellow member, he will be punished for six months (VII, 17–18). An expansive passage then indicates the procedure for managing someone who leaves the group and then wishes to return (he is effectively sent back to novice status; VII, 18–21) and for someone who leaves after having been a member for ten years or more (he can never return, nor can anyone who continues to interact with him; VII, 22–25).

The penal code of 1QS is vigorous and vivid in its treatment of transgressive behavior. A close reading of the text allows us to envision a particular character for the group associated with it and its expectations for its membership.[43] It is interesting to note in this context the nonstandardized quality of the presentation of these rules. Unlike a fully formulaic list of rules (for example, in the handbook of a condominium association or on the wall at a swimming pool), the treatment of the rules in 1QS speeds up when the transgressions are similar to one another, slows down to shift gears, and regroups in its conclusion. There is an almost ad hoc quality about the presentation here, as if the scribe is writing up the rules just as they come to mind.

The fragmentary evidence from Cave 4 both confirms and contradicts this perception. Three of the Serek manuscripts from Cave 4 retain portions of the penal code, and each has something interesting to tell us.

---

43. I have attempted such a reading in Maxine L. Grossman, "'Outside the True': Intimacy, Sectarian Identity, and Discursive Boundaries on the Study of the Dead Sea Scrolls," in *The T&T Clark Companion to the Dead Sea Scrolls*, ed. George J. Brooke and Charlotte Hempel (London: T&T Clark, forthcoming).

The first witness, 4Q258, contains just a single line (portions of only two words, in fact, although these words, "his hand from wi[thin]" are particularly distinctive).[44] However, this is the manuscript that preserves parallels to seven of the eleven columns of 1QS, and the presence of this parallel material allows the editors of the fragments to calculate (speculatively) the length of the 4Q manuscript and how much text it could contain. Based on the presence of material from before and after this brief line (paralleling 1QS VI, 12 and VIII, 6 respectively), they calculate that the intervening text must have been "shorter than the corresponding text of 1QS," perhaps by some six lines.[45] The missing lines may not come from the penal code itself (since they could be absent from some portion of 1QS VI, 12–24 or VIII, 1–6), but such an absence is certainly possible.

The textual evidence from 4Q259 is much more extensive, containing major portions of the penal code (paralleling 1QS VII, 8–15 and VII, 20–25).[46] Here again, the editors are able to line up the fragments with the penal code from 1QS, while suggesting the reconstruction of many small variations in wording to account for differences in available space.[47] Several specific points are notable. First, 4Q259 begins with a phrase that has been reconstructed as "[six mon]ths," in what is most likely a reference to the punishment for baseless animosity. This is helpful in light of the Cave 1 manuscript's treatment of this penalty, which includes a marginal correction from the text's six months to a period of one year. The penalty for indecent exposure in 4Q259 appears to be sixty days (although the first two letters of ששים are slightly unclear), as opposed to the thirty (שלושים) of 1QS. The editors question whether this reflects a scribal error or an accurate rendering of a different penalty statement.[48]

A third manuscript, 4Q261, contains similarly extensive evidence for the penal code,[49] including many places where the wording of this manuscript would have differed in small ways from that of 1QS.[50] It is difficult

44. 4Q258 V, 1; see Alexander and Vermes, *Qumran Cave 4:XIX*, 104.

45. Ibid., 104 ("Notes on Readings").

46. Ibid., 135–44.

47. A representative example is ibid., 140 n. 4, where the editors suggest a reconstruction of שנתים ("two years") in place of שנתים ימים ("two years of days" = "two years"), to fit within the available letter-space on the line.

48. See 4Q259 I, 13; see ibid., 138 n. 13.

49. 4Q261 II–VI; see ibid., 177–86.

50. See, for example, ibid., 180 n. 1, 181 nn. 2–3, 6, and also 182 ("Notes on Readings").

to detect any specific differences with respect to the ordering of transgressions or the content of penalties in this fragmentary material, but the editors indicate several occasions in which the text of 4Q261 would have been longer—and not shorter—than that of 1QS.[51]

The examples of the Cave 4 Serek material suggest some confirmation of our earlier suspicion, that the wording of the penal code in 1QS reflected not a fixed framing but a more ad hoc treatment.[52] However, these fragmentary manuscripts also suggest a consistency in the substantive content of the penal code, including at least tentative evidence for the presence of the specific transgressions and penalties in a specific order.

In light of these findings with regard to the Serek penal code, the evidence for the Damascus Document penal code (4QD) is particularly interesting. A few short lines of relevant material are preserved at the very end of one of the medieval Damascus Document manuscripts,[53] but much more material is preserved among the Cave 4 manuscripts of this text, which overlap extensively with the witnesses to the Serek tradition without merely reproducing the text as we have it there.[54] The 4QD penal code, in short order, articulates penalties for: lying about property, malice in a capital offense, rudeness toward a fellow member, pointless speech, interrupting a fellow member, lying down and sleeping in a meeting, leaving without permission three times in a session (with a different penalty if the group is standing), public nakedness, indecent exposure, frivolous laughter, rude gestures, and defamation of fellow covenanters and of the group as a whole. Additional penalties are asserted at the end of the penal code for one who takes food inappropriately, who "comes near to fornicate with

51. Ibid., 184 nn. 5–7.

52. Also potentially relevant is the fact that the 1QS copy of the penal code contains an unusual number of erasures and corrections. Joseph Baumgarten suggested that this might reflect ongoing editing in light of changes in the community's legal norms. See Baumgarten, "Cave 4 Versions of the Penal Code," 273; Tov, *Scribal Practices*, 229.

53. CD XIV, 20–22; a major textual variant is found here, in that lying about property is penalized by exclusion and a punishment of "six days." The editors of the 4QD material note that this "seems too short a penalty." See Joseph M. Baumgarten et al., eds., *Qumran Cave 4:XIII: The Damascus Document (4Q266–273)*, DJD 18 (Oxford: Clarendon, 1996), 73, 135.

54. 4Q266 10 I, 14–15; 10 II (4QD[a]); 4Q267 9 VI (4QD[b]); 4Q269 11 I–II (4QD[d]); 4Q270 7 I (4QD[e]); see Baumgarten et al., *Qumran Cave 4:XIII*, 72–75, 110–11, 134–35, 162–66; Hempel, "Penal Code Reconsidered," 338–41.

his wife contrary to the law," and one who murmurs, either against the "Fathers" or the "Mothers" of the congregation.[55]

The parallels to the Serek tradition here are striking, including not only specific transgressions (and sometimes specific details about them), but even at times the order and clustering of the transgressions. At the same time, the rendering of this material in the Damascus Document clearly represents evidence for a *different* penal code, associated with a different set of group norms and practices. The Damascus penal material is much more consistent about designating "exclusion" and "punishment" for each offense, with longer periods of "exclusion" (that generally line up with the Serek tradition penalties) and shorter periods of "punishment" for each offense.[56] Even more obviously, the Damascus material assumes the need to regulate the behavior of married couples (a social category absent from the Serek tradition) and regulates some kind of social status for "Fathers" and "Mothers" within the congregation.[57]

We may note one final example, from 4Q265, now labeled Miscellaneous Rules but formerly called 4QSD, in acknowledgment of its overlapping Serek and Damascus Document-like material. A fragmentary penal code within this manuscript preserves references to such transgressions as foolish laughter, rebelling against a higher-ranked sectarian, intentional rudeness, deception and intentional lying, and lies concerning property, as well as lying down and sleeping in the meeting, and dozing off three times. The order of these passages differs from that of 1QS, and not every transgression is paralleled, but the degree of similarity is striking. Significant differences, once again, arise specifically in terms of the designation of penalties; 4Q265 regularly specifies that punishment relates to the loss of "half one's bread."[58]

The penal codes of the Serek texts, the Damascus Document, and 4Q265 reflect distinct textual traditions. They assume different penalty structures and, in the case of the Damascus Document, a distinctly gendered set of rules for family and social order. But they also display remarkable parallels,

55. See Baumgarten et al., *Qumran Cave 4:XIII*, 72–75, 110–11, and esp. 162–66.

56. See Baumgarten, "Cave 4 Versions of the Penal Code," esp. 272, 274.

57. These expressions were probably "honorific titles applied to senior members" of the Damascus covenant group; see ibid., 271.

58. See Joseph M. Baumgarten, "Miscellaneous Rules," in *Qumran Cave 4:XXV: Halakhic Texts*, ed. Joseph M. Baumgarten et al., DJD 35 (Oxford: Clarendon, 1999), 57–78; on this particular penalty, see 4Q265 4 I, in ibid., 64–65.

in content, wording, and order. Some degree of overlap can be attributed to their shared genre, and we would certainly expect to find parallel genre conventions across the three texts. But our ability to line these texts up with one another and discover comparable listings of transgressions and penalties suggests something more than mere genre parallels, something connected with textual composition and transmission.

6. Textual Variations in Social and Historical Perspective

I have considered three distinct types of textual variation here: large-scale manuscript differences, significant differences in wording, and differences within shared textual material in separate literary works. In the process, I have paid particular attention to the Cave 1 Community Rule text (1QS) and several of the Cave 4 manuscripts (4Q256, 258, and 259). Although I have not had space here to deal comprehensively with differences related to orthography, wording, or scriptural citation, I can nevertheless make a few summary observations:

- The text of 1QS tends to be more expansive or wordy in its use of language, and it tends to include a greater number of references to scriptural material in support of its claims than does the Cave 4 material.
- The text of 1QS has a more developed sense of "Zadokite" identity within the leadership structure of the *yaḥad* community.
- The content of 1QS is more encyclopedic, containing evidence for nearly the entire Serek tradition, including 1Q28a and 1Q28b (but not the Otot text found in 4Q259).
- Literary sections of the Serek tradition, including its penal code, tend to have a modular quality, in which blocks of texts might be present or absent and might have independent lives, perhaps on their own (if we accept the cryptic evidence for 1Q28a) and certainly within other textual traditions.

On the whole, and in light of these points, 1QS appears to represent a more developed and more comprehensive witness to the Qumran Serek tradition than we find in our other key Serek manuscripts. From the perspective of textual transmission, it is therefore fascinating—and not a little bit confounding—to acknowledge that 1QS has been identified as one of the *earliest* manuscript witnesses to the Serek tradition. Unlike our three key Cave 4 manuscripts—which are identified as Early Herodian or Late Hasmonean/Early Herodian and have been dated paleographically to the second half of the first century BCE—the hand of 1QS is identified by paleographers as Hasmonean and has been dated a half century earlier.[59] The implications of this textual evidence are surprising. They indicate that the more expansive witness to the Serek tradition, with its fuller texts and its assumption of Zadokite priestly authority, could not have been a simple expansion of and replacement for the shorter text within the community in any sort of linear fashion. The expected textual relationship is not confirmed by the evidence of the manuscript witnesses.[60]

A variety of textual solutions have been recommended in response to this complicated situation. One possibility is that the less-expansive Cave 4 Serek material reflects a later summary and compression of the text of 1QS.[61] While valuable as the most straightforward treatment of the evidence, this argument does not explain why later editors would

59. The hand of 1QS, identified as Hasmonean Semiformal, has been dated to 100–75 BCE or earlier by its editors. Only two other Serek manuscripts are dated this early (4Q255, identified as Early Hasmonean Cursive, is dated to 125–100 BCE; 4Q257, identified as Hasmonean Semiformal, is dated to 100–75; both manuscripts are written on papyrus). The hands of 4Q256, 4Q258, and also 4Q260 and 4Q263, are identified as Early Herodian Formal and dated to 30–1 BCE, while the hand of 4Q259 is identified as Late Hasmonean/Early Herodian with a mixed style and dated to 50–25 BCE. See Alexander and Vermes, *Qumran Cave 4:XIX*, 20–21. For recent discussions of paleography see especially Frank M. Cross, "Paleography," in *Encyclopedia of the Dead Sea Scrolls*, ed. Lawrence H. Schiffman and James C. VanderKam (New York: Oxford University Press, 2000), 2:629–34; Schofield, *From Qumran to the Yaḥad*, 78–82; and Martin G. Abegg, "The Linguistic Analysis of the Dead Sea Scrolls: More Than (Initially) Meets the Eye," in Grossman, *Rediscovering the Dead Sea Scrolls*, 48–68. Paleographic scholarship has been critiqued, especially for its claims to identify very narrow dating ranges in texts, but radical rejection of paleographic dating remains a minority perspective in Qumran studies. See now Ada Yardeni, *Understanding the Alphabet of the Dead Sea Scrolls: Development, Chronology, Dating* (Jerusalem: Carta, 2015).

60. Sarianna Metso provides a comprehensive treatment of the Serek manuscript tradition, including a sophisticated stemmatic analysis of its textual development. See Metso, *Textual Development*, esp. 143–49; see also Schofield, *From Qumran to the Yaḥad*, 70–78.

61. See Alexander, "Redaction-History of *Serekh ha-Yaḥad*"; Devorah Dimant, "The Composite Character of the Qumran Sectarian Literature as an Indication of Its Date and Provenance," *RevQ* 22 (2006): 615–30; Schofield, *From Qumran to the Yaḥad*, 72–73.

remove scriptural supports for arguments (instead of adding them in). Also problematic, although perhaps possible historically, is the shift from a more complex Zadokite communal authority structure to a structure that looks simpler and less developed.

An alternative explanation is provided by Sarianna Metso, who argues that the later developments in the Serek tradition did not supercede its earlier witnesses. Instead, the earlier and later redactions were transmitted side-by-side with one another.[62] Thus, Metso argues, on the basis of the diverse manuscript tradition, "it is clear that there never existed a single, legitimate and up-to-date version of the Community Rule that supplanted all other versions."[63] Instead, "[t]he texts were 'cumulative' rather than 'up-to-date.'"[64] To put it another way, although the manuscript evidence for the Serek tradition may reflect a variety of stages of textual development, including development in a "supplementary" vein, the text itself never seems to have achieved the stage of a final "canonical form" of the sort that Rofé describes in his chapter on the book of Joshua.

Working toward an understanding of the textual development of the Serek tradition takes us back to Rofé's initial methodological suggestions. His historico-literary critical treatment moves from close attention to textual formation to the realm of the social world and questions of historical significance. In this context, then, Rofé would encourage us to ask: What was the social milieu in which this tradition arose? What was the social function of the text? How does it bear witness to a particular historical reality? It is to these questions that I now turn.

7. Locating the Serek Tradition in Social-Historical Perspective

As I noted at the opening of my discussion, the Essene hypothesis of the first generation of Qumran scholars provided the starting point for a social understanding of the scrolls. This view located the community of the Serek Hayaḥad at Qumran and identified it with the celibate Essenes described by Pliny and other classical sources, in contrast with the marrying covenanters of the Damascus Document, who lived "in camps" and were to be equated with the marrying Essenes described by Josephus.[65] This early

62. For this, see Metso, *Textual Development of the Qumran Community Rule*.

63. Metso, *Serekh Texts*, 69.

64. Ibid., 69.

65. See n. 31.

hypothesis tended to imagine Qumran as *the* habitation site of the Essenes and as the physical location in which the sectarian Dead Sea Scrolls were composed and the entire scrolls corpus was copied, read, and transmitted. We should note that this perspective was established when the majority of scholars had no access to the fragmentary Cave 4 material and in light of an archaeological view that dated the origins of sectarian habitation at Qumran to the last third of the second century or the very beginning of the first century, BCE. In light of the major Cave 1 manuscripts and this archaeological dating, such a view makes very good sense of the evidence.

The literary evidence of the sectarian scrolls, however, hints at a more complex historical process. The Damascus Document in particular provides important, if sometimes problematic,[66] evidence for social/historical events connected with a larger dynamic of sectarianism in Second Temple period Judaism. The text speaks of a two-stage process of development: first, with the establishment of a "righteous remnant" of Israel, and then, after a period of twenty years of "wandering" as blind men, the arising of a Righteous Teacher to lead the people in God's proper path.[67] Claims of a schism between the Teacher's group and the followers of the "Man of the Lie" are found both in this text and in examples from Qumran pesher.[68] Moreover, toward the end of the Damascus Document, we hear of other marginal groups, who appear to be loosely connected with the Damascus covenant group but who have rejected some aspects of their teachings.[69] A number of responses and correctives to the classical Essene hypothesis have taken precisely these social and historical complexities into account. Especially important among these have been the Groningen hypothesis

66. On the problems of writing history from sectarian texts like the Damascus Document, see Maxine L. Grossman, *Reading for History in the Damascus Document: A Methodological Study*, STDJ 45 (Leiden: Brill, 2002).

67. CD I, 4–5, 9–11.

68. CD I, 11–18 has the "Scoffer," who pours out "the water of lies"; CD XX, 15 references "the Man of Lies." This figure also appears in the pesher to the book of Psalms (4Q171 I, 26; IV, 14 [4QpPs[a]]).

69. CD XIX, 13–14 refers to individual apostates from the Damascus covenant, those who enter the group but do not remain faithful to it. Specific reference is also made to groups who are in opposition to the covenant group, including, "the builders of the wall" (CD XX, 31), whom God hates; "the men of war who turned back with the Man of Lies" (CD XX, 14–15); and the House of Peleg, whose participants are varied enough in their behavior that each member will be evaluated individually, rather than being subject to a single group judgment (CD XX, 22–25).

and the framing of the Qumran scrolls within the context of a larger Enochic Judaism.[70]

A revised understanding of the archaeological evidence and fragmentary scrolls from Qumran lends further nuance to the historical picture. Recent attention to the dating of the site of Khirbet Qumran suggests that the sectarians were present there no earlier than the beginning or first third of the first century BCE,[71] which means that the earliest Serek witnesses must have been composed and may have been copied in places other than the site of Qumran itself. The diversity of the Cave 4 Serek manuscripts challenges the notion of a unitary, unchanging Qumran *yaḥad* and contributes support for the picture of a network of related *yaḥad* communities, at Qumran and in other locations, as both Alison Schofield and John Collins have argued.[72] The overlapping penal code material from Cave 4 further reminds us that the *yaḥad* sectarians shared some specific rules, rather than just general values, with the Damascus

---

70. For an introduction to the Groningen hypothesis, see Florentino García Martínez, "Qumran Origins and Early History: A Groningen Hypothesis," *FO* 5 (1988): 113–36; Florentino García Martínez and Adam S. van der Woude, "A Groningen Hypothesis of Qumran Origins and Early History," *RevQ* 14 (1999): 521–41; García Martínez, "The Groningen Hypothesis Revisited," in *The Dead Sea Scrolls and Contemporary Culture: Proceedings of the International Conference held at the Israel Museum, Jerusalem (July 6–8, 2008)*, ed. Adolfo D. Roitman, Lawrence H. Schiffman, and Shani Tzoref, STDJ 93 (Leiden: Brill, 2011), 17–30. Enochic Judaism was first explored as a category by Gabriele Boccaccini in *Beyond the Essene Hypothesis: The Parting of the Ways Between Qumran and Enochic Judaism* (Grand Rapids: Eerdmans, 1998).

71. The adjusted dating of the sectarian habitation site at Khirbet Qumran is perhaps the least controversial aspect of a much larger and quite contested debate over the identity of the site and its connection to the scrolls and their owners. Some scholars have argued for identifying the site as a rural villa, a travelers' way station, or a pottery production site; some have attempted to completely divorce the site from the caves and the scrolls. For entrée into this sometimes contentious discussion, see Jodi Magness, *The Archaeology of Qumran and the Dead Sea Scrolls*, SDSS (Grand Rapids: Eerdmans, 2002); Katharina Galor, Jean-Baptiste Humbert, and Jürgen Zangenberg, *Qumran—The Site of the Dead Sea Scrolls: Archaeological Interpretations and Debates; Proceedings of a Conference Held at Brown University, November 17–19, 2002*, STDJ 57 (Leiden: Brill, 2006); and Magness's review of Galor et al., "Qumran, the Site of the Dead Sea Scrolls: A Review Article," *RevQ* 22 (2006): 641–64.

72. See Schofield, *From Qumran to the Yaḥad*; and John J. Collins, *Beyond the Qumran Community: The Sectarian Movement of the Dead Sea Scrolls* (Grand Rapids: Eerdmans, 2010).

covenanters, even as they articulated different understandings of themselves as bounded social groups.

Thinking in terms of a network of sectarian groups with complicated relationships to one another—rather than a binary of celibate Essenes at Qumran and marrying Essenes elsewhere—particularly transforms our understanding of the Serek tradition (since scholars already associated the Damascus Document with some sort of "network" of sectarian "camps"). How we locate the textual tradition in its larger social-historical world will in part be determined by how we understand the relationships of texts to communities and how we imagine the readers' expectations with regard to their textual traditions.

8. From Texts to Sects

Both in Qumran studies and in other related fields (especially the study of the New Testament gospels), there exists a confirmation bias that texts are distributed among movements in a one-to-one fashion,[73] with one gospel or sectarian rule per first century religious movement. Thus we might speak of Johannine Christians in contrast with Markan Christians or Damascus covenanters in contrast with *yaḥad* sectarians. Such an approach allows us to speculate in important ways about real social orders. It is possible, as well, to take this approach to the next level, by querying whether each *manuscript* of a particular tradition reflects the existence of a distinct social entity within the larger movement represented by the text tradition. Schofield demonstrates the possibilities for this sort of approach, envisioning a "radial relationship" of *yaḥad* sectarian groups (which she labels "little traditions"), growing outward from their shared "great tradition."[74] Textual development according to this model can be simultaneous and complicated.

---

73. On the methodological problems of such approaches to sectarianism, see Philip R. Davies, "Sects from Texts: On the Problems of Doing a Sociology of the Qumran Literature," in *New Directions in Qumran Studies: Proceedings of the Bristol Colloquium on the Dead Sea Scrolls, 8–10 September 2003*, ed. Jonathan G. Campbell, William John Lyons, and Lloyd K. Pietersen, LSTS 52 (London: T&T Clark, 2005), 69–82.

74. Schofield, *From Qumran to the Yaḥad*, 49–51.

The sectarian quality of our rule texts is an important factor in this discussion. From a sociological perspective,[75] both the *yaḥad* and the Damascus covenant group appear sectarian in their outlook: they view themselves as the only legitimate heirs of the larger Jewish heritage of Scripture and practice, and they separate themselves (psychologically, if not also physically) from sinful outsiders who make false claims upon that shared heritage. Certain hot-button issues are clearly a part of their sectarian frustration: management of the temple and improper ritual practices (as articulated in 4Q394–399 [4QMMT], among other texts),[76] possibly sacred calendar (again connected with MMT and a diversity of calendrical manuscripts),[77] and on-the-ground conflicts whose specifics remain at least partly beyond our interpretive reach.

Notably absent from this list of tensions with outsiders is any reference to the need for textual consistency at the level of words or redaction. Neither in the wording of the sectarian texts, nor indeed with respect to scriptural texts themselves, do we find evidence for sectarian schism based on the precise wording of shared texts. Thus, when the Damascus Document argues for a particular reading of one of the laws of forbidden unions from Lev 18 (in CD V, 7–11), for example, it does so not to choose one wording over another, but rather in order to argue for a particular social practice (here, related to marriage). A parallel phenomenon is reflected in the textual diversity of scriptural scrolls.[78] Among the Dead Sea Scrolls, we find biblical manuscripts that reflect the text type that was later preserved only within Jewish circles (the Masoretic Text), texts later only preserved

---

75. On the sociology of the sectarian scrolls, in addition to the sources cited in n. 10, see Albert I. Baumgarten, *The Flourishing of Jewish Sects in the Maccabean Era: An Interpretation*, JSJSup 55 (Leiden: Brill, 1997); Eyal Regev, *Sectarianism in Qumran: A Cross-Cultural Perspective*, RelSoc 45 (Berlin: de Gruyter, 2007); Jutta Jokiranta, *Social Identity and Sectarianism in the Qumran Movement*, STDJ 105 (Leiden: Brill, 2012); Jokiranta, "Social-Scientific Approaches to the Dead Sea Scrolls," in Grossman, *Rediscovering the Dead Sea Scrolls*, 246–63; and the chapters in "Part III: The Scrolls and Sectarianism," in Lim and Collins, *Oxford Handbook of the Dead Sea Scrolls*, 151–280.

76. For an introduction to the issues, see John Kampen and Moshe J. Bernstein, eds., *Reading 4QMMT: New Perspectives on Qumran Law and History*, SymS 2 (Atlanta: Scholars Press, 1996).

77. A brief and accessible entrée to the evidence for the calendar at Qumran is James C. VanderKam, *Calendars in the Dead Sea Scrolls: Measuring Time*, LDSS (London: Routledge, 1998).

78. See the relevant chapters in this volume.

among Christians (the Septuagint), and texts preserved within the Samaritan Pentateuch or not preserved at all. Although the Masoretic tradition is well represented among the biblical scrolls from Qumran, it is far from the only textual tradition found there. Instead, pluriformity of scriptural texts seems to have been the rule of the day.[79]

Recognition of textual pluriformity can point in the direction of a variety of possibilities with regard to social context. In concluding this discussion, I will consider three such scenarios.

The first possibility reflects the arguments that Eugene Ulrich has brought to bear on the pluriformity of the biblical scrolls. Ulrich argues that ancient Jewish readers, including our ancient sectarians, simply were not committed to particular editions of scriptural texts.[80] The commitment to a particular wording in a particular (potentially quite distinct) edition of Deuteronomy or Jeremiah or Samuel is the product of later communal-canonical thinking and is not a commonplace of late Second Temple period Judaism, he argues.

If the same dynamic held for the Community Rule, it might follow that *yaḥad* sectarians could understand two distinct editions of the rule to be saying the same thing, irrespective of whether the texts incorporated scriptural citations, expanded upon arguments with flowery language, or simply laid down the bare facts in blunter and less decorative fashion. From this perspective, a great many of the textual differences between, for example, the texts of 1QS and 4Q256/258 would not be treated as differences at all, but rather as representatives of the same premises, just differently clothed. Similar support for this argument comes from the wording of our witnesses to the penal code, to the extent that we follow the reconstruction of these fragmentary texts. While they appear to have conveyed many of the same rules, in much the same order, the evidence seems also to suggest that their wording could be highly variable and that specific

---

79. There is a vast literature on this subject. In addition to the chapters in this volume, see, for example, Eugene Ulrich, *The Dead Sea Scrolls and the Origins of the Bible*, SDSS (Grand Rapids: Eerdmans, 1999); Ulrich, "Methodological Reflections on Determining Scriptural Status in First Century Judaism," in Grossman, *Rediscovering the Dead Sea Scrolls*, 145–61; Emanuel Tov, *Textual Criticism of the Hebrew Bible*, 3rd ed. (Minneapolis: Fortress, 2012); Molly M. Zahn, *Rethinking Rewritten Scripture: Composition and Exegesis in the 4QReworked Pentateuch Manuscripts*, STDJ 95 (Leiden: Brill, 2011); and James C. VanderKam, *The Dead Sea Scrolls and the Bible* (Grand Rapids: Eerdmans, 2012).

80. See n. 79.

penalties might vary from manuscript to manuscript (and even within a single manuscript exemplar).

In their treatment of the sectarian rule scrolls, Schofield and Collins emphasize the presence of a network of *yaḥad* groups, and Schofield understands the diversity of the Serek tradition in light of that network of groups. An assumption of this type of social context allows us to envision a second, slightly different, treatment of textuality. The assumption here would be that sectarians would notice, and possibly care about, a higher proportion of the textual differences between manuscripts, but that they would have a social category for understanding those differences that would be relatively forgiving of them. Thus, a sectarian raised in the tradition represented by 1QS might hear a reading of 4Q256 or 4Q258 and think, "yes, well, ours is better, but that's fine, as far as it goes," while a sectarian in the reverse circumstance might think, "yes, fine, but they always were too fancy for their own good."

A third relationship to difference might reflect higher limits on permissiveness (or, in sociological terms, a greater degree of tension across social boundaries). Again, in this case, we might assume that some kinds of divergences in wording would be glossed over as unimportant, but it is possible that other differences—for example, with regard to the language of communal authority—could point to real moments of social tension, if not outright schism among *yaḥad* sectarians. The presence or absence of Zadokite priestly authority remains a key sticking point here. Did the distinct *yaḥad* subgroups, to the extent that we accept their presence, include contemporaneous groups that accepted Zadokite authority and those that did not? Or was this particular distinction reflective of a change over time? Is the presence in 4Q259 of the 4QOtot text, in a space generally given over to the Hymn of the Maskil, evidence for another such point of contention? A tentative parallel to this kind of distinction might be found in the differences within modern-day Jewish liturgy (admittedly a vast field to compare against the limited evidence of the Qumran texts). The classical Reform tradition removed references to resurrection from the Amidah, the central prayer in the standard liturgy; the contemporary Reconstructionist Jewish liturgy incorporates gender-inclusive language at regular points in that liturgical cycle. These are only two examples of differences in wording that would seem minimal to those outside the debate but could seem sharply transgressive among Jewish listeners with conflicting liturgical expectations.[81]

81. By way of introduction, see Ismar Elbogen, *Jewish Liturgy: A Comprehen-*

All of these examples assume the oral experience of the sectarian rules[82] in addition to their written transmission. All also assume a potential for contestation as well as an ability to read different wording as nominally the same. In addition, for all of these readings, a supplementary model is quite useful. We can imagine participants in a *yaḥad* community group bringing together divergent elements of their tradition and incorporating them into a master witness of the tradition like that of 1QS, a Zadokite redaction of the Serek material with an eye to the inclusion of as many relevant texts as possible. Within that supplementary model, a set of core texts (paralleling the material that begins at 1QS V) could appear on its own or in combination with any of a variety of additional texts.

Rofé's methodological suggestions with respect to a historico-literary critical treatment of Scripture provide a model for working with the sectarian rule texts that proves fruitful, both for engagement with their complex manuscript history and also for a speculative understanding of their social location. His understanding of textual growth in light of supplementation, rather than a straight documentary hypothesis, is similarly borne out in what I have identified as a modular quality in the evidence of the Serek tradition. Where I have diverged from his approach is in the possibility of engaging with a completed canonical text of the sort that he finds in the biblical book of Joshua.

It is possible that, under a different set of historical circumstances, a fixed and authoritative Serek text (or a set of fixed texts in a Serek tradition) might have developed. The text contained in 1QS may indeed have come to take on this role for some sectarians at some point in their history. But our evidence for the Rule of the Community indicates that at least in certain sectarian circles and possibly much more generally, such a notion of canonization was far from complete. Our evidence instead highlights the diversity that remains at the root of textual formation in this social and literary context. To the extent that a variety of very diverse

sive History, trans. Raymond P. Scheindlin (Philadelphia: Jewish Publication Society, 1993). For a recent presentation of the Reconstructionist liturgy, see, for example, David A. Teutsch, *Kol Haneshamah: Shabbat Veḥagim*, trans. Joel Rosenberg, Hebrew and English ed. (Wyncote, PA: Reconstructionist Press, 1994). Compare also the gendered liturgical language of, for example, Marcia Falk, *The Book of Blessings: A New Prayer Book for the Weekdays, the Sabbath, and the New Moon Festival* (San Francisco: HarperSanFrancisco, 1996).

82. See Metso, *Serekh Texts*, 63–71.

manuscripts—with different wording, content, and character—can be recognized not only as examples of the same *textual tradition* but in fact as copies of the same *literary text*, it becomes necessary to rethink our larger understanding of original texts and textual formation in an ancient Jewish setting.

Limited Efficacy in Reconstructing the Gospel Sources for Matthew and Luke

Joseph A. Weaks

1. Introduction

The Synoptic Gospels Matthew, Mark, and Luke share a literary dependency. One or two of the gospels was used as a source for another. These gospels, then, present the ideal situation for reconstructing an ancient textual source, a circumstance where the source critic would be most likely to succeed. Two redactors used the same source, all in the same language, each over a short period of time, and all within a close time span of each other (within five to thirty years). The results of reconstructing a source from this doubly attested ancient material should be as reliable as any source critic could hope to obtain.

A near consensus of gospel scholars conclude that Mark was written first among the canonical gospels and that Matthew and Luke are both dependent on Mark as a source.[1] But because the text of Mark is extant, relatively little work has been done discerning how well Mark could be reconstructed as a source for Matthew and Luke, until recently. In this author's previous work, "Mark without Mark,"[2] a complete reconstruction of Mark as used by Matthew and Luke is now available. This reconstructed text of Mark, referred to as MarQ,[3] provides the ideal analogue

1. For an outstanding summary of the current state of Markan priority, see M. Eugene Boring, *An Introduction to the New Testament: History, Literature, Theology* (Louisville: Westminster John Knox, 2012), 472–92.

2. Joseph Allen Weaks, "Mark without Mark: Problematizing the Reliability of a Reconstructed Text of Q" (PhD diss., Brite Divinity School, 2010). Much of the data presented in the current chapter comes from and is further explored in this work.

3. While the gospel non-Markan source Q is a source (*Quelle*) of an unknown

for assessing how well a source can be reconstructed from two texts that used it. In "Mark without Mark," the text of MarQ is derived by reconstructing the source text behind Matthew and Luke for every unit of material that they do share in common with Mark. The text of MarQ can then be compared (and contrasted!) with the text of canonical Mark. This provides an empirical model for assessing the efficacy of conducting source reconstruction among these gospel texts. Once MarQ has been reconstructed, it can be compared and contrasted with actual Mark to assess how well the reconstruction process has preserved the original text. This research has direct implications for evaluating gospel source criticism as a whole, especially in assessing what can be made of the additional source dependencies among the synoptics.

2. Using a Reconstructed Q Text

Matthew and Luke share a significant amount of material not derived from Mark.[4] One was either borrowing from the other, or they share a common source. Among the large majority of scholars that agree on the priority of Mark, a smaller majority of gospel source specialists also assert the independence of Matthew and Luke from each other, concluding that each utilized Mark as a primary source but also included material from an unknown source (referred to as Q) from which they both drew the traditions they share in common but that are not found in Mark. This majority solution to the synoptic data has had profound impact on the way other work has been done in early Christian history.

If it is the case that an additional source, Q, lies behind the text of Matthew and Luke, then this source text might even predate Mark. Such a text would be highly valued in historical inquiries such as Christian origins and the historical Jesus—and indeed it has been.

For more than a century, gospel scholars have been reconstructing a text of Q. After all, "five words in an original source are worth a thousand words in a secondary source."[5] Over the decades, the confidence with which

---

name, MarQ (pronounced "mar-cúe" or simply "reconstructed Mark") is a reconstruction of the Markan source.

4. Approximately 3,700 words, comprising about 20 percent of Matthew and of Luke.

5. Everett Ferguson, *Backgrounds of Early Christianity*, 2nd ed. (Grand Rapids: Eerdmans, 1993), xv.

scholars have studied, redacted, and stratified the reconstructed text of Q has increased.[6] The temptation in scholarship is to treat a reconstructed Q text in the same manner as extant texts that are multiply attested, such as the canonical gospels. Most works on early Christian backgrounds use a reconstructed text of Q as the primary starting point. John Dominic Crossan, for example, in his tome on *The Historical Jesus* treats a reconstructed Q as a source more reliable than any of the canonical gospels.[7] In much historical work on early Christian origins, the text of Q itself becomes further redacted into different strata in order to hypothesize the theology and ethos of the earliest Christian communities. For many, Q and the conclusions that derive from its reconstructed text are a starting place for the development of New Testament (NT) scholarship.[8]

The difficulty with relying so heavily on a reconstructed text of Q is that a reconstructed text is rife with imperfections. It is incomplete in extent and in content. When reconstructing a source from two texts that used it, only that material which is used by both redactors can be discovered with a meaningful degree of certainty. Because of individual redaction, the material that *is* preserved ends up presenting a poor replica of the actual source text that was used. So, how imperfect is it? How poor of a replica? Comparing MarQ with canonical Mark is a great analogue for modeling the results of textual source reconstruction.

3. The Reconstruction of MarQ

The text of MarQ is a reconstruction of the Markan material used by Matthew and Luke, often referred to as the triple tradition passages. It is constructed by considering every pericope or literary section where Matthew and Luke adopted material from Mark and then examining each section synoptically to reconstruct what can be identified from the source they

---

6. See Nicholas Perrin, "The Limits of a Reconstructed Q," in *Questioning Q: A Multidimensional Critique*, ed. Mark S. Goodacre and Nicholas Perrin (Downers Grove, IL: InterVarsity Press, 2004), 71–88 for a tracing of the gradual shift in affirming the text of Q.

7. John Dominic Crossan, *The Historical Jesus: The Life of a Mediterranean Jewish Peasant* (San Francisco: HarperSanFrancisco, 1991).

8. Raymond Edward Brown, *An Introduction to the New Testament*, ABRL (New York: Doubleday, 1997), 7. In Brown's 878-page tome, students are first introduced to Q on 7.

used.[9] The MarQ text is taken in Luke's order, in correspondence to the convention adopted in reconstructions of Q. Further, the text of MarQ as developed in "Mark without Mark" is as generous of a reconstruction as is possible. In other words, every time it was possible (though not necessarily likely) that a word or phrase that is actually from Mark could be retained, the text of MarQ includes that portion. In each section that Matthew and Luke share, there are many variants where only one of them will preserve a particular word or phrase from Mark. The text of MarQ, whenever possible through standard criteria, includes those words. Look, for example, at the reconstruction of MarQ 11:15–17. In the following alignment, the solid underscore highlights variants singly attested in Matthew that are included in the reconstruction, the broken underscore likewise from Luke. Each of those variants was chosen because they make the reconstruction best match the text of Mark. The ~~crossed out~~ text is the words unique to Matthew or Luke that were not brought into the reconstruction. The chapter and verse references in MarQ correspond to its parallel material in Mark's chapter and verse.

Table 1: Reconstructing MarQ from Matthew and Luke: "Cleansing of the Temple"

Matt 21:12–13	MarQ 11:15–17	Luke 19:45–46
12 Καὶ εἰσῆλθεν ~~Ἰησοῦς~~ εἰς τὸ ἱερὸν καὶ ἐξέβαλεν ~~πάντας~~ τοὺς πωλοῦντας καὶ ἀγοράζοντας ἐν τῷ ἱερῷ, καὶ τὰς τραπέζας τῶν κολλυβιστῶν κατέστρεψεν καὶ τὰς καθέδρας τῶν πωλούντων τὰς περιστεράς,	15 Καὶ εἰσελθὼν εἰς τὸ ἱερὸν ἤρξατο ἐκβάλλειν τοὺς πωλοῦντας καὶ ἀγοράζοντας ἐν τῷ ἱερῷ, καὶ τὰς τραπέζας τῶν κολλυβιστῶν κατέστρεψεν καὶ τὰς καθέδρας τῶν πωλούντων τὰς περιστεράς,	45 Καὶ εἰσελθὼν εἰς τὸ ἱερὸν ἤρξατο ἐκβάλλειν τοὺς πωλοῦντας

9. The section divisions derive from Kurt Aland, ed., *Synopsis Quattuor Evangeliorum: Locis parallelis evangeliorum apocryphorum et patrum adhibitis edidit*, 13th ed. (Stuttgart: Deutsche Bibelgesellschaft, 1985). The text used was that of NA^{27} (Eberhard Nestle and Kurt Aland, eds., *Novum Testamentum Graece*, 27th ed. [Stuttgart: Deutsche Bibelgesellschaft, 1993]).

13 καὶ λέγει αὐτοῖς· γέγραπται· ὁ οἶκός μου οἶκος προσευχῆς κληθήσεται, ὑμεῖς δὲ αὐτὸν ποιεῖτε σπήλαιον λῃστῶν.	17 καὶ λέγει αὐτοῖς· [] γέγραπται· [] ὁ οἶκός μου οἶκος προσευχῆς κληθήσεται, [] ὑμεῖς δὲ αὐτὸν ἐποιήσατε σπήλαιον λῃστῶν.	46 λέγων αὐτοῖς· γέγραπται· ~~καὶ ἔσται~~ ὁ οἶκός μου οἶκος προσευχῆς, ὑμεῖς δὲ αὐτὸν ἐποιήσατε σπήλαιον λῃστῶν.
12 And ~~Jesus~~ entered the temple and drove out ~~all~~ who were selling and those who were buying in the temple, and he overturned the tables of the money changers and the seats of those who sold doves.	15 And he entered the temple and began to drive out those who were selling and those who were buying in the temple, and the tables of the money changers he overturned and the seats of those who sold doves;	45 And he entered the temple and began to drive out those who were selling things there;
13 And he said to them, "It is written, 'My house shall be called a house of prayer'; but you are making it a den of robbers."	17 And he says to them, "It is written, 'My house shall be called a house of prayer'; but you have made it a den of robbers."	46 then he said, "It is written, 'My house shall be~~come~~ a house of prayer'; but you have made it a den of robbers."

Every variant that preserves Markan material within a triple-tradition section is included in the new reconstruction if it is possible that a standard reconstruction might have come to the same conclusion. This method preserves Mark at all points possible. By using a reconstruction of Mark that is "as good as is possible," any differentiations revealed between Mark and MarQ when compared become all the more reliable and profound.

4. An Overview of MarQ

4.1. The Extent

MarQ contains 418 verses made up of 5,754 words. This places its text at about half the size of canonical Mark.

Table 2: Size of MarQ and Mark

	Pericopes	Verses	Words	Characters
Mark	114	661	11,105	55,464
MarQ	83	418	5,754	28,555
	73%	63%	52%	51%

The table accentuates the difference between comparing the size of the two texts by artificial structural categories and actual content. MarQ contains at least a small portion of 73 percent of the literary units in Mark,[10] as well as 63 percent of the verses. However, a more accurate indication of the size of the text is word counts, since verses used by Matthew or Luke are typically only partially preserved. The reconstructed text of MarQ is only 52 percent of Mark. This result alone problematizes the reliability of MarQ as an indicator of the text of the actual source used by Matthew and Luke. If barely more than half of the text survives the reconstruction process, it is difficult to approach that text as if it is an accurate representative of the actual Mark text. A breakdown of the text into the amount that is doubly attested shows even further problems with the result.

Table 3: Attestation of MarQ

	Words	Percent of Mark	Percent of MarQ
All of Mark	11,105	100%	193%
All of MarQ	5,754	52%	100%
Partially doubly attested in MarQ	2,743	25%	48%
Completely doubly attested in MarQ	1,953	18%	34%
Non-Markan words in MarQ	383	3%	7%

10. Units or sections or pericope as defined in Aland, *Synopsis Quattuor Evangeliorum*.

While little more than half (52 percent) of the words of Mark are preserved in MarQ, less than half of those words (48 percent) are doubly attested in Matthew and Luke. A strict, conservative reconstruction of Mark would preserve only a little more than a fifth (21 percent) of the Mark text. When the text of Q is reconstructed from Matthew and Luke, scholars might be tempted to conclude that half of the reconstructed Q text being doubly attested is evidence of its reliability.[11] About half of the MarQ reconstruction is also doubly attested, but in comparing this to the text of actual Mark, one can see that a reconstructed text, even when half of its words are doubly attested, represents the preservation of only just over one-fifth of the original text.

4.2. The Content

The diagram on pages 338–39 provides an overview of the literary units that remain in MarQ. The synoptic diagram provides a complete list of pericopes in Mark. Each pericope that is not found in MarQ is marked by a strike-through in the pericope description. Regarding order, each pericope from MarQ is placed in Luke's order, parallel with the Markan section it corresponds to, when possible. For sections that occur out of Markan order, a box surrounds the text reference, and a line is drawn connecting the section between Mark and MarQ. A dashed line or box indicates that only a portion of the full verse reference is found in the corresponding match.

The synoptic diagram demonstrates that Luke maintained Mark's order on the whole. Thirteen sections (about 15 percent) of MarQ *are* located outside of Mark's order. However, even this small number of changes begins to alter the presentation of the text. John the Baptist's backstory (MarQ 6:17–18), though highly abbreviated, comes earlier in MarQ. Jesus is rejected at Nazareth early in the story (MarQ 6:1–6a). The anointing in Bethany is extremely early (MarQ 14:3–9), immediately after the twelve are chosen. Jesus's first utterance is no longer "Follow me," setting the tone for discipleship in the whole gospel, but rather "Prophets are not without

11. "It is worth noting that the average verbatim agreement of approximately 50 percent is significantly higher than what random probability would predict" (John S. Kloppenborg, *Excavating Q: The History and Setting of the Sayings Gospel* [Minneapolis: Fortress, 2000], 63).

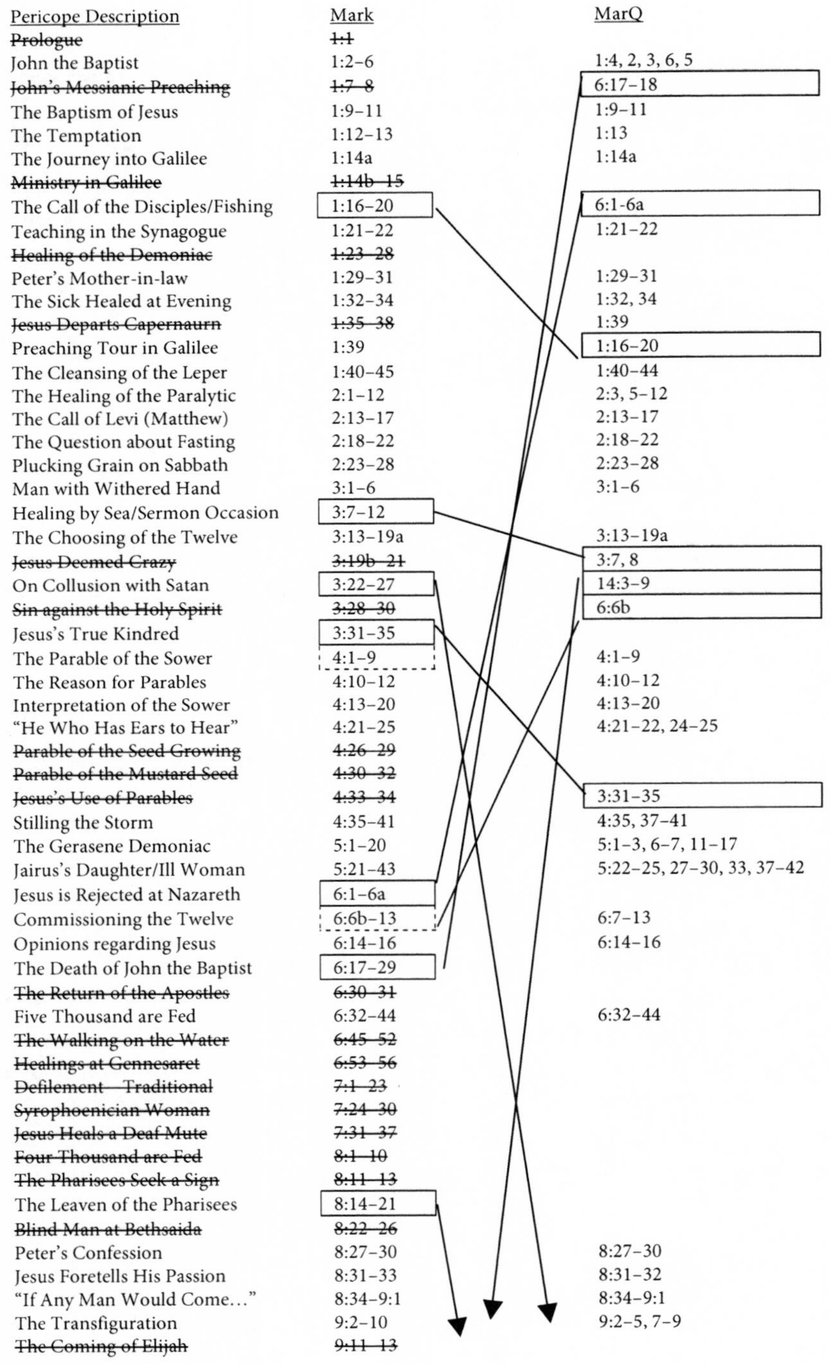

Pericope Description	Mark	MarQ
~~Prologue~~	~~1:1~~	
John the Baptist	1:2–6	1:4, 2, 3, 6, 5
~~John's Messianic Preaching~~	~~1:7–8~~	6:17–18
The Baptism of Jesus	1:9–11	1:9–11
The Temptation	1:12–13	1:13
The Journey into Galilee	1:14a	1:14a
~~Ministry in Galilee~~	~~1:14b–15~~	
The Call of the Disciples/Fishing	1:16–20	6:1–6a
Teaching in the Synagogue	1:21–22	1:21–22
~~Healing of the Demoniac~~	~~1:23–28~~	
Peter's Mother-in-law	1:29–31	1:29–31
The Sick Healed at Evening	1:32–34	1:32, 34
~~Jesus Departs Capernaurn~~	~~1:35–38~~	1:39
Preaching Tour in Galilee	1:39	1:16–20
The Cleansing of the Leper	1:40–45	1:40–44
The Healing of the Paralytic	2:1–12	2:3, 5–12
The Call of Levi (Matthew)	2:13–17	2:13–17
The Question about Fasting	2:18–22	2:18–22
Plucking Grain on Sabbath	2:23–28	2:23–28
Man with Withered Hand	3:1–6	3:1–6
Healing by Sea/Sermon Occasion	3:7–12	
The Choosing of the Twelve	3:13–19a	3:13–19a
~~Jesus Deemed Crazy~~	~~3:19b–21~~	3:7, 8
On Collusion with Satan	3:22–27	14:3–9
~~Sin against the Holy Spirit~~	~~3:28–30~~	6:6b
Jesus's True Kindred	3:31–35	
The Parable of the Sower	4:1–9	4:1–9
The Reason for Parables	4:10–12	4:10–12
Interpretation of the Sower	4:13–20	4:13–20
"He Who Has Ears to Hear"	4:21–25	4:21–22, 24–25
~~Parable of the Seed Growing~~	~~4:26–29~~	
~~Parable of the Mustard Seed~~	~~4:30–32~~	
~~Jesus's Use of Parables~~	~~4:33–34~~	3:31–35
Stilling the Storm	4:35–41	4:35, 37–41
The Gerasene Demoniac	5:1–20	5:1–3, 6–7, 11–17
Jairus's Daughter/Ill Woman	5:21–43	5:22–25, 27–30, 33, 37–42
Jesus is Rejected at Nazareth	6:1–6a	
Commissioning the Twelve	6:6b–13	6:7–13
Opinions regarding Jesus	6:14–16	6:14–16
The Death of John the Baptist	6:17–29	
~~The Return of the Apostles~~	~~6:30–31~~	
Five Thousand are Fed	6:32–44	6:32–44
~~The Walking on the Water~~	~~6:45–52~~	
~~Healings at Gennesaret~~	~~6:53–56~~	
~~Defilement—Traditional~~	~~7:1–23~~	
~~Syrophoenician Woman~~	~~7:24–30~~	
~~Jesus Heals a Deaf Mute~~	~~7:31–37~~	
~~Four Thousand are Fed~~	~~8:1–10~~	
~~The Pharisees Seek a Sign~~	~~8:11–13~~	
The Leaven of the Pharisees	8:14–21	
~~Blind Man at Bethsaida~~	~~8:22–26~~	
Peter's Confession	8:27–30	8:27–30
Jesus Foretells His Passion	8:31–33	8:31–32
"If Any Man Would Come…"	8:34–9:1	8:34–9:1
The Transfiguration	9:2–10	9:2–5, 7–9
~~The Coming of Elijah~~	~~9:11–13~~	

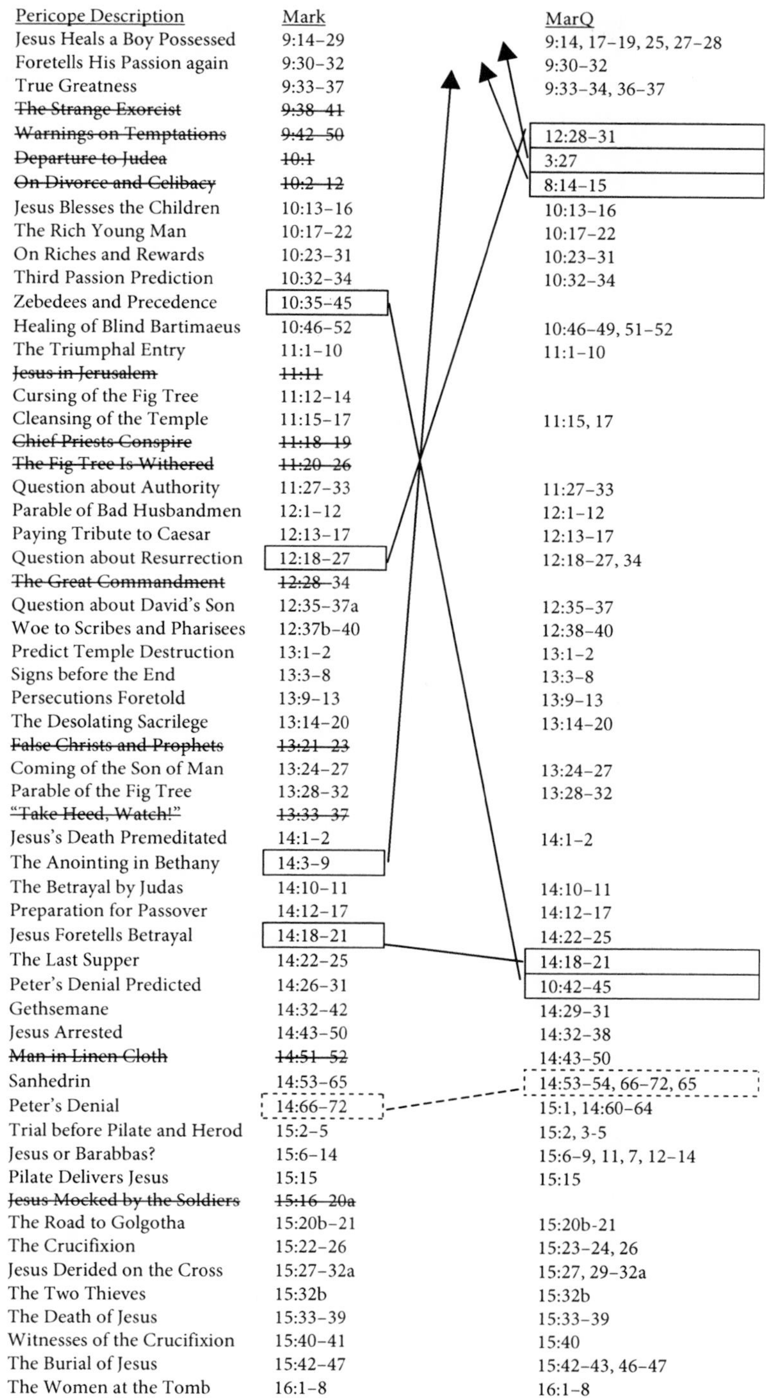

Pericope Description	Mark	MarQ
Jesus Heals a Boy Possessed	9:14–29	9:14, 17–19, 25, 27–28
Foretells His Passion again	9:30–32	9:30–32
True Greatness	9:33–37	9:33–34, 36–37
~~The Strange Exorcist~~	~~9:38–41~~	
~~Warnings on Temptations~~	~~9:42–50~~	12:28–31
~~Departure to Judea~~	~~10:1~~	3:27
~~On Divorce and Celibacy~~	~~10:2–12~~	8:14–15
Jesus Blesses the Children	10:13–16	10:13–16
The Rich Young Man	10:17–22	10:17–22
On Riches and Rewards	10:23–31	10:23–31
Third Passion Prediction	10:32–34	10:32–34
Zebedees and Precedence	10:35–45	
Healing of Blind Bartimaeus	10:46–52	10:46–49, 51–52
The Triumphal Entry	11:1–10	11:1–10
~~Jesus in Jerusalem~~	~~11:11~~	
Cursing of the Fig Tree	11:12–14	
Cleansing of the Temple	11:15–17	11:15, 17
~~Chief Priests Conspire~~	~~11:18–19~~	
~~The Fig Tree Is Withered~~	~~11:20–26~~	
Question about Authority	11:27–33	11:27–33
Parable of Bad Husbandmen	12:1–12	12:1–12
Paying Tribute to Caesar	12:13–17	12:13–17
Question about Resurrection	12:18–27	12:18–27, 34
~~The Great Commandment~~	~~12:28–~~34	
Question about David's Son	12:35–37a	12:35–37
Woe to Scribes and Pharisees	12:37b–40	12:38–40
Predict Temple Destruction	13:1–2	13:1–2
Signs before the End	13:3–8	13:3–8
Persecutions Foretold	13:9–13	13:9–13
The Desolating Sacrilege	13:14–20	13:14–20
~~False Christs and Prophets~~	~~13:21–23~~	
Coming of the Son of Man	13:24–27	13:24–27
Parable of the Fig Tree	13:28–32	13:28–32
~~"Take Heed, Watch!"~~	~~13:33–37~~	
Jesus's Death Premeditated	14:1–2	14:1–2
The Anointing in Bethany	14:3–9	
The Betrayal by Judas	14:10–11	14:10–11
Preparation for Passover	14:12–17	14:12–17
Jesus Foretells Betrayal	14:18–21	14:22–25
The Last Supper	14:22–25	14:18–21
Peter's Denial Predicted	14:26–31	10:42–45
Gethsemane	14:32–42	14:29–31
Jesus Arrested	14:43–50	14:32–38
~~Man in Linen Cloth~~	~~14:51–52~~	14:43–50
Sanhedrin	14:53–65	14:53–54, 66–72, 65
Peter's Denial	14:66–72	15:1, 14:60–64
Trial before Pilate and Herod	15:2–5	15:2, 3–5
Jesus or Barabbas?	15:6–14	15:6–9, 11, 7, 12–14
Pilate Delivers Jesus	15:15	15:15
~~Jesus Mocked by the Soldiers~~	~~15:16–20a~~	
The Road to Golgotha	15:20b–21	15:20b–21
The Crucifixion	15:22–26	15:23–24, 26
Jesus Derided on the Cross	15:27–32a	15:27, 29–32a
The Two Thieves	15:32b	15:32b
The Death of Jesus	15:33–39	15:33–39
Witnesses of the Crucifixion	15:40–41	15:40
The Burial of Jesus	15:42–47	15:42–43, 46–47
The Women at the Tomb	16:1–8	16:1–8

honor, except in their hometown." In addition to these alterations in order, a larger amount of material is missing altogether.

Recognizing that section divisions are an imprecise metric in their own right, thirty-two of the scriptural traditions are missing from MarQ. Further, many of those included pericopes contain only a few verses and words. These components of Mark, lost in its reconstruction, include the gospel's own beginning and ending. Mark 1:1 and the opening title for the gospel ("The beginning of the good news about Jesus Christ, God's Son"; CEB) are regarded as foundational for establishing Mark's genre,[12] as well as for summarizing the purpose and theology of the text to come.[13] This titular definition that so profoundly opens the Gospel of Mark is not a part of MarQ.

As for the ending, while MarQ does end with a verse 16:8, it is not the same verse found in Mark. Matthew and Luke share a common structure and only five key functional words in their parallels to 16:8:

> Καὶ <u>ἀπελθοῦσαι</u> ταχὺ <u>ἀπὸ τοῦ μνημείου</u> μετὰ φόβου καὶ χαρᾶς μεγάλης ἔδραμον <u>ἀπαγγεῖλαι τοῖς μαθηταῖς</u> αὐτοῦ.
> So <u>they left the tomb</u> quickly, with fear and great joy, and ran <u>to tell</u> his <u>disciples</u>.

In both Matthew and Luke, the women (1) "depart" or "return" (2) "from" (3) "the tomb" and then (4) "bring the news" (5) to "his disciples" or "the eleven" and the rest. Any reconstruction of Mark from Matthew and Luke will have the women leaving the tomb and telling the disciples, eradicating the peculiar ending of Mark. The ending of Mark punctuating the messianic secret that is so much a part of Markan theology is lost.

In addition to missing the original beginning and ending of Mark, MarQ is also missing many key narrative components that help define Mark as what it is. In MarQ, there is no opening title for the gospel of the son of God (Mark 1:1), no saying about one coming who is more powerful than I (1:7), no first exorcism (1:23–24), no roof entrance for the paralyzed

12. M. Eugene Boring, *Mark: A Commentary*, NTL (Louisville: Westminster John Knox, 2006), 6–9.

13. "It would seem, then, that the introductory sentence summarizes the content of the work as an account of how the early Christian proclamation about Jesus originated" (Adela Yarbro Collins, *Mark: A Commentary*, Hermeneia [Minneapolis: Fortress, 2007], 130; see also 130–32).

man (2:4), no temple bread for the disciples (2:26), no Sabbath made for humankind (2:27), no family thinking Jesus out of his mind (3:21), no Beelzebul saying (3:22), no Satan references (1:13; 3:23, 26; 4:15; 8:33), no getting the same measure that one gives (4:24), no secretly growing seed (4:26), no mustard seed (4:31), no backstory on the man possessed (5:3–5), no name for his demon Legion (5:9), no name for Jairus (5:22), no medical history for the hemorrhaging woman (5:26), no staff or sandals for the disciples sent out (6:8–9), no dancing daughter of Herodias (6:17–18), no walking on water (6:48), no dirty hands for the disciples (7:2), no teaching on what defiles (7:14–23), no debating a Syro-Phoenician woman (7:26), no Jesus spitting with his fingers in his ears (7:33), no second multitude feeding (8:1–2), no pleading for a sign (8:11), no blind man at Bethsaida (8:22), no deafness for the persistent possession (9:17), no one for us who was not against us (9:40), no special privilege for children or millstone punishments (9:42), no preemptively cutting off hand (9:43) or foot (9:45) or eye (9:47), no teaching on divorce (10:2–12), no extra commandment about defrauding (10:19), no asking to sit at Jesus's right hand (10:37), no name for Bartimaeus (10:46), no accursed fig tree (11:13–14), no preventing the carrying of things through the temple (11:16), no Shema (12:29), no widow's mite (12:42–43), no keeping watch in the night (13:34), no hymn-singing after the Last Supper (14:26), no desertion prediction in the passion (14:27), no second cock crow (14:30, 72), no Father ἀββά in Jesus's prayer (14:36), no second or third nap on the Mount of Olives (14:39–42), no certain young man in a linen cloth (14:51–52), no fire for Peter in the courtyard (14:54), no false testimonies against Jesus (14:56–57), no crown of thorns (15:17), no nine o'clock crucifixion time check (15:25), no death verification by Pilate's centurion (15:44), no Salome among the women (15:40; 16:1), and no saying nothing to anyone out of fear (16:8). With so much iconic Markan material missing from the MarQ text, can it be said to indicate the actual Mark source in any meaningful way?

4.3. The Preservation of Speech

Given that the doubly attested material in the reconstruction of Mark from Matthew and Luke is the most reliable, an observation regarding these doubly attested sections reveals the type of text that best survives the reconstruction process. The three longest passages of exact agreement between Matthew and Luke in the creation of MarQ are strings of nineteen, seventeen, and fifteen words.

MarQ 1:40–42 (18 words):
λέγων· κύριε, ἐὰν θέλῃς δύνασαί με καθαρίσαι. καὶ ἐκτείνας τὴν χεῖρα ἥψατο αὐτοῦ λέγων· θέλω, καθαρίσθητι· καὶ εὐθέως
saying, "Lord, if you choose, you can make me clean." He stretched out his hand and touched him, saying, "I do choose. Be made clean!" Immediately

MarQ 8:35 (16 words):
θέλῃ τὴν ψυχὴν αὐτοῦ σῶσαι ἀπολέσει αὐτήν· ὃς δ' ἂν ἀπολέσῃ τὴν ψυχὴν αὐτοῦ ἕνεκεν ἐμοῦ
want to save their life will lose it, and those who lose their life for my sake

MarQ 12:36 (15 words):
εἶπεν κύριος τῷ κυρίῳ μου· κάθου ἐκ δεξιῶν μου, ἕως ἂν θῶ τοὺς ἐχθρούς σου
The Lord said to my Lord, "Sit at my right hand, until I put your enemies"

The most obvious observation is that these passages are all speech. This trend continues with clauses of shorter verbatim agreement. It is speech content where Matthew and Luke share the largest amount of verbatim agreement in their Markan material. Analyzing the types of material that MarQ does in fact preserve of Mark renders similar results.

There are five places where MarQ and Mark match verbatim for more than twenty words in a row. Each of these places are speech text: twenty-nine words in MarQ 10:14–15 ("…it is to such as these that the kingdom of God belongs…"), twenty-seven words in MarQ 10:18–19 ("…you know the commandments…"), twenty-six words in MarQ 12:14 ("…is it lawful to pay taxes…"), twenty-three words in 8:34–35 ("…those who want to save their life will lose it…"), and twenty-three words in MarQ 13:29–30 ("…this generation will not pass away…"). Not only are these strings also speech text; each of these portions of speech is aphoristic, memorable speech text—especially quotable material as encountered by Matthew and Luke.

A third way to ask a similar question is to examine every verse from MarQ that has at least a ten-word string of verbatim, parallel agreements with Mark. This is where MarQ and Mark share at least ten words in a row without interruption, omission, or addition. In total, there are eighty-one verses containing a ten-word or longer string of matching text between

Mark and MarQ. Those verses are MarQ 1:3–4, 11, 16, 19, 22, 44; 2:10, 14–15, 17, 19–20, 22; 3:18; 4:8, 25; 5:7, 13–14; 6:4, 41; 8:31, 34–35, 38–9:2; 9:5, 19, 37; 10:14–15, 18–19, 21, 23, 25, 29, 33, 45; 11:1, 15, 28, 30–31, 33; 12:9–11, 14, 16, 19, 23, 26, 30, 36, 39–40; 13:4, 8, 12–14, 17, 24, 28–31; 14:18, 21–22, 25, 34, 38, 48–49; 15:2, 29, 33.

Similar to the previous investigations of matching strings, the bulk of the content in these sections is speech, either memorable sayings or portions of a longer speech. The third, fourth, and fifth most common words in those texts are *αὐτός* ("he/they"), ἐγώ ("I"), and λέγω ("say"), as in "he says" or "I say." Only thirteen of these eighty-one verses do not center around a saying; only 556 of the 1,959 words (28 percent) are not contained within speech. The combination of these results demonstrates a clear pattern: that speech material can be reconstructed from texts that used it much more reliably than other narrative material.

The Q source reconstructed from Matthew and Luke is often referred to as a sayings source.[14] The majority of its reconstructed content is sayings material.[15] The assumption has long been that the actual hypothetical Q text was a sayings source. However, these observations imply that the reconstructed text is not predominantly sayings material because the actual text was, but that a reconstructed text will result in a higher proportion of sayings material than was present in the original text. The sayings material in a reconstructed text is less a generic indicator than it is a byproduct of the reconstruction process. The MarQ text was an implausibly generous reconstruction: variants were included at all points that matched material from canonical Mark. A more realistic reconstruction process would not incorporate much of this singly attested connecting narrative material, with the result that the higher portion of remaining doubly attested material would produce a text that begins to look more and more predominantly like a sayings source as well. The original Q source could also be a narrative document to a degree undetected in its reconstructions. The implication is not necessarily that Q had narrative material that was lost since neither Matthew nor Luke reproduced it. Rather, the implication is that the narrative material could be to some extent present in Matthew and Luke, even though scholars lack the criteria for detecting it.

14. James M. Robinson, *The Sayings Gospel Q: Collected Essays*, BETL 189 (Leuven: Peeters, 2005).

15. Charles E. Carlston and Dennis Norlin, "Statistics and Q: Some Further Observations," *NovT* 41 (1999): 113.

4.4. The Stylometry of MarQ

4.4.1. Introduction

Another contribution in "Mark without Mark" is a stylometric survey of the newly reconstructed MarQ text, along with Mark, Matthew, Luke, and additional texts. Grammatical, syntactical, and lexical searches across different corpora allow the comparative analysis of relevant frequencies across similar, and different, texts. How does the frequency of a particular stylistic verb form or vocabulary choice compare between Mark and MarQ and other texts? The differences in frequencies between the newly constructed MarQ and the other gospels has some predictability.

4.4.2. The Disappearance of Distinctive Features

Among words and structures with a relatively low frequency in Mark compared to Matthew or Luke, one would expect the frequency in MarQ to rise above that found in Mark, since echoes of Matthew and Luke have been retained in the reconstruction process. Most often, this is the case. Take, for example, the occurrence of aorist passive participles. Aorist passive participles occur in Mark with a frequency of 2.65 per mil[16] while in Matthew and Luke they are found at a rate of 5.99 per mil and 4.41 per mil, respectively. In MarQ, aorist passive participles have a frequency of 4.00 per mil. Likewise, terms and structures that have a high frequency in Mark and a relatively low frequency in Matthew and Luke have frequencies in MarQ much lower than in Mark. The overall effect of this observable phenomenon is that once a text has been derived by reconstructing it from texts that used it, the result is a text that has had its unique characteristics stripped away to a large and measurable extent. Distinct vocabulary is watered down. Unique expressions and formulations have been lost. Avoidance of certain narrative features that other texts used has disappeared. In the end, it becomes somewhat impossible to reclaim the uniqueness of a text that has been reconstructed. This can be seen clearly in the occurrence of tenses in the gospel texts.

16. "Per mil" means how often an occurrence is found per one thousand words; the ‰ is the per mil symbol used in displaying frequency in text.

Table 4: Tenses in the Gospels and MarQ

Verb Tense	Mark ‰	MarQ ‰	Matthew ‰	Luke ‰
Present	86.27	77.34	77.27	76.89
Future	10.96	15.29	19.33	16.05
Imperfect	25.90	14.25	7.73	18.62
Aorist	101.03	120.09	106.95	107.20

The "watered down" effect can be visualized in table 4 by noting that the frequency of a feature in MarQ usually falls between that of Mark and that of the average of Matthew and Luke. One key interpretive feature of the Gospel of Mark that scholars regularly cite as a distinctive stylistic feature of Mark that sets it apart from the other gospels is its use of linear, continuous, durable, progressive verb aspect.[17] Often this is Mark's regular use of the historical present. The numbers in the above frequency chart demonstrate this feature of Mark. Mark's use of the Greek present (86.3 per mil) and imperfect (25.9 per mil) verb tenses is much higher than it is in Matthew and Luke. Present tense verbs occur nine times more often per thousand words in Mark than in either Matthew or Luke. But in the reconstructed MarQ, that distinctness is lost. The occurrence in MarQ falls right in line with the usage in Matthew and Luke, at around 77 per mil.

E. J. Pryke's volume on redactional features of Mark lists over a dozen distinctive syntactical features of Mark:

- Parenthetical clauses
- Genitive absolute
- Participle as a main verb
- πολλά ("many") in the accusative
- λέγω ὅτι ("I say that")
- ἄρχομαι ("begin") with an infinitive
- εὐθύς ("immediately")
- πάλιν ("back")

17. For a summary of Mark's key features, see Frank J. Matera, *What Are They Saying About Mark?* (New York: Paulist, 1987) and James Keith Elliott, *The Language and Style of the Gospel of Mark: An Edition of C. H. Turner's "Notes on Marcan Usage" Together with Other Comparable Studies*, NovTSup 71 (Leiden: Brill, 1993).

- Redundant participles
- Periphrastic tenses
- Impersonals
- ὥστε ("so that") with an infinitive
- Two or more participles before or after the main verb
- γάρ ("for") explanatory formula[18]

Nearly all of these distinctive features essentially disappear in MarQ. The frequency of the genitive absolute structure in MarQ drops to below that found in any of the gospels. The key terms such as πάλιν, πολλά, and εὐθύς drop to unremarkable levels. The immediacy motif in Mark, where Jesus "immediately" (εὐθύς) comes up from the water and "immediately" is driven into the wilderness before the disciples "immediately" drop their nets, is gone. From a frequency of 3.62 per mil in Mark to one of 0.70 per mil in MarQ, the reduction ensures that this characteristic would no longer be so prevalent in internal analysis of the reconstructed text of Mark. The same is the case for the key Markan words of "seeing" (ἰδέ and forms of βλέπω) and "teaching" (forms of διδάσκω). Their frequency in MarQ is again inconspicuous. A reconstructed source text, as a consequence of the reconstruction process, no longer bears these integral signs of the text. Some words in Mark disappear altogether.

Two dozen words from Mark never occur in MarQ. These words (and their number of occurrences in Mark) are ἴδε ("look!"; 9), καλῶς ("well"; 6), σατανᾶς ("Satan"; 6), Βεελζεβούλ ("Beelzebulb"; 1), συζητέω ("argue"; 6), εἶτα ("next"; 4), ἐκθαμβέω ("be alarmed"; 4), θαμβέω ("be amazed"; 3), ἐκθαυμάζω ("be amazed"; 1), ἄλαλος ("speechless"; 3), Ναζαρηνός ("Nazarene"; 4), Ναζαρά ("Nazareth"; 1), γέεννα ("Hell"; 3), κτίσις ("creation"; 3), φανερόω ("reveal"; 3), Τύρος ("Tyre"; 3), Σιδών ("Sidon"; 2), Βηθσαϊδά ("Bethsaida"; 2), Δεκάπολις ("Decapolis"; 2), θεάομαι ("see"; 2), διαβλέπω ("see clearly"; 1), ὄμμα ("eye"; 1), μονόφθαλμος ("one-eyed"; 1), and διδασκαλία ("teaching"; 1). Some of these words are by no means rare, and yet they never occur in MarQ. Clearly, when working with a reconstructed text, arguments from omission and negative evidence are a nonstarter.

These lexical and syntactical features missing from the reconstructed text point to the absence of larger thematic components as well. Because

18. E. J. Pryke, *Redactional Style in the Marcan Gospel: A Study of Syntax and Vocabulary as Guides to Redaction in Mark*, SNTSMS 33 (Cambridge: Cambridge University Press, 1978).

these significant terms and phrases lost their distinction in the reconstruction, the themes developed based on them also disappear. Many of the themes and motifs considered dominant in Mark end up being undetectable in MarQ.

The motif of "wonder" so distinctive in Mark[19] becomes unexceptional in MarQ, since only a third of the pertinent texts survives in the reconstruction, with every related key word frequency reducing in MarQ. In MarQ 6:6, Jesus is no longer amazed (θαυμάζω) at the crowd's unbelief. In MarQ 10:22, the rich young ruler is not shocked (στυγνάζω) at hearing what he must do. In Mark 14:33, Peter, James, and John become alarmed (ἐκθαμβέω), but in MarQ they become grieved (λυπέω).

The secrecy motif of Mark loses its prominence in MarQ. It appears in Mark primarily through commands of silence and the lack of understanding Jesus.[20] Of the nine commands from Jesus to keep silent (Mark 1:25, 34, 43–45; 3:12; 5:43; 7:36; 8:26, 30; 9:9), four remain. Of the passages that display misunderstandings on the part of the disciples (4:13, 40–41; 6:50–52; 7:18; 8:16–21; 9:5–6, 19; 10:24; 14:37–41), three remain. One of those missing is the fullest articulation of the disciples' misunderstandings, that found in Mark 8:16–21 where the disciples misconstrue the feeding of the multitudes.

The intercalation in Mark is all but lost in MarQ. This prevalent, unique literary device ascribed to the Gospel of Mark is the sandwiching of one story inside another, presumably for the powerful effect such intratextuality has on producing meaning in the text. Of the eight primary examples of Mark's intercalation (Mark 3:21, 22–30, 31–35; 4:1–9, 10–12, 13–20; 5:21–24, 25–34, 35–43; 6:7–13, 14–29, 30; 11:12–14, 15–19, 20–25; 14:1–2, 3–9, 10–11; 14:17–21, 22–26, 27–31; 15:40–41, 42–46; 15:47–16:8),[21] only three are left in nested form in MarQ. A large contingent of the thematic features characteristic of Mark are lost in the reconstruction from the texts that used it.

19. Timothy Dwyer, *The Motif of Wonder in the Gospel of Mark*, JSNTSup 128 (Sheffield: Sheffield Academic, 1996), 196.

20. Christopher M. Tuckett, *The Messianic Secret*, IRT 1 (Philadelphia: Fortress, 1983).

21. William R. Telford, *The Theology of the Gospel of Mark*, NTT (Cambridge: Cambridge University Press, 1999).

4.4.3. The Introduction of Anomalous Features

As was confirmed above, many of the frequencies in a stylometric analysis across dependent texts follow a logical pattern. For example, a distinctive feature of Matthew is the phrase βασιλεία τῶν οὐρανῶν ("kingdom of heaven"), which occurs nowhere else in the New Testament. This phrase has a slightly higher rate of occurrence in Matthean *Sondergut* ("unique") material (2.72 per mil) than in the material it took from Mark (1.13 per mil) or the material it shares with Luke (2.13 per mil). Logically, Matthew uses this phrase more often when relying on its own sources. But this type of pattern does not always hold true. For example, the word ἰδού ("Look!") occurs in Matthew more often than in Mark or Luke, but it occurs less in Mathew's unique material (1.94 per mil) than in either its Markan material (3.86 per mil) or the material it shares with Luke (2.93 per mil).

The reduction of Markan features in MarQ often follows a logical pattern, but some new features of a reconstructed text also appear with random, even illogical occurrence. The first-person singular personal pronoun ἐγώ occurs more often in MarQ (12.69 per mil) than it does in Mark (9.46 per mil), Matthew (12.04 per mil), or Luke (11.23 per mil). Even more unpredictably, the frequency of accusative nouns in MarQ (71.08 per mil) is 11 percent higher than in Mark (64.17 per mil) despite the fact that the two texts MarQ is reconstructed from each has a lower frequency of accusative nouns—Matthew (62.14 per mil) or Luke (60.11 per mil)! In a survey of over 580 structural and lexical searches in "Mark without Mark," the text of MarQ has a lower frequency than Mark, Matthew, or Luke, seventy-one times, and a higher frequency than any of the three, eighty-six times (15 percent!).

For example, as a result of these seemingly random anomalies, MarQ seems more preoccupied with authority figures than any of the synoptic gospels.

Table 5: Words for Authority Figures

Term	Mark ‰	MarQ ‰	Matthew ‰	Luke ‰
ἄρχων ("ruler")	0.09	0.53	0.27	0.41
ἑκατοντάρχης ("centurion")	0.00	0.18	0.22	0.15
τετραάρχης ("ruler")	0.00	0.18	0.05	0.10

ἡγεμών ("governor")	0.09	0.53	0.54	0.10
ἀρχιερεύς ("chief priest")	1.94	2.82	1.36	0.77
Καῖσαρ ("Caesar")	0.35	0.35	0.22	0.36

In every case, the frequency in MarQ is higher than in Mark and most often higher than in Matthew and Luke as well.

However, the most damning example of artificially introduced features was on display in table 4 showing frequency of tenses. That table shows the data behind Mark's propensity to use the present tense verbs nine times more than Matthew or Luke for each one thousand words. However, the table also shows that MarQ uses the aorist tense more than any of Mark, Matthew, or Luke. It does so to a greater differential than Mark uses the present tense. MarQ uses the aorist tense over twelve times more per thousand words than Matthew or Luke and nineteen times more than Mark. To restate it, MarQ is more distinctive in its use of aorist verbs than Mark is in its use of present verbs! Scholars studying the reconstructed MarQ text in order to know more about the source Matthew and Luke used would certainly conclude that one dominant feature of the source text was that it preferred the punctiliar, nonlinear aorist tense—and those scholars would be tragically wrong.

These unpredictable anomalies represent tremendous potential in the analysis of a reconstructed text for errantly ascribing a redactional feature to the original source simply because it is sufficiently differentiated from other texts. It then also represents tremendous opportunity to be wrong. This inevitably happens in the study of a reconstructed Q text. When the text of Q is reconstructed as a source for Matthew and Luke, many scholars point to distinct characteristics of the reconstructed Q text as evidence in support of the Q theory itself.

> At first sight such work may appear to be extremely hypothetical, being based on what some would argue is a very questionable presupposition (the very existence of Q as a single document). However, the very distinctiveness of the Q material as shown by the recent redaction-critical studies of Q is in itself an indication that this material did exist as a separate entity at some stage in the development of the synoptic tradition.[22]

22. Christopher M. Tuckett, *Q and the History of Early Christianity: Studies on Q* (Edinburgh: T&T Clark, 1996), 571.

The fact is that distinctive features found in the analysis of a reconstructed text have no definitive correlation with the original historical source it attempts to approximate. A reconstructed text is unreliable in that it is missing the very features and structures characteristic of the actual source text and, further, it contains features and structures that originate not from the actual source text but from the reconstruction process itself.

5. The Efficacy of a Reconstructed Gospel Source

5.1. Introduction

The goal of reconstructing a source is to use that reconstructed text as an approximation, a substitute for the actual text used as a source. One additional limitation of a reconstructed text is that it cannot be completely sifted from the text(s) that used it.

5.2. Correlations with MarQ

The 580 stylometric searches used in "Mark without Mark" to compare MarQ with each synoptic gospel were also used as a dataset for establishing correlation coefficients between each of the texts. These correlations become benchmarks for establishing how similar two texts are to each other, in comparison to two other sets of texts. When the conversation is about texts that were sources for each other, the correlations establish how indicative one text is of another. As the correlation coefficient between two texts approaches 1.000, it demonstrates that the two datasets are related and indicative of one another.

Table 6: Correlation Coefficients

	MarQ	Mark	Matthew	Luke	Synoptics	NT
MarQ	**1.000**	.9888	.9892	.9896	.9926	.9767
Mark	.9888	**1.000**	.9831	.9914	.9937	.9810
Matthew	.9892	.9831	**1.000**	.9928	.9964	.9885
Luke	.9896	.9914	.9928	**1.000**	.9986	.9892
Synoptics	.9926	.9937	.9964	.9986	**1.000**	.9903
NT	.9767	.9810	.9885	.9892	.9903	**1.000**

Many of the relationships here are as one would expect. Luke and Matthew correlate to each other higher (.9928) than either do to Mark (.9831 and .9914). Each of the gospels correlates more highly with the synoptics as a whole (above .99) than to the New Testament as a whole (below .99). However, the correlation patterns for MarQ are striking. If the reconstructed MarQ text were a good approximation of the Mark text, then the correlation between the two texts should be greater than it is with other texts. This is not the case. MarQ is more similar to Matthew (.9892) and to Luke (.9896) than it is to Mark (.9888). The reconstructed text of Mark is more indicative of Matthew and Luke than it is of Mark.

5.3. Agreement with MarQ

The amount of repetitive agreement can establish the close kinship between a text and its source as well. Mark and Luke have only two verses that share a sequence of fifteen or more words in the same form and order. Mark and Matthew share five verses with exact strings of at least fifteen words. In contrast, MarQ has fourteen verses with fifteen-word strings matching Luke and an overwhelming forty-one verses matching Matthew. When looking for long strings of shared material fifteen words or longer in a single verse, canonical Mark matches Luke twice and Matthew five times, but MarQ matches Luke fifteen times and Matthew forty-one times. This enormous disparity in agreements exposes how the reconstructed text has much longer, exact phrasing in common with Matthew and Luke than the source text does.

When searching for smaller phrases of just six words that do not need to match exactly, allowing for one intervening nonmatching word, MarQ has 317 verses matching a phrase in Matthew, but only 298 with Mark. The MarQ text, which was created at every point to be the best reconstruction of Mark that is possible, still looks more like, and is more indicative of, Matthew and Luke, the texts from which it is reconstructed.

5.4. The Skewed Result of a Reconstructed Text

After reconstructing Mark from Matthew and Luke, the resulting text is very dissimilar from the actual text of Mark. In summary:

- The reconstructed text of Mark is only half the size of the actual text of Mark.

- The content that disappears in MarQ leaves a text that largely loses the features that characterize the historical text it is attempting to approximate.
- The features that remain in the text of MarQ offer misleading pointers to what the text of Mark is like.
- The final text of MarQ remains more indicative of Matthew and Luke than of its Markan source.

Or, more simply, MarQ is a very poor representation of Mark.

When scholars work with a reconstructed text of Q as a source for Christian origins, they recognize the tenuous nature of its construction. Yet, the temptation is too great to gloss over the difficulties with the text and make the appeal to press on. Recognizing the possibility (inevitability!) that not all of a Q text can be reclaimed in reconstruction, detailed analysis proceeds as if the reconstructed text of Q can be treated as a smaller selection from the actual Q text. Recognizing that the text is inherently incomplete, the temptation remains to treat the text as a random sample, where the proportionate conclusions remain the same. The hope is that if the original text contained a particular thematic or grammatical or theological component, the reconstructed text might also include it in the same proportion. But this can now be seen as folly.

At the very least, a reconstructed text must be handled the way one treats the text of an ancient manuscript fragment, of which half the text is missing on account of disintegrating and missing pages and one whose content has no second attestation. Further, the analog should include the suspicion that the missing and changed content was done with a significant amount of intent by a later copyist, for the features of the reconstructed text bear the imprint of the text(s) that used it. Every empirical example of textual redaction would play this out. The redactor had an agenda, a set of interests and principles that (imperfectly and inconsistently) were applied as sources were used. The story was retold through a particular set of lenses, such that the version of the source that it is possible to reconstruct is not a random sample, but rather a selective and tainted result.

Take, for example, Mark's use of the thematic vocabulary of the Old Testament. Often the identity of the Jesus figure is shaped within the context of the vocabulary of the Old Testament. Naturally, not every quotation and allusion to the Old Testament within Mark survives in MarQ. However, it is not a random set of these quotations, but rather a systematic omission. Every quotation or allusion that is absent from MarQ is missing on account of Luke's omission. Every quotation that does not survive the reconstruction process is one that Luke decided to omit from its source. Luke did not like sheep without a shepherd from Num 27:17 (and 2 Chr 18:16) and Mark 6:34. Luke omitted the honoring with lips but turning hearts away from Isa 29:13 and Mark 7:6. Luke did not care for the creative mixing in Mark 7:10 of the commandment to honor father and mother (Exod 20:12 and Deut 5:16) with the putting to death of the one doing otherwise (Exod 21:17 and Lev 20:9). Luke had no use for a man leaving his father and mother to join his wife and become one flesh from Gen 2:24 and Mark 10:7–8. Luke thought not to mention the abomination of desolation from Dan 9:27, 11:31, 12:11, and Mark 13:14. Matthew did. Matthew preserved these texts from Mark, but a reconstruction of Mark will overlook them, not because they randomly were unused by either source, but because they were systematically omitted from one of them.

One can justifiably conclude that the same pattern likely holds for Luke's and Matthew's use of their non-Markan source, Q. Luke and Matthew share a significant Scripture quotation in only two places. First, in the temptation story (Matt 4:4–10 and Luke 4:4–12), Jesus quotes Deuteronomy (Deut 8:3, 6:16, and 6:13, while the tester responds with Ps 91:11). Second, when Jesus tells John's disciples to report what they see of the Messiah (Matt 11:5 and Luke 7:22), the response comes as various quotations and allusions from Isaiah (Isa 35:5–6; 61:1). But Matthew is loaded with so many more quotations and allusions to the scriptural world of the faith community.[23] Is it at all plausible to think that if Luke and Matthew were using a second common source, that texts would not have been omitted from it by Luke in the same way they were from Mark?

Far from an innocuous sampling, a reconstructed text bears the distinct marks of the witnesses that used it. Specifically, the present analogy of reconstructing Mark as a source from Matthew and Luke severely problematizes the manner in which a reconstructed Q text is analyzed as an ancient and primary source for studying Christian origins. A reconstructed text cannot sustain the same investigations, analyses, and methodologies that scholars bring to extant texts that are multiply attested. In the end, the ability to detect or demonstrate that a source is being used does not suggest that scholars have the ability and criteria to reliably

23. See Matt 1:23; 2:6, 15, 18; 4:15–16; 5:21, 27, 33, 38; 8:17; 9:13; 10:35–36; 12:7, 18–21, 40; 13:42, 50, 55; 16:17; 18:16; 21:5, 16; 27:9.

reconstruct that source. Even in the most ideal circumstances, as demonstrated in the empirical comparison between Mark and its reconstruction from Matthew and Luke, a text reconstructed from the writings that used it as a source remains in many significant ways an insufficient representation of the actual source text.

Bibliography

Abegg, Martin G. "The Linguistic Analysis of the Dead Sea Scrolls: More Than (Initially) Meets the Eye." Pages 48–68 in *Rediscovering the Dead Sea Scrolls: An Assessment of Old and New Approaches and Methods*. Edited by Maxine L. Grossman. Grand Rapids: Eerdmans, 2010.

Abusch, Tzvi. "Hunting in the Epic of Gilgamesh: Speculations on the Education of a Prince." Pages 11–20 in *Treasures on Camels' Humps: Historical and Literary Studies from the Ancient Near East Presented to Israel Eph'al*. Edited by Mordechai Cogan and Dan'el Kahn. Jerusalem: Magnes, 2008.

———. "Ishtar's Proposal and Gilgamesh's Refusal: An Interpretation of the Gilgamesh Epic, Tablet 6, lines 1–79." *HR* 26 (1986): 143–87.

Achenbach, Reinhard. "Der Pentateuch, seine theokratischen Bearbeitungen und Josua–2 Könige." Pages 225–53 in *Les dernières rédactions du Pentateuque, de l'Hexateuque et de l'Ennéateuque*. Edited by Thomas Römer and Konrad Schmid. BETL 203. Leuven: Peeters, 2007.

Aejmelaeus, Anneli. "Jeremiah at the Turning-Point of History: The Function of Jer. XXV 1–14 in the Book of Jeremiah." *VT* 52 (2002): 459–82.

———. *On the Trail of the Septuagint Translators: Collected Essays*. CBET 50. Kampen: Kok Pharos, 1993.

———. "Septuagintal Translation Techniques: A Solution to the Problem of the Tabernacle Account." Pages 381–402 in *Septuagint, Scrolls and Cognate Writings: Papers Presented at the International Symposium on the Septuagint and Its Relationship to the Dead Sea Scrolls and Other Writings*. Edited by George J. Brooke and Barnabas Lindars. SCS 33. Atlanta: Scholars Press, 1992.

———. "The Significance of Clause Connectors in the Syntactical and Translation-Technical Study of the Septuagint." Pages 361–80 in *VI Congress of the International Organization for Septuagint and Cognate Studies, Jerusalem 1986*. Edited by Claude E. Cox. SCS 23. Atlanta: Scholar's Press, 1987.

———. "What Can We Know about the Hebrew *Vorlage* of the Septuagint?" *ZAW* 99 (1987): 58–89.

Aland, Kurt, ed. *Synopsis Quattuor Evangeliorum: Locis parallelis evangeliorum apocryphorum et patrum adhibitis edidit*. 13th ed. Stuttgart: Deutsche Bibelgesellschaft, 1985.

Albertz, Rainer. "Bekehrung von oben als 'messianisches Programm': Die Sonderüberlieferung der Septuaginta in Dan 4–6." Pages 46–62 in *Theologische Probleme der Septuaginta und der hellenistischen Hermeneutik*. Edited by Henning Graf Reventlow. VWGTh 11. Gütersloh: Kaiser; Gütersloher Verlaghaus, 1997.

———. *Der Gott des Daniel: Untersuchungen zu Daniel 4–6 in der Septuagintafassung sowie zu Komposition und Theologie des aramäischen Danielbuches*. SBS 131. Stuttgart: Katholisches Bibelwerk, 1988.

Alexander, Philip S. "The Redaction-History of *Serekh ha-Yaḥad*: A Proposal." *RevQ* 17 (1996): 437–56.

Alexander, Philip S., and Géza Vermes, eds. *Qumran Cave 4:XIX: Serekh ha-Yaḥad and Two Related Texts*. DJD 26. Oxford: Clarendon, 1998.

Ambos, Claus. *Der König im Gefängnis und das Neujahrsfest im Herbst: Mechanismen der Legitimation des babylonischen Herrschers im 1. Jahrtausend v.Chr. und ihre Geschichte*. Dresden: ISLET, 2013.

Andersen, Francis I., and A. Dean Forbes. *The Vocabulary of the Old Testament*. Rome: Pontifical Biblical Institute, 1992.

Arnaud, Daniel. *Corpus des textes de bibliothèque de Ras Shamra-Ougarit (1936–2000) en sumérien, babylonien et assyrien*. AuOrSup 23. Sabadell: AUSA, 2007.

Auer, Anita, and Anja Voeste. "Grammatical Variables." Pages 253–70 in *The Handbook of Historical Sociolinguistics*. Edited by Juan Manuel Hernández Campoy and Juan Camilo Conde Silvestre. BHL. Chichester: Wiley-Blackwell, 2012.

Auld, A. Graeme. *I and II Samuel: A Commentary*. OTL. Louisville: Westminster John Knox, 2011.

Ausloos, Hans. "LXX's Rendering of Hebrew Proper Names and the Characterization of the Translation Technique of the Book of Judges." Pages 53–71 in *Scripture in Transition: Essays on Septuagint, Hebrew Bible and Dead Sea Scrolls in Honour of Raija Sollamo*. Edited by Anssi Voitila and Jutta Jokiranta. JSJSup 126. Leiden: Brill, 2008.

———. "The Septuagint's Rendering of Hebrew Hapax Legomena and the Characterization of Its 'Translation Technique': The Case of Exodus." *APB* 20 (2009): 360–76.

———. "The Septuagint's Rendering of Hebrew Toponyms as an Indication of the Translation Technique of the Book of Numbers." Pages 35–50 in *Textual Criticism and Dead Sea Scrolls Studies in Honour of Julio Trebolle Barrera: Florilegium Complutense*. Edited by Andrés Piquer Otero and Pablo A. Torijano Morales. JSJSup 157. Leiden: Brill, 2012.

Ausloos, Hans, and Bénédicte Lemmelijn. "Characterizing the LXX Translation of Judges on the Basis of Content-Related Criteria: The Greek Rendering of Hebrew Absolute Hapax Legomena in Judg 3:12–30." Pages 171–92 in *After Qumran: Old and Modern Editions of the Biblical Texts; The Historical Books*. Edited by Hans Ausloos, Bénédicte Lemmelijn, and Julio Trebolle Barrera. BETL 246. Leuven: Peeters, 2012.

———. "Content Related Criteria in Characterising the LXX Translation Technique." Pages 357–76 in *Die Septuaginta: Texte, Theologien, Einflüsse; 2. Internationale Fachtagung veranstaltet von Septuaginta Deutsch (LXX.D), Wuppertal 23.–27. Juli 2008*. Edited by Wolfgang Kraus, Martin Karrer, and Martin Meiser. WUNT 252. Tübingen: Mohr Siebeck, 2010.

———. "Faithful Creativity Torn between Freedom and Literalness in the Septuagint's Translations." *JNSL* 40 (2014): 53–69.

———. "Rendering Love: Hapax Legomena and the Characterisation of the Translation Technique of Song of Songs." Pages 43–61 in *Translating a Translation: The LXX and Its Modern Translations in the Context of Early Judaism*. Edited by Hans Ausloos, Johann Cook, Florentino García Martínez, Bénédicte Lemmelijn, and Marc Vervenne. BETL 213. Leuven: Peeters, 2008.

Ausloos, Hans, Bénédicte Lemmelijn, and Valérie Kabergs. "The Study of Aetiological Wordplay as a Content-Related Criterion in the Characterisation of LXX Translation Technique." Pages 273–94 in *Die Septuaginta: Entstehung, Sprache, Geschichte; 3. Internationale Fachtagung veranstaltet von Septuaginta Deutsch (LXX.D), Wuppertal 22.–25. Juli 2010*. Edited by Siegfried Kreuzer, Martin Meiser, and Martin Sigismund. WUNT 286. Tübingen: Mohr Siebeck, 2012.

Baden, Joel S. *The Composition of the Pentateuch: Renewing the Documentary Hypothesis*. AYBRL. New Haven: Yale University Press, 2012.

Baillet, Maurice, Józef T. Milik, and Roland de Vaux, eds. *Les "Petites Grottes" de Qumrân: Exploration de la falaise: Les grottes 2Q, 3Q, 5Q, 6Q, 7Q à 10Q: Le rouleau de cuivre*. 2 vols. DJD 3. Oxford: Clarendon, 1962.

Barr, James. "'Guessing' in the Septuagint." Pages 19–34 in *Studien zur Septuaginta: Robert Hanhart zu Ehren; Aus Anlaß seines 65. Geburtstages*. Edited by Detlef Fraenkel, Udo Quast, and John William Wevers. MSU 20. Göttingen: Vandenhoeck & Ruprecht, 1990.

———. "Reading a Script without Vowels." Pages 71–100 in *Writing without Letters*. Edited by William Haas. Manchester: Manchester University Press; Totowa, NJ: Rowman & Littlefield, 1976.

———. "Vocalization and the Analysis of Hebrew among the Ancient Translators." Pages 1–11 in *Hebräische Wortforschung: Festschrift zum 80. Geburtstag von Walter Baumgartner*. Edited by Benedikt Hartmann, Ernst Jenni, E. Y. Kutscher, Victor Maag, Isac Leo Seeligmann, and Rudolf Smend. VTSup 16. Leiden: Brill, 1967.

Barthélemy, Dominique. *Les devanciers d'Aquila: Première publication intégrale du texte des fragments du Dodécaprophéton trouvés dans le désert de Juda*. VTSup 10. Leiden: Brill, 1963.

———. "La qualité du texte massorétique de Samuel." Pages 1–44 in *The Hebrew and Greek Texts of Samuel: 1980 Proceedings IOSCS—Vienna*. Edited by Emanuel Tov. Jerusalem: Academon, 1980.

———, ed. *The Story of David and Goliath: Textual and Literary Criticism*. OBO 73. Fribourg: Editions Universitaires; Göttingen: Vandenhoeck & Ruprecht, 1986.

Baumgarten, Albert I. *The Flourishing of Jewish Sects in the Maccabean Era: An Interpretation*. JSJSup 55. Leiden: Brill, 1997.

Baumgarten, Joseph M. "The Cave 4 Versions of the Qumran Penal Code." *JJS* 43 (1992): 268–76.

———. "Miscellaneous Rules." Pages 57–78 in *Qumran Cave 4:XXV: Halakhic Texts*. Edited by Joseph M. Baumgarten, Torleif Elgvin, Esther Eshel, Erik Larson, Manfred R. Lehmann, Stephen J. Pfann, and Lawrence H. Schiffman. DJD 35. Oxford: Clarendon, 1999.

Baumgarten, Joseph M., Józef T. Milik, Stephen J. Pfann, and Ada Yardeni, eds. *Qumran Cave 4:XIII: The Damascus Document (4Q266–273)*. DJD 18. Oxford: Clarendon, 1996.

Beall, Todd S. *Josephus' Description of the Essenes Illustrated by the Dead Sea Scrolls*. SNTSMS 58. Cambridge: Cambridge University Press, 1988.

Becker, Uwe. *Richterzeit und Königtum: Redaktionsgeschichtliche Studien zum Richterbuch*. BZAW 192. Berlin: de Gruyter, 1990.

Ben-Hayyim, Zeev. עברית וארמית נוסח שומרון, כרך ד': מלי תורה [*The Literary and Oral Tradition of Hebrew and Aramaic amongst the*

Samaritans. Vol. 4: *The Words of the Pentateuch*]. Jerusalem: Academy of the Hebrew Language, 1977.

Ben-Hayyim, Zeev, and Abraham Tal. *A Grammar of Samaritan Hebrew: Based on the Recitation of the Law in Comparison with the Tiberian and Other Jewish Traditions*. Winona Lake, IN: Eisenbrauns, 2000.

Benz, Brendon C. "The Varieties of Sociopolitical Experience in the Late Bronze Age Levant and the Rise of Early Israel." PhD diss., New York University, 2012.

Berlin, Adele. Review of *Empirical Models for Biblical Criticism*, edited by Jeffrey H. Tigay. *JAOS* 107 (1987): 145–46.

Berner, Christoph. "The Redaction History of the Sinai Pericope (Exod 19–24) and Its Continuation in 4Q158." *DSD* 20 (2013): 378–409.

Bird, Graeme D. *Multitextuality in the Homeric Iliad: The Witness of the Ptolemaic Papyri*. Hellenic Studies 43. Washington, DC: Center for Hellenic Studies, 2010.

Block, Daniel I. *The Book of Ezekiel: Chapters 25–48*. NICOT. Grand Rapids: Eerdmans, 1998.

Blum, Erhard. "Der kompositionelle Knoten am Übergang von Josua zu Richter: Ein Entflechtungsvorschlag." Pages 181–212 in *Deuteronomy and Deuteronomic Literature: Festschrift C. H. W. Brekelmans*. Edited by Marc Vervenne and Johan Lust. BETL 133. Leuven: Peeters, 1997.

Boccaccini, Gabriele. *Beyond the Essene Hypothesis: The Parting of the Ways Between Qumran and Enochic Judaism*. Grand Rapids: Eerdmans, 1998.

Böck, Barbara. *The Healing Goddess Gula: Towards an Understanding of Ancient Babylonian Medicine*. CHANE 67. Leiden: Brill, 2014.

Bodine, Walter R. *The Greek Text of Judges: Recensional Developments*. HSM 23. Chico, CA: Scholars Press, 1980.

———. "Kaige and Other Recensional Developments in the Greek Text of Judges." *BIOSCS* 13 (1980): 45–57.

Bogaert, Pierre-Maurice. "De Baruch à Jérémie: Les deux rédactions conservées du livre de Jérémie." Pages 168–73 in *Le livre de Jérémie: Le prophète et son milieu; Les oracles et leur transmission*. Edited by Pierre-Maurice Bogaert. BETL 54. Leuven: Peeters, 1981.

———. "Les deux rédactions conservées (LXX et MT) d'Ézéchiel 7." Pages 21–47 in *Ezekiel and His Book: Textual and Literary Criticism and Their Interrelation*. Edited by Johan Lust. BETL 74. Leuven: Peeters, 1986.

———. "L'importance de la Septante et du 'Monacensis' de la Vetus Latina pour l'exégèse du livre de l'Exode (Chap. 35–40)." Pages 399–428 in

Studies in the Book of Exodus: Redaction, Reception, Interpretation. Edited by Marc Vervenne. BETL 126. Leuven: Peeters, 1996.

———. "Job latin chez les Pères et dans les Bibles: D'une version courte à des versions longues sur le grec et sur l'hébreu." *RBén* 122 (2012): 48–99, 366–93.

———. "La libération de Jérémie et le meurtre de Godolias: Le texte court (LXX) et la rédaction longue (TM)." Pages 312–22 in *Studien zur Septuaginta: Robert Hanhart zu Ehren: Aus Anlaß seines 65. Geburtstages*. Edited by Detlef Fraenkel, Udo Quast, and John William Wevers. MSU 20. Göttingen: Vandenhoeck & Ruprecht, 1990.

———. "Le livre de Jérémie en perspective: Les deux rédactions antiques selon les travaux en cours." *RB* 101 (1994): 363–406.

———. "Les mécanismes rédactionnels en Jér 10,1–16 (LXX et TM) et la signification des suppléments." Pages 222–38 in *Le livre de Jérémie: Le prophète et son milieu; Les oracles et leur transmission*. Edited by Pierre-Maurice Bogaert. BETL 54. Leuven: Peeters, 1981.

———. "Montagne sainte, jardin d'Éden et sanctuaire (hiérosolymitain) dans un oracle d'Ézéchiel contre le prince de Tyr (Éz 28,11–19)." Pages 131–53 in *Le Mythe, son langage et son message: Actes du Colloque de Liège et Louvain-la-Neuve de 1981*. Edited by Henri Limet and Julien Ries. Homo religiosus 9. Louvain la-Neuve: Centre d'Histoire des Religions, 1983.

———. "Relecture et déplacement de l'oracle contre les Philistins: Pour une datation de la rédaction longue (TM) du livre de Jérémie." Pages 139–50 in *La vie de la parole: De l'Ancien au Nouveau Testament; Études d'exégèse et d'herméneutique bibliques offertes à Pierre Grelot*. Paris: Desclée, 1987.

———. "Le témoignage de la Vetus Latina dans l'étude de la tradition des Septante: Ézéchiel et Daniel dans le Papyrus 967." *Bib* 59 (1978): 384–95.

———. "*Urtext*, texte court et relecture: Jérémie xxxiii 14–26 TM et ses préparations." Pages 236–47 in *Congress Volume: Leuven 1989*. Edited by John A. Emerton. VTSup 43. Leiden: Brill, 1991.

———. "La *vetus latina* de Jérémie: Texte très court, témoin de la plus ancienne Septante et d'une forme plus ancienne de l'hébreu (Jer 39 et 52)." Pages 51–82 in *The Earliest Text of the Hebrew Bible: The Relationship between the Masoretic Text and the Hebrew Base of the Septuagint Reconsidered*. Edited by Adrian Schenker. SCS 52 Atlanta: Society of Biblical Literature, 2003.

Boling, Robert G. *Joshua: A New Translation with Notes and Commentary*. AB 6. Garden City, NY: Doubleday, 1982.

———. *Judges: Introduction, Translation, and Commentary*. AB 6A. Garden City, NY: Doubleday, 1975.

Boring, M. Eugene. *An Introduction to the New Testament: History, Literature, Theology*. Louisville: Westminster John Knox, 2012.

———. *Mark: A Commentary*. NTL. Louisville: Westminster John Knox, 2006.

Boulluec, Alain Le, and Pierre Sandevoir. *L'Exode: Traduction du texte grec de la Septante*. BA 2. Paris: Cerf, 1989.

Brady, Monica. "Biblical Interpretation in the 'Pseudo-Ezekiel' Fragments (4Q383–391) from Cave Four." Pages 88–109 in *Biblical Interpretation at Qumran*. Edited by Matthias Henze. SDSS 6. Grand Rapids: Eerdmans, 2005.

Brisch, Nicole. "Mother Goddess (Ninmah, Nintud/r, Belet-ili)." *Ancient Mesopotamian Gods and Goddesses*. Oracc and the UK Higher Education Academy. http://oracc.museum.upenn.edu/amgg/listofdeities/mothergoddess/.

Brooke, George J. "Power to the Powerless: A Long-Lost Song of Miriam." *BAR* 20 (1994): 62–65.

———. "The Temple Scroll and the LXX Exodus 35–40." Pages 81–106 in *Septuagint, Scrolls and Cognate Writings: Papers Presented at the International Symposium on the Septuagint and Its Relationship to the Dead Sea Scrolls and Other Writings*. Edited by George J. Brooke and Barnabas Lindars. SCS 33. Atlanta: Scholars Press, 1992.

———. "Thematic Commentaries on Prophetic Scriptures." Pages 134–57 in *Biblical Interpretation at Qumran*. Edited by Matthias Henze. SDSS 6. Grand Rapids: Eerdmans, 2005.

Brown, Raymond Edward. *An Introduction to the New Testament*. ABRL. New York: Doubleday, 1997.

Budde, Karl. *Die Bücher Samuel*. KHC 8. Tübingen: Mohr Siebeck, 1902.

Burchard, Christoph. "Joseph and Asenath: A New Translation and Introduction." *OTP* 2:177–247.

Burrows, Millar. *The Dead Sea Scrolls of St. Mark's Monastery: 2.2. Plates and Transcription of the Manual of Discipline*. New Haven: American Schools of Oriental Research, 1951.

Butler, Sally A. L. *Mesopotamian Conceptions of Dreams and Dream Rituals*. AOAT 258. Münster: Ugarit-Verlag, 1998.

Campbell, Anthony F., and Mark A. O'Brien. *Unfolding the Deuteronomistic History: Origins, Upgrades, Present Text*. Minneapolis: Fortress, 2000.

Carlston, Charles E., and Dennis Norlin. "Statistics and Q: Some Further Observations." *NovT* 41 (1999): 108–23.

Carr, David M. *The Formation of the Hebrew Bible: A New Reconstruction*. New York: Oxford University Press, 2011.

———. *Writing on the Tablet of the Heart: Origins of Scripture and Literature*. New York: Oxford University Press, 2005.

Carroll, Robert P. *Jeremiah: A Commentary*. OTL. London: SCM; Philadelphia: Westminster, 1986.

Cavigneaux, Antoine. "A Scholar's Library in Meturan?" Pages 251–73 in *Mesopotamian Magic: Textual, Historical, and Interpretative Perspectives*. Edited by Tzvi Abusch and Karel van der Toorn. AMD 1. Groningen: Styx, 1999.

Chalcraft, David J., ed. *Sectarianism in Early Judaism: Sociological Advances*. BibleWorld. London: Equinox, 2007.

Charlesworth, James H. *The Old Testament Pseudepigrapha*. 2 vols. New York: Doubleday, 1983, 1985.

Charlesworth, James H., and Brent A. Strawn. "Reflections on the Text of *Serek ha-Yaḥad* Found in Cave IV." *RevQ* 17 (1996): 403–35.

Civil, Miguel. "Old Babylonian Proto-Lu: Types of Sources." Pages 24–73 in *The Series* lu_2 = *ša and Related Texts*. Edited by Miguel Civil and Erica Reiner. MSL 12. Rome: Pontifical Biblical Institute, 1969.

Cogan, Mordechai. "Some Text-Critical Issues in the Hebrew Bible from an Assyriological Perspective." *Text* 22 (2005): 1–20.

Collins, John J. *Beyond the Qumran Community: The Sectarian Movement of the Dead Sea Scrolls*. Grand Rapids: Eerdmans, 2010.

———. *Daniel: A Commentary on the Book of Daniel*. Hermeneia. Minneapolis: Fortress, 1993.

Collins, Nina L. "Evidence in the Septuagint of a Tradition in which the Israelites Left Egypt without Pharaoh's Consent." *CBQ* 56 (1994) 442–48.

Conrad, Joachim. "Die Entstehung und Motivierung alttestamentlicher Paraschen im Licht der Qumranfunde." Page 47–56 in *Bibel und Qumran: Beiträge zur Erforschung der Beziehungen zwischen Bibel- und Qumranwissenschaft; Hans Bardtke zum 22.9.66*. Edited by Siegfried Wagner. Berlin: Evangelische Haupt-Bibelgesellschaft, 1968.

Cooper, Jerrold S. "Bilinguals from Boghazköi I." *ZA* 61 (1971): 1–22.

———. “Gilgamesh Dreams of Enkidu: The Evolution and Dilution of Narrative.” Pages 39–44 in *Essays on the Ancient Near East in Memory of Jacob Joel Finkelstein*. Edited by Maria de Jong Ellis. MCAAS 19. Hamden, CT: Archon Books, 1977.

———. “Sumerian and Akkadian in Sumer and Akkad.” *Or* 42 (1973): 239–46.

———. “Symmetry and Repetition in Akkadian Narrative.” *JAOS* 97 (1977): 508–12.

Crane, Ashley S. *Israel's Restoration: A Textual-Comparative Exploration of Ezekiel 38–39*. VTSup 122. Leiden: Brill, 2008.

Crawford, Sidnie White. *Rewriting Scripture in Second Temple Times*. SDSS. Grand Rapids: Eerdmans, 2008.

———. “Understanding the Textual History of the Hebrew Bible: A New Proposal.” Pages 60–69 in *The Hebrew Bible in Light of the Dead Sea Scrolls*. Edited by Nóra Dávid, Armin Lange, Kristin De Troyer, and Shani Tzoref. FRLANT 239. Göttingen: Vandenhoeck & Ruprecht, 2012.

Crenshaw, James L. *Education in Ancient Israel: Across the Deadening Silence*. AYBRL. New York: Doubleday, 1998.

Cross, Frank M. “The Ammonite Oppression of the Tribes of Gad and Reuben: Missing Verses from 1 Samuel 11 Found in 4QSamuel[a].” Pages 148–58 in *History, Historiography, and Interpretation*. Edited by Hayim Tadmor and Moshe Weinfeld. Jerusalem: Magnes, 1983.

———. “Paleography.” Pages 629–34 in vol. 2 of *Encyclopedia of the Dead Sea Scrolls*. Edited by Lawrence H. Schiffman and James C. VanderKam. 2 vols. New York: Oxford University Press, 2000.

Cross, Frank M., Donald W. Parry, Richard J. Saley, and Eugene Ulrich, eds. *Qumran Cave 4:XII: 1–2 Samuel*. DJD 17. Oxford: Clarendon, 2005.

Crossan, John Dominic. *The Historical Jesus: The Life of a Mediterranean Jewish Peasant*. San Francisco: HarperSanFrancisco, 1991.

Davies, Philip R. “Biblical Hebrew and the History of Ancient Judah: Typology, Chronology and Common Sense.” Pages 150–63 in *Biblical Hebrew: Studies in Chronology and Typology*. Edited by Ian Young. JSOTSup 369. London: T&T Clark, 2003.

———. “Sects from Texts: On the Problems of Doing a Sociology of the Qumran Literature.” Pages 69–82 in *New Directions in Qumran Studies: Proceedings of the Bristol Colloquium on the Dead Sea Scrolls, 8–10 September 2003*. Edited by Jonathan G. Campbell, William John Lyons, and Lloyd K. Pietersen. LSTS 52. London: T&T Clark, 2005.

De Bruyne, Donatien. "Les anciennes versions latines du Cantique des Cantiques." *RBén* 38 (1926): 97–122.

Delnero, Paul. "Sumerian Extract Tablets and Scribal Education." *JCS* 62 (2010): 53–69.

———. *The Textual Criticism of Sumerian Literature*. JCSSup 3. Boston: American Schools of Oriental Research, 2012.

———. "Variation in Sumerian Literary Compositions: A Case Study Based on the Decad." PhD diss., University of Pennsylvania, 2006.

Dietrich, Walter. *Prophetie und Geschichte: Eine redaktionsgeschichtliche Untersuchung zum deuteronomistischen Geschichtswerk*. FRLANT 108. Göttingen: Vandenhoeck & Ruprecht, 1972.

"The Digital Dead Sea Scrolls." Israel Museum. http://dss.collections.imj.org.il/community.

Dimant, Devorah. "1 Enoch 6–11: A Fragment of a Parabiblical Work." *JJS* 53 (2002): 223-37.

———. "The Composite Character of the Qumran Sectarian Literature as an Indication of Its Date and Provenance." *RevQ* 22 (2006): 615–30.

Dolbeau, François. "Nouveaux sermons de saint Augustin pour la conversion des païens et des donatistes." *REAug* 37 (1991): 37–78.

Driver, Samuel R. *An Introduction to the Literature of the Old Testament*. 5th ed. Edinburgh: T&T Clark, 1894.

———. *An Introduction to the Literature of the Old Testament*. 9th ed. Edinburgh: T&T Clark, 1913.

Durham, John I. *Exodus*. WBC 3. Waco, TX: Word, 1987.

Dus, Jan. "Gibeon: Eine Kultstätte des Šmš und die Stadt des benjaminitischen Schicksals." *VT* 10 (1960): 353–74.

Dwyer, Timothy. *The Motif of Wonder in the Gospel of Mark*. JSNTSup 128. Sheffield: Sheffield Academic, 1996.

Ebeling, Erich, Franz Köcher, and Liane Rost. *Literarische Keilschrifttexte aus Assur*. Berlin: Akademie, 1953.

Edzard, Dietz Otto. *"Gilgamesh und Huwawa": Zwei Versionen der sumerischen Zedernwaldepisode nebst einer Edition von Version "B."* Munich: Bayerische Akademie der Wissenschaften, 1993.

Elbogen, Ismar. *Jewish Liturgy: A Comprehensive History*. Translated by Raymond P. Scheindlin. Philadelphia: Jewish Publication Society, 1993.

Elliott, James Keith. *The Language and Style of the Gospel of Mark: An Edition of C. H. Turner's "Notes on Marcan Usage" Together with Other Comparable Studies*. NovTSup 71. Leiden: Brill, 1993.

Emerton, John A. Review of *Empirical Models for Biblical Criticism*, edited by Jeffrey H. Tigay. *VT* 37 (1987): 508–9.

Eshel, Esther, and Hanan Eshel. "Dating the Samaritan Pentateuch's Compilation in Light of the Qumran Biblical Scrolls." Pages 215–40 in *Emanuel: Studies in Hebrew Bible, Septuagint, and Dead Sea Scrolls in Honor of Emanuel Tov*. Edited by Shalom M. Paul, Robert A. Kraft, Lawrence H. Schiffman, and Weston W. Fields. VTSup 94. Leiden: Brill, 2003.

Falk, Daniel K. *The Parabiblical Texts: Strategies for Extending the Scriptures among the Dead Sea Scrolls*. CQS 8. LSTS 63. London: T&T Clark, 2007.

Falk, Marcia. *The Book of Blessings: A New Prayer Book for the Weekdays, the Sabbath, and the New Moon Festival*. San Francisco: HarperSanFrancisco, 1996.

Ferguson, Everett. *Backgrounds of Early Christianity*. 2nd ed. Grand Rapids: Eerdmans, 1993.

Fernández Marcos, Natalio. "The Hebrew and Greek Texts of Judges." Pages 1–16 in *The Earliest Text of the Hebrew Bible: The Relationship between the Masoretic Text and the Hebrew Base of the Septuagint Reconsidered*. Edited by Adrian Schenker. SCS 52. Atlanta: Society of Biblical Literature, 2003.

———. *The Septuagint in Context: Introduction to the Greek Versions of the Bible*. Translated by Wilfred G. E. Watson. Leiden: Brill, 2000.

Fincke, Andrew. *The Samuel Scroll from Qumran: 4QSam*[a] *Restored and Compared to the Septuagint and 4QSam*[c]. STDJ 43. Leiden: Brill, 2001.

Fincke, Jeanette C. "The Babylonian Texts of Nineveh: Report on the British Museum's Ashurbanipal Library Project." *AfO* 50 (2003/2004): 111–49.

———. "The List of Nineveh Joins: Description and Explanation." http://www.fincke-cuneiform.com/nineveh/joins/description.htm.

Finkel, Irving L. "Adad-apla-iddina, Esagil-kīn-apli, and the Series SA.GIG." Pages 143–59 in *A Scientific Humanist: Studies in Memory of Abraham Sachs*. Edited by Erle Leichty, Maria de Jong Ellis, and Pamela Gerardi. OPSNKF 9. Philadelphia: University Museum, 1988.

Fishbane, Michael. *Biblical Interpretation in Ancient Israel*. Oxford: Oxford University Press, 1985.

Fleming, Daniel E. *The Legacy of Israel in Judah's Bible: History, Politics, and the Reinscribing of Tradition*. Cambridge: Cambridge University Press, 2012.

Fleming, Daniel E., and Sara J. Milstein. *The Buried Foundation of the Gilgamesh Epic: The Akkadian Huwawa Narrative*. CM 39. Leiden: Brill, 2010.

Flint, Peter W. *The Dead Sea Psalms Scrolls and the Book of Psalms*. STDJ 17. Leiden: Brill, 1997.

Foley, John Miles. "Analogues: Modern Oral Epic." Pages 196–212 in *A Companion to Ancient Epic*. Edited by John Miles Foley. Oxford: Blackwell, 2005.

———. *Homer's Traditional Art*. University Park: Pennsylvania State University Press, 1999.

———. *The Theory of Oral Composition: History and Methodology*. Folkloristics. Bloomington: Indiana University Press, 1988.

———. *Traditional Oral Epic: The Odyssey, Beowulf, and the Serbo-Croatian Return Song*. Berkeley: University of California Press, 1990.

Frechette, Christopher. *Mesopotamian Ritual-Prayers of "Hand-Lifting" (Akkadian* Šuillas*): An Investigation of Function in Light of the Idiomatic Meaning of the Rubric*. AOAT 379. Münster: Ugarit-Verlag, 2012.

Fretheim, Terence E. *Jeremiah*. SHBC. Macon, GA: Smyth & Helwys, 2002.

Friedman, Richard Elliott. "Foreword." Ten unnumbered pages in *Empirical Models for Biblical Criticism*. Edited by Jeffrey H. Tigay. Eugene, OR: Wipf & Stock, 2005.

———. Review of *Empirical Models for Biblical Criticism*, edited by Jeffrey H. Tigay. *JR* 67 (1987): 539–40.

Gadotti, Alhena. *"Gilgamesh, Enkidu, and the Netherworld" and the Sumerian Gilgamesh Cycle*. UAVA 10. Boston: de Gruyter, 2014.

Gall, August Freiherr von, ed. *Der hebräische Pentateuch der Samaritaner*. Giessen: Töpelmann, 1914–1918.

Galor, Katharina, Jean-Baptiste Humbert, and Jürgen Zangenberg. *Qumran—The Site of the Dead Sea Scrolls: Archaeological Interpretations and Debates; Proceedings of a Conference Held at Brown University, November 17–19, 2002*. STDJ 57. Leiden: Brill, 2006.

Galter, Hannes D. "Cuneiform Bilingual Royal Inscriptions." Pages 25–50 in *Language and Culture in the Near East*. Edited by Shlomo Izre'el and Rina Drory. IOS 15. Leiden: Brill, 1995.

García Martínez, Florentino. "The Groningen Hypothesis Revisited." Pages 17–30 in *The Dead Sea Scrolls and Contemporary Culture: Proceedings of the International Conference held at the Israel Museum, Jerusalem (July 6–8, 2008)*. Edited by Adolfo D. Roitman, Lawrence H. Schiffman, and Shani Tzoref. STDJ 93. Leiden: Brill, 2011.

———. "Qumran Origins and Early History: A Groningen Hypothesis." *FO* 25 (1988): 113–36.

García Martínez, Florentino, and Eibert J. C. Tigchelaar, eds. *The Dead Sea Scrolls Study Edition*. 2 vols. Grand Rapids: Eerdmans; Leiden: Brill, 1999.

García Martínez, Florentino, and Adam S. van der Woude. "A Groningen Hypothesis of Qumran Origins and Early History." *RevQ* 14 (1999): 521–41.

Geers, Frederick W. "Heft Ac." Cuniform Digital Library Initiative. http://www.cdli.ucla.edu/tools/cdlifiles/geers_ac.pdf.zip.

George, Andrew R. *The Babylonian Gilgamesh Epic: Introduction, Critical Edition and Cuneiform Texts*. 2 vols. Oxford: Oxford University Press, 2003.

———. *Babylonian Literary Texts in the Schøyen Collection*. CUSAS 10. Bethesda, MD: CDL, 2009.

———. "The Gilgameš Epic at Ugarit." *AuOr* 25 (2007): 237–54.

Gertz, Jan Christian, Angelika Berlejung, Konrad Schmid, and Markus Witte. *T&T Clark Handbook of the Old Testament: An Introduction to the Literature, Religion, and History of the Old Testament*. London: T&T Clark, 2012.

Goldman, Yohanan. *Prophétie et royauté au retour de l'exil: Les origenes littéraires de la forme massorétique du livre de Jérémie*. OBO 118. Fribourg: Editions Universitaires; Göttingen: Vandenhoeck & Ruprecht, 1992.

Gordon, Robert P. "Compositeness, Conflation and the Pentateuch." *JSOT* 51 (1991): 57–69.

Greenspoon, Leonard J. "The Kaige Recension: The Life, Death, and Postmortem Existence of a Modern—and Ancient—Phenomenon." Pages 5–16 in *XII Congress of the International Organization for Septuagint and Cognate Studies, Leiden, 2004*. Edited by Melvin K. H. Peters. SCS 54. Atlanta: Society of Biblical Literature, 2006.

———. *Textual Studies in the Book of Joshua*. HSM 28. Chico, CA: Scholars Press, 1983.

Greenstein, Edward L. "The Firstborn Plague and the Reading Process." Pages 555–68 in *Pomegranates and Golden Bells: Studies in Biblical, Jewish, and Near Eastern Ritual, Law, and Literature in Honor of Jacob Milgrom*. Edited by David P. Wright, David Noel Freedman, and Avi Hurvitz. Winona Lake, IN: Eisenbrauns, 1995.

Grelot, Pierre. "Le Chapitre V de *Daniel* dans la Septante." *Sem* 24 (1974): 45–66.

Gressmann, Hugo. "Die Aufgaben der alttestamentlichen Forschung." *ZAW* 42 (1924): 1–33.

Groß, Walter. *Richter*. HThKAT. Freiburg: Herder, 2009.

Grossman, Maxine L. "'Outside the True': Intimacy, Sectarian Identity, and Discursive Boundaries on the Study of the Dead Sea Scrolls." In *The T&T Clark Companion to the Dead Sea Scrolls*. Edited by George J. Brooke and Charlotte Hempel. London: T&T Clark, forthcoming.

———. *Reading for History in the Damascus Document: A Methodological Study*. STDJ 45. Leiden: Brill, 2002.

Guenther, Allen Robert. "A Diachronic Study of Biblical Hebrew Prose Syntax: An Analysis of the Verbal Clause in Jeremiah 37–45 and Esther 1–10." PhD diss., University of Toronto, 1977.

Gurney, Oliver R. "Scribes at Huzirīna." *NABU* 1997/17.

Gurney, Oliver R., and Jacob J. Finkelstein. *The Sultantepe Tablets*. Vol. 1. BIAAOP 3. London: British Institute of Archaeology at Ankara, 1957.

Gurney, Oliver R., and Peter Hulin. *The Sultantepe Tablets*. Vol. 2. BIAAOP 7. London: British Institute of Archaeology at Ankara, 1964.

Haelewyck, Jean-Claude. *Hester*. VL 7.3. Freiburg: Herder, 2003.

———. "The Relevance of the Old Latin Version for the Septuagint, with Special Emphasis on the Book of Esther." *JTS* 57 (2006): 439–73.

Hanhart, Robert. *Text und Textgeschichte des 2. Esrabuches*. MSU 25. Göttingen: Vandenhoeck & Ruprecht, 2003.

Hasel, G. F. *The Remnant: The History and Theology of the Remnant Idea from Genesis to Isaiah*. AUMSR 5. Berrien Springs, MI: Andrews University Press, 1972.

Heffron, Yağmur. "Gula/Ninkarrak (Goddess)." *Ancient Mesopotamian Gods and Goddesses*. Oracc and the UK Higher Education Academy. http://oracc.museum.upenn.edu/amgg/listofdeities/gulaninkarrak/.

Hempel, Charlotte. "The Damascus Document and 1QSa." Pages 47–62 in *The Qumran Rule Texts in Context: Collected Studies*. TSAJ 154. Tübingen: Mohr Siebeck, 2013.

———. "The Earthly Essene Nucleus of 1QSa." *DSD* 3 (1996): 253–69.

———. "'Haskalah' at Qumran: The Eclectic Character of Qumran Cave 4." Pages 303–37 in *The Qumran Rule Texts in Context: Collected Studies*. TSAJ 154. Tübingen: Mohr Siebeck, 2013.

———. "The Penal Code Reconsidered." Pages 337–48 in *Legal Texts and Legal Issues: Proceedings of the Second Meeting of the International*

Organization for Qumran Studies, Cambridge 1995. Edited by Moshe J. Bernstein, Florentino García Martínez, and John Kampen. STDJ 23. Leiden: Brill, 1997.

———. "Rewritten Rule Texts." Pages 137–50 in *The Qumran Rule Texts in Context*. TSAJ 154. Tübingen: Mohr Siebeck, 2013.

Hendel, Ronald S. "The Two Editions of the Royal Chronology in Kings." Pages 99–114 in *Textual Criticism and Dead Sea Scrolls Studies in Honour of Julio Trebolle Barrera: Florilegium Complutense*. Edited by Andrés Piquer Otero and Pablo A. Torijano Morales. JSJSup 157. Leiden: Brill, 2012.

Henze, Matthias. *The Madness of King Nebuchadnezzar: The Ancient Near Eastern Origins and Early History of Interpretation of Daniel 4*. JSJSup 61. Leiden: Brill, 1999.

Hess, Richard S. "The Dead Sea Scrolls and Higher Criticism of the Hebrew Bible: The Case of 4QJudg[a]." Pages 122–28 in *The Scrolls and the Scriptures: Qumran Fifty Years After*. Edited by Stanley E. Porter and Craig A. Evans. JSPSup 26. RILP 3. Sheffield: Sheffield Academic, 1997.

Hobson, Russell. *Transforming Literature into Scripture: Texts as Cult Objects at Nineveh and Qumran*. BibleWorld. Sheffield: Equinox, 2012.

Hoegenhaven, Jesper. "The First Isaiah Scroll from Qumran (1QIs[a]) and the Massoretic Text: Some Reflections with Special Regard to Isaiah 1–12." *JSOT* 28 (1984): 17–35.

Holladay, William L. *Jeremiah 1: A Commentary on the Book of the Prophet Jeremiah, Chapters 1–25*. Hermeneia. Philadelphia: Fortress, 1986.

———. *Jeremiah 2: A Commentary on the Book of the Prophet Jeremiah, Chapters 26–52*. Hermeneia. Minneapolis: Fortress, 1989.

Holm, Tawny L. *Of Courtiers and Kings: The Biblical Daniel Narratives and Ancient Story-Collections*. EANEC 1. Winona Lake, IN: Eisenbrauns, 2013.

Honko, Lauri. *Textualizing the Siri Epic*. FFC 264. Helsinki: Suomalainen Tiedeakatemia, Academia Scientiarum Fennica, 1998.

Hoop, Raymond de. "'Then Israel Bowed Himself…' (Genesis 47.31)." *JSOT* 28 (2004): 467–80.

Hornkohl, Aaron D. *Ancient Hebrew Periodization and the Language of the Book of Jeremiah: The Case for a Sixth-Century Date of Composition*. SSLL 74. Leiden: Brill, 2014.

Horrocks, Geoffrey. "Homer's Dialect." Pages 193–217 in *A New Companion to Homer*. Edited by Ian Morris and Barry Powell. MS 163. Leiden: Brill, 1997.

Hunger, Hermann. *Babylonische und assyrische Kolophone*. AOAT 2. Kevelaer: Butzon & Bercker; Neukirchen-Vluyn: Neukirchener, 1968.

Hunt, Joel H. *Mesopotamian Šuilla Prayers to Ea, Marduk, and Nabû: Exegetical Studies*. Lewiston, NY: Mellen, 2010.

Hurvitz, Avi. "The Evidence of Language in Dating the Priestly Code: A Linguistic Study in Technical Idioms and Terminology." *RB* 81 (1974): 24–56.

———. *A Linguistic Study of the Relationship between the Priestly Source and the Book of Ezekiel: A New Approach to an Old Problem*. CahRB 20. Paris: Gabalda, 1982.

———. "Terminological Modifications in Biblical Genealogical Records and Their Potential Chronological Implications." Pages 105–16 in *Hebrew in the Second Temple Period: The Hebrew of the Dead Sea Scrolls and of Other Contemporary Sources*. Edited by Steven E. Fassberg, Moshe Bar-Asher, and Ruth A. Clements. STDJ 108. Leiden: Brill, 2013.

Janssen, Kolet, and Rebekka Jonkers. *Mondeling Examen: Marc Vervenne*. Leuven: Acco, 2010.

Janzen, J. Gerald. *Exodus*. WC. Louisville: Westminster John Knox, 1997.

———. *Studies in the Text of Jeremiah*. HSM 6. Cambridge: Harvard University Press, 1973.

Japhet, Sara. *I and II Chronicles: A Commentary*. OTL. London: SCM, 1993.

Jastrow, Morris, Jr. *The Religion of Babylonia and Assyria*. Boston: Ginn, 1898.

Jeansonne, Sharon Pace. *The Old Greek Translation of Daniel 7–12*. CBQMS 19. Washington, DC: Catholic Biblical Association of America, 1988.

Jokiranta, Jutta. *Social Identity and Sectarianism in the Qumran Movement*. STDJ 105. Leiden: Brill, 2012.

———. "Social-Scientific Approaches to the Dead Sea Scrolls." Pages 246–63 in *Rediscovering the Dead Sea Scrolls: An Assessment of Old and New Approaches and Methods*. Edited by Maxine L. Grossman. Grand Rapids: Eerdmans, 2010.

Joosten, Jan. "L'excédent massorétique du livre de Jérémie et l'hébreu post-classique." Pages 93–108 in *Conservatism and Innovation in the Hebrew Language of the Hellenistic Period: Proceedings of a Fourth International Symposium on the Hebrew of the Dead Sea Scrolls and Ben Sira*. Edited by Jan Joosten and Jean-Sébastien Rey. STDJ 73. Leiden: Brill, 2008.

Joseph, Brian D., and Richard D. Janda, eds. *The Handbook of Historical Linguistics*. BHL. Malden, MA: Blackwell, 2003.

Josephus. *Les antiquités juives*. Translated by Etienne Nodet, Yohanan Lederman, and Serge Bardet. 5 vols. Paris: Cerf, 1995–2005.

Kabergs, Valérie. "Creativiteit in het spel? De Griekse weergave van expliciet Hebreeuws woordspel op basis van eigennamen in Pentateuch en Twaalf Profeten." PhD diss., Katholieke Universiteit Leuven, 2015.

———. "Puns Within the Context of Name Explanations in MT and LXX Exodus." Pages 215–33 in *Die Septuaginta: Text, Wirkung, Rezeption; 4. Internationale Fachtagung veranstaltet von Septuaginta Deutsch (LXX. D), Wuppertal 19.–22. Juli 2012*. Edited by Wolfgang Kraus and Siegfried Kreuzer. WUNT 325. Tübingen: Mohr Siebeck, 2014.

Kabergs, Valérie, and Hans Ausloos. "Paronomasia or Wordplay? A Babel-Like Confusion: Towards a Definition of Hebrew Wordplay." *Bib* 93 (2012): 1–20.

Kalimi, Isaac. *An Ancient Israelite Historian: Studies in the Chronicler, His Time, Place, and Writing*. SSN 46. Assen: Van Gorcum, 2005.

———. *The Reshaping of Ancient Israelite History in Chronicles*. Winona Lake, IN: Eisenbrauns, 2005.

Kampen, John, and Moshe J. Bernstein, eds. *Reading 4QMMT: New Perspectives on Qumran Law and History*. SymS 2. Atlanta: Scholars Press, 1996.

Katzin, David. "The Use of Scripture in 4Q175." *DSD* 20 (2013): 200–236.

Kellenberger, Edgar. "Textvarianten in den Daniel-Legenden als Zeugnisse Mündlicher Tradierung." Pages 207–23 in *XIII Congress of the International Organization for Septuagint and Cognate Studies: Ljubljana, 2007*. Edited by Melvin K. H. Peters. SCS 55. Atlanta: Society of Biblical Literature, 2008.

Kelley, Page H., Daniel S. Mynatt, and Timothy G. Crawford. *The Masorah of Biblia Hebraica Stuttgartensia: Introduction and Annotated Glossary*. Grand Rapids: Eerdmans, 1998.

Kim, Dong-Hyuk. Review of *Ancient Hebrew Periodization and the Language of the Book of Jeremiah: The Case for a Sixth-Century Date of Composition*, by Aaron D. Hornkohl. *RBL* 3 (2016): 1–9.

King, Leonard W., ed. *Babylonian Magic and Sorcery: "Being The Prayers of the Lifting of the Hand"; The Cuneiform Texts of a Group of Babylonian and Assyrian Incantations and Magical Formulae Edited with Transliterations and Full Vocabulary from Tablets of the Kuyunjik Collections Preserved in the British Museum*. London: Luzac, 1896.

———. "BMS 01." Cuniform Digital Library Initiative. http://cdli.ucla.edu/P393771.

———. "BMS 01 K 03332 dupl." Cuniform Digital Library Initiative. http://cdli.ucla.edu/P394701.

———. "BMS 06." Cuniform Digital Library Initiative. http://cdli.ucla.edu/P394195.

Klein, Ralph W. *1 Chronicles*. Hermeneia. Minneapolis: Fortress, 2006.

———. "New Evidence for an Old Recension of Reigns." *HTR* 60 (1967): 93–105.

Kloppenborg, John S. *Excavating Q: The History and Setting of the Sayings Gospel*. Minneapolis: Fortress, 2000.

Knoppers, Gary N. *1 Chronicles 1–9*. AB 12. New York: Doubleday, 2003.

———. *1 Chronicles 10–29*. AB 12A. New York: Doubleday, 2004.

Korpel, Marjo C. A. "Unit Delimitation in Ugaritic Cultic Texts and Some Babylonian and Hebrew Parallels." Pages 141–60 in *Layout Markers in Biblical Manuscripts and Ugaritic Tablets*. Edited by Marjo C. A. Korpel and Josef M. Oesch. Pericope 5. Assen: Van Gorcum, 2005.

Kouwenberg, N. J. C. "Diachrony in Akkadian and the Dating of Literary Texts." Pages 433–51 in *Diachrony in Biblical Hebrew*. Edited by Cynthia Miller-Naudé and Ziony Zevit. LSAWS 8. Winona Lake, IN: Eisenbrauns, 2012.

Kramer, Samuel Noah. "The Epic of Gilgameš and Its Sumerian Sources: A Study in Literary Evolution." *JAOS* 64 (1944): 7–23, 83.

Kratz, Reinhard, and Mladen Popovic. "Editorial Note." *DSD* 20 (2013): 347–48.

Kugler, Robert. "Of Calendars, Community Rules, and Common Knowledge: Understanding 4QS^{e}–4QOtot, with Help from Ritual Studies." Pages 215–28 in *Rediscovering the Dead Sea Scrolls: An Assessment of Old and New Approaches and Methods*. Edited by Maxine L. Grossman. Grand Rapids: Eerdmans, 2010.

Kuhl, Curt. "Die 'Wiederaufnahme': Ein literarkritisches Prinzip?" *ZAW* 64 (1952): 1–11.

Kunstmann, Walter G. *Die babylonische Gebetsbeschwörung*. LSS NS 2. Leipzig: Hinrichs, 1932.

Kutsch, Ernst. "Die Textgliederung im hebräischen Ijobbuch sowie in 4QTgJob und in 11QTgJob." *BZ* 27 (1983): 221–28.

Læssøe, Jørgen. *Studies on the Assyrian Ritual and Series Bit Rimki*. Copenhagen: Munksgaard, 1955.

Lambert, W. G. *Babylonian Creation Myths*. MC 16. Winona Lake, IN: Eisenbrauns, 2013.

Lambert, W. G., and Alan R. Millard. *Atra-ḫasīs: The Babylonian Story of the Flood*. Oxford: Clarendon, 1969. Repr., Winona Lake, IN: Eisenbrauns, 1999.

Langlamet, François. "Les divisions massorétiques du livre de Samuel: À propos de la publication du Codex du Caire." *RB* 91 (1984): 481–519.

Leichty, Erle, Jacob J. Finkelstein, and Christopher B. F. Walker. *Catalogue of the Babylonian Tablets in the British Museum*. Vol. 8: *Tablets from Sippar 3*. London: British Museum Publications, 1988.

Lemmelijn, Bénédicte. "As Many Texts as Plagues: A Preliminary Report of the Main Results of the Text-Critical Evaluation of Exod 7:14–11:10." *JNSL* 24 (1998): 111–25.

———. "Flora in Cantico Canticorum: Towards a More Precise Characterisation of Translation Technique in the LXX of Song of Songs." Pages 27–51 in *Scripture in Transition: Essays on Septuagint, Hebrew Bible and Dead Sea Scrolls in Honour of Raija Sollamo*. Edited by Anssi Voitila and Jutta Jokiranta. JSJSup 126. Leiden: Brill, 2008.

———. "Free and Yet Faithful: On the Translation Technique of LXX Exod 7:14–11:10." *JNSL* 33 (2007): 1–32.

———. "Influence of a So-Called P-Redaction in the 'Major Expansions' of Exodus 7–11? Finding Oneself at the Crossroads of Textual and Literary Criticism." Pages 203–22 in *Textual Criticism and Dead Sea Scrolls Studies in Honour of Julio Trebolle Barrera: Florilegium Complutense*. Edited by Andrés Piquer Otero and Pablo A. Torijano Morales. JSJSup 157. Leiden: Brill, 2012.

———. *A Plague of Texts? A Text-Critical Study of the So-Called "Plague Narrative" in Exodus 7:14–11:10*. OtSt 56. Leiden: Brill, 2009.

———. "Setting and Function of Ex 11:1–10 in the Exodus Narrative." Pages 443–60 in *Studies in the Book of Exodus: Redaction, Reception, Interpretation*. Edited by Marc Vervenne. BETL 126. Leuven: Peeters, 1996.

———. "The So-Called 'Major Expansions' in SamP, 4QpaleoExod^{m} and 4QExod^{j} of Exod 7:14–11:10: On the Edge between Textual Criticism and Literary Criticism." Pages 429–39 in *X Congress of the International Organization for Septuagint and Cognate Studies, Oslo 1998*. Edited by Bernard A. Taylor. SCS 51. Atlanta: Society of Biblical Literature, 2001.

———. "The So-Called 'Priestly' Layer in Exod 7:14–11:10: 'Source' and/or/nor 'Redaction'?" *RB* 109 (2002): 481–511.

———. "Two Methodological Trails in Recent Studies on the Translation Technique of the Septuagint." Pages 43–63 in *Helsinki Perspectives on the Translation Technique of the Septuagint*. Edited by Raija Sollamo and Seppo Sipilä. PFES 82. Helsinki: The Finnish Exegetical Society; Göttingen: Vandenhoeck & Ruprecht, 2001.

———. "What Are We Looking for in Doing Text-Critical Research?" *JNSL* 23 (1997): 69–80.

Lenzi, Alan. "Assyriology and Biblical Interpretation." Pages 42–52 in *The Oxford Encyclopedia of Biblical Interpretation*. Edited by Steven L. McKenzie. New York: Oxford University Press, 2013.

———. "A New Akkadian Shuila-Prayer to the Three Paths of Heaven and the Third Tablet of *Bīt salā' mê*." *Or* NS 82 (2013): 1–10. http://cdli.ucla.edu/P453575.

———. "A Shuilla: Gula 1a." Pages 243–56 in *Reading Akkadian Prayers and Hymns: An Introduction*. Edited by Alan Lenzi. ANEM 3. Atlanta: Society of Biblical Literature, 2011.

———. "A Shuilla: Sin 1." Pages 385–402 in *Reading Akkadian Prayers and Hymns: An Introduction*. Edited by Alan Lenzi. ANEM 3. Atlanta: Society of Biblical Literature, 2011.

Lenzi, Alan, Christopher Frechette, and Anna Elise Zernecke. "Introduction." Pages 1–68 in *Reading Akkadian Prayers and Hymns: An Introduction*. Edited by Alan Lenzi. ANEM 3. Atlanta: Society of Biblical Literature, 2011.

Levin, Christoph. "Das vorstaatliche Israel." *ZTK* 97 (2000): 385–403.

Levine, Baruch A. "More on the Inverted *Nuns* of Num. 10:35–36." *JBL* 95 (1976): 122–24.

———. *Numbers 1–20*. AB 4A. New York: Doubleday, 1993.

———. *Numbers 21–36*. AB 4B. New York: Doubleday, 2000.

Lieberman, Stephen J. "Canonical and Official Cuneiform Texts: Towards an Understanding of Assurbanipal's Personal Tablet Collection." Pages 305–36 in *Lingering Over Words: Studies in Ancient Near Eastern Literature in Honor of William L. Moran*. Edited by Tzvi Abusch, John Huehnergard, and Piotr Steinkeller. HSM 37. Atlanta: Scholars Press, 1990.

Lilly, Ingrid I. *Two Books of Ezekiel: Papyrus 967 and the Masoretic Text as Variant Literary Editions*. VTSup 150. Leiden: Brill, 2012.

Lim, Timothy H., and John J. Collins, eds. *The Oxford Handbook of the Dead Sea Scrolls*. OHRT. Oxford: Oxford University Press, 2012.

Lionarons, Joyce Tally. "Textual Appropriation and Scribal (Re)Performance in a Composite Homily: The Case for a New Edition of Wulfstan's *De Temporibus Anticristi*." Pages 67–94 in *Old English Literature in Its Manuscript Context*. Edited by Joyce Tally Lionarons. MES 5. Morgantown: West Virginia University Press, 2004.

Liverani, Mario. "Critique of Variants and the Titulary of Sennacherib." Pages 225–57 in *Assyrian Royal Inscriptions: New Horizons*. Edited by Frederick Mario Fales. OAC 17. Rome: Istituto per l'Oriente, 1981.

Lloyd, Seton, and Nuri Gokçe. "Sultantepe: Anglo-Turkish Joint Excavations, 1952." *AnSt* 3 (1953): 27–47.

Lloyd Jones, G. Review of *Empirical Models for Biblical Criticism*, edited by Jeffrey H. Tigay. *ExpTim* 98 (1986): 25.

Lord, Albert B. *Singer of Tales*. HSCL 24. Cambridge: Harvard University Press, 1960.

Loretz, Oswald, and Werner R. Mayer. *Šu-ila-Gebete: Supplement zu L. W. King; Babylonian Magic and Sorcery*. AOAT 34. Kevelaer: Butzon & Bercker; Neukirchen-Vluyn: Neukirchener, 1978.

Luraghi, Silvia, and Vit Bubenik, eds. *Continuum Companion to Historical Linguistics*. London: Continuum, 2010.

Lust, Johan. "Ezekiel 36–40 in the Oldest Greek Manuscript." *CBQ* 43 (1981): 517–33.

———. "Major Divergences between LXX and MT in Ezekiel." Pages 83–92 in *The Earliest Text of the Hebrew Bible: The Relationship between the Masoretic Text and the Hebrew Base of the Septuagint Reconsidered*. Edited by Adrian Schenker. SCS 52. Atlanta: Society of Biblical Literature, 2003.

———. "The Septuagint Version of Daniel 4–5." Pages 39–53 in *The Book of Daniel: In the Light of New Findings*. Edited by Adam S. van der Woude. BETL 106. Leuven: Peeters, 1993.

———. "The Story of David and Goliath in Hebrew and Greek." Pages 5–18 in *The Story of David and Goliath: Textual and Literary Criticism*. Edited by Dominique Barthélemy. OBO 73. Fribourg: Editions Universitaires; Göttingen: Vandenhoeck & Ruprecht, 1986.

———. "The Use of Textual Witnesses for the Establishment of the Text: The Shorter and Longer Texts of Ezekiel; An Example: Ez 7." Pages 7–20 in *Ezekiel and His Book: Textual and Literary Criticism and Their Interrelation*. Edited by Johan Lust. BETL 74. Leuven: Peeters, 1986.

Magness, Jodi. *The Archaeology of Qumran and the Dead Sea Scrolls*. SDSS. Grand Rapids: Eerdmans, 2002.

———. "Qumran, The Site of the Dead Sea Scrolls: A Review Article." *RevQ* 22 (2006): 641–64.

Matera, Frank J. *What Are They Saying About Mark?* New York: Paulist, 1987.

Matouš, Lubor. "Les rapports entre la version sumérienne et la version akkadienne de l'epopée de Gilgameš." Pages 83–94 in *Gilgameš et sa légende*. Edited by Paul Garelli. CRRAI 7. CahTD 1. Paris: Klincksieck, 1960.

Maul, Stefan M. "Die Tontafelbibliothek aus den sogenannten 'Haus des Beschwörungspriesters.'" Pages 189–228 in *Assur-Forschungen: Arbeiten aus der Forschungsstelle "Edition literarischer Keilschrifttexte aus Assur" der Heidelberger Akademie der Wissenschaften*. Edited by Stefan M. Maul and Nils P. Heeßel. Wiesbaden: Harrassowitz, 2010.

———. *Zukunftsbewältigung: Eine Untersuchung altorientalischen Denkens anhand der babylonish-assyrisches Löserituale (Namburbi)*. BaF 18. Mainz: von Zabern, 1994.

Maul, Stefan M., Rita Strauß, and Daniel Schwemer. *Ritualbeschreibungen und Gebete I*. WVDOG 133. KAL 4. Wiesbaden: Harrassowitz, 2011.

Mayer, Werner R. "Sechs Šu-ila-Gebete." *Or* NS 59 (1990): 449–90.

———. *Untersuchungen zur Formensprache der babylonischen "Gebetsbeschwörungen."* StPohl Series Maior 5. Rome: Pontifical Biblical Institute, 1976.

McCarter, P. Kyle, Jr. *I Samuel: A New Translation With Introduction, Notes and Commentary*. AB 8. Garden City, NY: Doubleday, 1980.

———. *II Samuel: A New Translation with Introduction, Notes, and Commentary*. AB 9. Garden City, NY: Doubleday, 1984.

McGregor, Leslie John. *The Greek Text of Ezekiel: An Examination of Its Homogeneity*. SCS 18. Atlanta: Scholars Press, 1986.

McKane, William. *A Critical and Exegetical Commentary on Jeremiah*. Vol. 1: *Introduction and Commentary on Jeremiah I–XXV*. ICC. Edinburgh: T&T Clark, 1986.

———. *A Critical and Exegetical Commentary on Jeremiah*. Vol. 2: *Commentary on Jeremiah XXVI–LII*. ICC. Edinburgh: T&T Clark, 1996.

McKenzie, Steven L. "The Chronicler as Redactor." Pages 70–90 in *The Chronicler as Author: Studies in Text and Texture*. Edited by M. Patrick Graham and Steven L. McKenzie. JSOTSup 263. Sheffield: Sheffield Academic, 1999.

———. "Why Didn't David Build the Temple? The History of a Biblical Tradition." Pages 204–24 in *Worship and the Hebrew Bible: Essays in Honour of John T. Willis*. Edited by M. Patrick Graham, Rick R. Marrs, and Steven L. McKenzie. JSOTSup 284. Sheffield: Sheffield Academic, 1999.

McLay, R. Timothy. "Daniel." Pages 991–1022 in *A New English Translation of the Septuagint*. Edited by Albert Pietersma and Benjamin G. Wright. Oxford: Oxford University Press, 2007.

———. *The OG and Th Versions of Daniel*. SCS 43. Atlanta: Scholars Press, 1996.

———. "Old Greek Translation of Daniel IV–VI and the Formation of the Book of Daniel." *VT* 55 (2005): 304–23.

Meadowcroft, Timothy J. *Aramaic Daniel and Greek Daniel: A Literary Comparison*. JSOTSup 198. Sheffield: Sheffield Academic, 1995.

Meer, Michaël N. van der. *Formation and Reformulation: The Redaction of the Book of Joshua in the Light of the Oldest Textual Witnesses*. VTSup 102. Leiden: Brill, 2004.

Metso, Sarianna. "Methodological Problems in Reconstructing History from Rule Texts Found at Qumran." *DSD* 11 (2004): 315–35.

———. *The Serekh Texts*. CQS 9. LSTS 62. New York: T&T Clark, 2007.

———. *The Textual Development of the Qumran Community Rule*. STDJ 21. Leiden: Brill, 1997.

———. "When the Evidence Does Not Fit: Method, Theory, and the Dead Sea Scrolls." Pages 11–25 in *Rediscovering the Dead Sea Scrolls: An Assessment of Old and New Approaches and Methods*. Edited by Maxine L. Grossman. Grand Rapids: Eerdmans, 2010.

Milik, Józef T. "Annexes à la Règle de la Communauté (1QS)." Page 107 in *Qumran Cave 1*. Edited by Dominique Barthélemy and Józef T. Milik. DJD 1. Oxford: Clarendon, 1955.

Milstein, Sara J. "Reworking Ancient Texts: Revision through Introduction in Biblical and Mesopotamian Literature." PhD diss., New York University, 2010.

———. *Tracking the Master Scribe: Revision through Introduction in Biblical and Mesopotamian Literature*. New York: Oxford University Press, 2016.

Montgomery, James A. *A Critical and Exegetical Commentary on the Book of Daniel*. ICC. Edinburgh: T&T Clark, 1927.

Moore, George Foot. "Tatian's Diatessaron and the Analysis of the Pentateuch." *JBL* 9 (1890): 201–15.

Mroczek, Eva. "Thinking Digitally about the Dead Sea Scrolls: Book History Before and Beyond the Book." *BH* 14 (2011): 241–69.

Müller, Reinhard, and Juha Pakkala, eds. *Insights into Editing in the Hebrew Bible and the Ancient Near East: What Does Documented Evidence Tell Us about the Transmission of Authoritative Texts?* CBET 84. Leuven: Peeters, forthcoming.

Müller, Reinhard, Juha Pakkala, and Bas ter Haar Romeny. *Evidence of Editing: Growth and Change of Texts in the Hebrew Bible.* RBS 75. Atlanta: Society of Biblical Literature, 2014.

Munnich, Olivier. "Texte massorétique et Septante dans le livre de Daniel." Pages 93–120 in *The Earliest Text of the Hebrew Bible: The Relationship between the Masoretic Text and the Hebrew Base of the Septuagint Reconsidered.* Edited by Adrian Schenker. SCS 52. Atlanta: Society of Biblical Literature, 2003.

Nagy, Gregory. *The Best of the Achaeans: Concepts of the Hero in Archaic Greek Poetry*. Rev. ed. Baltimore: Johns Hopkins University Press, 1999.

———. *Homer: The Classic.* Hellenic Studies 36. Washington, DC: Center for Hellenic Studies, 2009.

———. *Homer: The Preclassic.* SCL 67. Berkeley: University of California Press, 2010.

Nestle, Eberhard, and Kurt Aland, eds. *Novum Testamentum Graece.* 27th ed. Stuttgart: Deutsche Bibelgesellschaft, 1993.

Neumann, Siegfried. "The Brothers Grimm as Collectors and Editors of German Folktales." Pages 24–40 in *The Reception of Grimms' Fairy Tales: Responses, Reactions, Revisions.* Edited by Donald Haase. Detroit: Wayne State University Press, 1993.

Niditch, Susan. *Oral World and Written Word: Ancient Israelite Literature.* LAI. Louisville: Westminster John Knox, 1996.

Nihan, Christophe. "La mort de Moïse (Nb 20,1–13; 20,22–29; 27,12–23) et l'édition finale du livre des Nombres." Pages 145–82 in *Les dernières rédactions du Pentateuque, de l'Hexateuque et de l'Ennéateuque.* Edited by Thomas Römer and Konrad Schmid. BETL 203. Leuven: Peeters, 2007.

Noth, Martin. *The Deuteronomistic History.* Translated by David J. A. Clines. JSOTSup 15. Sheffield: JSOT Press, 1981.

———. *Überlieferungsgeschichte des Pentateuchs.* 2nd ed. Stuttgart: Kohlhammer, 1948.

O'Connell, Kevin G. *The Theodotionic Revision of the Book of Exodus: A Contribution to the Study of the Early History of the Transmission of the Old Testament in Greek*. HSM 3. Cambridge: Harvard University Press, 1972.

Oesch, Josef M. *Petucha und Setuma: Untersuchungen zu einer überlieferten Gliederung im hebräischen Text des Alten Testaments*. OBO 27. Fribourg: Editions Universitaires; Göttingen: Vandenhoeck & Ruprecht, 1979.

———. "Textgliederung im Alten Testament und in den Qumranhandschriften." *Henoch* 5 (1983): 289–321.

O'Hare, Daniel M. *"Have You Seen, Son of Man?" A Study in the Translation and Vorlage of LXX Ezekiel 40–48*. SCS 57. Atlanta: Society of Biblical Literature, 2010.

O'Keeffe, Katherine O'Brien. *Visible Song: Transitional Literacy in Old English Verse*. CSASE 4. Cambridge: Cambridge University Press, 1990.

Orlinsky, Harry M. "The Hebrew *Vorlage* of the Septuagint of the Book of Joshua." Pages 187–95 in *Congress Volume: Rome, 1968*. Edited by John A. Emerton. VTSup 17. Leiden: Brill, 1969.

Pakkala, Juha. "Gedaliah's Murder in 2 Kings 25:25 and Jeremiah 41:1–3." Pages 401–11 in *Scripture in Transition: Essays on Septuagint, Hebrew Bible, and Dead Sea Scrolls in Honour of Raija Sollamo*. Edited by Anssi Voitila and Jutta Jokiranta. JSJSup 126. Leiden: Brill, 2008.

———. *God's Word Omitted: Omissions in the Transmission of the Hebrew Bible*. FRLANT 251. Göttingen: Vandenhoeck & Ruprecht, 2013.

Parke-Taylor, Geoffrey H. *The Formation of the Book of Jeremiah: Doublets and Recurring Phrases*. SBLMS 51. Atlanta: Society of Biblical Literature, 2000.

Parpola, Simo. "Assyrian Library Records." *JNES* 42 (1983): 1–29.

———. *Letters from Assyrian and Babylonian Scholars*. SAA 10. Helsinki: Helsinki University Press, 1993.

Parunak, Henry Van Dyke. "Oral Typesetting: Some Uses of Biblical Structure." *Bib* 62 (1981): 153–68.

Pedersén, Olof. *Archives and Libraries in the Ancient Near East: 1500–300 B.C.* Bethesda, MD: CDL, 1998.

———. *Archives and Libraries in the City of Assur: A Survey of the Material from the German Excavations*. Vol. 1. SSU 6. Uppsala: Acta Universitatis Upsaliensis, 1986.

Perrin, Nicholas. "The Limits of a Reconstructed Q." Pages 71–88 in *Questioning Q: A Multidimensional Critique*. Edited by Mark S. Goodacre and Nicholas Perrin. Downers Grove, IL: InterVarsity Press, 2004.

Perrot, Charles. "*Petuhot* et *Setumot*: Étude sur les alinéas du Pentateuque." *RB* 76 (1969): 50–91.

Person, Raymond F., Jr. "II Kings 24,18–25,30 and Jeremiah 52: A Text-Critical Case Study in the Redaction History of the Deuteronomistic History." *ZAW* 105 (1993): 174–205.

———. "Biblical Historiography as Traditional History." Pages 73–83 in *Oxford Handbook of Biblical Narrative*. Edited by Danna Fewell. Oxford: Oxford University Press, 2016.

———. *The Deuteronomic History and the Book of Chronicles: Scribal Works in an Oral World*. AIL 6. Atlanta: Society of Biblical Literature, 2010.

———. *The Deuteronomic School: History, Social Setting, and Literature*. SBLStBL 2. Atlanta: Society of Biblical Literature, 2002.

———. *From Conversation to Oral Tradition: A Simplest Systematics for Oral Traditions*. RSRS 10. London: Taylor & Francis, 2016.

———. *In Conversation with Jonah: Conversation Analysis, Literary Criticism, and the Book of Jonah*. JSOTSup 220. Sheffield: Sheffield Academic, 1996.

———. *The Kings–Isaiah and Kings–Jeremiah Recensions*. BZAW 252. Berlin: de Gruyter, 1997.

———. "Orality Studies, Oral Tradition: Hebrew Bible." Pages 55–63 in vol. 2 of *The Encyclopedia of Biblical Interpretation*. Edited by Steven L. McKenzie. 2 vols. Oxford: Oxford University Press, 2013.

———. "A Reassessment of Wiederaufnahme from the Perspective of Conversation Analysis." *BZ* 43 (1999): 241–48.

———. *Second Zechariah and the Deuteronomic School*. JSOTSup 167. Sheffield: JSOT Press, 1993.

———. "Text Criticism as a Lens for Understanding the Transmission of Ancient Texts in Their Oral Environments." Pages 197–215 in *Contextualizing Israel's Sacred Writings: Ancient Literacy, Orality, and Literary Production*. Edited by Brian B. Schmidt. AIL 22. Atlanta: SBL Press, 2015.

Person, Raymond F., Jr., and Chris Keith. "Introduction." In *The Dictionary of the Bible and Ancient Media*. Edited by Tom Thatcher, Chris Keith, Raymond F. Person Jr., and Elsie Stern. London: Bloomsbury, forthcoming.

Pfann, Stephen J. "Cryptic Texts." Pages 515–74 in *Qumran Cave 4:XXVI: Cryptic Texts and Miscellanea Part 1*. Edited by Stephen J. Pfann, Philip S. Alexander, James C. VanderKam, Monica Brady, and Frank M. Cross. DJD 36. Oxford: Clarendon, 2000.

Pinault, David. *Story-Telling Techniques in the Arabian Nights*. SAL 15. Leiden: Brill, 1992.

Polzin, Robert. *Samuel and the Deuteronomist: A Literary Study of the Deuteronomic History*. Vol. 2: *1 Samuel*. ISBL. Bloomington: Indiana University Press, 1993.

Pryke, E. J. *Redactional Style in the Marcan Gospel: A Study of Syntax and Vocabulary as Guides to Redaction in Mark*. SNTSMS 33. Cambridge: Cambridge University Press, 1978.

Puech, Émile, ed., *Qumrân Grotte 4:XVIII: Textes hébreux (4Q521–4Q528, 4Q576–4Q579)*. DJD 25. Oxford: Clarendon, 1998.

Qimron, Elisha, and James H. Charlesworth. "Rule of the Community (1QS)." Pages 1–107 in *The Dead Sea Scrolls: Hebrew, Aramaic, and Greek Texts with English Translations*. Vol. 1: *Rule of the Community and Related Documents*. Edited by James H. Charlesworth. PTSDSSP. Louisville: Westminster John Knox; Tübingen: Mohr Siebeck, 1994.

Quant, John F. "Rewriting Scripture Inside and Out: A Typology of Rewriting in Variant Editions and Rewritten Scripture." PhD diss., Emory University, 2014.

Radner, Karen. *The Prosopography of the Neo-Assyrian Empire*. Vol. 1.1A. Helsinki: Neo-Assyrian Text Corpus Project, 1998.

Reade, Julian E. "Archaeology and the Kuyunjik Archives." Pages 213–22 in *Cuneiform Archives and Libraries: Papers Read at the 30e Rencontre Assyriologique Internationale, Leiden, 4–8 July, 1983*. Edited by Klaas R. Veenhof. PIHANS 57. Leiden: Nederlands Instituut voor het Nabije Oosten, 1986.

———. "Ninive (Nineveh)." *RlA* 9:388–433.

Regev, Eyal. *Sectarianism in Qumran: A Cross-Cultural Perspective*. RelSoc 45. Berlin: de Gruyter, 2007.

Rezetko, Robert. "Dating Biblical Hebrew: Evidence from Samuel–Kings and Chronicles." Pages 215–50 in *Biblical Hebrew: Studies in Chronology and Typology*. Edited by Ian Young. JSOTSup 369. London: T&T Clark, 2003.

———. "David over Saul in MT 2 Samuel 6,1–5: An Exercise in Textual and Literary Criticism." Pages 255–71 in *For and Against David: Story and History in the Books of Samuel*. Edited by A. Graeme Auld and Erik Eynikel. BETL 232. Leuven: Peeters, 2010.

———. "Diachrony in Biblical Hebrew: Review of an Approach from the Perspective of Paraleipomenon." *HS* 52 (2011): 397–409.

———. "'Late' Common Nouns in the Book of Chronicles." Pages 379–417 in *Reflection and Refraction: Studies in Biblical Historiography in Honour of A. Graeme Auld*. Edited by Robert Rezetko, Timothy H. Lim, and W. Brian Aucker. VTSup 113. Leiden: Brill, 2007.

———. "The Qumran Scrolls of the Book of Judges: Literary Formation, Textual Criticism, and Historical Linguistics." *JHS* 13 (2013): 1–68.

———. *Source and Revision in the Narratives of David's Transfer of the Ark: Text, Language, and Story in 2 Samuel 6 and 1 Chronicles 13, 15–16*. LHBOTS 470. New York: T&T Clark, 2007.

———. "The Spelling of 'Damascus' and the Linguistic Dating of Biblical Texts." *SJOT* 24 (2010): 110–28.

———. "What Happened to the Book of Samuel in the Persian Period and Beyond?" Pages 237–52 in *A Palimpsest: Rhetoric, Ideology, Stylistics and Language Relating to Persian Israel*. Edited by Ehud Ben Zvi, Diana V. Edelman, and Frank H. Polak. PHSC 5. Piscataway, NJ: Gorgias, 2009.

Rezetko, Robert, and Ian Young. *Historical Linguistics and Biblical Hebrew: Steps Toward an Integrated Approach*. ANEM 9. Atlanta: SBL Press, 2014.

"Rm 0096." Cuniform Digital Library Initiative. http://cdli.ucla.edu/P424619.

Robert, Ulysse, ed., *Heptateuchi partis posterioris versio latina antiquissima e Codice Lugdunensi*. Lyon: Rey, 1900.

Robinson, James M. *The Sayings Gospel Q: Collected Essays*. BETL 189. Leuven: Peeters, 2005.

Robson, Eleanor. "CAMS/Geography of Knowledge." University of Pennsylvania Museum of Archaeology and Anthropology. http://oracc.museum.upenn.edu/cams/gkab/.

———. "Reading the Libraries of Assyria and Babylonia." Pages 41–56 in *Ancient Libraries*. Edited by Jason König, Katerina Oikonomopoulou, and Greg Woolf. Cambridge: Cambridge University Press, 2013.

———. "The Tablet House: A Scribal School in Old Babylonian Nippur." *RA* 95 (2001): 39–66.

Rofé, Alexander. "The Acts of Nahash according to 4QSam[a]." *IEJ* 32 (1982): 129–33.

———. "The Battle of David and Goliath: Folklore, Theology, Eschatology." Pages 117–51 in *Judaic Perspectives on Ancient Israel*. Edited by Jacob Neusner, Baruch A. Levine, Ernest S. Frerichs, and Caroline McCracken-Flesher. Philadelphia: Fortress, 1987.

———. "The End of the Book of Joshua according to the Septuagint." *Henoch* 4 (1982): 17–36.

———. *Introduction to the Literature of the Hebrew Bible*. JBS 9. Jerusalem: Simor, 2009.

———. "Joshua 20: Historico-Literary Criticism Illustrated." Pages 131–47 in *Empirical Models for Biblical Criticism*. Edited by Jeffrey H. Tigay. Philadelphia: University of Pennsylvania Press, 1985.

———. "Studying the Biblical Text in the Light of Historico-Literary Criticism: The Reproach of the Prophet in Judg 6:7–10 and 4QJudg[a]." Pages 111–23 in vol. 1 of *The Dead Sea Scrolls in Context: Integrating the Dead Sea Scrolls in the Study of Ancient Texts, Languages, and Cultures*. Edited by Armin Lange, Emanuel Tov, and Matthias Weigold. 2 vols. VTSup 140. Leiden: Brill, 2011.

Rogerson, John W. Review of *Empirical Models for Biblical Criticism*, edited by Jeffrey H. Tigay. *JTS* 39 (1988): 532–35.

Römer, Thomas. "La construction du Pentateuque, de l'Hexateuque et de l'Ennéateuque: Investigations préliminaires sur la formation des grands ensembles littéraires de la Bible hébraïque." Pages 9–34 in *Les dernières rédactions du Pentateuque, de l'Hexateuque et de l'Ennéateuque*. Edited by Thomas Römer and Konrad Schmid. BETL 203. Leuven: Peeters, 2007.

Römer, Thomas, Jean-Daniel Macchi, and Christophe Nihan, eds. *Introduction à l'Ancien Testament*. 2nd ed. MdB 49. Geneva: Labor et Fides, 2009.

Rooker, Mark F. *Biblical Hebrew in Transition: The Language of the Book of Ezekiel*. JSOTSup 90. Sheffield: JSOT Press, 1990.

Rösel, Martin. *Übersetzung als Vollendung der Auslegung: Studien zur Genesis-Septuaginta*. BZAW 223. Berlin: de Gruyter, 1994.

Ryholt, Kim. "A New Version of the Introduction to the Teachings of 'Onch-Sheshonqy." Pages 113–40 in *A Miscellany of Demotic Texts and Studies*. Edited by Paul John Frandsen and Kim Ryholt. CP 3. CNIP 22. Copenhagen: University of Copenhagen, Museum Tusculanum Press, 2000.

———. *The Story of Petese, Son of Petetum and Seventy Other Good and Bad Stories (P. Petese)*. CP 4. CNIP 23. Copenhagen: University of Copenhagen, Museum Tusculanum Press, 1999.

Sadaqa, Abraham, and Ratzon Sadaqa. *Jewish and Samaritan Version of the Pentateuch: With Particular Stress on the Differences between Both Texts*. Tel Aviv: Mass, 1961–1965.

Saggs, Henry W. F. Review of *Empirical Models for Biblical Criticism*, edited by Jeffrey H. Tigay. *JSS* 32 (1987): 196–99.

Sanderson, Judith E. *An Exodus Scroll from Qumran: 4QpaleoExod*[m] *and the Samaritan Tradition*. HSS 30. Atlanta: Scholars Press, 1986.

Sasson, Jack M. "Prologues and Poets: On the Opening Lines of the Gilgamesh Epic." Pages 265–77 in *Beyond Hatti: A Tribute to Gary Beckman*. Edited by Billie Jean Collins and Piotr Michalowski. Atlanta: Lockwood, 2013.

Schäfer, Peter. "Tradition and Redaction in Hekhalot Literature." *JSJ* 14 (1983): 172–81.

Scheil, M. Vincent. *Une Saison de Fouilles à Sippar*. MIFAO 1. Le Caire: Imprimerie de Institut français archéologie orientale, 1902.

Schenker, Adrian. *Une Bible archétype? Les parallèles de Samuel–Rois et des Chroniques*. Edited by Michaël Langlois. L'Écriture de la Bible 3. Paris: Cerf, 2013.

———. "La rédaction longue du livre de Jérémie doit-elle être datée au temps des premiers Hasmonéens?" *ETL* 70 (1994): 281–93.

Schiffman, Lawrence H. "The Early History of Public Reading of the Torah." Pages 38–49 in *Jews, Christians, and Polytheists in the Ancient Synagogue: Cultural Interaction during the Greco-Roman Period*. Edited by Steven Fine. London: Routledge, 1999.

Schmid, Konrad. *The Old Testament: A Literary History*. Minneapolis: Fortress, 2012.

Schofield, Alison. *From Qumran to the Yaḥad: A New Paradigm of Textual Development for The Community Rule*. STDJ 77. Leiden: Brill, 2009.

Schorch, Stefan. "The Construction of Samari(t)an Identity from the Inside and from the Outside." Pages 135–50 in *Between Cooperation and Hostility: Multiple Identities in Ancient Judaism and the Interaction with Foreign Powers*. Edited by Rainer Albertz and Jakob Wöhrle. JAJSup 11. Göttingen: Vandenhoeck & Ruprecht, 2013.

———. "Gemeindeopfer oder Priesteropfer? Die späte Deuteronomisierung des samaritanischen Passaopfers." Pages 237–46 in *"Und das Leben ist siegreich!": Mandäische und samaritanische Literatur; Im Gedenken an Rudolf Macuch (1919–1993)*. Edited by Rainer Voigt. MF 1. Wiesbaden: Harrassowitz, 2008.

———. "The Septuagint and the Vocalization of the Hebrew Text of the Torah." Pages 41–54 in *XII Congress of the International Organization for Septuagint and Cognate Studies: Leiden, 2004*. Edited by Melvin K. H. Peters. SCS 54. Atlanta: Society of Biblical Literature, 2006.

——. *Die Vokale des Gesetzes: Die samaritanische Lesetradition als Textzeugin der Tora*. Vol. 1: *Das Buch Genesis*. BZAW 339. Berlin: de Gruyter, 2004.

——. "Which Bible, Whose Text? Biblical Theologies in Light of the Textual History of the Hebrew Bible." Pages 359–74 in *Beyond Biblical Theologies*. Edited by Heinrich Assel, Stefan Beyerle, and Christfried Böttrich. WUNT 295. Tübingen: Mohr Siebeck, 2012.

Seeligmann, Isac Leo. "Hebräische Erzählung und biblische Geschichtsschreibung." *TZ* 18 (1962): 305–25.

Segal, Michael. "4QReworked Pentateuch or 4QPentateuch?" Pages 391–99 in *The Dead Sea Scrolls: Fifty Years after Their Discovery: Proceedings of the Jerusalem Congress, July 20–25, 1997*. Edited by Lawrence H. Schiffman, Emanuel Tov, and James C. VanderKam. Jerusalem: Israel Exploration Society, 2000.

Seiler, Stefan. *Die Geschichte von der Thronfolge Davids (2 Sam 9–20; 1 Kön 1–2): Untersuchungen zur Literarkritik und Tendenz*. BZAW 267. Berlin: de Gruyter, 1998.

Shead, Andrew G. *The Open Book and the Sealed Book: Jeremiah 32 in Its Hebrew and Greek Recensions*. JSOTSup 347. HBV 3. London: Sheffield Academic, 2002.

Shenkel, James Donald. *Chronology and Recensional Development in the Greek Text of Kings*. HSM 1. Cambridge: Harvard University Press, 1968.

Skehan, Patrick W., Eugene Ulrich, and Judith E. Sanderson, eds., *Qumran Cave 4:IV: Palaeo-Hebrew and Greek Biblical Manuscripts*. DJD 9. Oxford: Clarendon, 1992.

Smend, Rudolf. *Die Entstehung des Alten Testaments*. 4th ed. Stuttgart: Kohlhammer, 1989.

——. "Das Gesetz und die Völker: Ein Beitrag zur deuteronomistischen Redaktionsgeschichte." Pages 494–509 in *Probleme biblischer Theologie: Festschrift für Gerhard von Rad zum 70. Geburtstag*. Edited by Hans Walter Wolff. Munich: Kaiser, 1971.

Smith, Colin J. "'With an Iron Pen and a Diamond Tip': Linguistic Peculiarities of the Book of Jeremiah." PhD diss., Cornell University, 2003.

Soggin, J. Alberto. *Judges: A Commentary*. OTL. Philadelphia: Westminster, 1981.

Soisalon-Soininen, Ilmari. *Ilmari Soisalon-Soininen: Studien zur Septuaginta-Syntax; zu seinem 70. Geburtstag am 4. Juni 1987*. Edited by

Anneli Aejmelaeus and Raija Sollamo. AASF Series B 237. Helsinki: Suomalainen Tiedeakatemia, 1987.

Sollamo, Raija. "The LXX Renderings of the Infinitive Absolute Used with a Paronymous Finite Verb in the Pentateuch." Pages 101–13 in *La Septuaginta en la investigación contemporanea: V Congreso de la IOSCS*. Edited by Natalio Fernández Marcos. TECC 34. Madrid: Instituto "Arias Montano," 1985.

———. *Renderings of Hebrew Semiprepositions in the Septuagint*. AASF Dissertationes Humanarum Litterarum 19. Helsinki: Suomalainen Tiedeakatemia, 1979.

Sommer, Benjamin D. *A Prophet Reads Scripture: Allusion in Isaiah 40–56*. Contraversions. Stanford, CA: Stanford University Press, 1998.

Stipp, Hermann-Josef. "Linguistic Peculiarities of the Masoretic Edition of the Book of Jeremiah: An Updated Index." *JNSL* 23 (1997): 181–202.

———. *Das masoretische und alexandrinische Sondergut des Jeremiabuches: Textgeschichtlicher Rang, Eigenarten, Triebkräfte*. OBO 136. Fribourg: Editions Universitaires; Göttingen: Vandenhoeck & Ruprecht, 1994.

———. "Zur aktuellen Diskussion um das Verhältnis der Textformen des Jeremiabuches." Pages 630–53 in *Die Septuaginta: Texte, Kontexte, Lebenswelten; Internationale Fachtagung veranstaltet von Septuaginta Deutsch (LXX.D), Wuppertal 20.–23. Juli 2006*. Edited by Martin Karrer and Wolfgang Kraus. WUNT 219. Tübingen: Mohr Siebeck, 2008.

Sweeney, Marvin A. "Introduction to Isaiah." Pages 974–77 in *The New Oxford Annotated Bible, with the Apocryphal/Deuterocanonical Books: New Revised Standard Version*. Edited by Michael D. Coogan, Marc Zvi Brettler, Carol A. Newsom, and Pheme Perkins. 3rd ed. New York: Oxford University Press, 2001.

———. "Jeremiah." in *Oxford Bibliographies Online: Biblical Studies*. http://www.oxfordbibliographies.com/view/document/obo-9780195393361/obo-9780195393361-0060.xml.

———. *The Prophetic Literature*. IBT. Nashville: Abingdon, 2005.

Tal, Abraham. *The Samaritan Pentateuch: Edited according to Ms 6(C) of the Shekhem Synagogue*. TSHLRS 8. Tel-Aviv: Tel Aviv University, 1994.

Talstra, Eep. "Deuteronomy 31: Confusion or Conclusion? The Story of Moses' Threefold Succession." Pages 87–110 in *Deuteronomy and Deuteronomic Literature: Festschrift C. H. W. Brekelmans*. Edited by Marc Vervenne and Johan Lust. BETL 133. Leuven: Peeters, 1997.

Telford, William R. *The Theology of the Gospel of Mark*. NTT. Cambridge: Cambridge University Press, 1999.

Teutsch, David A., ed. *Kol Haneshamah: Shabbat Vehagim*. Translated by Joel Rosenberg. Hebrew and English ed. Wyncote, PA: Reconstructionist Press, 1994.

Thackeray, Henry St. John. "The Greek Translators of the Four Books of Kings." *JTS* 8 (1907): 262–78.

Thomas, Christine M. "Stories Without Texts and Without Authors: The Problem of Fluidity in Ancient Novelistic Texts and Early Christian Literature." Pages 273–91 in *Ancient Fiction and Early Christian Narrative*. Edited by Ronald F. Hock, J. Bradley Chance, and Judith Perkins. SymS 6. Atlanta: Scholars Press, 1998.

Tigay, Jeffrey H. "Conflation as a Redactional Technique." Pages 53–95 in *Empirical Models for Biblical Criticism*. Edited by Jeffrey H. Tigay. Philadelphia: University of Pennsylvania Press, 1985.

———. "The Documentary Hypothesis, Empirical Models and Holistic Interpretation." Pages 116–43 in *Modernity and Interpretations of Ancient Texts: The Collapse and Remaking of Traditions*. Edited by Jun Ikeda. IIAS Reports 1102. Kyoto: International Institute of Advanced Studies, 2012.

———. "An Empirical Basis for the Documentary Hypothesis." *JBL* 94 (1975): 329–42.

———, ed. *Empirical Models for Biblical Criticism*. Philadelphia: University of Pennsylvania Press, 1985. Repr. with a new foreword by Richard Elliott Friedman. Eugene, OR: Wipf & Stock, 2005.

———. *The Evolution of the Gilgamesh Epic*. Philadelphia: University of Pennsylvania Press, 1982. Repr., Wauconda, IL: Bolchazy-Carducci, 2002.

———. "The Evolution of the Pentateuchal Narratives in the Light of the Evolution of the *Gilgamesh Epic*." Pages 21–52 in *Empirical Models for Biblical Criticism*. Edited by Jeffrey H. Tigay. Philadelphia: University of Pennsylvania Press, 1985.

———. "Introduction." Pages 1–20 in *Empirical Models for Biblical Criticism*. Edited by Jeffrey H. Tigay. Philadelphia: University of Pennsylvania Press, 1985.

———. "Preface and Acknowledgements." Pages xi–xii in *Empirical Models for Biblical Criticism*. Edited by Jeffrey H. Tigay. Philadelphia: University of Pennsylvania Press, 1985.

———. "The Samaritan Pentateuch as an Empirical Model for Biblical Criticism." *BM* 22 (1977): 348–61. [Hebrew]

———. "The Stylistic Criteria of Source-Criticism in the Light of Ancient Near Eastern Literature." Pages 67–91 in *Isac Leo Seeligmann Volume: Essays on the Bible and the Ancient World*. Vol. 3: *Non-Hebrew Section*. Edited by Alexander Rofé and Yair Zakovitch. Jerusalem: Rubinstein, 1983.

———. "The Stylistic Criterion of Source Criticism in the Light of Ancient Near Eastern and Postbiblical Literature." Pages 149–73 in *Empirical Models for Biblical Criticism*. Edited by Jeffrey H. Tigay. Philadelphia: University of Pennsylvania Press, 1985.

———. "Summary and Conclusions." Pages 239–41 in *Empirical Models for Biblical Criticism*. Edited by Jeffrey H. Tigay. Philadelphia: University of Pennsylvania Press, 1985.

Tinney, Steve. "On the Curricular Setting of Sumerian Literature." *Iraq* 59 (1999): 159–72.

Toorn, Karel van der. *Scribal Culture and the Making of the Hebrew Bible*. Cambridge: Harvard University Press, 2007.

Tov, Emanuel. "4QJer^{a-e}." Pages 145–207 in *Qumran Cave 4:X: The Prophets*. Edited by Eugene Ulrich, Frank M. Cross, Russell E. Fuller, Judith E. Sanderson, Patrick W. Skehan, and Emanuel Tov. DJD 15. Oxford: Clarendon, 1997.

———. "The Biblical Texts from the Judaean Desert: An Overview and Analysis of the Published Texts." Pages 139–66 in *The Bible as Book: The Hebrew Bible and the Judaean Desert Discoveries*. Edited by Edward D. Herbert and Emanuel Tov. London: The British Library; New Castle, DE: Oak Knoll, 2002.

———. "The Composition of 1 Samuel 16–18 in the Light of the Septuagint Version." Pages 97–130 in *Empirical Models for Biblical Criticism*. Edited by Jeffrey H. Tigay. Philadelphia: University of Pennsylvania Press, 1985.

———. "The Dead Sea Scrolls and the Textual History of the Masoretic Bible." Pages 41–53 in *The Hebrew Bible in Light of the Dead Sea Scrolls*. Edited by Nóra Dávid, Armin Lange, Kristin De Troyer, and Shani Tzoref. FRLANT 239. Göttingen: Vandenhoeck & Ruprecht, 2012.

———. "Did the Septuagint Translators Always Understand Their Hebrew Text." Pages 203–18 in *The Greek and Hebrew Bible: Collected Essays on the Septuagint*. VTSup 72. Leiden: Brill, 1999.

———. "Exegetical Notes on the Hebrew *Vorlage* of the LXX of Jeremiah 27 (34)." *ZAW* 91 (1979): 73–93.

———. *The Greek and Hebrew Bible: Collected Essays on the Septuagint*. VTSup 72. Leiden: Brill, 1999.

———. "The Growth of the Book of Joshua in Light of the Evidence of the Septuagint." Pages 321–39 in *Studies in the Bible*. Edited by Sara Japhet. ScrHier 31. Jerusalem: Magnes, 1986.

———. "Interchanges of Consonants between the Masoretic Text and the *Vorlage* of the Septuagint." Pages 255–66 in *Sha'arei Talmon: Studies in the Bible, Qumran, and the Ancient Near East Presented to Shemaryahu Talmon*. Edited by Michael Fishbane and Emanuel Tov. Winona Lake, IN: Eisenbrauns, 1992.

———. "Introduction to 4QCant[a–c]." Pages 195–98 in *Qumran Cave 4:XI: Psalms to Chronicles*. Edited by Eugene Ulrich, Frank M. Cross, Joseph A. Fitzmyer, Peter W. Flint, Sarianna Metso, Catherine M. Murphy, Curt Niccum, Patrick W. Skehan, Emanuel Tov, and Julio Trebolle Barrera. DJD 16. Oxford: Clarendon, 2000.

———. "The Literary History of the Book of Jeremiah in the Light of Its Textual History." Pages 211–37 in *Empirical Models for Biblical Criticism*. Edited by Jeffrey H. Tigay. Philadelphia: University of Pennsylvania Press, 1985.

———. "The 'Lucianic' Text of the Canonical and the Apocryphal Sections of Esther: A Rewritten Biblical Book." *Text* 10 (1982): 1–25.

———. "The Nature and Background of Harmonizations in Biblical Manuscripts." *JSOT* 31 (1985): 3–29.

———. "The Nature of the Differences between MT and the LXX in 1 Sam. 17–18." Pages 19–46 in *The Story of David and Goliath: Textual and Literary Criticism*. Edited by Dominique Barthélemy. OBO 73. Fribourg: Editions Universitaires; Göttingen: Vandenhoeck & Ruprecht, 1986.

———. "Recensional Differences between the MT and the LXX of Ezekiel." *ETL* 62 (1986): 89–101.

———. *Scribal Practices and Approaches Reflected in the Texts Found in the Judean Desert*. STDJ 54. Leiden: Brill, 2004.

———. "Sense Divisions in the Qumran Texts, the Masoretic Text, and Ancient Translations of the Bible." Pages 121–46 in *The Interpretation of the Bible: The International Symposium in Slovenia*. Edited by Jože Krašovec. JSOTSup 289. Sheffield: Sheffield Academic, 1998.

———. *The Septuagint Translation of Jeremiah and Baruch: A Discussion of an Early Revision of the LXX of Jeremiah 29–52 and Baruch 1:1–3:8*. HSM 8. Missoula, MT: Scholars Press, 1976.

———. "Some Aspects of the Textual and Literary History of the Book of Jeremiah." Pages 145–67 in *Le livre de Jérémie: Le prophète et son milieu, les oracles et leur transmission*, ed. Pierre-Maurice Bogaert. BETL 54. Leuven: Peeters, 1981.

———. *The Text-Critical Use of the Septuagint in Biblical Research*. JBS 3. Jerusalem: Simor, 1981.

———. *Textual Criticism of the Hebrew Bible*. 3rd ed. Minneapolis: Fortress, 2012.

———. "Textual Harmonizations in the Ancient Texts of Deuteronomy." Pages 271–82 in *Hebrew Bible, Greek Bible, and Qumran: Collected Essays*. TSAJ 121. Tübingen: Mohr Siebeck, 2008.

Tov, Emanuel, and Sidnie A. White. "4QRP[b] (4Q364)." Pages 197–254 in *Qumran Cave 4:VIII: Parabiblical Texts, Part 1*. Edited by Harold Attridge, Torleif Elgvin, Józef T. Milik, Saul Olyan, John Strugnell, Emanuel Tov, James C. VanderKam, and Sidnie A. White. DJD 13. Oxford: Clarendon, 1997.

———. "4QRP[c] (4Q365)." Pages 255–318 in *Qumran Cave 4:VIII: Parabiblical Texts, Part 1*. Edited by Harold Attridge, Torleif Elgvin, Józef T. Milik, Saul Olyan, John Strugnell, Emanuel Tov, James C. VanderKam, and Sidnie A. White. DJD 13. Oxford: Clarendon, 1997.

Trebolle Barrera, Julio. "4QJudg[a]." Pages 161–64 in *Qumran Cave 4:IX: Deuteronomy, Joshua, Judges, Kings*. Edited by Eugene Ulrich, Frank M. Cross, Sidnie White Crawford, Julie Ann Duncan, Patrick W. Skehan, Emanuel Tov, and Julio Trebolle Barrera. DJD 14. Oxford: Clarendon, 1995.

———. *Centena in libros Samuelis et Regum: Variantes textuales y composición literaria en los libros de Samuel y Reyes*. TECC 47. Madrid: Consejo Superior de Investigaciones Científicas, 1989.

———. "El estudio de 4QSam[a]: Implicaciones exegéticas e históricas." *EstBib* 39 (1981): 5–18.

———. *The Jewish Bible and the Christian Bible: An Introduction to the History of the Bible*. Translated by Wilfred G. E. Watson. Leiden: Brill; Grand Rapids: Eerdmans, 1998.

———. "Redaction, Recension, and Midrash in the Books of Kings." *BIOSCS* 15 (1982): 12–35.

———. *Salomón y Jeroboán: Historia de la recensión y redacción de I Reyes 2–12, 14*. BSalmD 3. Salamanca: Universidad Pontificia, 1980.

———. "Samuel/Kings and Chronicles: Book Division and Text Composition." Pages 96–108 in *Studies in the Hebrew Bible, Qumran, and the Septuagint Presented to Eugene Ulrich*. Edited by Peter W. Flint, Emanuel Tov, and James C. VanderKam. VTSup 101. Leiden: Brill, 2006.

———. "Testamento y muerte de David: Estudio de historia de la recensión y redacción de 1 Reyes II." *RB* 87 (1980): 87–103.

———. "Textual and Literary Criticism on Passages Attested by 4QSam[a,b] (1 Sam 6:4–5 and 1 Sam 23:11–12)." Pages 70–83 in *The Hebrew Bible in Light of the Dead Sea Scrolls*. Edited by Nóra Dávid, Armin Lange, Kristin De Troyer, and Shani Tzoref. FRLANT 239. Göttingen: Vandenhoeck & Ruprecht, 2012.

———. "Textual Criticism and the Composition History of Samuel: Connections between Pericopes in 1 Samuel 1–4." Pages 261–86 in *Archaeology of the Books of Samuel: The Entangling of the Textual and Literary History*. Edited by Philippe Hugo and Adrian Schenker. VTSup 132. Leiden: Brill, 2010.

———. "Textual Criticism and the Literary Structure and Composition of 1–2 Kings/3–4 Reigns: The Different Sequence of Literary Units in MT and LXX." Pages 55–78 in *Die Septuaginta: Entstehung, Sprache, Geschichte; 3. Internationale Fachtagung veranstaltet von Septuaginta Deutsch (LXX.D), Wuppertal 22.–25. Juli 2010*. Edited by Siegfried Kreuzer, Martin Meiser, and Martin Sigismund. WUNT 286. Tübingen: Mohr Siebeck, 2012.

———. "Textual Variants in 4QJudg[a] and the Textual and Editorial History of the Book of Judges." *RevQ* 14 (1989): 229–45.

Tsedaka, Israel. *Samaritanische Tora*. Holon: A. B. Institute of Samaritan Studies, 1998.

Tuckett, Christopher M. *The Messianic Secret*. IRT 1. Philadelphia: Fortress, 1983.

———. *Q and the History of Early Christianity: Studies on Q*. Edinburgh: T&T Clark, 1996.

Uhlig, Siegbert. *Das äthiopische Henochbuch*. JSHRZ 5.6. Gütersloh: Mohn, 1984.

Ulrich, Eugene. "4QJosh[a]." Pages 143–52 in *Qumran Cave 4:IX: Deuteronomy, Joshua, Judges, Kings*. Edited by Eugene Ulrich, Frank M. Cross, Sidnie White Crawford, Julie Ann Duncan, Patrick W. Skehan,

Emanuel Tov, and Julio Trebolle Barrera. DJD 14. Oxford: Clarendon, 1995.

———. "Clearer Insight into the Development of the Bible: A Gift of the Scrolls." Pages 119–37 in *The Dead Sea Scrolls and Contemporary Culture: Proceedings of the International Conference Held at the Israel Museum, Jerusalem (July 6–8, 2008)*. Edited by Adolfo D. Roitman, Lawrence H. Schiffman, and Shani Tzoref. STDJ 93. Leiden: Brill, 2011.

———. *The Dead Sea Scrolls and the Origins of the Bible*. SDSS. Grand Rapids: Eerdmans, 1999.

———. "Deuteronomistically Inspired Scribal Insertions into the Developing Biblical Texts: 4QJudg[a] and 4QJer[a]." Pages 489–506 in *Houses Full of All Good Things: Essays in Memory of Timo Veijola*. Edited by Juha Pakkala and Martti Nissinen. PFES 95. Helsinki: Finnish Exegetical Society; Göttingen: Vandenhoeck & Ruprecht, 2008.

———. "Impressions and Intuition: Sense Divisions in Ancient Manuscripts of Isaiah." Pages 279–307 in *Unit Delimitation in Biblical Hebrew and Northwest Semitic Literature*. Edited by Marjo C. A. Korpel and Josef M. Oesch. Pericope 4. Assen: Van Gorcum, 2003.

———. "Methodological Reflections on Determining Scriptural Status in First Century Judaism." Pages 145–61 in *Rediscovering the Dead Sea Scrolls: An Assessment of Old and New Approaches and Methods*. Edited by Maxine L. Grossman. Grand Rapids: Eerdmans, 2010.

———. "The Old Latin, Mount Gerizim, and 4QJosh[a]." Pages 361–75 in *Textual Criticism and Dead Sea Scrolls Studies in Honour of Julio Trebolle Barrera: Florilegium Complutense*. Edited by Andrés Piquer Otero and Pablo A. Torijano Morales. JSJSup 157. Leiden: Brill, 2012.

———. "The Old Latin Translation of the LXX and the Hebrew Scrolls from Qumran." Pages 121–65 in *The Hebrew and Greek Texts of Samuel, 1980 Proceedings IOSCS—Vienna*. Edited by Emanuel Tov. Jerusalem: Academon, 1980.

———. "The Parallel Editions of the Old Greek and Masoretic Text of Daniel 5." Pages 201–17 in vol. 1 of *A Teacher for All Generations: Essays in Honor of James C. VanderKam*. Edited by Eric F. Mason, Samuel I. Thomas, Alison Schofield, and Eugene Ulrich. 2 vols. JSJSup 153. Leiden: Brill, 2012.

———. *The Qumran Text of Samuel and Josephus*. HSM 19. Missoula, MT: Scholars Press, 1978.

———. "The Text of Daniel in the Qumran Scrolls." Pages 573–85 in volume 2 of *The Book of Daniel: Composition and Reception*. Edited by John J. Collins and Peter W. Flint. 2 vols. VTSup 83. Leiden: Brill, 2001.

———. "The Text of the Hebrew Scriptures at the Time of Hillel and Jesus." Pages 85–108 in *Congress Volume: Basel 2001*. Edited by André Lemaire. VTSup 92. Leiden: Brill, 2002.

Ulrich, Eugene, and Frank M. Cross, eds. *Qumran Cave 4:VII: Genesis to Numbers*. DJD 12. Oxford: Clarendon, 1994.

Van De Mieroop, Marc. *Cuneiform Texts and the Writing of History*. London: Routledge, 1999.

VanderKam, James C. *Calendars in the Dead Sea Scrolls: Measuring Time*. LDSS. London: Routledge, 1998.

———. *The Dead Sea Scrolls and the Bible*. Grand Rapids: Eerdmans, 2012.

———. *The Dead Sea Scrolls Today*. 2nd ed. Grand Rapids: Eerdmans, 2010.

Vattioni, Francesco. "Osservazioni ai papiri greci del Cantico dei Cantici." *SPap* 17 (1978): 89–95.

Veijola, Timo. *Das Königtum in der Beurteilung der deuteronomistischen Historiographie: Eine redaktionsgeschichtliche Untersuchung*. AASF Series B 198. Helsinki: Suomalainen Tiedeakatemia, 1977.

Veldhuis, Niek. "Elementary Education at Nippur: The Lists of Trees and Wooden Objects." PhD diss., Rijksuniversiteit Groningen, 1997.

Verbeke, Elke. "Hebrew Hapax Legomena and Their Greek Rendering in LXX Job." PhD diss., Katholieke Universiteit Leuven, 2011.

———. "The Use of Hebrew Hapax Legomena in Septuagint Studies: Preliminary Remarks on Methodology." Pages 507–21 in *Florilegium Lovaniense: Studies in Septuagint and Textual Criticism in Honour of Florentino García Martínez*. Edited by Hans Ausloos, Bénédicte Lemmelijn, and Marc Vervenne. BETL 224. Leuven: Peeters, 2008.

Vermes, Géza. "The History of the Community." Pages 49–66 in *The Complete Dead Sea Scrolls in English*. New York: Penguin, 1997.

Vermes, Géza, and Martin Goodman, eds. *The Essenes according to the Classical Sources*. OCTb 1. Sheffield: JSOT Press, 1989.

Vervenne, Marc. "Current Tendencies and Developments in the Study of the Book of Exodus." Pages 21–59 in *Studies in the Book of Exodus: Redaction, Reception, Interpretation*. Edited by Marc Vervenne. BETL 126. Leuven: Peeters, 1996.

———. "Tekst en teksten." Pages 25–39 in *Inleiding in het Oude Testament*. Edited by Henk Jagersma and Marc Vervenne. Kampen: Kok, 1992.

Vogelzang, Marianna E. *Bin Šar Dadmē: Edition and Analysis of the Akkadian Anzu Poem*. Groningen: Styx Publications, 1988.

———. "Repetition as a Poetic Device in Akkadian." Pages 167–82 in *Mesopotamian Poetic Language: Sumerian and Akkadian*. Edited by Marianna E. Vogelzang and Herman L. J. Vanstiphout. CM 6. Groningen: Styx Publications, 1996.

Wade, Martha Lynn. *Consistency of Translation Techniques in the Tabernacle Accounts of Exodus in the Old Greek*. SCS 49. Atlanta: Society of Biblical Literature, 2003.

Wahlde, Urban C. von. "Wiederaufnahme as a Marker of Redaction in Jn 6,51–58." *Bib* 64 (1983): 542–49.

Walker, Christopher B. F. "The Kouyunjik Collection of Cuneiform Texts: Formation, Problems, and Prospects." Pages 183–93 in *Austen Henry Layard tra l'Oriente e Venezia: Symposium Internazionale, Venezia, 26–28 Ottobre 1983*. Edited by Frederick Mario Fales and Bernard J. Hickey. La Fenice 8. Rome: "L'Erma" di Bretschneider, 1987.

Walters, Stanley D. "Hannah and Anna: The Greek and Hebrew Texts of 1 Samuel 1." *JBL* 107 (1988): 385–412.

Weaks, Joseph Allen. "Mark without Mark: Problematizing the Reliability of a Reconstructed Text of Q." PhD diss., Brite Divinity School, 2010.

Wenthe, Dean O. "The Old Greek Translation of Daniel 1–6." PhD diss., University of Notre Dame, 1991.

West, Martin L. *Textual Criticism and Editorial Technique: Applicable to Greek and Latin Texts*. Teubner Studienbücher: Philologie. Stuttgart: Teubner, 1973.

Westermann, Claus. *Genesis*. BKAT 1. Neukirchen-Vluyn: Neukirchener Verlag, 1982.

Wevers, John William. *Notes on the Greek Text of Exodus*. SCS 30. Atlanta: Scholars Press, 1990.

———. *Notes on the Greek Text of Genesis*. SCS 35. Atlanta: Scholars Press, 1993.

———, ed. *Septuaginta: Vetus Testamentum Graecum*. Vol. 2.1: *Exodus*. SVTG. Göttingen: Vandenhoeck & Ruprecht, 1991.

Wiener, Harold M. *The Composition of Judges II 11 to I Kings II 46*. Leipzig: Heinrichs, 1929.

Woods, Christopher. "Bilingualism, Scribal Learning, and the Death of Sumerian." Pages 91–120 in *Margins of Writing, Origins of Cultures*. Edited by Seth L. Sanders. OIS 2. Chicago: Oriental Institute of the University of Chicago, 2006.

Würthwein, Ernst. *Die Bücher der Könige, 1. Könige 1–16*. ATD 11.1. Göttingen: Vandenhoeck & Ruprecht, 1977.

———. *Die Bücher der Könige, 1. Kön. 17—2. Kön. 25*. ATD 11.2. Göttingen: Vandenhoeck & Ruprecht, 1984.

Yarbro Collins, Adela. *Mark: A Commentary*. Hermeneia. Minneapolis: Fortress, 2007.

Yardeni, Ada. *Understanding the Alphabet of the Dead Sea Scrolls: Development, Chronology, Dating*. Jerusalem: Carta, 2015.

Young, Ian, Robert Rezetko, and Martin Ehrensvärd. *Linguistic Dating of Biblical Texts*. 2 vols. BibleWorld. London: Equinox, 2008.

Zahn, Molly M. *Rethinking Rewritten Scripture: Composition and Exegesis in the 4QReworked Pentateuch Manuscripts*. STDJ 95. Leiden: Brill, 2011.

Zakovitch, Yair. "Assimilation in Biblical Narratives." Pages 175–96 in *Empirical Models for Biblical Criticism*. Edited by Jeffrey H. Tigay. Philadelphia: University of Philadelphia Press, 1985.

Zevit, Ziony. Review of *Biblical Hebrew: Studies in Chronology and Typology*, by Ian Young, ed. *RBL* 8 (2004): 1–15.

Ziegler, Joseph, ed. *Septuaginta: Vetus Testamentum Graecum*. Vol. 15: *Ieremias, Baruch, Threni, Epistula Ieremiae*. SVTG. Göttingen: Vandenhoeck & Ruprecht, 1957.

Ziegler, Joseph, and Olivier Munnich, eds., *Septuaginta: Vetus Testamentum Graecum*. Vol. 16.2: *Susanna, Daniel, Bel et Draco*. 2nd ed. SVTG. Göttingen: Vandenhoeck & Ruprecht, 1999.

Zimmern, Heinrich. *Beiträge zur Kenntnis der Babylonischen Religion*. AB 12. Leipzig: Hinrichs, 1901.

Contributors

Maxine L. Grossman is Associate Professor of Jewish Studies and Religious Studies in the Joseph and Rebecca Meyerhoff Center for Jewish Studies at the University of Maryland (College Park, Maryland). Her areas of research include the Dead Sea Scrolls and Second Temple Judaism, methods and theories in the study of religion, and gender studies. She is the author of *Reading for History in the Damascus Document: A Methodological Study* (2002) and the editor of *Rediscovering the Dead Sea Scrolls: An Assessment of Old and New Approaches and Methods* (2010). She is a founding coeditor of the *Journal of Ancient Judaism.*

Bénédicte Lemmelijn is Professor of Old Testament within the Research Unit Biblical Studies at the Katholieke Universiteit Leuven (Belgium) and Research Associate at the Faculty of Theology of the University of the Free State (Bloemfontein, South Africa). Her research centers mainly on the redaction and textual criticism of the Hebrew Bible, including especially the characterization of the translation techniques of the Septuagint. She is the author of *A Plague of Texts? A Text-Critical Study of the So-Called "Plagues Narrative" in Exodus 7,14–11,10* (2009) and a coeditor of *After Qumran: Old and Modern Editions of the Biblical Texts—The Historical Books* (2012), in addition to authoring or editing many other books and articles.

Alan Lenzi is Associate Professor and Chair in the Department of Religious Studies at the University of the Pacific (Stockton, California). His research interests center on ancient Mesopotamian cultural and intellectual history, especially of the first millennium BCE. He is the author of *Secrecy and the Gods: Secret Knowledge in Ancient Mesopotamia and Biblical Israel* (2008) and a coauthor of *Ludlul Bēl Nēmeqi: The Standard Babylonian Poem of the Righteous Sufferer* (2010).

Sara J. Milstein is Assistant Professor of Hebrew Bible and Ancient Near Eastern Studies in the Department of Classical, Near Eastern, and Religious Studies at the University of British Columbia (Vancouver, Canada). Her research interests include Near Eastern scribal culture, evidence for revision in biblical and Mesopotamian literature, and comparative studies in biblical and Mesopotamian law. She is the author of *Tracking the Master Scribe: Revision through Introduction in Biblical and Mesopotamian Literature* (2016), and a coauthor of *The Buried Foundation of the Gilgamesh Epic: The Akkadian Huwawa Narrative* (2010), as well as numerous recent articles.

Raymond F. Person Jr. is Professor of Religion at Ohio Northern University (Ada, Ohio). His current research interests focus on how conversation analysis and the comparative study of oral tradition can be combined in ways that illuminate how literature functioned in the ancient world as well as environmental hermeneutics. His most recent monographs are *Deuteronomy and Environmental Amnesia* (2014) and *From Conversation to Oral Tradition* (2016). He is a coeditor of the forthcoming *The Dictionary of the Bible and Ancient Media*.

Robert Rezetko is an independent scholar and an associated researcher of Radboud Universiteit Nijmegen (Netherlands) and the University of Sydney (Australia). His research interests relate to the literary, textual, and historical linguistic study of Biblical Hebrew and other premodern languages and writings. He is currently working on a second doctorate in Spanish historical sociolinguistics. He is the author of *Source and Revision in the Narratives of David's Transfer of the Ark: Text, Language and Story in 2 Samuel 6 and 1 Chronicles 13, 15–16* (2007) and a coauthor of *Linguistic Dating of Biblical Texts* (2 vols.; 2008) and *Historical Linguistics and Biblical Hebrew: Steps Toward an Integrated Approach* (2014).

Stefan Schorch is Professor of Hebrew Bible at Martin-Luther-Universität Halle-Wittenberg (Germany). His main areas of research are the textual history of the Hebrew Bible, Hebrew language, Jewish literature of the Second Temple period, and Samaritan literature. He is the author of *Euphemismen in der Hebräischen Bibel* (2000) and *Die Vokale des Gesetzes* (2004), as well as numerous articles.

Julio Trebolle Barrera is Professor Emeritus in the Department of Hebrew and Aramaic Studies at the Universidad Complutense de Madrid (Spain). His areas of research include the textual history of the Bible, textual criticism, Qumran, the Septuagint, and biblical exegesis. He is the author of *Centena in libros Samuelis et Regum: Variantes textuales y composición literaria en los libros de Samuel y Reyes* (1989) and *The Jewish Bible and the Christian Bible: An Introduction to the History of the Bible* (1998), among other books and about two hundred articles.

Joseph A. Weaks is pastor of First Christian Church (Disciples of Christ) in Odessa, Texas. He was the Leander Keck Fellow of New Testament Studies at Brite Divinity School during his doctoral work. His areas of research include gospel synoptic studies, computer-assisted textual analysis, and contemporary congregational church life.

Ian Young is Associate Professor in the Department of Hebrew, Biblical and Jewish Studies at the University of Sydney (Australia). His areas of research include the language and textual criticism of the Hebrew Bible, with a particular focus on the book of Daniel. He is the author of *Diversity in Pre-exilic Hebrew* (1993) and a coauthor of *Linguistic Dating of Biblical Texts* (2 vols.; 2008) and *Historical Linguistics and Biblical Hebrew: Steps Toward an Integrated Approach* (2014), as well as numerous articles.

Ancient Sources Index

Many contributors argue in this volume and in other works for how anachronistic many of our distinctions are between "biblical" and "nonbiblical" works, between "canonical" and "noncanonical," and between "standard" and "sectarian," arguing instead for a tremendous degree of textual plurality and fluidity. Thus the traditional structure of this index is intended to be simply more convenient for its users and in no way should be understood as undermining the necessity of questioning the very categories by which this index is organized.

Ancient Near Eastern Sources

Deuterocanonical Books

Dead Sea Scrolls

Other Ancient Jewish Sources

New Testament

Other Ancient Christian Sources

Other Greco-Roman Sources

Other Literature

Modern Authors Index